McDonnell Douglas

Volume I : Francillon

McDonnell Douglas Aircraft

since 1920 : Volume I

René J Francillon

Naval Institute Press

BY THE SAME AUTHOR

Japanese Aircraft of the Pacific War

Lockheed Aircraft since 1913

Tonkin Gulf Yacht Club

CONTENTS

vi

A forestaste of Volume II. Designed by the engineering team in Long Beach and bearing designations in the famous DC series, the DC-9-80 (redesignated MD-80 in 1983) and the DC-10 are McDonnell Douglas products which first flew long after the 1967 merger of the McDonnell Company and the Douglas Aircraft Company, Inc. (*MDC*)

Preface and Acknowledgments

When nearly twenty years ago we first discussed the content and format of this book, John Stroud, the General Editor of the Putnam Aeronautical Series, and I amost immediately realized that we had a problem on our hands if we attempted to compress within the covers of one volume the history of the 80 aircraft types which by then had been designed and built by the McDonnell Douglas Corporation and its forebears.

The temptation was great to cover each aircraft type in as much detail as in companion volumes of the Putnam Aeronautical Series devoted to manufacturers which put into production a substantially smaller number of designs and had shorter production runs. Giving in to this temptation whilst covering the history and products of both Douglas and McDonnell would, however, have resulted in a book of over 1,000 pages. Clearly, economic necessities precluded the production of such a mammoth volume as its price would have been beyond the reach of many readers. Therefore, after briefly consider publishing this work in two volumes, we decided to cover the history of both the Douglas and McDonnell branches of the McDonnell Douglas Corporation in a single volume but to keep down its size by taking the following steps:

1 In line with companion volumes in the Putnam Aeronautical Series, this book would cover only the aircraft-related activities of the company and would exclude missiles and space exploration.
2 As long as technical and historical integrity was preserved, details on each aircraft type would be kept down to manageable size. Thus, for example, only the original customer and civil registration or military serial number of each aircraft built by the firm were listed in Appendices B and C. In this respect, readers are reminded of the availability of specialized monographs on the DC-1, DC-2, DC-3, DC-4, DC-5, DC-6, DC-7 and DC-8 published by Air-Britain and the London Amateur Aviation Society (LAAS); duplicating or even expanding upon these specialized efforts was considered wasteful of time and money.
3 In almost sixty years of operations, the firm and its forebears generated, either as private ventures or in answer to customers' requests, a truly fantastic number of projects. For example, during the DC-10 design phase alone, the author was associated with the weekly appearance, over several months, of new configurations (some with two, some with three and some with four engines, and with all conceivable engine locations being considered); this rash of projects only ended when the existing DC-10 went into production. To limit

the size of this volume, only a few representative projects were illustrated in Appendix D.

Between 1979, when *McDonnell Douglas Aircraft since 1920* was first published, and the beginning of 1988, when the second edition was being finalized, the firm not only continued as a leader in military aircraft production but also, after surviving difficult times in its commercial activities, remained among the free world's three major jetliner manufacturers. Moreover, McDonnell Douglas acquired Hughes Helicopters, Inc in January 1984. Hence, with the need to incorporate details of new products, add the pre-merger history of Hughes and its products, and update other portions of the book, the feasibility of producing a single volume disappeared as, once again, we were faced with a 1,000-page behemoth.

We refused to consider compressing further the text or reducing the number or size of illustrations in order to reduce the number of pages and, reluctantly, were forced to accept the two-volume solution which had been rejected ten years earlier. How to divide the work in two volumes was not easily decided. In the end, we elected to go with the present volume devoted to the history of Douglas and its aircraft and to release later a second volume covering the aircraft and corporate history of the Hughes companies (Hughes Aircraft Company, Aircraft Division of the Hughes Tool Division, and Hughes Helicopters) since 1936, the McDonnell Aircraft Corporation from 1939 to 1966, the Platt-LePage Aircraft Company from 1940 until 1944, the McDonnell Company in 1966-67, and the McDonnell Douglas Corporation since 1967.

While such a division was logical as far as Hughes or McDonnell products were concerned, we were left with the trickier problem of deciding where to fit products developed by Douglas but produced by McDonnell Douglas Aircraft. A case in point is the DC-10. As its designation implies, the aircraft is a Douglas product. Yet, its development and production would not have taken place had not Douglas been saved from bankruptcy by its acquisition by McDonnell. Production go-ahead was given by the Board of Directors in St Louis and the first flight was made on 29 August, 1970, more than three years after the McDonnell Douglas Corporation had come into being. We ended up deciding to include the DC-10, and its KC-10 and MD-11 derivatives, in the McDonnell Douglas volume. Likewise, we decided to end the DC-9 history in Volume I with the Series 50 aircraft and to i5nclude the Series 80, a true McDonnell Douglas product which has since been redesigned MD-80, and its MD-90 derivatives in Volume II. We beg readers and reviewers to be tolerant. We could not come up with an ideal split between the two volumes and retained this solution as it appeared to be the least objectionable among unsatisfactory choices.

The selection of photographs presented more problems. The choice, when so many good and interesting photographs were available, took up many frustrating evenings. In selecting the photographs, I was guided by my belief that the history of an aircraft manufacturing firm and the history of its aircraft do not end with the initial delivery of such aircraft.

Furthermore, I was convinced that most readers would prefer to see photographs of aircraft in their operational markings rather than in their factory-fresh appearance. Consequently, I have selected as many photographs as possible showing the in-service appearance of the aircraft.

I have been greatly assisted by several individuals, airlines and government agencies throughout the world which supplied many of the photographs (as well as operation data). Contributors of photographs include: *Private individuals*: Jean Alexander, Richard Sanders Allen, John Beatty, Allan Bovelt, Peter Bowers, Jean Cuny, Jacques Chillon, Bunny Darby, Rowland Gill, Peter Keefe, Katsu Kori, Peter Lewis, Peter Mancus, David Menard, Karl Peters, Mervyn Prime, Frank Smith, Paul Stevens, Gordon Swanborough, Peter Westburg and Stan Wilkinson. *Aerospace companies*: Aviation Traders (Engineering) Ltd, Canadair Ltd, General Electric Co, Industrie Aeronautiche e Meccaniche he Rinaldo Piaggio SpA, Lockheed Aircraft Service Co, Northrop Corp, Pratt & Whitney Aircraft, Rolls-Royce (1971) Ltd, Saab-Scania AB, Teledyne Ryan, Aeronautical and Westinghouse Electric Corp. *Airlines:* Andes, Acromexico, AeroPeru, Aer Turas-Teoranta, Air Canada, Air France, Air New Zealand, Air Siam, Air Zaïre, Alitalia, American, Ansett, ALM Antillean, Austrian, Avensa, Braniff, British Airways, British Caledonian, British Midland, Cargolux, Continental, CP Air, Delta, Eastern, Ecuatoriana, Faucett, Finnair, Flying Tiger, IAS Cargo, Iberia, JAL, Kar-Air, KLM, Laker, Lanica, Loftleidir, Lufthansa, Northwest, ONA, Ozark, Pan American, PSA, Sabena, SAETA, SAN, SAS, Saudi, Seaboard, South African, Spantax, Swissair, TAME, Texas International, Thai, TIA, Trans-Australia, Trans World, United, UTA, Viasa, Western and World. *US Government Agencies:* Civil Aeronautics Board, Coast Guard, Dept of the Air Force (especially the Air Force Museum, the Magazine & Book Division of the Office of Information, and the 1361st Audiovisual Squadron of MAC), Dept of the Army, Dept of the Navy (especially the Media Services Branch of the Office of Information, the Naval Air Systems Command, the Naval Photographic Center, the Captain and crew of the USS *Coral Sea*, and the Office of Information of the Marine Corps), Federal Aviation Administration, Library of Congress, National Aeronautics and Space Administration, National Air & Space Museum of the Smithsonian Institution, and National Archives. *Foreign Government Agencies:* Argentina (air attaché); Australia (Australian War Memoral, RAAF, RAN); Canada (defence attaché, Public Archives, Dept of National Defence); Denmark (air attaché); Ecuador (Dirección de Aviación Civil); Finland (air attaché); France (ECA); Great Britain (MoD, RAF Museum); Israel (air attaché, Heyl Ha'Avir); Japan (air attaché); Netherlands (air attaché, RNethAF); New Zealand (RNZAF); Norway (air attaché, Luftforsvaret); and West Germany (air attaché). *Magazines;* Air Action, Air Fan, Air Force Magazine, Air International, Air Pictorial, Aviation Week & Space Technology, Aviation Magazine, Flight International, Interconair, Le Fanatique de l'Aviation, Koku Fan, and Naval Aviation News.

Although this book was undertaken as a private venture and was not sponsored by the McDonnel Douglas Corporation, it obviously could not have been written without help from the company and from several of my former colleagues who, acting in a private capacity, supplied me with a steady flow of information and data.

To all, within and without MDC, I wish to express my deep gratitude for their most generous co-operation. Special thanks must, however, go to five of my long-time friends—H. L. James, P. Mancus, R. C. Mikesh, R. K. Smith and M. C. Windrow—who played a major role in making this book possible. Their encouragement and support never let me down and, often, their enthusiasm saved me from dropping the project. Of a different nature, the help received from my former secretary, Mrs Elisa Klein, was equally important as her patience in going over many changes in the manuscript was a strong inducement to my continuing the task.

Most of the general arrangement drawings in this book were prepared by L. E. Bradford. Mr Bradford died before completing this task and I have to thank Michael Badrocke and Clem Watson for producing the remaining drawings to the same high standard.

Author's Notes

Some readers may question the name under which some of the later aircraft are described. For example, the DC-8 is commonly listed as a McDonnell Douglas type whereas in this book it is listed as the Douglas DC-8. This situation often arises following mergers such as that which took place in 1967 between Douglas and McDonnell. While there are good reasons to list former Douglas and McDonnell products still supported by McDonnell Douglas (eg DC-8, DC-9, A-4 and F-4) under the latter name, the practice, when extended to include older types still in service, has led to such a strange sounding appellation as McDonnell Douglas DC-3! The author decided to 'render unto Caesar the things which are Caesar's,' and to list aircraft under the name of the company responsible for their design and initial production.

Other will question the use of the terms s/n and serials (or serial numbers) to identify respectively the manufacturer's numbers and military serial numbers assigned to each aircraft. Usually, to avoid confusion between these numbering systems, aviation historians have adopted the abbreviations c/n (constructor's number) for the numbers assigned by the manufacturer, and s/n (serial number) for the numbers assigned by military customers. However, although changing over the years, the prevailing custom within the Douglas organization has been to designate company-assigned numbers as either s/n (serial numbers) or FSN (Factory Serial Numbers). The author elected to standardize on the use of s/n for the Douglas-assigned numbers, starting with 100 as given in 1920 to The Cloudster.

Vallejo, California, January 1988

xii

Between 1935, when the first DST flew on 17 December, and 1947, when the last
DC-3C was delivered to Sabena on 21 March, Douglas built 10,654 DC-3s
and derivatives. This VC-47A-20-DK (s/n 13047, 43-93166) of the
Wyoming Air National Guard bears the insignia of the 187th FIS
aft of its cockpit. (*Wyoming ANG*)

Origin and History of the Company

The Douglas Aircraft Company and its forebears–which, for many years
after 1924 when two World Cruisers accomplished the first round-the-
world flight, proudly displayed the motto 'First around the World'—have
produced a fascinating variety of aeroplanes which have greatly
contributed to the development of civil and military aeronautics throughout the world. Especially since World War II, commercial and military
transport aircraft built by Douglas or, in the case of the Li-2 *Colt*, built in
the Soviet Union have been operated by virtually every nation in the world
and have been flown under all climatic conditions from the heat of the
equatorial jungles to the bitter cold of the North and South Poles.

The Douglas companies also excelled over a period of almost half a
century in designing and producing a successful line of combat aircraft.
Notably, ever since 14 April, 1921, when the fledgling Davis-Douglas Co
was awarded its first military contract, $119,550 to build and test three DT-1
naval torpedo bombers, the name Douglas has been closely associated with
US Naval Aviation. Foremost among Douglas types which distinguished
themselves in USN service are the SBD Dauntless, the aircraft which
during the Battle of Midway in June 1942 helped turn the tide in the Pacific
War; the AD Skyraider, the outstanding attack aircraft which first gained
fame during the Korean War and flew its last combat sortie in Southeast
Asia on the eve of the fall of Saigon in April 1975; and the A-4 Skyhawk,
which nine years after it went out of production was gaining a new lease of
life in Singapore, through the installation of a modern engine, and New
Zealand, through the fitting of advanced electronic equipment.

1

To a large extent, these achievements were made possible by the unusual ability and drive of the founder, Donald W. Douglas, and by the creative genius of both John K. Northrop and Edward H. Heinemann. Jack Northrop not only organized what became the El Segundo Division of the Douglas Aircraft Company, the birthplace of so many great aircraft, but also contributed his multi-spar wing structure to assure the success of the DC-1/DC-3 series. Ed Heinemann, often called 'Mr Naval Aviation' in the United States, led the design teams for such outstanding aircraft as the Dauntless, Boston, Invader, Skyraider, Skyrocket, Skywarrior, and Skyhawk.

Donald Wills Douglas

Second son of an assistant cashier of the National Park Bank, Donald Wills Douglas was born in Brooklyn, New York, on 6 April, 1892, and received his early education at Trinity Chapel School in New York City. At the age of seventeen, by which time he had acquired a great love for the sea, Donald Douglas followed in the footsteps of his older brother and entered the US Naval Academy at Annapolis as a plebe in the autumn of 1909. Already, however, Donald Douglas was developing a strong interest in aviation and was using some of his spare time to build and test model aeroplanes powered by a whirling wheel filled with powder. In the life of Donald Douglas the love for the sea was to remain a consuming hobby but aviation was to become a most successful career. In 1912 he decided to resign as a midshipman before graduating from the US Naval Academy and to undertake a career in aeronautical engineering. Later, some of Douglas's friends and associates were to claim that his decision to leave Annapolis had come as a result of one of his model aeroplanes landing dangerously close to an Admiral; Donald Douglas has consistently denied any truth to this story but, none the less, it became part of the Douglas legend.

After leaving Annapolis, Donald Douglas attempted to obtain his first job in the budding aircraft industry but he was turned down by both Grover Loening and Glenn Curtiss. Undaunted, he enrolled as a student in aeronautical engineering at MIT. Among his MIT professors, Jerome C. Hunsaker—an Annapolis graduate who later, with the rank of Commander, became chief of the Bureau of Construction and Repairs Aircraft Division, US Navy—played an important part in shaping Donald Douglas's career and Douglas, after obtaining his Bachelor of Science diploma in the spring of 1914, remained at MIT for a year as Hunsaker's assistant. Design and construction, rather than teaching, attracted the energy of the young engineer and in 1915 he left to join the Connecticut Aircraft Co as a consultant. The professional aviation career of Donald W. Douglas had begun.

Donald Douglas's association with the Connecticut Aircraft Co, during which he participated in the design of the DN-1—the first dirigible for the US Navy—, was brief. In August 1915, when only 23-years old, he joined the Glenn Martin Company in Los Angeles as chief engineer and worked on a number of early Martin designs until November 1916 when, following

2

the consolidation in August 1916 of the Wright Company and the Glenn Martin Company into the Wright-Martin Aircraft Corporation with operations on the east coast of the United States, he resigned to accept a position with the US Army. This short stay in Southern California and his marriage in 1916 to Miss Charlotte Marguerite Ogg in Riverside, California, had convinced Douglas that the Golden State was where he wanted to raise his family and where prevailing weather conditions were particularly favourable for aircraft construction and testing.

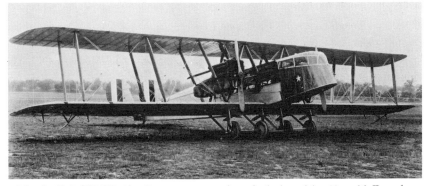

Martin T-1 (GMP), the first transport aircraft designed by Donald Douglas when he was Chief Engineer of the Glenn Martin Company. (*Martin*)

When leaving the Wright-Martin Aircraft Corporation Douglas agreed to become chief civilian aeronautical engineer for the Aviation Section of the US Army Signal Corps. Once again his employment was of short duration as Glenn Martin, following the organization of a new Glenn Martin Company in Cleveland, Ohio, asked him to resume his function as chief engineer. With Glenn Martin, Douglas was responsible for the design of the large twin-engined MB-1 or GMB bomber for the US Army, of its transport derivative—the T-1 or GMP—and of its naval version, the TM-1 or MTB. Of these, the T-1 transport, with accommodation for a crew of two in a glassed-in enclosure and ten passengers, was the one which was of greatest interest to Donald Douglas who, already, had great faith in the future of commercial air transport.

Still Douglas was restless and anxious to become his own master. In March 1920 he resigned his $10,000 a year position with the Glenn Martin Company and again set off for California where, soon after, he was able to form the first of the four aircraft companies which have borne his name. The Douglas Aircraft saga was beginning.

From then on the life of Donald Wills Douglas was closely associated with the history of the Davis-Douglas Company, the Douglas Company, the Douglas Aircraft Company and the McDonnell Douglas Corporation and with the aircraft they have built since 1920. As a result, Donald Douglas has earned an impressive list of awards and honours, including the Robert J. Collier Trophy in 1936, the Guggenheim Medal in 1939, an LL.D

Donald Wills Douglas (1892-1981), founder of the Douglas Aircraft Company and Honorary chairman of the McDonnell Douglas Corporation after 1967 (*left*), and John Knudsen Northrop (1895-1981), who worked for Douglas between 1923 and 1927 and was President of Northrop Corporation, a Douglas subsidiary, from 1932 until 1937. (*MDC* and *Northrop*)

(Doctor of Laws) degree from the University of California at Los Angeles in 1947, the US Certificate of Merit in 1948, the Commander's Cross of the Order of Orange-Nassau in 1950, the Légion d'Honneur in 1951, the USAF Exceptional Service Award in 1953, the Royal Order of Dannebrog in 1955, and the Elmer A. Sperry Award in 1956. Donald Douglas died on 1 February, 1981.

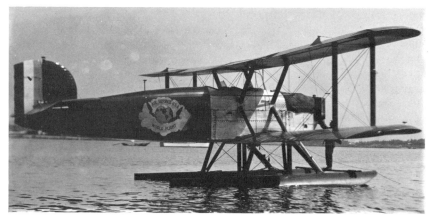

Boston, the DWC bearing the side number 3, capsized while under tow to the Faroe Islands. The World Cruiser was the first type of Douglas aircraft on which John K. Northrop worked.

4

Davis-Douglas Company

While living in Cleveland, Donald Douglas and his wife often missed the mild winter climate of Southern California, and in January 1920 Mrs Douglas and their two sons left for Los Angeles. Two months later Donald Douglas, who had just completed the design of the Martin MTB, was able to join his family. In the event, it turned out to be a permanent move as Douglas decided to leave the security of the chief engineer's job in the cold of Cleveland for an as yet uncertain future in the warmth of Los Angeles.

With only $600 savings, his enthusiasm and his ability as a designer at his disposal, Donald Douglas needed urgently to find a financial sponsor. Some of his hopes and reasons for this move were set forth in a letter dated 1 April, 1920, which Douglas wrote to his old mentor and former colleague, Cdr Jerome Hunsaker, the chief of the Bureau of Construction and Repairs Aircraft Division of the US Navy: '. . . I have perhaps vain hopes of interesting capital in Southern California in an aircraft venture. California has long been a place where I wanted to live not only because of personal reasons, but because I have felt that if there is to be any civilian aeronautics it will be there that it will first attain real success . . .'. In his answer Cdr Hunsaker encouraged Douglas to join William Boeing in Seattle, and expressed his regrets that the US Navy would not have the benefit of Douglas's services through any of the contractors with whom the Navy expected to do business in the near future. Douglas was not prepared to work again for another company but within a year he was able to obtain some of the US Navy business which Hunsaker had mentioned.

Donald Douglas hoped to be able to undertake the design and construction of transport aircraft inspired by his work on the Martin T-1 but, during the spring of 1920, it appeared that his efforts to raise capital to finance his venture were doomed to fail. However, as the result of earlier conversations with Bill Henry—a young sports writer on the staff of the *Los Angeles Times* who, for a short time, had been advertizing manager for the Glenn Martin Company in Cleveland—Douglas was introduced to David R. Davis.* This wealthy sportsman, who had become interested in aviation, did not wish to finance the production of transport aircraft but was willing to provide capital of $40,000 to form a company with Douglas if the latter was prepared to design and build a single aircraft for an attempt on the first nonstop flight across the United States. This was not the big start Douglas had hoped for but it was a start, and on 22 July, 1920, David R. Davis and Donald W. Douglas formed the Davis-Douglas Company.

Upon reaching an agreement with Davis, in June 1920 Donald Douglas rented the first office space for his company, a single room in the back of a barber shop on Pico Boulevard in Los Angeles, and invited five of his former colleagues at the Glenn L. Martin Co—Ross Elkins, James Goodyear, George Borst, Henry Guerin and George Strompl—to join him

---

*David R. Davis was to become known for his design of the Davis wing used in such aircraft as the Consolidated B-24.

5

The barber's shop on Pico Boulevard, Los Angeles, in the back of which Donald Douglas rented space for the grandiosely-named Engineering Department of the Davis-Douglas Company. (*MDC*)

in his new venture. While the back-room of the barber shop, inadequate as it was as an office and draughting room, would have to do for the time being, Douglas and his associates had to find a suitable place to build their aircraft. Eventually in late July, the Davis-Douglas Company rented the loft of an old factory, the Koll Planing Mill, in Los Angeles where the assembly of the aircraft intended for the first nonstop flight across the United States was undertaken. Before the completion of the still unnamed aircraft, Eric Springer—who had learned to fly in 1913–14 at the Glenn L. Martin flying school in Griffith Park, Los Angeles, and who had gone on to become Martin's chief test pilot, in which capacity he had taken the Douglas-designed Martin MB-1 twin-engined bomber on its maiden flight on 17 August, 1918—joined the Davis-Douglas Company as test pilot. Upon seeing the almost completed aircraft Eric Springer is said to have exclaimed: 'You've got a real cloud duster there, Doug'. The phrase caught on and the aircraft, the first produced in the Douglas family, was named The Cloudster.

Components for The Cloudster were completed in February 1921 and, after being lowered in sections down a lift shaft from the loft of the Koll Planing Mill, the aircraft was trucked to the Goodyear Blimp hangar at South Park and Florence Boulevards in Los Angeles where the Davis-Douglas Company had rented space to assemble its Cloudster. On 24 February the aircraft made its first 30-minute flight with Eric Springer at the controls. With the appearance of The Cloudster, the first aeroplane in history capable of lifting a useful load exceeding its own weight, Donald Douglas had accomplished his part in the agreement between Davis and himself. At that time David Davis was most pleased with The Cloudster and was anxious to attempt, with Eric Springer, the nonstop link between the Pacific and Atlantic coasts. However, as told in detail in the main part of this volume, the flight was cut short over Texas due to an engine failure.

Meanwhile Donald Douglas, who had taken an active part in the actual construction of The Cloudster, did not remain inactive but undertook the design of a single-engined torpedo bomber for the US Navy. However, as efforts were being made to prepare The Cloudster for a new attempt at the nonstop crossing of the United States, David R. Davis lost interest in the project and showed little enthusiasm in financing the production of three experimental torpedo bombers for which the Davis-Douglas Company had received a contract from the Navy in April 1921. There thus remained no choice but to dissolve the company and once again Donald Douglas had to search for financial backing for his expanded operations. Should such financial support be forthcoming, a new company would have to be formed. This time it would bear only the name of Donald W. Douglas.

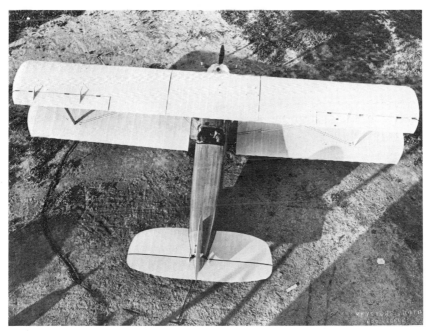

The Cloudster photographed in February 1921 shortly after its completion. It had side-by-side accommodation and ailerons only on the upper wing.
(*Keystone*)

Douglas Company

Following the withdrawal of David Davis's financial backing, Donald Douglas again turned to his friend Bill Henry for assistance. With the promise of partial payments by the US Government for work in progress on the DT-1, Douglas needed only $15,000 to launch his company and begin construction of the Navy torpedo bombers. He was, however, still a relatively unknown aircraft designer and bankers were not prepared to advance the needed funds without proper guarantees. To help his friend, Bill Henry introduced Douglas to his employer, Harry Chandler, the publisher of the *Los Angeles Times*. When approached by Douglas, Chandler, anxious to promote new business ventures in Southern California, agreed to co-guarantee a $15,000 bank loan if Douglas was able to obtain a similar guarantee from nine other California businessmen. Within a few days Donald Douglas obtained the nine additional signatures and received the requisite $15,000 bank loan. In July 1921 The Douglas Company was incorporated in the State of California.

The DT-1 (A6031) as originally completed. With this aircraft began an unbroken client-supplier relationship between the US Navy and Douglas.
(*US National Archives*)

After settling the financial affairs of the new company, Douglas and his small team were able to concentrate on the detailed design of the DT-1, which took place in the rented hangar of the Goodyear Blimp Company. Delivered in late 1921, the sole single-seat DT-1 was followed by two DT-2s which had a crew of two and a modified radiator installation. After the successful testing of the DT-2 prototypes in competition with three other American designs and the imported Blackburn Swift F, in the spring of 1922 The Douglas Company was awarded its first production contract, with the Navy Department's initial order for eighteen production DT-2s.

One of the two Curtiss HS-2Ls which were rebuilt and modified by the Davis-Douglas Company for Pacific Marine Airways. The flying-boats received Douglas s/ns 104 and 105. (*Western Airlines*)

At the same time, to supplement the limited production capacity of The Douglas Company, the Navy placed complementary orders for six DT-2s to be built by the Naval Aircraft Factory in Philadelphia, and eleven DT-2s to be built by the Dayton-Wright Company in Dayton—the first Douglas-designed aircraft to be produced by other contractors. Two years later the type won a new success for Douglas when the modified DT-2B was ordered by the Norwegian Government which also acquired the licence manufacturing rights for the aircraft. These achievements were, indeed, quite spectacular considering the fact that the DT-1 and first two DT-2s were designed and built by a company which, at the time, had less than a dozen employees, limited facilities, and other difficulties.

While the DT-1 and DT-2s were being evaluated by the Navy, The Douglas Company undertook to overhaul and modify two Boeing-built Curtiss HS-2L flying-boats for Pacific Marine Airways. These two aircraft became the last aeroplanes handled by Douglas in the original premises. With the award of the first DT-2 production contract it had become imperative for Donald Douglas to find better and larger facilities in which to house the expanded activities of his company. Douglas planned to move to the Long Beach area—where eventually a large Douglas plant was built in 1941—but in the summer of 1922 went on to lease the abandoned buildings of the Herrman Film Corporation at 2435 Wilshire Boulevard in Santa Monica where a vacant field was available for flight operations. In these newly acquired facilities, the production of DT-2s was followed by the construction of some of the most famous of the Douglas aeroplanes, the World Cruisers. The Douglas World Cruiser was derived from the naval DT-2 and was ordered by the War Department for the specific purpose of

Aerial view of the plant at 2435 Wilshire Boulevard, Santa Monica. The aircraft parked in front is a DT 2. (*MDC*)

attempting the first round-the-world flight. For that purpose four US Air Service DWCs left Santa Monica on the first leg of their flight on 17 March, 1924. One hundred and seventy-five days and 28,945 miles (46,580 km) later, two of these DWCs—supplemented by a third aircraft replacing one of the original machines which had been lost in the North Atlantic—arrived in Seattle. The Douglas Company had earned its proud motto 'First around the World'.

The success obtained with the naval DT-2s and with the Air Service's World Cruisers ·solidly established the reputation of The Douglas

Running up the Liberty engine of the O-2 s/n 212, 25-377 of the Air Service Training Corps. The top part of the cowling has been removed. (*USAF*)

10

Company which then grew rapidly. The next major achievement for Donald Douglas was the winning of the 1924 observation aircraft competition for the Air Service which was held at McCook Field and where The Douglas Company entered its Liberty-powered XO-2. From this victory The Douglas Company, and its successor the Douglas Aircraft Company Inc, went on to build a total of 778 observation biplanes for the US Armed Forces and 101 observation biplanes for the export market. Douglas's first commercial transport aircraft, the M series of mailplanes, was also derived from this successful line of military observation biplanes.

An M-4 built for the US Mail and bearing on its tail the early logo of the Douglas Company. (*MDC*)

During its existence, The Douglas Company also produced the Commuter and DA-1 Ambassador two-seat sporting monoplanes, the C-1 series of military cargo and personnel transport aircraft, the DT-2B torpedo bombers for Peru and the T2D-1 twin-engined torpedo bombers for the US Navy. At that time The Douglas Company employed several designers who achieved fame either while with Douglas or with other companies. Among these early Douglas employees was Arthur E. Raymond who joined The Douglas Company in 1924 and became Vice-President (Engineering) of the Douglas Aircraft Company Inc ten years later. Perhaps even better known is John K. Northrop who first joined Douglas in 1923 and left in 1927 to join Lockheed where he designed the famous Vega single-engined transport; in 1932 he rejoined the Douglas team to form the Northrop Corporation, a subsidiary of the Douglas Aircraft Co Inc. Equally famous is James H. 'Dutch' Kindelberger who was Douglas's chief engineer from 1924 until 1934 when he resigned to become President of General Aviation Manufacturing Corporation; soon thereafter Kindelberger became President and General Manager of North American Aviation Inc, in which capacity he was credited with initiating the design of the P-51 Mustang of World War II.

In 1922, its first full year of operations, The Douglas Company had delivered a total of six aircraft for a total value of $130,890. Four years later, in 1926, the company's production had risen to 120 aircraft, a twenty-fold increase, for a total value of $1,662,724 and an increase in dollar value of 1,270 per cent! With production increasing at such a pace, the facilities of the Wilshire plant in Santa Monica soon became insufficient. At first it was the flying activities which had to be curtailed and after the early part of 1927 all aircraft built in the Wilshire plant had to be towed at night from the plant to Clover Field, also in Santa Monica but some two miles away. This in itself proved to be a major impediment to normal operations but, at the same time, it was becoming clear that the maximum production capacity of the Wilshire plant—the lease of which was due to expire in July 1929—was soon to be reached. Fortunately, the City of Santa Monica was anxious to retain The Douglas Company in its midst and was prepared to expand the facilities available at Clover Field and to co-operate with Douglas. However, to take advantage of this opportunity more capital was required and thus, once again, in 1928, Donald W. Douglas had to reorganize his company.

Douglas Aircraft Company Inc
Prior to World War II

Up to that time Donald W. Douglas, initially with Bill Henry and later with his father, William E. Douglas, had controlled the capital of The Douglas Company and had relied, whenever necessary, on loans from the Security Trust & Savings Bank. At the same time all but $40,000 of the net profit made since 1922 had been re-invested in The Douglas Company; as a result of this prudent management policy, the net worth of The Douglas Company had risen to $2,500,000 by the autumn of 1928. This was a spectacular achievement for a company which, seven years earlier, had needed a $15,000 loan to begin operations. Excellent as the cash position of The Douglas Company was—about $1,400,000 was held in cash and marketable securities—Donald Douglas, advised by the brokerage firms of E. A. Pierce & Company and Bancamerica Blair Corporation, elected to revamp the capital structure of his company.

Accordingly a new company, the Douglas Aircraft Company Inc, was organized on 30 November, 1928, to purchase the assets of The Douglas Company with an authorized capital stock issue of 1,000,000 shares. The new company, which retained Santa Monica as the location of the corporate office and production facilities, was incorporated in the State of Delaware to benefit from that state's more favourable tax laws. Only 300,000 shares were initially issued, of which the Douglases received 200,000 shares for the assets of The Douglas Company, whilst the balance was taken by Bancamerica Blair and E. A. Pierce for $1,000,000 and distributed to the public. Some $650,000 of this new money went into the company's cash account while the balance was spent on the acquisition of property and the construction thereon of a new plant. Completed in 1929, the new plant was located on the fringe of Clover Field, alongside Ocean Park Boulevard, in Santa Monica, and occupied seven and three-quarter

Dolphin 114 of Wilmington-Catalina Airlines on the pier at Avalon.
(*NA & SM*)

acres owned in fee by the Douglas Aircraft Company Inc. At the same time, the City of Santa Monica expanded and improved the facilities available at Clover Field and permitted the company its use for experimental flying under a ten-year renewable contract, at a nominal rental.

After moving to its new facilities, the Douglas Aircraft Company continued the production of its series of observation biplanes and began the production of its first flying-boat, the PD-1 series. Douglas also began to build a new series of twin-engined amphibians, the Dolphins, for which the Sinbad, completed in 1930, acted as prototype, in anticipation of a booming market for luxury transport aircraft. Unfortunately for Douglas, the timing of the project was bad as the October 1929 stock market crash triggered the Great Depression and with it the anticipated civilian market for Dolphins all but vanished (eventually, and including the Sinbad prototype, a total of only 59 amphibians of this type was produced by Douglas; of these, 45 were delivered to the US Armed Forces). Production and design of military aircraft—including the series of observation biplanes which remained in production until 1936, the new series of observation monoplanes, the XO-35/XB-7 line of twin-engined aircraft, the P2D-1 series, the XT3D-1 and XT3D-2 experimental torpedo bomber aircraft and the XFD-1 naval fighter—continued at a satisfactory rate and kept the Douglas Aircraft Company alive and financially sound at a time when so many other US companies of all kinds were going bankrupt.

Douglas Y1B-7 of the 88th Observation Squadron. (*NA & SM*)

Considering the staggering problems faced by the American economy (unemployment in the United States increased from 3·2 per cent of the labour force in 1929 to a high of 24·9 per cent in 1933), it is surprising to note that this was the period selected by Douglas to abandon his conservative financial policy and to relax the dividend policy of his company. Between 1930 and 1932, while the company earned a net profit of $1,311,000, dividends totalling $1,153,000 were paid out. None the less, and in spite of the fact that net sales dropped from a record of $4,088,595 in 1930 to $2,294,295 in 1933, the financial position of the company remained sound with cash and marketable securities, about $1,521,000 in 1933, substantially exceeding current liabilities, about $200,000 at the end of the same year. Meanwhile, net working capital increased from about $2,000,000 in 1928 to $3,300,000 in 1933. The financial soundness of the Douglas Aircraft Company was to prove particularly valuable in enabling Donald Douglas to launch his company into a new, and yet untried by him, market: the manufacture of passenger transport aircraft for the airlines. This factor, in the opinion of the author, has often been neglected in explaining the spectacular success of the DC series; the Douglas Aircraft Company had the right capital at the right time.

On 2 August, 1932, Jack Frye—then Vice President in charge of Operations for Transcontinental & Western Air Inc in Kansas City, Missouri—wrote a letter to Donald Douglas in which he informed the Douglas Aircraft Corporation (*sic*) that TWA was 'interested in purchasing ten or more trimotored transport planes'. To this letter Jack Frye attached a copy of TWA performance specifications and concluded by asking Donald Douglas to advise whether his company was 'interested in this manufacturing job' and, if so, 'approximately how long would it take to turn out the first plane for service tests'. This letter was to mark a new birth for the Douglas Aircraft Company, and the start of the world's most famous family of transport aircraft.

When Douglas received Jack Frye's letter, preliminary studies for an aircraft capable of meeting TWA's specifications were undertaken. At that time, Douglas's engineering staff—with James 'Dutch' Kindelberger as

14

chief and Arthur Raymond as assistant chief engineer—was well aware of the potential of the Boeing Model 247, a modern twin-engined transport aircraft then under development in Seattle. The risks inherent in competing with such a formidable design combined with the anticipated small market for this type of aircraft—in view of the precarious economic conditions then prevailing and the resultant problems faced by the airline industry, Douglas foresaw the need for less than 100 aeroplanes of this type—acted as a strong damper on the early enthusiasm of the Douglas team. This brief hesitancy, however, soon ended when Donald Douglas received the visit of Harold E. Talbott Jr, then Chairman of North American Aviation Inc which owned 89,000 shares of Douglas stock. Not only did Talbott represent the largest stockholders apart from Douglas himself but he was also a director of Transcontinental & Western Air. His convincing arguments were heard and, a few days later, Douglas sent his Vice-President and General Manager Harry H. Wetzel, and Arthur E. Raymond to New York with the responsibility of presenting to TWA the initial proposal for the design and construction of the Douglas Commercial One, the DC-1. With Harry Wetzel negotiating all contractual and financial questions and Arthur Raymond discussing all technical matters with the engineering staff of TWA and their Technical Adviser, Charles A. Lindbergh, the Douglas representatives were able to impress the management of TWA and, on 20 September, 1932, Douglas received a contract for a DC-1 prototype with options for a further sixty aircraft. The DC saga was beginning.

While working on the detail design of the DC-1, the Douglas team, already well experienced, benefited from the valuable assistance of several individuals and companies. Among these many contributions, the

The DC-1 during early flight trials, as indicated on the rudder by the taped over NC prefix of its registration which reads 223Y. (*MDC*)

15

following must be noted. John K. Northrop, after returning to the Douglas fold to form the Northrop Corporation in January 1932, contributed to the DC-1 design his multi-cellular wing construction which was both comparatively cheap to make and extremely strong and thus accounted greatly for the longevity of the DC-1 and its descendants, the DC-2 and DC-3. A team from the California Institute of Technology, led by Drs Clark B. Millikan and Arthur L. Klein, after conducting extensive wind-tunnel testing of DC-1 models, helped the Douglas team by pointing out the need to move the aircraft's centre of gravity forward and to change the radius of curvature of the fillet joining the wing to the fuselage to improve lift and reduce drag. From the National Advisory Committee for Aeronautics (NACA) Douglas obtained information necessary for the design of more efficient engine nacelles and cowlings and for the use of an improved wing aerofoil. From a consultant, Stephen J. Zand of the Sperry Corporation, came new ideas and techniques to reduce noise level inside the passenger cabin. Finally, from the work of Frank W. Caldwell, chief engineer of the Hamilton Standard Propeller Company, came the design of the variable-pitch propellers without which the DC-1 would not have been able to meet TWA's stringent single-engined requirements. The combined talents of the Douglas engineers and their outside associates resulted in an aircraft which exceeded all TWA's original performance specifications.

Due to the combined effects of the limited new programmes sponsored by the US Armed Forces during this period of tight budget control, of the heavy workload imposed on the Douglas team by the design, construction and testing of the DC-1 and its production variant, the DC-2, and of the heavy drain on Douglas's finances imposed by this programme, only one new design—that of the XO2D-1 naval observation biplane—was undertaken by the company during the period from 1932 to early 1934. The design and testing of the DC-1 and the placing in production of the DC-2

The XO2D-1, the last Douglas biplane design.

16

tied up more than $2,000,000, of which $450,000 was raised by loans. Hence cash and marketable securities held by the Douglas Aircraft Company dropped from $2,000,000 in 1932 to $650,000 in November 1934, with $166,000 from this amount pledged as collateral for the loans. At the same time, disappointing results achieved with the Dolphin programme and reduced government orders resulted in a drop in net income from an all-time high of $690,000 in 1930 to a low of $38,753 in 1934. Furthermore, the heavy costs of the DC-1 and DC-2 development programme forced Douglas to modify for the first time his company's policy of writing off the development cost of each aircraft type within one year, and the development cost of this programme was spread over the fiscal years 1934 and 1935. Fortunately for Douglas, these heavy financial outlays were offset by a promising future, as evidenced in the 1934 balance sheet on which appeared two unusually large asset accounts: 'contracts in progress' with $1,500,000 and 'accounts receivable' with $603,000.

Among the 142 aircraft produced in 1934 by the Douglas Aircraft Company and its subsidiary, the Northrop Corporation, were the first fifty-nine DC-2s. In 1935, DC-2s accounted for 53 of the 130 aircraft delivered by Douglas. However, the years 1934 and 1935 also saw the inception of the design of a number of new aircraft types including the XTBD-1 and XP3D-1 for the US Navy, and the DST (Douglas Sleeper Transport), the first model in the DC-3 series. In the case of the DST and its day transport version, the DC-3, the company failed to foresee the true potential market for the aircraft.

This weakness in Douglas's commercial market research—which had already resulted in the failure of the Commuter and Ambassador, and in the limited success of the Dolphin—was to remain characteristic of the company throughout its existence and, eventually in 1967, contributed significantly to the disappearance of the Douglas Aircraft Company following the underestimation of the potential market for the DC-9 twin-jet transport. Throughout the history of the DC series, Douglas combined brilliant engineering work with poor market intelligence, and the design of most DC types resulted mainly from reaction to customers' specific requests rather than from Douglas's own anticipation of future airline needs. Thus, the DC-1 and DC-2 stemmed from a request from TWA, the DST/DC-3 was designed in answer to a request from American Airlines, the DC-4 (C-54) design was sponsored by American, Eastern and United, the DC-6 was born to satisfy the needs of American and United in meeting the competition from TWA's Constellation fleet, and the DC-7 and DC-10 originated with requests from American Airlines. As regards the DC-8 and DC-9, they were designed to counteract the competition from the Boeing Airplane Company with the 707 and from British Aircraft Corporation with the BAC One-Eleven.

When, on 5 May, 1934, American Airlines began its transcontinental service from New York to Los Angeles over a route longer than those flown by Transcontinental & Western Air and United Air Lines, it offset the

NC16001 and NC16006, two of the early DSTs of American Airlines, on the ramp at Newark Airport, New Jersey. (*American Airlines*)

competitive disadvantage of the longer route by operating Curtiss Condor twin-engined biplanes equipped with sleeping berths. However, with United operating the faster Boeing Model 247D and TWA the still faster DC-2, it soon became imperative for American to replace the obsolescent Condor. To obtain such an aircraft, the airline approached Douglas in late 1934 with a request for a version of the DC-2 with a wider fuselage to accommodate sleeping berths. Initially, this request was received with only lukewarm enthusiasm as the company underestimated the market for this type of aircraft and because American Airlines was short of cash. However, following a long telephone conversation between C. R. Smith, President of American Airlines, in Chicago and Donald Douglas in Santa Monica during which C. R. Smith promised that his company would buy twenty of the new aircraft, Douglas went ahead with the design of the 'wide-body' version of the DC-2. It is interesting to note that this telephone conversation, followed by a telegram from C. R. Smith confirming his intent to order twenty and to take an option for twenty more, was the basis on which Douglas launched the DST/DC-3 series; the formal contract, which went back and forth between Santa Monica and Chicago for modifications, was in fact signed only after the delivery of many DSTs. Aviation was still a gentleman's business.

At first Douglas and American planned the DST as a minimum-change version of the DC-2 with the two aircraft having 85 per cent common parts. It soon, however, became necessary to abandon this conservative approach and, ultimately, the DC-3 used only 15 per cent of the parts and components used by the DC-2. While this design philosophy resulted in substantially higher engineering and manufacturing costs, it enabled Douglas to produce an aircraft capable of a great variety of civil and military roles, and production of the series exceeded 10,000 aircraft, the largest production run of any transport aircraft in the world. First flown on 17 December, 1935—exactly thirty-two years after the historic flight of the

Wright brothers at Kitty Hawk—, the initial DST (s/n 1494, X14988) was followed by only 37 other aircraft fitted as sleeper transports (DST and DST-A). This limited production, which could be regarded as a justification for Douglas's initial doubts on the size of the market, was, however, followed by a large production run of pre-war commercial DC-3 versions and by truly massive production of the aircraft in its myriad military models. As a result, DC-3s—including mostly ex-military C-47s as well as other versions of the basic type—were still among the most numerous civil and military transport aircraft in the world thirty-five years after the maiden flight of the first DST.

Continued production of the DC-2 and its military derivatives—the last civil DC-2 was delivered in July 1937 and the last C-39 in September 1939— and increasing DST/DC-3 production contributed greatly to the net sales of the Douglas Aircraft Company which increased from $8,591,114 in 1935 to $60,970,774 in 1940. During the same period, net income rose from $1,262,967 to $10,831,971, while cash and marketable securities held by the company went up from $1,722,000 to $26,675,000. Also significant was the fact that, due to the increasing volume of commercial business, sales to the US Armed Forces, which up to and including 1933 represented some 90 per cent of Douglas's total sales, accounted for only 54 per cent of the $125,632,000 revenue of the company between 1922 and 1939. The war, however, was to change this picture drastically. While sales and income figures for the company during World War II will be discussed in another chapter, it is worth pointing out that the profit margin on wartime contracts was, contrary to common belief, much lower than on peacetime, mainly commercial, contracts and net income, which accounted for a record 17·76 per cent of net sales in 1940, dipped to a low of 0·59 per cent of net sales in 1943.

The Santa Monica plant as it appeared in May 1938. Aircraft on the apron include Dolphin, B-18, DC-3 and TBD-1. (*MDC*)

19

In August 1937, the Douglas Aircraft Company acquired the remaining 49 per cent of the shares of the Northrop Corporation—of which Douglas had owned 51 per cent of the stock since January 1932—and began operating the facilities of its former subsidiary as the El Segundo Division. While the history of the Northrop Corporation and the aircraft it built are described in the following chapter, the design and production of the El Segundo Division is included here. The Douglas engineering teams in Santa Monica and El Segundo were responsible during the late thirties for a series of new designs. Of these designs, the Douglas DF, DC-4 (DC-4E), DC-5 and B-23 had only limited success while the XB-19, of which only one example was built, later made a significant contribution to the design of large aircraft in the United States. More successful was the B-18 which, first delivered in its production form in February 1937, became the standard heavy bomber of the Army Air Corps until replaced by the Boeing B-17. Even more successful were two designs stemming from the El Segundo team, the SBD—first delivered to the US Marine Corps in June 1940—and the DB-7/A-20 series—first delivered to France in late 1939. These last two types, together with the C-54 (DC-4) and A-26 series, became—with the military variants of the DC-3, the Boeing-designed B-17 and the Consolidated-designed B-24—the major types of aircraft produced by Douglas during the war years.

Assembly line in the Santa Monica plant during production of the initial batch of B-18As. (*USAF*)

Northrop Corporation

Three years younger than Donald Douglas, John Knudsen Northrop was born in Newark, New Jersey, in 1895 and went to California with his parents in 1904. This move was to have a profound effect on his professional career as he later steadfastly refused to work in another state and it was this which in 1932 led to his association with Douglas to form the Northrop Corporation.

First working with the Loughead (later changed to Lockheed) brothers in Santa Barbara, California, beginning in 1916, John K. Northrop designed for them the F-1, a ten-seat flying-boat of large dimensions, and the S-1, a two-seat sports aircraft. However, in 1921 the Loughead brothers had to fold up their operations and, eventually, John Northrop found his way to the Douglas Company where he was employed from 1923 to 1926 and where his first assignment was to work on the engineering of the World Cruiser. This first association with Douglas came to an end in 1926 when the Lockheed team was re-constituted. Joining Lockheed as chief engineer, Northrop was then responsible, with the assistance of 'Gerry' Vultee, for the design of the Lockheed Vega, a single-engined transport aircraft of exceptionally clean design for the period. A little over a year later Northrop again left the employ of Lockheed and formed his own company, the Avion Corporation, to experiment with the design of flying wing aircraft and develop his multi-cellular all-metal construction technique. However, lacking sufficient capital to continue on its own, the Avion Corporation was absorbed in 1929 by the United Aircraft & Transport Corporation and operated until 1931 as the Northrop Aircraft Corporation, a division of UA & T Corp.

During this period Northrop designed the Alpha, a single-engined passenger- and mail-carrying aircraft of all-metal construction with open cockpit behind an enclosed cabin, and the Beta, a small two-seat all-metal sports aircraft. However, in September 1931 the United Aircraft & Transport Corporation decided to consolidate its two subsidiaries—the Northrop Aircraft Corporation and Stearman Aircraft—into a single corporate entity and to centre all the operations of the enlarged company in Wichita, Kansas. Desirous of remaining in California, John Northrop had provided in his contract with UA & T Corp a clause which released him if his company should be moved away. Accordingly, he decided to try once again to form a new company in California. With the assistance of his friend and former employer, Donald Douglas, John Northrop achieved his goal.

The Northrop Corporation was formed in January 1932 with the Douglas Aircraft Company holding 51 per cent of the stock and with John K. Northrop as its President. To house the new company Douglas initially obtained the use of facilities located alongside Mines Field (now Los Angeles International Airport) in Inglewood, California. There the fledgling Northrop Corporation undertook the design and construction of two developments of the Northrop/Stearman Alpha series, the Gamma and the Delta. Both were single-engined all-metal aircraft which were among the first types to be fitted with split flaps and made use of Northrop's own multi-cellular construction techniques. While only sixty Gammas were built, these aeroplanes appeared in many versions fulfilling many missions including record breaking, mail carriage, polar exploration, advanced training, light bombing, and engine testing. Most famous of all Gammas was the Gamma 2B, the first aircraft delivered in 1932 by the Northrop Corporation, with which the noted explorer Lincoln Ellsworth made a spectacular flight across Antarctica in November–December 1935. Also spectacular were the record flights made by Frank Hawks, first using the Gamma 2A and later the Gamma 2C. The Gamma design also played a significant yet less glamorous role as 49 aircraft were completed by Northrop as light bombers for the Chinese Nationalist Government, a long-time Douglas customer, and the type was developed into the A-17 series of attack aircraft for the Army Air Corps.

The Northrop Gamma 2B of Lincoln Ellsworth, during its trans-Antarctic flight.
(*NA & SM*)

Production of the Delta, the other design undertaken by the Northrop Corporation during 1932, was even more limited as sales of this passenger transport were impeded by the decision of the Civil Aeronautics Authority to forbid the use of single-engined aircraft on scheduled passenger flights. Consequently, with the exception of four aircraft delivered to airlines and one to the US Coast Guard, all Deltas were sold as luxury private transports. However, the type was developed by Canadian Vickers into a general reconnaissance bomber while one of the original Northrop-built Deltas was impressed into the Royal Australian Air Force as a transport.

Although it did not achieve success, the next type of aeroplane designed by the Douglas subsidiary, the XFT-1 experimental naval fighter, marked the beginning of the association between the Northrop Corporation and the US Armed Forces, particularly the US Navy. Blessed with better luck was the XBT-1, prototype of a series of carrier-borne bombers which culminated in the SBD Dauntless, and the A-17 series of attack bombers which, along with its 8A export versions, were derived from the Northrop 2F (XA-16), itself a development of the basic Gamma design. During this

Northrop A-17s in production at Mines Field, Los Angeles. The aircraft had blue fuselages and yellow wing and tail surfaces. (*USAF*)

period several other designs were begun but these types either failed to go into production or were produced in quantities only after the Northrop Corporation had been re-organized into the El Segundo Division of the Douglas Aircraft Company.

While production of the first series of one hundred A-17As for the Army Air Corps was under way, the Northrop Corporation began to experience serious labour problems and the War Department refused to accept any more Northrop-built aircraft until the problems were resolved. In an attempt to correct this situation Douglas decided to acquire the remaining 49 per cent of the stock of the Northrop Corporation and this was done on 5 April, 1937. Continuing labour troubles led to an employee strike in disregard of a wages agreement signed with the Committee of Industrial Organization in the previous March and forced Douglas to dissolve the Northrop Corporation on 8 September, 1937. Soon after work was resumed under the direct aegis of the Douglas Aircraft Company, the facilities of the Northrop Corporation being operated from then on as the El Segundo Division of Douglas. Meanwhile, Jack Northrop went on to form a new independent company, Northrop Aircraft Inc, which began operation in 1939.

By the time the Northrop Corporation was dissolved a total of only 278 aircraft had been delivered by this subsidiary of Douglas. More significant for the future of the Douglas Aircraft Company were the contributions made by Northrop in terms of technical experience—the multi-cellular construction method contributing greatly to the reputation of longevity and reliability earned by the DC series of commercial transports—and design skill—the team led by Edward A. Heinemann in the El Segundo Division developing for Douglas an uninterrupted series of very successful carrier-borne bombers beginning with the BT-1 and culminating with the A-4 Skyhawk.

Douglas Aircraft Company Inc
During World War II

On 30 November, 1939, the war in Europe was already in its third month, but for the Douglas Aircraft Company, which was just completing its eleventh and so far most profitable year (a net income of $2,884,197 was realized during the period 1 December, 1938, to 30 November, 1939), the future appeared full of promise. A record backlog of $68,987,717 had been secured (since the inception of the Douglas Aircraft Company the year-end backlog had steadily increased from $2,341,338 in 1929 to $31,256,498 in 1937 and stood at $23,500,926 on 30 November, 1938) and this substantial order book was broken down as follows: 57·9 per cent represented military export orders, 34·6 per cent orders placed by the War and Navy Departments, and 7·5 from domestic and foreign civil customers.

At that time DC-2s and DC-3s were used by all major airlines in the United States and by eighteen foreign airlines, and Douglas had the following types in full production: DC-3 (with the exception of the single C-41A, military versions of the DC-3 were yet to be ordered), DC-5 in civil and military versions, 8A and DB-7 bombers for export, A-20 and B-23 bombers for the Air Corps and SBD dive-bombers for the Navy and the Marine Corps, while new designs under construction included the DC-4 four-engined transport and the very large XB-19 bomber. With the world situation worsening rapidly, production and development of these aircraft were soon accelerated as massive orders were placed by the US Armed Forces and it soon became obvious that existing facilities would soon become inadequate to meet wartime requirements of the US Government and its Allies.

An impressive row of SBD-4 fuselages in the El Segundo plant on 1 January, 1943. (*MDC*)

24

To assist in solving this problem which affected not only Douglas but also most other manufacturers of aircraft and related equipment—on 16 May, 1940, President Roosevelt had called for the production of 50,000 aircraft a year in the United States—the US Government implemented its Emergency Plant Facilities programme which provided that construction of new facilities would be financed by the manufacturers themselves with the Government reimbursing them over a period of five years and then assuming title to the facilities. By this method the Government did not have to face an immediate and massive outlay of funds while the manufacturers were effectively relieved from assuming the risk of possession of excess factory space after the war. To take advantage of this programme Douglas organized a wholly-owned subsidiary, Western Land Improvement Co, which undertook the construction of a new plant in Long Beach, adjacent to the Long Beach Municipal Airport.

While construction of the Long Beach plant was proceeding apace the Douglas Aircraft Company began to receive several major production orders covering military versions of the DC-3 and additional A-20 aircraft to be produced in both the Santa Monica and Long Beach plants, while production of SBDs in the El Segundo plant was accelerated. Finally in November 1941 the Long Beach plant was ready to begin operation and the first aircraft assembled there, a C-47-DL,* was delivered on 23 December, 1941, sixteen days after the United States had been forced into the war. During the next three and a half years, the Long Beach plant was the scene of feverish activities and the following types were produced: C-47-DL, C-47A-DL, C-47B-DL, A-20B-DL, A-26B-DL, A-26C-DL, B17F-DL and B-17G-DL. In accordance with the terms of the Emergency Plant Facilities programme, ownership of the Long Beach plant was transferred in 1944 from the Douglas Aircraft Company to the US Government, but Douglas, leasing it back, continued using it throughout the war. Eventually, Douglas re-acquired title to parts of it in November 1946.

Meanwhile Douglas's main plant in Santa Monica continued to house most of the company's design facilities and contributed to the overall war effort by producing large numbers of C-47s and other DC-3 military variants, C-54s and A-20s. New designs undertaken at Santa Monica during the war included the novel XB-42 and XB-43 bombers and the XC-112 (DC-6 prototype) and C-74 (construction of which was undertaken in Long Beach). Similarly, design and production at the other Douglas pre-war plant, the El Segundo Division, proceeded at an accelerated pace with production centring on the SBD carrier-borne bombers. Also built in El Segundo during the war were the three prototypes for the A-26 series and some XSB2D-1s, XTB2D-1s, BTD-1s, XBTD-2s

---

*The use of two letters to identify the manufacturer and the factory was introduced at that time by the War Department; the plants of the Douglas Aircraft Company were assigned the following codes: DL, Long Beach; DO, Santa Monica; DE, El Segundo; DC, Chicago; DK, Oklahoma City; and DT, Tulsa.

The third C-54-DO (41-20139), one of the aircraft originally ordered as a commercial DC-4, as it appeared on 17 May, 1942, in USAAF markings. (*USAF*)

and XBT2D-1s (prototypes of the AD Skyraider series) while design work on the D-558-1 jet-powered research aircraft was begun.

Impressive as it was, the combined production capability of the Santa Monica, El Segundo and Long Beach plants was still insufficient to meet the urgent needs of the Allied forces, and Douglas, which had become the main supplier of transports for the Allies, had to turn to the US Government to obtain additional facilities. Already the Government had taken action to provide for production of war materiel by organizing, initially to supplement but eventually to supplant the Emergency Plant Facilities programme, the Reconstruction Finance Corporation. According to this scheme, the Defense Plant Corporation, a subsidiary of the Reconstruction Finance Corporation, undertook the construction of a series of factories which were to be leased to manufacturing companies. At the termination of the lease, titles for these were either to remain in the hands of the Reconstruction Finance Corporation, be transferred to the War or Navy Department, or sold to private companies. Taking advantage of this programme Douglas obtained leases on facilities in Chicago, Oklahoma City and Tulsa.

Used exclusively to supplement the Santa Monica plant in the production of Skymasters, the plant located in Chicago delivered the first of 655 C-54s on 1 October, 1943. Likewise the Oklahoma City plant was used solely for the production of military variants (C-47 and C-117) of the DC-3 series. On the other hand the Tulsa plant, also located in Oklahoma, which initially had been intended for Douglas production of B-24 Liberators assembled from components manufactured in Willow Run, Michigan, by the Ford Motor Company, was used for producing three types of aircraft. In addition to B-24 four-engined bombers, the Tulsa plant was used to build A-26 twin-engined attack bombers and A-24 single-engined attack bombers.

At the end of the war the Douglas Aircraft Company was able to boast of a brilliant record. In terms of airframe weight and based on the period from

26

1 January, 1940, to 31 December, 1944, the company could claim to be the largest aircraft manufacturer in the United States with total production representing 306,573,000 lb or 15·3 per cent of the industry's total. In terms of number of aircraft built between 1 July, 1940, and 31 August, 1945, Douglas, with 30,980 aircraft delivered, ranked second behind North American which had produced 41,188 aircraft. During this period total production of aircraft by Douglas was broken down by plants as follows:

	Number of aircraft	Percentage of total
Long Beach	9,439	30·5
Santa Monica	7,309	23·6
El Segundo	5,414	17·5
Oklahoma City	5,319	17·2
Tulsa	2,870	9·2
Chicago	629	2·0

In terms of financial results the company also had good reason to be satisfied as the much lower profit margin on wartime government contracts had been partially offset by the substantially increased volume of production. During the fiscal years 1940 and up to the end of 1944 net sales consistently increased, from $60,970,774 to $1,061,407,485, while net income achieved a peak of $18,176,971 in 1941 but dropped to $5,952,257 in 1943. Results for the fiscal year 1945 (net sales of $744,682,664 and net income of $8,955,754) reflected the cancellation of many contracts at the end of the war.

The Chicago plant where 655 C-54-DCs were built between 1943 and 1945.
(*MDC*)

27

Following VJ-Day the leases on the Chicago, Oklahoma City and Tulsa plants were allowed to expire as all their production orders were cancelled by the US Government but Douglas continued to lease some in Long Beach as orders for the C-74 transport made their use desirable. Eventually, in November 1946, Douglas purchased the major part of the Long Beach plant. Meanwhile, most post-war operations were concentrated in the company's own facilities in Santa Monica and El Segundo.

Destruction of much surface and maritime transport material and factories in many parts of the world during the war, coupled with the significantly increased capability—notably as regards overwater operations—achieved by air transport during the conflict, represented a tremendous potential for the world's airlines which thus needed a large number of aircraft with which to rebuild their fleets. To capture this market British manufacturers, benefiting from the forward planning of the Brabazon Committee, and American manufacturers competed fiercely for orders. However, the reputation and leadership which Douglas had achieved before the war as the major supplier of civil transports (DC-2s and DC-3s) and during the war as prime producer of military transports (C-47 variants and C-54s) placed the company in a most favourable position to supply the pressing needs of the world's airlines.

In this market Douglas had to face two major sources of competition. The first, and principal one in terms of number of aircraft, stemmed from its own successes as large numbers of C-54s, C-47s and other military variants of the DC-3 series became available as surplus following the end of the war when the US Armed Forces were considerably reduced and when many lend-lease aircraft were returned or disposed of abroad. Thus, a substantial number of C-54s and military versions of the DC-3 were converted for airline use, both by specialized companies and by Douglas itself, while Douglas was only able to sell 28 new DC-3Ds and 79 new DC-4s during the immediate post-war years. Douglas's other major competitor was its rival from across town, the Lockheed Aircraft Corporation, which on 9 January, 1943, had first flown its XC-69, the military prototype of the Constellation series. For Douglas the Constellation represented a major threat as it was not only fitted with a pressurized cabin which the DC-4 lacked but was also substantially faster (cruising speed of 300 mph EAS versus 250 mph EAS for the DC-4) and carried a thirty per cent heavier payload over longer distances.

While Douglas could do little to compete against its own surplus aircraft—an attempt at modernizing the DC-3 as the Super DC-3 failed to succeed in the civil market—the company met the competition of the Lockheed Constellation head on with its DC-6 series. The prototype for this series, the XC-112 ordered by the Army Air Forces, made its first flight on 15 February, 1946, when the Constellation was entering airline service with Pan American Airways and TWA. However, as the DC-6 was a progressive development of the DC-4/C-54 series, Douglas was able to deliver the first DC-6s to American Airlines and United Air Lines on 24 November, 1946, and the type entered service with both airlines on 27 April, 1947. It then appeared that Douglas would be able to compete successfully with Lockheed. Unfortunately, the DC-6 had to be taken out of service in November 1947. After suitable modifications had been devised, the cost of which was borne by Douglas, the DC-6 was returned to service in March 1948 and the Lockheed/Douglas competition characterized the market for commercial four-engined transports during the late forties and fifties. Douglas met all increases in range and payload offered by Lockheed's Constellation/Super Constellation/L-1649A series with similar and often superior increases in payload and range of the DC-6 and DC-7 series. In the process, Douglas developed the DC-6 into the DC-6A, DC-6B, DC-7, DC-7B and DC-7C series of which, by late 1958, a grand total of 1,042 was produced including C-118 and R6D military transport versions. Lockheed, meanwhile, produced a total of 899 Constellation/Super Constellation/L-1649A aircraft for the civil and military markets. Thus, even excluding the DC-4s and civil conversions of C-54s sold to the airlines Douglas was able to claim victory in the long battle for the production of four-reciprocating engine transports. More significant even than the number of aircraft produced was the fact that Douglas could justly claim with the DC-6B to have built the most economical transport aircraft of the piston era.

The YC-124-DL (42-65406), modified from the fifth C-74 airframe, at Long Beach in November 1949. (*USAF*)

In the military market the second half of the forties was a lean period for Douglas with quantity production being limited to three types: the AD Skyraider carrier-borne attack aircraft and the C-74 and C-124 transport aircraft. As regards new developments, work on current prototypes and new projects was limited to the D-558-1, D-558-2 and X-3 research aircraft, the F3D Skyknight naval night fighter, the F4D Skyray carrier-borne interceptor, the A2D Skyshark turbine-powered carrier-borne attack aircraft and the A3D Skywarrior twin-jet carrier-borne bomber. However, following the outbreak of hostilities in Korea in 1950 Douglas again received orders for large quantities of military aircraft.

In terms of financial results the post-war period was also rather difficult, with total sales dropping from $744,682,664 in 1945 to an average of less than $120,000,000 for the period 1946–49 and total net income for these four years—including a loss of $2,140,579 in 1947, the first loss experienced by the Douglas Aircraft Company—reached only $11,385,849 or an average of only $2,846,462 per year. These financial results were also reflected in the small number of aircraft delivered during this period (127 aircraft during 1946, the smallest number since 1933) and by the low employment figure (an average of 25,000 employees worked for Douglas during the late forties).

On 25 June, 1950, a year after US troops had been withdrawn from Korea, the forces of the Democratic People's Republic of Korea invaded South Korea in an effort to unify the country under communist control and the US Government reacted swiftly. Among the first types of aircraft used in Korea by the American forces were a number of World War II Douglas veterans: the B-26 (previously A-26) bomber and the C-47 and C-54 transports and during the next three years these aircraft were joined in

The first D-558-1 Skystreak (BuNo 37970) at Muroc Dry Lake, California.
(*NA & SM*)

30

Douglas F4D-1 Skyray of VMF-115 in March 1957. (*USMC*)

action by the following Douglas-built aircraft: AD Skyraiders, C-74s, C-117s, C-118s, C-124s and F3D Skyknights. On the production scene the combined effects of the Korean War and of the Cold War resulted in increased production orders for the AD Skyraider, the A3D Skywarrior, the F4D Skyray and the C-124 Globemaster, while orders were placed for Douglas's own new designs, the B-66 Destroyer and the A4D Skyhawk, and for the Boeing-designed B-47 jet bomber which was also to be built by Douglas. To fulfil these orders production rates were stepped up at the Santa Monica plant, where the C-118s were built, at the El Segundo plant, where F3Ds, F4Ds, ADs, A3Ds and A4Ds were produced, and at the Long Beach plant, where B-66s and C-124s were built. In addition, the Government-owned plant in Tulsa was re-activated for use by Douglas to produce B-66 and B-47 bombers for the USAF.

As a result of increased military aircraft production and continued strong demand for the DC-6 and DC-7 commercial transports in the first half of the fifties, Douglas experienced a period of steady financial growth with net income reaching $18,586,305 in 1953 and $36,156,861 in 1954 (the previous high was $18,176,971 achieved in 1941) while employment grew steadily (employees at the end of the fiscal years 1950, 1952 and 1954 were respectively, 25,500, 62,200 and 71,900). Having accumulated a record backlog of $2,213,833,000 (of which $1,983,109,000 or 89·6 per cent represented military orders) by 30 November, 1953, Douglas was able to continue showing encouraging financial results (a next to record-high net income of $33,202,304 was realized in 1956 while net sales set an all-time record of $1,209,920,338 in 1958) for a number of years after the end of the Korean War. However, the inability of the company to secure production orders for new types of military aircraft and the initial lack of decision as regards Douglas's entry into the commercial jet era were to lead to new difficulties and, eventually, to the demise of the Douglas Aircraft Company.

Aerial view of the Long Beach plant in the 1960s. To the right is one of the buildings specially erected to house the DC-8, and later DC-9 and DC-10, lines whilst across Lakewood Boulevard can be seen the administrative tower and World War II-vintage manufacturing halls. (*MDC*)

The award on 13 September, 1952, of a contract for the development of the XA4D-1 marked the last time that Douglas was able to secure an order leading to quantity production for a new type for the US Navy and Marine Corps, as a later development contract for the F5D-1 Skylancer led to the construction of only four prototypes while the development contract for the F6D-1 Misseleer was cancelled before completion of a single prototype. As, meanwhile, production of the other types built by the El Segundo Division, the F3D Skyknight, the AD Skyraider, the F4D Skyray and the A3D Skywarrior were respectively completed in October 1953, March 1957, December 1958 and January 1961, the company was forced in 1962 to transfer production of the Skyhawk to the Long Beach plant (with final

The Tulsa plant in the 1950s with some B-47E-DTs on the flight ramp. (*MDC*)

32

assembly and testing in Palmdale, California, in Government-owned facilities) and to close its El Segundo plant.

Douglas faired little better with the USAF as anticipated orders for a turbine-powered tanker version of the C-124 failed to materialize and the XC-132 programme was cancelled. Thus Douglas received its last Air Force contract for a new type (the C-9A cannot be regarded as a new type but rather as a version of the existing DC-9-30CF) on 5 May, 1954, when the C-133 Cargomaster was first ordered. However, the Tulsa plant was retained as modification contracts were received covering the Boeing-designed B-47, B-52 and C-135 and because Douglas also used this plant to manufacture components for its commercial transports.

The third D-558-2 Skyrocket (BuNo 37975) being checked at Edwards AFB. It is seen with a screen in front of the fuselage intake for the J34 turbojet. (*Aero Digest*)

More than five years after the Germans had flown the world's first turbojet-augmented aircraft (the Heinkel He 118 V2 fitted with an HeS 3A beneath the fuselage) Douglas flew its first aircraft partially powered by a turbojet (two XBTD-2s were fitted with a Westinghouse 19A turbojet mounted obliquely in their rear fuselage and supplementing their nose-mounted Wright R-3350-14s). This historic event was followed in May 1946—more than 3½ years after Bell had flown its XP-59A, the first US jet-powered fighter aircraft—by the first flight of the Douglas XB-43, the first US jet-powered bomber, and in March 1948 by the first flight of the XF3D-1, the prototype of the first jet-powered Douglas aircraft to be put into quantity production. Meanwhile Douglas also designed three types of high-speed research aircraft, the jet-powered D-558-1 and X-3 and the rocket-powered D-558-2 which, on 21 November, 1953, became the world's first aircraft to exceed Mach 2·0. Yet, in spite of these achievements and of the fact that its position as the world's prime supplier of commercial transports was being challenged by the development in Britain of the de Havilland Comet (first flown on 27 July, 1949), the company remained cool towards the idea of developing a turbojet-powered airliner. Repeatedly Donald Douglas and his Vice President for Engineering, Arthur Raymond, pronounced themselves in favour of first developing propeller-turbine powered aircraft. To this effect, several design studies of propeller-turbine powered developments of the DC-6, DC-7 and C-74 series were made while development of jet-powered transports was pursued as a low-key effort.

In April 1954, following a series of accidents, the commercial operation of Comet Is was suspended and Douglas's prudence appeared justified. However, in April 1952, the Boeing Company had embarked on an ambitious private venture to develop a jet-powered aircraft capable of fulfilling both the role of tanker aircraft for the USAF and of commercial passenger transport aircraft. Following the successful first flight of the Boeing 367-80 on 15 July, 1954, the airlines began to show considerable interest in acquiring jet transports, and Douglas, which since 1952 had been working more actively on a number of design studies, had no other choice but to throw itself wholeheartedly into a new competitive battle. These efforts, made public in June 1955 when Douglas announced itself ready to enter the jet transport field, were rewarded on 25 October of that year when Pan American World Airways announced an initial order for twenty-five DC-8s and for only twenty of the competitive Boeing 707. In fact the Douglas–Boeing competition appeared to initially turn in favour of the California-based company; for the first eleven months following Pan American's historic order, the DC-8 order book was ahead of the 707's.

This success, however, was achieved at a heavy price in terms of Douglas financial resources as sales price for the DC-8 had to be kept low due to Boeing's strenuous efforts to enter the commercial market and due to the need for Douglas to build new facilities, as those available at Santa Monica—where so far all production of commercial aircraft had been centred—were inadequate (runway too short and major noise disturbance at an airfield surrounded by residential areas). Capitalizing on its existing facilities at Long Beach and on the willingness of the municipality to enlarge its airfield, Douglas announced in April 1956 the construction of new facilities on a 55-acre site adjacent to the existing plant. Intended initially only to house the DC-8 production line, these new facilities were anticipated to cost some $19,000,000 when fitted with the necessary machinery and equipment, but the actual cost was much higher as in 1957 alone the company spent $30,800,000 (an amount just exceeding the net income of $30,665,252 realized during the year) for property, plant and equipment. Meanwhile, Boeing had been authorized to produce KC-135 military tankers on the same line as the 707s and was thus able indirectly to spread part of the commercial cost overruns on the military contracts.

While Douglas and Boeing were developing their commercial jets, the world's airlines had been experiencing a period of rapid growth with increases in passenger-miles of 17·3 per cent in 1955, 16·4 per cent in 1956 and 14·7 per cent in 1957 while the economy of the Western nations was progressing rapidly. However, when the Boeing 707-120 and Douglas DC-8-10 entered service in October 1958 and September 1959, respectively, airline traffic had slumped (passenger miles growth rate was only 4·9 per cent in 1959) and follow-on orders for 707s and DC-8s did not reach their anticipated rate. At the same time the DC-8 initially failed to achieve its guaranteed range, the same problem also affecting the Bocing 707, and Douglas had to spend further funds to correct this deficiency. These problems resulted in a sharp reduction in DC-8 sales which dropped from 73 in 1955, to 40 in 1956, 10 in 1957, 11 in 1958, 18 in 1959 (the year during which the aircraft entered service and thus a period when, normally, new commercial aircraft types obtain substantial sales) and only three in 1960. Meanwhile, Douglas's net income kept dropping from the $33,202,304 achieved in 1956 (the company's second highest profit figure) to $16,847,028 in 1958—the year during which the company recorded its all-time net sales record of $1,209,920,338—and eventually in 1959 Douglas recorded its second net loss ($33,822,229). The following year saw Douglas recording a net loss of $19,429,437 with profitability being again achieved in 1961 when the company obtained a net income of $5,956,909.

The old and the new: a DC-8-11 (N804E) and a DC-3-201G (N15849, ex C-49D 41-7720) of Delta Air Lines. (*Delta Air Lines*)

The losses suffered in 1959 and 1960 together with disappointing DC-8 sales (by the end of 1961 the company had sold 176 DC-8s while Boeing had sold 320 Model 707s and 720s), prevented the company from being able to develop other commercial jetliners with which to complement the DC-8 line. However, to counter Boeing which had already developed the 720 series from the 707 and was known to be working on a smaller medium-range jet transport, Douglas announced in 1960 an agreement with Sud-Aviation of France which gave the company the sales rights and product support responsibilities for the Caravelle twin-jet transport in the Western Hemisphere, Great Britain, Australia and large portions of Africa, Asia and the Middle East. Douglas also obtained an option to manufacture Caravelles in the United States should sales justify this operation. Already in February 1960 Sud-Aviation had been able to sell 20 Caravelles to United Air Lines, a long-time Douglas customer, and with the assistance of

35

Douglas obtained from TWA a contract for 20 Caravelles in September 1961. By that time, however, Boeing had launched its 727 programme—initial orders for 40 aircraft each had been announced in December 1960 by Eastern Air Lines and United Air Lines—and TWA joined the 727 customers in March 1962 when it ordered ten aircraft of this type. Three months later TWA cancelled its Caravelle order thus sounding the end of the French aircraft's inroad into the US market. Soon the Douglas–Sud-Aviation agreement was cancelled and Douglas was effectively locked out from the very profitable medium-range transport market (by mid-1977 the Boeing Company, with only nominal competition from the Hawker Siddeley Trident to contend with, had sold over 1,461 Model 727s).

While working with Sud-Aviation to sell Caravelles, Douglas had kept its eyes on the potential market for short-range jet aircraft and had made a series of design studies for aircraft of this type. Eventually in February 1963, as a net profit of $10,205,248 had been realized during 1962, the management authorized the start of detailed engineering work on the design of a twin-jet transport and in May of the same year the sale of fifteen DC-9s to Delta Air Lines was announced. Unbeknown to all at that time, this was the last type of aircraft developed solely by the Douglas Aircraft Company. Partially due to the slow initial rate of sales (only 58 DC-9s had been sold by the time the first aircraft made its maiden flight at Long Beach on 25 February, 1965) and partially due to a management failure to believe market estimates, Douglas planned on producing only about 500 DC-9s over a ten-year period. However, following its first flight, the DC-9 obtained much success and in 1965 alone 170 aircraft were sold while by the end of 1966 total sales reached 424 aircraft. To produce these aircraft Douglas had conceived an original risk-sharing programme with other manufacturers involving an intricate network of plants: the nose of the aircraft was built in Santa Monica, the wing and tail assemblies by de Havilland of Canada, fuselage panels by Aerfer in Italy and other components were manufactured in various parts of the United States. The Long Beach plant was responsible for the production of the fuselage, final assembly—this operation taking place on a single assembly line producing jointly DC-8s and DC-9s—and testing of the DC-9.

As the DC-9 was in the midst of its flight trial programme Douglas announced in April 1965 the development of a series of stretched versions of the DC-8 offering either substantially increased payload (Series 61 and 63) or much longer range (Series 62). All three versions of the Super DC-8 achieved considerable success and soon the joint DC-8/DC-9 production line proved inadequate to achieve a delivery rate compatible with the substantial order book obtained and the company was forced into an urgent and ill-planned expansion programme.

During 1965 Douglas was producing DC-8s and DC-9s for commercial customers and A-4 Skyhawks for the Armed Forces while a steady volume of modifications was handled in the Tulsa plant. Douglas, which had entered the missile age at the beginning of World War II when the beam-

The parallel final assembly lines for the DC-8 and DC-9 at the Long Beach plant. (*MDC*)

guided Roc I air-to-surface missile had been conceived, also continued to be very active in this field. While details of the design and production of missiles fall outside the scope of this book, mention should be made here of some of the most significant types of missiles and space launchers developed by Douglas. These included the Nike Ajax, Nike Hercules and Nike Zeus surface-to-air missiles, the Sparrow and nuclear-armed Genie air-to-air missiles, the Roc and Skybolt air-to-surface missiles, the Honest John and Thor surface-to-surface missiles, and the Thor, Delta and Saturn S-IV/S-IVB launch vehicles. Most of the company's missile and space activities were centred in a new plant in Huntington Beach, California, where during 1965 a design team was able to win for Douglas an Air Force contract—unfortunately, later cancelled when the Department of Defense had to re-allocate funds to support operations in Southeast Asia—for the MOL (Manned Orbiting Laboratory). While Douglas was fortunate, initially at least, to win the MOL contract it lost to Lockheed the hard-fought competition for the very big C-5A military cargo aircraft.

The loss of the C-5A contract, on which the company depended to restore its position as one of the major manufacturers of military aircraft, was followed by Douglas's failure to match Boeing's impetus in developing a very large jet based on the technology acquired during the C-5A competition. Then, in an ill-conceived effort to outpace Boeing and their 747, Douglas hurriedly marketed a double-deck, 650-seat transport but the projected aircraft failed to gain airline acceptance on account of its excessive capacity. The back to back losses to the Lockheed C-5A and Boeing 747 proved for Douglas to be the last straw.

During the annual stockholders' meeting in April 1966, just days before Boeing announced the first order for its 747, an official of the Douglas Aircraft Company confidently stated that the company was 'in one of the most satisfactory phases of its history'. However, faced with rising costs, labour shortages, delays in delivery by key suppliers and the urgent need to expand production facilities—the joint DC-8/DC-9 production line at Long Beach was replaced by a single DC-8 line and two parallel DC-9 lines while a new subsidiary, Douglas Aircraft Company of Canada, had to assume responsibility for the production of wing and tail assemblies for the DC-9 in Canada and to that effect leased and operated parts of the de Havilland plant at Malton, Ontario, from 1 December, 1965—Douglas lost control of its costs. Earnings which had been expected to reach about $20,000,000 during the fiscal year 1966 gave place to a deficit, after tax credits, of $27,560,067. Having a substantial backlog of orders, the company hoped to obtain sufficient additional working capital and, while attempts were made to raise $50 million of equity capital, Douglas negotiated with its bankers for an increase in its line of credit. On the banker's advice Douglas then approached the Wall Street firm of Lazard Frères to obtain assistance in finding a solution to the problems.

Lazard Frères set up headquarters in Santa Monica to assist in sorting out various offers of financial assistance and direct merger. Eventually on 9 December, 1966, Lazard Frères made clear that, in their opinion, a merger was necessary and that what Douglas needed was not only capital but also new management. During the next few weeks merger offers were received from Sherman Fairchild, a dominant figure in both Fairchild Hiller and Fairchild Camera, General Dynamics, Martin Marietta, McDonnell, North American Aviation and Signal Oil & Gas.

Among these offers, that made by McDonnell—which already in January 1963 had attempted to merge with Douglas by offering one-half share of McDonnell stock for each share of Douglas stock and which at the time owned 300,000 shares of Douglas common stock—was unanimously recommended on 13 January, 1967, by the joint negotiating committee set up by Douglas and Lazard Frères to advise the Board of Directors of the ailing Santa Monica firm. The offer made by the McDonnell Company consisted of the immediate purchase for $68,700,000 of 1·5 million of new Douglas common shares and then, should the proposed merger be approved by the Justice Department, all shares of Douglas stock would be exchanged for $1\frac{3}{4}$ shares of McDonnell common stock.

Government approval followed swiftly as continuation of operations by Douglas was important to sustain the US war effort in Vietnam and, on 28 April, 1967, the Douglas Aircraft Company Inc gave place to the McDonnell Douglas Corporation. An important page in the history of the American aviation industry had been turned but with it yet another Douglas commercial aircraft—the DC-10 which was in danger of becoming stillborn—was saved to carry on the DC tradition. The story of the McDonnell Douglas Corporation since 1967 is dealt with in Volume II.

Annual Aircraft Deliveries, Net Sales and Net Income
Douglas, 1922 to 1966

Fiscal Year	Number of aircraft delivered	Net Sales	Net Income
1922	6	$130,890	N.A.
1923	33	745,028	N.A.
1924	11	429,087	$9,116
1925	11	358,804	47,838
1926	120	1,662,724	375,870
1927	98	1,970,961	356,027
1928	97	1,863,502	415,089*
1929	134	2,546,025	403,364
1930	189	4,088,595	689,850
1931	245	3,825,270	549,331
1932	70	2,347,569	145,953
1933	92	2,294,295	46,112
1934	142	7,526,705	38,753
1935	130	8,591,114	1,262,967
1936	228	10,087,371	976,342
1937	303	20,950,361	1,081,513
1938	410	28,347,474	2,147,392
1939	314	27,866,657	2,884,197
1940	579	60,970,774	10,831,971
1941	1,233	180,940,110	18,176,971
1942	3,416	489,781,985	9,229,620
1943	9,017	987,687,196	5,952,257
1944	11,598	1,061,407,485	7,685,227
1945	5,353	744,682,664	8,955,754
1946	127	106,720,701	2,180,522
1947	361	128,458,597	(2,140,579)
1948	270	118,581,847	5,829,206
1949	289	117,421,934	5,516,700
1950	246	129,892,551	7,214,440
1951	312	225,173,226	6,912,829
1952	755	522,619,409	10,792,285
1953	735	874,515,463	18,586,305
1954	840	915,216,705	36,156,861
1955	672	867,504,228	28,215,262
1956	677	1,073,515,406	33,202,304
1957	682	1,091,366,415	30,665,252
1958	652	1,209,920,338	16,847,028
1959	331	883,884,228	(33,822,229)
1960	374	1,174,041,175	(19,429,437)
1961	231	791,312,495	5,956,909
1962	222	749,920,706	10,205,248
1963	197	698,341,099	11,790,666
1964	199	650,127,609	13,694,988
1965	146	766,790,535	14,598,313
1966	190	1,048,011,571	(27,560,067)†

From 1922 to 1927, figures are for 1 January to 31 December; for the year 1928, figures are for 1 January to 30 November; from 1929 to 1965, figures are for 1 December to 30 November; for the year 1966, figures are for 1 December, 1965, to 31 December, 1966.
*Eleven months only.   †Thirteen months.

Painted as Western Air Express' first M-2, this is the rebuilt Douglas M-4 which was flown across the United States in 1977. (*Harry S. Gann, Jr/MDC*)

DC-6A (PP-LFA, s/n 45527) over the Los Angeles metropolis before being delivered to Lóide Aéreo in Brazil. (*MDC*)

NZ6210 and NZ6203, the third and tenth A-4Ks, in the markings of No.75 Squadron, RNZAF. (*Alain Crosnier*)

40

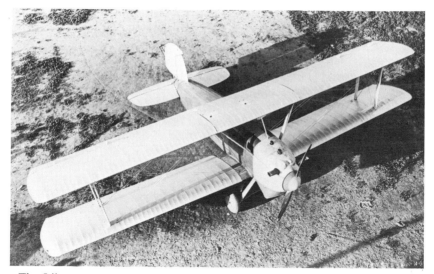

The Liberty-powered Cloudster, view showing the close cowling and fabric covering over the wings. (*Keystone*)

Davis-Douglas Cloudster

In June 1920 Donald Douglas, alone in the back room of a barber shop, began to design The Cloudster with which his partner, David R. Davis, intended to make the first nonstop flight between the west and east coasts of the United States. Within a month he was joined by five former colleagues from the Glenn L. Martin Co, George Borst, Ross Elkins, James Goodyear, Henry Guerin and George Strompl, and construction of the aeroplane was undertaken in the second-storey loft of the Koll Planing Mill in downtown Los Angeles. The Cloudster was a single-bay tractor biplane powered by a 400 hp Liberty water-cooled engine and had a fuselage of comparatively large diameter. The forward section of the wooden fuselage was covered with veneer panels and housed the engine and its radiator which was faired into the lower section of the fuselage. Two fuel tanks holding a total of 660 US gallons (2,498 litres) and a 50-US gallon (189-litre) oil tank, with which the aircraft had a design range of 2,800 miles (4,505 km), were housed behind the engine compartment. Behind these tanks and aft of the wings there was an open cockpit with side-by-side seating for a crew of two. The rear fuselage section, tail unit and wings were of wood with fabric covering.

As airframe components were being completed in the loft of the Koll Planing Mill, they were lowered to the ground down a lift shaft and the wings, tail unit and fuselage went separately by truck to the Goodyear Field where the aircraft was assembled in an airship hangar. Bearing the serial number 100—no lower serial number being assigned by Douglas—The Cloudster was completed in February 1921 and, shortly after, Eric Springer attempted a first flight from Goodyear Field. However, even though the aircraft was lightly loaded, this attempt almost ended tragically as the field was quite short and Springer had to ground loop the aircraft to prevent its complete destruction. Fortunately damage was slight and on 24 February, 1921, after the aircraft had been duly named The Cloudster, Eric Springer and David Davis took it on an uneventful first flight which lasted thirty minutes. A series of test flights was then made to determine the optimum cruise performance, and during this period, on 19 March, The Cloudster broke the Pacific Coast altitude record by climbing to 19,160 ft (5,840 m). Finally, in early June, Springer and Davis were satisfied that the aeroplane was ready for their attempt to cross the United States from March Field—an Air Service base near Riverside, California—to Curtiss Field, Long Island, New York.

To benefit from the maximum number of daylight hours whilst the aircraft was heavily laden with fuel and more difficult to handle, it was decided to take off at dawn, but for several days the flight had to be postponed due to the prevailing seasonal early morning fog at March Field. At last, on 27 June, 1921, the fog cleared early enough and Springer and Davis took off at 06·00 and The Cloudster headed southeast towards Yuma, Arizona. By noon on the same day the aircraft was 6,000 ft (1,830 m) above Tucson, Arizona, flying towards El Paso, Texas, which was reached at 15·45. The good luck, which had held so far, finally disappeared when the engine stopped because of a failure of the timing gear and forced Springer to make an emergency landing at Fort Bliss, Texas. Within three weeks temporary repairs had been made and the aircraft was flown back to March Field, where it was intended to fit a slightly modified Liberty engine for a new attempt. However, David Davis had lost his enthusiasm for the project and the small Douglas team was busy on their first military aeroplane, the DT series of torpedo bombers, and no serious effort was

The Cloudster in the configuration in which it was originally operated by T. Claude Ryan in 1925. (*Ryan*)

42

Final Cloudster configuration with cockpit moved forward and enclosed cabin for ten passengers. (*Ryan*)

made to ready the aircraft. Eventually, on 2 and 3 May, 1923, Lieutenants Kelly and Macready, in an Air Service Fokker T-2 (serial A.S.64233), completed the first successful flight across the United States by flying from New York to San Diego. The Cloudster had lost its raison d'être and Douglas was glad to find a buyer for it.

Shortly after the Fokker T-2's transcontinental flight, The Cloudster was acquired by two businessmen, T. Kinney and B. Brodsky, who intended to use it for flying passengers over Venice, California, a beach resort which they were actively promoting. For this the aircraft was extensively modified and normal accommodation for five passengers and a pilot was provided in three rows of open cockpits, with the first two cockpits replacing one of the fuselage fuel tanks. On occasions, the first two cockpits were used to each carry four passengers, thus raising the total number of people lifted by The Cloudster to ten. The scheme, however, did not achieve much success and The Cloudster was sold in 1925 to T. Claude Ryan in San Diego. With Ryan's Los Angeles-San Diego Air Line the aircraft was used to carry passengers on the route and to fly prospective real estate buyers to San Clemente Island off the coast of Southern California. However, the upper wings and propeller of the aircraft were damaged during a landing mishap.

While the upper wings were being repaired by Douglas, Ryan modernized the passenger accommodation of the aircraft. The crew's two-seat open cockpit was moved forward to a position just beneath the leading edge of the upper wings, and an enclosed cabin accommodating ten passengers—five passengers on each side of a central aisle—was fitted behind the pilot's cockpit. At the same time, the Liberty engine was equipped with a large exhaust stack carrying the exhaust fumes over the wings and away from the open cockpit. Later, Ryan further modified the engine installation by fitting a circular radiator around the propeller shaft and eliminating the original large propeller spinner and the radiator installation beneath the engine. After modification the aircraft was used to

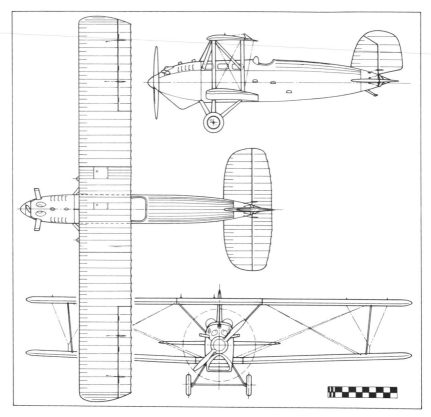

Douglas Cloudster before final modifications.

fly passengers between Los Angeles and San Diego on a scheduled basis. Later, following the demise of Ryan's Los Angeles-San Diego Air Line, The Cloudster was used for charter flights.

Since the ratification on 16 January, 1919, of the eighteenth article of amendment to the Constitution of the United States—which prohibited the manufacture, sale, or transport of intoxicating liquors—towns across the borders were making a profitable business by providing a way for Americans to quench their thirst. Noteworthy amongst these towns was Tijuana, in Mexico's Baja California, which depended on a mountain road linking it to Mexicali for its supply of beer. However, shortly before Christmas 1926 this road was washed out and the bars of Tijuana were in danger of losing a substantial Christmas bonus. To overcome this problem several aircraft were chartered and The Cloudster found itself involved in this unusual airlift.

As other Mexican roads had also been washed out by heavy rains The Cloudster was diverted from the beer airlift when a wealthy Chinese businessman chartered it for a flight from Tijuana to Ensenada, further down the coast of Baja California. Arriving over Ensenada after dusk, the pilot, J. J. Harrigan, had no alternative but to attempt a landing on the beach. Unfortunately, he miscalculated his approach and hit the water before managing to stop the aircraft. The pilot and passengers walked out unhurt but, during the night, rising tide and high waves caught the stranded Cloudster and it was totally destroyed.

Span 55 ft 11 in (17·04 m); length 36 ft 9 in (11·2 m); height 12 ft (3·66 m).
Loaded weight 9,600 lb (4,354 kg); power loading 24 lb/hp (10·9 kg/hp).
Maximum speed 120 mph (193 km/h); cruising speed 85 mph (137 km/h); absolute ceiling 19,160 ft (5,840 m); normal range 550 miles (885 km); maximum range 2,800 miles (4,505 km); maximum endurance 33 hr.

Douglas DT

Cdr Hunsaker—then chief of the US Navy's Bureau of Construction and Repairs Aircraft Division—shortly after learning that Donald Douglas, his former assistant at MIT, had moved to the West Coast, hinted in a letter to him that he hoped the Navy would help develop the aviation facilities on the Pacific Coast. Little did he know that less than ten months later his friend would submit on behalf of the Davis-Douglas Company the specification for a new type of single-engined torpedo seaplane. From this specification dated 1 February, 1921, would evolve the first Douglas production type, forging a strong relationship between Douglas and US Naval Aviation which has remained unbroken for more than half a century.

The DT-1 (A6031), displaying its folded wings for carrier storage.
(*US National Archives*)

45

The aircraft proposed by Douglas in February 1921 was similar to The Cloudster but, whereas the first Douglas had an all-wood structure, the torpedo bomber was of mixed construction. Built in three sections, the fuselage was of welded steel with aluminium covering on the forward and centre sections and fabric covering on the rear section, and the horizontal tail surfaces were also of welded steel with fabric covering. Wooden structure with fabric covering was used for the vertical surfaces and the wings which, for shipboard storage, could be folded horizontally alongside the fuselage. As originally proposed, the aircraft was a single-seater with the pilot in an open cockpit in the centre section of the fuselage behind the wing trailing edge. Twin wooden floats were to be fitted for operations from water and a 1,835 lb (832 kg) torpedo could be carried in a recess beneath the fuselage.

After completing the plans for his torpedo bomber, Donald Douglas went to Washington where he submitted his proposal to the Bureau of Construction and Repairs of the Navy Department. At that time the Navy wanted to test several types of torpedo-carrying aircraft before signing production contracts. Prototypes of the Curtiss CT-1, Stout ST-1, Fokker FT-1 and Blackburn Swift F were ordered for competitive evaluation whilst on 14 April, 1921, the Davis-Douglas Company was awarded Contract No. 53305, its first military contract. For the sum of $119,550 the company contracted to build and test three experimental aircraft designated DT-1s and to supply complete engineering information as well as three sets of wheel undercarriages for operation from shore bases or aboard aircraft carriers.

Built in the Goodyear airship hangar in East Los Angeles, the first aircraft (s/n 101, Navy serial A6031) was completed as a single-seater in October 1921 and was powered by a standard 400 hp Liberty water-cooled engine enclosed in a cowling of rectangular cross-section with radiators attached externally to the firewall on each side of the fuselage. At the time of its completion the DT-1 was fitted with twin floats but for its test flight had a land undercarriage and was tested by Eric Springer from Goodyear Field in early November 1921. On the 10th of the same month, Springer flew the aircraft to the Naval Air Station, San Diego, where it satisfactorily completed its acceptance trials, with both wheels and floats, in mid-December 1921.

Successful as it was, the DT-1 did not fully satisfy naval aviators, who felt that torpedo bombers should carry a crew of two or three. Accordingly, the Douglas Company received instructions to modify the second and third aircraft (A6032 and A6033) as two-seaters. To accommodate an observer/gunner, the pilot's cockpit was moved forward to a position immediately beneath the upper wings whilst the second crew member, who manned a flexible 0·3-in machine-gun, sat in a separate cockpit behind the trailing edge of the wings.

For a while it seemed that the future of the Douglas torpedo bomber was in jeopardy because on 8 March, 1922—by which time it had been flown for

The DT-1 on floats at NAS San Diego, with torpedo beneath the fuselage. (*USN*)

a total of 22 hr 25 min—the DT-1 struck the water and nosed over during a high-speed flight over San Diego Bay. Even less fortunate was the first of the two modified prototypes, designated DT-2s, which was destroyed in a landing accident on 19 July, 1922, at Anacostia after being tested for a total of only 6 hr 23 min. Fortunately for Douglas, the third aircraft, which had made its maiden flight on 18 April, 1922, and had been ferried to San Diego four days later, fared better as it successfully completed its final Board of Inspection and Survey (BIS) trials and served briefly with Torpedo Squadron One (VT-1) before being struck off the Navy List.

Douglas DT-2 (A6408) of VT-19 over Oahu in 1925. An auxiliary tank is fitted beneath the fuselage in place of the torpedo. (*US National Archives*)

47

This third aircraft (A6033) had a modified engine installation with the two external water-cooling units of the DT-1 replaced by a nose radiator mounted within the engine cowling. It had originally been fitted for factory trials with a standard 400 hp Liberty engine; however, to offset the heavier weight of the two-seat DT-2, it had been decided to fit a higher compression 450 hp Liberty engine and this was installed in San Diego before beginning preliminary Service trials. With this engine, however, oil cooling problems were experienced and the Navy returned the aircraft to have a modified oil radiator mounted externally over the left hand walk-way. Further tests were then made in Los Angeles and San Diego until finally the aircraft was transferred to Naval Air Station, Anacostia, where it was received in October 1922 and where full BIS trials were successfully completed in January 1923.

First DT-2 built by the Dayton-Wright Company in Dayton, Ohio.
(*US National Archives*)

In spite of the accidents suffered by A6031 and A6032, and before completion of the BIS trials with A6033, the Navy Department had already decided to order the DT-2 into quantity production as, during competitive trials, it had been found superior to its four competitors on almost all counts—its ease of maintenance and handling and its strong structure being particularly praised. Accordingly, Contract Nos. 55991 and RNAF-62, respectively covering eighteen DT-2s (A6405 to A6422) and six DT-2s (A6423 to A6428), were awarded to the Douglas Company and to the Naval Aircraft Factory (NAF) Philadelphia, while eleven additional DT-2s (A6085 to A6095) were ordered from the Dayton-Wright Company at Dayton.

In anticipation of its first production contract, the Douglas Company, which in July 1921 had succeeded the Davis-Douglas Company, had to find larger quarters to house its expanded activities, and the DT-2s became the first aircraft to be built in the Wilshire Boulevard plant in Santa Monica. Five DT-2s were delivered in 1922, and the initial production contract—during the course of which the shape of the aircraft's vertical tail surfaces

Bearing the Marine Corps insignia on its engine cowling, this DT-5 was powered by a Wright T-2B liquid-cooled engine. (*USMC*)

was changed when a balanced rudder of increased height and area was fitted—was completed in the following year. By that time, however, the DT-2 had won an enviable reputation and a repeat order for twenty aircraft (A6563 to A6582) had been awarded to Douglas, while twenty additional DT-2s (A6583 to A6602) were ordered from the Lowe-Willard-Fowler (LWF) Engineering Co of College Point, New York.

An improved version of the aircraft designated DT-3 was proposed by Douglas in 1923, but was not ordered by the Navy, and the DT-1 and DT-2 were the only two versions of the aircraft to be built. However, four other versions were produced by modifying existing airframes. First of these developments was the DT-4 developed by the NAF which re-engined four of its DT-2s (A6423, A6424, A6427 and A6428) with 650 hp direct-drive Wright T-2 twelve-cylinder liquid-cooled engines. Intended primarily as a bomber rather than a torpedo bomber, the DT-4 had a cone-shaped engine cowling and external radiators mounted on the bracing struts between the lower wings and the fuselage. The DT-4s saw limited service, but one of them, which had been entered in the 1923 Merchants Exchange of St Louis Trophy Race in St Louis distinguished itself by making the fastest lap in the load-carrying competition with a speed of 115 mph (185 kmh).

Two of the DT-4s (A6427 and A6428) were again modified a year later and, with 650 hp geared Wright T-2B engines, redesignated DT-5s.

In addition to producing eleven DT-2s, the Dayton-Wright Co modified three LWF-built DT-2s (A6593, A6596 and A6597) as long-range scout floatplanes. Designated SDW-1s, these three aircraft had their torpedo racks removed and could be recognized by their deeper centre fuselage and engine cowling accommodating additional fuel tanks.

The fourth modified DT version, the DT-6, was the penultimate Douglas-built DT-2 (s/n 142, A6581) in which a 450 hp Wright P-1 air-cooled radial was experimentally substituted for the water-cooled 450 hp Liberty.

The soundness of the DT design, which had already attracted the attention of the Air Service—the Douglas World Cruiser being a direct derivative of the DT-2—, won for Douglas its first export orders and

49

SDW-1 (BuNo A6597) modified by Dayton-Wright from an LWF-built DT-2.
(*NA & SM*)

The experimental DT-6 which was modified from a Douglas-built DT-2 to test
the Wright P-1 air-cooled radial. (*USN*)

Douglas-built prototype of the DT-2B which was acquired by the Norwegian
Government. (*US National Archives*)

resulted also in the first construction under licence by a foreign manufacturer of a Douglas-designed aircraft. This notable event was achieved in 1924 when the Norwegian Government placed an order for one DT-2B and acquired a manufacturing licence. Powered by a 450 hp Liberty engine, the Douglas-built DT-2B was fitted with the nose radiator and tail surfaces developed for the DWC and was followed by seven other machines

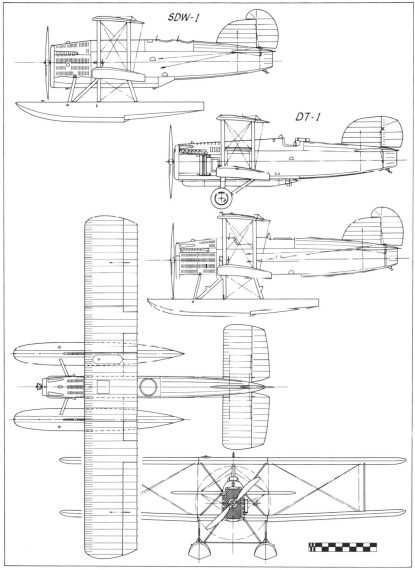

Douglas DT-2, with side views of DT-1 and SDW-1.

built under licence by the Marinens Flyvebåtfabrik (Naval Flying-Boat Factory) in Norway. Another export order was received by Douglas from the Peruvian Navy, and four DTBs (s/n 253, 254, 384 and 385)—similar to the DT-2B but powered by a 650 hp Wright Typhoon liquid-cooled engine—were built in 1927 and 1929 to bring to a close the production of DT-type aircraft.

The first production DT-2 (A6405) was accepted by the US Navy on 19 October, 1922, and delivered to Torpedo Squadron Two (VT-2) which had taken delivery of its first four aircraft (A6406 to A6409) on 12 December, 1922. Deliveries continued during 1923 and the last Douglas-built DT-2s from the second production batch were accepted in October of that year. In the months following their operational debut, DT-2s set a number of world records including the following:

Class C landplanes:
Altitude of 3,538 m (11,609 ft) with payload of 1,000 kg (2,204·6 lb). Lt R. Irvine at McCook Field, Dayton, on 17 April, 1923.

Class C seaplanes:
Speed of 116 km/h (72 mph) over a 500 km (310·6 miles) course. Lt (jg) M. A. Schur at San Diego on 6 June, 1923.
Distance of 330·2 km (205·2 miles) and endurance of 2 hr 45 min 9 sec with payload of 1,000 kg (2,204·6 lb). Lt R. L. Fuller at San Diego on 6 June, 1923.
Altitude of 3,307 m (10,850 ft) with payload of 250 kg (551·2 lb). Lt E. B. Brix at San Diego on 7 June, 1923.
Altitude of 4,239 m (13,908 ft) without payload. Lt C. F. Harper at San Diego on 7 June, 1923.
Speed of 113·5 km/h (70·5 mph) over a 1,000 km (621·4 miles) course without payload. Lt (jg) M. A. Schur at San Diego on 12 June, 1923.
Distance of 1,275 km (792·25 miles) and endurance of 11 hr 16 min 59 sec without payload. Lt (jg) M. A. Schur at San Diego on 12 June, 1923.

In service with the US Navy, the DT-2s were flown primarily as floatplanes from seaplane tenders and shore bases and were operated in this capacity by five Torpedo Squadrons (VT-1, VT-2, VT-5A, VT-19 and VT-20) serving with the Atlantic, Pacific and Asiatic Fleets. They also served with Utility Squadron One (VJ-1) and Observation Squadron Six (VO-6) and were operated by station flights at Anacostia, Coco Solo, the Edgewood Arsenal, Pearl Harbor, Pensacola and San Diego. Finally, other DT-2s—mainly LWF-built aircraft—were operated from the first US carrier, the USS *Langley*, to develop free and catapult-assisted take-off techniques while anchored or under way. Highlights of these tests occurred on 2 May, 1924, when a DT-2 carrying a dummy torpedo was launched by catapult from the USS *Langley* then anchored in Pensacola Bay, and on 2 April, 1925, when another DT-2 demonstrated the feasibility of using flush-mounted deck catapults to launch aircraft from a moored aircraft carrier.

Marinens Flyvebåtfabrik DT-2B dropping a torpedo.
(*Royal Norwegian Armed Forces*)

Service use of the DT-2s was not limited to the US Navy; a number of LWF-built aircraft were briefly operated by the First Aviation Group of the US Marine Corps, while two other DT-2s, one Douglas-built (A6577) and one NAF-built (A6426), were loaned to the Air Service for parachute dropping experiments. This type of test was also extensively conducted by the US Navy which operated a number of DT-2s for that purpose. The Peruvian Navy operated its DTBs as floatplanes for a number of years while the Norwegian Marinens Flyvevaben (Naval Flying Service) still had a number of DT-2Bs in second line service as late as 1940.

One of the two DT-2s which was transferred to the Air Service. The aircraft is finished overall in olive drab and carries the tail striping adopted by the Army Air Corps in November 1926. (*US National Archives*)

53

With the US Navy, however, the DT-Series had a comparatively short Service life as the wood used extensively in their structure deteriorated rapidly due to salt water contamination. The last Douglas-built DT-2 to be struck off the Navy list was A6579 which ended its useful life on 21 November, 1928, while the experimental DT-6 (A6581) was struck off at the end of January 1927. While other types of Douglas aircraft were to have a much longer Service life and obtain a wider acclaim, the DT series proved nevertheless to be one of the most significant aircraft built by Douglas. Particularly significant were the facts that the design of this aircraft led to the establishment of a strong relationship between Douglas and the US Navy and that it enabled the company to secure its first overseas licence production rights and to obtain its first export orders.

DT-1 floatplane
Span 50 ft (15·24 m); length 37 ft 8 in (11·48 m); height 15 ft 1 in (4·6 m); wing area 707 sq ft (65·683 sq m). Empty weight 4,367 lb (1,981 kg); loaded weight 6,895 lb (3,128 kg); wing loading 9·8 lb/sq ft (47·6 kg/sq m); power loading 17·2 lb/hp (7·8 kg/hp). Maximum speed at sea level 101 mph (163 km/h); climb to 5,000 ft (1,524 m) 15·6 min; service ceiling 8,700 ft (2,650 m); normal range 232 miles (373 km).

DT-2 floatplane
Dimensions as DT-1. Empty weight 4,528 lb (2,054 kg); loaded weight 7,293 lb (3,308 kg); wing loading 10·3 lb/sq ft (50·4 kg/sq m); power loading 16·2 lb/hp (7·4 kg/hp). Maximum speed at sea level 99·5 mph (160 km/h); climb to 5,000 ft (1,524 m) 14·5 min; service ceiling 7,400 ft (2,255 m); normal range 274 miles (441 km).

DT-2 landplane
Span and wing area as floatplane. Length 34 ft 2 in (10·41 m); height 13 ft 7 in (4·14 m). Empty weight 3,737 lb (1,695 kg); loaded weight 6,502 lb (2,949 kg); wing loading 9·2 lb/sq ft (44·9 kg/sq m); power loading 14·4 lb/hp (6·6 kg/hp). Maximum speed at sea level 101 mph (163 km/h); climb to 5,000 ft (1,524 m) 13·6 min; service ceiling 7,800 ft (2,315 m); normal range 293 miles (472 km).

DT-4 floatplane
Dimensions as DT-1. Empty weight 4,976 lb (2,257 kg); loaded weight 7,741 lb (3,511 kg); wing loading 10·9 lb/sq ft (53·5 kg/sq m); power loading 11·9 lb/hp (5·4 kg/hp). Maximum speed at sea level 107 mph (172 km/h); climb to 5,000 ft (1,524 m) 12·8 min; service ceiling 6,050 ft (1,845 m); normal range 226 miles (364 km).

DT-4 landplane
Span and wing area as DT-1. Length 34 ft 5⅜ in (10·5 m); height 13 ft 5 in (4·09 m). Empty weight 4,224 lb (1,916 kg); loaded weight 6,989 lb (3,170 kg); wing loading 9·9 lb/sq ft (48·3 kg/sq m); power loading 10·8 lb/hp (4·9 kg/hp). Maximum speed at sea level 108 mph (174 km/h); climb to 5,000 ft (1,524 m) 10 min; service ceiling 11,025 ft (3,375 m); normal range 240 miles (386 km).

DT-5 floatplane

Dimensions as DT-1. Empty weight 5,226 lb (2,370 kg); loaded weight 7,991 lb (3,625 kg); wing loading 11·3 lb/sq ft (55·2 kg/sq m); power loading 12·3 lb/hp (5·6 kg/hp). Maximum speed at sea level 110·5 mph (178 km/h); climb to 5,000 ft (1,524 m) 9·6 min; service ceiling 10,200 ft (3,110 m); normal range 233 miles (375 km).

DT-5 landplane

Dimensions as DT-4 landplane. Empty weight 4,474 lb (2,029 kg); loaded weight 7,239 lb (3,284 kg); wing loading 10·2 lb/sq ft (50 kg/sq m); power loading 11·1 lb/hp (5·1 kg/hp). Maximum speed at sea level 112 mph (180 km/h); climb to 5,000 ft (1,524 m) 7·4 min; service ceiling 12,700 ft (3,870 m); normal range 246 miles (346 km).

DT-6 landplane

Span and wing area as DT-1. Length 34 ft 1⅝ in (10·4 m); height 13 ft 7 in (4·14 m). Empty weight 3,674 lb (1,666 kg); loaded weight 6,439 lb (2,921 kg); wing loading 9·1 lb/sq ft (44·5 kg/sq m); power loading 14·3 lb/hp (6·5 kg/hp). Maximum speed at sea level 102 mph (164 km/h); climb to 5,000 ft (1,524 m) 12 min; service ceiling 9,550 ft (2,910 m); normal range 295 miles (475 km).

Douglas World Cruiser

The two decades separating the two World Wars were marked by a series of spectacular long-distance flights, but few can equal the significance of the 28,945-mile (46,580-km) flight round the world made in 1924 by a formation of single-engined aircraft. Yet, whereas Lindbergh's flight between New York and Paris remains well known to the general public, the first flight round the world by two US Air Service's Douglas World Cruisers is no longer remembered. None the less, Donald Douglas had good reason to remember with pride the epic flight which earned for his company the motto 'First around the world'.

The association between The Douglas Company and the Air Service, later between the Douglas Aircraft Company and the Army Air Corps/Army Air Forces, can be traced back to a memorandum written on 25 October, 1922, by the Acting Chief of the Engineering Division, Air Service. Aware of the fact that the US Navy had ordered the Douglas DT-2 into quantity production, this officer recommended the purchase of a modified aircraft to be powered by a Packard 2025 engine for the purpose of arriving 'at some definite conclusions as to the advantages and disadvantages of a single engine bombardment airplane, similar in performance and weight carrying to twin-engined airplanes in use'. While this recommendation was not endorsed by the War Department, it did attract the attention of the Army to the new Douglas aircraft.

During the spring of 1923 the Air Service began to show considerable interest in a flight round the world by a formation of military aircraft, and a group of officers was assigned the task of finding suitable equipment and of planning the entire venture. As none of the aircraft already operated by the Air Service was found satisfactory, a search began for a machine which

Bearing the Wright Field number P318 on its rudder, the DWC prototype (23-1210) was substituted for the *Boston* during the last stages of the round-the-world flight. (*USAF*)

could be easily fitted with interchangeable land and water type under-carriages. In the process the War Department instructed the Air Service on 24 June, 1923, 'to take necessary actions to procure all available data on the Fokker F-5 Transport and the Davis-Douglas Cloudster ... and to procure one of these planes for test' and thus set the round-the-world project into motion.

Rather than providing information on a modified Cloudster, Douglas submitted on 5 July, 1923, specifications for a much modified DT-2

The folding wings of the *New Orleans* reveal the DT ancestry of the DWC. (*US National Archives*)

56

aeroplane—then designated D-WC (for Douglas-World Cruiser) but later becoming the DWC when the hyphen was dropped—which the company claimed could be delivered at a price of $23,721 within 45 days of receiving a contract. As the basic DT-2 design had already been proven and as it had the requisite interchangeable wheels and floats, the Douglas project appeared to show the greatest promise. Accordingly, Lt Erik Nelson, one of the officers on the round-the-world planning group, was sent to Los Angeles with instructions to negotiate the construction of a specialized aircraft based on the DT-2 design.

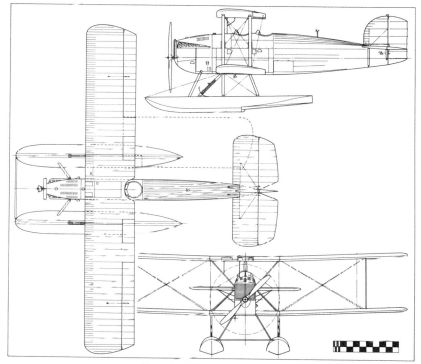

Douglas World Cruiser.

The confidence shown by the Air Service, which had not previously acquired Douglas aircraft, was of major importance for the future of the still struggling company. Consequently, Donald Douglas, assisted by John Northrop, immediately began to plan the necessary modifications of the DT-2 to meet the Air Service requirements. Structurally there was no need to modify the aircraft but, whereas in the DT-2 a substantial portion of the useful load was taken up by the torpedo and other military equipment, fuel was to account for a much larger share of the new aircraft's useful load.

To give the aircraft the necessary range with reserves for long over-water flights, the fuel system was completely modified and comprised a 60-US gallon (227-litre) tank in the centre section of the upper wings, a 62-gallon

(235-litre) tank in the root of each lower wing, a 150-gallon (568-litre) tank behind the engine firewall, a 160-gallon (606-litre) tank beneath the pilot's cockpit and a 150-gallon (568-litre) tank beneath the observer's seat. With these installed total petrol capacity was increased from the 115 gallons (435 litres) in the DT-2 to 644 gallons (2,438 litres) in the World Cruiser, and with full fuel load the maximum still-air range was calculated to be 2,200 miles (3,540 km). The DT-2's 420 hp Liberty engine was retained but the radiator arrangement was modified to facilitate maintenance, and two different sizes of radiators were provided, the larger one being specially intended for use in tropical areas. Other modifications included a change in shape and area of the vertical tail surfaces and the addition of external bracing struts beneath the tailplane. Finally, to improve communication in flight, the observer's cockpit was moved forward to a position immediately behind the pilot's cockpit, and a cut-out was incorporated in the trailing edge of the centre section of the upper wing to provide upward visibility for navigational purposes.

As soon as Donald Douglas had completed his drafting work his proposal was taken to Washington by Lt Nelson, where it was submitted to General Mason M. Patrick, Chief of the Air Service, United States Army. On 1 August, 1923, General Patrick gave his approval and the War Department awarded a contract for the construction of a prototype. As much of the aircraft was similar to the DT-2, work progressed rapidly and before the end of the year—after completion of manufacturer's trials by Eric Springer—the aircraft (s/n 144) had been tested by the Air Service at McCook Field, where it was flown with wheel undercarriage, and at Hampton Roads, Virginia, where seaplane trials were conducted. As the test results were fully satisfactory, the War Department gave the final go-ahead for the projected round-the-world flight on 19 November, 1923, and eight days later The Douglas Company received a $192,684 contract for the construction of four aircraft and spares. The last of these aircraft was delivered on 11 March, 1924.

Two DWCs at Sand Point Flying Field, Lake Washington, in early April 1924. One aircraft has already been fitted with its floats whilst the other retains the undercarriage with which it was flown from Santa Monica. (*USAF*)

By that time the plans for the flight had been completed and spares—including fifteen Liberty engines, fourteen extra sets of floats and about 200 per cent airframe replacement parts—had been positioned in various parts of the world. With everything ready, the flight crews and their aircraft left Santa Monica, the unofficial starting point for their history-making flight, on the morning of 17 March, 1924, en route to Seattle for the official start.

While in Seattle the aircraft were fitted with their floats and were officially named after four major American cities. The name, serial number and respective crews of these aircraft were as follows:

Douglas s/n	Serial number	Side number	Name	Crew
145	23-1229	1	*Seattle*	Major Frederick L. Martin (Flight Commander) and Staff Sgt Alva L. Harvey
146	23-1230	2	*Chicago*	Lt Lowell Smith and Lt Leslie Arnold
147	23-1231	3	*Boston*	Lt Leigh Wade and Staff Sgt Henry H. Ogden
148	23-1232	4	*New Orleans*	Lt Erik Nelson (Engineer Officer) and Lt John Harding.

After a delay of two days—first because of fog and then a broken propeller—the four DWCs left Sand Point on Lake Washington on 4 April, 1924, for Prince Rupert in Canada, on the first leg of their journey. From there they flew to Alaska, with stops in Sitka, Cordova, and Chignik where the *Seattle*, piloted by Major Martin, was forced to stay behind. After repairs had been made to their aircraft Martin and Harvey set out to catch up but were caught in fog and crashed on a mountainside. The *Seattle* was destroyed but Martin and Harvey, after a ten-day ordeal in a blizzard, managed to reach Port Moller on foot.

Chicago, Boston and *New Orleans* continued and, avoiding the USSR which had not granted overflight rights, arrived in Yokohama on 24 May. Still fitted with floats, the aircraft then continued via Korea, the Chinese coast, Hong Kong, Indo-China, Thailand and Burma to Calcutta, where

New Orleans, Chicago and *Boston II* lined-up on 23 September, 1924, five days before completing their epic flight. (*Raymond Vignolle*)

59

the floats were replaced with wheels. Flying westward across India, the three DWCs continued their journey and after flying over the Middle East and Southern and Central Europe arrived in Paris in time to celebrate Bastille Day. From the French capital the three crews took their aircraft to London and thence to Brough near Hull, where floats were fitted for the Atlantic crossing.

After leaving Scapa Flow, in Orkney, Lt Wade and Sgt Ogden, in *Boston*, experienced oil pump failure which compelled them to alight at sea. Luck was with them, for after drifting for hours, they were spotted by the light cruiser USS *Richmond*. The two men were taken aboard and the *Richmond* undertook the difficult task of towing the aircraft to the Faroe Islands. Unfortunately, a mile from safe harbour, rough water capsized the *Boston*. In the meantime, the remaining two aircraft, *Chicago* and *New Orleans*, successfully crossed the Atlantic via Iceland and Greenland, and Smith, Arnold, Nelson and Harding were reunited with Wade and Ogden at Picton in Nova Scotia. Again fitted with wheels, and joined by the prototype DWC which had been delivered to Wade and Ogden and named *Boston II*, they flew southward to Washington where the crews were given a hero's welcome. It then remained only to fly across the United States, and the *Chicago* and *New Orleans* completed the round-the-world flight on 28 September when they landed back in Seattle.

From Santa Monica the two aircraft had flown round the world in 175 days and covered 28,945 miles (46,580 km) in 371 hr and 7 min at an average flying speed of 78 mph (125 km/h). The longest leg had been the 875-mile (1,408-km) flight between Reykjavik and Frederiksdal, but the flight between Attu Island and Paramushiru Island—a distance of 900 miles (1,448 km) flown with an intermediate alighting at sea for refuelling from a tanker vessel—had been the longest one in terms of duration: 11 hours.

The *New Orleans* (s/n 148, 23-1232) on display in the Air Force Museum at Wright-Patterson AFB, Ohio. (*USAF*)

Douglas DOS observation aircraft with twin 0·30-in machine-guns in the rear cockpit. (*Northrop Institute of Technology*)

Eventually the *Chicago* was donated to the National Air Museum of the Smithsonian Institution in Washington and the *New Orleans* was given to the Los Angeles County Museum which, in 1957, handed it on long-term loan to the Air Force Museum at Wright-Patterson AFB, Ohio.

The story of the Douglas World Cruiser did not end, however, with the successful completion of the first flight around the world. The Air Service purchased six externally similar aircraft for use as observation aircraft. Initially designated DOS (Douglas Observation Seaplane), these aircraft (serials 24-2 to 24-7) retained the interchangeable wheel/float undercarriage of the DWC but had fuel capacity reduced to 110 gallons (416 litres), while twin 0·30-in machine-guns were mounted in the rear cockpit. Redesignated O-5s in May 1924, they were operated by the 2nd Observation Squadron from Kindley Field, Corregidor, on behalf of the Philippine Aviation Department.

DWC landplane

Span 50 ft (15.24 m); length 35 ft 6 in (10·82 m); height 13 ft 7 in (4·14 m); wing area 707 sq ft (65·683 sq m). Empty weight 4,380 lb (1,543 kg); loaded weight 6,995 lb (3,173 kg); wing loading 9·9 lb/sq ft (48·3 kg/sq m); power loading 16·7 lb/hp (7·6 kg/hp). Maximum speed at sea level 103 mph (166 km/h); service ceiling 10,000 ft (3,050 m); maximum range 2,200 miles (3,701 km).

DWC floatplane

Span and wing area as landplane. Length 39 ft (11·89 m); height 15 ft 1 in (4·6 m). Empty weight 5,180 lb (1,825 kg); loaded weight 7,795 lb (3,536 kg); wing loading 11 lb/sq ft (53·8 kg/sq m); power loading 18·6 lb/hp (8·4 kg/hp). Maximum speed at sea level 100 mph (161 km/h); service ceiling 7,000 ft (2,135 m); maximum range 1,650 miles (2,655 km).

Douglas XO-2 (23-1254) with 1A-1500 engine as entered in the 1925 competition for Packard-powered Corps Observation aircraft. (*US National Archives*)

Douglas Observation Biplanes

With a total of 879 aircraft delivered between 1924 and 1936— comprising one civil aircraft, 108 aircraft sold to foreign air forces and 770 machines which served with all US Services (Air Service/Air Corps/USAAF, National Guard, Navy, Marine Corps and Coast Guard)—the series of Douglas observation biplanes was one of the most important types of American military aeroplanes of the twenties and early thirties.

Amongst the last contracts drawn against Fiscal Year 1923 funds by the War Department, on behalf of the Air Service, were Contracts 728 and 821 which were awarded to The Douglas Company for the design and manufacture of two experimental observation aircraft. Both designated XO-2, these were identical with the exception of powerplant, the first (s/n 157, serial 23-1251) was to be powered by a 420 hp Liberty V-1650-1 water-cooled engine whereas the second (s/n 167, serial 23-1254) was to be fitted with a 510 hp Packard 1A-1500 liquid-cooled engine. Together with competitive designs ordered from American and foreign manufacturers, these two machines were intended to be entered in a series of trials at McCook Field for the purpose of selecting a Corps Observation aircraft with which to replace the aging DH-4Bs and DH-4Ms. In view of the large number of surplus Liberty engines available to the Air Service—of which an excessive number had been ordered during the war and delivered too late to be used during that conflict—the War Department further instructed the competitors to complete first the version of their aircraft powered by this type of engine, and competition trials were set for November 1924.

Completed in the Wilshire Boulevard plant during the autumn of 1924, the Liberty-powered XO-2 was tested by Eric Springer before being delivered to McCook Field. During the competitive trials, the XO-2 was evaluated with two sets of equal-span wings—a set of 36 ft 3 in (11·05 m) wings with an area of 370 sq ft (34·373 sq m) being substituted for the original 39 ft 8 in (12·09 m) wings with an area of 411 sq ft (38·182 sq m)—but the long-span wings were found to provide better handling characteristics, lower landing speed and higher ceiling and were adopted as standard. Proving to be 22 mph (35 kmh) faster than the similarly powered DH-4B which it was to supplant and being found superior to all of its competitors, the Douglas XO-2 was recommended unanimously by the members of the Evaluation Board for Air Service adoption and was the object of the largest contract yet obtained by The Douglas Company. Awarded by the War Department on 25 February, 1925, Contract 25-421 called for the production of seventy-five aircraft which were delivered in 1925–26 as O-2s, O-2As, O-2Bs, O-7s, an O-8, an O-9 and an XA-2.

In the competition for Packard-powered Corps Observation aircraft held early in 1925 at McCook Field, the Douglas design was less successful and lost to the Curtiss XO-1 which had come in second in the competition for Liberty-powered aircraft. This defeat, however, proved to be a blessing in disguise as the Packard engine failed to live up to expectation and, ultimately, Douglas production of O-2s and derivatives exceeded that by Curtiss of O-1s and versions thereof. In fact, following the delivery in 1925 of the first production model in the O-2 series, the Douglas observation biplanes were built in more than fifty versions culminating in the O-2MC-10 delivered to China during 1936.

O-2: First production version of which forty-five (serials 25-335 to 25-379) were delivered. Generally identical to the Liberty-powered XO-2 with long span wings, production O-2s had a simplified engine installation with a large tunnel-type radiator of modified design mounted further back beneath the propeller shaft of the 435 hp Liberty V-1650-1 engine. A 30-US gallon (113·6-litre) petrol tank was located in the centre section of each

The twenty-first O-2 (25-355), with the characteristic Liberty engine installation of the first Douglas observation biplanes. (*USAF*)

lower wing and could be jettisoned in emergency. The undercarriage consisted of two oleo legs and two Vs hinged at the centreline of the underside of the fuselage. One fuselage-mounted forward-firing 0·30-in machine-gun and one flexible rear-firing 0·30-in machine-gun were fitted as standard armament and the aircraft carried bombs of up to 100 lb (45·4 kg) on four wing racks. Provision was also included for the installation of one 0·30-in machine-gun over each lower wing and photographic equipment in the rear cockpit.

O-2A: Eighteen aircraft (serials 25-387 to 25-404) identical to the O-2s but fitted with night flying equipment.

Bearing two stars on its rudder, this O-2B was assigned to the Chief of the Air Service. (*USAF*)

O-2B: Six machines (serials 25-381 to 25-386) fitted with dual control for use as command aircraft. Armament removed. Some of these aircraft were fitted with a propeller spinner.

O-2BS: One specially modified aircraft (s/n 265) ordered in 1926 by James McKee, a Pittsburgh businessman and pilot, for the first single-aircraft single-pilot trans-Canada flight. As few landing fields were available across Canada, McKee requested that the aircraft be fitted with twin floats for use on the many Canadian rivers and lakes. This requirement also necessitated the replacement of the ventral radiator with a new frontal unit mounted higher up to prevent water ingestion. Armament and all military equipment were dispensed with. For the trans-Canada flight the O-2BS (O-2B Special, US civil registration C236) was fitted as a two-seater and powered by a 400 hp Liberty 12 engine. In 1927, however, the aircraft was modified as a three-seater—a third open cockpit being fitted in the forward fuselage ahead of the wings—and a 410 hp Pratt & Whitney Wasp A air-cooled radial was substituted for the original Liberty water-cooled engine.

O-2C: Forty-six observation aircraft (serials 26-001 to 26-014 and 26-386 to 26-417) of which nineteen were delivered to the Air Corps while twenty-seven were delivered to the Militia Bureau for use by National

Guard units. The aircraft differed from the earlier O-2s in being fitted with the flat radiator first installed on the O-2BS and in minor armament installation modifications. Two additional aircraft were delivered to the US Marine Corps as OD-1s. Eight similar aircraft (s/n 358 to 365) were ordered by the Mexican Government.

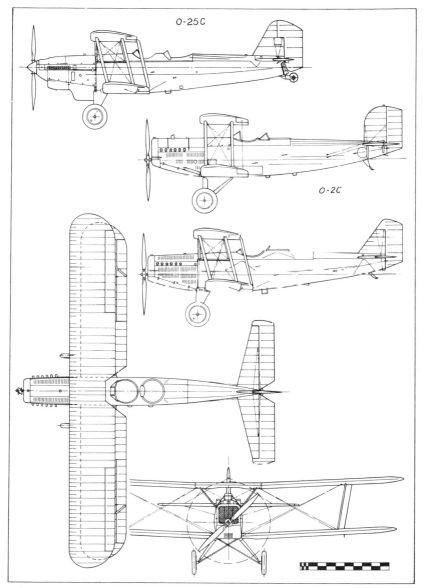

Douglas O-2H, with side views of O-2C and O-25C.

XO-2C: Designation applying to one O-2C (26-387) which was modified for testing experimental wireless equipment installed in a ventral pannier. A large rectangular frame aerial was attached on the starboard wing struts and landing lights were mounted in fairings at the tips of the lower wings.

O-2D: Unarmed staff transports similar to the O-2Cs of which two were built (serials 26-419 and 26-420).

O-2E: One aircraft (serial 26-418) basically similar to the O-2Cs but fitted with modified vertical tail surfaces and with a strut between upper and lower ailerons instead of the steel wire used on all previous models.

O-2F and **O-2G:** Designations not used.

O-2H: Although retaining a designation in the O-2 series, the O-2H was virtually a new design with revised fuselage construction, new tail surfaces, streamlined undercarriage and staggered wings of unequal span (40 ft 10 in upper wings and 38 ft 6 in lower wings) and reduced area (362 sq ft). The interplane struts, which were vertical on earlier O-2 variants, were slanted inward from top to bottom and the struts between upper and lower ailerons tested on the O-2E were adopted as standard. The modified wings no longer housed the petrol tanks and a single tank of 110-US gallon (416-litres) capacity was installed in the fuselage ahead and below the pilot's cockpit. Still powered by a 435 hp Liberty V-1650-1 engine enclosed in a cowling similar to that used on the O-2BS to O-2E versions, the O-2H was normally fitted with a two-blade metal propeller in place of the wooden unit previously used. Late production O-2Hs were fitted with shorter but broader vertical tail surfaces and revised horizontal tail surfaces. A total of 140 O-2Hs were built by Douglas comprising ninety aircraft for the Air Corps (27-288 to 27-297, 28-128 to 28-187, 29-158 to 29-163, and 29-165 to 29-178) and fifty aircraft for the National Guard (28-349 to 28-358, 29-342 to 29-351, and 29-375 to 29-404).

O-2J: Unarmed staff transport version of the O-2H fitted with dual controls and a sliding writing table in the rear cockpit. Tail surfaces as on early O-2H. For fire protection the entire engine compartment could be

Early production O-2H (28-158) with the tall vertical tail surfaces. This 91st Observation Squadron aircraft was photographed at Mather Field, Sacramento, California, during Air Corps Manoeuvres. (*USAF*)

The Douglas O-2J, specially built for General Fechet, Chief of the Air Corps, was delivered on 6 June, 1928. (*USAF*)

flooded with pyrene under pressure. Three O-2Js were built (28-127, 28-188 and 29-209).

O-2K: Improved version of late production O-2Hs of which thirty-seven (29-179 to 29-183, 29-185 to 29-208, and 29-210 to 29-217) were built for the Air Corps while twenty (29-413 to 29-432) were produced for the National Guard. Forty O-2Ks were modified as basic trainers by fitting dual controls and were redesignated BT-1s. These BT-1s should not be confused with the Northrop BT-1 carrier bombers built by the subsidiary of the Douglas Aircraft Company in 1937–38.

O-6: All-metal version of the original O-2 built in the mid-twenties by Thomas-Morse. The five experimental XO-6/O-6 (25-435 to 25-439) were heavier than the O-2 but the sixth aircraft, the XO-6B 25-440, was smaller and led to the production of the much modified O-19 series retaining little of the Douglas design.

O-7: Three experimental aircraft (25-405 to 25-407) produced under the original contract for 75 aircraft awarded Douglas after the 1924 McCook Field competition. The O-7s had airframes identical to those of the O-2s but were powered by a direct-drive 510 hp Packard 1A-1500 engine driving a two-blade wooden propeller. Externally, these aircraft could be distinguished from the O-2s as they had only three exhaust stubs on each side of the cowling. Converted back to O-2 (25-406 and 407) and O-2C (25-405) configurations.

O-8: One experimental aircraft (25-408) produced under the original contract and initially intended to be powered by an inverted Packard 1A-1500 but completed with a 400 hp Curtiss R-1454 nine-cylinder radial. Aircraft later modified back to O-2A standard.

O-9: Similar to O-7 but powered by a geared 500 hp Packard 1A-1500 driving a four-blade propeller. Modified later to O-2A configuration (serial 25-409).

XO-14: Experimental scaled-down version of the O-2H powered by a 225 hp Wright R-970-5 radial. One aircraft (s/n 477, serial 28-194) completed in November 1928. The XO-14 had a span of 30 ft 1 in (9·17 m)

Douglas O-8 (25-408) on 18 October, 1926. (*Peter Westburg*)

O-9 (25-409) with geared Packard 1A-1500 engine and four-blade propeller. (*USAF*)

The XO-14 (28-194) bearing the Wright Field number XP539 on its rudder. (*USAF*)

The O-22 (29-371) with experimental NACA cowling. (*Peter Westburg*)

compared with the O-2H's 40 ft 10 in (12·45 m) and a length of 23 ft 1 in (7·26 m) instead of 30 ft (9·14 m) while the gross weight was reduced from 4,557 lb (2,067 kg) to 2,500 lb (1,134 kg). The XO-14, the first Douglas aeroplane to be fitted with wheel brakes, was delivered to the Air Corps in February 1929 and remained in service until July 1933 when it was sold to a private owner.

O-22: Experimental version with sweptback upper wings and N interplane struts substituted for the two parallel I struts fitted to previous Douglas observation biplanes. The aircraft had corrugated metal covering on its vertical tail surfaces and was fitted with a tailwheel instead of a skid. Powered by a 450 hp Pratt & Whitney R-1340-9 radial and tested without cowling, with a Townend ring and with early NACA-type cowling. Two aircraft built (29-371 and 29-372) and delivered in late 1929; also known as YO-22s.

O-25: One airframe (29-164) taken from an O-2H contract and powered by a 600 hp Curtiss Conqueror V-1570-5 liquid-cooled engine. A new swinging-arm type machine-gun mounting developed by Douglas was installed in the rear cockpit.

XO-25A: Designation applied to the O-25 modified to test the 600 hp Curtiss Conqueror V-1570-27 engine with Prestone cooling system enclosed in a much revised cowling.

O-25A: Production version of the O-25 powered by the geared 600 hp Curtiss V-1570-7. Tailwheel instead of a tailskid. Fifty aircraft (30-160, 30-164 to 30-195, and 30-354 to 30-370) built for the Air Corps.

O-25B: Three staff transports (30-161 to 30-163) identical to O-25As but unarmed and fitted with dual controls.

O-25C: Production model of the XO-25A with Prestone-cooled geared Curtiss V-1570-27 in a streamlined cowling. Radiator moved further back beneath the forward fuselage and spinner fitted over the propeller hub. Thirty (32-181 to 32-210) built for the Air Corps. These aircraft were the last Douglas observation biplanes to be powered by liquid-cooled engines.

O-25A (30-167) with Curtiss V-1570-5 engine. (*USAF*)

O-29: One aircraft (29-184) with airframe similar to that of the O-2Ks but powered by a 525 hp Wright R-1750 air-cooled radial. Later re-engined with a 575 hp Wright R-1820-1 radial and first redesignated Y1O-29A and, finally, O-29A.

O-32: Similar to the O-29A but powered by an uncowled 450 hp Pratt & Whitney R-1340-3 radial, this aircraft (serial 29-218) was subsequently fitted with dual controls and operated as a basic trainer under the designation BT-2.

O-32A: Production version of the O-32 with minor changes. Modified as BT-2A bàsic trainers. Thirty built (30-196 to 30-225) for the Air Corps.

YO-34: One aircraft (29-373) with airframe similar to that of the two YO-22s but powered by a 600 hp Curtiss Conqueror V-1570-11 liquid-cooled engine.

O-25C of the 91st Observation Squadron operating from Crissy Field, San Francisco. (*USAF*)

70

O-38: Using an airframe similar to that on aircraft of the O-25 series and fitted with a tailwheel, forty-five O-38s (30-408 to 30-419, 31-349 to 31-379, 31-406 and 31-407) were delivered to National Guard units and were powered by a 525 hp Pratt & Whitney R-1690-3 radial fitted with a Townend ring and driving a two-blade metal propeller.

O-38A: Unarmed staff transport version of the O-38 of which only one (30-407) was built for the National Guard.

O-38B (31-424) bearing the markings of Bolling Field, Washington DC, on its rear fuselage. (*William Balogh*)

O-38B: Identical to the O-38s but powered by a 525 hp Pratt & Whitney R-1690-5 radial, thirty O-38Bs (31-409 to 31-438) went to the Air Corps while a further thirty-three (32-102 to 32-116, and 32-325 to 32-342) were delivered to National Guard units. One of the California National Guard's O-38Bs was experimentally powered by a 600 hp Pratt & Whitney Hornet C radial and fitted with a canopy similar to that devised for the O-38S. Two O-38Bs (31-411 and 433) were used by the Bureau of Air Commerce and received civil registrations.

O-38C: One aircraft ordered in January 1932 by the War Department for use by the US Coast Guard (Air Corps serial 32-394 changed to USCG serial CG-9, later V-108). Identical to the O-38B but powered by a 525 hp R-1690-7 radial.

O-38D: Military designation given to the private venture O-38S which, after being tested by the Matériel Division at Wright Field, was acquired in October 1932 by the War Department for use by the Militia Bureau and was assigned the military serial 33-001.

O-38E: The thirty-seven O-38Es (33-002 to 33-016, and 34-001 to 34-022), with the exception of a slightly modified cowling enclosing a 625 hp Pratt & Whitney R-1690-13 radial, the use of a three-blade propeller, provision for the standard armament and an open rear canopy section, were identical to the wide-fuselage O-38S and were ordered for the National Guard. Contract 5911 awarded on 10 August, 1933, covering

71

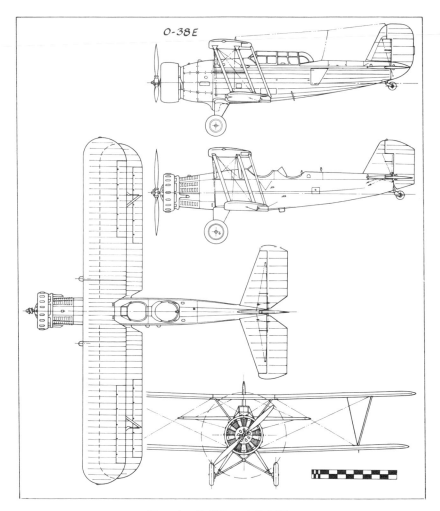

Douglas O-38B and O-38E.

aircraft 34-001 to 34-022 (initially assigned serials 33-298 to 33-319) was the last War Department contract for Douglas observation biplanes. At least one O-38E operated by the 113th Observation Squadron, Indiana National Guard, was fitted with twin Edo floats and had its canopy removed.

O-38F: Last War Department designation assigned to aircraft in the Douglas observation biplanes series. Eight O-38Fs (33-322 to 33-329) were delivered to the National Guard and were powered by a 625 hp Pratt & Whitney R-1690-9 radial. A new fully enclosed canopy was fitted over the cockpit of this unarmed version derived from the O-38E.

72

A Peruvian Navy O-38P at Santa Monica before delivery. (*Peter Westburg*)

O-38P: Designation applied to six aircraft ordered in 1932 by the Aviacion Naval Peruana. Basically similar to the O-38Es of the National Guard, the O-38Ps were powered by a 640 hp Wright R-1820-F radial. The standard undercarriage could be replaced by twin floats.

O-38S: Developed as a private venture, the O-38S (unofficial designation standing for O-38 Special) was an improved O-38 with a much wider fuselage, streamlined interplane struts and a sliding canopy covering the tandem cockpits. Powered by a 575 hp Wright R-1820-E radial enclosed in a smooth cowling, the aircraft was tested with two-blade and three-blade propellers. Following evaluation by the Matériel Division, the O-38S (s/n 1121, civil registration X12267) was purchased for use by the Militia Bureau and was officially designated O-38D. The O-38E, O-38F and O-38P were production versions of the experimental O-38S.

XA-2: In 1925, Douglas was instructed to complete one of the forty-six O-2s ordered under the original contract for seventy-five machines as a prototype for an attack aircraft. The XA-2 (serial 25-380) was powered by a 420 hp Liberty V-1410 twelve-cylinder, inverted-vee, air-cooled engine and was armed with six forward-firing 0·30-in machine-guns—two in the upper

Bearing the civil registration X12267, the O-38S was developed as a private venture. It was later used by the Militia Bureau as the O-38D with the serial NG33-1. (*USAF*)

73

The heavily-armed XA-2 (25-380). Note 0·30-in guns in each wing panel, above the cowling and on twin-mounting in the rear cockpit. (*USAF*)

engine cowling, two in the upper wings, and two in the lower wings—and twin flexible 0·30-in machine-guns in the rear cockpit. Completed in 1926, the aircraft was tested against the Curtiss XA-3. The competition was won by the Curtiss aircraft and the XA-2 was not proceeded with.

BT-1: Designation applied to forty O-2Ks modified as basic trainers for use by Air Corps and National Guard units. Flight controls and instruments were fitted in the rear cockpit and the armament was removed. At least one BT-1 had a full canopy over the rear cockpit.

BT-2: Basic trainer with dual controls obtained by modifying the sole O-32 (29-218).

BT-2A: Designation applied to the thirty O-32As (30-196 to 30-225) after modification to basic trainer standards and removal of armament.

BT-2B: First basic trainer model ordered as such by the Air Corps. Airframe similar to that of the O-38 but fitted with the less powerful Pratt & Whitney R-1340-11 rated at 450 hp at sea level. A total of 146 BT-2Bs (31-001 to 31-146) was ordered in June 1930. Aircraft 31-034 was experimentally fitted with twin Edo floats.

BT-2BI: Designation applied to fifty-eight BT-2Bs modified as instrument trainers in 1932. Collapsible blind flying hood fitted over the rear cockpit.

BT-2BG and **BT-2BR:** Initial designations applied respectively to two BT-2BIs and fifteen BT-2Bs modified as radio-controlled aerial targets. *See* A-4 designation.

BT-2C: Improved BT-2B with modified undercarriage and overall length reduced from 31 ft 2 in (9·50 m) to 30 ft 4 in (9·25 m). Twenty (31-439 to 31-458) ordered in December 1930.

BT-2CI: Thirteen BT-2Cs fitted as instrument trainers.

BT-2CR: Designation given to seven BT-2Cs modified in 1940 as drone control aircraft for use in connection with the A-4 aerial targets.

BT-2BI with collapsible blind-flying hood over the rear cockpit. (*USAF*)

A-4: Seventeen aircraft (31-1, -36, -39, -49, -56, -58, -60, -72, -76, -78, -91, -99, -101, -114, -116, -127, and 31-135)—initially designated BT-2BGs and BT-2BRs—modified in 1940 as radio-controlled anti-aircraft targets. The rear cockpit was faired over and, for checking purposes only, the aircraft were flown as single-seaters. To facilitate landings under radio control, the aircraft were fitted with tricycle undercarriages with steerable nosewheels and mainwheels moved aft, while ballast was installed to restore the centre of gravity.

A-6: Designation applied to a projected radio-controlled target conversion of O-38 series aircraft.

OD-1: Identical to the O-2Cs, the OD-1s (BuNos A7103 and A7104) were ordered by the Navy Department and delivered to the US Marine Corps in 1929.

O-2M: In 1929, following its order for eight O-2Cs, the Mexican Government placed an order for nine aircraft (s/n 608 to 616) generally similar to the O-32A but powered by a 525 hp Pratt & Whitney Hornet A

The A-4 radio-controlled drone with tricycle undercarriage was brightly painted with red fuselage and silver wings. (*USAF*)

75

Two OD 1s were ordered by the Navy Department. The first (BuNo A7203) of these aircraft is shown in the markings of Marine Observation Squadron One (VO-1M). (*USMC*)

radial. Various modifications, including the fitting of a tailwheel, were incorporated in the O-2Ms and these modifications were adopted as standard on the O-38s for the Air Corps and the National Guard. A repeat order for three aircraft (s/n 925, 926 and 946) was placed and these machines, which differed only in minor details, were designated O-2M-2s.

O-2MC: Next to the US War Department, the Chinese Government was the largest customer for Douglas observation biplanes and a total of 82 machines was delivered to China between 1930 and 1936. With the exception of the single O-2MC-10 which was similar to the O-38s and powered by a 670 hp Wright R-1820-F21 radial, the various versions of the

A Chinese O-2MC photographed at Santa Monica before delivery. (*Peter Westburg*)

The Chinese O-2MC2 was one of four versions of the Douglas observation biplanes powered by Pratt & Whitney Hornet A engines. (*MDC*)

O-2MC were essentially identical to the O-38. Ten O-2MCs (s/n 915 to 924) were powered by uncowled 525 hp Pratt & Whitney Hornet A radials, twenty O-2MC-2s (s/n 1049 to 1068) had a similar engine but were fitted with a Townend ring, five O-2MC-3s (s/n 1127 to 1131) had the 575 hp Pratt & Whitney Hornet B1 radial, twelve O-2MC-5s (s/n 1336 to 1347) were powered by the 420 hp Pratt & Whitney Wasp C1, and twenty-two O-2MC-6s (1379 to 1400) had 575 hp Wright R-1820-E radials.

Preceded in late 1925 by the delivery of the six unarmed O-2Bs—two went to Bolling Field, DC, and four to Kelly Field, Texas—, the first operational Douglas observation biplanes, forty-five O-2s and eighteen O-2As, were delivered during the first four months of 1926 to Observation Squadrons and other units of the Air Service based at Biggs, Bolling, Chanute, Crissy, Fairfield, Kelly, Langley, Marshall, Maxwell, Mitchel, Post and Sam Houston Fields. Later on in the same year, as the Air Service gave place to the US Army Air Corps, the improved O-2C observation aircraft was delivered and two O-2Ds were handed over for use by Maj-Gen Mason D. Patrick, Chief of the Air Corps, and F. Trubee Davison, Secretary of War for Aviation. Beginning in 1928, these early Douglas observation biplanes were supplemented in squadron operations by the much improved O-2Hs while the other two major variants, the O-25/O-25C and O-38 series, respectively entered service in 1930 and 1931. Strong and reliable, these Douglas observation biplanes served alongside the Curtiss-designed observation biplanes until replaced by more modern equipment such as the Douglas observation monoplanes.

The reliability and pleasant flying characteristics of the Douglas observation biplanes led to the development of a series of basic trainers which began with the forty BT-1s obtained in 1930 by fitting dual controls and instrumentation to a like number of O-2Ks from which the armament had been removed. These aircraft, supplemented by some O-2Hs similarly modified but not redesignated, were operated by the Air Corps and the National Guard until 13 September, 1935, when a BT-1 made the last

The last Liberty-powered aircraft to be operated by the Army Air Corps, the BT-1 remained in service until September 1935. (*USAF*)

military flight on the power of the veteran Liberty engine which had been developed during the First World War. Longer lived were the R-1340 Wasp-powered BT-2s, BT-2As, BT-2Bs and BT-2Cs which remained in service with the Air Corps until the early forties.

While the Douglas observation biplanes and their trainer derivatives gave a good account of themselves during their career with Air Corps units, these machines are mainly remembered for their sterling service with all pre-war National Guard units. Their association with the National Guard began in late 1926 when the 101st (Mass NG), 102nd (NY), 103rd (Penn), 104th (Maryland), 105th (Tenn), 106th (Alabama), 109th (Minn), 115th (Calif), 116th (Wash), 118th (Conn), and 154th (Arkansas NG) Observation Squadrons each received two O-2Cs while the 107th (Michigan), 110th (Missouri), 111th (Texas), 113th (Ind), and 120th (Colorado NG) Observation Squadrons each received one O-2C. In later

An O-38F at Langley Field, Virginia, on 29 April, 1939. (*USAF*)

years, National Guard units were assigned directly from the production line fifty O-2Hs, twenty O-2Ks (BT-1s), forty-five O-38s, one O-38A, thirty-three O-38Bs, one O-38D, thirty-seven O-38Es and eight O-38Fs while a number of other Douglas observation biplanes and basic trainers were transferred to the National Guard after serving with Air Corps units. As late as 1940, when additional units were formed, some late model Douglas observation biplanes were assigned to these new units and the type was not phased out from the National Guard inventory until 1942 as they were easy to fly and maintain, qualities which were just what was needed for service with militia units.

In addition to performing with distinction the lacklustre duties associated with peacetime operations of observation and training units, these Douglas biplanes played a significant role during the 1934 Air Mail Emergency when for a period of seventy-eight days the Army Air Corps operated the Nation's air mail routes. For the carriage of mail, a number of aircraft in the O-25, O-38 and BT-2 series, including aircraft requisitioned from the National Guard, were modified by fairing over the rear cockpit and fitting in its place a box with a capacity of 150–160 lb (68–73 kg) of mail and by installing improved radio equipment. Unfortunately, the Douglas biplanes were found to be space-limited when carrying mail, while the aircraft c.g. was moved too far back, thus forcing the pilots to maintain a constant forward pressure on the control column. Furthermore, the exhaust of the radial engined versions was found too dazzling for safe night landings and, consequently, the O-38s and BT-2s were used during the last phase of the Air Mail Emergency only when no other aircraft were available. The BT-2BIs and BT-2CIs, on the other hand, were used extensively to provide instrument flying and radio range training for the pilots assigned to the project.

In Mexico, the O-2Cs, O-2Ms and O-2M-2s gave equally good service and some survived until well into the 1940s. In China, however, the O-2MCs had a much shorter career as they were faced by the much superior

BT-2C modified for use during the 1934 Air Mail Emergency. It had a faired-over rear cockpit and the side fuselage access door was marked US Mail. (*USAF*)

The O-2BS as flown across Canada in September 1926 by James McKee.
(*US National Archives*)

fighter aircraft of the Imperial Japanese Army and Navy, and little or no
data on their operations filtered back to their manufacturers.

The single aircraft in the series to be ordered as a civil machine, the
O-2BS, had by far the most colourful life. Ordered in 1926 by James Dalzell
McKee, the aircraft made the first single-plane flight across Canada.
Between 11 September and 19 September, 1926, and with the help of the
Canadian authorities which provided all necessary support facilities and
assigned Squadron Leader Earl Godfrey as liaison officer and navigator,
McKee flew the 3,000 miles (4,830 km) between Montreal and Vancouver
in 35 hr 8 min at an average air speed of 85 mph (137 km/h).

Following his successful flight, McKee returned his aircraft to the
Douglas factory where he had it modified as a three-seater and fitted with a
410 hp Pratt & Whitney Wasp A radial. He then intended to use it—
redesignated MO-2B for modified O-2B—for a series of flights in the
Canadian North but, following his death in the crash of a Canadian
Vickers Vedette flying-boat, the aircraft was taken over by the Canadian
Government and, as G-CYZG, was operated until January 1930 as a high-
altitude photographic survey aircraft.

The MO-2B in RCAF service. ZG are the last two letters of its civil registration,
G-CYZG. (*Public Archives of Canada*)

	O-2	O-2H	O-25A	O-38	BT-2B	O-2MC-4
Span, ft in	39 8	40 10	40 0	40 0	40 0	40 0
(m)	(12·09)	(12·45)	(12·19)	(12·19)	(12·19)	(12·19)
Length, ft in	28 9	30 0	30 8	31 0	31 2	30 4
(m)	(8·76)	(9·14)	(9·35)	(9·45)	(9·50)	(9·25)
Height, ft in	10 6	10 0	10 10	10 8	10 6	10 10
(m)	(3·20)	(3·05)	(3·30)	(3·25)	(3·20)	(3·30)
Wing area, sq ft	411	352	364·1	362	362	362
(sq m)	(38·182)	(33·630)	(33·825)	(33·630)	(33·630)	(3·630)
Empty weight, lb	3,032	2,857	3,400	3,070	2,918	3,003
(kg)	(1,375)	(1,296)	(1,542)	(1,393)	(1,324)	(1,362)
Loaded weight, lb	4,650	4,484	4,805	4,343	4,063	4,144
(kg)	(2,109)	(2,034)	(2,180)	(1,970)	(1,843)	(1,880)
Maximum weight, lb	4,785	4,550	—	4,456	4,067	—
(kg)	(2,170)	(2,064)	—	(2,021)	(1,845)	—
Wing loading, lb/sq ft	11·3	12·4	13·2	12·0	11·2	11·4
(kg/sq m)	(55·2)	(60·5)	(64·4)	(58·6)	(54·5)	(55·6)
Power loading, lb/hp	10·7	10·3	8·0	8·3	9·0	9·2
(kg/hp)	(4·8)	(4·7)	(3·6)	(3·8)	(4·1)	(4·2)
Maximum speed,* mph	128·5	134·5	156·6	150	134	135
(km/h)	(207)	(216)	(252)	(241)	(216)	(217)
Cruising speed, mph	103	110	125	120	117	113
(km/h)	(166)	(177)	(201)	(193)	(188)	(182)
Climb rate, ft/min	807	1,075	1,515	1,500	1,130	1,130
(m/min)	(246)	(328)	(426)	(457)	(344)	(344)
Service ceiling, ft	16,275	16,900	22,180	19,000	19,200	19,000
(m)	(4,960)	(5,150)	(6,760)	(5,790)	(5,850)	(5,790)
Normal range, miles	360	512	—	275	320	—
(km)	(580)	(824)	—	(442)	(515)	—

*At sea level.

81

A C-1, the first Douglas military transport, seen on 28 April, 1926. (*USAF*)

Douglas C-1

Douglas obtained its first contract for transport aircraft when funds from the 1925 Fiscal Year budget of the War Department were set aside, under Contract AC810, for the acquisition of nine large single-engined aircraft.

Designated C-1s and powered by a Liberty V-1650-1 water-cooled engine rated at 435 hp at 1,785 rpm, these aircraft (serials 25-425 to 25-433) were similar in construction to the DWC and O-2 series—welded steel fuselage structure with aluminium covering forward of the wing leading edges and fabric covering on the centre and rear fuselage sections and wooden wing structure with fabric covering—but were substantially larger and heavier. The pilot and co-pilot or flight mechanic sat side by side in an open cockpit located forward of the wings, and a 10 ft (3·05 m) long enclosed cabin having a clear cross-section 46 in (1·17 m) wide and 50 in (1·27 m) high was fitted in the centre fuselage. Normally six passenger seats were installed within this cabin but, alternatively, eight seats could be fitted. For freight carrying, the seats were removed and large pieces of cargo, such as a Liberty engine, could be loaded through an opening in the floor. Maximum cargo load was 2,500 lb (1,140 kg).

The first C-1 (s/n 158, serial 25-425) made its maiden flight at Santa Monica on 2 May, 1925, and, later in the month, successfully completed Service trials at McCook Field. Before the end of the same year all nine aircraft had been delivered to the Air Service, and one (25-426) was experimentally fitted with an epicyclic-geared 420 hp Liberty V-1650-5 and redesignated C-1A. For several months the C-1A was tested with a variety of cowlings and engine installations as well as with a ski-undercarriage before being returned to the standard, V-1650-1 powered, C-1 configuration for operational use. This aircraft, however, retained the modified vertical tail surfaces with enlarged rudder with which it had been fitted in its

A Douglas C-1C serving as base transport at March Field, California. (*USAF*)

original C-1A configuration.

The C-1B was a 1925 projected version which was not built but seven improved C-1Cs (serials 26-421 to 26-427) were ordered in 1926 under Contract AC26377. The C-1C had increased span, a longer fuselage and a redesigned balanced rudder. The Liberty V-1650-1 engine as fitted to the C-1 version was retained but silencing exhaust manifolds were fitted. The split-axle undercarriage was modified and the radius rods attached in front of the axles instead of behind them as on the C-1. Internally, the C-1C differed from the C-1 in having a metal floor instead of the wooden floor of the earlier version and in having provision for the carriage of four stretchers for ambulance use. Ten additional C-1Cs (serials 27-203 to 27-212) were ordered with 1927 Fiscal Year funds and all C-1Cs were delivered by Douglas before the end of 1927.

In service, the C-1s and C-1Cs were attached singly or in small detachments to major Army fields and air depots, rather than in batches to specialized transport squadrons. In addition, one C-1 (25-432) distinguished itself in 1929 when it was used as a tanker aircraft during early

The C-1A (25-426) was the second C-1 modified to test an epicyclic-geared Liberty V-1650-5 engine. (*USAF*)

83

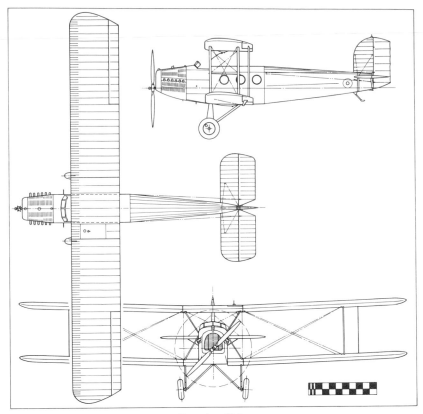

Douglas C-1.

flight-refuelling experiments with the Fokker C-2 and Boeing Hornet Shuttle. As transports, some of the C-1s and C-1Cs were still operated by the Air Corps in the mid-thirties. Furthermore, the Approved Type Certificate No.14 was issued in October 1927 to the Douglas C-1 but it is not known whether surplus C-1s found their way onto the civil market.

C-1

Span 56 ft 7 in (17·25 m); length 35 ft 4 in (10·77 m); height 14 ft (4·27 m); wing area 805 sq ft (74·787 sq m). Empty weight 3,836 lb (1,740 kg); loaded weight 6,443 lb (2,922 kg); wing loading 8 lb/sq ft (39·1 kg/sq m); power loading 14·8 lb/hp (6·7 kg/hp). Maximum speed at sea level 116 mph (187 km/h); cruising speed 85 mph (137 km/h); initial rate of climb 645 ft/min (197 m/min); service ceiling 14,850 ft (4,525 m); range 385 miles (620 km).

C-1C

Span 60 ft (18·29 m); length 36 ft (10·97 m); height 14 ft (4·27 m); wing area 800 sq ft (74·323 sq m). Empty weight 3,900 lb (1,769 kg); loaded weight 7,412 lb (3,362 kg); wing loading 9·3 lb/sq ft (45·2 kg/sq m); power loading 17 lb/hp (7·7 kg/hp). Maximum speed at sea level 121 mph (195 km/h); cruising speed 85 mph (137 km/h); service ceiling 15,950 ft (4,860 m).

The DAM-1 (s/n 169) at Santa Monica on 7 July, 1925. (*MDC*)

Douglas Mailplanes (M Series)

Donald Douglas followed with interest the progress of, and difficulties experienced by, the US Aerial Mail Service operated by the Post Office Department and believed that a new and more reliable aircraft was needed to replace the modified DH-4s which had operated since 1921. As the Post Office shared this conviction, negotiations between the Douglas Company and postal authorities led in early 1925 to the development of a specialized mailplane derived from the Douglas O-2.

Sponsored by the Post Office Department and bearing the company's designation DAM-1 (Douglas Air Mail One), the aircraft was virtually identical to the Liberty-powered O-2, but for military equipment and armament and having an entirely revised cockpit arrangement. Basically, it was a single-seater with an open cockpit located in the same position as the cockpit of the observer/gunner in the O-2. A fire-proof, aluminium-and-asbestos lined compartment with a capacity of 58·5 cu ft (1·66 cu m) was located forward of the cockpit and up to 1,000 lb (454 kg) of mail could be loaded into it through two hatches in the top of the fuselage.

As could be expected, since it was a direct derivative of the successful O-2, the DAM-1 (s/n 169) successfully passed its manufacturer's trials which began on 6 July, 1925, in the hands of Eric Springer. Soon after the aircraft was handed over to the Post Office Department under a one-year lease agreement. Operated primarily on the Chicago–Elko (Nevada) segment of the transcontinental air mail route, the DAM-1 was fitted with two 150,000 candle power landing lights under each lower wingtip and two 30,000 candle power parachute flares, and collective exhaust pipes extending well aft along the fuselage sides were installed. Proving faster, having longer range, and being capable of lifting two and a half times as much mail as the old Post Office DH-4s, the aircraft gave complete satisfaction and its success led to the adoption in March 1926 of the Douglas M-3 as the new Post Office aircraft. However, before expiry of the one-year lease, the DAM-1 was damaged in an accident and returned to Douglas. Rebuilt and brought up to M-2 standard, the original Douglas mailplane was redesignated M-1 and was delivered to Western Air Express in June 1926 to supplement its previously ordered fleet of M-2s.

Western Air Express's interest in the Douglas mailplane series began in October 1925 when this company was awarded Contract Air Mail Four (CAM 4), one of the first mail contracts issued by the Post Office Department pursuant to the 1925 Kelly Air Mail Act. To operate CAM 4 between Salt Lake City and Los Angeles via Las Vegas, in December 1925 Western Air Express (WAE) ordered an initial batch of five Douglas M-2s (s/n 244 to 248). Still powered by 400 hp Liberty engines, the M-2s were fitted with a radiator installation similar to that used on the O-2BS and subsequent models in the O-2 series and differed further from the original

One of the M-2s with which Western Air Express began mail operations between Los Angeles and Salt Lake City on 17 April, 1926. (*Western Airlines*)

DAM-1 in having provision for two passenger seats and cockpit openings for the forward mail compartment and hatches. On 17 April, 1926, WAE began mail operations on the route when a Douglas M-2 flown by Charles James left Salt Lake City for Los Angeles while, later in the day, another M-2 piloted by Maury Graham flew the reverse leg. A little over a month later, on 23 May, the first two passengers, who each paid a $90 fare, were flown between Salt Lake City and Los Angeles. By the end of 1926, in the M-2s, Western Air Express had carried 209 passengers, 71,414 lb (32,393 kg) of mail and 263 lb (119 kg) of express over Contract Air Mail route 4. WAE demonstrated its satisfaction by acquiring the modified M-1 prototype and ordering a sixth M-2 (s/n 254) which was delivered in 1927, and later acquired an M-4A.

In early 1926, the Post Office Department invited bids for a Liberty-powered mailplane to replace the DH-4s on the transcontinental mail routes. Having already developed and demonstrated an aircraft meeting all the requirements of the Post Office, Douglas entered an improved version,

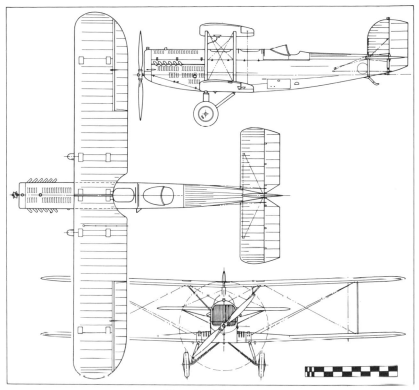

Douglas M-2.

the M-3. The M-3 had streamlined wires between the flying surfaces, instead of the cables used on the DAM-1 and M-2s, and other changes included improvements in engine accessories, instruments and night flying equipment. The long exhaust pipes added to the earlier Douglas mailplanes became standard while, for use by the Post Office Department, there was provision for only one passenger seat. Capable of carrying 1,000 lb (454 kg) of mail as opposed to only 400 lb (181 kg) for the similarly powered Air Mail DH-4 which it was intended to replace, the M-3 was selected by the Post Office in preference to the Boeing Model 40, and in March 1926 Douglas was awarded a contract for ten aircraft (s/n 255 to 264). Within a year, the Post Office Department ordered an additional forty (s/n 303 to 342) which, designated M-4s, differed from the M-3s in having wings of larger area and overall span increased from 39 ft 8 in (12·09 m) to 44 ft 6 in (13·56 m) to enable them to lift a heavier load from the smaller airfields.

When the Douglas M-4s were ordered, however, the Post ·Office Department already planned to discontinue its own air mail operations and, as provided in the Air Mail Act of 1925 and Air Commerce Act of 1926, was progressively relinquishing its routes to commercial carriers.

An M-3 in service with National Air Transport. The aircraft is fitted with a tall radio mast on the rear fuselage. (*United Air Lines*)

Finally, on 31 August, 1927, by which time many of the M-4s were still in their delivery crates, the Post Office made a final mail flight between New York and Chicago. For a while indecision prevailed with regard to the disposition of aircraft no longer needed by the postal authorities and consideration was given to modifying sixteen of the Post Office's Douglas mailplanes for use by the Air Corps as 'cross-country airplanes'. However, the airlines needed them urgently and the Post Office fleet was put up for auction. Largest user of surplus M-3s and M-4s was National Air Transport (NAT) which acquired eighteen of these aircraft for use on the New York–Chicago route.

In addition to the forty M-4s ordered by the Post Office Department, Douglas built two modified aircraft. The M-4A (s/n 357) differed from the M-4 only in minor detail and was ordered by Western Air Express to bring its fleet of Douglas mailplanes to a total of nine (six M-2s, one M-1, one surplus M-4, and the M-4A). The final aircraft in the series, the M-4S (s/n 383), was ordered by National Air Transport and was a three-seater

The M-4S ordered by National Air Transport, photographed at Santa Monica before delivery. (*MDC*)

In 1977 this rebuilt M-4 was flown across the United States to be placed on permanent display in the National Air & Space Museum. (*Western Airlines*)

powered by a 410 hp Pratt & Whitney Wasp A nine-cylinder radial. For use in NAT's pilot training programme, the aircraft was fitted with dual controls and instruments in the centre cockpit.

Before obtaining the M-4S, NAT had fitted a Wasp A radial to one of the M-3s acquired from the Post Office Department while another of its M-3s was experimentally fitted with an enclosed pilot's cockpit. NAT operated its fleet of M-3s and M-4s until October 1930 while WAE disposed of its Douglas mailplanes shortly after. One of these aircraft, the M-4 acquired by WAE from the Post Office, was later re-acquired by Western Airlines for display and publicity purposes. Restored once again, this aircraft was donated in 1977 to the National Air & Space Museum.

A further development was planned and construction of one aircraft—designated M-5 and bearing the s/n 925—began. However, before completion, the project was terminated and the s/n and some of the parts already built were used on one of the O-2Ms built for the Mexican Government.

M-2

Span 39 ft 8 in (12·09 m); length 28 ft 11 in (8·81 m); height 10 ft 1 in (3·07 m); wing area 411 sq ft (38·183 sq m). Empty weight 2,885 lb (1,309 kg); loaded weight 4,755 lb (2,157 kg); wing loading 11·6 lb/sq ft (56·5 kg/sq m); power loading 11·9 lb/hp (5·4 kg/hp). Maximum speed at sea level 145 mph (233 km/h); cruising speed 118 mph (188 km/h); initial rate of climb 1,100 ft/min (335 m/min); service ceiling 17,000 ft (5,180 m); range 650 miles (1,045 km).

M-4

Span 44 ft 6 in (13·56 m); length 28 ft 11 in (8·81 m); height 10 ft 1 in (3·07 m); wing area 465 sq ft (43·2 sq m). Empty weight 3,405 lb (1,544 kg); loaded weight 4,900 lb (2,223 kg); wing loading 10·5 lb/sq ft (51·2 kg/sq m); power loading 12·3 lb/hp (5·6 kg/hp). Maximum speed at sea level 140 mph (225 km/h); cruising speed 110 mph (177 km/h); initial rate of climb 1,000 ft/min (305 m/min); service ceiling 16,500 ft (5,030 m); range 700 miles (1,125 km).

The Commuter, the first Douglas venture in the light aircraft field, at Santa Monica on 20 January, 1926. (*MDC*)

Douglas Commuter

Like several other designers, Donald Douglas believed that a large number of pilots who had left the Air Service at the end of the war wanted to continue flying as a sport and that a market existed for an inexpensive light aircraft. In an attempt to capture a share of this market, Douglas designed a small two-seat aircraft which could be powered by either a 35 hp Anzani three-cylinder air-cooled radial or a 60 hp Wright Gale engine of similar configuration. Named the Commuter and completed in 1926, the aircraft was unusual in several respects. In particular, this aircraft, the first monoplane designed by Douglas, had high-mounted, externally braced, wings which could be manually folded along the fuselage to enable it to be stored in a garage. It was also the first aeroplane to make use of the new Clark Y aerofoil. Of wooden construction, the machine had fabric covering overall with the exception of the engine cowling which had quickly detachable aluminium panels and from which protruded the cylinder heads.

In spite of its appeal the Commuter (s/n 150), which was completed in January 1926 and tested by Eric Springer, remained experimental, as competition in this field was fierce and because the Douglas Company had by then sufficient military work on hand to occupy its limited work force.

Span 37 ft 3 in (11·35 m). Empty weight 800 lb (363 kg); loaded weight 1,250 lb (567 kg); power loading 35·5 lb/hp (16·1 kg/hp) Anzani, 20·8 lb/hp (9·1 kg/hp) Wright. Maximum speed 76 mph (122 km/h).

Douglas T2D and P2D

The first twin-engined Douglas product and the first twin-engined aircraft intended to operate from the decks of aircraft carriers, the T2D-1 had an unusual development history going back to an original Naval Aircraft Factory design for a multi-purpose single-engined aircraft. Developed into a three-seat, land-based or seaplane torpedo bomber and powered by a 525 hp Wright T-2 liquid-cooled engine, this large machine was initially built by the Curtiss Aeroplane and Motor Co as the CS-1 (six aircraft) and was later produced by the Glenn L. Martin Co as the SC-1 (35 aircraft).

While Martin continued to develop the Naval Aircraft Factory design and produced a series of torpedo bombers (SC-2, T3M-1, T3M-2, XT3M-3, XT3M-4, XT4M-1 and T4M-1) which culminated in the TG-1 and TG-2 built by the Great Lakes Aircraft Corporation, the engineering staff at the Naval Aircraft Factory studied various possibilities of improving the performance of its basic design. From these studies were evolved an improved single-engined model, of which three examples were built as TB-1s by the Boeing Airplane Co, and two twin-engined models, the NAF-built XTN-1 and the Douglas-built XT2D-1s.

At the time the Bureau of Aeronautics greatly favoured multi-purpose aircraft so as to make the best possible use of an aircraft carrier's limited space, and insisted on procuring aircraft capable of fulfilling alternatively the level bombing, torpedo bombing and scouting roles. At the same time it favoured types with either wheel undercarriages for aircraft carrier or land based operations or with floats. However, these conflicting requirements imposed serious performance restrictions and thus led the Naval Aircraft Factory to study various ways of improving the performance of this class of multi-purpose aircraft. Whereas with the Boeing-built TB-1s this goal was

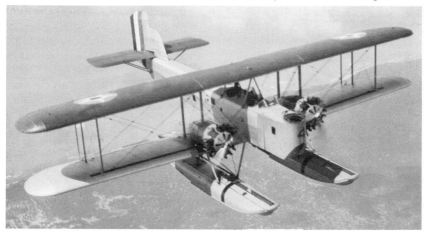

T2D-1 in flight over Oahu, Hawaii, on 25 April, 1929, (USN)

91

partially reached through the use of one of the most powerful engines then available, the liquid-cooled 770 hp Packard 1A-2500, the NAF design team elected to study concurrently the possibility of producing a twin-engined version, as the use of two motors instead of one promised not only an improvement in performance but also an improvement in reliability and safety during long overwater missions.

With the development by Pratt & Whitney and Wright of new radial, air-cooled, engines developing more than 500 hp and weighing substantially less than contemporary liquid-cooled engines of similar power, the NAF team had at its disposal ideal powerplants for the new twin-engined, multi-purpose, land-, carrier-, or sea-based aircraft. Taking advantage of the availability of these engines and wishing to ascertain the possible advantages of twin-engined aircraft, in May 1925 the Bureau of Aeronautics instructed the NAF to undertake the construction of one experimental XTN-1 (BuNo A7027) while, two months later, it awarded to the Douglas Company a contract for the construction of three generally similar XT2D-1s (BuNos A7051 to A7053).

Naval Aircraft Factory XTN-1 (BuNo A7027), the prototype of the Douglas T2D-1/P2D-1 series. (*John J. Ide*)

Completed in January 1927, the first XT2D-1 was powered by two 500 hp Wright P-2 nine-cylinder, air-cooled, radials mounted on the lower wing and driving two-blade propellers. Like the XTN-1, the Douglas-built aircraft bore a strong resemblance, particularly in the shape of the rear fuselage and tail sections, to the single-engined Martin T3M-1, a progressive development of the original NAF design built by Curtiss as the CS-1. Like the T3M-1, the XTN-1 and XT2D-1 had two tandem open cockpits for the pilots, but on the two twin-engined designs the rear-gunner/wireless operator cockpit was moved forward while a fourth open cockpit was provided in the extreme nose and fitted with a single flexible ring-mounted machine-gun and a transparent bomb-aiming panel. Located forward of the wings and fitted with a slanted transparent panel on each side of the fuselage, the cockpit of the command pilot offered an exceptional forward and downward field of view—a valuable asset during landings aboard aircraft carriers. For use from shore bases or, as intended, from aircraft carriers the XT2D-1 was fitted with a split-axle under-carriage. For operations from water the aircraft could be fitted with floats.

Following its maiden flight on 27 January, 1927, the first XT2D-1 (BuNo A7051) was flown to San Diego for shipment aboard the USS *Argonne* to Hampton Roads, Virginia, where in late March 1927 it was fitted with its floats for Service trials at Anacostia. Efforts were also made at that time to prepare the aircraft for deck trials aboard the USS *Langley* which was scheduled to return from exercises off Cuba in late April. Unfortunately, due primarily to the poor reliability of its two Wright P-2 engines, the XT2D-1 could not be got ready on time and instead of performing carrier qualification trials was sent to the Naval Aircraft Factory to be re-engined with two 525 hp Wright R-1750 radials. Progressively this type of engine

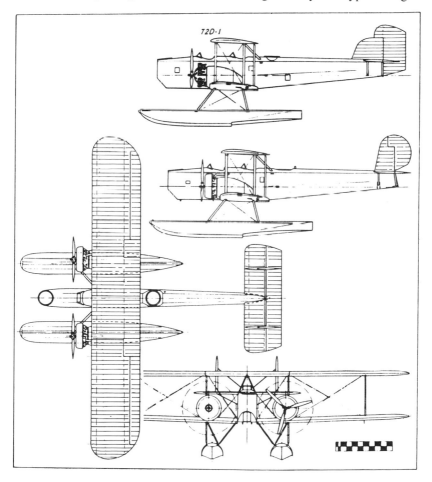

Douglas P2D-1 and T2D-1.

93

was also fitted to the two other prototypes (BuNos A7052 and A7053) and A7053 demonstrated the good qualities of the XT2D-1 design during a multi-stop ferry flight from San Diego to Anacostia between 27 December, 1927, and 5 January, 1928.

Already, on the basis of limited operational trials conducted by Torpedo Squadron Two (VT-2) beginning in May 1927, the Navy had decided to place a limited production order for nine T2D-1s (BuNos A7587 to A7595) which differed from the XT2D-1s is a number of respects. The use of the lighter Wright R-1750 radials driving three-blade propellers necessitated a redesign of the engine nacelles and the powerplants were mounted further forward of the wing leading edge. At the same time, the length of the fuselage was reduced by almost 3 ft (91.4 cm) to improve balance, and various improvements were incorporated in the two forward cockpits. Later, beginning with the second production aircraft (A7588), a new balanced rudder of increased height and area was fitted to improve directional stability and this modification was retro-fitted to the first production T2D-1 and to at least one of the XT2D-1s.

The first T2D-1 (BuNo A7587), with original tail surfaces as seen as Santa Monica on 17 May, 1928. (*MDC*)

In service the T2D-1s were liked by crews as, when fitted with land undercarriages, they were some 15 per cent faster than the contemporary single-engined Martin T3M-2s and because the pilots benefited from a clear field of vision, a significant asset for carrier operations. However, contemporary engines being unreliable, the T2D-1 was regarded by many as twice as prone as the T3M-2 to engine failure and liable to presents pilots with a major directional stability problem when attempting a single-engined landing aboard a carrier.Moreover, the Navy felt that performance advantages would be negated while operating from carriers by the aircraft's large size and heavier weight which reduced the number of machines which could be embarked. As the Martin T4M-1, powered by a single 525 hp Pratt & Whitney R-1690-24 radial, was only 10 per cent slower than the T2D-1, the Navy decided to standardize on this type for carrier operations and to assign the T2D-1s to operations from shore bases and coastal waters.

Bomb-carrying P2D-1 with flexible guns installed in the front and rear cockpits.
(*US National Archives*)

This decision, however, led to major inter-Service squabbling as the Army Air Corps considered that operations by shore-based T2D-1s conflicted with its own operations. None the less, the T2D-1s were assigned in late 1928 to the Commander Aircraft Squadrons and Attending Craft, Pearl Harbor, where they were operated by Patrol Squadrons One and Six (VP-1 and VP-6) until struck off the Navy List in April 1933. During operations in Hawaii, the T2D-1s were operated from shore bases to obtain a detailed topographic survey of the islands. However, more often than not, they were operated as seaplanes for maritime reconnaissance and in

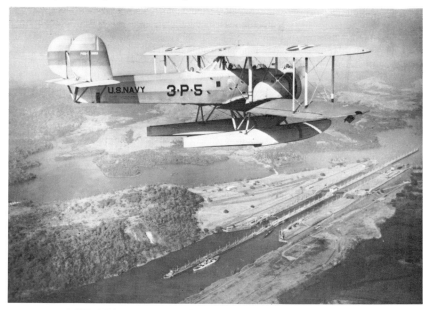

A VP-3 P2D-1 over the Gatun locks of the Panama Canal.
(*US National Archives*)

this role endeared themselves to their crews because of their ability to take off easily and to climb quickly with heavy loads.

Results obtained with the T2D-1s operating in the Hawaiian Islands led to the placing in June 1930 of a new order for 18 aircraft specially intended for maritime reconnaissance. Originally designated T2D-2s but delivered as P2D-1s to reflect their new mission, these aircraft incorporated a number of modifications dictated by experience. Major changes included the use of twin fins and rudders to improve controllability while flying on one engine and an increase in normal fuel capacity from 250 US gallons (946 litres) for the T2D-1s to 350 gallons (1,325 litres) for the P2D-1s, while the new aircraft were powered by a pair of 575 hp Wright R-1820-E nine-cylinder radials driving three-blade propellers and fitted with Townend rings. Delivered during 1931, the P2D-1s were operated by Patrol Squadron Three (VP-3) in the Canal Zone until 1937 when the first Douglas-built twin-engined aircraft were finally retired.

XTN-1 floatplane

Span 57 ft (17·37 m); length 44 ft 10 in (13·67 m); height 15 ft 7 in (4·75 m); wing area 886 sq ft (82·312 sq m). Empty weight 6,003 lb (2,723 kg); loaded weight 10,413 lb (4,723 kg); maximum weight 11,926 lb (5,410 kg); wing loading 11·8 lb/sq ft (57·4 kg/sq m); power loading 10·4 lb/hp (4·7 kg/hp). Maximum speed at sea level 123 mph (182 km/h); climb to 5,000 ft (1,524 m) 7·1 min; service ceiling 12,600 ft (3,840 m); normal range 375 miles (604 km); maximum range 764 miles (1,230 km).

XT2D-1 floatplane

Span and wing area as XTN-1. Height 15 ft 6¾ in (4·74 m). Empty weight 6,475 lb (2,937 kg); maximum weight 10,800 lb (4,899 kg). Maximum speed at sea level 121 mph (179 km/h); normal range 587 miles (945 km).

XT2D-1 landplane

Span and wing area as XTN-1. Length 44 ft 11$\frac{15}{32}$ in (13·71 m). Empty weight 5,733 lb (2,600 kg); maximum weight 9,778 lb (4,435 kg). Maximum speed at sea level 123 mph (182 km/h); normal range 596 miles (959 km).

T2D-1 floatplane

Span and wing area as XTN-1. Length 44 ft 4 in (13·51 m); height 16 ft 11 in (5·16 m). Empty weight 6,528 lb (2,961 kg); loaded weight 10,503 lb (4,764 kg); maximum weight 11,040 lb (5,008 kg); wing loading 11·9 lb/sq ft (57·9 kg/sq m); power loading 10 lb/hp (4.5 kg/hp). Maximum speed at sea level 124 mph (183 km/h); climb to 5,000 ft (1,524 m) 7·7 min; service ceiling 11,400 ft (3,475 m); normal range 384 miles (618 km); maximum range 454 miles (732 km).

T2D-1 landplane

Span and wing area as XTN-1. Length 42 ft (12·8 m); height 15 ft 11 in (4·85 m). Empty weight 6,011 lb (2,726 kg); loaded weight 9,986 lb (4,530 kg); maximum weight 10,523 lb (4,773 kg); wing loading 11·4 lb/sq ft (55 kg/sq m); power loading 9·5 lb/hp (4·3 kg/hp). Maximum speed at sea level 125 mph (185 km/h); climb to 5,000 ft (1,524 m) 5·9 min; service ceiling 13,830 ft (4,155 m); normal range 457 miles (735 km).

P2D-1 floatplane

Span 57 ft (17·37 m); length 43 ft 11 in (13·39 m); height 17 ft 6 in (5·33 m); wing area 909 sq ft (84·449 sq m). Empty weight 7,486 lb (3,395 kg); loaded weight 12,611 lb (5,720 kg); maximum weight 13,052 lb (5,920 kg); wing loading 13·9 lb/sq ft (67·7 kg/sq m); power loading 11 lb/hp (5 kg/hp). Maximum speed at sea level 136 mph (203 km/h); cruising speed 108 mph (174 km/h); climb to 5,000 ft (1,524 m) 8 min; service ceiling 11,200 ft (3,415 m); maximum range 1,010 miles (1,625 km).

P2D-1 landplane

Span and wing area as floatplane. Length 40 ft 11 in (12·47 m); height 16 ft 2 in (4·93 m). Empty weight 6,685 lb (3,032 kg); maximum weight 12,251 lb (5,557 kg). Maximum speed at sea level 138 mph (206 km/h); climb to 5,000 ft (1,524 m) 6·8 min; service ceiling 12,700 ft (3,870 m).

Douglas DA-1

As in their first attempt with the Commuter, Douglas elected to use the monoplane configuration for a new attempt at penetrating the private aircraft market. However, whereas the Commuter had high-mounted wings, the DA-1 marked Douglas's first experience with the parasol monoplane configuration.

Design work on the DA-1 was begun in 1926 but progressed at a slow pace, as the company's limited engineering staff was kept busy with the basic design of new military types and the modification and improvement of aircraft already in production. Compared with the Commuter, which had just begun flight trials, the DA-1 was conceived as a markedly different aeroplane, with emphasis on sturdy construction and dependability rather than on low manufacturing and operating costs.

The newly completed DA-1 at Santa Monica on 7 September, 1928. The new Douglas logo appears beneath the rear cockpit. (*MDC*)

Twice as heavy as the Commuter, the DA-1 was powered by a 220 hp Wright Whirlwind nine-cylinder radial enclosed in a conical-shaped cowling with protruding cylinder heads and a two-blade propeller with large spinner. The fuselage was of chrome-molybdenum structure, the wings had Russian birch spars and ribs with plywood covering, whilst the fabric-covered tail surfaces and the cabin floor were of duralumin. Accommodation was provided for one pilot and one or two passengers in tandem open cockpits, and quickly disconnected dual controls were fitted in the front cockpit for pilot training.

Ordered by Ambassador Airways Inc, the DA-1 (s/n 503, X7281) was first flown in September 1928 and, after completing its tests at Santa Monica, was flown to El Paso, Texas, to be demonstrated during the air races held there in the autumn of 1928. After the races the aircraft, piloted by Eric Springer and carrying Donald Douglas, took off from El Paso for Santa Monica. However, shortly after take-off the engine stopped. Springer succeeded in making an emergency landing and he and his passenger walked out unhurt. Unfortunately, as one of the undercarriage legs had been torn off and one wing damaged, the aircraft was not repaired and Douglas did not pursue his second attempt at producing a private aircraft.

Span 35 ft (10·67 m); length 22 ft 6 in (6·86 m); wing area 212 sq ft (19·695 sq m). Empty weight 1,750 lb (794 kg); loaded weight 2,530 lb (1,148 kg); wing loading 11·9 lb/sq ft (58·3 kg/sq m); power loading 11·5 lb/hp (5·2 kg/hp). Maximum speed 140 mph (225 km/h); initial rate of climb 900 ft/min (274 m/min); service ceiling 14,500 ft (4,420 m).

Douglas PD-1

One of the most interesting examples of progressive aircraft development, although rather complicated, originated in the autumn of 1914 when the British Admiralty ordered two experimental twin-engined Curtiss flying-boats. Derived from the Curtiss H *America* which had been financed by Rodman Wanamaker and intended for a flight across the Atlantic by John Cyril Porte, these two aircraft were successfully tested and led to the production of sixty-two Curtiss H-4 Little Americas for the British Royal Naval Air Service. From these H-4s Curtiss developed the larger and more powerful H-8 and H-12 Large Americas which were operated by the RNAS during the First World War. Development of these series of twin-engined flying-boats continued in the United Kingdom where in 1915 John Porte fitted improved hulls of his own design to Curtiss H-4s to produce the Felixstowe F.1. The Porte hull's better seaworthiness led to a decision to fit a larger hull of similar design to the Curtiss H-12. This new flying-boat, the Felixstowe F.2, was further improved and was put into production in England as the F.2A. A year later, a version with new wing structure and other refinements went into production as the Felixstowe F.5.

A VP-4 PD-1. Note flattened rear engine nacelles and hull which was much wider than the fuselage. (*US National Archives*)

In the United States, the Navy, after obtaining twenty Curtiss H-12/H-12Ls, ordered 274 larger H-16s which used Porte's improved hull. In addition, the US Navy ordered a version of the Felixstowe F.5 which was powered by two Liberty engines. Designated F-5Ls, later PN-5s, 228 of these flying boats were built by Curtiss, Canadian Aeroplanes Ltd and the Naval Aircraft Factory. Two generally similar machines, the F-6Ls (PN-6s) were built by the Naval Aircraft Factory and were characterized by new parallel-chord ailerons. The next version designed at the NAF in 1923, the PN-7, introduced a new thicker wing of reduced span but retained the hull, fuselage and tail assembly of the F-5L and F-6L. Powered by two Wright T-2 engines with pusher propellers, the two PN-7s were followed by two PN-8s which, retaining the new wing design, had metal hulls and were powered by Packard 1A 2500 engines. One of the PN-8s was modified after delivery to PN-9 configuration with redesigned tail surfaces and revised engine nacelles. Four PN-10s similar to the PN-9 were then ordered but the last two were completed as PN-12s with radial engines, one being powered by two Wright Cyclones whilst the other had a pair of Pratt & Whitney Hornets.

On 31 December, 1927, the US Navy had only three serviceable flying-boats as the F-5Ls ordered at the end of the war had reached the end of their useful lives, whilst the various PN designs were retained for experimental purposes. However, in the PN-12 the Navy had an excellent design which benefited from the greater reliability of its radial engines. Accordingly, the Navy Department decided to place production orders for PN-12 variants with a number of civil contractors, and amongst them was the Douglas Company which on 29 December, 1927, received a $1,553,505 contract for the production of 25 patrol flying-boats which were to be delivered in nine months' time.

Before undertaking production of its first flying-boat, the Douglas Company modified the PN-12 design and introduced a number of improvements. In particular, the Douglas team streamlined the

99

wing struts and bracing wires and adopted ailerons of improved design without the external flying balance tabs used on the PN-12, although the external tabs were retained for the rudder in order to reduce control loads on the rudder pedals. At the same time the rear of the nacelles housing the 525 hp Wright R-1750A nine-cylinder radials were sharply tapered to smooth the airflow, and three-blade metal propellers with preflight adjustable-pitch were selected. Improvements were also introduced in equipment and instruments, and the Douglas-built flying-boats, designated PD-1s, were fitted with a gyroscopically stabilized automatic pilot, generators, electric engine starters and improved radio equipment. These 'boats were of metal construction with metal clad hulls and fabric covered wings and tails.

Problems encountered in tooling up for production and in finalizing design changes delayed completion of the first PD-1 (s/n 478, BuNo A7979) until the spring of 1929. As the Douglas plant was too far inland for flight tests, the aircraft had to be taken unassembled to NAS North Island in San Diego. There the first aircraft made its maiden flight in May 1929 off the sheltered waters of San Diego Bay. No significant problem was

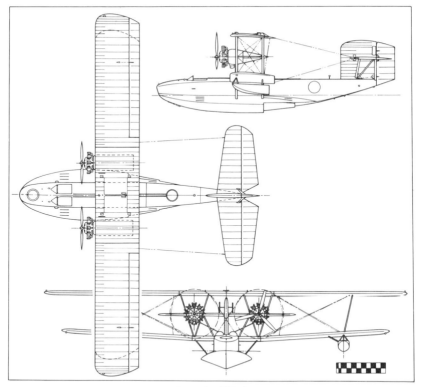

Douglas PD-1.

100

PD-1 of VP-7B taking off from San Diego bay on 15 September, 1930.
(*US National Archives*)

encountered during manufacturer's and Service trials but further delays were incurred while production was transferred from the Wilshire plant to the new Santa Monica plant. The last PD-1 was finally delivered in June 1930.

Entering service with VP-7B in July 1929, the PD-1s proved reliable and demonstrated regular endurance of up to 24 hours whilst serving with Patrol Squadrons One, Four, Six and Seven. In service, these aircraft were re-engined with 575 hp Wright R-1820-64 nine-cylinder radials. However, the basic design had been initiated in the early years of the war and the aircraft rapidly became obsolete. In October 1936, only six years after the last aircraft had been delivered, the PD-1s were withdrawn from squadron service. At that time fifteen PD-1s were transferred to NAS Pensacola, Florida, as trainers, the last PD-1 being struck off charge at Pensacola on 31 March, 1939.

Span 72 ft 10 in (22·2 m); length 49 ft 2 in (14·99 m); height 16 ft 4 in (4·98 m); wing area 1,162 sq ft (107·954 sq m). Empty weight 7,453 lb (3,381 kg); loaded weight 14,122 lb (6,406 kg); wing loading 12·2 lb/sq ft (59·3 kg/sq m); power loading 13·4 lb/hp (6·1 kg/hp). Maximum speed at sea level 114 mph (183 km/h); cruising speed 94 mph (151 km/h); climb to 5,500 ft (1,675 m) 10 min; service ceiling 10,900 ft (3,320 m); range 1,309 miles (2,107 km). Crew of five with, for long-range patrol, relief crew of five.

Armament: one flexible 0·30-in machine-gun in open bow position and one in open midship position. Up to 2,000 lb (907 kg) of bombs, torpedoes or mines on external wing racks.

The Douglas Sinbad at Santa Monica on 28 July, 1930. (*MDC*)

Douglas Sinbad and Dolphin

Ten years after founding the Davis-Douglas Company, Donald Douglas, for whom the sea always retained its fascination, combined his vocation and his avocation by building the first flying-boat of his own design, the Sinbad. Prototype of the Dolphin series, the twin-engined Sinbad was conceived in the economic boom of the late 1920s as a luxury 'air yacht'. Unfortunately, in the civil market, the aircraft was a victim of the Great Depression and Douglas was saved from incurring a telling financial blow only through the fortuitous success of the military versions of the Dolphin.

At the time of its completion in July 1930, the Sinbad (s/n 703, X145W) bore a remarkable resemblance to the smaller Saunders-Roe A.17 Cutty Sark which had made its first flight at Cowes in the Isle of Wight a year earlier. In fact, the dimensions, accommodation, powerplant type and installation, and external appearance of the Sinbad were strikingly similar to those of the prototype Saunders-Roe A.19 Cloud, a scaled-up version of the Cutty Sark which was also built in 1930. Like its British contemporary, the Douglas flying-boat was a high-wing cantilever monoplane of wood and metal construction, with all-metal hull and wood-covered cantilever wing. Both aircraft had accommodation for two pilots in an enclosed cabin, that of the Sinbad being located just forward of the wing whilst that of the Cloud was located further forward, and for eight passengers in a cabin within the hull and beneath the wing. Other similarities between the two contemporary aircraft included the use of a pair of 300 hp Wright J-5C Whirlwind radials mounted above and forward of the wing on multiple struts—the struts of the Sinbad's engine pylons being initially faired over to reduce drag—, and of tube-braced tailplanes. Finally, whereas the Sinbad was a flying-boat and as such was only fitted with a beaching gear, its Dolphin production version was an amphibian which was fitted with an undercarriage of similar geometry to that of the Cloud.

The Sinbad was first tested from Santa Monica Bay in July 1930. At that time its engines were enclosed in metal covered cowlings which sloped rearward and downward for attachment to the wing upper surface. However, flight trials soon revealed the need for a number of major modifications to the airframe and powerplant installation. In particular, it was found necessary to mount the engines higher and the extensive fairings were replaced by conical nacelles of welded chrome-molybdenum steel which were attached to the wing upper surface by six bracing struts. At the same time a small auxiliary aerofoil between the engine nacelles was added to increase rigidity and smooth out the airflow. Less drastic modifications included the addition of twin auxiliary tail fins and the relocation of the fixed floats further outboard. So modified, the Sinbad flying-boat was purchased for $31,500 by the US Coast Guard. Entering service with the USCG in February 1931, the aircraft initially received the serial number 27 (changed to 227 in February 1935 and to V106 in October 1936). It was phased out of service in November 1939.

While the Sinbad was being tested, Douglas was planning the production of the Dolphin, an amphibian version based on the modified Sinbad and intended for military and civil markets. These aircraft were fitted with retractable undercarriages comprising a main gear attached to the hull by hinged V struts and to the wing undersurface by an oleo leg. A tailwheel replaced the skid of the Sinbad and was attached to the hull aft of the rear step. In flight, or for water operation, the main gear was raised by shortening the oleo legs, thus lifting the wheels above the waterline, while the tailwheel pivoted upward until it was close to the hull. All production Dolphins were fitted with this gear but, as described later, one OA-4B of the Air Corps was later fitted for test purposes with a non-retractable tricycle undercarriage.

While only 58 Dolphins were built between 1931 and 1934, this total included not less than 17 variants and models as the Dolphins were either custom-built for each civil customer or produced in small batches for military customers. Furthermore, progressive improvements, modifications and/or engine changes were introduced on the line. Thus, the production and service history of the Dolphins is best summarized by providing details for each individual aircraft or batch of aircraft.

S/n 999 and 1002: Registered NC967Y and NC12212 respectively, these amphibians were powered by 300 hp Wright J-5C Whirlwinds and acquired by Wilmington-Catalina Airline Ltd. In addition to being fitted with the retractable undercarriage, they differed from the Sinbad flying-boat in having a longer, deeper and sharper bow. Initially designated Model 1s and fitted out to carry six passengers and two pilots, they later had seats for eight passengers and were redesignated Model 1 Specials. Both were

Douglas Dolphin 1 (s/n 999, NC967Y) of Wilmington-Catalina Airlines. (*NA & SM*)

operated on the 20-mile route between Wilmington, in the Los Angeles harbour area, and Avalon, a resort on Santa Catalina Island, beginning in 1931.

S/n 1000: Ordered by the US Navy and designated XRD-1, this aircraft (BuNo A8876) differed from the first commercial Dolphin in being powered by two 435 hp Wright R-975Es and fitted with military instrumentation and equipment. Accepted on 1 August, 1931, the RD-1 (ex XRD-1) was operated as a staff transport until struck off at Norfolk, Virginia, on 12 July, 1938.

S/n 1001: The third commercial Dolphin (NC982Y) was built in 1931 as a luxurious six-seater (two pilots and four passengers) for Powell Crosley Jr, a noted industrialist. Designated Model 3, it differed from the two Wilmington-Catalina Dolphins in having two 300 hp Pratt & Whitney Wasp Junior A engines. Interestingly, NC982Y found its way to Australia where, with Australian military serial A35-3, it was impressed into the

The Dolphin 1 Special on 17 July, 1932. It was painted in Coast Guard markings but had not been delivered. (*MDC*)

104

RAAF on 5 October, 1942. Assigned successively to No.9 Squadron and No.3 OTU the veteran Dolphin survived the war and was sold to a Mr Whittle on 3 May, 1945.

S/n 1003: Built and demonstrated as a civil Model 1 Special (NC12243), this aircraft was acquired in August 1932 by the USCG. Re-engined with two 435 hp Wright R-975Es, it was designated Douglas RD under the Navy system but without model number. It successively bore the serials 28, 128 (from January 1935) and V109 (from October 1936), and was decommissioned in November 1939.

Douglas Y1C-21 (32-279) at Luke Field, Hawaii, in June 1933. (*USAF*)

S/n 1075 to 1082: Ordered as Y1C-21s for the Army Air Corps under Contract AC-4460 of 10 August, 1931, these eight aircraft (32-279 to 286) were generally similar to the Navy's XRD-1 and powered by two 350 hp Wright R-975-3 engines. Initially, the Air Corps intended to assign one or two of them to each Bombardment Group with the idea that they would fly along with the bombers during overwater flights to act as navigators and rescue aircraft. However, mainly due to their relatively low speed, which prevented them from keeping up with the bombers, the idea was soon dropped. Later, they were redesignated plain C-21s, in the transport category, and then OA-3s, in the observation amphibian category. So designated, they were used as transport and rescue aircraft, and an OA-3 assigned to the 7th Bombardment Group at Hamilton Field, California, pioneered for the Air Corps the technique of air-sea rescue operations. Some of these aircraft, temporarily designated FP-1s, were also loaned to the Treasury Department for use on border patrols during Prohibition. Eventually, the OA-3s, with the exception of 32-281 which was destroyed on 23 November, 1938, in a taxying accident at West Point, were assigned to the Panama Canal Zone, the Territory of Hawaii, and the Philippine Islands. The last was withdrawn in March 1940.

S/n 1083 and 1084: Ordered on 7 May, 1932, as an addendum to Contract AC-4460, the two Y1C-26s (later redesignated C-26s and OA-4s) underwent a series of major redesigns which became characteristic of all subsequent military and civil Dolphins. On these aircraft (32-396 and

Douglas OA-3 of Major-Gen Drum, over Oahu, Hawaii, on 22 April, 1935.
(*USAF*)

32-397) the wing area was increased from the original 562 sq ft (52·212 sq m) to 592 sq ft (54·999 sq m), the overall length was increased from 43 ft 10 in (13·36 m) to 45 ft 5 in (13·84 m), and the height and area of the vertical tail surfaces were increased, thus enabling the removal of the two auxiliary fins first introduced during testing of the Sinbad. Fuel capacity was increased from 180 to 240 US gallons (681 to 908 litres). Powered by two 300 hp Pratt & Whitney R-985-1 radials, these aircraft also served briefly with the Treasury Department under the FP-2 designation. Back with the Air Corps, both aircraft were overhauled and modernized in 1936 when their ply-covered wings were replaced with new wings built of stainless steel. At that time, 400 hp R-985-9s were installed and their designation changed to OA-4Cs.

S/n 1122: Ordered by the Air Corps for the USCG, this aircraft was designated RD-2, under the Navy system, and successively bore the Coast Guard serials 29, 129 (from January 1935) and V111 (from October 1936). It was similar to the Y1C-26s, but was powered by two 500 hp Pratt & Whitney R-1340-10s.

S/n 1123 to 1126 and 1132 to 1135: Initially designated Y1C-26As, these

A Y1C-26A in service with the Army Air Corps. (*USAF*)

106

The first US Presidential aircraft was this RD-2 (BuNo 9347). (*NA & SM*)

aircraft (32-403 to 32-410) were ordered on 10 June, 1932, in two batches of four under Contract AC-5100. They differed from the similarly-powered Y1C-26 only in minor details and were successively redesignated C-26As and OA-4As while serving with the Air Corps. The designation FP-2A was used when some of them were on loan to the Treasury Department. Like the OA-4s, four OA-4As (32-403 and 32-406 to 32-408) were modernized in 1936 and redesignated OA-4Cs.

S/n 1138: Ordered as a VIP-barge and placed at the disposal of President Franklin Roosevelt, this RD-2 (BuNo 9347) was structurally similar to the Y1C-26As but had luxurious accommodation for five passengers and was initially powered by two 410 hp Pratt & Whitney R-1340-1s. These engines were later replaced by two 500 hp R-1340-10s. Accepted on 6 June, 1933, this RD-2 was transferred to NACA on 4 December, 1939.

S/n 1139 and 1140: Powered by two 450 hp R-1340-96s, these two RD-2s (BuNos 9348 and 9349) had somewhat less luxurious accommodation and were intended for use by senior Navy and Marine officers. Both were struck off in March 1940.

S/n 1183 and 1184: Powered by two 550 hp Pratt & Whitney R-1340-29s, the two C-29s (33-292 and 33-293) were the most powerful Dolphins; in other respects they were similar to the Y1C-26As. When used by the Treasury Department they were designated FP-2Bs.

OA-4B fitted experimentally with a fixed tricycle undercarriage. (*USAF*)

S/n 1185 to 1188: Like the C-29s, the four C-26Bs (33-294 to 33-297) were ordered on 2 March, 1933, under Contract AC-5745. Powered by two 400 hp R-985-9s, they were redesignated OA-4Bs. One of them was fitted experimentally with a non-retractable tricycle undercarriage, while another one, 33-295, was brought up to OA-4C standard in 1936.

S/n 1262 to 1267: Delivered to the US Navy in 1934–35, the six RD-3s (BuNos 9528 to 9533) were a utility transport version of the RD-2. They were powered by two 450 hp Pratt & Whitney R-1340-4s or R-1340-96s.

An RD-3 (BuNo 9529) at Santa Monica on 17 October, 1934. (*USAF*)

S/n 1268 to 1277: Bringing to a close the production of US military Dolphin variants, the ten RD-4s (USCG serials 130 to 139, later V125 to V134) were generally similar to the RD-3s but were powered by two 420 hp Pratt & Whitney Wasp C1s and their fuel tankage was increased to 252 US gallons (954 litres). The first of these aircraft was commissioned in November 1934 and the type was extensively used before the war on search and rescue missions. Four RD-4s were still in service in December 1941 when the Coast Guard, which in peacetime operated under the control of the Treasury Department, was transferred to Naval control. The RD-4s were then assigned to security patrols along the American coastline and the last of them (serial V132) was finally decommissioned in June 1943.

S/n 1278: With this aircraft Douglas resumed Dolphin production for the civil and export markets. Powered by two 550 hp Wasp S1D1s and using an airframe similar to that of the RD-4s, this aircraft was registered NC14203 before being sold to M. Armand Esders, a French industrialist. Registered F-ANJT and named *Jade Blanc V*, this Dolphin 113 received its French certificate of airworthiness on 19 October, 1934.

S/n 1279 to 1284: Basically similar to the preceding aircraft but powered by Pratt & Whitney engines of the Wasp or Wasp Junior series (450 hp Wasp Junior SB was typical), these aircraft were custom-built. The Dolphin 114 (s/n 1279, NC14204) was ordered by Philip K. Wrigley, the owner of the Santa Catalina resort, and was operated by his Wilmington-Catalina Airline. It was power by two 450 hp Wasp SC1s. On 8 April, 1943, this aircraft was impressed into the RAAF as A35-4 but, after serving with No.3 OTU and No.4 Communication Flight, it crashed at Rose Bay, Sydney, on 29 July, 1943.

The Dolphin 117 (NC14205) private transport of William Boeing.
(*Peter M. Bowers*)

The Dolphin 117 (s/n 1280, NC14205) was purchased in 1934 by William E. Boeing, the founder of The Boeing Company. Still registered, as N26K, in 1977, this aircraft is the last known survivor of the Dolphin series. The next aircraft, s/n 1281, was an export model sold in 1934 to the Armada Argentina in the service of which it bore the serial T 203.

Ordered in 1934 by Standard Oil of New Jersey, s/n 1282, NC14286, was a Dolphin 136 with 450 hp Wasp Junior SBs. Later transferred by Standard Oil to its subsidiary Australian Petroleum Company Ltd, on 7 June, 1940, this aircraft became the first Dolphin to be impressed into the RAAF (serial A35-1). In Australian military service A35-1 was joined by the previously mentioned A35-3 and A35-4, and A35-2, a Dolphin of unknown origin. Following accidents, A35-1 and A35-2 were converted to components on 15 July, 1943, and 14 July, 1944, respectively, and parts of these two aircraft were used to rebuild A35-3, the only Australian Dolphin to survive the war.

Two Dolphin 119s (s/n 1282 and 1283, NC14207 and NC14208) were also built in 1934 for A. G. and W. K. Vanderbilt.

S/n 1348 and 1349: Bringing production to a close, these two Dolphin 129s were ordered by Pan American Airways for use by its subsidiary, China National Aviation Corporation (CNAC), on Route No.3, from Shanghai to Canton, via Wenchow, Foochow, Amoy and Swatow. They were powered by 450 hp Pratt & Whitney Wasp S3D1s.

While the Cloudster and M-series had been used to carry passengers, neither type had been originally conceived for that purpose. Thus, the Dolphin—even though it was produced in small numbers and was eclipsed by later Douglas commercial designs—occupies a special place in the

109

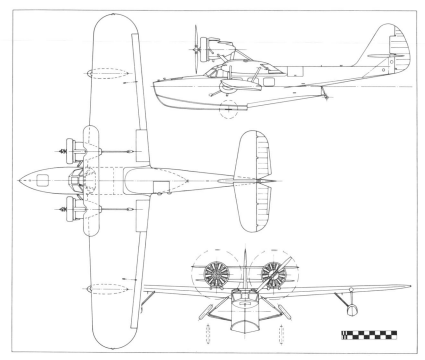

Douglas Dolphin.

company's history as it was its first passenger-carrying commercial transport to be put into production. Furthermore, during its many years of service with the USAAC, USCG, USMC, USN and RAAF, the Dolphin earned a solid reputation for its reliability and good handling.

Sinbad
Span 60 ft (18·29 m); length 42 ft 6 in (12·95 m); height 13 ft 6 in (4·11 m); wing area 562 sq ft (52·212 sq m).

Y1C-21
Span and wing area as Sinbad. Length 43 ft 10 in (13·36 m); height 14 ft 1 in (4·29 m). Empty weight 5,861 lb (2,659 kg); loaded weight 8,583 lb (3,893 kg); wing loading 15·3 lb/sq ft (74·6 kg/sq m); power loading 12·3 lb/hp (5·6 kg/hp). Maximum speed at sea level 140 mph (225 km/h); cruising speed 119 mph (192 km/h); climb to 10,000 ft (3,050 m) 18·5 min; service ceiling 14,200 ft (4,330 m).

Y1C-26A
Span 60 ft (18·29 m); length 45 ft 5 in (13·84 m); height 15 ft 2 in (4·62 m); wing area 592 sq ft (54·999 sq m). Empty weight 5,992 lb (2,718 kg); loaded weight 8,571 lb (3,888 kg); wing loading 14·5 lb/sq ft (70·7 kg/sq m); power loading 14·3 lb/hp (6·5 kg/hp). Maximum speed at sea level 137 mph (220 km/h); climb to 10,000 ft (3,050 m) 21·1 min; service ceiling 13,200 ft (4,025 m).

XRD-1

Span and wing area as Y1C-21. Length 43 ft 3 in (13·18 m); height 14 ft 1 in (4·29 m). Empty weight 6,127 lb (2,779 kg); loaded weight 8,347 lb (3,786 kg); wing loading 14·9 lb/sq ft (72·5 kg/sq m); power loading 9·6 lb/hp (4·4 kg/hp). Maximum speed at 5,000 ft (1,524 m) 151 mph (243 km/h); rate of climb 860 ft/min (262 m/min); service ceiling 17,300 ft (5,275 m); normal range 466 miles (750 km).

RD-3

Span and wing area as Y1C-26A. Length 45 ft 3 in (13·79 m); height 15 ft 2 in (4·62 m). Empty weight 6,764 lb (3,068 kg); loaded weight 9,734 lb (4,415 kg); wing loading 16·4 lb/sq ft (80·3 kg/sq m); power loading 10·8 lb/hp (4·9 kg/hp). Maximum speed at sea level 149 mph (240 km/h); cruising speed 105 mph (169 km/h); climb to 5,000 ft (1,524 m) 6·2 min; service ceiling 15,100 ft (4,600 m); normal range 692 miles (1,114 km).

Dolphin 114

Span and wing area as Y1C-26A. Length 45 ft 3 in (13·79 m); height 15 ft 2 in (4·62 m). Empty weight 6,730 lb (3,053 kg); loaded weight 9,500 lb (4,309 kg); wing loading 16 lb/sq ft (78·3 kg/sq m); power loading 10·6 lb/hp (4·8 kg/hp). Maximum speed 156 mph (251 km/h); cruising speed 140 mph (225 km/h); rate of climb 710 ft/min (216 m/min); service ceiling 19,800 ft (6,035 m); normal range 720 miles (1,159 km).

Douglas Observation Monoplanes

Ever since the XO-2 had made its first flight in 1924, Douglas had been improving its series of observation biplanes by using a variety of liquid-cooled and air-cooled engines offering increased power and reliability and/or lighter installed weight instead of the O-2 series' Liberty. Numerous structural and aerodynamic improvements were also progressively introduced. Yet, as the twenties turned into the thirties, the Douglas observation biplanes were beginning to show their age and the development of observation aircraft offering substantially improved performance ranked high amongst priority programmes sponsored by the Air Corps.

In an endeavour to retain its position as prime supplier of observation aeroplanes to the Air Corps, Douglas—capitalizing on the experience acquired with the Commuter and DA-1—designed an all-metal aircraft with high-mounted wings of gull form. On 7 January, 1930, these efforts were rewarded when Contract AC-2822 covering two experimental aircraft was signed by the War Department. Designated XO-31 by the Air Corps, the first aircraft (s/n 721, serial 30-229) was completed and first flown at Santa Monica in mid-December 1930. The aircraft, which was unarmed, had tandem open cockpits for the pilot and observer and corrugated duralumin skin panels on the centre and rear fuselage sections and on the vertical tail surfaces. Its high-mounted gull wings were attached to a tubular cabane mounted on top of the fuselage and braced by steel wires. Powered by a 600 hp direct-drive Curtiss Conqueror V-1570-25 twelve-cylinder liquid-cooled engine, the XO-31 had a split-axle fixed under-carriage and over the wheels large fairings could be fitted.

111

The XO-31 (30-229) as it appeared at Wright Field, Ohio, in August 1933. The auxiliary fins mounted above the horizontal tailplane were to improve directional stability. (*USAF*)

The manufacturer's flight trials revealed that handling left much to be desired, while problems were encountered with parasite drag around the radiator installation. In a first round of modifications a variable-incidence tailplane was substituted for the fixed unit previously used and the radiator was moved further back beneath the engine cowling. So modified, the aircraft was delivered in February 1931 to Wright Field for Service trials. The modifications made while the aircraft was still in Santa Monica had proved fairly successful but the directional instability—a problem which was to plague all versions of the O-31—was still affecting the aircraft's handling. Consequently, while at Wright Field, between 1931 and 1937, the XO-31 was tested with auxiliary fins mounted on the tailplane and with various shapes of enlarged tail surfaces.

Delivered to the Air Corps in May 1931, the second aircraft (s/n 722, serial 30-230) of the original contract was designated YO-31 and powered by a 600 hp geared Curtiss V-1570-7 driving a two-blade propeller turning in the opposite direction to that of the XO-31. Externally, the YO-31 differed from the XO-31 only in having a 3 in (7·6 cm) longer cowling of modified contour—this stemming from the YO-31's geared engine—and, initially at least, in having a modified vertical fin of broader chord.

In October 1931, Douglas also submitted to the US Navy's Bureau of Aeronautics a proposal covering a two-seat carrier-based fighter based on the YO-31. To be powered by a 700 hp radial engine (Pratt & Whitney Hornet or Wright R-1670 series) and carrying armament consisting of two forward-firing 0·30-in machine-guns and one flexible rear-firing gun of the same calibre, this aircraft was estimated to have a top speed of 214 mph at 16,000 ft (344 km/h at 4,875 m) and to possess a normal range of 505 miles (813 km) and a maximum range of 770 miles (1,239 km). This first Douglas proposal for a naval fighter did not attract the interest of the Bureau of Aeronautics and its development was not funded. Thus, the next Douglas gull-wing monoplanes were the six aircraft built under Contract AC-4326 which had been awarded on 23 June, 1931.

112

YO-31A: Powered by Curtiss V-1570-53 engines driving three-blade propellers, four YO-31As (serials 31-604 to 31-607) were accepted by the Air Corps between January and May 1932. The corrugated metal skin fuselage and tail of the XO-31 and YO-31 was replaced by semi-monocoque construction with smooth metal covering and a canopy was fitted over the pilot's cockpit and the forward section of the observer's cockpit. The YO-31As also had revised tail surfaces, with the tailplane and elevators attached to the vertical fin and braced to the rear fuselage by supporting struts. A smoother contoured engine cowling was adopted and a spinner was fitted over the hub of the propeller. The most important modification, however, was that affecting the span, area and geometry of the gull-wings as the parallel leading and trailing edges of the YO-31 wings gave way to the YO-31A's wings of elliptical planform.

The first YO-31A (31-604) seen while on test at Wright Field under the designation XYO-31A. The temporary fin extension was riveted to the original vertical surfaces. (*USAF*)

During tests at Wright Field with the Air Corps, then at Langley with NACA and finally back at Santa Monica with Douglas, the first aircraft of this type (31-604)—temporarily redesignated XYO-31A—was used to test four different wing positions and led to a progressive growth of the vertical tail surfaces culminating in a unit with a tall pointed fin and inset rudder. Another YO-31A was tested in April 1932 against the Curtiss YO-40A but the YO-31A was found inferior to the Curtiss type in almost all respects; however, the experimental Wright Y1R-1820-F powering the YO-40A was extremely unreliable and, on 20 May, 1932, the Curtiss crashed and left the field to Douglas. Following completion of Service tests, the four YO-31As were redesignated O-31As.

Y1O-31A: Designation given to five aircraft ordered on 26 August, 1931, under Contract AC-4534. Before completion these aircraft were redesignated Y1O-31Cs but, eventually, they were completed as Y1O-43s in 1933.

YO-31B: Sixth aircraft ordered under Contract AC-4326, the YO-31B (serial 32-231) was a two-seat unarmed staff aircraft built for the Militia Bureau of the War Department. Powered by a 600 hp Curtiss V-1570-29, it was basically similar to the YO-31A but was fitted with a sliding canopy faired back into the vertical fin. Later this aircraft was fitted with the larger tail surfaces and modified wing installation tested on the XYO-31A and served until May 1942 under the O-31B designation.

YO-31C: Fifth aircraft ordered under Contract AC-4326, the sole YO-31C (31-608) was delivered to the Air Corps in July 1932 and had the same powerplant installation as the YO-31A. The aircraft could be distinguished by the addition of a blister beneath the rear cockpit to give more standing room for the observer while manning the flexible rear-firing machine-gun, and by the substitution of a cantilever undercarriage for the split-axle unit used on all previous versions of the O-31. During its trial programme the aircraft was designated XYO-31C but eventually was simply designated O-31C.

YO-31C (31-608) with flexible 0·30-in machine-gun in the rear cockpit. (*USAF*)

Y1O-31C: Temporary designation applying to five aircraft ordered as Y1O-31As but delivered as Y1O-43s.

Y1O-43: As a result of extensive tests conducted with the XYO-31A and XYO-31C to determine the best wing position and most effective shape of vertical tail surfaces, the five aircraft (serials 32-291 to 32-295) ordered as Y1O-31As in August 1931 were completed as Y1O-43s. Combining a powerplant installation and fuselage similar to those of the YO-31C with parasol wings and shorter vertical tail surfaces with full height rudder, the Y1O-43s were accepted by the Air Corps between February and April 1933 and, after completion of flight tests, were designated O-43s.

O-43A: The first full-scale production contract was awarded on 2 March, 1933, when the War Department ordered twenty-four aircraft derived from the Y1O-43s. Twenty-three of these aircraft (33-268 to 33-290) were designated O-43As and were powered by the 675 hp Curtiss V-1570-59 driving a three-blade propeller. Delivered between July and November 1934, the O-43A differed from the O-43 in having a deeper fuselage to eliminate the need for a blister beneath the observer's cockpit, in being fitted with taller vertical surfaces with inset rudder, in dispensing with the large propeller spinner first used on the YO-31As and in having a sliding canopy which fully enclosed the tandem cockpits.

114

Douglas O-43 with Wright Field markings on the rear fuselage. The tubular cabane is well detailed in this view *(USAF)*

O-43A bearing the tail code of the San Antonio Air Depot.
(MSgt David Menard)

XO-46: Delivered in October 1934, the last airframe (serial 33-291) ordered under the O-43A contract was fitted with a 725 hp Pratt & Whitney R-1535-7 fourteen-cylinder air-cooled radial driving a three-blade propeller. The tubular cabane mounted on the centre section and supporting the parasol wings of the O-43A by means of steel wires was replaced by parallel streamlined struts beneath the wings.

O-46A: When awarded on 29 April, 1935, Contract AC-7342 covered seventy-one aircraft derived from the XO-46 but two contract changes, dated 31 October, 1935, and 6 March, 1936, added respectively seventeen and two aircraft. Thus, a total of ninety O-46As (serials 35-161 to 35-231, 36-128 to 36-144 for the Air Corps, and 36-147 to 36-148 for the National Guard) were delivered between May 1936 and April 1937. These aircraft

115

The XO-46 (33-291) was the first Douglas observation monoplane to be powered by a radial engine and to have its wing braced to the fuselage by two parallel struts. (*USAF*)

differed from the XO-46 in having their Pratt & Whitney R-1535-7 engines moved forward 8½ in (21·6 cm) to improve cg location and in having their canopies faired into the vertical fin.

YO-48: Projected version which was to have had an airframe similar to that of the O-46A but powered by a 775 hp Wright R-1670-3 radial. A 1936 contract covering this version and calling for the modification of the XO-46 (33-291) was cancelled and no YO-48 was built.

Besides being flown in protracted tests alongside the XO-31 and YO-31, three of the four O-31As and the O-31C were operated successively for short periods by the 1st, 12th, 22nd and 99th Observation Squadrons. Beginning during the second half of 1940, the last two surviving aircraft from this batch ended their useful lives as instructional airframes. These early aircraft were followed in Air Corps service by the five O-43s and twenty-three O-43As which from 1933 were actively operated until transferred to the National Guard or used as instructional airframes. Still longer lived were the O-46As which entered service in 1936. Most of these

O-46A (35-164) in service with the Army Air Corps. (*William Balogh*)

116

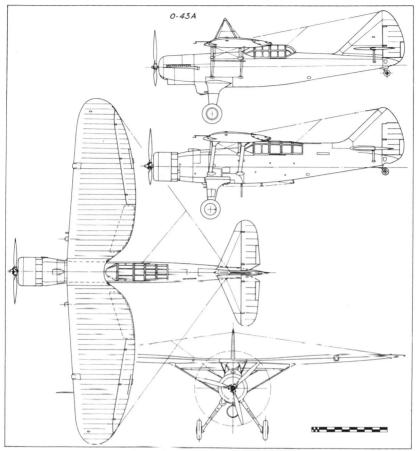

Douglas O-46A and O-43A.

were transferred to National Guard units in the late thirties and early forties, but a handful of O-46As were still operated by the 2nd Observation Squadron at Nichols Field, Luzon, when Japan attacked the Philippines in December 1941 and these aircraft were the only Douglas observation monoplanes to see action, brief as it was.

In National Guard service in 1932 the O-31B became the first machine in this series to be operated and, after being flown by command personnel of the Militia Bureau, was transferred to the 108th Observation Squadron, Illinois National Guard, until assigned as a ground instructional airframe in May 1942. This aircraft was followed by a number of O-43As which, after serving with Air Corps units, were assigned to the 111th Observation Squadron, Texas National Guard. Later, O-46As transferred from the Air Corps served until 1942 with the 102nd, 104th, 105th, 110th, 118th, 124th and 127th Observation Squadrons of the National Guard. Notable among

117

these were 35-177 which accumulated the highest number of flying hours—4,123—of any aircraft in the O-31/O-43/O-46 series, and 35-217, which was the last surviving Douglas observation monoplane in service, and was finally donated to a school in January 1946. Aircraft 35-179 is now preserved in the collection of the United States Air Force Museum at Wright-Patterson AFB, Ohio.

For Douglas, the O-46A marked the end of an important chapter in its corporate history as its final type of observation aircraft; the O-53, a derivative of the Douglas A-20B of which 1,489 (serials 41-3670 to 41-5158) had been ordered in 1940, was not built because changes in requirements led to the cancellation of the contract.

YO-31

Span 46 ft 4 in (14·12 m); length 33 ft 5 in (10·19 m); height 10 ft 7 in (3·23 m); wing area 308·2 sq ft (28·633 sq m). Empty weight 3,496 lb (1,586 kg); loaded weight 4,654 lb (2,111 kg); wing loading 15·1 lb/sq ft (73·7 kg/sq m); power loading 7·8 lb/hp (3 5 kg/hp). Maximum speed at sea level 182·5 mph (294 km/h); cruising speed 157 mph (253 km/h); rate of climb 1,700 ft/min (518 m/min); service ceiling 24,300 ft (7,435 m).

YO-31C

Span 45 ft 11 in (14 m); length 34 ft (10·36 m); height 11 ft 6¾ in (3·53 m); wing area 339·9 sq ft (31·578 sq m). Empty weight 3,888 lb (1,763 kg); loaded weight 4,982 lb (2,260 kg); wing loading 14·6 lb/sq ft (71·7 kg/sq m); power loading 8·3 lb/hp (3·8 kg/hp). Maximum speed at sea level 195 mph (314 km/h); cruising speed 160 mph (257 km/h); climb to 10,000 ft (3,050 m) 7·2 min; service ceiling 22,700 ft (6,920 m); range 260 miles (418 km).

O-43A

Span 45 ft 11 in (14 m); length 33 ft 11 in (10·34 m); height 12 ft 3 in (3·71 m); wing area 335 sq ft (31·123 sq m). Empty weight 4,135 lb (1,876 kg); loaded weight 5,300 lb (2,404 kg); wing loading 15·8 lb/sq ft (77·2 kg/sq m); power loading 7·9 lb/hp (3·6 kg/hp). Maximum speed at sea level 190 mph (306 km/h); cruising speed 163 mph (262 km/h); climb to 5,000 ft (1,524 m) 3·3 min; service ceiling 22,400 ft (6,830 m).

O-46A

Span 45 ft 9 in (13·94 m); length 34 ft 6¾ in (10·54 m); height 10 ft 8⅛ in (3·25 m); wing area 332 sq ft (30·844 sq m). Empty weight 4,776 lb (2,166 kg); loaded weight 6,639 lb (3,011 kg); wing loading 20 lb/sq ft (97·3 kg/sq m); power loading 9·2 lb/hp (4·2 kg/hp). Maximum speed at 4,000 ft (1,220 m) 200 mph (322 km/h); cruising speed 171 mph (275 km/h); rate of climb 1,765 ft/min (541 m/min); service ceiling 24,150 ft (7,360 m); range 435 miles (700 km).

YI B-7 of the 12th Observation Squadron over the Great Salt Lake during the 1934 Air Mail Emergency (*USAF*)

Douglas O-35 and B-7

In June 1929 the US War Department ordered two prototypes of the Fokker XO-27, a design which made use of several advanced features and which promised to offer a substantial improvement in performance and operational flexibility over those obtained with the Curtiss, Douglas and Thomas-Morse observation biplanes then operated by the Air Corps. To obtain an aircraft better suited for night operations and offering improved range, the Fokker design team had selected a twin-engined monoplane configuration and made use of a retractable undercarriage.

In spite of having received, in January 1930, a contract for two XO-31 single-engined observation monoplanes, the Douglas Aircraft company became concerned that the appearance of the new twin-engined Fokker XO-27s would seriously affect its leading position as supplier of observation aircraft for the Air Corps. Therefore Douglas submitted a proposal for the design and construction of a twin-engined observation aeroplane. On 26 March, 1930, Douglas's efforts were rewarded when the War Department approved Contract AC2851 for one XO-35 and one XO-36. Both aircraft were generally similar and, having high-mounted braced gull wings and metal construction with corrugated duralumin covering on the fuselage and tail surfaces, bore a strong family resemblance to the single-engined XO-31 ordered earlier in the year. The Curtiss Conqueror liquid-cooled engines powering these aircraft were enclosed in nacelles attached to the wing under-surfaces and fuselage sides by a series of struts. The main undercarriage units retracted backwards into the engine

The XO-35 (30-227) displaying its defensive armament and corrugated metal fuselage and tail covering. (*USAF*)

nacelles with the lower portion of each wheel protruding to reduce damage in the event of a wheels-up landing. The crew of four comprised an observer/gunner in an open cockpit in the nose of the aircraft, a pilot in an open cockpit just forward of the wings, a gunner in an open cockpit in the rear fuselage and a radio-operator in an enclosed station amidship.

When first ordered, the two aircraft were intended to differ only in the models of engines used with the XO-35 having two geared 600 hp GIV-1570C (military designation V-1570-29) Conquerors driving three-blade metal propellers while the XO-36 was to be fitted with two direct-drive 600 hp V-1570C (military designation V-1570-23) Conquerors driving two-blade metal propellers. As the propellers fitted to the XO-36 had a smaller diameter than those of the XO-35, the engine nacelles were to be mounted 8 inches (20·3 cm) closer to the aircraft centreline. However, before the XO-36 was ready, the Air Corps decided to have it completed as a light bomber as its calculated performance substantially exceeded that of the then standard Air Corps light bombers, the Keystone B-3A, B-4A, B-5A and B-6A twin-engined biplanes. At the same time, the Air Corps instructed that the second Fokker XO-27 be completed as a light bomber under the designation XB-8 while the XO-36 was redesignated XB-7.

Bomb-laden XB-7 (30-228) at Wright Field, Ohio, in the autumn of 1932. (*USAF*)

120

Carrying the same defensive armament as the XO-35—a flexible 0·30-in machine-gun and a similar weapon in the midship open cockpit—the XB-7 could lift 1,200 lb (544 kg) of bombs on racks beneath the fuselage.

Completed and tested at Santa Monica in the spring of 1931, the XO-35 (s/n 913, serial 30-227) was delivered to Wright Field on 24 October, 1931, and the XB-7 (s/n 914, serial 30-228), which was subjected to longer manufacturer's trials, was received at Wright Field in July 1932. Already on 22 August, 1931, the Air Corps had placed an order for seven Y1B-7s (32-308 to 32-314) and five Y1O-35s (32-315 to 32-319) and these were delivered between August and November 1932. Standardizing on geared variants of the Conqueror engines—640 hp V-1570-33 of 675 hp V-1570-53 models being fitted to the Y1B-7s while 650 hp V-1570-39 or 675 hp V-1570-53 models were fitted to the Y1O-35s—, the Service test aircraft differed from the two prototypes in having smooth metal covering on their

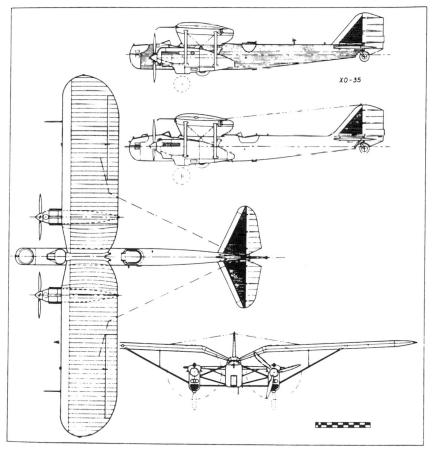

Douglas Y1B-7 and XO-35.

121

fuselages and fabric covering on the movable portions of the tail surfaces. To improve the cg location, overall length was increased from 45 ft (13·72 m) to 45 ft 11 in (14·0 m). An adjustable tab was also added to the rudder to improve engine-out handling, and the tailplane, which on the XO-35 and XB-7 was wire-braced, was now supported by metal struts. Fuel capacity was increased by 116 US gallons (439 litres) in compliance with a Directive which required that new Air Corps machines be given a minimum of two hours' endurance plus two hours' reserve. Other changes introduced on the Service trials aircraft included a modified fuel distribution system, improved engine controls and oil cooler, and modified equipment.

While undergoing flight trials at Wright Field the XO-35 was extensively damaged on 11 July, 1932. Repaired and overhauled, the aircraft was flown again from Wright Field and, including a short assignment to the Western Zone during the Air Corps' 1934 air mail operations, it was flown for a total of 999 hours until surveyed on 28 October, 1938. Surveyed* six months later, the XB-7 had been flown for a total of 450 hours from Santa Monica, and from Wright, Patterson and Langley Fields. More actively used were the twelve Service evaluation aircraft but no O-35 quantity production followed as the Air Corps had lost interest in twin-engined observation aircraft, while the B-7 was rapidly made obsolete by the more advanced Martin B-10.

Shortly after being accepted by the Air Corps, the seven Y1B-7s, later designated B-7s, were assigned to the 11th and 31st Bombardment Squadrons at March Field, California. Within ten months one of these aircraft was lost in a crash but, in early 1934, the remaining six B-7s were assigned to the Western Zone for air mail operations. The two aircraft which survived this episode were operated until surveyed in 1938–39. Similarly, the five O-35s were first assigned to Observation Squadrons at Crissy and Mitchel Fields before operations in the Western Zone during the 1934 Air Mail Emergency. All O-35s survived the air mail interlude and the last of these aircraft was surveyed in February 1939.

*Surveyed is a US military term indicating that the aircraft has been found unsuitable for further service.

For the 1933 Army manoeuvres at Ft Knox, Kentucky, this Y1B-7 of the 31st Bombardment Squadron was camouflaged with water-soluble paints. (*USAF*)

Bearing the insignia of the 31st Bombardment Squadron, this Y1B-7 is seen at Elko, Nevada, during the 1934 Air Mail Emergency. (*USAF*)

On 9 February, 1934, President Roosevelt cancelled the Air Mail Contracts and asked Gen Benjamin D. Foulois, Chief of the Army Air Corps, to have his Service take over air mail operations throughout the United States. Few Air Corps aircraft were suited for this task but the Douglas O-35s and B-7s appeared better suited than most. Accordingly, the XO-35, five O-35s and six B-7s were assigned to the Western Zone to carry the mail over the area west of Cheyenne, Wyoming, to the Pacific Coast. This was the most difficult zone because of the mountainous terrain and pilots assigned to it urgently needed to familiarize themselves with the routes they were to fly. Unfortunately, on 16 February, 1934, while flying one of these familiarization flights over the Salt Lake City–Boise–Pasco–Portland–Seattle route, 2nd Lt James Easthman flying a B-7 (serial 32-309) was caught in a snowstorm while attempting to land at Jerome, Idaho. While circling the aerodrome Easthman stalled and was killed in the crash. Four days later, the Air Corps began carrying mail and did so until 1 June, 1934, when the last military aircraft was scheduled for an air mail flight. While assigned to the Western Zone, the XO-35, O-35s and B-7s had flown a total of 1,412 hours but, in addition to 2nd Lt Easthman's machine, three B-7s had been lost for an overall loss ratio of one aircraft per 353 flying hours.

XO-35

Span 65 ft (19·81 m); length 45 ft (13·72 m); height 11 ft 7 in (3·53 m); wing area 621·2 sq ft (57·711 sq m). Empty weight 7,296 lb (3,309 kg); loaded weight 9,494 lb (4,306 kg); maximum weight 10,254 lb (4,651 kg); wing loading 15·3 lb/sq ft (74·1 kg/sq m); power loading 7·1 lb/hp (3·6 kg/hp). Maximum speed at sea level 178 mph (286 km/h); cruising speed 156 mph (251 km/h); climb to 10,000 ft (3,050 m) 8·4 min; service ceiling 21,750 ft (6,630 m).

XB-7

Dimensions as XO-35. Empty weight 6,865 lb (3,114 kg); loaded weight 10,537 lb (4,780 kg); maximum weight 11,287 lb (5,119 kg); wing loading 17 lb/sq ft (82·8 kg/sq m); power loading 8·7 lb/hp (4 kg/hp). Maximum speed at sea level 169 mph (272 km/h); cruising speed 147 mph (237 km/h); climb to 10,000 ft (3,050 m) 11·3 min; service ceiling 18,950 ft (5,775 m).

Y1B-7

Dimensions as XO-35 except length 45 ft 11 in (14 m). Empty weight 5,519 lb (3,411 kg); loaded weight 9,953 lb (4,515 kg); maximum weight 11,177 lb (5,070 kg); wing loading 16 lb/sq ft (78·2 kg/sq m); power loading 7·4 lb/hp (3·3 kg/hp). Maximum speed at sea level 182 mph (293 km/h); cruising speed 158 mph (254 km/h); climb to 10,000 ft (3,050 m) 8·7 min; service ceiling 20,400 ft (6,220 m); normal range 411 miles (661 km); maximum range 632 miles (1,017 km).

Douglas XT3D

Even though it was flown for ten years, the XT3D-1/XT3D-2 remains one of the least known of Douglas aircraft. Ordered on 30 June, 1930, as a potential successor to the Martin T4M and Great Lakes TG torpedo bombers of the US Navy, the XT3D-1 was an unstaggered fabric-covered metal biplane powered initially by a 575 hp Pratt & Whitney Hornet S2B1-G nine-cylinder air-cooled radial driving a two-blade metal propeller. The crew of three consisted of a bomb-aimer/gunner in an open cockpit ahead of the wing, a pilot in an open cockpit beneath the wing trailing edge, and a gunner in an open cockpit aft of the wings. The gunners each manned a single flexible 0·30-in machine-gun and the bomb-aimer aimed the 1,835 lb (832 kg) torpedo or bombs through an optically-flat,

The XT3D-1 at NAS Anacostia. Note forward location of bomb-aimer/gunner cockpit with aiming window in the forward part of the deepened fuselage. (*Northrop Institute of Technology*)

For stowage aboard carriers, the XT3D-1 was fitted with folding wings which gave it an unusual appearance. (*MDC*)

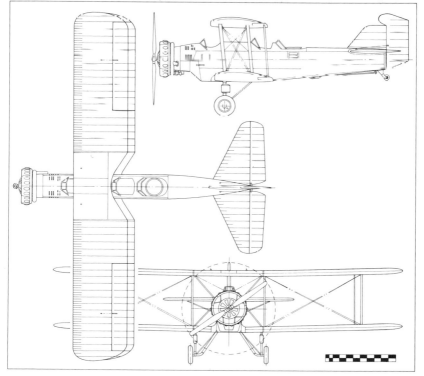

Douglas XT3D-1.

The XT3D-2 with arrester gear extended and enclosed cockpits.
(*US National Archives*)

forward-looking, window in the lower part of the deepened fuselage aft of the engine. The fixed undercarriage was of the split-axle type, and an arrester hook was installed beneath the rear fuselage.

Following completion of brief manufacturer's trials at Santa Monica during the early summer of 1931, the XT3D-1 (s/n 927, BuNo A8730) was shipped to NAS Anacostia where it was received on 19 September. Board of Inspection and Survey (BIS) trials were conducted at NAS Anacostia and Hampton Roads and at the Dahlgreen Naval Proving Ground between 14 October, 1931, and 8 April, 1932, but the results were disappointing as the trials' report concluded that the XT3D-1, particularly in the fuselage and undercarriage, was not 'streamlined to the best advantage and performance sacrificed thereby' and that the engine operation was not satisfactory 'with continuous minor troubles being experienced'. Consequently, the aircraft was returned to Douglas for modifications.

In an attempt to improve the aircraft's performance, Douglas installed an 800 hp Pratt & Whitney XR-1830-54 fourteen-cylinder air-cooled radial with a full NACA cowling—whereas the Hornet S2B1-G of the XT3D-1 had a simple Townend ring—and added wheel spats. In addition, a sliding canopy was added over the bomb-aimer's cockpit whilst a large canopy was fitted over the pilot's and rear gunner's cockpits. So modified and redesignated XT3D-2, the aircraft was ferried from NAS San Diego to NAS Anacostia during February 1933. However, by that time the USN was more interested in dive-bombers than in torpedo bombers. Thus, full BIS trials were not considered necessary and the XT3D-2 was put through a more limited trial programme. Doubts about the aircraft's structural strength, particularly for carrier operations, its disappointing perform-ance, partially due to the fact that neither controllable-pitch propeller nor cowling flaps were used, and continuous engine troubles marred these tests.

To improve its engine's performance, the XT3D-2 was repeatedly returned to Pratt & Whitney at Hartford, Connecticut, for modifications but no satisfactory solution could be found. Consequently, the XT3D-2 was rejected as a Service type and used on a limited basis as an engine testbed. In this capacity, the aircraft was fitted in October 1936 with an 800 hp R-1830-58. Soon after, the XT3D-2 was to have been used for testing the new 1,500 hp Wright XR-2600-2 engine but this plan was not implemented. Finally, the XT3D-2, still powered by an R-1830-58, made its last flight at NAS Philadelphia on 22 April, 1941. Two weeks later, on 5 May, the aircraft was struck off strength and sent to NAS Norfolk for use as an instructional airframe.

XT3D-1

Span 50 ft (15·24 m); length 35 ft 5 in (10·8 m); height 13 ft 2½ in (4·03 m); wing area 624 sq ft (57·971 sq m). Empty weight 4,238 lb (1,922 kg); loaded weight 7,639 lb (3,465 kg); maximum weight 7,857 lb (3,564 kg); wing loading 12·2 lb/sq ft (59·8 kg/sq m); power loading 13·3 lb/hp (6 kg/hp). Maximum speed at 6,000 ft (1,830 m) 128 mph (206 km/h); climb to 5,000 ft (1,524 m) 7·7 min; service ceiling 14,000 ft (4,265 m); range 558 miles (898 km).

XT3D-2

Maximum speed at sea level 153 mph (246 km/h); climb to 5,000 ft (1,524 m) 6·6 min; service ceiling 15,700 ft (4,785 m); range 778 miles (1,252 km).

Northrop Gamma

When, in January 1932, John K. Northrop and Donald W. Douglas joined forces to set up the Northrop Corporation as a partially-owned subsidiary of the Douglas Aircraft Company, the two friends and associates agreed to capitalize on Northrop's experience as a designer of exceptionally clean all-metal aircraft. Thus, the initial objective of the new company was to design and build two series of aircraft, which, continuing the previously established Northrop tradition of naming its aircraft after Greek letters, became the Gammas and the Deltas. Whereas, the Deltas were conceived initially as passenger-carrying aircraft, the Gammas were designed as special-purpose and mail-carrying aircraft. Eventually, the development of the Gamma led to a series of military light attack aircraft.

First to be built in the Mines Field factory specially acquired to house the Northrop Corporation were two unique Gammas, the Gamma 2A for the well known pilot Frank Hawks and the Gamma 2B for the Lincoln Ellsworth Trans-Antarctic Expedition. Each had an enclosed cockpit set in the fuselage aft of the wings and both were completed in August 1932. They were followed by six other aircraft for civil customers (Gamma 2D, 2G, 2H and 2L), one prototype of a military advanced trainer (Gamma 2J), and fifty-three military light attack aircraft (Gamma 2C, 2E and 2F). As these Gammas were custom-built, with the exception of the forty-nine Gamma 2Es produced for the Chinese Government, details of their production and service history are given later for each individual aircraft or batch of aircraft. They are listed by factory serial numbers beginning with s/n 1 as the Northrop-built, later the El Segundo-built, aircraft were assigned factory serial numbers independent from those given to aircraft built in other plants or divisions of Douglas.

S/n 1: Powered by a 785 hp geared Wright Whirlwind GR-1510 fourteen-cylinder air-cooled radial driving a three-blade propeller, the Gamma 2A (initially registered X12265) was a single-seater with pilot's cockpit located aft of the wing and enclosed by a streamlined canopy. A large compartment, not normally used, was provided in the fuselage forward of the cockpit. Initially, the Gamma 2A was fitted with full-span flaps and park bench ailerons above the wing outer panels. Later, when conventional ailerons were installed, flaps of reduced length and area were adopted. The wings were of typical Northrop multi-spar construction with the centre section built integrally with the fuselage and outer panels bolted to the centre section. The main undercarriage was housed in large streamlined trousers, from which only about one-third of the wheels protruded, and the tailwheel was spatted.

The aircraft was purchased by The Texas Company (Texaco) on 6 December, 1932, for $40,000 and was delivered on 17 December. Assigned to Texaco's Domestic Sales as Texaco No. 11 *Sky Chief*, the aircraft was put at the disposal of Frank Hawks for record breaking and advertizing purposes. Among the records set by the Gamma 2A, then registered NR12265, flown by Frank Hawks, were nonstop flights between Los Angeles and New York (in 13 hr 27 min at an average speed of 181 mph/291 km/h on 2 June, 1933); Regina, Saskatchewan, and Bridgeport, Connecticut (7 hr 55 min); and Los Angeles and Atlanta (11 hr 45 min).

On 21 August, 1934, Texaco sold the Gamma 2A to industrialist Gar Woods who entered the aircraft in the 1936 Bendix Trophy Race from New York to Los Angeles. On this occasion, the Gamma 2A was flown by Joseph P. Jacobson but caught fire in the air. The pilot baled out

The single-seat Gamma 2A with which Captain Frank Hawks broke several speed records. (*Rees Van Dossen*)

128

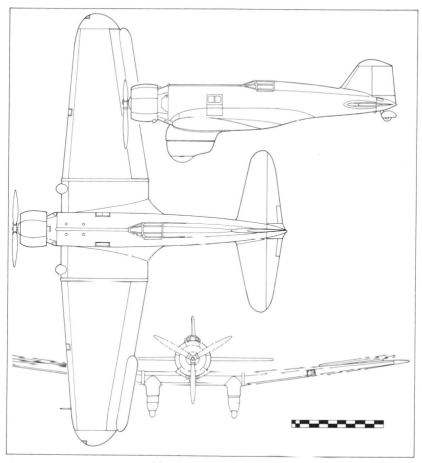

Northrop Gamma 2A.

successfully, but the Gamma crashed near Stafford, Kansas, and was completely destroyed.

S/n 2: Handed over to Lincoln Ellsworth on 29 November, 1932, the Gamma 2B (initially registered X12269) was the first aircraft of the new Northrop Corporation to be delivered. Named *Polar Star*, this aircraft had been ordered for a proposed flight across the Antarctic continent. It differed from the Gamma 2A in having its cockpit and canopy extended rearward to house a passenger/co-pilot, in addition to the pilot, and in being powered by a 500 hp Pratt & Whitney Wasp SD nine-cylinder radial driving a two-blade propeller. For use on its polar venture, the Gamma 2B could be fitted with skis in place of the main and tailwheels, and, for use as a floatplane, could be equipped with twin Edo floats replacing the trousered main undercarriage. First fitted with full-span flaps and park bench

Northrop Gamma 2B in its original configuration with park-bench ailerons and short vertical tail surfaces. (*Pratt & Whitney*)

ailerons, the aircraft was fitted with conventional ailerons before being shipped for its first polar venture.

Shipped via New Zealand aboard the *Wyatt Earp*, the *Polar Star* and its famous Norwegian pilot, Bernt Balchen, reached the Bay of Whales on the Ross Sea in January 1934 as part of the first trans-antarctic expedition led by Lincoln Ellsworth and Sir George Hubert Wilkins. Unfortunately, before undertaking its mission, the aircraft became jammed in the ice floes and had to be taken back to Northrop for repairs. In September 1934, Ellsworth, Wilkins and Balchen and their *Polar Star* were back in Antarctica. From its base on Snow Hill Island in the Weddell Sea, the *Polar Star* then flew a number of reconnaissance flights during which five islands, three fjords and several mountain peaks were added to the mapped area of the Antarctic. However, worsening weather conditions and a feud between Ellsworth and Balchen—the pilot insisting that a three-man crew would be needed for the multi-stop flight across Antarctica whereas Ellsworth, as leader of the expedition, wanted only a two-man crew—forced back an attempt started on 3 January, 1935. At that time, the expedition was postponed and the *Polar Star* and expedition members were taken to Montevideo aboard the *Wyatt Earp*. The third expedition set up base camp on Dundee Island in the Weddell Sea, in the latter part of the austral spring. By then, Bernt Balchen had been replaced by Herbert Hollick-Kenyon as the *Polar Star*'s pilot, and the new pilot and Lincoln Ellsworth were all set to embark upon their mission, a multi-stop flight across Antarctica to determine what lay between 60 and 120 degrees longitude. On 23 November, 1935, the *Polar Star* took off from Dundee Island bound for Admiral Byrd's base at Little America, 2,140 miles (3,445 km) away. To cross the Hearst Land mountains, Ellsworth and Hollick-Kenyon had to climb to 13,000 ft (3,960 m) and, as their radio failed, they dropped an American flag to record their passage. Later in the day, when high winds and dense cloud threatened to obscure their vision and divert their course, they made a landing, 13 hr from their start, on a bleak plateau 6,400 ft (1,950 m) above sea level. They had flown 1,450 miles (2,335 km). After camping for 17 hr, they took off, but found visibility so poor that they landed 60 miles (97 km) further on. After a lapse of 57 hr, during which they endeavoured unsuccessfully to repair their radio, they took off and covered another 100 miles (161 km), landing once more to check their course. A blizzard forced them to remain there for eight days. On 4 December, they flew on for 660 miles (1,062 km), landing again to make observations and plot their course. They learned they were within 150 miles (240 km) of their destination but were very low on fuel. The next day they made their final take off and flew until the engine gave its last splutter, then glided into a safe landing, 25 miles (40 km) short of Little America. Again, they pitched their tent and made everything snug and on 9 December set out on foot, reaching Byrd's deserted camp in six days of sledging.

On 15 January, 1936, a month after their arrival, the British Royal Research Society ship *Discovery II*, which had steamed as close as possible to Little America, sighted Hollick-Kenyon, and a few hours later Ellsworth was found safe at Byrd's camp. Later in the month, the *Wyatt Earp* took the two men and their *Polar Star* on board for the voyage home. The aircraft, which had suffered little damage in its 2,400 mile (3,860 km) journey, was eventually donated to the Smithsonian Institution. Today, the *Polar Star* is in the collection of the National Air & Space Museum.

Gamma 2B *Polar Star* as fitted with twin floats in the summer of 1934. (*MDC*)

131

The Gamma 2C prototype of a two-seat bomber. (*USAF*)

S/n 5: Begun as a private venture and completed in May 1933, the Gamma 2C was the prototype of a two-seat attack bomber. Initially bearing the civil registration X12291, the aircraft was powered by a 735 hp Wright SR-1820-F2 nine-cylinder radial driving a two-blade propeller. In addition to being fitted to carry bombs externally between its trousered undercarriage units, the Gamma 2C differed from the previous two Gammas in having its two-seat enclosed cockpit moved forward, with the pilot sitting slightly behind the wing leading edge. After being tested at Wright Field, beginning in July 1933, the Gamma 2C was purchased by the Army Air Corps on 28 June, 1934. Details of its subsequent military career will be found in the chapter devoted to the Northrop A-17 and Douglas 8A series.

S/ns 8–10: Three mail-carrying single-seat Gamma 2Ds (initially registered X13757, X13758 and NR13759 respectively) were purchased by Transcontinental and Western Air. Delivered on 30 April, 11 June and 18 July, 1934, and assigned fleet numbers TWA 16, 17 and 20 respectively, these aircraft were initially powered by 710 hp Wright SR-1820-F3 radials driving two-blade propellers. The pilot's cockpit, enclosed under a simplified sliding canopy, was located aft of the wing, and two cargo holds (combined capacity, 110 cu ft—3·10 cu m; maximum payload, 1,396 lb—633 kg) were provided in the fuselage forward of the cockpit.

The first Gamma 2D (s/n 8, NR13757) was used by TWA's Jack Frye on 13–14 May, 1934, to set a transcontinental, one-stop, record (Los Angeles–Kansas City–Newark in 11 hr 31 min) while carrying a payload comprising 335 lb (152 kg) of mail and 85 lb (39 kg) of express, and constituting the first consignment to be flown following resumption of air mail operations by the commercial carriers. This aircraft remained in TWA service for two years until sold in 1936 to Charles Babb, an aircraft broker. Apparently, Babb intended to sell it to the Spanish Republican Government, but the deal did not materialize. Its subsequent fate is unclear but, apparently, the aircraft was sold in early 1942 to the US Corps of Engineers and, according to unconfirmed reports, was wrecked in Africa during World War II.

The next Gamma 2D (s/n 9, NR13758) had a more interesting career, as TWA modified it as an 'Overweather Experimental Laboratory' for research into problems which would be encountered by later airliners operating at high altitudes. For this purpose, the aircraft was re-engined with a 775 hp SR-1820-F52 engine driving a three-blade propeller and fitted, under a three-way contract between TWA, General Electric and the Army Air Corps, with a GE turbosupercharger. At the same time, a flight engineer's station with a special set of 36 instruments was fitted in the cargo compartment. In this form, the aircraft was flown extensively for TWA by D. W. 'Tommy' Tomlinson with James Heistand as research engineer, until 11 October, 1940, when it was sold to the Texas Company. Now powered by a 735 hp SR-1820-F53 without the turbosupercharger, this Gamma 2D

Transcontinental & Western Air's second Gamma 2D was used for research into high-altitude operations. (*TWA*)

was assigned as Texaco No.36 to Aubrey Keif, General Domestic Sales Department, for testing oil temperatures and flows. Two years later, on 15 October, 1942, Texaco sold the aircraft to the Army Air Forces which designated it UC-100 in the utility transport category. On 17 January, 1943, the UC-100 (serial 42-94140) was damaged in a landing accident at Duncan Field, Texas. Repaired and flown briefly, 42-94140 was finally surveyed at Kelly Field, Texas, on 11 August, 1943, due to shortage of parts.

If less spectacular, the career of the third Gamma 2D (s/n 10, NR/NC13759) was none the less colourful. After being operated by TWA, beginning in July 1934, this aircraft was purchased by the Texas Company on 11 October, 1935. As Texaco No.20, it was assigned to Aubrey Keif for sales promotion in the northern United States and Canada. In December 1935, when Ellsworth and Hollick-Kenyon were believed lost in Antarctica, Texaco entrusted this Gamma 2D to Frank Hawks for a fast flight from the United States, via the West Coast of South America, to Antarctica. However, Ellsworth and Hollick-Kenyon were found before Frank Hawks arrived in Antarctica and his Gamma 2D was shipped back to the United States. On 18 February, 1937, it was sold to Frank Cordova in New York and delivered to Col Gustavo Leon in Mexico where it was registered XA-ABJ. This, however, was a cover for the ultimate destination of the aircraft as in December 1937 the Gamma 2D was shipped aboard the Spanish steamship ss *Ibai*. The aircraft was last reported in use as a bomber by the Spanish Republican forces, in which service it bore a code in the TG series.

S/n 11: Ordered by the already famous aviatrix Jacqueline Cochran, the Gamma 2G (X13761/NC13761) was the sole Gamma to be powered by a liquid-cooled engine, a 700 hp Curtiss Conqueror SGV-1570F-4 driving a two-blade propeller. The aircraft was fitted as a two-seater and did not have a forward cargo compartment, but in other respects it was generally similar to the Gamma 2Ds. However, the aircraft was extensively damaged during its delivery flight on 30 September, 1934, when the ferry pilot, Wesley Smith, was forced by the overheating Conqueror engine to make a forced landing near Tucumcari in New Mexico. This accident forced Jacqueline Cochran to abandon her plan to enter the Gamma 2G in the Mac.Robertson race from England to Australia and the aircraft had to be rebuilt with parts from s/n 13, an uncompleted Gamma 2D. At that time, the aircraft was re-engined with a Pratt & Whitney engine and Jacqueline Cochran entered it in the 1935 Bendix Trophy Race; bad luck struck again as Jacqueline Cochran was forced out of the race by rapidly deteriorating weather conditions. She then leased the Gamma 2G to Howard Hughes who had a 1,000 hp Wright SR-1820-G2 radial engine, driving a three-blade constant-speed propeller, installed. As the most powerful Gamma, the aircraft was used by Howard Hughes to set a new transcontinental nonstop record on 13–14 January, 1936, (Burbank to Newark in 9 hr 26 min 10 sec; average speed, 259 mph—417 km/h). Less than six months later, on 10 July, the Gamma 2G was destroyed when engine failure on take off from Indianapolis forced Jackie Odlum to attempt an emergency landing. The aircraft nosed over, ground looped and was damaged beyond repair.

The Gamma 2G awaiting delivery at Mines Field, Los Angeles, on 29 September, 1934. (*Karl W. Peters*)

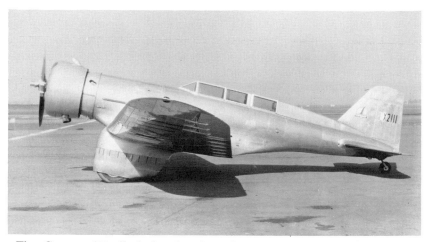

The Gamma 2H displaying its clean lines, broad wings and trousered undercarriage. (*Karl W. Peters*)

S/n 12: Similar to the Gamma 2G, but powered by a 710 hp Wright SR-1820-F3 engine, the Gamma 2H (successively X2111, NR2111 and NC2111) was delivered to Marion P. Guggenheim on 2 December, 1934. It was later operated by Russel M. Thaw, who with William H. Klenke as mechanic, set out in December 1935 to fly to Antarctica to help in the search for Ellsworth and Hollick-Kenyon. However, on 9 December the Gamma 2H was badly damaged in a take off accident at Atlanta. After being repaired, the aircraft was acquired by Bernarr MacFadden who flew it until early in 1942 when it was acquired by the US Corps of Engineers. Subsequent fate unknown.

S/n 14–27, 30–37, 45 and 46: These 24 aircraft were purchased by the Chinese Government as light bombers. Powered by 710 hp Wright SR-1820-F3 engines driving two-blade propellers, they were externally similar to the Gamma 2C in its original configuration. However, a major recognition feature was the addition of a partially retractable bomb-aimer's tub beneath the fuselage just aft of the wing. During normal operations, the bomb-aimer/gunner sat facing forward, behind the pilot, under the canopy which covered the two cockpits. To man the flexible 0·30-in machine-gun, he swivelled his seat to face aft. From this position, he could also slide down into the tub to aim the bombs through a forward-facing window. Forward-firing armament consisted of four wing-mounted 0·30-in machine-guns, and the maximum bombload carried beneath the fuselage was 1,600 lb (726 kg). With minor modifications differentiating each model, two of these aircraft were completed as Gamma 2Es, seven as Gamma 2ECs, and fifteen as Gamma 2EDs. The first aircraft was delivered on 19 February, 1934, and the last on 21 September, 1934.

S/n 44: The Gamma 2F was the second link, after the Gamma 2C, in the development of the A-17 series for the Army Air Corps.

135

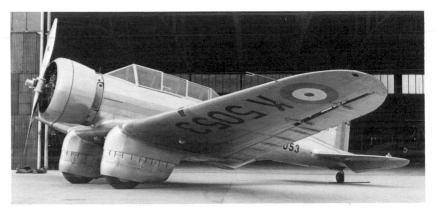

The Gamma 2ED-C which was tested by the A & AEE at Martlesham Heath.
(*Flight International*)

S/n 47: First flown with the US civil experimental registration X13760, this Gamma 2ED-C powered by a 735 hp SR-1820-F53 radial was completed in July 1934 as a demonstration aircraft. In early 1935, piloted by Frank Hawks and G. H. Irving, it was used for a 20,000 mile (32,200 km) tour through Central and South America to locate suitable landing fields and control stations for use in the proposed 'Round America Air Race'. Countries visited included Cuba, Panama, Peru, Chile, Argentina, Brazil, Uruguay, Ecuador, Colombia, Venezuela, El Salvador and Mexico. Total flying time was 101·23 hr at an average speed of slightly over 200 mph (320 km/h). Purchased in 1935 by the British Air Ministry for evaluation by the A & AEE at Martlesham Heath, the aircraft received the serial K5053 upon delivery to the United Kingdom. Its subsequent fate is unknown.

S/n 48–72: Components and subassemblies for these twenty-five Gamma 2Es were built by Northrop in the Mines Field plant and shipped to China. They were assembled by the Central Aircraft Manufacturing Company (CAMCO) at Loiwing and joined the twenty-four Northrop-assembled Gamma 2Es, 2ECs and 2EDs in service with the Chinese Army Air Arm. All 49 aircraft were rapidly destroyed in training accidents and during the early phase of the second Sino-Japanese conflict.

S/n 186: After a long hiatus in Gamma production, during which Northrop built mostly A-17 attack bombers for the Army Air Corps, a unique aircraft was produced as a demonstrator to be entered in the Army Air Corps competition for basic and advanced trainers. Designated Gamma 2J and registered X18148, the aircraft was a two-seater powered by a 600 hp Pratt & Whitney Wasp S3H1-G engine driving a three-blade propeller. The aircraft retained the standard Gamma wings but had a new fuselage and a fully retractable main undercarriage folding inward into the wing leading edge. This undercarriage design was also used in the A-17As, the first of which appeared seven months after the Gamma 2J. Delivered on 10 January, 1936, the Gamma 2J lost the competition to the North

Gamma 2J as used by Douglas as a company hack. (*MDC*)

American NA-26 (Air Corps BC-1). Retained by Douglas as a company hack, the aircraft suffered an engine failure, stalled and crashed at El Paso Municipal Airport on 19 May, 1945. The pilot, Aubrey S. Taylor, was killed but the two passengers were only injured.

S/n 347: The last Gamma was specially built for the Bristol Aeroplane Co for use as a flying test-bed for the new fourteen-cylinder sleeve-valve Hercules engine. Delivered without engine on 4 June, 1937, and registered G-AFBT, the Gamma 2L was fitted initially with a 1,290 hp Bristol Hercules Mk 1SM driving a three-blade propeller. With this engine, the aircraft made its first flight at Filton, Bristol, during September 1937. Later, the Gamma 2L was used to test the Hercules Mk 1M(a), Mk 3SM, and Mk 6SM. It was dismantled at Filton towards the end of World War II. Externally, the Gamma 2L was easily recognizable because of the characteristic Bristol exhaust collector ring in the forward portion of the

G-AFBT, the Gamma 2L used by the Bristol Aeroplane Co to test the Hercules engine, seen here during the war with dark earth/dark green upper surfaces and yellow under surfaces. (*Rolls-Royce*)

137

cowling and the fixed undercarriage and vertical tail surfaces similar to those of the Northrop A-17. The pilot and flight engineer sat in tandem, with the pilot above the wing, under a canopy fairing into the rear fuselage.

Gamma 2A

Span 48 ft (14·63 m); length 29 ft 9 in (9·07 m); wing area 363 sq ft (33·724 sq m). Empty weight 3,500 lb (1,588 kg); loaded weight 7,000 lb (3,175 kg); wing loading 19·3 lb/sq ft (94·1 kg/sq m); power loading 8·9 lb/hp (4 kg/hp). Maximum speed 248 mph (399 km/h) at 7,000 ft (2,135 m); cruising speed 220 mph (354 km/h); range 2,500 miles (4,025 km).

Gamma 2D

Span 47 ft 9½ in (14·57 m); length 31 ft 2 in (9·5 m); height 9 ft (2·74 m); wing area 363 sq ft (33·724 sq m). Empty weight 4,119 lb (1,868 kg); loaded weight 7,350 lb (3,334 kg); wing loading 20·2 lb/sq ft (98·9 kg/sq m); power loading 10·4 lb/hp (4·7 kg/hp). Maximum speed 223 mph (359 km/h) at 6,300 ft (1,920 m); cruising speed 204 mph (328 km/h); initial rate of climb 1,390 ft/min (424 m/min); service ceiling 23,400 ft (7,130 m); range 1,970 miles (3,170 km).

Gamma 2ED-C

Span and wing area as Gamma 2A. Length 28 ft 10 in (8·79 m); height 9 ft 1 in (2.77 m). Empty weight 3,850 lb (1,746 kg); loaded weight 7,600 lb (3,447 kg); wing loading 20·9 lb/sq ft (102·2 kg/sq m); power loading 10·3 lb/hp (4·7 kg/hp). Maximum speed 228 mph (367 km/h) at 11,500 ft (3,505 m); initial rate of climb 1,175 ft/min (358 m/min); service ceiling 29,300 ft (8,930 m).

Douglas XFD-1

Even though the quest for higher performance was beginning to render the low-wing monoplane configuration more attractive, in the early thirties the US Navy was showing little eagerness to accept monoplane designs for use as carrier-based fighters. Thus, when in the spring of 1932 the Bureau of Aeronautics issued its Design No.113 calling for a two-seat carrier-based fighter, it once again requested proposals for aircraft of biplane configuration. Seven manufacturers, including the Douglas Aircraft Company, submitted designs and, in June 1932, Douglas and Vought were each selected to build a prototype.

Designed under the supervision of J. Kindelberger and A. Raymond, the XFD-1 (s/n 1136, BuNo 9223) was a two-seat externally-braced fabric-covered metal biplane of conventional design and was the last aircraft submitted to the US Navy to use a faired spreader-bar for its fixed under-carriage. The aircraft was powered by a 700 hp Pratt & Whitney R-1535-64 fourteen-cylinder air-cooled radial housed in a long-chord NACA cowling and drove a fixed-pitch two-blade propeller. Small split-flaps were installed on the upper wings inboard of the ailerons and a large one-piece split-flap extended between the ailerons beneath the lower wings. The crew of two sat in tandem under a long enclosed canopy, and armament consisted of two forward-firing 0·30-in machine-guns mounted

The XFD-1 (BuNo 9223) at Santa Monica. Ailerons were fitted on both upper and lower wings but flaps were only below the upper wings. (*MDC*)

in the engine cowling and one hand-held 0·30-in machine-gun in the rear cockpit. Completed in January 1933, the aircraft was test flown by Eddie Allen but was nearly lost during high-speed diving trials when the engine cowling slid forward. Fortunately for Eddie Allen, the cowling broke off before crashing into the propeller and he was able to land the aircraft without too much damage to the airframe.

After a slightly modified cowling with stronger attachment clamps had been fitted, the aircraft was delivered to NAS Anacostia for competitive trials with the Vought XF3U-1. In its final report issued at the completion of Service Acceptance Trials which had taken place at Anacostia between 18 June, 1933, and 14 August, 1934, the Board commented favourably on the aircraft's excellent flying characteristics and on a number of its outstanding features, particularly the flexible gun installation which had been found to be the best so far submitted for test. In spite of the fact that the XFD-1 did not fulfil its performance guarantees—top speed was 208 mph (335 km/h) versus a guarantee of 216 mph (348 km/h)—the Board recommended that the XFD-1, with changes incorporated to correct performance and other deficiencies, be accepted as a Service type. Meanwhile however, the Navy had lost interest in the two-seat fighter class and the XFD-1 was not proceeded with whilst the slightly faster XF3U-1

The XFD-1 was Douglas's only piston-engined fighter biplane to be tested but it was not put into production. (*MDC*)

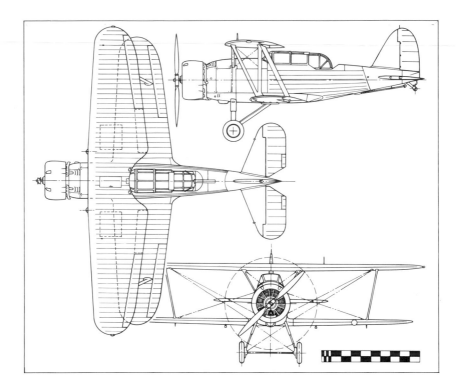

was developed into the Vought SBU scout-bomber series.

Having failed US Navy acceptance, the Douglas XFD-1 was returned to the manufacturer. Eventually in 1936 the aircraft was fitted with a 750 hp Wright 1820-F53 nine-cylinder radial and offered for export as a two-seat scout bomber. However, the aircraft was by then obsolete as a combat aircraft and, as no customer could be found, was handed over to Pratt & Whitney to be used as an engine test-bed.

After failing to obtain a production contract for the XFD-1, its first venture in the naval fighter business, Douglas did not enter designs in any carrier-based fighter competition until the XF3D-1 Skyknight of 1946. Thus, the XF2D-1 designation did not apply to a Douglas-designed aircraft but was assigned to the prototype of the F2H Banshee series.

Span 31 ft 6 in (9·6 m); length 25 ft 4 in (7·72 m); height 11 ft 1 in (3·38 m); wing area 295 sq ft (27·689 sq m). Empty weight 3,227 lb (1,464 kg); loaded weight 4,672 lb (2,119 kg); maximum weight 5,000 lb (2,268 kg); wing loading 15·8 lb/sq ft (76·5 kg/sq m). Maximum speed 208 mph (335 km/h) at 8,000 ft (2,440 m); cruising speed 170 mph (274 km/h); climb to 5,000 ft (1,524 m) 3·3 min; service ceiling 23,700 ft (7,225 m); range 576 miles (927 km).

Above weights and performance with R-1535-64 engine. Performance with 1820–F53 engine: maximum speed 211 mph (339 km/h) at 8,000 ft (2,440 m); cruising speed 175 mph (282 km/h); service ceiling 28,200 ft (8,595 m); range 460 miles (740 km).

Northrop Delta

Developed in parallel with the Gamma series, the Delta was initially intended as a transport and differed from the first product of the Northrop Corporation in having a wider fuselage joined to the Gamma wings. However, on 1 October, 1934, an amendment to the United States 1926 Air Commerce Act became effective. It required that, for transport of passengers at night or over terrain not readily permitting emergency landings, the airlines use only multi-engined aircraft capable of flying with one engine inoperative. This new stringent requirement, not anticipated when John Northrop had undertaken the design of the Delta series, effectively wiped out the potential market for this aircraft as no US airline was prepared to purchase aircraft which could be used only during daytime and over certain areas. Thus, as its military applications were limited, the Delta was soon restricted to the small executive market.

Before promulgation of this new regulation, three passenger-carrying Deltas were sold to the airlines, and Swedish Air Lines (ABA) bought a version specially modified as a mailplane. Eight other Deltas were sold as executive transports whilst the last (Delta 1D-8) built by Northrop was delivered unassembled to Canadian Vickers to serve as a pattern for the production of a general-purpose bomber version in Canada. The production, development and operational records of each of these thirteen aircraft are reported here in the order of their production.

The Delta 1A before delivery to Transcontinental & Western Air. (*NA & SM*)

S/n 3: Completed and first flown in May 1933, the Delta 1A (X12292/NC12292) had accommodation for a pilot in a cockpit located behind the engine firewall and enclosed by a sliding canopy, and for eight passengers in an enclosed cabin behind the cockpit. The aircraft was powered by a 710 hp Wright SR-1820-F3 radial driving a two-blade propeller and was licensed under ATC Group 2-456 in August 1933. The aircraft was then leased to TWA for use as a mailplane on the Kansas City–Los Angeles route. On 24 October of that year, the Delta 1A was damaged in a forced landing near Grants, New Mexico, but was repaired and put back into service. Less than three weeks later, on 10 November, the engine caught fire in flight. The pilot, Harlan Hull, successfully baled out but the aircraft crashed near Moriarty, some 65 miles east of Albuquerque.

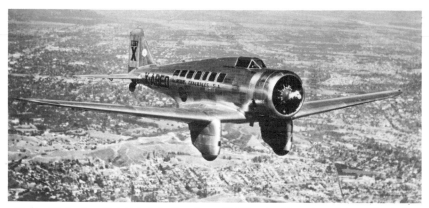

Delta 1B during flight trials in Southern California. The aircraft bears both its permanent Mexican registration (X-ABED) and temporary US experimental registration (X236Y). (*Pratt & Whitney*)

S/n 4: The Delta 1B (initially registered X236Y) had only a slightly longer service life as it was destroyed by fire on 5 May, 1934, just ten months after being completed. Ordered by Pan American for its subsidiary Aerovías Centrales SA, this aircraft was delivered on 20 August, 1933, and was registered in Mexico as X-ABED. It was powered by a 660 hp Pratt & Whitney Hornet T2D-1 driving a two-blade propeller, and its crew and passenger accommodation was similar to that of the Delta 1A.

S/n 7: Purchased by AB Aerotransport (Swedish Air Lines), the Delta 1C was registered SE-ADI and named *Halland*. It was generally similar to the first two Deltas but was powered by a 700 hp Pratt & Whitney T1D1 driving a two-blade propeller. Delivered in April 1934, the aircraft was used for a special dash between Paris and Stockholm and it linked the two capitals in 4 hr 40 min, averaging better than 198 mph (319 km/h).

Delta 1C (*left*) and Delta 1E (*right*) of AB Aerotransport. (*SAS*)

Following this noteworthy flight, the aircraft was entered in the October 1934 Mac.Robertson Race from England to Australia but became a non-starter and, instead, was put into scheduled passenger operation on the Gothenburg–Copenhagen–Malmö and Malmö–Copenhagen–Hanover routes. In May 1937 ABA sold the Delta 1C to Mrs Beryl Markham who had it registered in the United Kingdom as G-AEXR. Apparently, the aircraft never reached England and reports on its subsequent history are conflicting. According to some sources, the Delta 1C may have been registered in Iraq as YI-OSF while other sources give the aircraft's ultimate owners as the Spanish Republicans. Still others claim that the Delta 1C was still in Sweden during the war and that in 1943 it was operated as a target-tug for or by Flygvapnet.

S/n 28: Originally delivered to the Richfield Oil Corporation on 21 July, 1934, the Delta 1D (NC13777) was fitted as a six-passenger executive aircraft. The crew of two, pilot and co-pilot, was housed in a widened cockpit, and the aircraft was powered by a 710 hp Wright SR-1820-F3 driving a three-blade propeller. While operated by Richfield, the Delta 1D established some remarkable point-to-point records such as Seattle to Los Angeles in 5 hr 12 min, and San Francisco to Los Angeles in 1 hr 38 min. Later owners included Baker Oil Tools Inc, Le Tourneau Co, and Minneapolis-Honeywell Regulator Co. In April 1945, the Delta 1D was re-engined with a 735 hp SR-1820-F53. As late as 1973, this Delta was still FAA-registered, although not in flying condition, to Richard M. Davis of Shawnee Mission, Kansas.

S/n 29: Although designated Delta 1E, this aircraft's external appearance was closer to that of the Gammas than to that of other Deltas. It was acquired by AB Aerotransport as a night mailplane and was fitted with a cargo compartment behind the engine firewall. The crew of two sat in tandem in an enclosed cockpit in the rear of the fuselage. Powered by a 660 hp Pratt & Whitney Hornet T2D1 driving a two-blade propeller, the Delta 1E was tested in the United States as X13755 and registered SE-ADW *Småland* in Sweden. On 6 July, 1934, less than one month after its delivery, SE-ADW crashed at Almhut in Småland, due to rudder flutter. The crew of two baled out successfully.

S/n 38: This Delta 1D-1 (NC14241), powered by a 710 hp SR-1820-F3 driving a two-blade propeller, was delivered to Powell Crosley Jr, on 23 August, 1934. In December 1936 the Delta 1D-1 and Delta 1D-4 (s/n 41, ex NC14266) were purchased by the Vimalert Co Ltd on behalf of the Spanish Republicans and, on 5 January, 1937, were shipped from Brooklyn on board the ss *Mar Cantábrico*. The ship was intercepted at sea by Nationalist warships and its cargo of aircraft (including the two Deltas, four Vultee V-1As, one Fairchild 91, and one Lockheed 10 Electra) was confiscated for use by Franco's forces. Thus, during the Spanish civil war, the Delta 1D-1 and 1D-4 served in the transport role with Grupo 43 as 43-5 and 43-4 respectively. The Delta 1D-1 No. 43-5 was last reported in 1939, without wings and engine, on the airfield at León.

With Nationalist markings and the code 43-5 on its fuselage, this Delta 1D-1 was one of eight aircraft obtained by General Franco's forces when the ss *Mar Cantábrico* was captured at sea. (*USAF*)

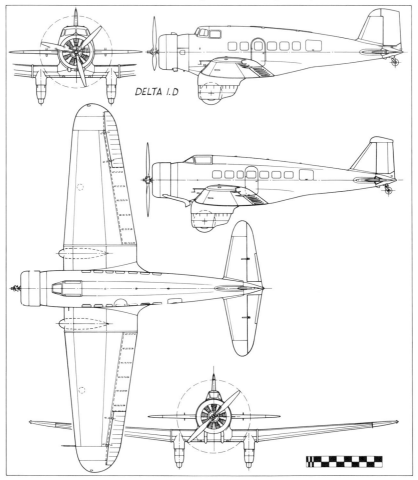

DELTA I.D

Northrop Delta 1B and 1D.

144

S/n 39: Delivered to Hal Roach Studios Inc on 18 August, 1934, the Delta 1D-2 (NC14242) was sold to Earle P. Halliburton Inc on 8 January, 1935. Less than two years later the SR-1820-F3 powered aircraft was acquired by Charles H. Babb. Also intended for ultimate delivery to the Spanish Republicans, the Delta 1D-2 was sold to Rudolf Wolf on 14 December, 1936, and its wings were shipped tò Le Havre aboard the SS *Waalhaven* whilst its fuselage was loaded on the SS *President Harding*. Reassembled in France, where it was registered F-AQAQ, the aircraft was flown to Spain sometime before July 1937. With the Spanish Republicans, the Delta 1D-2 was registered EC-AGC and operated by LAPE (Líneas Aéreas Postales Españolas) until evacuated to Algeria at the end of the civil war. Handed back to Spain, the aircraft was operated briefly by Grupo L-12 of the Ejército del Aire.

The Delta 1D-2 which was operated as EC-AGC by LAPE (Líneas Aéreas Postales Españolas) during the Spanish Civil War. (*Captain Pedro Tonda*)

S/n 40: The Delta 1D-3 (NC14265) was delivered to William H. Danforth. Originally powered by a 650 hp Hornet S4D1, the aircraft was re-engined in August 1936 with a 650 hp Hornet S9E, but was destroyed in a hangar fire at Miami on 1 January, 1938.

S/n 41: Powered by a 710 hp SR-1820-F3, the Delta 1D-4 (NC14266) was delivered to Morton May on 5 December, 1934. Four months later it was transferred to Wilbur D. May for use as an executive transport by the May Company. Acquired in late 1936 by Vimalert, the aircraft found its way to Spain, as already mentioned. The Delta 1D-4 survived the Spanish Civil War and was subsequently operated by Grupo L-12 of the Ejército del Aire.

S/n 42: Sold to George F. Harding, President of the Chicago Real Estate Loan &Trust Company, the Delta 1D-5 (NC14267) was delivered on 30 July, 1935, and was powered by a 735 hp SR-1820-F2. After being used by Harding as an executive transport, it was acquired by Lincoln Ellsworth on 27 April, 1938, and was fitted with a long-range tank in the cabin to increase the total fuel capacity from 328 US gallons (1,242 litres) to 533 gallons (2,093 litres). Shipped to Antarctica aboard the *Wyatt Earp*, the Delta ID-5 (now registered NX14267) made one flight on 14 January, 1939, with

The Delta 1D-5 in RAAF markings after being impressed in December 1942. (*Australian War Memorial*)

Canadian pilot J. H. Lymburner at the controls. After the Ellsworth expedition returned to Australia in February 1939, the Commonwealth Government purchased the aircraft which was then stored until August 1940. At that time, it was registered VH-ADR and operated by the Department of Civil Aviation for testing radio installations, navigational aids, and equipment. In December 1942, the Delta 1D-5 was impressed and delivered to No.1 Aircraft Depot, RAAF, at Laverton, Victoria. With the serial number A61-1, the aircraft was flown as a military transport successively by Nos.35, 34 and 37 Squadrons. While operated by No.37, it was damaged beyond repair in a take off accident on 30 September, 1943.

S/n 73: Powered by a 710 hp SR-1820-F3 and initially delivered to Bruce Dodson on 22 December, 1934, the Delta 1D-6 (NC14220) was sold in May 1935 to Seward Webb Pulitzer, in September 1938 to Joyland Enterprises Inc, and finally on 5 September, 1942, to the US Corps of Engineers. With the Corps of Engineers, the aircraft was operated out of Edmonton, Alberta, as a transport aircraft for the Canol Project. It was either destroyed or scrapped in Canada during the war.

The sole Delta 1D-7 was operated by the Coast Guard under the designation RT-1. (*NA & SM*)

S/n 74: Ordered by the US Coast Guard and designated Northrop RT-1 (serial 382 and, from October 1936, V150), the Delta 1D-7 was delivered on 20 February, 1935. Initially used as the personal transport of Henry Morgenthau, the Secretary of the Treasury, and later as a USCG staff transport, it was powered by a 735 hp SR-1820-F2. Following an accident, it was purchased in damaged condition for $1,400 (original price had been $41,909) by Charles Babb. The aircraft, after being repaired, was licensed as NC28663 and transferred on 10 December, 1941, to Airmotive Inc. Subsequent fate unknown.

S/n 185: The last aircraft in the series, a Delta 1D-8, was ordered by the Canadian Department of National Defence to serve as a pattern for the production of a photographic survey version to be built by Canadian Vickers. Parts and subassemblies were built by Northrop and assembled by Canadian Vickers. Powered by a 775 hp SR-1820-F52, the Delta 1D-8 was first flown at the Fairchild Airport, Longueuil, Quebec, on 16 August, 1936. To suit the aircraft for its intended role as a photographic survey aircraft operating under the harsh conditions of Canada's northern territories, its fuselage was strengthened and adapted to house a crew of three and a trio of Fairchild A3 automatic cameras, while the oleo-pneumatic legs of its undercarriage were lengthened. Alternatively, the aircraft could be fitted with Vickers Type F streamlined skis or Type 75 floats. Equipped with these floats and bearing the Canadian military serial 667, the aircraft was taken on charge by the RCAF on 1 September, 1936, at Ottawa Air Station, Rockliffe. Serving successively with No.8 (GP) Squadron and No.120 (BR) Squadron, the Delta I (RCAF serial 667, Canadian Vickers c/n 177) was retired in late 1941 and became Instructional Airframe A143 on 6 June, 1942. It was struck off strength on 26 April, 1944.

Delta II of No.8 Squadron about to be launched at RCAF Station Ottawa, Ontario, on 26 August, 1939. (*Canadian Armed Forces*)

Bearing the Canadian military serial 683, this aircraft was the first of eight Delta IIIs delivered in 1940 by Canadian Vickers. (*Canadian Armed Forces*)

Two more Delta Is (RCAF 668 and 669, c/ns 178 and 179) built by Canadian Vickers were delivered in October 1936. These, together with the original aircraft, were later fitted with additional cockpit side and floor windows and redesignated Delta IAs. Nine Delta IIs (RCAF 670 to 677 and 682, c/ns 180 to 183 and 191 to 195) on the assembly lines were fitted with the additional windows and had provision for armament including two wing-mounted, forward-firing 0·30-in machine-guns, one 0·30-in gun in a semi-enclosed dorsal position, one 250-lb (113·4-kg) bomb under each wing and four 20-lb (9·1-kg) bombs beneath the fuselage. However, the installation of the dorsal gun turret resulted in severe tail buffeting and, consequently, it was found necessary to install new vertical tail surfaces. This was first accomplished on RCAF 676 which, redesignated Delta III, was tested with the new tail surfaces during the summer of 1940. Although successful when the aircraft operated on wheels or skis, when floats were fitted the new surfaces necessitated the addition of an auxiliary ventral fin. The last eight Canadian Vickers-built aircraft (RCAF 683 to 690, c/ns 196 to 203) were completed in 1940 as Delta IIIs. The last six Canadian Deltas were struck off strength on 14 February, 1945, after serving with Nos.1, 6, 8 and 120 Squadrons, with the Western Air Command, 13 OTU and 3 Training Command.

Delta 1B

Span 47 ft 9 in (14·55 m); length 34 ft 3 in (10·44 m); height 9 ft 8 in (2·95 m); wing area 363 sq ft (33·724 sq m). Empty weight 4,100 lb (1,860 kg); loaded weight 7,000 lb (3,175 kg); wing loading 19·3 lb/sq ft (94·1 kg/sq m); power loading 10·6 lb/hp (4·8 kg/hp). Maximum speed at sea level 210 mph (338 km/h); cruising speed 187 mph (301 km/h); initial rate of climb 1,000 ft/min (305 m/min); service ceiling 20,000 ft (6,095 m); range 1,550 miles (2,495 km).

Delta 1D-5

Span and wing area as 1B. Length 33 ft 1 in (10·08 m); height 10 ft 1 in (3·07 m). Empty weight 4,540 lb (2,059 kg); loaded weight 7,350 lb (3,334 kg); wing loading 20·2 lb/sq ft (98·9 kg/sq m); power loading 10 lb/hp (4·5 kg/hp). Maximum speed 219 mph (352 km/h) at 6,300 ft (1,920 m); cruising speed 200 mph (332 km/h); initial rate of climb 1,200 ft/min (366 m/min); service ceiling 20,000 ft (6,095 m); range 1,650 miles (2,655 km).

148

Douglas DC-1

Technical obsolescence of existing equipment and competitive pressures are among the most important instruments of progress in the airline industry. Significantly, both factors were behind the inception of the Douglas DC-1, the progenitor of the world's most famous family of commercial transport aircraft. Delivered to its sponsors— Transcontinental & Western Air—in December 1933, the DC-1 marked the beginning of a long and still uninterrupted association between the DC-series and most of the world's airlines.

Following the crash of the TWA Fokker F-10A NC999E on 31 March, 1931, the Bureau of Air Commerce instructed the operators of this and all other types of airliners with wooden spars and ribs to periodically inspect the internal wing structure. Such inspections proved excessively costly and time consuming for the fledgling US airlines and resulted in the early phasing-out of most wooden airliners. As a result of this directive, a year later TWA found it necessary to look for new aircraft and decided to negotiate with Boeing Aircraft Company the purchase of a number of Model 247 all-metal twin-engined monoplane transports. When negotiations between Boeing and TWA began, the Model 247, which was fitted with a retractable undercarriage and could accommodate ten passengers in a fully enclosed cabin, was still under development. However, Boeing's

The DC-1 photographed on 1 July, 1933, at Clover Field, Santa Monica, just before its first flight. (*MDC*)

insistence on first completing the delivery of all sixty Model 247s ordered by United Air Lines, a company then partially owned by Boeing and TWA's prime competitor, placed TWA in a precarious position. Either TWA had to accept initial delivery of Model 247s long after its competitors or had to initiate the design of a comparable aircraft. The latter solution was the one TWA adopted.

Under the impetus of Jack Frye, then its Vice President in charge of Operations, TWA decided to gamble its future on a new aircraft equal or superior to the Boeing 247. To that effect TWA drafted a specification calling for a three-engined aircraft, preferably of all-metal construction and monoplane configuration, to be powered by 500 to 550 hp supercharged engines. A crew of two and at least twelve passengers were to be carried over a distance of 1,080 miles (1,738 km) at a cruising speed of 150 mph (241 km/h). Other performance requirements were as follows:—top speed at sea level: at least 185 mph (298 km/h); cruising speed at sea level: at least 146 mph (235 km/h); landing speed: not more than 65 mph (105 km/h); rate of climb at sea level: at least 1,200 ft/min (6 m/sec); service ceiling: at least 21,000 ft (6,400 m); and service ceiling on any two engines: 10,000 ft (3,050 m). Gross weight was not to exceed 14,200 lb (6,396 kg) and payload with full equipment and fuel for maximum range was to be at least 2,300 lb (1,043 kg). However, the most stringent requirements in TWA's specification read as follows: 'This plane, fully loaded, must make satisfactory take-offs under good control at any TWA airport on any combination of two engines.' Considering the fact that one of TWA's major airports on its transcontinental route was Albuquerque, which is located at an elevation of 4,954 ft (1,510 m) and where summer temperatures often exceed 90 deg F (32 deg C), this requirement appeared, at the time, difficult to meet.

On 2 August, 1932, TWA sent its specification and an invitation to bid for the new transport design to Consolidated, Curtiss, General Aviation, Martin and Douglas. In the midst of the depression years, with only lean military contracts available, the opportunity to obtain new commercial contracts was an effective spur to the creative talent of Donald Douglas and his team of engineers. Within a few days the Douglas Aircraft Company expressed its intention to submit a proposal to TWA.

From the inception of the project the Douglas team decided to depart somewhat from the specification, to improve their competitive chances and achieve performance superior to that of the Boeing 247. The availability of supercharged engines in the 700 hp-class and the use of NACA cowlings and engine nacelles into which the main undercarriage retracted made possible the design of an all-metal twin-engined low-wing monoplane meeting all requirements. Other far-reaching decisions taken during the early design phase included the selection of a multi-spar wing structure—a feature inspired by the work of John K. Northrop and which was to give to the DC-1 and later DC aircraft an exceptional strength and fatigue-free life—and the adoption of a fuselage of sufficient diameter to enable the

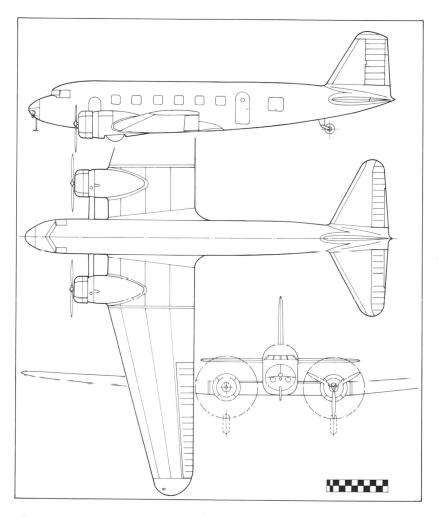

taller passengers to stand upright in the aisle. This last feature combined with the method of construction with the wing centre-section built integrally with the fuselage—thus avoiding the need to have spars obstructing the passenger cabin as in the Boeing 247—and with effective cabin sound-proofing, were to offer greater passenger appeal and make it more competitive.

Ten days after the receipt of the TWA specification, Arthur Raymond and Harry Wetzel left Santa Monica for New York to present the Douglas proposal. Discussions and negotiations lasted more than three weeks during which the major stumbling block proved to be TWA's insistence on obtaining a guarantee that the aircraft would be able to take-off on one engine with full payload from any airport on its network. Even though the use of split flaps was contemplated, this requirement appeared difficult to meet. Yet the Douglas design, which had been designated DC-1, for Douglas Commercial One—a misnomer as the modified Cloudster had been used for commercial purposes by Ryan as had been the Mailplanes, and rebuilt Curtiss HS-2Ls of the Pacific Marine Airways and some Douglas Dolphins—appeared sufficiently promising for TWA to sign a contract on 20 September, 1932. Under the terms of the contract TWA would pay $125,000 for the first aircraft and had an option to buy all or part of sixty additional aircraft in lots of ten, fifteen or twenty at a unit price, less engines, of $58,000. However, as a safeguard against the possibility of the twin-engined DC-1 failing to meet requirements, the General Motors Corporation—which then controlled TWA and owned General Aviation—ordered General Aviation to undertake the construction of a new trimotor. The DC-1 flew when the General Aviation aeroplane was 80 per cent complete and, as the DC-1 exceeded its performance requirements, General Aviation did not complete its design.

Detailed engineering work began at once in the Santa Monica plant and Douglas called upon several new techniques—including extensive use of wind-tunnel tests, fuselage mock-up and independent test models for various systems such as fuel and hydraulics—to optimize the aircraft's design. As the DC-1 was taking shape, it became clear that it would be substantially heavier than originally estimated and thus would not be able to meet the single-engine take-off requirements unless variable-pitch propellers were installed. At that time the selection of engines for the DC-1 led to intense competition between Pratt & Whitney and Wright which respectively offered variants of their Hornet and Cyclone engines. Soon,

The DC-1 in TWA markings during initial trials. (*MDC*)

however, TWA and Douglas agreed initially to install two 690 hp Wright SGR-1820-F nine-cylinder air-cooled radials driving three-blade Hamilton Standard propellers. To begin with fixed-pitch propellers were installed but were soon replaced by variable-pitch units.

With this powerplant and bearing the experimental registration X223Y, the DC-1 (s/n 1137) was completed a mere nine months after the historic contract had been signed. With Carl Cover and Fred Herman at the controls, the DC-1 made its first flight on 1 July, 1933, at Clover Field, Santa Monica. To the Douglas staff's dismay, the maiden flight was almost the last flight as the engines failed each time the DC-1 reached its climbing attitude and the aircraft was saved only through Cover's skilful piloting. Fortunately, there was nothing wrong in the DC-1 design, and the trouble, traced to a design fault of the carburettor's fuel lines, was easily corrected. Returned to flight status the aircraft soon proved a complete success and TWA placed an initial order for twenty DC-2s, a derivative of the DC-1 with fuselage length increased by two feet (0·61 m) to accommodate an additional row of two seats.

During the three months following its eventful maiden flight the DC-1 was intensively tested by pilots from Douglas, TWA and the Bureau of Air Commerce. With the exception of modifications to the vertical tail surfaces to increase the rudder area, few changes were found necessary. Yet, the flight-test programme was marked by a series of memorable incidents including the almost complete jamming of the control surfaces due to the use of the wrong type of hydraulic fluid in the automatic pilot system and an accidental wheels-up landing when a crew member forgot to lower the mainwheels. Finally, on 4 September, 1933, the aircraft was put through its most difficult test to demonstrate its ability to meet TWA's most stringent requirement: a flight from Winslow, Arizona, to Albuquerque, New Mexico, with one engine shut down from take-off to landing. After one of its engines had been switched off during the take-off run, the DC-1 climbed slowly from 4,500 ft (1,370 m) to its cruising altitude of 8,000 ft (2,440 m) and, single-engined, successfully flew the 280 miles (451 km) between the two points. Douglas had proved the DC-1's ability to meet all requirements demanded by TWA in its original request of 2 August, 1932.

Having lost the initial competition to power the DC-1, Pratt & Whitney kept trying to interest Douglas in the use of the nine-cylinder air-cooled Hornet for comparative tests. With interest expressed by certain possible customers of the DC-1 for a Hornet-powered version, the promise of an improved and more powerful Hornet (the E Series), and the supplying of engines and a technical team by Pratt & Whitney, Douglas was persuaded to design, construct and test a Hornet installation in the DC-1.

In late September 1933 the installation of two 700 hp Pratt & Whitney Hornet SD-Gs was ready for testing. With these engines the aircraft was redesignated DC-1A and made its first flight on 6 October, 1933, piloted by Edmund T. Allen and D. W. Tomlinson. Ground and flight tests were extensively conducted and the Hornets were in and out of the aircraft

The port Hornet SD-G installation in the DC-1A, (*Pratt & Whitney*)

several times as various improvements were incorporated. In any event, the Wright Cyclone was eventually selected, it is said, on the basis of price and other non-technical considerations. Possibly another consideration may have been the lack of growth potential of the smaller Hornet engine. However, the DC-2 was available with the Hornet, and several Hornet-powered DC-2As were sold. One of these DC-2As—NC14285, s/n 1328, sold to Standard Oil of California—initially used the two Hornet SD-G radials which had been experimentally fitted to the DC-1A.

In December 1933 the DC-1, which had cost Douglas $306,778 to design, build and test, was officially delivered to TWA for, according to the terms of the contract, only $125,000. The $182,000 of company funds spent by Douglas on the DC-1 project were, however, to bring in substantial dividends as the DC-2 programme broke even following the delivery of some fifty aircraft. Having taken delivery of the DC-1, then registered NC223Y, TWA used it as a flying laboratory over its entire network and, occasionally, operated it for a few scheduled passenger runs pending the delivery of DC-2s. During this period the aircraft had two 710 hp SGR-1820-F3s substituted for the original 690 hp SGR-1820-Fs; still later the DC-1 was fitted with two 760 hp SGR-1820-F52s. With TWA the aircraft is best remembered for its spectacular record flight on 19 February, 1934, when, with Jack Frye and Eddie Rickenbacker, it flew coast to coast, from Los Angeles to Newark, in 13 hr 4 min. On the eve of the 1934 Air Mail

Emergency, when private air mail contracts were cancelled, this dramatized the airlines' ability to carry mail rapidly.

During the early part of 1935 the DC-1 was extensively modified before being lent by TWA to the National Aeronautical Association for an attempt at various US and world speed, distance and weight carrying records. For this purpose, the aircraft was fitted with two 875 hp Wright SGR-1820-F25s, and additional fuel tanks were installed in the fuselage to bring total capacity up from 510 US gallons (1,931 litres) to 2,100 gallons (7,949 litres) thus leading to the elimination of most cabin windows. As a result of these modifications, maximum take-off weight rose to 28,500 lb (12,927 kg), and dump valves, allowing the whole load of fuel to be dumped in three minutes, had to be installed to enable the aircraft, should the need arise, to make an emergency landing without exceeding its maximum landing weight.

The DC-1 after its transcontinental speed record for transport aircraft on 19 February, 1934. (*NA & SM*)

On its way to the East Coast where the attempts at setting world records were to take place, the DC-1 broke its own transcontinental speed record on 30 April, 1935, when, flown by D. W. Tomlinson, H. B. Snead and F. R. Redpath, it flew nonstop from Burbank to New York in 11 hr 5 min. Between 16 and 19 May, 1935, flown by D. W. Tomlinson and J. S. Bartles, it set or broke 22 records including eight world records. The most significant of these was set on 16 and 17 May when the aircraft, carrying a 1,000 kg (2,205 lb) load, flew over a 5,000 km (3,107 miles) course in 18 hr 22 min 49 sec at an average speed of 272·03 km/h (169·03 mph).

Having completed its time with TWA, the DC-1 was acquired by Western Aero & Radio Co of Burbank for Howard Hughes. Hughes had the aircraft modified further and planned to use it for at least three record attempts: a Hollywood to New York flight (via Nome, Khabarovsk, Vladivostok, Shanghai, Khabarovsk, Nome, and Edmonton, Canada); a New York to Moscow flight via Paris; and a round-the-world

Seen on take-off from Oakland, California, the DC-1 was then owned by
Western Aero & Radio Co on behalf of Howard Hughes.
(*International News Photo*)

flight. Authorization for these flights was requested of the Department of
Commerce and the Department of State but delays were incurred and,
eventually, Howard Hughes lost interest in the DC-1 and used a faster
Lockheed 14 for his round-the-world flight. The DC-1 then appeared on a
Shipper's Export Declaration dated 4 January, 1937, which was submitted
by the Vimalert Company Ltd. According to this document the aircraft,
along with seven Vultee V-1As, six Boeing 247s, two Northrop Deltas, one
Lockheed Model 10 Electra and one Fairchild 91, was to be shipped aboard
the ss *Mar Cantábrico* from New York to Bilbao. Intended for use by the
Azaña (the Spanish Republican Government), for some still unexplained
reason the DC-1 was not shipped. Eventually, however, the aircraft found
its way to Spain via Great Britain and France, having been in May 1938
acquired by Viscount Forbes, the Earl of Granard, and registered G-AFIF.

When he had acquired the DC-1, Lord Forbes planned to fly it across the
Atlantic but this plan was also dropped and the aircraft was shipped to
England where it was assembled at Croydon. At that time the long-range
fuselage tanks were removed and the cabin furnishing and windows re-
installed. Within a few months Lord Forbes sold the aircraft to a French
company acting as agents for LAPE (Líneas Aéreas Postales Españolas),
the airline operated for the Spanish Republican Government. From
October 1938 until the end of the Spanish Civil War the aircraft was flown
by LAPE as EC-AGJ. It then changed hands once more and was registered
EC-AAE as part of the fleet of SATA (Sociedad Anonima de Transportes
Aereos). Finally, while operating a scheduled flight between Seville,
Malaga and Tetuan in December 1940, the DC-1 suffered an engine failure
immediately after taking off from Malaga and had to be crash landed. The
passengers and crew walked out of the wreckage but the DC-1 was
damaged beyond repair.

Two crew and 12 passengers.

Span 85 ft (25·91 m); length 60 ft (18·29 m); height 16 ft (4·88 m); wing area 942 sq ft (87·515 sq m). Empty weight 11,780 lb (5,343 kg); loaded weight 17,500 lb (7,938 kg); wing loading 18·6 lb/sq ft (90·7 kg/sq m); power loading 12·3 lb/hp (5·6 kg/hp). Maximum speed 210 mph (338 km/h); cruising speed 190 mph (306 km/h) at 8,000 ft (2,440 m) and 200 mph (322 km/h) at 14,000 ft (4,270 m); initial rate of climb 1,050 ft/min (320 m/min); service ceiling 23,000 ft (7,010 m); normal range 1,000 miles (1,609 km).

Performance with SGR-1820-F3 engines.

Northrop XFT

The XFT-1, although itself unsuccessful, did herald the beginning of an uninterrupted and fruitful association between the Northrop Corporation and the US Navy. Having issued Specification No. SD-204 on 24 January, 1933, calling for new fighter designs and being impressed by the results obtained by Northrop with its Gamma and Delta series, the Navy ordered an XFT-1 prototype on 8 May, 1933, as its second type of experimental low-wing monoplane fighter.

Initial design was done directly by John K. Northrop who conceived the aircraft as a scaled-down version of the Delta single-engined transport and detailed design was done by a team led by Ed Heinemann acting as Project Engineer. The XFT-1 was of typical Northrop all-metal construction with three-spar wing and its fixed undercarriage was enclosed in large fairings from which the lower part of the wheels protruded. A sliding canopy was fitted over the cockpit, and the 625 hp Wright R-1510-26, which drove a two-blade metal propeller with pitch adjustable on the ground only, was enclosed in a large NACA-type cowling. Armament consisted of either two 0·30-in machine-guns or one 0·30-in and one 0·50-in machine-gun mounted in the cowling in front of the cockpit, and two 116 lb (52·6 kg) bombs could

The XFT-1 at Mines Field on 10 February, 1934. (*US National Archives*)

157

be carried under the wings. Split-flaps extending across the wings and centre-section from the inner ends of the ailerons were fitted to reduce landing speed and externally-balanced control tail surfaces were adopted.

Completed in early January 1934, the XFT-1 (s/n 6, BuNo 9400) was first flown on the 16th of that month with Vance Breese at the controls. Following completion of manufacturer's trials, the aircraft was delivered in March 1934 to NAS Anacostia for Service evaluation. At Anacostia the XFT-1, which reached a top speed of 235 mph at 6,000 ft (378 km/h at 1,830 m), was found to be the fastest aircraft yet tested by the Navy, but its handling characteristics were loathed by the Service test pilots. Even though with the aid of flaps the aircraft's landing speed had been demonstrated not to exceed 65 mph (105 km/h), the Service pilots often preferred to land it at much higher speeds as at around 65 mph it was very difficult to control. This failing and the poor forward visibility, were major shortcomings for an aircraft intended to operate aboard aircraft carriers, and it did not win much favour from naval pilots, who preferred the more pleasant handling of biplane fighters. More serious, however, were the aircraft's spinning characteristics as severe tail buffeting occurred during prolonged spins and resulted in increasingly heavy stick forces.

During diving trials at NAS Norfolk, Virginia, the XFT-1's fuel tank was extensively damaged and in August 1934 the aircraft was sent back to Northrop for repairs, modifications and additional manufacturer's trials. Re-engined with a 650 hp Wright XR-1510-8, the aircraft was tested by Northrop and Wright until April 1935 when it was returned to Anacostia for four months of Naval evaluation. Still found unsatisfactory, the XFT-1 was again sent back to Northrop where modification work progressed at a slow pace. At that time a 650 hp Pratt & Whitney R-1535-72 double-row radial was installed in a modified cowling, while fuel capacity was reduced from 120 US gallons (454 litres) to 80 gallons (303 litres) to offset the heavier engine weight. At the same time the shape of the vertical tail

The small overall dimensions of the XFT-2 made its R-1535-72 engine appear much larger than it was. (*MDC*)

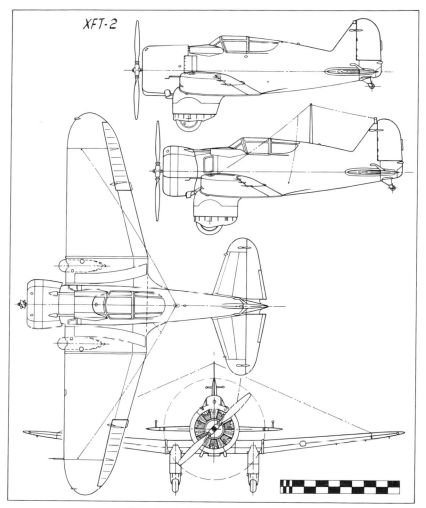

Northrop XFT-1 and XFT-2.

surfaces was modified to increase the area of the fin and rudder, but little else could be done to improve the aircraft's handling.

In this form the aircraft was designated XFT-2 and delivered to Anacostia in April 1936. During Service tests it was found to have only slightly improved performance but the vicious spin continued to plague it. Once again in July 1936 the aeroplane, having failed to satisfy the Navy, was ordered back to the factory. Plans were made to ship the aircraft back to El Segundo but test pilot Mosher ignored his instructions and took off for California. During the ferry flight, on 21 July, 1936, turbulence was encountered over the Allegheny mountains and the aircraft went into a spin and crashed.

159

Span 32 ft (9·75 m); length 21 ft 11 in (6·68 m); height 9 ft 5 in (2·87 m); wing area 177 sq ft (16·444 sq m). Empty weight 2,469 lb (1,120 kg); loaded weight 3,756 lb (1,704 kg); maximum weight 4,003 lb (1,816 kg); wing loading 21·2 lb/sq ft (103·6 kg/sq m); power loading 6 lb/hp (2·7 kg/hp). Maximum speed 235 mph (378 km/h) at 6,000 ft (1,830 m); climb to 6,000 ft (1,830 m) 2·6 min; service ceiling 26,500 ft (8,075 m); range 976 miles (1,570 km).

XFT-2

Dimensions as XFT-1 except length 21 ft 3 in (6·48 m). Empty weight 2,730 lb (1,238 kg); loaded weight 3,770 lb (1,710 kg); maximum weight 4,017 lb (1,822 kg); wing loading 21·3 lb/sq ft (104 kg/sq m); power loading 5·8 lb/hp (2·6 kg/hp). Maximum speed 240 mph (386 km/h) at 7,500 ft (2,285 m); climb to 5,000 ft (1,524 m) 2·2 min; service ceiling 27,500 ft (8,380 m).

Douglas XO2D-1

The XO2D-1 was the last Douglas biplane design and was to remain one of the least-known of the company's naval aircraft. Ordered in June 1933, this aircraft was powered, like its competitors the Curtiss XO3C-1 (BuNo 9413)—the prototype of the SOC Seagull series which saw extensive service with the US Navy until 1944—and the Vought XO5U-1 (BuNo 9399), by a 550 hp Pratt & Whitney R-1340-12 nine-cylinder air-cooled radial driving a two-blade propeller. The two-seat XO2D-1 was a conventional single-bay sesquiplane, with ailerons on the upper wing only and flaps beneath both wings. It was an all-metal aircraft with fabric-covered centre and rear fuselage, wings and control surfaces. Intended to replace the Vought O3U Corsair series as a standard scout-observation biplane aboard US Navy battleships, cruisers and aircraft carriers, the XO2D-1 was fitted with an amphibious undercarriage with twin retractable mainwheels incorporated in the central main float. For carrier operations an arrester hook was flush-

The XO2D-1 was a sesquiplane with narrow-chord lower wings. It is seen at NAS Anacostia during evaluation. (*NA & SM*)

mounted beneath the rear fuselage, and, for storage aboard ships, the wings could be folded manually alongside the fuselage.

Bearing the s/n 1236, the sole XO2D-1 (BuNo 9412) was completed and flown at Santa Monica in late March 1934 before being shipped to Anacostia, where the aircraft was received on 23 April, 1934. However, less than ten days after arrival, the XO2D-1 suffered substantial damage when the number three cylinder-head burned through the outside structure. At that time, rather than sending the aircraft back to Douglas for repairs, the Navy decided to use the Brewster Company facilities on Long Island. Following repairs, the aircraft was returned to flight status on 7 July, 1934. Service trials were conducted by Detachment Five of Experimental Squadron One (VX1D5) at NAS Norfolk, in August and September 1934, with further tests taking place at Anacostia during the latter part of 1934 and the first two months of 1935. By that time, however, the Curtiss XO3C-1 had been found to be superior and, on 23 March, 1935, the Navy ordered 135 Curtiss floatplanes under the designation SOC-1.

Five days before the award of the production contract to Curtiss, the XO2D-1 was shipped back to Douglas which subsequently used the aircraft for limited company trials. Finally, on 13 September, 1935, it was

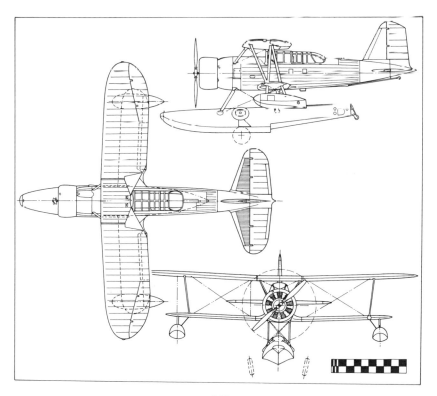

The XO2D-1 at NAS Anacostia on 2 May, 1934. (*USN*)

returned to the Navy at NAS North Island, San Diego. By then, though it had accumulated only 89 hours, the aircraft was in need of overhaul. Rather than incurring this additional expense, the Navy decided to survey the XO2D-1.

Span 36 ft (10·97 m); span folded 13 ft 6 in (4·11 m); length 32 ft (9·75 m); height, wheels down, 16 ft 4¼ in (4·98 m); wing area 302·8 sq ft (28·131 sq m). Empty weight 3,460 lb (1,569 kg); loaded weight 5,109 lb (2,317 kg); wing loading 16·9 lb/sq ft (82·4 kg/sq m); power loading 9·3 lb/hp (4·2 kg/hp). Maximum speed at sea level 162 mph (261 km/h); climb to 5,000 ft (1,524 m) 6 min; service ceiling 14,300 ft (4,390 m); range 798 miles (1,284 km).

Armament. One forward-firing 0·30-in machine-gun and one flexible rear-firing 0·30-in machine-gun, and two 100-lb (45-kg) bombs.

Douglas DC-2

Stretching the fuselage of an airliner to increase its accommodation and payload, and thus improve its operating economics—a technique which has found widespread application in the jet era—is a method long favoured by Douglas. In fact, when in 1933 TWA had exercised its option to purchase production models of the DC-1, the airline and the manufacturers had agreed to increase the fuselage length of the production aircraft by two feet (0·61 m) and to add a row of seats, to give a total of fourteen. Thus, with more powerful Cyclone SGR-1820-F3s the aircraft went into production as the DC-2 on the strength of a TWA initial order for twenty. The first of these (NC13711, s/n 1237) made its maiden flight on 11 May, 1934.

Three main commercial versions and eight military transport models were produced by Douglas. In addition, distribution and production rights for the DC-2 were the subject of negotiations between Douglas and Fokker (NV Nederlandsche Vliegtuigenfabriek Fokker) in the Netherlands; Amtorg, the Russian trading company; and Nakajima Hikoki KK (Nakajima Aeroplane Co Ltd) in Japan; and between Fokker and Airspeed Ltd in the United Kingdom.

These activities began in the autumn of 1933 when the flight test results of the DC-1 and the promise of the DC-2 attracted the interest of the Dutch aviation community. Independently of each other, KLM Royal Dutch Airline and Fokker negotiated with Douglas for construction and distribution rights for the DC-2. KLM intended to have the aircraft built either by Fokker, not knowing that Anthony Fokker was already negotiating on his own with Douglas, or Aviolanda (Maatschappij Voor Vliegtuigbouw NV). Eventually, in January 1934 Fokker was able to sign a contract with Douglas granting his company rights to build the DC-2 under licence and to sell it in Europe. As it turned out, Fokker did not build the DC-2 but assembled and sold in Europe 39 Douglas-built aircraft. In January 1935, Fokker negotiated with Airspeed a sub-licence under which the British firm acquired rights to build and sell a number of Fokker designs in Britain, as well as the Douglas DC-2. Airspeed assigned its type number A.S. 23 to the proposed licence-built version of the DC-2 and reserved the registration G-ADHO for its first aircraft but the project failed to materialize. More productive was the agreement signed in March 1934 by which Douglas granted to Nakajima Hikoki KK rights to build and sell the DC-2 in the Empire of Japan and Manchukuo. One fully-assembled DC-2 and parts for a second were delivered by Douglas, while five more DC-2s were built by Nakajima in 1936–37 and operated by Dai Nippon Koku KK

Swissair's DC-2 HB-ITE. (*Swissair*)

163

The DC-2 cabin, looking forward towards the cockpit access door. (*Fokker*)

Cockpit details of a DC-2-115F. (*Fokker*)

164

(Greater Japan Air Lines Co Ltd) on routes linking Japan with Formosa. One of these aircraft, which received the Allied code name Tess, was operated during the war by the Imperial Japanese Army. Douglas also negotiated with the Soviet trading agency Amtorg which wished to obtain DC-2 manufacturing rights for the USSR. These were not granted, but Amtorg purchased one DC-2 (s/n 1413, NC14949, URSS-M25).

Three major versions of the DC-2—one powered by Wright Cyclones, one by Pratt & Whitney Hornets, and one by Bristol Pegasus—were built. When powered by Cyclone engines (SR-1820-F2, -F2A, -F3, -F3A, -F3B, -F52 or -F53 ranging from 710 hp to 875 hp for take off) the commercial aircraft were generically known as DC-2s, with specific models being designated DC-2-112, DC-2-115 (-115A, -115B, -115D, -115E, -115G, and -115J to -115M), -118A, -118B, -120, -123, -124, -152, -171, -172, -185, -190, -192, -193, -199, -200, -210, -211 and DC-2-221 depending upon the engine model fitted and other special minor modifications requested by customers. With Hornet SD-G, S1E-G or S2E-G engines, the DC-2-115B, DC-2A-127, DC-2-115H and DC-2-165H were commonly known as DC-2As. Finally, two DC-2-115Fs powered by Bristol Pegasus VIs were unofficially designated DC-2Bs.

In addition to the commercial models, Douglas developed the following series of military transport versions:

R2D-1: Identical to the civil DC-2, five R2D-1s (BuNos 9620–9622, and 9993–9994) were acquired by the US Navy and operated as staff transports. Two 710 hp Wright R-1820-12s.

XC-32: Ordered with Fiscal 1936 funds, the XC-32 (serial 36-1) differed from the commercial aircraft in minor equipment details and in being powered by 750 hp Wright R-1820-25s.

C-32A: In 1942, the USAAF impressed a total of twenty-four commercial DC-2s (including five aircraft previously acquired by the British Purchasing Commission and operated by the RAF) which received the following serials: 42-53527–42-53532, 42-57154–42-57156, 42-57227–42-57228, 42-58071–42-58073, 42-61095–42-61096, 42-65577–42-65579, 42-68857–42-68858, 42-70863, 42-83226 and 42-83227. Most aircraft retained their original civil powerplants but some were fitted with military 740 hp Wright R-1820-33s. Not all were actually taken on strength by the USAAF and, in several instances, the assignment of a US military serial was merely a paper transaction.

C-33: Military cargo version of the DC-2 series, the C-33 had enlarged vertical tail surfaces, reinforced cabin floor and a 63-in high by 69-in wide (1·60-m by 1·75-m) cargo-loading door on the port side. Normal load consisted of either 2,400 lb (1,089 kg) of cargo or twelve passengers. Eighteen were built and assigned serials 36-70 to 36-87. Two 750 hp Wright R-1820-25s.

C-33A: Designation given to a projected modification of one C-33; redesignated C-38.

YC-34: Two personnel transports (36-345 and 36-346) similar to the

C-33 of the 63rd Transport Group during the 1941 War Games. (*USAF*)

XC-32 except for minor revisions in interior arrangements. Later redesignated C-34s.

C-38: Prototype of the series of aircraft sometimes referred to as DC-$2\frac{1}{2}$s due to the fact that they combined features of both DC-2 and DC-3. The C-38 was the first C-33 (serial 36-70) fitted with DC-3 type tail surfaces. Powered by two 975 hp Wright R-1820-45s, the C-38 served as the aerodynamic prototype for the C-39.

C-39: Thirty-five aircraft (serials 38-499–38-501 and 38-504–38-535) combining C-33 fuselage and wings with DC-3 centre-section, tail unit and

Army Air Corps C-39 photographed on 30 September, 1939. (*USAF*)

166

undercarriage. Two 975 hp Wright R-1820-55s. On delivery in September 1939, 38-535 became the last aircraft of the DC-2 series to come off the Douglas assembly lines.

C-41: One aircraft (serial 38-502) generally similar to C-39, but fitted as staff transport for use by the Chief of Staff, Army Air Corps. Two 1,200 hp Pratt & Whitney R-1830-21s. This should not be confused with the C-41A.

C-42: One aircraft (serial 38-503) similar to C-41 but powered by two 1,000 hp Wright R-1820-53s. Ordered for use as a staff transport by the Commanding General of the Air Force GHQ. Two C-39s (38-513 and 38-528) were later brought up to a standard approximating that of the C-42.

Out of a total production of 193 civil and military DC-2s, 78 were originally delivered to United States customers (31 to TWA, 16 to

The sole C-41 (38-502), used as a personal transport by General Henry H. Arnold, Air Corps Chief of Staff, at Bolling Field on 12 July, 1940. (*USAF*)

American Airlines, ten to Eastern Air Lines, nine to Pan American, five to Panagra, four to General Air Lines, and three to private customers). TWA, the largest operator of DC-2s, took delivery of the first aircraft (NC3711 *City of Chicago*) three days after its maiden flight and put it into scheduled service on its Colombus–Pittsburgh–Newark route on 18 May, 1934. Soon after, DC-2s went into service on the Chicago–Newark run and within eight days broke the speed record on this route four times. Finally, on 1 August, the DC-2 inaugurated transcontinental service by making 18-hour westbound and 16 hr 20 min eastbound flights over the New York–Los Angeles (Glendale) route via Chicago, Kansas City and Albuquerque. As its DC-2s were faster (almost 2 hours were saved on the transcontinental run), more comfortable and more economic than United Air Lines' Boeing 247s, TWA obtained the edge on this very competitive route. Thus, as public acceptance of the DC-2 was very encouraging, TWA had reasons to congratulate itself for initiating the development of the aircraft. TWA, however, was not to remain for long the sole DC-2 operator as Douglas— learning from Boeing's mistake of refusing to give prompt delivery of Model 247s to customers other than United Air Lines—had reserved for itself the right to sell DC-2s to other customers as long as its production

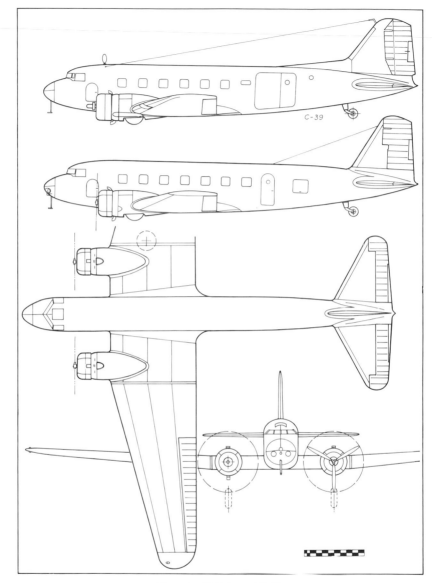

Douglas DC-2 and C-39.

capacity was sufficient to meet the contractual delivery schedule agreed with TWA. This arrangement was to prove beneficial for Douglas as, in spite of an agreed increase in unit price of $7,000 over the initial $58,000 agreed upon the signing of the original DC-1 contract, the company was to show a loss on the construction of the TWA fleet of DC-2s. Fortunately, other airlines had noted the remarkable performance of the DC-1 and, shortly after testing this aircraft, had ordered a substantial number of DC-2s. Among these early US customers was Eastern Air Lines which—including an order placed originally by General Air Lines—eventually operated a fleet of fourteen DC-2s on its East Coast flights to Florida; Pan American which, with its associate Pan American Grace, operated DC-2s on Latin American services and ordered more for its other associate CNAC (China National Aviation Corporation); and American Airlines which in 1934 had become the third competitor on the transcontinental routes linking major cities of the United States' East and West Coasts.

DC-2A-127 (NC14285) which was operated for less than a year by Standard Oil Co of California as a corporate transport. (*MDC*)

Non-airline customers in the United States included the Swiftlite Corporation which operated a Cyclone-powered DC-2-124 (s/n 1324, NC1000) from October 1934 to November 1936 until it was sold to Pan American. A Hornet-powered DC-2A-127 (s/n 1328, NC14285) was delivered to Standard Oil of California on 15 November, 1934, but, on 6 October, 1935, the aircraft crashed in the Great Salt Lake, Utah, due to fuel starvation. Finally, Captain George Whittell took delivery of a DC-2-190 (s/n 1586, NC16048) on 11 August, 1936.

First and largest foreign customer, Fokker initially acquired one aircraft, as well as European manufacturing and distribution rights. Several European airlines were eventually to fly the 39 Fokker-distributed DC-2s but the best remembered are those of KLM and Swissair. KLM, in particular, won fame for itself and the DC-2 when it entered its first aircraft of the type (PH-AJU, s/n 1317) in the October 1934 Mac.Robertson Race from England to Australia. Bearing the racing number 44 and named *Uiver* (*Stork*), the aircraft, with a crew of four commanded by K. D. Parmentier and J. J. Moll, three paying passengers and mail, came in first in the transport division and second in overall speed after covering the 11,123 miles (17,901 km) between Mildenhall and Melbourne, in 90·17 hours. PH-AJU's spectacular placing second to one of the three specially-built de Havilland Comet racers, established the reputation of the Douglas Aircraft Company as a manufacturer of commercial airliners. With KLM and its subsidiary KNILM, PH-AJU was joined by twenty other DC-2s (including

169

one DC-2A) and amongst major routes served by these aircraft was the Amsterdam–Batavia (now Jakarta) run linking the Netherlands to the Netherlands East Indies (now Indonesia). The DC-2s operating the KLM/KNILM Amsterdam–Batavia services, which began on 12 June, 1935, were initially fitted with only five fully-reclining seats, and were equipped with a special cabin cooling system; later, passenger accommodation was increased to eight fully-reclining seats. The six-day service to Batavia was operated twice weekly by DC-2s until October 1937 when DC-3s were introduced.

Next to KLM, Swissair and LAPE (Líneas Aéreas Postales Españolas), which acquired five and four DC-2s respectively from Fokker, were the most notable operators of Fokker-distributed DC-2s. In addition to the five DC-2s ordered directly from Fokker, Swissair also purchased another aircraft (HB-ISA, s/n 1320, ex A-500) which had been ordered in 1934 by the Austrian Government for use by Chancellor Engelbert Dollfuss. However, s/n 1320's career on Swissair's European routes lasted only a few months before it was sold to LAPE and registered EC-AAA. Operated on behalf of the Republicans during the Spanish Civil War, the four LAPE DC-2s (a fifth aircraft had been captured by the Nationalists and served as 42-1, *Capitán Vara de Rey*, in Grupo 42) primarily flew transport missions but also, in August–September 1936, some bombing sorties. For this role, the aircraft were armed with three flexible light machine-guns (one above and behind the cockpit, and one on each side of the rear cabin) and bombs were suspended on a rail running the length of the cabin, before being dropped through the opening left by the removal of the main entrance door. Shortly before the end of the Civil War, two of these DC-2s were used to fly—from Barcelona to Paris, via Toulouse—the gold reserves of the Republican Government. Finally, at war's end, the three surviving aircraft were transferred to Iberia.

On 18 July, 1936, EC-BBE, one of LAPE's DC-2s, was damaged by small-arms fire at Tablada. Captured by the Nationalists it then served as 42-1 *Capitán Vara de Rey* until the end of the Spanish Civil War. (*USAF*)

Pegasus-powered DC-2 of LOT-Polish Air Lines leaving Warsaw on 3 October, 1936, on the inaugural flight to Athens. (*Fokker*)

Among other European DC-2 operators, LOT (Polskie Linie Lotnicze) must be singled out as it was responsible for the development of the Bristol Pegasus powered DC 2B. As Bristol engines were built under licence by the Skoda Company and were in widespread use in Poland, LOT ordered through Fokker two 750 hp Pegasus VI powered aircraft (SP-ASK and SP-ASL, respectively s/n 1377 and 1378). The Pegasus VI installation was jointly developed in early 1935 by Douglas and Bristol. Lufthansa, which had acquired only one DC-2 from Fokker but had resold it to LOT, operated during World War II a fleet of some ten DC-2s captured from Dutch, Polish and Czechoslovak airlines. During the same period, another ex-KLM DC-2 (PH-ALE, s/n 1584) appeared on the British civil register as G-AGBH; the ex-LOT DC-2B SP-ASL was to have joined it as G-AGAD but was interned by the Rumanian Government.

Less wellknown is the fact that the French Government acquired through Fokker a single DC-2 (s/n 1333, F-AKHD) for which the car and aero-engine manufacturers Renault contributed $\frac{1}{16}$th of the purchase price. The aircraft was tested by the CEMA (Centre d'Essais du Matériel Aérien) in the autumn of 1935 and Renault contemplated acquiring the manufacturing rights to produce a version which would have been powered by two nine-cylinder engines of its design. Even though its flight trials were successful, the DC-2 was not adopted by the French.

In addition to the 39 Fokker-distributed aircraft and the two previously-mentioned DC-2s supplied to Nakajima in Japan and Amtorg in the USSR, DC-2 foreign sales made directly by Douglas included three aircraft for KNILM and two aircraft each for the Nanking Government, CNAC, Holyman's Airways, and Australian National Airways.

Before reviewing the use of DC-2 military variants by the US Navy and the USAAC, details of the wartime operations of ex-civil DC-2s by Ilmavoimat in Finland, the RAF in the Middle East and India, and the

RAAF in the South West Pacific Area are provided. The most famous of these aircraft was s/n 1354 which had originally been sold to KLM and registered PH-AKG. Later sold to AB Aerotransport in Sweden and registered SE-AKE, the aircraft was eventually purchased by Count Carl Gustav von Rosen who placed himself and the aircraft at the disposal of the Finnish Air Force then in combat with Soviet forces. Arriving in Finland in January 1940, the aircraft was fitted with a dorsal turret housing a single hand-held 7·7 mm machine-gun and with bomb racks for twenty-four 12 kg (26 lb) bombs beneath the wing centre-section. Bearing the military serial DC-1—later changed to DO-1 for obvious reasons—, the aircraft flew at least one bombing sortie against a Russian airfield. During the Continuation War, this aircraft, joined by two other DC-2s which had been captured by the Germans, flew more conventional transport missions and DO-1 was retained in service by Ilmavoimat until 1955. At least one of the Finnish aircraft was re-engined with Russian 1,000 hp M-62 radials.

The DC-2 *Hanssin Jukka* of Ilmavoimat with forward-firing nose gun, dorsal turret and external bomb racks beneath the fuselage. (*Finnish Air Force*)

During 1941, the British Purchasing Commission acquired from US airlines twenty-five DC-2s which were assigned the serial numbers AX755, AX767–AX769, DG468–DG482, HK820, HK821, HK837, HK847, HK867 and HK983. Three of these aircraft (DG480 to DG482) were not actually taken over by the RAF, and one crashed at Bathurst in Gambia during its ferry flight. Beginning in April 1941, the other RAF DC-2s were operated by No.31 Squadron in India and by Nos.117 and 267 Squadrons in the Middle East. Before being struck off charge, some of these aircraft were leased to Indian National Airways and Tata Air Lines (later Air-India). Ten other ex-Eastern Air Lines DC-2s were also acquired by the

Ex-Eastern Air Lines DC-2 in RAAF service with the Australian military serial A30-5. (*Australian War Memorial*)

British Purchasing Commission acting on behalf of the Royal Australian Air Force. Assigned the Australian serials A30-5 to A30-14 and delivered between November 1940 and May 1941, these DC-2s were operated in the southwest Pacific by Nos.1, 2 and 3 WAGS (Wireless Air Gunner School), Signals School, No.1 Service Flying Training School, the Paratroop Training Unit, No.1 Communication Flight, and Nos.34, 36 and 37 Squadrons, RAAF. Seven more DC-2s, including three ex-KNILM aircraft and the four aircraft acquired before the war by Holyman's Airways and ANA, as well as three ex-USAAF C-39s, were operated in the same theatre by Australian National Airways on behalf of the Allied Directorate of Air Transport.

As already related, commercial companies and foreign governments were not the only customers for the DC-2, and the US Army Air Corps, later the US Army Air Forces, was by far the biggest single customer, with a total of 58 military derivatives of the DC-2 and an additional 24 commercial DC-2s impressed as C-32As. Yet the first order for the American Armed Forces had been placed by the US Navy, which acquired five R2D-1s. No repeat order was placed by the Navy Department but, following the single XC-32, the War Department acquired several versions of the aircraft which became the principal type of military transport aircraft in the United States before World War II. Until the arrival of the C-47/R4D series, these aircraft provided the backbone of military logistic air transport but, by the time of the American entry into the war, they had outlived their prime importance and were rapidly supplanted by C-47s.

When the Defense Supplies Corporation, following the entry of the United States into the war, took over from US airlines a large number of DC-2s and DC-3s, the airlines found themselves hard pressed for equipment. To enable them to carry on limited operations under military control, the USAAF released back some of the impressed aircraft and the airlines exchanged some aircraft among themselves to meet the national defence needs. Several DC-2s/C-32As were involved in such exchanges. On occasions, however, DC-2s also changed hands for different reasons. One such example took place in 1941–42 when Northeast Airlines, due to financial problems, exchanged three new DC-3s for five used TWA DC-2s (NC13717, 13720, 13783, 13784 and 13787). In service with Northeast Airlines, these DC-2s were fitted with DC-3 wings and were unofficially known as DC-Twees. Later, these aircraft were taken over by the USAAF which assigned them the designation C-32A, the same as standard DC-2s in Army Air Forces service.

After the end of the war, the USAAF sold its DC-2 derivatives as surplus and released its impressed DC-2s (C-32As). These aircraft, augmented by some civil DC-2s which had outlived their usefulness with major airlines, were acquired by small non-scheduled carriers in various parts of the world. At least two DC-2s (N4867V, s/n 1368, ex-TWA NC14296; and s/n 1376, ex KNILM PK-AFL), one R2D-1 (N39165, s/n 1404, ex BuNo 9993), and one C-39 (s/n 2072, 38-515, now kept as part of the collection of the Air Force Museum at Wright-Patterson Air Force Base, Ohio) were known still to be in existence in the United States in 1977. Possibly other DC-2s or ex-military aircraft still survive in Australia and Latin America.

Although Douglas had already built several types of commercial aircraft, it was only with the advent of the DC-2 that the company acquired its reputation in this field. On 1 July, 1936, exactly three years after the maiden flight of the DC-1, the Collier Trophy was presented to Donald Douglas by President Roosevelt who stated: '. . . this airplane by reason of its high speed, economy, and quiet passenger comfort, has been generally adopted by transport lines throughout the United States. Its merits have been further recognized by its adoption abroad and its influence on foreign design is already apparent . . .'. Furthermore, thanks to the success of the commercial and military DC-2s, the company was able to recoup the loss of $266,000 incurred on the original TWA order and the programme ended with a substantial profit.

Accommodation: Crew of two and 14 passengers (all except C-33, C-38, C-39, C-41 and C-42).
Crew of two and 2,400 lb (1,089 kg) cargo or 12 passengers (C-33 and C-38).
Crew of three and 3,600 lb (1,633 kg) cargo or 12 passengers (C-39).

	DC-2*	DC-2B**	R2D-1	C-33	C-38	C-39	C-41	C-42
Span, ft in	85 0	85 0	85 0	85 0	85 0	85 0	85 0	85 0
(m)	(25·91)	(25·91)	(25·91)	(25·91)	(25·91)	(25·91)	(25·91)	(25·91)
Length, ft in	61 11¼	61 11¼	61 9	61 11¼	61 6	61 6	61 10	61 6
(m)	(18·89)	(18·89)	(18·82)	(18·89)	(18·75)	(18·75)	(18·85)	(18·75)
Height, ft in	16 3¾	16 3¾	16 3¾	16 3⅝	19 7	18 8	18 8	18 8
(m)	(4·97)	(4·97)	(4·97)	(4·97)	(5·97)	(5·69)	(5·69)	(5·69)
Wing area, sq ft	939	939	939	939	939	939	939	939
(sq m)	(87·236)	(87·236)	(87·236)	(87·236)	(87·236)	(87·236)	(87·236)	(87·236)
Empty weight, lb	12,408			12,476	12,475	14,287	17,525	15,712
(kg)	(5,628)			(5,559)	(5,658)	(6,481)	(7,949)	(7,127)
Loaded weight, lb	18,560	18,200	18,220	17,560	18,200	21,000	21,000	21,000
(kg)	(8,419)	(8,255)	(8,255)	(7,965)	(8,255)	(9,526)	(9,526)	(9,526)
Maximum weight, lb				18,588	18,500		26,300	23,625
(kg)				(8,432)	(8,391)		(11,929)	(10,716)
Wing loading, lb/sq ft	19·8	19·4	19·4	18·7	19·4	22·4	22·4	22·4
(kg/sq m)	(96·5)	(94·6)	(94·6)	(91·3)	(94·6)	(109·2)	(109·2)	(109·2)
Power loading, lb/hp	12·2	12·1	12·8	11·7	9·3	10·8	8·75	10·5
(kg/hp)	(5·5)	(5·5)	(5·8)	(5·3)	(4·2)	(4·9)	(4·0)	(4·8)
Maximum speed, mph at ft	210/8,000	198/6,500	210	202/2,500	208/2,500	210/5,000	225/7,500	214/5,000
(km/h at m)	(338/2,440)	(319/1,065)	(338)	(325/760)	(335/760)	(338/1,524)	(362/2,285)	(344/1,524)
Cruising speed, mph at ft	190/8,000	185/12,000		171	170	156/5,000	204/5,000	170/5,000
(km/h at m)	(306/2,440)	(298/3,660)		(275)	(274)	(251/1,524)	(328/1,524)	(274/1,524)
Climb, ft in min	1,000/1	5,000/3		1,110/1	10,000/9·7	1,480/1	10,000/8	1,230/1
(m in min)	(305/1)	(1,524/3)		(338/1)	(3,048/9·7)	(451/1)	(3,048/8)	(375/1)
Service ceiling, ft	22,450			20,000		20,600		22,000
(m)	(6,845)			(6,095)		(6,280)		(6,705)
Normal range, miles	1,000			916	1,100	1,170	1,285	1,000
(km)	(1,609)			(1,475)	(1,770)	(1,885)	(2,070)	(1,609)
Maximum range, miles						1,600	2,350	1,600
(km)						(2,575)	(3,780)	(2,575)

*with SGR-1820-F52   **with Bristol Pegasus VI

175

Douglas YOA-5 and XP3D

During 1932, the US Navy and Army Air Corps began to show an interest in the development of improved twin-engined patrol and bombing seaplanes, with the Navy indicating a preference for flying-boats with a patrol range of 3,000 miles (4,830 km) whilst the Air Corps favoured a small and, possibly, faster amphibian capable of operating over water alongside standard land-based bombers. This latter requirement stemmed from a unique concept, then being tried with Douglas Y1C-21s, which called for the use of amphibians to fly with formations of conventional bombers to act as navigational leaders and rescue aircraft. To meet these conflicting requirements, Douglas developed two very similar aircraft which, to a large extent, began as substantially scaled-up Dolphins. However, in spite of a major redesign of the Navy prototype, neither of these experimental aircraft received a production order.

The first to be developed was the Army Air Corps prototype which was ordered on 18 November, 1932, under Contract AC5450. Initially designated YB-11 in the bomber category, this amphibian was powered by two 670 hp Wright R-1820-13 nine-cylinder radials mounted à la Dolphin in individual nacelles above the cantilever wing. The aircraft had fixed floats and a two-step hull, and its main landing gear retracted into the fuselage sides just beneath the wing leading edge. The aircraft was armed with three flexible 0·30-in machine-guns—one in each hatch behind the wings and one in an enclosed bow turret, the first to be fitted to an American seaplane, located behind the mooring hatch and forward of the enclosed cabin.

While the aircraft was under construction, the concept of using mixed formations of amphibians and land-based bombers had proved to be impractical. Thus, the experimental aircraft was first redesignated YO-44, in the observation category, and then YOA-5, in the observation amphibian category. As the YOA-5, the aircraft (s/n 1174, serial 33-17) was completed and flown at Santa Monica during January 1935. On 24 February, 1935, the YOA-5 was delivered to Wright Field, Ohio, the Army Air Corps paying $192,348.79 for the aircraft. Following test and evaluation at Wright Field, it was assigned in October 1935 to the 1st Air Base Squadron at Langley Field, Virginia. While operated by that squadron, the aircraft set two world distance records for amphibians, the first being set on 12 December, 1935, when flown by Lt H. MacCaffery, Capt A. Y. Smith and Lt H. S. Hansell, it flew 1,033·2 miles (1,662·778 km) nonstop. Six and a half months later, on 29 June, 1935, the YOA-5 flown by Maj-Gen F. M. Andrews and Maj J. Whittey, broke its own record by flying nonstop from San Juan, Puerto Rico, to Langley Field, a distance of 1,429·685 miles (2,300·86 km). To set these records, the aircraft had been re-engined with two experimental 930 hp Wright YR-1820-45s but, during 1936, 750 hp R-1820-25s were installed. Powered by the R-1820-25, the

The YOA-5 (33-17) in the markings of the 1st Air Base Squadron. (*USAF*)

YOA-5 remained at Langley Field until June 1941 when it was transferred to Elmendorf Field, Alaska. Finally, after being flown for a total of 1,075·8 hours, the YOA-5 was condemned at Elmendorf on 31 December, 1943.

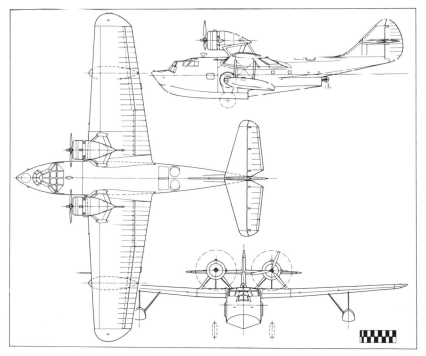

Douglas YOA-5.

177

The XP3D-1 (BuNo 9613) in Santa Monica Bay on 9 March, 1935. (*MDC*)

Larger and more powerful than the Army Air Corps aircraft, the XP3D-1 made its first flight on 6 February, 1935, and was delivered to NAS San Diego, California, on 6 March, 1935. Like its competitor, the Consolidated XP3Y-1 prototype of the wartime Catalina series, the Douglas XP3D-1 (s/n 1235, BuNo 9613) was powered by two 825 hp Pratt & Whitney R-1830-58 fourteen-cylinder radials. But, whereas the XP3Y-1 had its engines mounted ahead of the wing leading edge, the XP3D-1 had its engines in nacelles above and ahead of the wings in a similar manner to the powerplant installation of the YOA-5. In fact, the XP3D-1 and YOA-5 bore a very close family resemblance, but the XP3D-1 was characterized by taller and larger tail surfaces and by the substitution of beaching gear, which folded rearward alongside the fuselage, for the retractable undercarriage of the YOA-5.

With nearly identical performance, a choice between the XP3D-1 and XP3Y-1 was a difficult one. However, on the basis of an order for sixty aircraft, Consolidated quoted a $90,000 unit price, whereas Douglas's price

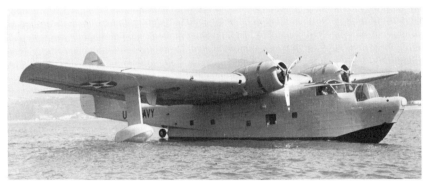

The much improved BuNo 9613 as it appeared after being modified as the XP3D-2. (*MDC*)

178

was $110,000 per aircraft. Consequently, on 29 June, 1935, Consolidated was awarded a contract for sixty P3Y-1s later redesignated PBY-1s, while the XP3D-1 remained in service with Detachment One of Patrol Squadron Three (VP3D1). Anticipating a chance to win a follow-on contract, Douglas decided to undertake wind-tunnel tests with a scale-model of a modified XP3D-1. The results showed that performance of the Douglas flying-boat could be substantially improved by raising the wing approximately 27 in (69 cm), eliminating the overhead nacelle mounting of the engines and putting 900 hp Pratt & Whitney R-1830-64s in the leading edge of the wing, and substituting partially retractable floats for the existing fixed floats. Consequently, the Bureau of Aeronautics agreed to return the XP3D-1 to Douglas for modification to the XP3D-2 configuration incorporating these changes, as well as the installation of a nose turret. After these modifications had been made, the XP3D-2 was redelivered to San Diego on 15 May, 1936.

Unfortunately for Douglas, Consolidated had also improved its aircraft and the 1936 contract went to fifty PBY-2s for which the Navy paid $97,960 per aircraft. Nonetheless, the Navy decided to retain the XP3D-2 which was then assigned to VP-11F at San Diego for use as an 'airboat flagship'. A few months later, on 8 February, 1937, the XP3D-2 crashed on take-off in Acapulco Bay in Mexico, while operated by VP-11F.

YOA-5
Crew of four. Span 89 ft 9 in (27·36 m); length 69 ft 6 in (21·18 m); height 22 ft (6·71 m). Loaded weight 20,000 lb (9,072 kg); power loading 13·3 lb/hp (6 kg/hp). Maximum speed at sea level 169 mph (272 km/h).
Armament. Three flexible 0·30-in machine-guns in two fuselage hatches and open bow position.

XP3D-1
Crew of five to seven. Span 95 ft (28·96 m); length 69 ft 10½ in (21·3 m); height 22 ft 5¼ in (6·84 m); wing area 1,295 sq ft (120·31 sq m). Empty weight 12,813 lb (5,812 kg); loaded weight 20,356 lb (9,233 kg); maximum weight 25,748 lb (11,679 kg); wing loading 15·7 lb/sq ft (7·1 kg/sq m); power loading 12·3 lb/hp (5·6 kg/hp). Maximum speed at sea level 165 mph (266 km/h); climb to 5,000 ft (1,524 m) 6·1 min; service ceiling 17,800 ft (5,425 m); normal range 1,628 miles (2,620 km); maximum range 3,010 miles (4,845 km).
Armament. One flexible 0·30-in in bow and one 0·50-in in open hatch on each side of hull, and up to 3,000 lb (1,361 kg) of bombs.

XP3D-2
Crew and dimensions as XP3D-1 except length 69 ft 7½ in (21·22 m). Empty weight 15,120 lb (6,858 kg); loaded weight 22,909 lb (10,391 kg); maximum weight 27,946 lb (12,676 kg); wing loading 17·7 lb/sq ft (8 kg/sq m); power loading 12·7 lb/hp (5·8 kg/hp). Maximum speed 183 mph (295 km/h) at 8,000 ft (2,440 m); climb to 5,000 ft (1,524 m) 6·1 min; service ceiling 18,900 ft (5,760 m); normal range 2,050 miles (3,300 km); maximum range 3,380 miles (5,430 km).
Armament. Three flexible 0·50-in machine-guns in two hull hatches and nose turret, and up to 3,000 lb (1,361 kg) of bombs

179

A TBD-1 of Torpedo Squadron Six over its carrier, the USS *Enterprise*, on 14 January, 1939. (*USN*)

Douglas TBD Devastator

The XTBD-1 (s/n 1285, BuNo 9720), ordered on 30 June, 1934, was an all-metal low-wing cantilever monoplane with a retractable main under-carriage and power-folding wings. Carrying a crew of three—pilot, navigator/torpedo officer, and radio-operator/gunner—in tandem cock-pits enclosed by a continuous canopy, it was powered by an 800 hp Pratt & Whitney XR-1830-60 fourteen-cylinder air-cooled radial driving a three-blade propeller. Defensive armament consisted of a forward-firing 0·50-in machine-gun mounted on the right side of the cowling and firing through the propeller disc and one flexible rear-firing 0·30-in machine-gun. Offensive load included either a 21-in (53·34-cm) torpedo semi-recessed beneath the fuselage or up to 1,200 lb (544 kg) of bombs. The XTBD-1 made its first flight at Santa Monica on 15 April, 1935, and was transferred nine days later to Anacostia to begin performance trials.

Various handling, performance and torpedo trials were made at Anacostia, Norfolk and the Naval Proving Ground at Dahlgreen, all these bases being located on the East Coast, until 26 November, 1935, when the aircraft was ordered back to the West Coast. After arriving at NAS North Island, California, the XTBD-1 successfully underwent carrier qualification trials aboard the USS *Lexington,* CV-2. However, it was found that the original canopy restricted visibility during landing. Consequently, when in the autumn of 1936 the aircraft was returned to Douglas for overhaul and minor modifications, the opportunity was taken to substitute a new domed canopy similar to that to be fitted to production aircraft. In this form, the aircraft was returned to the Navy on 13 December, 1936, and from then on was used for a variety of tests. It was finally scrapped at NAS Norman, Oklahoma, on 10 September, 1943.

The XTBD-1 displaying its folding wings and ventral bomb racks. This photograph was taken after the original flat canopy had been replaced with a higher one. (*US National Archives*)

Production of TBD-1s was begun on 3 February, 1936, when Douglas was awarded a contract for 114 (BuNos 0268 to 0381). These aircraft, bearing the type name Devastator, differed from the prototype in being powered by 900 hp R-1830-64 engines and in having revised vertical tail surfaces; empty and loaded weights were respectively increased from 5,046 lb (2,289 kg) to 5,600 lb (2,540 kg) and from 8,385 lb (3,803 kg) to 9,289 lb (4,213 kg). The first TBD-1 (BuNo 0268) was flown to Anacostia on 25 June, 1937, and, together with the second production aircraft, was used for Service tests. Eventually, the first aircraft was assigned on 14 August, 1939, to the Naval Torpedo Station at Newport, Rhode Island, to be fitted by the Naval Aircraft Factory with twin Edo floats. Redesignated TBD-1A, the aircraft was tested by VX-4 Detachment 4 until scrapped on 23 September, 1943.

The TBD-1A at the Naval Torpedo Station Newport, Rhode Island, in the autumn of 1939. (*US National Archives*)

A follow-on order for a further fifteen TBD-1s (BuNos 1505 to 1519) was placed on 16 August, 1938, and BuNo 1519, the last Devastator built was delivered in November 1939. No further developments of the Devastator were undertaken but for almost five years it was the standard carrier-borne torpedo-bomber of the Navy.

In November 1937, Torpedo Squadron Three (VT-3), attached to the aircraft carrier USS *Saratoga*, received its first TBD-1 (BuNo 0270). Soon after, VT-3 had a full complement of eight Devastators and undertook to put the aircraft through accelerated in-service tests. However, the TBD-1s had to be grounded after a few weeks in service as the rudder hinge was found to need modifications and because corrosion necessitated the re-skinning of the wings. Back in service, the Devastators of VT-3 took part in the 1938 Fleet Exercise during which they simulated an attack against Pearl Harbor. The success of this exercise did not go unnoticed by the Japanese military attachés and it played a decisive role in the planning of the 7 December, 1941, attack.

TBD-1s of VT-3 during prewar operations aboard the USS *Saratoga*.
(*US National Archives*)

Three more squadrons, VT-2 on the *Lexington*, VT-5 on the *Yorktown* and VT-6 on the *Enterprise*, were re-equipped with TBD-1s during 1938. These were followed in 1940–41 by VS-71 (Scouting Squadron Seventy-One) and VT-7 on the *Wasp*, VS-42 and VT-4 on the *Ranger* and VT-8 on the *Hornet*, while others were kept in reserve or assigned to Naval Air Station flights. Moreover, one TBD-1 (BuNo 1518) was operated for target-towing work by Marine Scouting Squadron Two between March and June 1941.

At the time of the Japanese attack against Pearl Harbor, sixty-nine TBD-1s were assigned to operational squadrons while thirty-one were serving with second-line units or were in the process of being overhauled. Thus, pending the availability of the new Grumman TBF-1 Avenger, this meagre force had to help stem the Japanese advance, perform anti-submarine patrols in the Pacific and Atlantic and train new torpedo-bomber crews. Offensive operations began on 1 February, 1941, when the

182

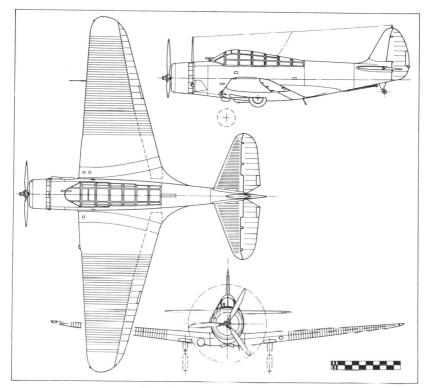

Douglas TBD-1 Devastator.

TBD-1s of VT-5 and VT-6, respectively embarked aboard the *Yorktown* and the *Enterprise*, successfully attacked shipping, airfields and land targets in the Japanese-held islands of Kwajalein, Jaluit and Taroa. Other raids were mounted in February and March 1942 against Japanese facilities on Wake, Wilkes and Marcus islands (VT-6), and at Lae and Salamaua (VT-2 and VT-5). In spite of intense anti-aircraft fire, all these torpedo and bomb attacks were made without loss.

Unfortunately, the luck of the Douglas torpedo-bomber had run out and, in the space of a month, the small force of Devastators was all but wiped out. This dramatic turn of events began during the Battle of the Coral Sea (4 to 8 May, 1942) when Devastators of VT-5 aboard the *Yorktown* and VT-2 aboard the *Lexington* encountered the carriers of the Japanese Navy. During the course of the battle, these aircraft sank the minesweeper *Tama Maru* in Tulagi harbour and helped sink the light carrier *Shoho*. However, they failed to hit the battle carriers *Shokaku* and *Zuikaku*, and aircraft from these succeeded in inflicting fatal blows to the *Lexington* which, with thirteen Devastators on board, sank during the evening of 8 May, 1942.

While the Battle of the Coral Sea had ended in a draw, the US Navy suffering the heaviest losses, but succeeding in turning back the Japanese invasion fleet which had been bound for Port Moresby, Papua, the Battle of Midway (4 to 6 June, 1942) ended in a clear American victory and marked the turning point in the Pacific War. This victory, however, was obtained at a heavy price including the loss of the *Yorktown* and not less than 36 out of 41 Devastators which had been embarked aboard that carrier (VT-5), on the *Enterprise* (VT-6) and the *Hornet* (VT-8) at the onset of battle. Furthermore, the tragic loss of these TBD-1s had taken place without any of them succeeding in scoring a hit on the Japanese carriers. However, on the last day of the battle, the three surviving Devastators of VT-6 helped sink the heavy cruiser *Mikuma* and seriously damage its sister ship *Mogami*.

After Midway, TBD-1s remained in service for a few weeks with VT-4 and VT-7 until they were replaced by TBF-1s. Thus, when the next major carrier battle was fought in October 1942 off Santa Cruz Island, the Douglas torpedo-bomber had disappeared from the decks of the US carriers to end its life in mechanics' schools. Furthermore, the use of torpedo-bombers had been found to be rather ineffective and the Devastator's successor, the Grumman Avenger, was seldom used to carry torpedoes. The last-known use of torpedoes, however, involved another Douglas-built aircraft, the ubiquitous AD Skyraider of VA-195 which, on 1 May, 1951, used torpedoes to attack the Hwachon Dam in Korea.

TBD-1

Span 50 ft (15·24 m); length 35 ft (10·67 m); height 15 ft 1 in (4·6 m); wing area 422 sq ft (39·205 sq m). Empty weight 5,600 lb (2,540 kg); loaded weight 9,289 lb (4,213 kg); maximum weight 10,194 lb (4,624 kg); wing loading 22 lb/sq ft (107·5 kg/sq m); power loading 10·3 lb/hp (4·7 kg/hp). Maximum speed 206 mph (332 km/h) at 8,000 ft (2,440 m); cruising speed 128 mph (206 km/h); initial rate of climb 720 ft/min (219 m/min); service ceiling 19,500 ft (5,945 m); range with torpedo 435 miles (700 km); range with 1,000 lb (454 kg) bomb 716 miles (1,152 km).

Douglas B-18 Bolo

For the development of military aviation in the United States, the early thirties were years of major drought. The effects of the depression which were weakening the American economy resulted in serious budgetary limitations, while prevailing sentiments among American citizens were strongly pacifist and isolationist, much as they came to be in the early seventies. Thus, in spite of the efforts of far sighted Air Corps officers, the role of this Service was being limited to air support of ground forces and to coastal defence, while the Baker Board set up in 1934 to study the role of military aviation in the United States was unanimous in stating 'Independent air missions have little effect upon the issue of the battle and none upon the outcome of the war'. It was in the midst of this money-conscious, non-airminded and strategically limited atmosphere that Army officers and officials of the War Department gathered at Wright Field during the summer of 1935 to select the next bomber for the Air Corps.

In May 1934, one month before taking delivery of the first Martin YB-10, the Service trials version of the Army's first all-metal monoplane bomber to be placed in quantity production, the Air Corps announced a new competition for multi-engined bombers capable of carrying 2,000 lb (907 kg) of bombs for not less than 1,020 miles (1,640 km) and if possible 2,200 miles (3,540 km), at a top speed of at least 200 mph (322 km/h) and if possible 250 mph (402 km/h). To meet this requirement, Douglas undertook to develop a twin-engined bomber based on its successful DC-2 transport. Designated DB-1 (Douglas Bomber One), this aircraft was basically designed around the wings of the DC-2 and was fitted with a deeper and fatter fuselage with a bomb bay located beneath the centre section. The bomber design also used enlarged tail surfaces, and the span and area of its wings were slightly increased by adding rounded tips. The aircraft was planned for operation by a six-man crew including two pilots, a navigator/bomb-aimer, and three gunners, and was to be armed with three hand-held 0·30-in machine-guns in nose and dorsal turrets and a ventral hatch.

Completed in April 1935 and powered by two 850 hp Wright R-1820-G5s with single collector exhausts exiting over the wing to render the aircraft less visible at night, the Douglas-owned prototype s/n 1353 underwent four months of manufacturer's trials before being ferried to Wright Field in August 1935. At Wright Field, the DB-1 was exhaustively tested in competition with the Martin 146, an enlarged and more streamlined development of the twin-engined B-10, and the Boeing 299, the prototype of the four-engined B-17 Flying Fortress. While the Boeing was substantially faster, had longer range and carried more bombs and heavier defensive armament than the DB-1, the Douglas bomber—based on a production lot of 220 aircraft—was priced at less than 59 per cent of the

Betraying its origin, the DB-1 looked more like a transport than a bomber. None the less, primarily due to budgetary considerations, the aircraft was selected in preference to the Boeing 299. (*USAF*)

Boeing ($58,500 versus $99,620 per aircraft). Thus the competition soon boiled down to a choice between quality and quantity, with the technical staff recommending the acquisition of a smaller number of Boeing bombers while the General Staff—pointing out that the DB-1's performance, with a top speed of 220 mph (354 km/h) and a range of 1,030 miles (1,660 km) with 2,532 lb (1,148 kg) of bombs, fully met the specification set by the Air Corps in May 1934—favoured the purchase of a larger number of Douglas bombers. Citing the crash at Wright Field of the Boeing 299 prototype as further justification for its more conservative approach to procurement, the General Staff finally decided in January 1936 to order 133 Douglas B-18s and thirteen Boeing YB-17s.

The selection of the B-18 over the Boeing B-17 was seriously criticized by officers of the time and by historians since as the B-17 was to become one of the most effective bombers of World War II while the B-18 was hopelessly obsolete by the time of America's entry into the war. However, it should be remembered that early B-17 models, up to and including the B-17D version, were also judged obsolete in 1941. On the other hand, the availability during the late thirties of a large number of B-18s and B-18As enabled the Air Corps to train sufficient cadres for the Army Air Forces bomber crews who flew late B-17 models with conspicuous success during the war years.

Before detailing the production models of the Douglas bomber, mention must be made of the fate of the DB-1 prototype. Following completion of its Air Corps evaluation, this aircraft was returned to Douglas to be brought up to B-18 production standard and, bearing the Air Corps serial

B-18 (37-51) at the Bolling Field Exhibit, 19 January, 1940. This aircraft was experimentally fitted with a 75-mm cannon beneath the fuselage. In this view, the cannon installation can be discerned under a protective security cover. (*USAF*)

37-51, it was redelivered on 28 February, 1937. Two years later, the aircraft was modified to test the feasibility of firing large cannon from aircraft. For this purpose, an M1898 75 mm field-piece was mounted in a fixed position in the bomb bay of 37-51 and the nose of the aircraft was scalloped down to enable the weapon to be fired forward in the axis of flight. Following initial ground firing trials, the aircraft was used for in-flight firing tests over Lake Erie and at the Aberdeen Proving Ground at Phillips Field, Maryland. Vibration, when the cannon was fired, proved excessive and the experiment with the B-18 was discontinued. However, the results of these tests proved most useful when the B-25G and H versions of the North American Mitchell were developed during the war. Whilst the cannon-armed B-18 remained experimental, other versions were produced in quantities as now detailed.

B-18: Differing from the DB-1 prototype in being powered by two 930 hp Wright R-1820-45s which drove propellers with wider blades and were housed in revised cowlings, the 131 production B-18s (serials 36-262 to 36-343, 36-431 to 36-446, and 37-1 to 37-33) also had a 7-inch (17·8 cm) shorter nose cone which incorporated additional lateral windows and a bomb-aiming window located in its forward lower portion. The first production aircraft was delivered to Wright Field on 23 February, 1937, and the DB-1, after being brought up to full B-18 standard, was redelivered five days later.

The DB-2 at Wright Field. The aircraft was later brought back to B-18 standard before delivery to the 18th Reconnaissance Squadron. (*USAF*)

DB-2: Bearing serial 37-34 which identified it as the last aircraft ordered under the original AC8307 contract, the DB-2 was completed out of sequence and thus became the 36th B-18 to be delivered when it was received at Wright Field on 8 November, 1937. It differed from standard production B-18s in being fitted with a modified nose incorporating a power-operated turret and extensively glazed lower bomb-aimer's position. The modified nose did not prove satisfactory and the aircraft was modified back to B-18 standard before being delivered to the 18th Reconnaissance Squadron at Mitchel Field, New York.

B-18A: Under contract AC9977, a total of 217 B-18As were procured in three batches (177 aircraft—serials 37-458 to 37-634—being ordered in June 1937, and 40 aircraft—38-585 to 38-609, and 39-12 to 39-26—being ordered a year later with FY1938 and 1939 funds). The most noticeable

B-18A of the 18th Reconnaissance Squadron operating from Mitchel Field, New York, on 8 August, 1940. (*USAF*)

modification was the introduction of yet another change in the nose arrangement, with the bomb-aimer's station being moved upward under an extended glazed housing, whilst the flexible forward-firing gun, now mounted in a globular ball turret, was installed further back and below. Other modifications included the installation of two 1,000 hp Wright R-1820-53 engines with fully-feathering hydromatic propellers. The first B-18A was flown on 15 April, 1938, and was delivered six weeks later.

B-18AM: Designation given in 1940 to seventeen B-18As from which D-3 and B-7 bomb shackles were removed to enable larger bombs to be carried.

B-18B: To provide the Army Air Forces with urgently needed maritime reconnaissance bombers for anti-submarine operations, 122 B-18As were modified in 1942 as B-18Bs by installing an SCR-517-T-4 ASV radar in a radome located in place of the bomb-aimer's station. In addition, Mk IV MAD (Magnetic Anomaly Detection) equipment was installed in a 'sting' tail. Offensive load normally included depth charges carried in the fuselage bomb bay, but tests and limited operations were also made with retro-bombtracks beneath the wings which fired the bombs backward in a pattern.

Radar-equipped B-18B (37-530) on patrol in the Caribbean. (*USAF*)

188

B-18M: Designation given in 1940 to 22 B-18s from which D-3 and B-7 bomb shackles were removed to enable larger bombs to be carried.

B-22: Projected development of the B-18A which was to have been powered by two 1,600 hp Wright R-2600-3s. Not proceeded with.

C-58: Designation applied to two B-18As modified as unarmed cargo transports.

Digby Mk 1: During 1938, a delegation of the British Air Ministry visited Douglas to investigate the purchase of a version of the B-18 for use by the Royal Air Force as a maritime reconnaissance-bomber. The aircraft, however, was found to be under-powered and to have poor airfield performance and unsatisfactory defensive armament. Furthermore, price — $109,000 per aircraft on the basis of a batch of 200 — and delivery rate — 58 weeks for 200 aircraft — were not attractive and the British order went to Lockheed which supplied its Model 214 Hudson.

The third Digby for the Royal Canadian Air Force, at Santa Monica before delivery. (*MDC*)

In spite of failing to obtain the RAF order, Douglas succeeded at about the same time in securing an order for twenty aircraft from the RCAF. Designated Digby Mk Is and assigned the Canadian military serials 738 to 757, these general reconnaissance bombers were externally similar to the B-18As of the US Army Air Corps. However, they were armed with 0·303-in flexible machine-guns and other British and Canadian equipment. The twenty Digby Mk Is were taken on strength by the RCAF between 29 December, 1939, and 22 May, 1940. Interestingly, these aircraft which followed the B-18s and B-18As on Douglas's assembly lines were given earlier serial numbers (1630 to 1649) previously assigned to a batch of cancelled aircraft of unrelated design.

Deliveries of B-18s, bearing the type name Bolo, began in the first half of 1937 with the assignment of four test and evaluation aircraft respectively to the Matériel Division at Wright Field, Ohio, the Technical Training Command at Chanute Field, Illinois, the Aberdeen Proving Ground, and to Lowry Field, Colorado. The 5th, 6th and 7th aircraft (36-266 to 36-268) were the first B-18s to be delivered to an operational unit, the 7th Bombardment Group at Hamilton Field, California, where they were later joined by thirty additional aircraft. The remaining 94 B-18s were initially assigned to the 5th Bombardment Group at Luke Field, Oahu, the 19th Bombardment Group and 38th Reconnaissance Squadron at March Field, California, the 18th Reconnaissance Squadron at Mitchel Field and the 21st Reconnaissance Squadron at Langley Field. Most of these units later had their B-18s supplemented or supplanted by B-18As while the 2nd Bombardment Group at Langley Field also operated some B-18As. As, beginning in 1940, new Bombardment Groups were being formed with cadres from the older units, their initial equipment often consisted of B-18s and B-18As. However, the days of the Douglas twin-engined bomber

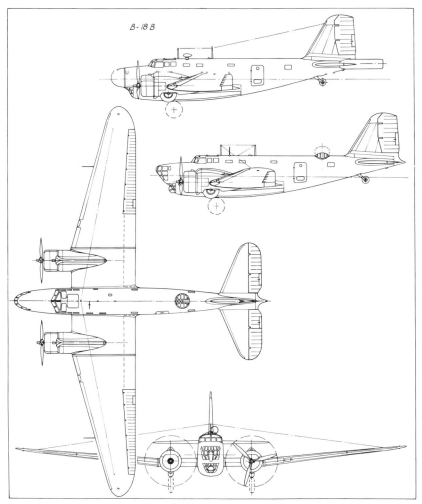

Douglas B-18A and B-18B.

190

as a first-line aircraft were numbered because the Boeing B-17 and Consolidated B-24 had finally been recognized as better suited for the new strategic role given to the Army Air Forces.

The B-18s and B-18As, even though obsolete, were the most numerous bombers deployed outside the continental United States at the time of America's entry into the war. In early December 1941, the 5th and 11th Bombardment Groups at Hickham Field had thirty-three B-18s, which represented 55 per cent of the bomber force in the Hawaiian Islands, while at Clark Field, the 28th Bombardment Squadron had twelve, a quarter of all US bombers in the Philippines. In the Panama Canal Zone and the Caribbean, B-18/B-18As were operated by the 6th Bombardment Group (3rd and 25th Squadrons at France Field and 74th Squadron at Howard Field, both in the Canal Zone), and by the 9th Bombardment Group (1st Squadron at Waller Field, Trinidad, 5th Squadron at Beane Field, Sta Lucia, and 99th Squadron at Zandery Field, Surinam). However, most of the B-18/B-18As based at Hickham and Clark Fields were destroyed on the ground during the initial Japanese attack on these aerodromes and the few remaining aircraft in these theatres did not play any significant role in subsequent operations.

7th Bombardment Group's B-18As lined up at March Field, California, in 1940.
(*USAF*)

Immediately following the Japanese surprise attacks, the B-18/B-18As in the continental United States, in the Canal Zone and the Caribbean were deployed in a defensive role in anticipation of possible attacks against the mainland and Panama. However, these did not materialize and the Douglas bombers were used mostly for anti-submarine operations in American and Caribbean waters. For this purpose, new units designated Sea Search Attack (SSA) Squadrons were formed, and the 2nd SSA Squadron at Langley Field developed new operating techniques while using the specially modified B-18Bs with ASV radar and MAD equipment.

Surplus B-18 modified after the war as a cargo transport. (*William Balogh*)

The operational use of the B-18Bs did not last more than a year as in August 1943 they were superseded by B-24s which had longer endurance, and shortly after responsibility for anti-submarine operations was transferred from the Army Anti-submarine Command to the Navy. Consequently, a few B-18Bs were used to develop radar bombing techniques but most B-18/B-18A and B-18Bs ended their useful life in the training and transport roles. Some postwar surplus B-18s of various models were operated as cargo or crop-spraying aircraft by small commercial operators.

Besides being operated by the Army Air Forces, wartime use of B-18s was limited to the Força Aérea Brasileira, which received two aircraft in 1942, and to the Royal Canadian Air Force which, as previously related, had received twenty Digbys in 1939–40. Most of these aircraft were operated by No.10 (BR) Squadron until replaced by Consolidated Liberators. The last Douglas Digby (serial 745) was struck off strength by the RCAF on 22 November, 1946.

DB-1

Span 89 ft 7 in (27·31 m); length 57 ft 3 in (17·45 m); height 15 ft 4 in (4·67 m); wing area 959 sq ft (89·094 sq m). Empty weight 14,806 lb (6,716 kg); loaded weight 20,159 lb (9,144 kg); wing loading 21 lb/sq ft (102·6 kg/sq m); power loading 11·9 lb/hp (5·4 kg/hp). Maximum speed 220 mph (354 km/h) at 10,000 ft (3,050 m); cruising speed 173 mph (278 km/h); climb to 10,000 ft (3,050 m) 8·8 min; service ceiling 25,000 ft (7,620 m); normal range 1,030 miles (1,660 km).

B-18

Span 89 ft 6 in (27·28 m); length 56 ft 8 in (17·27 m); height 15 ft 2 in (4·62 m); wing area 959 sq ft (89·094 sq m). Empty weight 15,750 lb (7,144 kg); loaded weight 23,200 lb (10,523 kg); maximum weight 27,087 lb (12,286 kg); wing loading 24·2 lb/sq ft (118·1 kg/sq m); power loading 12·5 lb/hp (5·7 kg/hp). Maximum speed 217 mph (349 km/h) at 10,000 ft (3,050 m); cruising speed 167 mph (269 km/h); climb to 10,000 ft (3,050 m) 9·1 min; service ceiling 24,200 ft (7,375 m); normal range 850 miles (1,370 km); maximum range 2,200 miles (3,540 km).

B-18A

Dimensions as B-18 except length 57 ft 10 in (17·63 m). Empty weight 16,320 lb (7,403 kg); loaded weight 24,000 lb (10,886 kg); maximum weight 27,673 lb (12,552 kg); wing loading 25 lb/sq ft (122·2 kg/sq m); power loading 12 lb/hp (5·4 kg/hp). Maximum speed 216 mph (348 km/h) at 10,000 ft (3,050 m); cruising speed 167 mph (269 km/h); climb to 10,000 ft (3,050 m) 9·9 min; service ceiling 23,900 ft (7,285 m); normal range 900 miles (1,450 km); maximum range 2,100 miles (3,380 km).

Armament. One flexible 0·30-in (B-18/B-18A) or 0·303-in (Digby) machine-gun in nose and dorsal turrets and ventral hatch. Bomb load. Normal 2,000 lb (907 kg), maximum 4,400 lb (1,996 kg).

Northrop 3A

In early 1935, the US Matériel Division announced a design competition for single-seat fighters to replace the Boeing P-26s, then the most advanced aircraft equipping Army Air Corps Pursuit Groups. Manufacturers were invited to submit private venture prototypes for evaluation at Wright Field beginning on 27 May, 1935. Initially, three companies decided to enter prototypes in the forthcoming competition: the Curtiss-Wright Corporation which designed its Model 75, the prototype of the P-36 and H75 series; the Seversky Aircraft Corporation which planned to develop a single-seat variant but initially delivered · a two-seat prototype, the SEV-2XP, the forebear of the P-35 series; and the Northrop Corporation which proposed its Model 3A.

To obtain the necessary performance while hastening the development of the new aircraft, an engineering team led by Ed Heinemann decided to design a retractable undercarriage variant of the XFT-1/XFT-2 naval fighter prototype. In spite of this time-saving approach, the Northrop 3A

The Northrop 3A photographed on what is believed to have been its last take-off. (*MDC*)

193

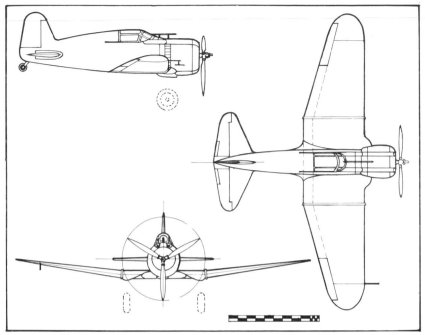

Northrop 3A

was too late to be delivered to Wright Field and the Matériel Division decided to adjourn the competition until August 1935 rather than award a production contract to Curtiss whose Model 75 had been the only entry available on the specified date. However, the stroke of luck which appeared to give a new lease of life to the Northrop 3A was of short duration.

The 3A (s/n 184), powered by a 700 hp Pratt & Whitney Twin Wasp Jr SA-G fourteen-cylinder radial driving a three-blade propeller, was completed in July 1935. Finished in contemporary Air Corps colours, blue fuselage with yellow wings and empennage, the aircraft was unarmed but had provision for two fuselage-mounted 0·30-in or 0·50-in machine-guns. After completing preliminary manufacturer's trials at Mines Field, it was ferried to Wright Field in July 1935. However, limited evaluation by Air Corps personnel confirmed the Northrop test pilot's report that the aircraft was rather unstable and prone to spinning. Accordingly, the 3A was returned to Mines Field where Northrop hoped to find some quick solution to the stability problem before entering the aircraft in the August 1935 competitive trials. Intent on testing the modifications made to the aircraft before its scheduled return to Wright Field, First Lieutenant Frank Scare took off on 30 July, 1935, for a test flight over the Pacific and failed to return. No trace of the Northrop 3A or its pilot was ever found.

The loss of the prototype effectively removed Northrop from consideration as supplier of the next generation of fighter aircraft for the Army

Air Corps. Consequently, to recoup some of its investment in the project, the company sold its design to Chance Vought Aircraft which developed it into the equally unsuccessful V-141 and V-143.

Span 33 ft 6 in (10.21 m); length 21 ft 10 in (6.65 m). Loaded weight 3,900 lb (1,769 kg). Maximum speed at sea level 279 mph (449 km/h); climb to 10,000 ft (3,050 m) 3·3 min; service ceiling 31,600 ft (9,630 m); endurance 3 hr.

Northrop A-17 and Douglas 8A

On Christmas Eve 1934, the mail brought to the fledgling Northrop Corporation a particularly appreciated yuletide present: official notification that the testing of their Gamma 2C and 2F had led to a War Department decision to allocate $2,047,774 for the purchase of one hundred and ten A-17 attack-bombers. While Contract AC7326 was not officially signed until 1 March, 1935, the Christmas Eve letter of intent insured the future of Northrop and concluded an often frustrating 18-month period which had begun on 18 July, 1933, when the company had delivered its fifth aircraft for evaluation by the Army Air Corps at Wright Field.

As the performance of its Gamma 2A and 2B exceeded substantially that of the Curtiss Shrike, the Army Air Corps' then current attack aircraft, Northrop had decided early in 1933 to undertake as a private venture, the development of an attack version of the Gamma. Retaining the wings and trousered undercarriage of the earlier aircraft, the Gamma 2C (s/n 5) was fitted with a new fuselage housing a pilot and radio operator/gunner under an enclosed canopy located further forward to improve forward visibility. Powered by a 735hp Wright SR-1820F-2 nine-cylinder radial driving a two-blade propeller, the Gamma 2C was armed with four wing-mounted 0·30-in machine-guns and one flexible 0·30-in machine-gun firing either upward from the rear cockpit or downward through a ventral hatch. Up to 1,100 lb (499 kg) of bombs was carried externally on racks beneath the fuselage and centre section. Bearing the experimental registration X12291, the aircraft was first flown in the spring of 1933 before being delivered, under a bailment contract, to the Army Air Corps for evaluation at Wright Field. These tests, however, indicated the need for several modifications and the Gamma 2C was returned to Northrop in February 1934.

YA-13: When the Gamma 2C was returned to Northrop, a number of minor internal modifications were incorporated. However, a more noticeable modification was made to the vertical tail surfaces, which were changed from the original trapezoidal shape to a triangular shape with the top and rudder trailing edge rounded. In this form, the aircraft was purchased by the Army Air Corps on 28 June, 1934, under Contract AC6811 and was designated YA-13 with Air Corps serial 34-27.

The XA-16 modified from the Gamma 2C/YA-13. (*NA & SM*)

XA-16: With the aim of improving the aircraft's performance and the pilot's forward visibility, the YA-13 was returned to Northrop in January 1935 to be re-engined with the smaller diameter 950 hp Pratt & Whitney R-1830-7 fourteen-cylinder radial, with a three-blade propeller. Redesignated XA-16, the aircraft was first flown in this form in March 1935. The test results indicated that the aircraft was over-powered and that production aircraft should either have a smaller engine or larger tail surfaces. Already, a less powerful engine had been retained for the Gamma 2F, the production prototype for the A-17 series, and the XA-16 remained unchanged. Later, however, the XA-16 was fitted with a 950 hp R-1830-9. So powered, it ended its life at an aircraft mechanics' school at Roosevelt Field, London Island.

Gamma 2F: Powered by a 750 hp Pratt & Whitney R-1535-11 fourteen-cylinder radial driving a three-blade propeller, the Gamma 2F (s/n 44) company-owned prototype was delivered on 6 October, 1934, for evaluation by the Army Air Corps. In addition to being powered by an engine of smaller diameter than either the R-1830-7 or 9 of the XA-16, the aircraft embodied several improvements which rendered it more attractive to its potential military users. In particular, the Gamma 2F was fitted with a smaller and longer canopy – the radio-operator/gunner being moved further aft – a more streamlined fuselage and revised tail surfaces. Furthermore, its main undercarriage was made to retract rearward into large fairings. Evaluation of the aircraft by the Army, which began on 6 October, 1934, when the Gamma 2F was delivered, proved generally successful but also indicated the need for additional streamlining. Modifications incorporated when the aircraft was returned to Northrop included the substitution of a fixed undercarriage, with struts and open-sided wheel fairings, for the original semi-retractable units, and extensive revisions to cowling, fuselage lines and tail shape. In addition, the canopy shape was extensively revised and an unglazed section was added between the sliding canopies covering the pilot's and radio-operator/gunner's

The Gamma 2F, prototype of the A-17 series, in its original configuration. (*Karl W. Peters*)

cockpits. In this form, the aircraft was delivered to the Army Air Corps on 27 July, 1935, as the first A-17 (serial 35-51) under Contract AC7326.

A-17: Like the modified Gamma 2F/A-17 (35-51), the 109 production A-17s (35-52 to 35-160) were powered by the 750 hp R-1535-11 and armed with four wing-mounted and one flexible rear-firing 0·30-in machine-guns. They differed from the production prototype in being fitted with three-segment perforated dive-brakes extending between the ailerons. Production delays due to the time required to complete the necessary tooling and obtain engineering releases on design features which would be acceptable to the Government, resulted in the first aircraft's delivery taking place only on 23 December, 1935. Furthermore, in spite of major efforts to increase production rate, the last aircraft on the contract was delivered a month late, on 5 January, 1937.

A-17A: While the A-17 production was underway, Northrop proposed to the Army Air Corps the development of a version with fully retractable main undercarriage similar to that fitted to the Gamma 2J experimental

A-17 (35-78) with the insignia of the Air Corps Technical School painted aft of the pilot's cockpit. (*Richard W. Seely via NA & SM*)

197

Two A-17s from the first batch of aircraft which entered service with the 3rd Attack Group in 1936. (*USAF*)

advanced trainer. While the use of the retractable undercarrige, which required the extension of the inboard wing leading edge to provide space for the wheels, was expected to result in an increase in empty weight of some 230 lb (104 kg), Northrop pointed out that speed and range would be significantly increased. Thus, even though the Army Air Corps was satisfied with the performance of the fixed undercarriage A-17, the promise of the retractable undercarriage version was such that Fiscal Year 1936 funds were used to place an initial order for one hundred A-17As (36-162 to 36-261). The first of these made its maiden flight on 16 July, 1936, and was delivered on 12 August. Production of the aircraft to follow was delayed by retraction mechanism problems and by labour troubles at Northrop, and they were delivered between April and December 1937. A further order for twenty-nine A-17As (38-327 to 38-355) was placed during the second half of 1937 and these last were delivered between June and September 1938. All

Northrop A-17A of the 90th Attack Squadron, 3rd Attack Group, on 7 June, 1938. (*USAF*)

A-17As were powered by 825 hp R-1535-13s and were armed with one flexible 0·30-in and four wing-mounted machine-guns. Normal bomb load consisted either of four external 100 lb (45 kg) bombs or twenty internally-carried 30 lb (13·6 kg) anti-personnel bombs. This standard load, similar to

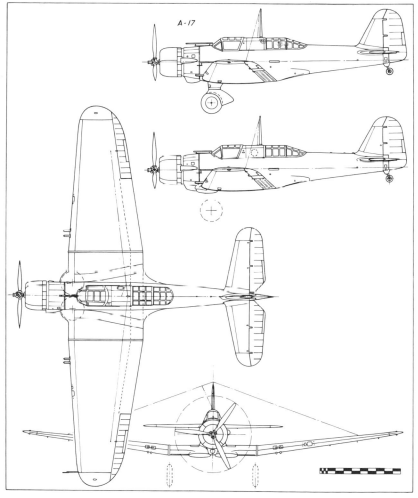

Northrop A-17A, with side view of A-17.

that of the A-17s, could be increased to a maximum of 1,200 lb (544 kg). Ninety-three A-17As were returned to Douglas on 20 June, 1940, for redelivery to the French Armée de l'Air.

A-17AS: These two aircraft, although they bore manufacturer's serial numbers s/n 289 and 290, following those assigned to the first batch of A-17A attack bombers, were built and delivered before the

A-17As. Processing an airframe similar to that of the A-17A, the first A-17AS (36-349) was a three-seat unarmed staff transport powered by a 600 hp direct-drive Pratt & Whitney R-1340-41 nine-cylinder radial driving a three-blade propeller. It was delivered on 17 July, 1936, to serve as the personal aircraft of Maj-Gen Oscar Westover, Chief of the Air Corps. On 21 September, 1938, the aircraft crashed and burned at Burbank and Gen Westover was killed. The second A-17AS (36-350) differed from its sister ship in being powered by a 600 hp geared R-1340-45 driving a two-blade propeller. Delivered on 12 July, 1936, it was assigned to Brig-Gen Henry H. Arnold who, upon the death of Gen Westover, became the new Chief of the Air Corps.

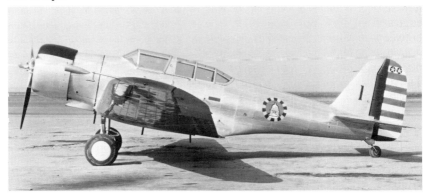

The first A-17AS (36-349), before delivery as Major-Gen Westover's personal transport. (*MDC*)

A-33-DE: Designation given in 1942 to thirty-one Douglas 8A-5s ordered by the Norwegian Government but taken over by the US Army Air Forces. Powered by the 1,200 hp Wright R-1820-87, these aircraft were operated as trainers in the Zone of the Interior and were assigned the serials 42-13584 to 42-13601 and 42-109007 to 42-109019.

Following the usual period of test and evaluation by the Matériel Division at Wright Field and by the Technical Training Command at Chanute Field, Illinois, in 1936 the Northrop A-17s were delivered to the 3rd Attack Group (8th, 17th and 90th Squadrons) at Barksdale Field, Louisiana, and to the 17th Attack Group (34th, 37th and 95th Squadrons) at March Field, California. One year later, the A-17s began to be supplemented in these two groups by the faster A-17As and, soon after, they were transferred to training and auxiliary units. Although, the A-17A had several notable features, such as its retractable undercarriage and comparatively heavy forward-firing armament, and although it had been pronounced at the end of the 1938–39 war manoeuvres to be the most effective ground attack aircraft yet devised, the Army Air Corps decided that twin-engined aircraft would offer substantial advantages. Thus, its first-line career was relatively short and, after less than three years' service with the 3rd and 17th Attack Groups, the bulk of the Air Corps' remaining A-17As were declared surplus and returned to Douglas for resale to France. Other A-17As, together with A-17s and A-33s, were used during the early war years as advanced trainers and hacks before ending up in mechanics' schools.

Two of the Northrop attack bombers, an A-17 (35-122) and an A-17A (36-184) were used by the National Advisory Committee for Aeronautics (NACA) for interesting experiments at Langley Field. To investigate the characteristics of the new laminar-flow aerofoil, 35-122 was extensively modified and new surfaces were built over and around the existing wing structure. Extending over approximately fifty per cent of the span, these new surfaces were highly polished and protruded forwarded of the leading edge and rearward of the trailing edge, thus nearly doubling the wing chord between the fuselage and the ailerons. In addition, a two-blade propeller driven by a small auxiliary engine was mounted on each side forward of the new leading edge to increase the speed of the airflow over the new surfaces. The results of this experiment, however, were disappointing as NACA was able to obtain more accurate data through conventional wind-tunnel tests.

In early 1939, NACA borrowed an Air Corps A-17A (36-184) to make engine cowling experiments. The chief object of the test was to determine the cooling characteristics of various forms of radial engine cowlings, particularly for ground and low-speed operations. Of secondary interest was the effect on the speed or drag of the aircraft. Initially, the aircraft was fitted with a large spinner completely covering the engine intake and giving the appearance of an aircraft powered by a liquid-cooled engine. For cooling the engine, large ducts were built into the wing-roots. Ground tests, however, resulted in excessive engine temperature and NACA decided not to flight test the aircraft in this configuration. Instead, NACA removed the wing ducts and replaced the oversizes spinner with a ducted spinner incorporating impeller blades. The tests showed that the nose-blower cowling was definitely superior to the NACA cowling as fitted to standard A-17As from the standpoint of ground cooling, since the engine was operated at full throttle for fifteen minutes with cylinder temperatures well below the recommended upper limits. Although there was a slight decrease in speed with the nose blower for the particular installation tested, the results of the speed tests were considered inconclusive. The original nose-blower cowling was definitely more powerful as a blower than it needed to be for satisfactory ground cooling, and consequently the power absorbed was excessive. Some improvements were obtained when the front opening area was reduced to 46 per cent of the original value, by means of an extension to the nose of the blower.

Capitalizing on the success of the earlier Northrop 2Es and of the A-17 series, the company developed a number of fixed and retractable undercarriage models for sale to overseas customers. However, these, Northrop Model 8s were produced after Northrop had become the El Segundo Division of Douglas and, consequently, were known as Douglas

8As.. The history of these versions and of the refurbished A-17As which were exported is detailed here.

8A-1: Generally similar to the A-17, the Model 8A-1 was developed for the Swedish Government, which ordered one prototype and parts for a second machine, the latter being intended to serve as a pattern aircraft for licence production by ASJA (AB Svenska Järnvägsverkstaderna) in Linköping. The Douglas-built prototype (s/n 378) was powered by an 875 hp Bristol Pegasus XII driving a three-blade propeller – the choice of this powerplant being dictated by the fact that the generally similar Bristol Mercury was being built under licence in Sweden by SFA – and was shipped on 22 April, 1938. In Sweden, the aircraft was designated B 5A by Flygvapnet and was assigned the serial number 7001. It was later modified for the target-towing role and redesignated B 5D. Parts for the second aircraft were assigned the Northrop s/n 410 and shipped on 8 August, 1938, to ASJA which used them in assembly of the first B 5B

Powered by a 980 hp SFA-built Mercury XXIV nine-cylinder air-cooled radial, this aircraft (Flygvapnet serial 7002) differed from the Northrop-built B 5A in having a domed canopy over the pilot's cockpit and the radio mast moved forward to the engine cowling. Fitted with Swedish armament (two 8 mm machine-guns in each wing and one flexible rear-mounted 8 mm

The A-17A (36-184) used by NACA during 1939 for engine cowling experiments. (*NASA*)

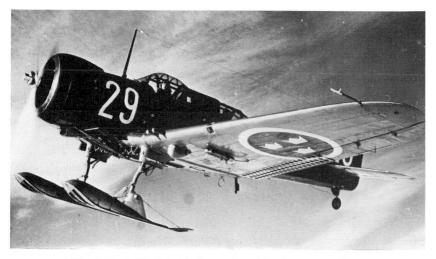

ASJA-built B 5B with skis, in service with Flygvapnet. (*SAAB*)

gun), this aircraft was followed by sixty-three ASJA-built B 5Bs (serials 7003 to 7065) which were delivered in 1940. A further contract for thirty-nine similar B 5Cs (serials 7066 to 7104) was completed in 1941 by SAAB (Svenska Åeroplan AB), the successor to ASJA. One of the Swedish built B 5s was fitted with twin floats during 1940 to obtain engineering data for the development of the SAAB S 17BS reconnaissance floatplanes.

In service with Flygvapnet, B 5s equipped Flottiljer F 4 at Östersund and F 12 at Kalmar until supplanted, beginning in 1944, by the more advanced SAAB B 17 single-engined light bomber of Swedish design.

8A-2: Thirty aircraft (s/n 348 to 377) powered by 840 hp Wright R-1820-G3s were built as Model 8A-2s for the Fuerza Aérea Argentina and were shipped between 22 February and 17 May, 1938. These aircraft were armed with two 12·7 mm and two 7·6 mm wing-mounted machine-guns and one flexible rear-firing 7·6 mm machine gun. Unlike the otherwise similar fixed-undercarriage A-17s of the Air Corps and the Swedish 8A-1, the Argentine 8A-2s were fitted with a partially retractable bomb-aiming tub beneath the radio-operator/gunner's cockpit. The 8A-2s were operated by the Regimiento de Ataque No.3, first from El Palomar and then from El Plumerillo, until this unit was re-equipped with locally-designed I.Ae.24 Calquin twin-engined bombers.

8A-3P: During 1938 the Cuerpo de Aeronáutica del Perú (CAP) ordered ten aircraft (s/n 412 to 421) differing from the Air Corps A-17A in being powered by the 1,000 hp Wright GR-1820-G103 and in being fitted with the partially retractable bomb-aiming tub. The first of these aircraft flew on 21 November, 1938, and three 8A-3Ps were flown from El Segundo to Lima, covering the 4,790 miles (7,709 km) in 24 hr 45 min at an average speed of almost 194 mph (312 km/h). The seven other 8A-3Ps were shipped. The

Powered by a Wright R-1820-G3, this aircraft was one of thirty 8A-2s ordered for the Fuerza Aérea Argentina. (*MDC*)

CAP used its DB-8A-3Ps during the 1941 war against Ecuador and the last was finally retired during the late 1950s.

8A-3N: Generally similar to the Peruvian 8A-3PS, the eighteen 8A-3Ns (s/n 531 to 548) ordered by the Netherlands Government were powered by 1,100 hp Pratt & Whitney Twin Wasp S3C-Gs and, following the maiden flight of the first aircraft on 31 July, 1939, were shipped between August and November 1939. When on 10 May, 1940, German forces mounted their three-prong attack on the Western Front, the Army Air Service had twelve serviceable DB-8A-3Ns based at Ypenburg with the 5th Fighter Squadron, 2nd Air Regiment. Caught by surprise, the 2nd Air Regiment immediately lost one of its DB-8A-3Ns on the ground but was able to put eleven aircraft into the air. Seven were then shot down by Bf 110s, while the Dutch claimed the destruction of one Ju 52. Shortly after landing,

Peruvian 8A-3P on a test flight off the coast near Los Angeles. (*H. Jackson*)

204

however, the four surviving Douglas attack bombers were again caught on the ground by the Luftwaffe and destroyed.

8A-4: Ordered by the Government of Iraq, fifteen 8A-4s (s/n 613 to 627) were shipped by Douglas between April and June 1940. In most respects they were similar to the 8A-3Ps and, like the Peruvian aircraft, were powered by 1,000 hp GR-1820-G103s. All DB-8A-4s are believed to have been destroyed by the Royal Air Force in actions taken to crush the Iraqi uprising which had started on 2 May, 1941, under the leadership of Rashid Ali.

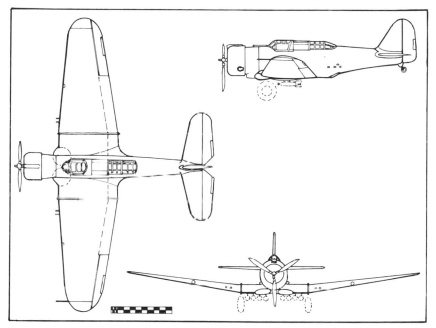

Douglas 8A-4

Iraqi 8A-4 at Mines Field before delivery. (*Northrop Institute of Technology*)

8A-5: Powered by the 1,200 hp Wright GR-1820-G205A, the Model 8A-5 was the last, the most powerful, and the most heavily armed variant of the Northrop/Douglas series of attack bombers. Thirty-six (s/n 715 to 750) were ordered by the Norwegian Government early in 1940. Their heavy armament consisted of four wing-mounted 0·30-in machine-guns, two 0·50-in machine-guns in pods beneath the wings, twin flexible rear-firing 0·30-in guns and up to 1,800 lb (816 kg) of bombs. Intended for use by the Heerens Flyvevåben (Army Flying Service), these aircraft were completed between October 1940 and January 1941. However, by that time Norway had been occupied by German forces and the 8A-5s were delivered to Island Airport, Lake Ontario, where the exiled Norwegian Government had set up a flying training centre known as Little Norway. However, as arrangements were later made for the training of Norwegian flying personnel in RAF and RCAF schools, the 8A-5s became surplus to Norwegian requirements and thirty-one of them were taken over by the USAAF as A-33-DEs.

In addition to the specially-built export versions described above, 93 ex-Army Air Corps A-17As found their way to Canada, South Africa and the United Kingdom. Initially, these aircraft were intended for delivery to France as the Armée de l'Air, greatly impressed by the Luftwaffe's success in Poland with the Ju 87Bs, had an urgent requirement for dive-bombers. As by then the US Army considered the A-17As to be obsolescent, the French Purchasing Commission was able to obtain 93 of these aircraft which were returned to Douglas on 20 June, 1940, to be refurbished and re-engined with 825 hp Pratt & Whitney Twin Wasp JrS2A5-Gs. However, by

Northrop 8A-5 at Little Norway, the Norwegian training centre at Island Airport, Ontario, Canada. (*Luftforsvaret*)

Northrop Nomad in service with the RCAF as a target-tug.
(*Canadian Armed Forces*)

then it was too late and, following the fall of France, the contract was taken over by the British Purchasing Commission. Named Nomads, sixty-one were to be delivered to the United Kingdom while the other aircraft were to go to Canada. The Nomads intended for the RAF received the following British military serials: AS440 to AS462, AS958 to AS976, and AW420 to AW438. However, the RAF shared the USAAF's opinion and considered the Nomad obsolete for combat operations. Consequently, with the exception of AS958, AS967, AS971 and AW421, the British Nomads were redelivered to South Africa for use in the flying schools operated by the SAAF as part of the Empire Air Training Scheme. In Canada, the thirty-two suplus A-17As delivered in August 1940 were assigned the serials 3490 to 3521 and operated as trainers and target-towing aircraft by Nos.4, 6 and 9 Bombing and Gunnery Schools.

XA-13

Span 48 ft (14·63 m); length 29 ft 2 in (8·89 m); height 9 ft 2 in (2·79 m); wing area 363 sq ft (33·724 sq m). Empty weight 3,600 lb (1,633 kg); loaded weight 6,463 lb (2,932 kg); maximum weight 6,575 lb (2,982 kg); wing loading 17·8 lb/sq ft (86·9 kg/sq m); power loading 9·1 lb/hp (4.1 kg/hp). Maximum speed 207 mph (333 km/h) at 3,300 ft (1,005 m); cruising speed 198 mph (319 km/h); rate of climb 1,300 ft/min (396 m/min); service ceiling 21,750 ft (6,630 m); maximum range 1,100 miles (1,770 km).

Data for other Models appear on page 208.

A-17
Span 47 ft 8½ in (14·54 m); length 31 ft 8⅝ in (9·67 m); height 11 ft 10¼ in (3·62 m); wing area 363 sq ft (33·724 sq m). Empty weight 4,874 lb (2,211 kg); loaded weight 7,337 lb (3,328 kg); wing loading 20·2 lb/sq ft (98·7 kg/sq m); power loading 9·8 lb/hp (4·4 kg/hp). Maximum speed at sea level 206 mph (332 km/h); cruising speed 170 mph (274 km/h); rate of climb 1,530 ft/min (466 m/min); service ceiling 20,700 ft (6,310 m); normal range 650 miles (1,046 km); maximum range 1,240 miles (1,995 km).

A-17A
Span 47 ft 9 in (14·55 m); length 31 ft 8 in (9·65 m); height 12 ft (3·66 m); wing area 363 sq ft (33·724 sq m). Empty weight 5,106 lb (2,316 kg); loaded weight 7,550 lb (3,425 kg); wing loading 20·8 lb/sq ft (101·6 kg/sq m); power loading 9·2 lb/hp (4·2 kg/hp). Maximum speed 220 mph (354 km/h) at 2,500 ft (760 m); cruising speed 170 mph (274 km/h); rate of climb 1,350 ft/min (411 m/min); service ceiling 19,400 ft (5,915 m); normal range 730 miles (1,175 km); maximum range 1,195 miles (1,923 km).

8A-1 (Saab B 5C)
Span 47 ft 9 in (14·55 m); length 31 ft 9⅞ in (9·7 m); height 12 ft 4 in (3·76 m); wing area 363·2 sq ft (33·75 sq m). Empty weight 5,368 lb (2,435 kg); loaded weight 7,496 lb (3,400 kg); wing loading 20·6 lb/sq ft (100·7 kg/sq m); power loading 7·6 lb/hp (3·5 kg/hp). Maximum speed 205 mph (330 km/h) at 6,235 ft (1,900 m); cruising speed 186 mph (300 km/h); climb to 9,845 ft (3,000 m) 8 min; service ceiling 22,475 ft (6,850 m); normal range 932 miles (1,500 km).

8A-3N
Span and wing area as A-17A. Length 32 ft 5 in (9·88 m); height 9 ft 9 in (2·97 m). Empty weight 5,508 lb (2,498 kg); loaded weight 7,848 lb (3,560 kg); maximum weight 8,948 lb (4,059 kg); wing loading 21·6 lb/sq ft (105·6 kg/sq m); power loading 7·1 lb/hp (3·2 kg/hp). Maximum speed 260 mph (418 km/h) at 12,000 ft (3,660 m); cruising speed 205 mph (330 km/h); rate of climb 1,430 ft/min (436 m/min); service ceiling 29,600 ft (9,020 m); normal range 910 miles (1,465 km).

8A-5 (A-33)
Span and wing area as A-17A. Length 32 ft 6 in (9·91 m); height 9 ft 4 in (2·84 m). Empty weight 5,510 lb (2,499 kg); loaded weight 8,600 lb (3,901 kg); maximum weight 9,200 lb (4,173 kg); wing loading 23·7 lb/sq ft (115·7 kg/sq m); power loading 8·6 lb/hp (3·9 kg/hp). Maximum speed 248 mph (399 km/h) at 15,700 ft (4,785 m); climb to 10,000 ft (3,050 m) 5·8 min; service ceiling 29,000 ft (8,840 m).

Armament. Four wing-mounted 0·30-in machine-guns and one flexible rear-firing 0·30-in machine-gun (Gamma 2C and 2F, A-17, A-17A, 8A-1, 8A-3P, 8A-3N and 8A-4); two 12·7 mm and two 7·6 mm wing-mounted machine-guns and one flexible rear-firing 7·6 mm machine-gun (8A-2); two 0·50-in forward-firing, four wing-mounted 0·30-in and two flexible rear-firing 0·30-in machine-guns (8A-5 and A-33).
Bomb load. Typical normal load included 20 internally-carried 30 lb (13·6 kg) and four external 100 lb (45 kg) bombs. Maximum load 1,200 lb (544 kg) or for the 8A-5 1,800 lb (816 kg).

Northrop BT-1 (BuNo 0595) of Bombing Squadron Five at the factory on 1 April, 1938. (*USN*)

Northrop BT-1

During 1934, after completing a detailed Type Specification for a new series of carrier-based dive-bombers, the US Bureau of Aeronautics invited a number of aircraft contractors to bid on the design and construction of experimental dive-bombers. Among the six manufacturers which submitted proposals three offered biplane designs—the Curtiss XSBC-3, the Great Lakes XB2G-1 and the Grumman XSBF-1, but the other three entered monoplanes—the Brewster XSBA-1, the Northrop XBT-1 and the Vought XSB2U-1. Noteworthy was the fact that the Northrop and Great Lakes designs were offered as pure bombers (VB class) whereas the other four designs were offered as scout bombers (VSB class).

Upon receiving the Navy's Invitation to Bid on 1 June, 1934, the Northrop Corporation selected Ed Heinemann to serve as Project Engineer for the programme. Under the general supervision of Jack Northrop, Heinemann prepared the initial general arrangement drawings and design layouts together with the details of the proposal for the Navy's evaluation, in competition with the proposals submitted by the other five contractors. Like the XFT-1 designed a year earlier by Northrop and Heinemann, the new dive-bomber was an all-metal low-wing monoplane with three-spar wing but, whereas the undercarriage of the XFT-1 was of the non-retractable type with large trouser fairings, the dive-bomber's undercarriage retracted backward into large fairings beneath the wings. Split flaps were provided on the trailing edge and could be used either as conventional flaps in the landing configuration or as dive-brakes with the upper section opening upward while the lower section was depressed. Pilot and observer were accommodated in tandem cockpits covered with a large glazed canopy incorporating sliding hatches, and provision was made for defensive armament comprising a fixed forward-firing 0·50-in machine-gun and a flexible rear-firing 0·30-in machine-gun. Offensive load included a 1,000 lb (454 kg) bomb on a Mk 35 rack beneath the fuselage which swung the bomb down and forward to clear the propeller, and two 100 lb (45·4 kg) bombs on Mk 41 racks beneath the wings. The aircraft was to be powered by a Pratt & Whitney R-1535-64 fourteen-cylinder air-cooled radial rated at 700 hp at 8,900 ft (2,715 m), and with this powerplant loaded weight was estimated at 6,208 lb (2,816 kg) and top speed calculated as 212 mph (341 km/h).

The Northrop proposal was favourably received by the Bureau of Aeronautics and, even though two of its competitors—the Vought XSB2U-1 and the Brewster XSBA-1—had substantially better calculated performance, one prototype of the Northrop XBT-1 was ordered on 12 November, 1934, under Contract 39004. Completed at the El Segundo plant in July 1935, the XBT-1 (s/n 43, BuNo 9745) made its first flight on 19 August and went through the initial phase of its flight trial programme without any major problems. However, when the XBT-1 was tested in dives, severe buffeting of the tail surfaces was experienced with the dive-brakes in the fully open position. It was determined that the buffeting was caused by turbulence induced by the split flaps in their open position and that this struck the horizontal tail surfaces. Numerous modifications were tested without success to reduce this disturbance without reducing the effectiveness of the dive-brakes. Finally, Heinemann decided to call on the staff of the aerodynamic section of NACA for assistance. After a series of wind-tunnel tests, NACA suggested that the single wave generated by the open flaps be broken into smaller eddies by perforating the upper and lower surfaces of the flaps.

The XBT-1 (BuNo 9745) on 14 April, 1936. (*US National Archives*)

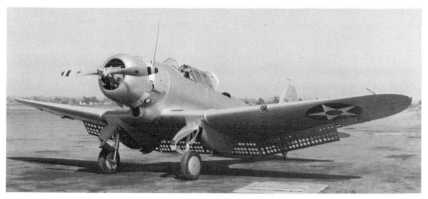

BT-1 (BuNo 0590) with perforated flaps in landing position. (*USN*)

With a series of holes drilled into them, the modified flaps were fitted on the prototype and flight tests resumed. Immediately, test pilot Vance Breese was able to report that the NACA suggestion was entirely successful, as not only was the tail surface buffet eliminated but also the aircraft's diving speed could be still further reduced by increasing the opening of the dive-brakes without re-inducing tail surface buffet. Furthermore, it was determined that, contrary to some pessimistic predictions, the total lift of the wings was not significantly affected by the new hole-pattern with the flaps in the closed position. However, other troubles crept in, and inflight fires, due to weaknesses in the engine and fuel system installation, were experienced. Local strengthening of the airframe was then made and the XBT-1 was readied for delivery to the Navy.

On 12 December, 1935, the XBT-1 was accepted by the Navy and four days later was delivered to Anacostia for final demonstration and acceptance trials. The Navy completed its trials programme in approximately two months and the Trial Board recommended that a number of

BuNo 0606 with flaps in dive position. (*USN*)

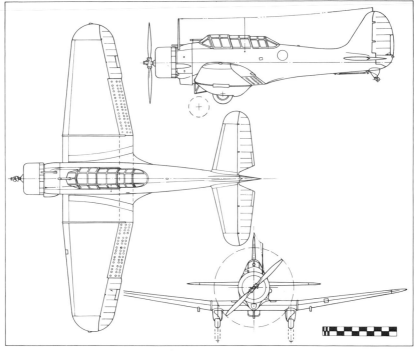

Northrop BT-1.

minor changes be incorporated. As soon as the effectiveness of these modifications had been tested, the aircraft was accepted as a satisfactory Service type and a contract for fifty-four BT-1s was awarded on 18 September, 1936.

The first production BT-1 (s/n 293, BuNo 0590), which was completed in September 1937, differed from the XBT-1 in being fitted with a tubular structure between the two cockpits to protect the crew in case of a crash, in having internal fuel capacity reduced from 184 US gallons (697 litres) to 180 gallons (681 litres), and an 825 hp Pratt & Whitney R-1535-94 substituted for the 700 hp R-1535-64. This first BT-1 was delivered to the Navy on 16 November, 1937, but a strike at the El Segundo plant delayed the delivery of the next until 21 March, 1938, and the fifty-second and last standard BT-1 was delivered on 5 August, 1938. Two other aircraft from the production contract for fifty-four BT-1s became respectively the XBT-2 and the BT-1S. Issued primarily to Navy Squadrons VB-5 (USS *Yorktown*) and VB-6 (USS *Enterprise*), the standard BT-1s were retained in first-line service until early in 1941, when they were replaced by SBD-2s and transferred to advanced training units before being surveyed.

On 28 November, 1936, Northrop was instructed to modify one of the fifty-four BT-1s in order to test a fully-retractable undercarriage. The

212

aircraft selected for this experiment (s/n 330, BuNo 0627) was designated XBT-2 and became the prototype of the famous SBD series.

Another BT-1 (s/n 346, BuNo 0643), the last aircraft from the 1936 production contract, was modified to assist in developing a satisfactory tricycle undercarriage for use aboard aircraft carriers. This project involved the installation of a jury-rigged, non-retractable nose unit incorporating an anti-shimmy device on the wheel, while the main legs were moved aft and braced in the down position. Other modifications included the lengthening of the arrester hook and the addition of tubular steps for cockpit access. First flown on 12 October, 1938, this experimental aircraft was unofficially designated BT-1S and was tested by the manufacturer at Mines Field—now Los Angeles International Airport—before being delivered to the Navy at Anacostia. During simulated carrier landings, a naval pilot was overcome by oil and petrol fumes infiltrating the cockpit

The experimental BT-1S (BuNo 0643) with non-retractable tricycle under-carriage, photographed at the factory on 19 October, 1938. (*MDC*)

following an engine failure. Only semi-conscious, the pilot made a successful power-off landing under crosswind conditions and thus demonstrated the advantages of the tricycle gear; before the landing run was completed, however, the pilot lost consciousness and his BT-1S collided with another aircraft taking off on a cross runway. Fortunately the pilot was not seriously injured but the BT-1S was badly damaged, bringing the experimental programme to an end. The wreck, re-acquired by Douglas, was repaired and brought back to a configuration similar to the original BT-1 standard. Then designated DB-19, the aircraft, which was now owned by Douglas, was offered for export and eventually found its way to Japan where it was tested by the Japanese Navy under the designation Navy Experimental Type D Attack Plane (DXD1).

Among other interesting planned developments was the aircraft's contemplated use as a parasite aircraft to be carried by large airships. Under one scheme advanced by the Bureau of Aeronautics, nine BT-1s

BT-1 (BuNo 0593) of Bombing Squadron Five (VB-5). The tail surfaces are red indicating that the aircraft was assigned to the USS *Yorktown* (CV-5). (*USN*)

were to be carried by a large airship; a still greater scheme was also studied involving the carriage of three Vought V-143 fighters and seven BT-1s. However, neither of these was implemented.

XBT-1
Span 41 ft 6 in (12·65 m); length 31 ft 10 in (9·7 m); height 12 ft 6 in (3·81 m); wing area 315 sq ft (29·265 sq m). Empty weight 4,183 lb (1,897 kg); loaded weight 6,410 lb (2,907 kg); maximum weight 6,972 lb (3,162 kg); wing loading 20·3 lb/sq ft (99·4 kg/sq m); power loading 9·2 lb/hp (4·2 kg/hp). Maximum speed 230 mph (370 km/h) at 8,900 ft (2,715 m); climb to 5,000 ft (1,524 m) 4·1 min; serving ceiling 23,500 ft (7,165 m); range with 1,000 lb (454 kg) bomb 564 miles (908 km); range without bomb 1,063 miles (1,711 km).

BT-1
Span and height as XBT-1. Length 31 ft 8 in (9·65 m); wing area 319 sq ft (29·636 sq m). Empty weight 4,473 lb (2,029 kg); loaded weight 6,527 lb (2,961 kg); maximum weight 7,075 lb (3,209 kg); wing loading 20·5 lb/sq ft (99·9 kg/sq m); power loading 7·7 lb/hp (3·5 kg/hp). Maximum speed 223 mph (357 km/h) at 9,500 ft (2,895 m); cruising speed 192 mph (309 km/h); initial rate of climb 1,270 ft/min (387 m/min); service ceiling 25,500 ft (7,770 m); range with 1,000 lb (454 kg) bomb 550 miles (885 km); range without bomb 1,150 miles (1,851 km).

Northrop 5

Bridging the gap between the Northrop 2E attack bombers exported to China and Britain and the Douglas 8A sold to several overseas air forces, the three Northrop 5s were designed in parallel with the Air Corps A-17 series. Thus, although intended for export markets, these three experimental aircraft closely corresponded to various models in the progressive development of the attack bombers produced for the US Army.

The first of these aircraft, the Northrop 5A, bore a marked resemblance to the YA-13 from which it differed in being powered by a 775 hp Wright SR-1820F-52 driving a three-blade propeller and in having a shallower canopy. Bearing the s/n 187 and assigned the temporary experimental registration X14997, the 5A was completed in October 1935. A month later, after completing its manufacturer's trials at Mines Field, the aircraft was shipped to Japan where it was evaluated by the Japanese Navy. It was then dismantled to provide useful engineering data for Japanese aircraft manufacturers. The Northrop 5B, which was also completed in October 1935, retained the trousered undercarriage of the Northrop YA-13 and 5A but was initially powered by a 700 hp Pratt & Whitney Twin Wasp Jr SB-1G fitted in a longer chord cowling and driving a three-blade propeller. Reigstered NR14998 and bearing the s/n 188, this aircraft was flown in late 1935 to Argentina where it was demonstrated to the Fuerza Aérea Argentina. While it was in Buenos Aires, it was re-engined with a 775 hp SR-1820-F52 and its testing eventually led to the Argentine Government placing an order for thirty Model 8A-2s. In February 1937, the Northrop

Northrop 5A at Mines Field on 16 October, 1935. (*MDC*)

215

5B was once again re-engined, this time with an 820 hp Wright R-1820G, before being recertificated by the Civil Aeronautics Authority's representative in Buenos Aires. With the registration X14498, the aircraft was then flown to México City, apparently having been sold to a Mr Henry G. Fletcher. It is believed that the aircraft was registered in México as XA-ABI and that it became the property of a Lt-Col Montero. The Northrop 5B's

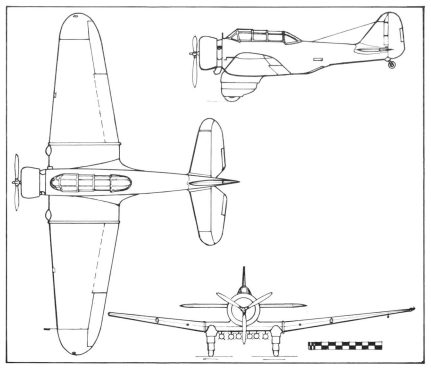

Northrop 5B

The Northrop 5D which provided Japan with useful information on the design and operation of retractable undercarriages. (*MDC*)

fate is unknown but possibly it may have found its way to Spain for use by Republican forces.

Completed in August 1936, the Northrop 5D (s/n 291, X16091) corresponded closely to the Northrop A-17AS. Like the A-17AS, the 5D was fitted with a retractable main undercarriage and was powered by a Pratt & Whitney nine-cylinder radial – in this instance a 600 hp Wasp S3H1 driving a two-blade propeller. The aircraft was exported to Japan where, following testing by the Navy, it provided Nakajima and Mitsubishi with valuable information on the design and operation of retractable undercarriages.

Northrop 5B

Span 47 ft 8¾ in (14·55 m); length 30 ft (9.14 m). Loaded weight 6,995 lb (3,173 kg). Power plant one 775 hp Wright SR-1820-F52 nine-cylinder air-cooled radial driving a three-blade Hamilton Standard propeller. Armament one 0.50-in fixed machine-gun in each wing, outboard of undercarriage, one 0.30-flexible dorsal gun, one 0.30-in flexible ventral gun, and six 100 lb (45.4 kg) bombs carried beneth the wing centre section.

Douglas DC-3 and Derivatives

On 17 December, 1935 – exactly thirty-two years after the Wright brothers had made the first powered, sustained and controlled flights in an aeroplane – Carl Cover, Ed Stineman and Frank Collbohm became the first men to fly a new twin-engined transport aircraft, the Douglas Sleeper Transport (DST). While the first flight of the DST initially attracted as little attention as the Wright brothers' spectacular achievement, this event was later regarded as a turning point in the history of aviation, as the type has since performed for virtually all nations a vast array of duties ranging from news-making feats to unsung routine labours, from luxury transcontinental passenger transport to tramp cargo, and from corporate flying office to night flying gun battery. In so doing it has received many names and designations: DC-3, Dakota, C-47, R4D, Li-2, PS-84, Skytrain, Skytrooper, Dak, Tabby, Gooney Bird, Spooky, Puff the Magic Dragon.

Development of this most famous of all Douglas aircraft was undertaken in late 1934 as a result of a request from American Airlines. Following resumption of US commercial airline operations after the 1934 Air Mail Emergency, this recently formed carrier had begun on 5 May, 1934, to operate transcontinental sleeper services. however, as its southern transcontinental route was longer than the more direct route flown by TWA, and as its Curtiss Condor twin-engined biplanes were substantially slower than TWA's DC-2s, American Airlines soon found itself in a poor competitive position in spite of the superior comfort of its sleeper service. Thus, during the summer of 1934 Cyrus R. Smith, President of American Airlines, and his Chief Engineer William Littlewood, defined their need for an aircraft combining the performance and economic characteristics of the DC-2 − then operated by TWA but already ordered by American Airlines − with the roominess and comfort of the Curtiss Condor. From these early discussions the airline established four requirements for the new aircraft: 1) more payload than the DC-2 in order to achieve reasonable seat-mile costs in spite of the higher aircraft-mile costs of the larger aeroplane; 2) more

The first of all the DC-3s. American Airlines' DST-114 NC14988 at Grand Central Air Terminal, Glendale, California, in 1936.

cabin volume to provide for the installation of berths on each side; 3) more range to enable nonstop New York–Chicago service in either direction (due to prevailing winds from the west, the DC-2 could fly nonstop from Chicago to New York but westbound had to land for fuel) and four-stop transcontinental service; and 4) more positive directional control to correct the DC-2's fishtailing tendency.

With the promise of early availability of the new Wright SGR-1820-G which was expected to develop some 35 per cent more power than the DC-2's SGR-1820-Fs, Bill Littlewood and his assistant Kirchner conceived a widened and stretched DC-2. In their initial calculations, the American Airlines' engineers anticipated that the new aircraft would have a 26-in (66 cm) wider fuselage to take a double berth on each side of the aisle or three seats abreast, and would be stretched by the equivalent of one row of seats, for a maximum of 21. It was to use 85 per cent parts and components common to the DC-2 and only 15 per cent new items.

Informal discussions between Littlewood and Douglas engineers took place during the late spring of 1934 but did not result in a commitment to build the new aircraft as Donald Douglas had doubts about both American Airlines' financial ability to back its development and about the size of the potential market for an aircraft larger than the DC-2 and designed for sleeper services. However, in the autumn of 1934, C. R. Smith's insistence led to a two-hour Chicago–Santa Monica telephone conversation with Donald Douglas and to a verbal commitment from American Airlines to order up to twenty 'wide-bodied', stretched developments of the DC-2. Shortly after, C. R. Smith obtained a $4,500,000 loan from the Reconstruction Finance Corporation and, thus, made credible his airline's ability to purchase the new aircraft. Donald Douglas was convinced and authorized his staff to begin design work in close co-operation with Bill Littlewood.

Whereas Littlewood and his American Airlines' colleagues had envisaged a fairly straightforward development of the DC-2, detailed design work − by a team led by Arthur Raymond, with basic layout under Ed Burton, stress analysis under Lee Atwood, and aerodynamics under Dr Bailey Oswald − soon established the need for a major redesign. Not only was the fuselage widened by 26 in (66 cm) and lengthened by 2 ft 6¼ in (77 cm) when compared with that of the DC-2, but its sides were rounded and the shape of the nose was altered by relocating the landing lights in the wing

NC33347 (s/n 6322) of Delta Air Lines. This aircraft was ordered by American Airlines as a DC-3-454 but was delivered as a C-49J to the USAAF on 14 January, 1943. Delta received it from the USAAF in October 1944. (*Delta Air Lines*)

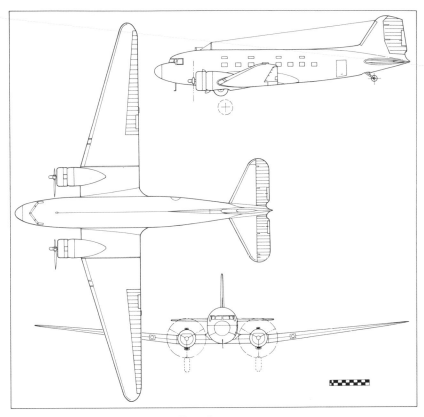

Douglas DST.

leading edge. Other major modifications included strengthened and longer wings (95 ft vs 85 ft; 28·96 m vs 25·91 m) of greater area (987 sq ft vs 939 sq ft; 91·696 sq m vs 87·236 sq m) which provided additional space for fuel tanks and resulted in good airfield performance in spite of higher operating weights. The tail surfaces were also redesigned and enlarged whilst the undercarriage was strengthened and its operation rendered less stiff on landing by increasing the effective travel of the oleo legs by 7 in (17·8 cm). The net result was an almost complete new design with only slightly less than 10 per cent of DC-2 interchangeable parts.

Construction of the first aircraft—s/n 1496, X14988, later NC14988— was undertaken in December 1934 while detailed engineering, pricing studies and contract negotiations were still underway. By the middle of 1935, however, Douglas was able to make firm technical and financial proposals to American Airlines, and on 8 July, 1935, C. R. Smith confirmed his airline's initial order for ten DSTs at a unit price of $79,500. Five months were then necessary to complete the first of these DSTs and the aircraft made its first flight on 17 December.

By the end of December 1935 the first DST had been flown 26 times and had accumulated a total of 25 hr 45 min in the air under the command of Carl Cover, then Douglas's Vice President for Sales, Elling Veblen, company test pilot, and Dan Beard, American Airlines' engineering test pilot. During the first months of 1936 flight trials continued with a brief interruption from 1 to 9 February when the aircraft was exhibited at the National Pacific Aircraft and Boat Show in Los Angeles where it was first shown to the public. For the most part, performance and handling characteristics had lived up to expectations but take-off roll at the design gross weight of 24,000 lb (10,886 kg) exceeded the stipulated 1,000 ft (305 m) and this caused some concern. Fortunately, Wright engineers found that the SGR-1820-G5s were not delivering their full take-off power and devised a minor crankcase modification which fully corrected this deficiency. The modified engines were fitted in mid-February 1935 and the aircraft was about to complete its flight trial programme when, on 5 March, it was damaged in a landing accident at Mines Field, a complete write-off being narrowly avoided by Dan Beard's quick reaction. Damage sustained was relatively small and, while it was being repaired, the first DST was also fitted with a small dorsal fin—a characteristic feature of all subsequent civil and military variants of the aircraft—to improve stability on the approach. Following resumption of flight testing on 27 March, the aircraft completed all certification requirements and on 21 May, 1936, was granted the first (ATC.607) of eight US Approved Type Certificates to be bestowed upon the DST and its numerous commercial progeny.

Five distinct series were built for civil customers before World War II. The original model, the one covered by ATC.607, was the DST which was fitted as a sleeper transport with fourteen 36-in (91·4-cm) wide double seats which could be made up into seven lower berths, and seven 30-in (76·2-cm) upper berths which folded up into the ceiling when not in use. Thus, the DST could accommodate either 14 passengers in night configuration or up to 28 passengers as a day transport, and there were four small upper windows on each side of the fuselage above the first, third, fifth and seventh main windows. The aircraft was powered by two 1,000 to 1,200 hp Wright SGR-1820-G2, -G2E, -G102, -G103 or -G202A engines and, depending upon the type of engines installed, was certificated at all-up weights of 24,000 to 25,000 lb (10,886 to 11,340 kg). A similar sleeper transport, the DST-A powered by Pratt & Whitney engines, received ATC.647 when fitted with 1,000 hp Twin Wasp SB-G or SB3-G radials and certificated at an all-up weight of 24,000 lb (10,886 kg), and ATC.671 when fitted with 1,050 to 1,200 hp Twin Wasp S1C-G, S1C3-G, SC-G, SC3-G or S4C4-G radials and certificated at an all-up weight of 25,200 lb (11,431 kg).

Day transport versions, without sleeping berths and without the small upper windows, were covered by ATC.618 and designated DC-3s when powered by various sub-types of Wright SGR-1820 radial engines and certificated at all-up weights of 24,000 to 25,200 lb (10,886 to 11,431 kg). Typical accommodation provided for 21 passengers in seven rows of seats

Twin Wasp-powered DST-A-207 of Western Air Express. This aircraft was operated on an interchange service with United Air Lines, hence the latter's tradename *The Mainliner* painted on the fuselage. (*Western Airlines*)

(double-seats on the left side of the aisle, single-seats on the right), but other arrangements seated either 14 (single swivelling seats on each side of the aisle) or 28 (seven rows of double-seats on each side of the aisle). When weighing 24,000 lb (10,886 kg) and powered by 1,000 hp Pratt & Whitney Twin Wasps, the day transports were designated DC-3As and received ATC.619 whilst other DC-3As with more powerful Twin Wasp engines and gross weight of 25,200 lb (11,431 kg) were covered by ATC.669.

Another prewar version of the Wright Cyclone-powered model of the aircraft was the DC-3B of which ten were built for TWA. Weighing 25,200 lb (11,431 kg), powered by 1,100 hp SGR-1820-G102s or 1,200 hp SGR-1820-G202As, and covered by ATC.635, these aircraft were combination sleeper/daytime transports with convertible seats/berths in the forward half of the cabin and seats in the rear to accommodate a maximum of 28 day passengers. They were recognizable by two small upper windows on each side above the first and third main windows.

Cyclone-powered DC-3-322 of Chicago and Southern Airlines at the Chicago Municipal Airport. (*Delta Air Lines*)

222

On 29 April, 1936, some three weeks before being granted its Approved Type Certificate, the first DST had been officially accepted by American Airlines at Phoenix, Arizona, so that the airline could avoid having to pay the California sales tax. The aircraft, however, was immediately returned to Santa Monica for 50 hours of route proving flights before its début in scheduled service. The original DST was eventually taken over by American Airlines on 11 July, 1936 and was operated by this carrier until February 1942 when it was purchased by the USAAF. Leased to TWA for one month it was then operated as a C-49E (serial 42-43619) until 15 October, 1942, when it crashed whilst trying to land at Chicago (Midway) in foul weather. By the time American Airlines had finally received NC14988 the airline already had four other DSTs in its fleet, the first being s/n 1495, NC16001, which had been accepted on 7 June, 1936—and, after a demonstration nonstop Chicago–Newark–Chicago flight in 8 hr 7 min on 21 June, began scheduled operations on 25 June, 1936.

The second DST (NC16001, s/n 1495) seen on 14 May, 1936, at Lakehurst, New Jersey, with the *Hindenburg* in the background.
(USN via Dr Richard K. Smith)

Within six months of entering service the new airliner was already on its way toward equalling, and eventually surpassing, the commercial success of the DC-2. By the end of 1936, American Airlines had received seven DSTs and thirteen DC-3s, Fokker had received the first export aircraft, the Soviet Amtorg had taken delivery of one, and Eastern Air Lines had obtained two. United had been the recipient of the first Twin Wasp-powered aircraft: five DC-3As and two DST-As. The following year, in July, Douglas suspended DC-2 production and concentrated on the DC-3/DST series, delivering 69 to US customers and exporting a further 31. Corresponding domestic and foreign deliveries respectively reached 12 and 31 during 1938. In 1939 the start of the war in Europe dried up an important source of sales as, up to then, Fokker—which held the agency and construction rights for the Continent—had accepted a total of sixty-three DC-3s and DC-3As. Nevertheless, production of civil versions continued at a fast pace until the US entry into the war when the manufacture of commercial aircraft was suspended. Douglas had delivered to US and foreign airlines and a few other civil customers a total of 430 aircraft, comprising 21 DSTs, 19 DST-As, 266 DC-3s, 114 DC-3As and 10 DC-3Bs. A further 149 aircraft ordered before the war by US airlines were taken over by the USAAF while still under construction and were delivered under military designations.

On 18 September, 1936, American Airlines began transcontinental coast-to-coast sleeper service between Newark, the airport then serving the New York area, and Grand Central Terminal in Glendale, the airport then handling most of the Los Angeles traffic. The impact of the DST upon this very competitive route can be judged from a comparison of the August 1934, 1935 and 1937 schedules of American Airlines which show that in 1934 the flight between New York and Los Angeles required 25 hr 55 min, a change of airlines, two changes of aircraft and fifteen stops; the following year the total time had been reduced to 23 hr 23 min but still required one aircraft change from Curtiss Condor to DC-2 in Fort Worth, and nine stops; however, following the introduction of the DST, American Airlines was able to offer a single-plane, three-stop service to a 17 hr 30 min schedule, a saving of almost one third over the 1934 schedule! As the airline received more DSTs and DC-3s, it kept adding new services, amongst which one of the most interesting routes was a feeder service linking Lakehurst, New Jersey—the US terminal point of the German Zeppelin *Hindenburg*—and Newark.

In the United States, American Airlines was followed as a DST/DC-3 operator by Eastern and United in 1937; TWA and Western in 1938; Braniff, Canadian Colonial, Northwest and Pennsylvania Central in 1939; and Chicago & Southern, Delta and Northeast in 1940. Thus, by the time of the Japanese attack on Pearl Harbor, 260 of the 322 aircraft operated by US domestic airlines were DC-3s or DSTs. Outside the United States, other

NC16070, the eleventh DC-3A for United Air Lines. The main entry door is on the starboard side. (*NASA*)

DC-3B-202 (NC17312, s/n 1922) of Transcontinental & Western Air over the Grand Canyon. (*NA & SM*)

American or American-controlled carriers operating DC-3s included China National Aviation Corporation in Southeast Asia, Hawaiian Airlines in the Territory of Hawaii, Pacific Alaska Airways in Alaska, and Pan American and Panagra in Latin America.

Overseas, KLM became the first DC-3 operator and, in association with KNILM, used the aircraft as a replacement for the DC-2 on the Amsterdam–Batavia route. Like the Dutch carrier, AB Aerotransport

Cabin arrangement of a KLM DC-3, with the special reclining seats fitted for use on the long Amsterdam–Batavia route. (*Lufthansa*)

SE-BAF, a DC-3-268 of AB Aerotransport, in early neutrality markings.
(*Fokker*)

(Sweden), Air France, ČSA (Czechoslovakia), LARES (Rumania), Sabena and Swissair acquired their prewar DC-3s through Fokker, Douglas's European agent, which assembled and test flew aircraft flown from Santa Monica to New York and then shipped across the Atlantic. In Europe, another airline almost became a prewar DC-3 operator, as in 1936 British Continental Airways requested that Airspeed exercise its option with Fokker to build the DC-3; lack of finance caused the projected order for 12 of these aircraft to be abandoned. Other major overseas customers for the DC-3 included Japan and the USSR—which purchased a substantial number as well as manufacturing rights—and Australia.

All these airlines had ample reason to congratulate themselves for selecting the DC-3 as their prime equipment as it proved not only reliable and safe but also became the first airliner to return a profit without the support of mail contracts or other forms of government subsidies. At the same time the aircraft was immensely popular with air travellers and, particularly in the United States, it introduced a whole new segment of the population to this then still new mode of transportation. This is shown by the fact that between 1935—the year preceding the DST/DC-3's entry into service—and 1941 the US domestic trunk carriers increased their passenger-mileage more than five times from 267 to 1,369 million. Unfortunately, the war was then engulfing a great deal of the world and, in most areas airline operations, where they had not been totally cancelled, became a mere extension of the military and government transport system. In the process, many of the airlines' DSTs and DC-3s were impressed by air forces where they were joined by thousands of their military derivatives. Other DC-3s, especially in the United States and in the neutral countries, continued airline operation until, at the end of the war, they were supplemented by an impressive flock of surplus C-47s, Dakotas and Li-2s to launch the industry into a still more impressive period of rapid growth.

As the Army Air Corps was already operating a number of military variants of the DC-2, it was natural for it to show considerable interest in the DC-3, as its load carrying ability substantially exceeded that of the older aircraft. However, funding limitations prevented the Air Corps from

226

acquiring more than one military derivative of the DC-3, the Santa Monica-built C-41A. This aeroplane (s/n 2145, 40-70) had been ordered on 17 August, 1939, and was delivered less than four weeks later. Serving as a command transport, powered by two 1,200 hp Pratt & Whitney R-1830-21s and fitted with swivelling seats, the C-41A was essentially a standard DC-3A with military instruments and communications equipment. It should not be confused with the similarly-powered C-41 which was essentially a re-engined C-39 combining DC-3 features—such as larger tail surfaces, more powerful engines and reinforced centre section—with those of the DC-2—including shorter-span wing and narrow fuselage.

Whereas the Army Air Corps had only been a nominal customer, its successor, the Army Air Forces, became the largest purchaser of DC-3 military derivatives. In addition to handling lend-lease contracts and orders for the Navy Department, it acquired some 10,000 aircraft through three processes: 1) direct contracts for new aircraft designed for military operations and built in the Long Beach, Oklahoma City and Santa Monica plants; 2) purchases of civil orders still under construction in the Santa Monica plant; and 3) impressment of Santa Monica-built DST/DC-3 airliners.

The first military derivative of the DC-3, the C-41A, at Wright Field in 1939. (*USAF*)

The first contract (AC15847) for fully militarized versions was awarded on 16 September, 1940, when 147 C-47s to be built in the new Long Beach plant were ordered. A year later the Oklahoma City plant was added as a second source when 1,900 C-47A-DKs were ordered under contract AC28405, while the Santa Monica plant was involved when on 24 June, 1941, ninety-two C-53s were ordered under contract AC18393. Brief details of these and other military DC-3s under Army Air Forces contracts are given below.

C-47-DL: Named Skytrain by the USAAF, this was the first fully militarized version of the DST/DC-3 series. Powered by two 1,200 hp Pratt & Whitney R-1830-92s, it differed from the generally similar DC-3A in incorporating a number of modifications to adapt the aircraft for military cargo. The main modifications were the provision of a large two-panel cargo door on the port side incorporating in its forward portion a standard door, and reinforced fuselage floor with tie-down fittings. The C-47s also

C-47A-90-DL and C-47A-65-DL of the 81st Troop Carrier Squadron, 436th Troop Carrier Group, over Southern France during *Operation Anvil*, 15 August, 1944. (*USAF*)

C-47A-80-DL of Luftforsvaret during a paratroop training sortie in Norway. (*Luftforsvaret*)

Skytrain of the Fuerza Aérea del Peru at Jorge Chavez Airport, Lima, in May 1977. (*René J. Francillon*)

had 6-in (15·2-cm) greater span and their fuel tank arrangement differed slightly from the DC-3A's with a normal capacity for 804 US gallons (3,043 litres) against the civil aircraft's 822 gallons (3,112 litres); in addition, for ferrying purposes, the C-47s could be fitted with up to nine 100-gallon (378·5-litre) fuselage tanks. An astrodome was added behind the flight deck. A total of 965 C-47s were built in Long Beach—the first being completed in November 1941 and delivered on 23 December, 1941—and, during the course of production, provision was added for the fitting of cargo hooks beneath the wing centre section to carry large items or for their release by parachute. Another modification was the removal of the tail cone to mount a cleat for glider towing. The normal crew consisted of pilot, co-pilot and radio operator, and the aircraft could carry 6,000 lb (2,725 kg) of cargo, or up to 28 airborne or parachute troops in folding canvas seats on the sides of the cabin, or 14 stretchers and three attendants.

SC-47 with Pratt & Whitney R-2000 engines at Thule, Greenland, in May 1958. (*MSgt David Menard*)

C-47A-DL and **C-47A-DK:** Produced both in Long Beach (2,954 -DLs) and Oklahoma City (2,299 -DKs), the C-47A was the most prolific version of the entire family, and, alone, accounted for almost 50 per cent of the whole Douglas production of DSTs, DC-3s and military derivatives. The C-47As differed from the C-47s primarily in being fitted with a 24-volt instead of 12-volt electrical system and with improved cabin heating.

Postwar modification of C-47As led to the development of the RC-47As fitted with limited reconnaissance equipment and used in Korea to drop flares to assist tactical aircraft; the SC-47As (redesignated HC-47As in 1962) for search and rescue operations; and the VC-47As which were fitted with conventional seats and other specialized items for use as staff transports.

229

C-47B-DL and **C-47B-DK**: Specially powered by 1,200 hp R-1830-90C engines with two-stage blowers and fitted with improved heaters, the C-47Bs were evolved for high-altitude operations such as the Hump route in the China–India–Burma theatre. However, the performance of the R-1830-90C engines proved disappointing and most C-47Bs were eventually modified as C-47Ds by omitting the engine blower. A total of 300 C-47B-DLs and 2,932 C-47B-DKs was built and the last C-47 delivered was a C-47B-50-DK (s/n 34409, 45-1139) which was handed over to the USAAF on 23 October, 1945. A number of C-47Bs were modified as staff transports under the designation VC-47B.

TC-47B-DK: Produced at Oklahoma City in parallel with the C-47Bs, the 133 TC-47Bs were equipped as navigational trainers, with the appropriate specialized equipment.

The XC-47C-DL (42-5671), showing details of its Edo amphibious floats. (*US National Archives*)

XC-47C-DL: One of the most interesting developments of the basic aircraft involved the installation of twin Edo Model 78 floats. Each single-step metal float was fitted with two retractable wheels and could carry 300 US gallons (1,136 litres) of fuel. The R-1830-92 powered XC-47C (s/n 7365, 42-5671) handled satisfactorily in the air and on smooth water but had several deficiencies, including inability to operate from all but the smoothest water, a high rate of tyre failures, excessive sensitivity on crosswind landings, and a greatly reduced payload when compared to standard C-47s. None the less, Edo received a contract for 150 sets of floats and C-47C amphibians were reported to have seen limited service in New Guinea and Alaska.

C-47D: Designation given to C-47Bs after removal of the engine high blower. Large numbers of C-47Ds were modified as staff transports (VC-47Ds), search and rescue aircraft (SC-47Ds, later HC-47Ds), reconnaissance aircraft (RC-47Ds), and trainers (TC-47Ds). The designation AC-47D was given twice to modified versions of the C-47D, the first time the prefix A standing for Airways Check and the second time for Attack. In 1953 twenty-six aircraft, modified by Hayes for airways checks, were designated AC-47Ds and operated by the Airways and Air Communication Service of MATS but, in 1962, they were redesignated EC-47Ds. Thus, when in 1965 the old faithful C-47 was modified as a heavily armed gunship for use in the Southeast Asia War, the designation AC-47D was resurrected. Most were armed with three General Electric 7·62 mm Miniguns firing through the open door and the fifth and sixth port side windows; they were aimed and fired remotely by the pilot and were loaded in flight by armourers who also dispensed flares. A few gunships, unofficially designated FC-47s, were armed with ten 0·30-in machine-guns instead of Miniguns.

C-47E: This designation was first reserved for modernized C-47s which were to have been powered by 1,475 hp Wright R-1820-80 engines but were not completed. It was given later to eight aircraft modernized for the USAAF by Pan American which re-engined them with 1,290 hp Pratt & Whitney R-2000-4s and fitted them out for airways checks.

YC-47F: This aircraft, which had first been designated YC-129, was a Super DC-3 tested briefly by the USAF, and is more fully described later.

The C-47s with series letters H to M (eg, LC-47H and VC-47J) were USN/USMC R4Ds which were designated in 1962 under the new Triservice system; they are described in the appropriate section of this narrative. The series letters N, P and Q were assigned to electronic reconnaissance versions of the C-47A (EC-47N) and C-47D (EC-47P), and to R-2000-4 powered aircraft (EC-47Q) developed for use in Vietnam.

C-53-DO: Whereas the C-47 versions were cargo transports built at Long Beach and Oklahoma City, the C-53 Skytroopers were troop transports built at Santa Monica. Powered by 1,200 hp R-1830-92s, the 221 C-53-DOs did not have the large cargo loading door, reinforced floor or astrodome of the C-47s. They were fitted with 28 fixed metal seats and a towing cleat for use as glider tugs.

XC-53A-DO: One C-53-DO (s/n 4932, 42-6480) was modified in March 1942 to test full-span slotted-flaps and was fitted with hot-air wing de-icing in place of the standard pneumatic de-icer boots of the other military derivatives of the DC-3. The aircraft remained experimental and, at the end of the war, was stored for the USAAF Museum; in 1949, however, it was sold as surplus and modified to a standard close to that of the DC-3C.

C-53B-DO: Eight C-53-DOs (41-20047 to -20050, 41-20052, and 41-20057 to -20059) were modified in 1942 for operations in the Arctic, with winterized equipment, extra fuselage fuel tanks and an astrodome.

C-53C-DO: Aircraft ordered by the airlines but taken over by the USAAF while under construction.

C-53D-DO: These 159 aircraft differed from the initial batch of C-53-DOs in being fitted with side seats intead of conventional seats.

C-53-DO of the 10th Transport Group at Patterson Field, Ohio, in 1941. (*USAF*)

C-117A-DK: Towards the end of the war the USAAF, with enough operational transports, felt a need for less spartan staff transports. Accordingly seventeen C-117A-DKs were built in 1944–45 with a 21-seat airline-type interior. They were generally identical to late series C-47B-DKs and were also powered by R-1830-90Cs with two-stage blowers, but they did not have the large cargo door and the reinforced floor. The final C-117A, which was accepted by the USAAF on 29 December, 1945, was the last new military derivative of the DST/DC-3 to be built.

C-117B-DK: Eleven C-117As were modified by removal of the engine high-blowers.

C-117C: Redesignated VC-47s which were overhauled and brought up to C-117B standard.

C-117D: Post-1962 designation of the USN/USMC R4D-8s (Super DC-3s).

XCG-17: Competing with the XC-47C for the title of most unusual DC-3 derivative, the XCG-17 was an experimental troop-transport glider obtained by removing the engines and fairing over the nacelles of a

The XCG-17 (41-18496, s/n 4588) during tests at Clinton County Army Base, Ohio, in 1944. (*USAF*)

232

C-47-DL (s/n 4588, 41-18496). This successful experiment—the XCG-17 had a flatter gliding angle, lower stalling speed and higher towing speed than conventional cargo gliders of the time—was made during the summer of 1944 from Clinton County Army Base in Ohio. However, by then the USAAF no longer needed combat gliders and the aircraft was stored at Davis Monthan, Arizona, until re-engined and sold as surplus.

The operational history of the C-47s, C-53s, C-117s and impressed DSTs/DC-3s in US service could easily warrant a book of its own as it spans a period of 35 years during which the United States were involved in three major wars and stood on guard during the Cold War. It is therefore possible to give here only a glimpse.

When the war began for the United States, the USAAF only had an embryonic transport element and lacked sufficient trained crews. Thus, to absorb the large numbers of C-47s and C-53s which were coming off the production lines and the impressed airliners of all types, the USAAF had initially to rely on the airlines which were called upon to supplement as well as train its personnel. The airlines were asked to perform special emergency missions—such as the airlift of supplies to the West Coast undertaken by Western immediately after Pearl Harbor, and the transport to Brazil of fifteen loads of troops by American Airlines in December 1941—and to help set up an effective overseas ferry and transport system. Among other airline aircraft types, the DC-3s and derivatives dominated the field; depending upon the period and the operational areas, these aircraft were finished either in standard airline markings or in full military garb.

The development of the routes, often entailing difficult flights over water or in areas with few or even no navigational aids or accurate maps, was successfully accomplished partly because of the reliability of the DC-3. One of these routes linked the United States with the United Kingdom and was developed by Northeast Airlines. On 2–4 July, 1942, the C-47-DL s/n 4332, 41-7833, flew from Presque Isle, Maine, to Prestwick, Scotland, via Labrador, Greenland, Iceland and the Hebrides, with Milton Anderson as pilot, Wilfred Lord as co-pilot, William Burns as radio-operator, and Samuel Solomon as steward; Anderson and Solomon were respectively Vice-President of Operations and President of Northeast, an indication of the airline's interest in this venture. Other major overseas routes were developed by American (Alaska, North and South Atlantic, Middle East and India); Eastern (Caribbean and South Atlantic); Northwest (Alaska and Aleutians); Pan American (South and Central Atlantic, Africa and the Middle East); TWA (North and South Atlantic, and Africa); United (Alaska and Pacific); and Western (Alaska).

On 20 June, 1942, the USAAF activated its Air Transport Command (ATC) and progressively took over an increasing share of these operations. The ATC was organized into six regional wings (North West, North Atlantic, South Atlantic, Caribbean, South Pacific and CBI), equipped primarily with military DC-3s, with Douglas C-54s and Curtiss C-46s. Three C-47/C-53 squadrons began to fly supplies from India to China over the Hump route during the summer of 1942, returning with wounded and other personnel. Substantial numbers of C-47s and other military DC-3 derivatives were operated throughout the war in a variety of support roles such as staff transport, training and communications. Whilst these aircraft and those of ATC were not normally involved in combat operations, the Skytrains and Skytroopers of Troop Carrier Squadrons took part in all major airborne operations including those in Sicily, New Guinea, Normandy, Southern France and Nijmegen.

After the war the USAAF needed only a few of these aircraft, and many of them were therefore sold to the world's airlines and to provide operators and foreign governments, whilst others were placed in storage. Those remaining with the USAAF/USAF served transport squadrons—for example, MATS had 239 C-47s when it was formed on 1 June, 1948—, and as hacks, staff transports and support aircraft with Regular, Reserve and ANG units. MATS C-47s, soon supplemented by other military DC-3s taken out of storage, flew their first Berlin Airlift sorties on 26 June, 1948, and 105 of these aircraft eventually played a major role in this operation.

After a period of relative calm during which the number of C-47s in USAF service dwindled rapidly, the type was recalled twice to take part in combat operations. During the first phase of the Korean War they equipped several USAF and Allied squadrons and were flown for general transport duties, airborne operations and medical evacuations, and although supplemented by more modern aircraft went on to serve for the duration. RC-47Ds were used to drop flares for tactical aircraft flying night interdiction and ground support sorties. During the Southeast Asia War, Gooney Birds were flown by the USAF not only in conventional transport duties—notably, resupply of isolated outposts—but also in the electronic reconnaissance and psychological warfare roles (EC-47) and in the night

EC-47N of the 360th Tactical Electronic Warfare Squadron over South Vietnam on 9 April, 1970. (*USAF*)

234

attack role (AC-47 coded Spooky and nicknamed Puff the Magic Dragon).

In spite of the loss of the European market with the start of the war in September 1939, Douglas continued to receive substantial airline orders, primarily in the United States but also in other still peaceful areas. Thus, when Japan attacked Pearl Harbor, the USAAF was able to obtain a quick supply of transport aircraft by simply taking over civil DC-3s and DC-3As then on the Santa Monica line. A total of 137 aircraft was involved, and as they had been started to different airline specifications and were powered by a variety of engines, they were assigned twenty-two different designations, while twelve of them were taken over but remained undesignated. Details of these aircraft are tabularized below and their military serial numbers are listed in Appendix B.

USAAF designation	No. of aircraft	Original customer	Douglas Spec. No.	Engines	Seats
C-48-DO	1	United	DC-3A-377	R-1830-82	21
C-48A-DO	3	—	DC-3A-368	R-1830-82	10
C-48C-DO	7	Pan Am & associates	DC-3A-414	R-1830-51	21
C-49-DO	6	TWA	DC-3-384	R-1820-71	24
C-49A-DO	1	Delta	DC-3-385	R-1820-71	21
C-49B-DO	3	Eastern	DC-3-387	R-1820-71	21
C-49C-DO	2	Delta	DC-3-386	R-1820-71	28
C-49D-DO	6	Eastern	DC-3-389	R-1820-71	28
C-49J-DO	34	sundry	DC-3-454	R-1820-71	28
C-49K-DO	23	sundry	DC-3-455	R-1820-71	28
C-50-DO	4	American	DC-3-396	R-1820-85	21
C-50A-DO	2	American	DC-3-401	R-1820-85	28
C-50B-DO	3	Braniff	DC-3-397	R-1820-81	21
C-50C-DO	1	Penn Central	DC-3-391	R-1820-79	21
C-50D-DO	4	Penn Central	DC-3-392	R-1820-79	28
C-51-DO	1	Can Col	DC-3-390	R-1820-83	28
C-52-DO	1	United	DC-3A-398	R-1830-51	28
C-52A-DO	1	Western	DC-3A-394	R-1830-51	28
C-52B-DO	2	United	DC-3A-395	R-1830-51	28
C-52C-DO	1	Eastern	DC-3A-402	R-1830-51	29
C-53C-DO	17	sundry	DC-3A-453	R-1830-92	28
C-68-DO	2	—	DC-3A-440	R-1830-92	21
Undesignated	12	Pan Am & associates	DC-3A-414	R-1830-92	28

The USAAF impressment of DST/DC-3 variants directly from the airlines constituted a third source of military DC-3s. A total of 93 of these aircraft was obtained in this manner but many were leased back for use on government approved routes; more often than not, however, an aircraft was not necessarily leased to the airline from which it had come. According to engine types and internal configuration, these aircraft were given the following designations and military serial numbers (serial numbers of aircraft ordered by the USAAF or taken over by this Service before their completion were not given in the preceding sections as they appear in Appendix B):

USAAF designation	No. of aircraft	Engines	AAF serial numbers
C-48B-DO	16	R-1830-51	42-38324/42-42-38326, 42-56089/42-56091, 42-56098/42-56102, 42-56609/42-56612, 42-56629
C-48C-DO	9	R-1830-51	42-38258/42-38260, 42-38327, 42-78026/42-78028, 44-52990/44-52991
C-49D-DO	5	R-1820-71	42-38256, 42-43624, 42-65583, 42-68860, 44-52999
C-49E-DO	22	R-1820-79	42-43619/42-43623, 42-56092/42-56097, 42-56103/42-56107, 42-56617/42-56618, 42-56625/42-56627, 42-56634
C-49F-DO	9	R-1820-71	42-56613, 42-56616, 42-56620/42-56621, 42-56623, 42-56628, 42-56633, 42-56636/42-56637
C-49G-DO	8	R-1820-97	42-38252, 42-38255, 42-56614/42-56615, 42-56630/42-56632, 42-56635
C-49H-DO	19	R-1820-97	42-38250/42-38251, 42-38253/42-38254, 42-38257, 42-38328/42-38331, 42-57506, 42-65580/42-65582, 42 68687/42-68689, 42-102422, 44-83228/44-83229
C-52D-DO	1	R-1830-51	42-6505
C-84-DO	4	R-1820-71	42-57157, 42-57511/42-57513

Even though, since March 1941, the US Navy and US Marine Corps have operated a total of at least 567 military versions of the DST and DC-3 series, the Navy Department directly ordered only 78. All other R4Ds—as the Navy version was originally designated—were ordered on behalf of the Navy by the USAAF or were subsequently transferred from the USAAF/USAF inventory. The USN/USMC versions of the aircraft were designated as follows:

R4D-1: The R4D-1s were generally similar to the C-47-DLs but differed only by the installation of some Navy instruments and communications equipment. They were cargo aircraft powered by Pratt & Whitney R-1830-92s and were delivered beginning in February 1942. The first 66 aircraft (BuNos 3131/3143, 4692/4706, 01648/01649, 01997/01990 and 05051/05072) were ordered under Navy contract while an additional forty R4D-1s (BuNos 12393/12404, 30147, 37660/37685 and 91104) came from USAAF contracts.

Early R4D-1 with the type of national markings applied to US Navy aircraft between January and May 1942. (*USN*)

236

R4D-2: Two DC-3-388s (BuNos 4707 and 4708) which had been ordered by Eastern Air Lines were taken over by the Navy while still under construction and became the Navy's first variant. Lacking the reinforced floor and cargo door of the R4D-1s, they were used as staff transports. They were powered by Wright R-1820-71s and corresponded to the C-49 series of the USAAF. They were later redesignated successively R4D-2Fs and R4D-2Zs to indicate their VIP flagship interior.

R4D-3: These 20 personnel transports (BuNos 05073/05084 and 06992/06999) were C-53-DOs transferred from the USAAF.

R4D-4: Ordered by Pan American as DC-3A-447s but taken over by the Navy while still under construction, then ten R4D-4s (BuNos 07000/07003 and 33815/33820) were flown as personnel transports. They were generally similar to the C-53C-DOs of the USAAF. Some were fitted with electronic countermeasure equipment and redesignated R4D-4Qs.

R4D-5: Eighty-one C-47A-DLs, ordered by the USAAF, were transferred to the Navy and assigned the BuNos 12405/12446 and 39057/39095. They were supplemented by 157 C-47A-DKs which received BuNos 17092/17248. In 1962 the surviving R4D-5s were redesignated C-47Hs in accordance with the new Triservice system. Many R4D-5s were modified for special purposes and were redesignated as follows:

Designations	Purposes
R4D-5E	Special electronic operations
R4D-5L (LC-47H)	Operations in Antarctica and the Arctic
R4D-5Q (EC-47H)	Radar countermeasures
R4D-5R (TC-47H)	Personnel transport
R4D-5S (SC-47H)	Air-sea warfare training
R4D-5T	Navigation training
R4D-5Z (VC-47H)	Staff transport

R4D-6: Corresponding to the C-47B-DK, under which designation they were ordered, the surviving aircraft from batches totalling 150 R4D-6s (BuNos 17249/17291, 39096/39098, 39100, 39109, 50740/50839, 99850 and 99852) were redesignated C-47Js in 1962. Special modifications co-

R4D-6L (BuNo 17274 *Charlene*) of Air Development Squadron Six (XV-6 during operations in the Antarctic in 1956, with retractable ski undercarriage and JATO bottles beneath the fuselage. (*US National Archives*)

responding to equivalent versions of the R4D-5 (C-47H) were designated R4D-6E, R4D-6L (LC-47J), R4D-6Q (EC-47J), R4D-6R (TC-47J), R4D-6S (SC-47J), R4D-6T and R4D-6Z (VC-47J).

R4D-7: In addition to the transport models, the Navy operated forty-one R4D-7 trainers (BuNos 39099, 39101/39108, 99824/99849, 99851 and 99853/99857) obtained from the USAAF contract for TC-47B-DKs. These aircraft were redesignated TC-47Ks in 1962.

C-47M: This designation was given to a number of C-47Hs and C-47Js which were fitted with special electronic equipment during the Southeast Asia War period.

Beginning in 1942, the R4Ds were operated by the Naval Air Transport Service (NATS) in the logistic role to deliver parts, supplies and personnel to naval facilities and Fleet forces all over the world and especially in the Pacific which was the Navy's main theatre of operations. In addition, starting during the fighting for Guadalcanal in the Solomons, R4Ds operated by USN and USMC units flew combat resupply missions in support of Marine land forces and this type of operation was done successfully throughout the long island-hopping campaign in the Pacific. Postwar, Navy and Marine R4Ds continued their support and became the standard US Navy staff transports. These R4Ds, too, went back to war twice in support of operations during the Korean and Southeast Asia wars.

While their wartime operations and postwar routine activities did not attract much attention, the Navy R4Ds gained much fame after the war during a series of flights in support of US Antarctic expeditions. A first group of six ski-equipped R4D-5Ls was launched, with the assistance of JATO—jet assisted take-off—from the deck of the USS *Philippine Sea* on 29 January, 1947, and operated from Little America, on the edge of the Antarctic continent, until 21 February. Others, including seven R4D-5Ls (LC-47Hs), four R4D-6Ls (LC-47Js) and six R4D-8Ls (LC-117Ds, Super DC-3s), were used in support of a series of Operations Deep Freeze and one of these aircraft, the R4D-5L BuNo 12418 *Que Sera Sera*, became the first aircraft to land at the South Pole, on 31 October, 1956. This aircraft has now joined an Eastern Air Lines DC-3* in the Smithsonian Institution's National Air & Space Museum.

Between September 1939 and July 1940 No.8 Squadron, RAAF, flew two DC-3-232s and two DC-3-232As leased from Australian National Airways. These aircraft were assigned the military serial numbers A30-1 to A30-4 (former identity being s/ns 2002/2003 and 2029/2030, VH-UZJ, VH-UZK, VH-ABR and VH-ACB). This use of DC-3s by the Royal Australian Air Force was significant as it was to mark the beginning of the long association—which has remained unbroken since April 1942 when No.31 Squadron, RAF, received its first DC-3s while operating in India—of Commonwealth air forces with impressed DC-3s and military C-47s and C-53s.

*DC-3-201 s/n 2000 N18124 (ex-NC18124). Delivered to EAL on 7 December, 1937. It flew a total of 56,782 hr.

With these air forces the military DC-3s became known as Dakotas, the name continuing the British tradition of assigning geographical names to transport and bomber aircraft and representing a clever acronym of the letters DACoTA—Douglas Aircraft Company Transport Aircraft. Mark numbers were assigned only to aircraft corresponding to genuine military C-47s and C-53s received under lend-lease, the Dakota Mk I to IV respectively being C-47-DL, C-53-DO, C-47A-DL/DK and C-47B-DK. The impressed DC-3s were named simply Dakotas, and the name came to be used after the war for DC-3s and surplus military derivatives in many parts of the world.

During the war the Royal Air Force received a total of 1,928 Dakotas including eight ex-civil DC-3s (LR230/LR235 and MA925/MA926) acquired from US airlines by the British Purchasing Commission, 53 Dakota Is (FD768/FD818, HK983 and HK993), nine Dakota IIs (FJ709/FJ712, HK867, MA928/MA929 and TJ167/TJ170), 962 Dakota IIIs (FD819/FD967, FL503/FL652, FZ548/FZ698, KG310/KG809, TS422/TS427 and TS431/TS436), and 896 Dakota IVs (KJ801/KJ999, KK100/KK220, KN200/KN701, KP208/KP279, TP181 and TP187). However, a number of these aircraft were transferred during the war to other Commonwealth and Allied air forces as well as to BOAC.

With the RAF, Dakotas were operated during the war by squadrons of No.45 Group, Ferry Command, on routes across the North Atlantic as well as in Canada and the United States. The most unusual flight across the Atlantic by a Ferry Command aircraft was made by FD900, between 24 June and 1 July, 1943, from Montreal to Prestwick towing a Waco Hadrian glider loaded with vaccines for the USSR. Other ferry units, including Nos. 45 and 47 Squadrons and No.2 Aircraft Delivery Unit, flew Dakotas on routes over the South Atlantic and across Africa. In the war zones the Dakotas became the RAF's most important transport aircraft and performed regular supply missions and took part in many famous glider-towing airborne and paratrooping operations. The first major use of the Dakota in this spectacular role was made during July 1943 in Sicily and this was followed in August and November 1943 and September 1944 by paratrooping operations on islands in the Aegean Sea, in June 1944 in Italy and Normandy, in August 1944 in Southern France, in September 1944 at Arnhem—during which Flt Lieut David Lord won a posthumous Victoria Cross in Dakota III KG734—, in March 1945 in support of the Rhine crossing, and in March and May 1945 in Burma.

After VE-Day several RAF fighter and bomber squadrons were scheduled to be converted to Dakota transport squadrons for use in the final stage of the war against Japan. However, Japan surrendered while most of these squadrons were still being converted; the RAF quickly disbanded several of its existing transport squadrons and disposed of many of its Dakotas. None the less, this did not mark the end of its Service life as the remaining aircraft, supplemented by several civil aircraft which were temporarily impressed, took an active part in Operation Plainfare—the

FL618, a Dakota III which was operated by the RCAF between 11 January, 1944, and 5 December, 1945. (*Canadian Armed Forces*)

RAF contribution to the Berlin Airlift. Other RAF Dakotas were involved in operations in Malaya and Kenya. The RAF finally retired its last Dakota, KN645, on 4 April, 1970.

The Royal Canadian Air Force, by then renamed Canadian Armed Forces, flew Dakotas until the 1970s. It had received its first aircraft in March 1943 and had a total of 169 Dakotas, including 60 (of which nine were ex-RAF aeroplanes and 51 were ex-USAAF C-47s) which received the Canadian military serials 650/664, 960/994, 1000 and 10910/10918, and 109 aircraft which retained their British serials. In addition to normal RCAF duties and, during World War II, in support of Allied operations in the CBI theatre, the Canadian Dakotas flew support missions for the United Nations in at least eight countries.

As mentioned earlier, the Royal Australian Air Force first operated four leased DC-3s in 1939–40. This Service later received three Dakota Is (A65-1, -3 and -4), 56 Dakota IIIs (A65-2 and A65-5/-59) and 65 Dakota IVs (A65-60/-124) and also operated on wartime loan twenty-four C-47s, C-49s, C-50s and C-53s which retained their USAAF serials. They were operated during the war by Nos.33, 35, 36, 37 and 38 Squadrons, No.1

Dakota III (N2-43) operated by the Royal Australian Navy at RANAS Nowra, New South Wales, as a radar-operator trainer. (*Mervyn Prime*)

240

Communication Unit and No.9 LASU and continued in RAAF service until the mid 1970s. Other Australian Dakotas were flown by the Royal Australian Navy. These RAAF and RAN Dakotas were outlived by those of the neighbouring Royal New Zealand Air Force, which until 1976 was still flying survivors from the 49 Dakotas (NZ3501/NZ3506 and NZ3516/NZ3558) it had received during the war to equip Nos.40 and 41 Squadrons.

Continuing its Douglas association begun with the DC-2, Fokker acquired from the onset the DC-3 European distribution and manufacturing rights, but did not exercise the latter and only assembled and serviced Douglas-built aircraft.

Captured L2D3 of the Japanese Navy at Zamboanga in the Philippines in May 1945. It has extended cockpit windows and Kinsei 51 engine installation. (*US National Archives*)

Mitsui and Company Ltd, the US-based subsidiary of Mitsui Bussan Kaisha (Mitsui Trading Company), acquired on 24 February, 1938, the licence rights to build and sell the DC-3 in Japan and Manchukuo. Moreover, it purchased thirteen Cyclone-powered DC-3s (s/ns 1979, 2025/2026, 2049/2052 and 2096/2101) and seven Twin Wasp powered DC-3As (s/ns 2009, 2037/2041 and 2048) which were shipped with wings, tail surfaces and propellers unassembled, and two DC-3As (s/ns 2005/2006) which were delivered unassembled to serve as patterns for Japanese production. Production was entrusted to Showa Hikoki Kogyo KK which, as well as assembling in 1939–40 the two imported aircraft, built 414 for the Japanese Navy. Designated Navy Type 0 Transports (short designation L2D), these aircraft were built in six models.

Short designation	Engines	Remarks
L2D2	1,000 hp Kinsei 43	Personnel transport
L2D3	1,300 hp Kinsei 51	Personnel transport
L2D3a	1,300 hp Kinsei 53	Personnel transport
L2D3-1	1,300 hp Kinsei 51	Cargo transport with reinforced floor and cargo door
L2D3-1a	1,300 hp Kinsei 53	Cargo transport with reinforced floor and cargo door
L2D4	1,300 hp Kinsei 51	Personnel transport with dorsal turret housing a flexible 13·2-mm machine-gun
L2D4-1	1,300 hp Kinsei 51	Cargo transport with reinforced floor, cargo door and dorsal turret
L2D5	1,560 hp Kinsei 62	Same as L2D4 but fitted with more powerful engines and partially built of wood and steel

Nakajima Hikoki KK also produced seventy-one L2D2s between 1940 and 1942. The L2D became the standard wartime transport aircraft of the Japanese Navy and was known to the Allies by the code name Tabby.

The USSR, too, obtained through Amtorg twenty-two DC-3s (s/ns 1589, 1974, 1987/1988, 2031/2035, 2042/2048 and 2112/2117)—of which at least two were delivered unassembled to serve as pattern aircraft—and the manufacturing rights for the Soviet Union. In preparation for production in State Aircraft Plant No.84, the Russians sent Boris P. Lisunov to Santa Monica in 1938 for a period of almost two years to study Douglas's production methods. Lisunov then returned to the Soviet Union where he was put in charge of adapting the DC-3 to Soviet production methods and operating conditions. Initially powered by two 900 hp Shvetsov M-62 radials (a Russian development of the M-25 which was a licence-built version of the Wright SGR-1820F powering the DC-2) and later by ASh-62 engines with various and increased ratings, the Russian version was first designated PS-84 but on 17 September, 1942, it was redesignated Lisunov Li-2. Production of the PS-84 began in 1940 in Moscow but was transferred to Tashkent when in 1941 the aircraft industry had to be relocated further

Soviet Air Force PS-84s with dorsal turrets.

242

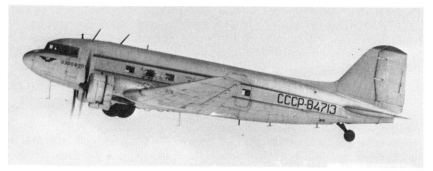

An Aeroflot Lisunov Li-2.

from the German forces. Over 2,000 PS-84/Li-2s were built from 1940 to 1945.

In service with Aeroflot and with the VVS (Voenno-vozdushnye sily, Military Air Forces) the PS-84/Li-2s were supplemented by 707 lend-lease C-47s which, like other military equipment similarly obtained, were never returned. Li-2s—including some armed with a 7·62-mm gun in a dorsal turret, as well as specialized versions such as the Li-2P passenger transport, the Li-2G cargo transport, the Li-2PG passenger/cargo transport, and the Li-2V for high-altitude operations which was fitted with RK-19 turbo-superchargers for its M-61IR engines—and C-47s continued in Soviet military and civil service until the early 1970s whilst others served the satellites. The air forces of over 85 other nations have flown—and many are still flying—Douglas C-47s and Lisunov Li-2s. Mention can be made of only four other air forces which flew C-47s under combat conditions: the French Armée de l'Air received its first C-47s during World War II and operated the type during the Indochinese and Algerian wars; the Royal Vietnamese Air Force flew C-47s and specialized EC-47s and AC-47s against communist forces until the fall of South Vietnam; the Dutch Koninklijke Luchtmacht operated C-47s in the East Indies during World War II and, later, against Indonesian insurgents; and the Greek Elliniki Vassiliki Aeroporia, which amongst other military DC-3s received in 1949 thirty rebuilt C-47s with special USAF serials (49-2612/49-2641), used its aircraft as makeshift bombers during the Greek civil war and as transports in Korea.

At the end of World War II over 200 prewar civil DC-3s were still in airline service or were soon returned to the airlines. In addition, thousands of surplus C-47s and C-53s were sold by the US Government. So urgent was the need for these aircraft that many were put into commercial service still with their military interiors, including the folding seats along the sides of the cabin. However, most ex-military aircraft were rapidly brought up to airline standard.

To supplement the large numbers of surplus aircraft, which in the communist bloc included many Lisunov Li-2s, and to make use of partially completed C-117 airframes, Douglas produced in Oklahoma City twenty-eight DC-3Ds (s/ns 42954/42981) for the civil market. These new transports were followed by twenty-one DC-3Cs produced for the commercial market by completely overhauling and partially rebuilding surplus C-47As and C-47Bs. The last of these (s/n 43154, OO-AWH; ex C-47A-5-DK, 42-92472, s/n 12276) was delivered to Sabena on 21 March, 1947, but crashed at London Airport Heathrow on 2 March, 1948. Efforts by Douglas to modernize its most successful aircraft led to the development of the Super DC-3 series but this failed to succeed with the airline industry.

While most DC-3s and surplus C-47s were used commercially with only a minimum of modifications—for example, even in passenger service the ex-C-47s often retained their double cargo doors—various companies attempted to improve their performance since more stringent certification standards had been imposed by the Federal Aviation Agency. In fact, the FAA considered withdrawal of the existing Approved Type Certificates for all versions of the DC-3 but the impracticality of such a decision was obvious and DC-3s went on flying safely even though they did not meet the new CAA standards. Two methods of improving the DC-3 performance without major and costly redesign are given as examples. One involved the installation of faster undercarriage retraction mechanism coupled with doors which completely faired over the wheels which, in all other DC-3s, when retracted were left partially exposed. The resultant drag reduction during the critical climb phase brought about appreciable gains in airfield performance. Another was the so-called 'Hi-Per DC-3' which was engineered at Miami by Pan American World Airways and Panagra and certificated in 1952. The 'Hi-Per DC-3', developed to improve performance at high-altitude airports, was obtained by installing a new powerplant package consisting of 1,450 hp Pratt & Whitney R-2000-D5 engines, new propellers, and improved exhaust, air intake and fire extinguishing equipment. However, neither of these modifications saw widespread use.

The open cargo doors of Papuan Airlines' VH-PNA reveal the military origin of this aircraft (ex C-47B-30-DK, 44-76771, which served with the RAAF as A65-99). (*Mervyn Prime*)

244

HC-AOP at Quito's Mariscal Sucre International Airport in February 1977. It has extended, square-tipped, wings and fairings which fully enclose the mainwheels. (*René J. Francillon*)

In postwar commercial passenger operations the DC-3s had first been assigned, particularly outside the United States, to relatively major short- and medium-haul routes. However, as more modern aeroplanes became available, the type was relegated to less important routes. Yet, in the early seventies, the world's airlines were still flying more DC-3s than any other type of aircraft (for example ICAO reported that on 31 December, 1971, its member states still had 1,470 DC-3s in service and that the fleet of Boeing 727s, which came in second place, then totalled 831 aircraft); but during 1975 there were only some 400 DC-3s in commercial service.

In addition to being operated by the airlines for passenger and cargo service, DC-3s have been and are still used as corporate transports and for aerial top dressing, geological survey, pest control and countless other tasks.

Lady Ann, owned by Morrison-Knudsen Company, was a typical example of a surplus C-47 converted for corporate use. It is seen at Boise Municipal Airport, Idaho. (*MK*)

245

Dakota IV (KJ839) fitted with Armstrong Siddeley Mamba propeller-turbines, landing at Northolt in September 1949. (*Flight International*)

Several attempts have been made to fit turbine engines to DC-3s. The first of these conversions was made in the United Kingdom and entailed the replacement of the Twin Wasp engines of the Dakota IV KJ839 (s/n 25623) with 1,425 shp Armstrong Siddeley ASMa.3 Mamba propeller-turbines (later replaced by 1,590 hp ASMa.6s). First flown on 27 August, 1949, the Mamba-Dakota was used as an engine test-bed until 1958 when the Twin Wasps were re-installed and the aircraft sold as G-APNX.

Three Dakota IVs were fitted with Rolls-Royce Dart propeller-turbines beginning with KJ829 (s/n 25613), an RAF aircraft which made its first Dart-powered flight on 15 March, 1950. In 1956 it was purchased by Rolls-

G-AMDB, one of the two Rolls-Royce Dart powered Dakotas of British European Airways. (*British Airways*)

Royce and was successively registered G-37-2 and G-AOXI. Whilst this Dart-Dakota was strictly used for experimental purposes, the other two aircraft (s/n 26106, G-ALXN, ex KJ934, and s/n 26432, G-AMDB, ex KJ993) were British European Airways aircraft which in 1951 were fitted with Rolls-Royce Darts by Field Aircraft Services to assist in the engine development programme for the BEA V.701 Viscounts. Besides being operated as engine test-beds and to gain experience with turbine operations and maintenance, these two aircraft were used for scheduled cargo service beginning on 15 August, 1951, when G-ALXN carried 1½ tons of freight from Northolt to Hanover.

During the late 1960s and early 1970s, Conroy Aircraft of Santa Barbara, California, proposed a number of schemes involving the fitting of surplus Dart 512s from ex-Continental Airlines Viscount 812s to low-time DC-3 airframes. One aircraft was test flown, and even demonstrated at the Salon de l'Aéronautique in Paris, but the projected modifications of a series of aircraft did not materialize. In 1977 TAMCO (Turbo-Airliner Manufacturing Company) proposed a major modification which would entail the fitting of either 1,535 shp Dart RDa.6s or 1,835 shp Dart RDa.7s to a modified and zero-timed DC-3 airframe with tricycle undercarriage, enlarged tail surfaces and longer, pressurized cabin accommodating 30 passengers. A prototype, named Turbo-Commuter, was certificated to FAR Part 298. However, at a price of $800,000, ten times the unit price of the first DSTs, it failed to gain acceptance. Ten years later, Aero Modification International marketed a similar scheme with 1,230 shp Pratt & Whitney PT6A-65Rs, five-blade propellers, and stretched fuselage. In 1951, an attempt was made in France to improve the DC-3's airfield performance by fitting one or two 362-lb (160-kg) thrust Turboméca Palas turbojets (one below the fuselage or one beneath each wing) but the scheme remained experimental.

Accommodation: Normal crew of three (pilot, co-pilot and radio-operator). Normal accommodation for 14 (DST), 21 to 28 (standard DC-3s) or 32 (maximum seating DC-3s) passengers or troops. Cargo version carried from 3,725 to 4,500 lb (1,690 to 2,040 kg) of freight or military supplies.

Powerplants used in civil and military DC-3s

Type	Maximum rating	Take-off rating	Aircraft versions
Wright Cyclone (9-cyl radial)			
SGR-1820-G2	850 hp at 5,800 ft (1,770 m)	1,000 hp	DST, DC-3
SGR-1820-G2E	—	1,000 hp	DST, DC-3
SGR-1820-G5	—	1,000 hp	First DST
SGR-1820-G102	—	1,100 hp	DST, DC-3
SGR-1820-G102A	900 hp at 6,700 ft (2,040 m)	1,100 hp	DST, DC-3
SGR-1820-G103A	—	1,100 hp	DC-3
SGR-1820-G202A	1,050 hp at 7,500 ft (2,285 m)	1,200 hp	DST, DC-3, DC-3B

Engine	Power at altitude	Power	Aircraft
R-1820-71	1,000 hp at 6,900 ft (2,105 m)	1,200 hp	C-49, C-49A, C-49B, C-49C, C-49D, C-49F, C-49J, C-49K, C-84, R4D-2
R-1820-79	—	1,100 hp	C-49E, C-50C, C-50D
R-1820-81	—	1,100 hp	C-50B
R-1820-83	900 hp at 6,700 ft (2,040 m)	1,100 hp	C-51
R-1820-85	900 hp at 6,700 ft (2,040 m)	1,100 hp	C-50, C-50A
R-1820-97	1,000 hp at 25,000 ft (7,620 m)	1,200 hp	C-49G, C-49H
Pratt & Whitney Twin Wasp			
(14-cyl radial)			
Twin Wasp SC-G	900 hp at 11,000 ft (3,355 m)	1,050 hp	DST-A, DC-3A
Twin Wasp SC3-G	900 hp at 12,000 ft (3,660 m)	1,050 hp	DST-A, DC-3A
Twin Wasp S1C-G	1,050 hp at 7,500 ft (2,285 m)	1,200 hp	DST-A, DC-3A
Twin Wasp S1C3G	1,050 hp at 7,500 ft (2,285 m)	1,200 hp	DC-3A, DC-3C, DC-3D
Twin Wasp S4C4-G	900 hp at 15,400 ft (4,695 m)	1,200 hp	DST-A, DC-3A
R-1830-21	1,050 hp at 6,500 ft (1,980 m)	1,200 hp	C-41A
R-1830-51	1,050 hp at 7,500 ft (2,285 m)	1,200 hp	C-48A, C-48B, C-48C, C-52, C-52A, C-52B, C-52C
R-1830-82	1,050 hp at 7,500 ft (2,285 m)	1,200 hp	C-48
R-1830-90C	1,000 hp at 14,500 ft (4,420 m)	1,200 hp	C-47B, TC-47B, R4D-6, R4D-7, C-117A
R-1830-90D	1,100 hp at 6,100 ft (1,860 m)	1,200 hp	C-47B, TC-47B, XC-47C, C-47D, C-117B, R4D-6, R4D-7
R-1830-92	1,050 hp at 7,500 ft (2,285 m)	1,200 hp	C-47, C-47A, C-53, XC-53A, C-53B, C-53C, C-53D, C-68, R4D-1, R4D-3, R4D-4, R4D-5
R-2000-4	1,100 hp at 7,000 ft (2,135 m)	1,290 hp	C-47E
R-2000-D5	1,200 hp at 6,400 ft (1,950 m)	1,450 hp	Hi-Per DC-3
Armstrong Siddeley			
(axial-flow			
propeller-turbine)			
Mamba ASMa.3	—	1,425 shp	Mamba-Dakota
Mamba ASMa.6	—	1,590 shp	Mamba-Dakota
Rolls-Royce			
(centrifugal-flow			
propeller-turbine)			
Dart 504	—	1,540 shp	Dart-Dakota
Dart 505	—	1,540 shp	Dart-Dakota
Dart 510	—	1,640 shp	Dart-Dakota
Dart 525	—	1,990 shp	Conroy modification
Mitsubishi Kinsei			
(14-cyl radial)			
Kinsei 43	990 hp at 9,185 ft (2,800 m)	1,000 hp	L2D2
Kinsei 51	1,200 hp at 9,845 ft (3,000 m)	1,300 hp	L2D3, L2D3-1, L2D4, L2D4-1
Kinsei 53	1,200 hp at 9,845 ft (3,000 m)	1,300 hp	L2D3a, L2D3-1a
Kinsei 62	1,180 hp at 19,030 ft (5,800 m)	1,560 hp	L2D5
Shvetsov			
(9-cyl radial)			
M-62	—	900 hp	PS-84, Li-2
ASh-62	—	1,200 hp	Li-2

	DST	DC-3A	DC-3C	C-47A-DL	C-47B-DK	C-49K-DO	C-117A-DK	Li-2
	(SGR-1802–G2)	(S1C3-G)	(R-1830-92)	(R-1830-92)	(R-1830-90C)	(R-1820-71)	(R-1830-90C)	(M-62)
Span, ft in	95 0	95 0	95 0	95 6	95 6	95 0	95 0	94 10 3/16
(m)	(28·96)	(28·96)	(28·96)	(29·11)	(29·11)	(28·96)	(28·96)	(28·81)
Length, ft in	64 5½	64 5½	64 5	63 9	63 9	64 6	64 6	64 5⅝
(m)	(19·65)	(19·65)	(19·65)	(19·43)	(19·43)	(19·66)	(19·66)	(19·65)
Height, ft in	16 3⅝	16 11⅛	16 11	17 0	17 0	17 0	16 8	—
(m)	(4·97)	(5·16)	(5·16)	(5·18)	(5·18)	(5·18)	(5·08)	—
Wing area, sq ft	987	987	987	987	987	987	987	983
(sq m)	(91·695)	(91·695)	(91·695)	(91·695)	(91·695)	(91·695)	(91·695)	(91·330)
Empty weight, lb	16,060	16,865	18,300	17,865	18,135	16,295	17,840	16,976
(kg)	(7,285)	(7,650)	(8,301)	(8,103)	(8,226)	(7,391)	(8,092)	(7,700)
Loaded weight, lb	24,000	25,200	25,200	26,000	26,000	24,400	26,000	23,589
(kg)	(10,886)	(11,431)	(11,431)	(11,793)	(11,793)	(11,068)	(11,793)	(10,700)
Maximum weight, lb	—	—	28,000	31,000	31,000	29,000	30,000	24,868
(kg)	—	—	(12,701)	(14,061)	(14,061)	(13,154)	(13,608)	(11,280)
Wing loading, lb/sq ft	24·3	25·5	25·5	26·3	26·3	24·7	26·3	24·0
(kg/sq m)	(118·7)	(124·7)	(124·7)	(128·6)	(128·6)	(120·7)	(128·6)	(117·2)
Power loading, lb/hp	12·0	10·5	10·5	10·8	10·8	10·2	10·8	13·1
(kg/hp)	(5·4)	(4·8)	(4·8)	(4·9)	(4·9)	(4·6)	(4·9)	(5·9)
Maximum speed, mph at ft	212/6,800	230/8,500	237/8,800	230/8,800	224/10,000	218/5,500	230/12,500	174
(km/h at m)	(341/2,075)	(370/2,590)	(381/2,680)	(370/2,680)	(360/3,050)	(351/1,675)	(370/3,810)	(280)
Cruising speed, mph	192	207	170	160	160	156	160	137
(km/h)	(309)	(333)	(274)	(257)	(257)	(251)	(257)	(220)
Climb rate, ft/min or time	850/1	1,130/1	—	10,000/9·6	10,000/9·5	10,000-10·0	10,000/9·4	—
(m/min or time)	(259/1)	(344/1)	—	(3,050/9·6)	(3,050/9·5)	(3,050/10·0)	(2,050/9·4)	—
Service ceiling, ft	20,800	23,200	—	24,000	26,400	22,750	26,400	18,375
(m)	(6,340)	(7,070)	—	(7315)	(8,045)	(6,935)	(8,045)	(5,600)
Normal range, miles	2,125	2,125	1,025	1,600	1,600	1,650	1,600	—
(km)	(3,420)	(3,420)	(1,650)	(2,575)	(2,575)	(2,655)	(2,575)	—
Maximum range, miles	—	—	—	3,800	3,600	1,800	3,600	—
(km)	—	—	—	(6,115)	(5,795)	(2,895)	(5,795)	—

Douglas built a total of 10,654 DC-3s and derivatives between 1935 and 1947. This total was broken down as follows:

	Santa Monica	Long Beach	Oklahoma City	Total by models	Total by categories
Prewar civil aircraft					430
DST	21	—	—	21	
DST-A	19	—	—	19	
DC-3	266	—	—	266	
DC-3A	114	—	—	114	
DC-3B	10	—	—	10	
Civil aircraft impressed before delivery					149
C-48	1	—	—	1	
C-48A	3	—	—	3	
C-48C	7	—	—	7	
C-49	6	—	—	6	
C-49A	1	—	—	1	
C-49B	3	—	—	3	
C-49C	2	—	—	2	
C-49D	6	—	—	6	
C-49J	34	—	—	34	
C-49K	23	—	—	23	
C-50	4	—	—	4	
C-50A	2	—	—	2	
C-50B	3	—	—	3	
C-50C	1	—	—	1	
C-50D	4	—	—	4	
C-51	1	—	—	1	
C-52	1	—	—	1	
C-52A	1	—	—	1	
C-52B	2	—	—	2	
C-52C	1	—	—	1	
C-53C	17	—	—	17	
C-68	2	—	—	2	
Undesignated	12	—	—	12	
R4D-2	2	—	—	2	
R4D-4	10	—	—	10	
Original military contracts					10,047
C-41A	1	—	—	1	
C-47	—	965	—	965	
C-47A	—	2,954	2,299	5,253	
C-47B	—	300	2,932	3,232	
TC-47B	—	—	133	133	
C-53	221	—	—	221	
C-53D	159	—	—	159	
C-47	—	—	17	17	
R4D-1	—	66	—	66	
Postwar civil aircraft					28
DC-3D	—	—	28	28	
	960	4,285	5,409		10,654

250

ZK-CQA operated by James Aviation Ltd for aerial top-dressing in New Zealand. During minimum turnround operations, such as that illustrated, the engines were kept running while chemical was loaded through a roof hatch. (*H. L. James*)

In addition, licensed-production in Japan totalled 485 including 414 L2Ds built by Showa Hikoki KK between 1941 and 1945, and 71 L2Ds built by Nakajima Hikoki KK between 1940 and 1942, but excluding two L2D-1s assembled by Showa from parts and components supplied by Douglas and already included among the 114 Santa Monica built DC-3As.

Licensed-production in the USSR was undertaken in 1939–40 and continued until at least 1945. Some 2,000 PS-84/Li-2s were built in Moscow and Tashkent.

Douglas DF

During the 1930s Pan American Airways and its subsidiaries used a large fleet of flying-boats and amphibians including Consolidated Commodores, Douglas Dolphins, Fairchild 91s, and Sikorsky S-38s, S-40s, S-41s, S-42s and S-43s. The airline also sponsored the development of two large long-range flying-boats, the Martin M-130 and Boeing 314 which entered service in November 1935 and May 1939 respectively.

Douglas, having recently been successful in selling three of its products to Pan American—the airline had acquired the Delta 1B and two Dolphins for two subsidiaries and had become the second airline to acquire DC-2s—, the company was hoping to attract the airline's interest in its new DF (Douglas Flying-boat) twin-engined flying-boat. Development of the DF was begun in 1935 and based to a large extent on experience gained with the design of the XP3D-2. The DF was intended as a replacement for Pan American's S-38s, S-41s and Commodores and, offering comparable capacity but less range than its Martin M-130, to complement the airline's newest four-engined flying-boats.

The DF was an all-metal high-wing monoplane with fabric-covered control surfaces. Smooth sheet metal skin was used except on the forward two-thirds of the wing which had corrugated skin. The hull was of the two-

The first DF flying-boat, photographed at Santa Monica on 10 September, 1936. (*MDC*)

step type and the single-step stabilizing floats were hydraulically-retracted inward and partially recessed into the underside of the wing. Power was supplied by two nine-cylinder 1,000 hp Wright SGR-1820G-2s driving three-blade constant-speed propellers. Accommodation was for a maximum of 32 passengers in four 8-seat compartments and for night service the normal seating could be replaced by 16 berths. The crew of four consisted of pilot, co-pilot, navigator and stewardess. The aircraft was equipped with galleys, two lavatories, and an aft cargo compartment.

Completed in September 1936, the first DF was successfully tested. However, as Pan American was not interested in operating a twin-engined flying-boat on relatively long overwater flights, Douglas found itself without a domestic customer for the prototype and the three additional DFs it had under construction. Fortunately, the company obtained

DF-151 under evaluation in Japan. (*Komori*)

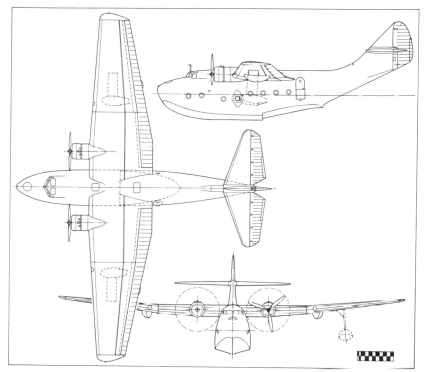

government authorization to sell them to any interested foreign customer.

Two of the Douglas flying-boats, which had been completed to Specification DF-151 standards, were shipped to Japan in 1936–37. Officially, as J-ANES and J-ANET, they were for Dai Nippon Koku KK (Greater Japan Air Lines). In fact, they were procured for evaluation by the Japanese Navy and designated HXD-1 and HXD-2, Navy Experimental Type D flying-boat. One of the two aircraft was quickly dismantled by Kawanishi to obtain engineering data later used in the design of its four-engined H8K flying-boat. The other aircraft was operated on survey flights, and on 10 August, 1938, during one of these, it crashed at sea.

The last two aircraft (Specification DF-195) were purchased by the Soviet Government and in 1937 were flown to the USSR via Alaska and across the Bering Sea. At least one, registered SSSR-N-205, was operated by Aeroflot on the Leningrad–Sevastopol route until about 1940.

Span 95 ft (28·96 m); length 69 ft 10 $\frac{9}{16}$ in (21·3 m); height 24 ft 6$\frac{1}{4}$ in (7·47 m); wing area 1,295 sq ft (120·31 sq m). Empty weight 17,315 lb (7,854 kg); loaded weight 28,500 lb (12,927 kg); wing loading 22 lb/sq ft (107·4 kg/sq m); power loading 14·25 lb/hp (6·5 kg/hp). Maximum speed 178 mph (286 km/h) at 6,800 ft (2,075 m); cruising speed 160 mph (257 km/h); initial rate of climb 800 ft/min (243 m/min); service ceiling 13,900 ft (4,235 m); range with 32 passengers 1,500 miles (2,415 km); range with 12 passengers 3,300 miles (5,310 km).

SBD-5s of Marine Scouting Squadron Three (VMS-3) on patrol off Bourne Field, St Thomas, Virgin Islands, in May 1944. (*USMC*)

Douglas SBD and A-24 Dauntless

On 28 November, 1936, a change to Contract 50517—which itself covered the production of 54 Northrop BT-1s—was approved by the US Navy. Under its terms Northrop was authorized to proceed with the modification of a BT-1 (s/n 330, BuNo 0627) to incorporate a fully-retractable main undercarriage folding laterally into flush wing wells. So modified the aircraft was redesignated XBT-2 and was the immediate forerunner of the well-known Dauntless two-seat carrier-borne dive-bomber series.

Completed and test flown on 22 April, 1938, the XBT-2 was initially powered by the same 825 hp Pratt & Whitney R-1535-94 as the production BT-1s. However, following an unfortunate wheels-up landing accident, Douglas decided, under authority of a new contract change dated 21 June, 1938, to install the 1,000 hp Wright R-1820-G133 with a three-blade constant-speed propeller. Other modifications incorporated at the same time included catapult hooks. In this form the aircraft was delivered on 24 August, 1938, to Anacostia for its Final Demonstration and Trials. In spite of minor problems, Navy personnel were enthusiastic as the XBT-2 reached a maximum speed of 265·5 mph (429 km/h) versus a guaranteed top speed of 258 mph (415 km/h) and a top speed of 223 mph (359 km/h) for the standard BT-1s.

Following these tests, the XBT-2 was delivered to the Langley Memorial Aeronautical Institute in February 1939 for full-scale wind-tunnel tests designed to investigate means of further increasing maximum speed and to improve stall characteristics. As a result NACA recommended that numerous wing and fuselage changes be made. Most of these changes, such as the fairing out of the neck-in section of the fuselage aft of the engine section—necessary because of the larger powerplant—and general improvement of exterior finish, were incorporated in the production design. However, the perforated dive-flaps—which NACA had suggested be removed, a recommendation reversing the one they had made for the BT-1—were retained at the cost of a slight loss in top speed, to eliminate tail buffeting with flaps extended.

One of the items included in the recommended changes was improvement in stability and control. These modifications stemmed from more stringent naval requirements. This improvement programme resulted in the manufacture and testing of twenty-one different sets of tail surface combinations and more than twelve lateral control surface configurations. Improvements in the aircraft's flying qualities were accomplished by changing control surface area, plan form and chord, leading-edge elevator balance, balance tab travel ratio, control surface gap and tail cone design and by introducing a dorsal fin.

To maintain aileron control after a stall, fixed leading-edge slots were also investigated and adopted. The results of these numerous modifications were rewarding and the XBT-2 was now representative of the production model which had been ordered on 8 April, 1939.

The thirty-six aircraft covered by the initial contract, No.65969, were designated SBD-1, reflecting both the change in mission to scout-bombing and the change in manufacturer's name, since in late 1937 the Northrop Corporation had given place to the El Segundo plant of the Douglas Aircraft Company. Eventually the number of aircraft covered by this contract was increased to 144 and included both SBD-1s and SBD-2s.

The first production SBD-1 (s/n 549, BuNo 1596), completed in April 1940 and first flown on 1 May, was delivered to the Navy on 6 September, 1940. This aircraft was generally identical to the XBT-2 in its final form but

The XBT-2 at Mines Field, Los Angeles, on 23 August, 1938.
(*US National Archives*)

The second SBD-1 (BuNo 1597) assigned to the Commanding Officer of VMB-2. (*USAF*)

incorporated a number of modifications including the installation of a 1,000 hp Wright R-1820-32, the addition in the centre section of two auxiliary 15-US gallon (56·8-litre) fuel tanks bringing total capacity to 210 US gallons (795 litres), and a second 0·50-in machine-gun in the engine cowling. This first aircraft was immediately followed by fifty-six identical aircraft—the last being delivered on 18 December, 1940—and by eighty-seven SBD-2s, the first of which was also delivered on 18 December. From then on the Dauntless, as the aircraft had been named, remained in production until 22 July, 1944, when the last SBD-6 (s/n 6563, BuNo 55049) was completed.

SBD-1: A total of fifty-seven SBD-1s (BuNos 1596 to 1631 and 1735 to 1755) were delivered in 1940 for use by the US Marine Corps. One 1,000 hp Wright R-1820-32 nine-cylinder air-cooled radial driving a constant-speed propeller. Two forward-firing 0·50-in machine-guns in the engine cowling and one flexible rearward-firing 0·30-in machine-gun. Total internal fuel capacity: 210 US gallons (795 litres). A swinging bomb cradle with a maximum capacity of 1,000 lb (454 kg) was located beneath the fuselage and a fixed rack for one 100 lb (45 kg) bomb was mounted under each outer wing section.

SBD-1P: Designation applying to eight SBD-1s modified after delivery to mount camera equipment.

SBD-2: Generally similar to the SBD-1s, eighty-seven SBD-2s (BuNos 2102 to 2188) were produced between December 1940 and May 1941 for Navy units. The auxiliary fuel tanks in the centre section were replaced by a 65-US gallon (246-litre) tank in each outer wing panel bringing total fuel capacity to 310 US gallons (1,173 litres); later on, some SBD-2s were retrofitted with self-sealing tanks reducing total capacity to 260 US gallons (984 litres). Armament was reduced by removal of one of the two 0·50-in machine-guns in the engine cowling. The second SBD-2 crashed during company acceptance tests and was replaced by an SBD-3 (s/n 1003).

SBD-2P: Camera-equipped SBD-2s modified after delivery (at least fifteen aircraft).

256

SBD-3: First ordered in September 1940, the SBD-3 was the first fully combat-worthy version of the Dauntless and a total of 585 SBD-3s (BuNo 2109—replacement aircraft for the eighth SBD-2 which had crashed during company's tests; the original BuNo was transferred to the replacement SBD-3 accepted by the US Navy—and BuNos 4518 to 4691, 03185 to 03384, and 06492 to 06701) were built under three different contracts. The SBD-3 differed from the SBD-2 in being powered by a 1,000 hp Wright R-1820-52, in the use of alclad alloy in lieu of dural, in the removal of flotation gear, and in having the same forward-firing armament as the SBD-1. Later, the rearward-firing armament was increased by the installation of twin belt-fed 0·30-in machine-guns in place of the earlier version's single drum-fed 0·30-in weapon. The self-sealing tanks, retrofitted on the SBD-2, were standard on the SBD-3. Armour protection was also introduced on this version. The first SBD-3 (s/n 751, BuNo 4518) was delivered on 18 March, 1941.

SBD-3A: Contractual designation applied to a version of the SBD-3, the A-24, delivered to the USAAF but ordered under Navy contract. *See* A-24-DE.

SBD-3P: Designation applied to some forty-seven camera-equipped SBD-3s.

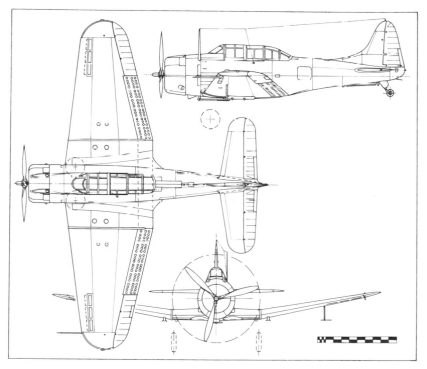

Douglas SBD-6 Dauntless

257

SBD-4: Due to the numerous changes introduced on the SBD-3, demands on the aircraft's 12-volt electrical system became excessive. Consequently, on the next version a 24-volt electrical system was installed and an electrical pump replaced the hand-operated fuel booster pump. The 1,000 hp R-1820-52 engine was retained but a new Hydromatic constant-speed propeller was installed. A total of 780 SBD-4s (BuNos 06702 to 06991 and 10317 to 10806) were built, the first (s/n 1547) being delivered on 18 October, 1942.

SBD-4A: Contractual designation applying to the A-24A-DEs ordered for the USAAF under US Navy contract.

SBD-4P: Designation applied to some sixteen SBD-4s fitted with camera equipment after delivery.

SBD-5: Main production version, the SBD-5 had a 1,200 hp Wright R-1820-60 enclosed in a redesigned cowling without the air intake on its upper lip, a feature identifying all previous versions. The increased power enabled the offensive load to be increased to a maximum of 2,250 lb (1,021 kg)—one 1,600 lb (726 kg) bomb under the fuselage and two 325 lb (147·5 kg) bombs under wings. The twin rearward-firing machine-guns were no longer a service change but installed at manufacture. All other features were identical to those of the SBD-4. First SBD-5 delivery took place on 21 February, 1943, (s/n 2236, BuNo 10807) and a total of 2,964 aircraft were built (BuNos 10807 to 11066, 28059 to 28829, 28831 to 29213, 35922 to 36421, 36433 to 36932, and 54050 to 54599).

SBD-5A: Contractual designation applied to sixty aircraft intended for the USAAF. Initially these aircraft were assigned USAAF serial numbers (42-60882 to 42-60941) and designated A-24B-DEs. Eventually they were accepted as SBD-5As (BuNos 09693 to 09752) beginning on 29 April, 1943, and operated by the Marine Corps. These aircraft differed from the standard SBD-5s in having a pneumatic tailwheel and in being fitted with Army equipment and instruments. No arrester hook was fitted to these land-based aircraft.

XSBD-6: In July 1943 one aircraft (s/n 4177, BuNo 28830), built in a batch of SBD-5s at the El Segundo plant, was singled out to serve as prototype for a modernized and more powerful version. A Wright R-1820-66 delivering 1,350 hp for take-off and rated at 1,200 hp at 5,500 ft (1,675 m) was installed and the metal fuel tanks with self-sealing liner were replaced by non-metallic self-sealing tanks with a total capacity of 284 US gallons (1,075 litres). The aircraft was accepted by the US Navy on 8 February, 1944.

SBD-6: Before accepting the XSBD-6, the Navy amended an existing contract for 3,000 SBD-5s to include instead 1,549 SBD-5s (included in SBD-5 numbers given above), the XSBD-6 and 1,450 SBD-6s. Eventually 1,000 SBD-6s were cancelled from this contract in February 1944 and only 450 production SBD-6s (BuNos 54600 to 55049) were delivered by the El Segundo plant between March and July 1944. These were virtually identical to the XSBD-6 and were fitted with ASV radar as had been many SBD-5s.

SBD-6A: Designation applied to a single aircraft (s/n 4561, BuNo 35922) which was originally intended to serve as prototype for a USAAF version equivalent to the SBD-6. The project was not realized and the aircraft was delivered as an SBD-5 against existing contract.

A-24-DE: Impressed with the results initially obtained by German dive-bombers during operations in Europe, the Army Air Corps obtained the loan of a number of Marine Corps SBD-1s and in July 1940 had them tested by the 24th Bombardment Squadron. After successful evaluation, the War Department approved on 27 September, 1940, the acquisition of seventy-eight A-24-DEs (serials 41-15746 to 41-15823); the order was placed by means of a Navy contract as the US Navy had jurisdiction over the El Segundo plant. The A-24-DE was essentially similar to the Navy's SBD-3 but featured Army instrumentation and radio equipment. A pneumatic tyre was fitted to the tailwheel instead of the naval aircraft's solid rubber tyre. The first aircraft was delivered on 17 June, 1941, (s/n 802, serial 41-15746) and until completion of this contract the A-24-DEs and SBD-3s came alternatively from the assembly lines at the El Segundo plant. Later, ninety similar aircraft—designated SBD-3As for contract purposes—were diverted from Navy contracts and received USAAF serials 42-6682 to 42-6771 and were delivered to the Army between July and October 1942.

The RA-24A-DE showing installation of recording equipment in fairings above the cowling and beneath the fuselage, and of a special antenna beneath the starboard wing. (*USAF*)

A-24A-DE: Counterpart of the Navy SBD-4s, the A-24A-DEs were built at El Segundo as SBD-4As as they were diverted from USN contracts. Upon delivery they received USAAF serials 42-6772 to 42-6831 and 42-60772 to 42-60881; acceptance took place between October 1942 and March 1943. Basically, the A-24A-DEs incorporated the changes introduced on the A-24-DEs (tailwheel tyre, instrumentation, etc.) in SBD-4 airframes. One aircraft (s/n 1538, serial 42-6783) was modified at Wright Field as a radio-controlled drone and designated RA-24A-DE; in 1948, when the A designation category was dropped by the USAF, it was redesignated QF-24A-DE and given a new serial number, 48–044. At the same time, all surviving A-24A-DEs became known as F-24A-DEs in the F for fighter designation category.

A-24B-DE: Designation applied to sixty aircraft (42-60882 to 42-60941) ordered for the USAAF under Navy contract but delivered to the Marine Corps (see SBD-5A).

A-24B-DT: Basically similar to the Navy SBD-5s, 1,200 A-24B-DTs were ordered directly by the USAAF (Contract AC-28716 dated 12 November, 1942) and were the only Dauntlesses built in the Tulsa plant. A total of 615 A-24B-DTs (585 of the 1,200 being cancelled) were built and received USAAF serials 42-54285 to 42-54899. Like the SBD-5s they were powered by the 1,200 hp Wright R-1820-60 whereas both A-24-DEs and A-24A-DEs used the 1,000 hp R-1820-52. In 1948 the few remaining aircraft of this variant became F-24B-DTs and one of these used as a drone control aircraft in connection with the tests of the QF-24A-DE, was redesignated DF-24B-DT and given a new serial number, 48-045.

Dauntless D.B. Mk.I: Designation given to nine SBD-5s delivered to the United Kingdom for tests. British serial numbers and corresponding BuNos were: JS997 and JS998 (ex-BuNos 36022 and 36023), JS999 (ex 36456), and JT923 to JT928 (ex 54191 to 54196).

The first unit to take delivery of its Dauntlesses was Marine Bomber Squadron Two (VMB-2, later VMSB-232) in San Diego, which acquired their SBD-1s in late 1940. Within a year, in time to face the Japanese onslaught, four more squadrons—VMB-1 (VMSB-132) of the Marine Corps, VS-6 and VB-6 aboard the USS *Enterprise* and VB-2 aboard the USS *Lexington*—were flying SBD-1s and SBD-2s. On the first day of the war the Dauntless got its baptism of fire as a number of SBD-2s were surprised by Japanese aircraft during a flight between the USS *Enterprise* and Pearl Harbor while SBD-1s of VMSB-232 were caught on the ground at Ewa, Hawaii. The losses sustained on 7 December, 1941, were promptly avenged

SBD-3 landing aboard the USS *Charger* (CVE-30); the tail hook has already engaged the arresting wire but the wheels are still off the deck.
(*US National Archives*)

VMSB-231's SBD-6 en route to bomb Vunakanau Airfield at Rabaul on 22 April, 1944. The aircraft is fitted with radar beneath its port wing. (*USMC*)

when Dauntlesses operating from the USS *Enterprise* contributed to the sinking of the first Japanese submarine. They also played an active role in raids against Japanese bases and shipping in the Gilbert and Marshall Islands during February 1942 and at Marcus and Wake Islands during the following month.

From then on, in spite of a shortage of aircraft which necessitated the retention of veteran SBDs in the Pacific whenever a carrier was sent to the United States, they were part of all major operations of the Fleet. After distinguishing themselves during the Battle of the Coral Sea, the SBDs obtained their most notorious success during the action in and around Midway in early June 1942 when, for the loss of 40 out of 128 taking part in this battle, they sank the Japanese aircraft carriers *Akagi, Kaga, Soryu* and *Hiryu*. Shortly after they were again in the thick of the action when they took part first in the opening strikes in support of the Marines landing on Guadalcanal and then, primarily flown by Marine squadrons, operated from Henderson Field during the six-month battle for that island.

As the war went on the SBDs equipped no less than twenty Marine squadrons and were retained until late 1944 as the main type of carrier-borne dive-bomber of the US Navy, which used the aircraft not only in the Pacific but also during the Allied landings in North Africa and in the Battle of the Atlantic. The Navy had planned to replace the SBDs with the newer Curtiss SB2C Helldiver but its teething troubles, combined with the SBDs' intrinsic qualities of reliability and toughness and their ability to operate from the deck of the smaller escort carriers, led to their retention until the end of the war. Shortly after the SBDs became surplus to Navy requirements.

With the USAAF the land-based versions of the Dauntless, the A-24 series, did not match the record of achievements of the carrier-borne versions. The first operational A-24 unit was the 27th Bombardment Group which was being shipped to the Philippines when the war broke out. Operating in the Netherlands East Indies and later in New Guinea, where it was joined by the similarly-equipped 8th Bombardment Group, this unit suffered heavy losses in the face of the then victorious Japanese forces. Nothing was basically wrong with their A-24-DEs but, whereas the Navy always tried to provide the SBDs with adequate fighter escort and had pilots highly trained in dive-bombing operations, the USAAF often had to send their A-24s without escort and in the hands of pilots trained only in level and glide bombing operations. Due to the disappointing results obtained by the 8th and 27th Bombardment Groups and their A-24-DEs, tentatively named Banshee by the Army, the aircraft never became popular with USAAF crews and most A-24A-DEs and A-24B-DTs were retained in the United States for training and other ancillary duties. However, in late 1943 the 531st Fighter-Bomber Squadron operated their A-24B-DTs briefly but successfully from bases in the Makin Islands. No attempt was made by the USAAF to deploy A-24s to the CBI, ETO or MTO theatres. Yet, in spite of their poor showing during the war, a number of A-24s, or F-24s as they had been redesignated, were still in the USAF inventory some two and a half years after the organization of that Service.

In addition to being operated primarily by USN, USMC and USAAF units, the Dauntless served with the air forces of four nations. First nation to receive it was the United Kingdom which obtained nine SBD-5s (JS997 to JS999 and JT923 to JT928) for RAF and Fleet Air Arm tests and evaluation, but by the mid-war years British requirements had changed and neither Service adopted them for squadron use.

New Zealand obtained on loan from the US Marine Corps eighteen SBD-3s (serials NZ5001 to NZ5018, the first six of which initially bore the serials NZ205 to NZ210), twenty-seven SBD-4s (NZ5019 to NZ5045) and twenty-three SBD-5s (NZ5046 to NZ5068). The first SBD-3s were taken on charge on 29 July, 1943, and two days later were assigned to No.25 Squadron upon its formation at Seagrove, near Auckland. After training

NZ5049, one of twenty-three SBD-5s delivered to the RNZAF, in service with No.25 Squadron in the spring of 1944. (*RNZAF*)

SBD-5 of Flotille 3F about to land on the French carrier *Arromanches*. (*ECPA*)

with SBD-3s and SBD-4s in New Zealand and Espiritu Santo Island in the New Hebrides, No.25 Squadron re-equipped with SBD-5s and on 22–23 March, 1944, the unit flew to Piva on Bougainville Island in the Solomons. The squadron's first strike was flown on 24 March but No.25 Squadron remained operational for only eight weeks. At that time their seventeen serviceable SBD-5s were returned to the US Marine Corps and No.25 Squadron was disbanded.

Shortly after the RNZAF had received its first SBD-3s a number of A-24B-DTs were handed over to France to equip units of the Armée de l'Air. Initially assigned in small numbers to existing fighter units to serve as advanced trainers and squadron hacks, A-24B-DTs were also operated by the École de Chasse (Fighter School) at Meknès in Morocco. Other aircraft were delivered to an escadrille of Groupe de Bombardement I/17 (GB I/17 *Picardie*) for use in the desert police role from a base at Riyak then in Syria More important was the use of A-24B-DTs made by GB I/18 *Vendée* which, between September 1944 and VE-Day, flew their Dauntlesses in support of French and American ground forces operating against German strongholds along the Atlantic coast of France and in the French Alps. After VE-Day GBI/18 was disbanded and its aircraft were handed over to the Fighter School in Meknès, the Gunnery School at Cazaux and a desert police escadrille in Morocco. The last of these was finally grounded in 1953.

Delivery of additional Dauntlesses to equip units of the French Aéronautique Navale had been planned to take place in time for them to participate in landing operations in Southern France. However, delays occurred and the two SBD-5 equipped units—initially designated Flotilles 3B and 4B but soon redesignated 3FB and 4FB—did not receive their aircraft until autumn 1944. After training at Agadir in Morocco, these two flotillas moved to Cognac, in Southwestern France, from where the first combat sorties against German targets on the Pointe de Grave took place on 9 December, 1944. Providing air support to Allied ground forces operating along the Atlantic coast of France, the two units flew their last combat sorties on 30 April, 1945. At the end of the war the surviving SBD-5s were assigned to Flotille 4F which served aboard the escort carrier *Dixmude* (ex-HMS *Bitter*) and to a training unit. In 1947–48, operating both from aboard the *Dixmude* and from Haiphong airfield, the SBD-5s of Flotille 4F were flown in support of French troops operating against Viet-Minh forces in Indo-China. In this role they were replaced in November 1948 by SBD-5s from Flotille 3F which was based aboard the light carrier *Arromanches* (ex-HMS *Colossus*). By that time the aircraft were war-weary and had to be brought back to France, to be retired in July 1949.

Mexico, unlike the United Kingdom and other major US Allies, could not afford to be difficult with regard to aircraft selection. Thus, beginning in 1944, a number of A-24B-DTs was operated by the Fuerza Aérea Mexicana on anti-submarine patrols in the Caribbean. Later these aircraft were used as trainers and for border patrol until retired in 1959.

Reliable, strong and capable of surviving heavy battle damage, the Dauntless was one of the best aircraft produced by the Douglas Aircraft Company. The role it played during the first two years of the war in the Pacific, and in particular the remarkable success of its operations during the Battle of Midway, have earned it a commendable place in history.

XBT-2

Span 41 ft 6 in (12·65 m); length 31 ft 9 in (9·68 m); height 12 ft 10 in (3·91 m); wing area 320 sq ft (29·729 sq m). Empty weight 5,037 lb (2,285 kg); loaded weight 7,018 lb (3,183 kg); maximum weight 7,560 lb (3,429 kg); wing loading 21·9 lb/sq ft (107·1 kg/sq m); power loading 8·5 lb/hp (3·9 kg/hp). Maximum speed 265·5 mph (427 km/h) at 16,000 ft (4,875 m); cruising speed 155 mph (249 km/h); initial rate of climb 1,450 ft/ min (442 m/min); service ceiling 31,000 ft (9,175 m); normal range 604 miles (972 km); maximum range 1,458 miles (2,345 km).

SBD-2

Span 41 ft 6⅜ in (12·66 m); length 32 ft 1¼ in (9·79 m); height 13 ft 7 in (4·14 m); wing area 325 sq ft (30·194 sq m). Empty weight 5,652 lb (2,564 kg); loaded weight 8,643 lb (3,920 kg); maximum weight 10,360 lb (4,699 kg); wing loading 26·6 lb/sq ft (129·8 kg/sq m); power loading 8·6 lb/hp (3·9 kg/hp). Maximum speed 256 mph (412 km/h) at 16,000 ft (4,875 m); cruising speed 148 mph (238 km/h); initial rate of climb 1,080 ft/min (329 m/min); service ceiling 27,260 ft (8,310 m); normal range 1,225 miles (1,970 km); maximum range 1,370 miles (2,205 km).

SBD-5

Dimensions as SBD-2 except length 33 ft 1¼ in (10·09 m). Empty weight 6,404 lb (2,905 kg); loaded weight 9,359 lb (4,245 kg); maximum weight 10,700 lb (4,853 kg); wing loading 28·8 lb/sq ft (140·6 kg/sq m); power loading 7·8 lb/hp (3·5 kg/hp). Maximum speed 255 mph (410 km/h) at 14,000 ft (4,265 m); cruising speed 185 mph (298 km/h); initial rate of climb 1,700 ft/min (518 m/min); service ceiling 25,530 ft (7,780 m); normal range 1,115 miles (1,795 km); maximum range 1,565 miles (2,520 km).

SBD-6

Dimensions as SBD-5. Empty weight 6,554 lb (2,973 kg); loaded weight 9,465 lb (4,293 kg); maximum weight 10,882 lb (4,936 kg); wing loading 29·1 lb/sq ft (142·2 kg/sq m); power loading 7 lb/hp (3·2 kg/hp). Maximum speed 262 mph (422 km/h) at 18,500 ft (5,640 m); cruising speed 143 mph (230 km/h); initial rate of climb 1,710 ft/min (521 m/min); service ceiling 28,600 ft (8,715 m); normal range 1,230 miles (1,980 km); maximum range 1,700 miles (2,735 km).

A-24-DE

Dimensions as SBD-5 except length 32 ft 8 in (9·96 m). Empty weight 6,181 lb (2,804 kg); loaded weight 8,934 lb (4,052 kg); maximum weight 10,200 lb (4,627 kg); wing loading 27·5 lb/sq ft (134·2 kg/sq m); power loading 8·9 lb/hp (4·1 kg/hp). Maximum speed 250 mph (402 km/h) at 17,200 ft (5,245 m); cruising speed 173 mph (278 km/h); climb to 10,000 ft (3,050 m) 7 min; service ceiling 26,000 ft (7,925 m); normal range 950 miles (1,530 km); maximum range 1,300 miles (2,090 km).

Douglas DC-4E

Initial discussions regarding the possible development of a four-engined transport aircraft with twice the capacity of the DC-3—the prototype of which had yet to make its first flight—and a range of 2,200 miles (3,540 km)—were held between Douglas and United Air Lines in the second half of 1935. Douglas was somewhat wary of committing itself to such a complex and expensive project; United Air Lines likewise, did not have the financial resources to underwrite the project and was in no position to guarantee sufficient orders on its own behalf. William Patterson, the President of United Air Lines, was convinced that such an aircraft was needed and tried to persuade other airlines to back Douglas. By February 1936 Douglas's initial design studies were sufficiently advanced and Patterson's efforts

The DC-4E during its evaluation by United Air Lines in the summer of 1939. (*United Air Lines*)

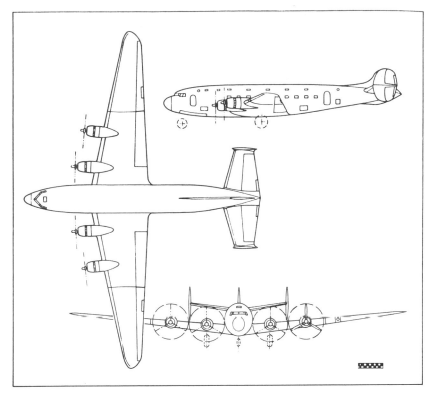

convincing enough for four other airlines to show considerable interest. A month later, American, Eastern, Pan American, TWA and United each committed $100,000 towards the design and construction of one prototype DC-4 (later designated DC-4E).*

As the DC-4E began taking shape, the aircraft appeared even more revolutionary than the earlier DC aircraft. It was big—the aircraft was planned to accommodate 42 passengers by day in two rows of seats on each side of a central aisle or 30 passengers by night with full sleeping accommodation including a private bridal room. Impressive as it was externally, the DC-4E was even more impressive from the technical point of view. The aircraft was powered by four 1,450 hp Pratt & Whitney R-2180-S1A1-G fourteen-cylinder air-cooled radials which were canted outward from the line of flight. The wings, fitted with slotted flaps, were of typical Northrop/Douglas construction with three spars and housed the inward-retracting main undercarriage. This main undercarriage was complemented by a nosewheel, the first to be used on an aircraft of this size. To obtain adequate stability and control with two inoperative engines on

*Fourth in the series of Douglas Commercial transports, this aircraft was logically designated DC-4, but when it was shelved in favour of a less complex type—the DC-4/C-54 series—the original DC-4 became the DC-4E (DC-4 Experimental).

266

one side the tailplane was given a substantial degree of dihedral and there were triple fins and rudders. Other major technical innovations included the use of power-boosted controls, an auxiliary power system consisting of two small reciprocating engines, AC electrical system and air-conditioned cabin. Full pressurization—not installed in the prototype—was to be incorporated into production aircraft.

Whilst initially impressed by the Douglas proposal, the sponsoring airlines began to show concern over the aircraft's complexity and by mid-1936 both Pan American and TWA decided to withdraw their support and to sponsor the smaller and somewhat less complex Boeing 307 Stratoliner. The decision of these two airlines left Douglas with only $300,000 in airline funds to develop a complex and costly aircraft.

Registered NX18100, the single DC-4E prototype (s/n 1601) was completed in May 1938, and on 7 June from Clover Field, Santa Monica, made an uneventful first flight with Carl Cover in command. However, due to numerous minor teething troubles with its intricate systems, the aircraft did not receive its ATC (Approved Type Certificate) until 5 May, 1939. The DC-4E was then handed over to United Air Lines and, painted in that airline's livery made numerous proving flights on United's network. During this period the aircraft demonstrated its ability to take-off on the power of only two engines when Benny Howard, a project pilot with United Air Lines, lifted the aircraft from Cheyenne Airport, Wyoming, located 6,200 ft (1,860 m) above sea level.

On the ground and in the air the aircraft was reported to be pleasant to handle and to possess no vices, but performance left something to be desired. The complexity of the systems presented excessive maintenance problems and operating economics were disappointing in spite of an increase in passenger capacity from 42 to 52 and an increase in gross weight from 61,500 lb (27,896 kg) to 65,000 lb (29,483 kg). Accordingly, the sponsoring airlines agreed with Douglas to suspend development in favour of a new, less complex, DC-4 project, which was to lead to the military C-54 and to the DC-4s still in service in many parts of the world.

NC18100 after receiving its Approved Type Certificate. (*United Air Lines*)

The DC-4E landing at Tokyo after being re-assembled in Japan. (*Katsu Kori*)

NC18100 was returned to Douglas and in late 1939 was acquired by Mitsui Trading Company ostensibly for Dai Nippon Koku (Greater Japan Air Lines). Re-assembled in Japan by Douglas personnel, the aircraft was flown for a brief period until reported as having crashed in Tokyo Bay. In fact the aircraft had been quietly dismantled by Nakajima at the behest of the Japanese Navy—for which the airline had acted as cover—to be used as basis for the design of a four-engined long-range bomber, the Nakajima G5N1 Shinzan (Mountain Recess).

After deducting the $300,000 received from the three sponsoring airlines (American, Eastern and United) but including the unspecified amount paid by Mitsui, Douglas lost a total of $1,344,600 on the DC-4E project.

Span 138 ft 3 in (42·14 m); length 97 ft 7 in (29·74 m); height 24 ft 6½ in (7·48 m); wing area 2,155 sq ft (200·207 sq m). Empty weight 42,564 lb (19,308 kg); loaded weight 61,500 lb (27,896 kg); maximum weight 66,500 lb (30,164 kg); wing loading 28·5 lb/sq ft (139·3 kg/sq m); power loading 10·6 lb/hp (4·8 kg/hp). Maximum speed 245 mph (394 km/h) at 7,000 ft (2,135 m); cruising speed 200 mph (322 km/h); initial rate of climb 1,175 ft/min (358 m/min); service ceiling 22,900 ft (6,980 m); range 2,200 miles (3,540 km).

Douglas DB-7 and A-20 Havoc/Boston

The DB-7/A-20 and A-26 attack bombers were among the most important aircraft types contributed by Douglas to the Allied war effort. In particular, the DB-7 and A-20 series combined good performance with exceptionally good handling and rugged construction enabling them to survive major battle damage. Development of the series was undertaken in March 1936 as a private venture when Ed Heinemann, under the supervision of John Northrop, began to design the Northrop 7A. Intended to fulfil observation and attack missions, the Northrop 7A was twin-engined, with wings mounted high on the fuselage sides and with a tricycle undercarriage. On the power of two 425 hp Pratt & Whitney R-985 Wasp Jr radials, it was anticipated to have a top speed of 250 mph (402 km/h) and was to be armed with one forward-firing 0·30-in machine-gun and similar guns on flexible mounts in dorsal and ventral positions. For the attack role forty 17 lb (7·7 kg) bombs were to be carried in a bomb bay in the fuselage beneath the wing centre section while, for the observation role, the bomb bay was to be replaced by an extensively glazed compartment. Northrop built a full-scale mock-up of the 7A but work was suspended in December 1936, at a time when fifty per cent of the engineering drawings had been completed, as the US Army requirements were rapidly changing.

Work on a more powerful and larger twin-engined attack bomber began anew in the autumn of 1937 to meet the requirements of the Army Air Corps which wanted an aircraft to be operated solely in the attack role and possessing a range of 1,200 miles (1,930 km) with a 1,200 lb (544 kg) bomb load. Designated 7B, the new aircraft was designed at El Segundo by a team led by Project Engineer Weidenheimer. Retaining the high-wing configuration of the 7A, the 7B was powered by two 1,100 hp Pratt & Whitney

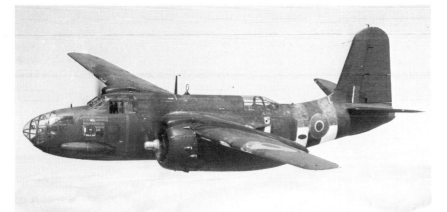

Boston IIIA B-Beer of No.88 Squadron, RAF. (*Public Archives of Canada*)

The Model 7B at Mines Field before installation of its armament. (*MDC*)

R-1830-S3C3-G fourteen-cylinder air-cooled radials and had an internal fuel capacity of 370 US gallons (1,401 litres), compared with the 7A's 200 gallons (757 litres). While the dorsal and ventral 0·30-in machine-guns were retained on the 7B, the aircraft, which had no provision for the 7A's ventral observation compartment, could be fitted with either a glazed nose with accommodation for a bomb-aimer and his sighting equipment or an unglazed nose carrying two 0·50-in and six 0·30-in machine-guns firing

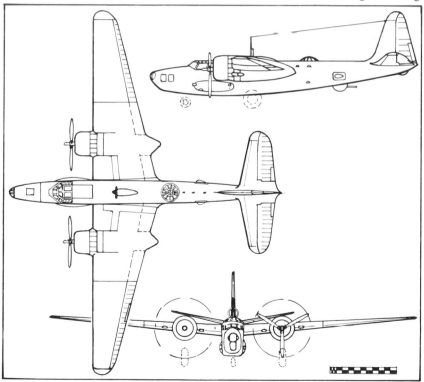

Douglas Model 7B.

forward. Bomb load was doubled to include eighty 17 lb (7·7 kg) bombs or one 2,000 lb (908 kg) bomb.

First flown at Mines Field, Los Angeles, on 26 October, 1938, the 7B (s/n 379) soon attracted the attention of the French Purchasing Commission in the United States. As a result of this French interest, and in spite of the Air Corps' own urgent requirements, Douglas was permitted to demonstrate it to French representatives. Unfortunately, while being flown with a French officer on board, the 7B crashed on 23 January, 1939, during a single-engine fly-past and its Douglas pilot, John Cable, was killed. The French staff, however, had seen enough to recommend acquisition of a modified version.

Redesign had already begun and, to meet the needs of the Armée de l'Air, Douglas accelerated its efforts to complete engineering drawings for the modified aircraft which was designated DB-7 (Douglas Bomber 7). A first contract for one hundred DB-7s was signed by the French Purchasing Commission on 15 February, 1939, and was increased by 170 aircraft in October of that year following the outbreak of war in Europe. The first DB-7 was completed in August 1939 and derivative aircraft were built until October 1944 when the last A-20 was delivered. In the following pages, details of every variant of the DB-7 and A-20 series are grouped in two sections: 1) the DB-7 family for export; and 2) the USAAF and USN aircraft. Details pertaining to Havocs and Bostons operated by Commonwealth air forces are included, where appropriate, in each of these two sections.

DB-7: Retaining the 7B's wing geometry, the wings of the DB-7 were mounted lower on a completely redesigned and larger fuselage. The first one hundred DB-7s were each powered by two 1,000 Pratt & Whitney R-1830-SC3-G radials enclosed in revised nacelles attached beneath the wings, whereas the engines of the 7B had been enclosed in nacelles partially extending above the wings. No provision was made in the DB-7 for the installation of an unglazed nose containing a battery of forward-firing

DB-7 of Groupe de Bombardement I/19 near Algiers in 1941. (*Jean Cuny*)

271

guns, but it was fitted with a glazed nose incorporating a bomb-aimer's station and housing four forward-firing 7·5 mm machine-guns. Defensive armament included a flexible 7·5 mm machine-gun in a dorsal position and a similar weapon firing through a ventral hatch. All instruments, guns, bomb sight and racks, and equipment were of French manufacture, with metric calibration. Dual controls with limited instrumentation were fitted in the rear cockpit.

The first aircraft made its maiden flight on 17 August, 1939, and DB-7 were first accepted by the French Purchasing Commission at Santa Monica on 31 October with deliveries being made by ship to Casablanca. The last 170 aircraft—built in Santa Monica but with fuselages produced in El Segundo whereas earlier aircraft were entirely built in the El Segundo plant—differed from the first production batch of one hundred DB-7s in having two 1,100 hp Pratt & Whitney R-1830-S3C4-Gs with two-speed superchargers instead of the single-speed supercharger of the first aircraft's R-1830-SC3-Gs.

Bearing the French military designation DB-7 B-3 (B-3 indicating that the aircraft was a three-seat bomber), the aircraft were operated by the Armée de l'Air starting in January 1940. One of these aircraft—the 131st built under French contract—was modified by Douglas to test twin fins and rudders in an effort to improve directional stability and increase the field of fire for the dorsal machine-gun but this modification was not retained. Late production DB-7s were fitted with self-sealing tanks and some armour plating for crew protection. Before the fall of France in June 1940 about half of the DB-7 order had been accepted; but a number of these never reached the Armée de l'Air as they were still en route at the time of the French collapse while some sixteen DB-7s from the first production batch were diverted for use by Belgium's Aviation Militaire. France thus actually took possession of only seventy DB-7s.

The 131st DB-7, experimentally fitted with twin fins and rudders. (*MDC*)

When France fell, the United Kingdom took over the DB-7s, including those intended for Belgium before that country, too, was occupied by the Germans, and these aircraft were modified as follows:

Boston I: Twenty DB-7s powered by 1,000 hp Pratt & Whitney R-1830-SC3-Gs were taken over by the RAF as Boston Is and were assigned serials AE457 to AE472 and DK274 to DK277. After throttle modification made to reverse their operation—forward to open instead of to close as in the French aircraft—the Boston Is were used as trainers by the RAF.

Boston II: Designation tentatively given to ex-French DB-7s with 1,100 hp R-1830-S3C4-G engines. Upon arrival in the United Kingdom the aircraft became Havoc Is.

Havoc I (Intruder) and *Havoc I (Night Fighter):* As the DB-7s taken over by the United Kingdom lacked the range necessary for bombing operations from British bases, the decision was taken to modify the R-1830-S3C4-G powered aircraft (including some early production aircraft which were re-engined) for night intruder and night fighter duties. Serials assigned to the British night intruder and fighter versions covered 181 aircraft (AW392 to AW 414, AX848 to AX851, AX910 to AX975, BB890 to BB912, BD110 to BD127, BJ458 to BJ501, BK882 and BK883, BL227 and BL228, BT460 to BT465, BV203 and DG554 and DG555). Conversion of these DB-7s was undertaken at the Burtonwood Aircraft Repair Depot, and British armament, equipment and instruments were fitted at that time. The Havoc Is were completed in two basic versions: the Havoc I (Intruder) version, which earlier was successively designated Moonfighter, Ranger and Havoc IV, was fitted with a glazed nose and armed with four forward-firing 0·303-in machine-guns in the lower part of the nose, one flexible 0·303-in rearward-firing machine-gun and a bomb load of 2,400 lb (1,089 kg); and the Havoc I (Night Fighter) version which had an unglazed nose housing AI Mk IV radar and eight forward-firing 0·303-in machine-guns but no rear-defence or provision for bombs. The Havoc I (Intruder) was a three-seater whereas the Havoc I (Night Fighter) was a two-seater.

Havoc I (Pandora): Some twenty Havoc I (Intruders) were modified to carry in the bomb bay a Long Aerial Mine. This device contained an explosive charge and, when dropped, was attached to the aircraft by a 2,000 ft (610 m) cable which was to be trailed in the path of enemy bomber formations. Operational tests were made by No.93 Squadron but proved disappointing and the aircraft were modified back to Havoc I (Intruder) standard.

Havoc I (Turbinlite): Twenty-one Havoc I (Night Fighters) with armament removed but retaining the AI Mk IV radar, were fitted with a 2,700 million candle-power Helmore/GEC searchlight in the nose. The object was to detect enemy bombers with the help of the AI radar and then to illuminate them for the benefit of single-seat night fighters which had to rely on visual interception. The advent of radar-equipped night fighters

273

Havoc I (Turbinlite) with Helmore/GEC searchlight in the nose. (*USAF*)

with performance equal or superior to the Hurricane rapidly rendered them obsolete.

Havoc III: Designation initially given to the Havoc I (Pandora).

Havoc IV: Designation initially given to the Havoc I (Intruder).

DB-7A: One hundred DB-7As were ordered by France on 20 October, 1939. Basically the aircraft was a more powerful, minimum-change version of the DB-7 with modified undercarriage, local structural strengthening and enlarged vertical tail surfaces. The aircraft was powered by two 1,600 hp Wright R-2600-A5B fourteen-cylinder air-cooled radials enclosed in longer nacelles. In the original French specification the aircraft was intended to carry similar armament to that of the DB-7 but with a fixed aft firing 7·5-mm machine-gun mounted within each engine nacelle. In the event all DB-7As were taken over by the United Kingdom. All but the first aircraft (British serial AH430), which crashed when on a company test flight, were flown by the RAF as Havoc IIs.

Havoc II: The 100 French DB-7As taken over by the RAF were converted to Havoc Night Fighter standard and assigned the serials AH430 to AH529. A new unglazed nose housing twelve 0.303-in machine-guns was

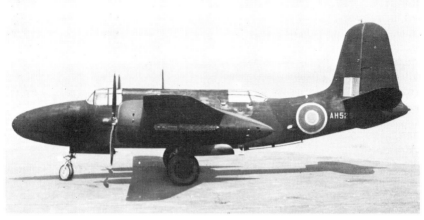

Havoc II (AH525) with Martin Baker-designed twelve-gun installation. (*The Aeroplane*)

274

designed by Martin Baker Limited, and the aircraft were sent to Burtonwood for conversion and to have AI radar fitted. Before delivery to Britain one of these aircraft, AH463, was experimentally fitted with a mock-up of a Boulton Paul dorsal turret.

Havoc II (Turbinlite): Designation applied to thirty-nine Havoc IIs which were fitted with Helmore/GEC searchlight but no armament.

DB-7B: Only version of the DB-7/A-20 series directly ordered by Britain, the DB-7B had revised systems and introduced a bomb-aimer nose extending six inches and possessing 25 per cent more Plexiglass. An initial order for 150 aircraft, later increased to 300, was placed on 20 February, 1940, and are described under the Boston III designation.

DB-73: Similar to the DB-7B but fitted with French armament, equipment and instruments, 480 DB-73s were ordered by France on 18 May, 1940—hence the change of designation to avoid confusion with the British-ordered DB-7Bs. All DB-73s, including 240 aircraft built by Boeing (c/n 2130 to 2203 and 2718 to 2883), were completed to DB-7B standard following the French defeat and intended for delivery as Boston IIIs.

Boston III: Designation applied to 300 British-ordered DB-7Bs (W8252 to W8401 and Z2155 to Z2304), one DB-7B (AH740) delivered as a replacement for the DB-7A (AH430) which had crashed while under test with the manufacturer, to 240 ex-French DB-73s built by Douglas (AL263 to AL502) and to 240 ex-French DB-73s built by Boeing (AL668 to AL907). However, 132 Boeing-built DB-73s, 75 Douglas-built DB-73s and six British-ordered DB-7Bs were retained by the US Army Air Forces when the original British and French contracts were transferred to the Lend-Lease programme. Deliveries of Boston IIIs began in the spring of 1941 and these aircraft were fitted with British instruments, radio equipment, bomb racks and 0·303-in machine-guns. Like the earlier DB-7A/Havoc II the Boston III was powered by two 1,600 hp Wright R-2600-A5B radials. Compared with the DB-7 and DB-7A ordered by France, the Boston III had improved self-sealing tanks and armour protection. Whereas the French aircraft were intended for short-range tactical sorties, the British aircraft needed longer range to operate against targets in occupied Europe and total fuel capacity was increased from 205 US gallons (776 litres) to 394 gallons (1,491 litres). At least two Boston IIIs were used for special armament experiments—W8315, an aircraft of No.88 Squadron, which was fitted with a Boulton Paul power-operated four-gun dorsal turret, and W8268/G which was fitted with four rocket projectile rails beneath each wing. The Boston IIIs became the first version of the DB-7/A-20 series to be operated in its intended role but at least twenty went to the Soviet Air Force whilst others saw service with the RCAF, the RAAF and the SAAF or were modified to Intruder and Turbinlite configurations.

Boston III (Intruder): A number of Boston IIIs were modified for night intruder operations over occupied Europe and were so redesignated. A gun pack, containing four 20-mm cannon and fitted beneath the fuselage, supplemented the standard Boston III armament.

Boston III (Turbinlite): At least three other Boston IIIs were fitted with a Helmore/GEC searchlight in the nose in a manner similar to the installation on the Havoc I/II (Turbinlite).

DB-7C: When in October 1941 the Netherlands Government in exile ordered forty-eight DB-7Cs (serials DO-101 to DO-148) for use in the East Indies by the Koninklijke Marine, they requested that these aircraft—which had airframes similar to that of the DB-7B—include provision for the following equipment: 1) interchangeable glazed nose with bomb-aimer station and unglazed nose housing four 20-mm cannon; 2) automatic life raft; and 3) special racks enabling the aircraft to be used as torpedo bombers. To meet these requirements Douglas ground-tested a special nose section housing four forward-firing 20-mm cannon. However, the DB-7Cs, which were powered by a pair of 1,600 hp Wright R-2600-A5Bs, were eventually completed with glazed nose to a standard similar to that of the USAAF A-20Cs. Only about half the Dutch order for DB-7Cs could be delivered to Java before the Japanese occupation and the remainder was taken over for redelivery under the Lend-Lease programme.

As already related, Douglas had in early 1939—prior to the signing of the first contract for 100 French DB-7s—undertaken a complete redesign of the 7B to meet the latest Air Corps requirements and on 30 June, 1939, 63 A-20s and 123 A-20As were ordered under Contract AC12967. Eventually a further twenty were ordered under AC15093 and these 206 aircraft built at Santa Monica were delivered as A-20, A-20As, P-70s and YF-3s.

A-20: Initially sixty-three A-20s were ordered and were to be powered by two 1,700 hp Wright R-2600-7s fitted with turbosuperchargers mounted on the outboard side of the engine nacelles; however, only the fifteenth aircraft under Contract AC12967 (serial 39-735) was actually powered by these engines because of cooling difficulties and troubles with the turbosupercharger. Also there was no need for increased power at high altitudes in an aircraft which was intended to operate at low and medium altitudes. Eventually, the sole A-20 was modified and became the XP-70. Like the A-20A, P-70 and YF-3, the A-20 had a redesigned and stronger airframe similar to that of the DB-7B. Compared with the French DB-7A, the A-20 differed in using steel forgings instead of dural for its main wing attachment fittings, in having strengthened wing and fuselage structure to cope with a 3,750 lb (1,701 kg) increase in gross weight, in being fitted with a six inch (15·2 cm) longer nose offering 25 per cent more glazed area, and in having self-sealing fuel tanks with a total capacity of 394 US gallons (1,491 litres). Armament planned for the A-20 and A-20A consisted of four forward-firing 0·30-in machine-guns—mounted two each in external side blisters instead of within the lower nose section—, twin flexible 0·30-in machine-guns in an open dorsal position and one flexible 0·30-in machine-gun in a ventral tunnel position. Provision was also made for a fixed aft-firing weapon of similar calibre mounted in each engine nacelle. However, these two machine-guns, which were fired by the pilot by means of a foot trigger, were not normally mounted.

A-20A of the 58th Bombardment Squadron off Oahu, Hawaii, on 29 May, 1941. (*USAF*)

A-20A: First major production version of the A-20 series for the Air Corps/Air Forces, the A-20A differed from the A-20 in being powered by two 1,600 hp Wright R-2600-11 engines without turbosuperchargers. One hundred and forty-three A-20As (serials 39-721 to 39-724, 40-071 to 40-179 and 40-3143 to 40-3162) were delivered to the USAAC/USAAF and were first operated by the 3rd Bombardment Group stationed at Savannah, Georgia.

XA-20B: Designation applied to the one A-20A which was modified in July 1941 to test three power-operated, remotely controlled, turrets. The experiment was not entirely successful and was discontinued.

A-20B-DL: Ordered on 2 October, 1940, under Contract AC15948, 999 A-20Bs (serials 41-2671 to 41-3669) were built in the new Long Beach plant. Powered by two 1,600 hp Wright R-2600-11 engines, the A-20Bs had a glazed nose of modified geometry and modified rear bomb bays with horizontal instead of vertical bomb racks. For ferrying purposes an auxiliary tank with a capacity of 200 US gallons (757 litres) could be installed in the bomb bay. Two forward-firing 0·50-in machine-guns, one on each side of the forward fuselage, one flexible 0·50-in gun in the dorsal station and one flexible 0·30-in machine-gun in the ventral tunnel constituted the normal defensive armament but the two nacelle guns could also be fitted. In the field many A-20Bs had the Plexiglass nose area faired over to house four to six 0·50-in forward-firing machine-guns. Eight A-20Bs (serials 41-2771 to 41-2778) were transferred to the US Navy as BD-2s.

A-20C-DO: As part of the Lend-Lease programme, 375 A-20C-DOs (serials 41-19088 to 41-19462) were built in Santa Monica under Contract DA2 while an additional 433 (serials 42-32951 to 42-33383) were built under Contract DA934. These were primarily intended for delivery to the

RAF as Boston IIIAs and to the Soviet Air Force but a substantial number of A-20Cs were taken over by the USAAF after 7 December, 1941, to establish A-20 training groups in the United States. The A-20Cs were identical to the DB-7Bs built under British contract but US 0·30-in machine-guns were substituted for British 0·303-in weapons and the exhaust collector ring for the 1,600 hp R-2600-23 engines was replaced by individual exhaust stacks which resulted in an increase in top speed of some 15 mph (24 km/h). On the last 433 aircraft combat fuel capacity was increased to 540 US gallons (2,044 litres) by adding a 140-gallon (530-litre) self-sealing tank in the bomb bay. Various minor modifications were introduced during production and included the substitution of continuous belt feed for magazines previously used for the twin 0·30-in machine-guns in the dorsal position as well as the installation of improved wing flap mechanism. At least fifty-six A-20Cs taken over by the USAAF, starting on 1 January, 1942, were fitted with racks for a torpedo under the belly of the aircraft. Several aircraft were modified in the field, as had been A-20As and A-20Bs, to mount a battery of six 0·50-in machine-guns in the glazed nose which, in this case, was either painted over or covered with light metal. Experimental projects using A-20C airframes included the testing of an experimental caterpillar track main undercarriage on serial 41-19158; the experimental installation on the second A-20C-5-DO (42-33201) of a Martin twin-gun dorsal turret similar to that later fitted to all aircraft beginning with the A-20G-20-DO block; the experimental conversion of an A-20C's rear cockpit and aft part of the rear bomb bay to install a bomb-aimer's station such as was planned, but not realized, for the A-20G and A-20H equipped with gun noses; finally, one A-20C had all its combat equipment removed and had aluminium alloy armour plates installed over 75 per cent of its airframe to modify it as an armament target aircraft against which frangible bullets fired by gunnery students would shatter.

Line-up of Havocs from a USAAF training unit; the aircraft in the foreground is an A-20C-10-DO. (*USAF*)

278

An A-20C-DO (41-19158) and an A-20H-10-DO (44-466, *illustrated*) were experimentally fitted with tracked main undercarriages. (*Harold G. Martin*)

Boston IIIA: Ordered as A-20Cs under Lend-Lease contracts, 200 Boston IIIAs were reserved for delivery to the United Kingdom (British serials BZ196 to BZ352, BZ355 to BZ378 and BZ381 to BZ399) while other Boston IIIAs were taken over in the field with some of them retaining their original US serials (*eg* 41-19406 operated in the Western Desert by No.114 Squadron) while others received new British serials (HK869, HK870, HK872 to HK879, HK912, HK918, HK923, HK924, HK934, HK960, HK962, HK964, HK967, HK969, HK970, HK972 and HK973). The Boston IIIAs differed from the Boston IIIs in being powered by Wright R-2600-23s with individual exhaust stacks instead of R-2600-A5Bs and in having total fuel capacity increased to 540 US gallons (2,044 litres).

A-20C-BO: One hundred and forty A-20Cs built under Lend-Lease Contract DA-1 by Boeing (serials 41-19589 to 41-19728, c/n 2885 to 3024).

A-20D-DO: Projected lightweight version which was to have been powered by R-2600-7 engines with turbosuperchargers and which would have had non-self-sealing fuel tanks of increased capacity. Contract cancelled.

A-20E-DO: Designation applied to seventeen modified A-20As with minor internal changes.

XA-20F-DO: Designation applied to one A-20A modified at the factory to test two General Electric remotely-controlled turrets—one above and one beneath the fuselage—housing twin 0·50-in machine-guns. Later the aircraft was modified at Wright Field and a fixed forward-firing 37-mm cannon was installed in the nose. The experimental turret installation was not retained for A-20 production but provided useful data for the A-26 Invader programme.

A-20G-DO: Built in larger numbers than any other version, the A-20G had an unglazed nose housing a battery of forward-firing guns. A total of 2,850 A-20Gs (for list of serials refer to Appendix B), powered by R-2600-23s were built at Santa Monica. A number of changes were

A-20G-1-DO of the 90th Bombardment Squadron, 3rd Bombardment Group, at Hollandia, New Guinea, on 27 June, 1944. (*USAF*)

common to all blocks (A-20G-1 to A-20G-45) and included: 1) removal of dual controls from the rear gunner's compartment; 2) installation of carburettor de-icing equipment; and 3) use of heavier gauge armour plate adding some 400 lb (181 kg) to the weight. On the A-20G-1-DO armament consisted of four forward-firing 20-mm cannon in the nose, one 0·50-in machine-gun in the dorsal position and one 0·30-in gun in the ventral position, while 2,000 lb (908 kg) of bombs were carried internally. Beginning with the A-20G-5-DO block six 0·50-in machine-guns replaced the four cannon which had a slower rate of fire and were found less accurate than the heavy machine-guns. Starting with the 751st aircraft in the series, the first A-20G-20-DO, the single hand-held machine-gun in the dorsal position was replaced by a Martin turret housing twin 0·50-in machine-guns and an 0·50-in gun substituted for the 0·30-in weapon in the ventral tunnel. At the same time two bomb racks stressed to carry 500 lb (227 kg) bombs were fitted beneath the outer wing panels. Several other modifications were added throughout the A-20G production life and included improved carburettor air filter (A-20G-10), heating for winter operations (A-20G-15), increased internal fuel capacity from 540 US gallons (2,044 litres) to 725 gallons (2,744 litres) and provision for a 374-gallon (1,416-litre) drop tank beneath the fuselage (A-20G-20), improved collecting system for spent cartridges (A-20G-30), heavier-gauge skin on stabilizer (A-20G-35), modified engine exhaust system (A-20G-40). Most of the A-20G-1-DOs, as well as a large number of later A-20G variants, were delivered to the Soviet Union under Lend-Lease arrangements. An experimental nose gun installation housing two 37 mm cannon and two 0·50-in machine-guns was fitted to an A-20G but not retained for production, while engineering design for the installation of a 75 mm cannon in the nose of an A-20G was cancelled before completion of a test vehicle.

A-20H-DO: Basically the A-20Hs were identical to the A-20G-45-DOs but were powered by 1,700 hp R-2600-29s. The change in powerplant was made necessary by the discontinued production of the 1,600 hp R-2600-23

A pair of A-20Hs from the 410th Bombardment Group, Ninth Air Force. (*USAF*)

and by the need to increase the power available as take-off weight had increased from 21,500 lb (9,752 kg) for the A-20C to 24,170 lb (10,963 kg) for the A-20H-10-DO. A total of 412 A-20Hs was built (for list of serial numbers refer to Appendix B). One A-20H-10-DO (44-466) was also tested with a caterpillar track main undercarriage.

A-20J-DO: Early in the summer of 1943 the Air Matériel Command at Wright Field requested that Douglas study the possibility of installing a bomb-aimer's nose in approximately one out of each ten A-20Gs, to enable these aircraft to be used as formation leaders on bombing runs. To meet this requirement, Douglas designed an entirely new nose, which was covered by a frameless, moulded Plexiglass canopy, adding seven inches (17·8 cm) to the aircraft's length and incorporating a Norden bomb sight and two forward-firing 0·50-in machine-guns. Four hundred and fifty

Although bearing the serial number (43-21751) of an A-20J-15-DO, this aircraft was fitted with an A-20C type nose and was a CA-20J bearing the Air Transport Command logo on its aft fuselage. (*USAF*)

281

A-20Js (see Appendix B for list of serials) were built and these, which included 169 Boston IVs delivered to the RAF, had airframes similar to that used on the A-20G-25 and later variants.

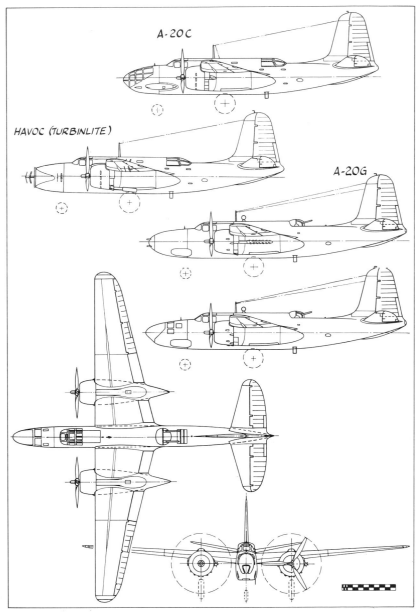

Douglas A-20J, with side views of A-20C, Havoc (Turbinlite) and A-20G.

Boston IV: Delivered under Lend-Lease, 169 A-20Js were designated Boston IVs by the RAF and assigned the serials BZ400 to BZ568. Powered by R-2600-23s, the Boston IVs retained the same armament, including the twin-gun Martin dorsal turret, as their USAAF counterparts.

A-20K-DO: Similar to the A-20Js but using A-20H airframes and powerplant installation, 413 A-20Ks were built and ninety of these were operated by the RAF as Boston Vs. The A-20K-15-DO, serial 44-825, was delivered on 20 September, 1944, and was the last aircraft in the DB-7/A-20 series to be built.

Boston V: Last version delivered to the RAF, the Boston V, of which ninety (BZ580 to BZ669) were operated, was identical to the A-20K of the USAAF.

XF-3: Prior to completion of the first of sixty-three A-20s ordered in June 1939, the Air Corps instructed Douglas in March 1940 to modify three of these as prototypes for a photographic reconnaissance aircraft. The first of the three (serial 39-741) was designated XF-3 and, like the sole A-20, was powered by two turbosupercharged Wright R-2600-7s. T-3A cameras were installed in the rear bomb bay, all bomb racks were removed and the standard defensive armament of the A-20 was retained. Following completion of the flight trial programme, which was marred by teething troubles with the superchargers, the aircraft was re-engined with 1,600 hp R-2600-3s and delivered to the US Navy as the BD-1 (BuNo 4251).

YF-3: Ordered as A-20 serials 39-745 and 39-748, two aircraft were completed as YF-3 experimental photographic reconnaissance aircraft. The YF-3, powered by turbosupercharged R-2600-7s, differed from the XF-3 in having a tail turret—the only one fitted to aircraft in the DB-7/A-20 series—in which a gunner manned twin flexible 0·30-in machine guns. No production development.

F-3A: Designation applied to forty-six A-20Js and A-20Ks with either two 1,600 hp R-2600-23s or two 1,700 hp R-2600-29s modified as night photographic-reconnaissance aircraft. Five A-20Js were so modified at the Daggett Modification Center starting in February 1944 and forty-one additional aircraft were brought up to the same standard at the factory starting in June 1944. To enable the installation of cameras in the nose the two forward-firing 0·50-in machine-guns of the A-20J and A-20K were removed. Additional cameras were fitted in the bomb bay and photo flash bombs were carried in the forward section of the bomb bay.

O-53: A contract for 1,489 O-53 observation aircraft (serials 41-3670 to 41-5158) was placed on 2 October, 1940. These were to be built at Long Beach alongside the generally similar A-20Bs but the contract was cancelled before completion of a single O-53 as the Air Corps no longer had a requirement for heavy observation aircraft.

XP-70: Difficulties experienced with the turbosupercharged R-2600-7 engines, particularly with respect to engine cooling, led to an Air Corps decision to have sixty of the A-20s on order modified as night fighters. To test the necessary equipment, the sole A-20 (serial 39-735) was modified as a night fighter prototype. Two 1,600 hp Wright R-2600-11s replaced the turbosupercharged R-2600-7s and British AI Mk IV radar was fitted in the nose with radar antennae on the fuselage sides and wings. All bomb racks and defensive armament were removed and four 20 mm cannon with 60 rpg were installed in a ventral tub.

P-70: Fifty-nine P-70s, originally ordered as A-20s (serials 39-736 to 39-740, 39-742 to 39-744, 39-746 and 39-747, and 39-749 to 39-797), were completed with R-2600-11s as night fighters and were identical to the XP-70 except for minor equipment changes.

P-70A-1: Thirty-nine A-20Cs were modified by the USAAF in 1943 to serve as night fighters. The P-70A-1s were powered by two 1,600 hp R-2600-23s and were armed with six to eight 0·50-in machine-guns in a ventral tray. Improved radar equipment was also installed in the nose.

P-70A-2: Sixty-five P-70A-2s were obtained by modifying a similar number of A-20Gs. The aircraft retained the standard battery of forward-firing guns but all flexible weapons were removed.

P-70B-1: One A-20G-10-DO was modified as an experimental night fighter and fitted with SCR720 centimetric radar in the nose. Armament consisted of six 0·50-in machine-guns in three blisters on each side of the fuselage.

P-70B-2: Designation applying to 105 A-20Gs and A-20Js modified as night fighter trainers and fitted with SCR720 or SCR729 centimetric radar in the nose. Six to eight 0·50-in machine-guns could be carried in a ventral tray but were not always fitted.

BD-1: Designation applied to the XF-3 after it had been re-engined with 1,600 hp Wright R-2600-3s and transferred to the US Navy for target towing and general utility duties. The aircraft was assigned the BuNo 4251.

BD-2: Designation given to eight A-20B-DLs which were transferred to the US Navy (BuNos 7035 to 7042) and used for target towing and general utility duties. Provision for offensive and defensive armament removed.

The first P-70 (39-736), with antennae for AI Mk. IV radar and ventral tub housing four 20 mm cannon. (*USAF*)

A pair of BD-1s being delivered to a US Navy Utility Squadron.
(*US National Archives*)

First accepted at the factory, beginning on 31 October, 1939, the French-ordered DB-7s were ferried to Floyd Bennett Field in New York before being shipped to Casablanca where they were re-assembled, camouflaged and flight tested before delivery to operational units of the Armée de l'Air. Five Groupes de Bombardement, GB I/19, II/19, II/61, I/32 and II/32, had been scheduled to be equipped with DB-7s but only the first three had fully converted to the type by the time of the German invasion. Rushed from North Africa to France, GB I/19, II/19 and II/61 were able to fly some seventy sorties against troops and panzer concentrations, supply convoys and depots, and road bridges before being evacuated to North Africa shortly before the Armistice.

In North Africa the surviving aircraft and the additional DB-7s which had been received from America were redistributed to GB I/32 and II/32 in Morocco and to GB I/19 and II/61 in Algeria. In November 1942, during Operation Torch, US Navy carrier-borne fighters caught the DB-7s of GB I/32 on the ground and inflicted severe losses to this unit, thus preventing it from attacking the Allied landing forces. Shortly after, the North African-based French forces sided with the Allies and the DB-7s were relegated to training and ancillary duties. However, from October 1944 to April 1945, a handful of DB-7s was operated by GB 1/34 *Béarn* and 1/31 *Aunis* against German strongholds along the Atlantic Coast of France.

More significant to the overall Allied war effort was the contribution of another Free French unit, GB I/120 *Lorraine*, which operated under RAF

A GB I/19 DB-7 in Algeria; the aircraft bears the yellow and red cowling and tail stripes imposed in 1941-42. (*Jean Cuny*)

control as No.342 Squadron. After operating with Bristol Blenheim IVs in the Western Desert, No.342 Squadron had been re-formed at West Raynham, Norfolk, on 7 April, 1943. Equipped with Boston IIIAs, this unit flew its first operational mission, an attack against the power station in Rouen, on 12 June, 1943. As part of No.137 Wing, Second Tactical Air Force, the French unit was successively equipped with Boston IIIAs and Boston IVs and took an active part in bombing operations against targets in occupied Europe.

In RAF service the French-flown Boston IIIAs and Boston IVs (Lend-Leased A-20Cs and A-20Js) had long been preceded by British-flown, French-ordered, Havoc Is and IIs and Boston Is and IIIs (of the 781 Boston IIIs which were assigned British serials 480 had been initially ordered by France). First to go into combat with RAF units were the Havoc I (Intruders) of No.23 Squadron and, beginning during the winter of 1940–41, this unit distinguished itself during night interdiction sorties over France. In the night intruder role, No.23 Squadron was later supplanted by Nos.418 (RCAF) and 605 Squadrons with the more powerful and longer-ranged Boston III (Intruders), while in the night fighter role Havoc Is and IIs were flown by No.85 Squadron—which became operational with the type on 7 April, 1941—and, more briefly, by Nos.25 and 93 Squadrons. This last mentioned unit also gained some attention by being the only squadron to operate, though with limited success, Havoc I (Pandoras). Not significantly more successful were the Turbinlite versions of the Havoc I, Havoc II and Boston III which were operated by No.1422 Flight (Air Target Illumination Unit)—formed at Heston in early 1941 to train crews and supply specially modified Havocs and Bostons—and by Nos.1451 to 1460 Flights (later re-numbered Nos.530 to 539 Squadrons) which were operational with Turbinlite aircraft from July 1941 until January 1943.

In its intended light bombing role, the aircraft was first operated in Britain by No.88 Squadron which, after training with Boston Is while still flying operational sorties with Bristol Blenheim IVs, received its Boston IIIs in October 1941. First combat sorties with this type were flown by Nos.88 and 226 Squadrons in February 1942 during the attempt to prevent the dash through the English Channel by the German warships *Scharnhorst* and *Gneisenau*. In Britain, and later Northern Europe, these two units were joined in 1942 by No.107 Squadron and in 1943 by No.342 (Free French) Squadron. Operations flown by RAF Boston IIIs included a number of spectacular low-altitude missions—*eg* attack against the Matford works at Poissy on 8 March, 1942, numerous daylight Circus operations, and smoke-laying sorties for the invasion fleet on D-Day. In 1944 and 1945 only Nos.88 and 342 Squadrons were still flying Boston IIIs, IIIAs and IVs but in April 1945 they were respectively disbanded.

In the Western Desert and Mediterranean area, Bostons were flown operationally by Nos.13, 18, 55 and 114 Squadrons of the RAF and by Nos.12 and 24 Squadrons of the South African Air Force. The SAAF squadrons, which preceded the RAF Boston squadrons in the area, distinguished themselves during raids known as 'Boston Tea Parties' against enemy airfields in the Western Desert. Beginning with Nos.18 and 114 Squadrons, which became operational in April 1943 from Souk-el-Khemis, Tunisia, the four RAF squadrons flew Boston IIIs, IIIAs, IVs and Vs in support of Allied operations in Tunisia, Sicily and Italy, and all four squadrons retained their Bostons until early 1946 when they were either disbanded or re-equipped with Mosquitos.

Havocs also saw service with the Fleet Requirements Unit of the Fleet Air Arm which operated BD121, BD122 and BL227 in 1940–41, while the Royal Canadian Air Force acquired one Boston III (AL672), one Boston IIIA (BZ385) and one Boston IV (BZ410).

F-Freddie, a Havoc I (Intruder) of No.23 Squadron, RAF.
(*British Official photograph*)

Boston III (A28-5, ex-AL895) of No.22 Squadron, RAAF, near Port Moresby in November 1942. (*Frank F. Smith*)

In the war against Japan, No.22 Squadron of the Royal Australian Air Force operated a total of sixty-nine DB-7/A-20 aircraft between March 1942 and October 1944. All known as Bostons to the RAAF, these aircraft were of varied origin—some being ex-USAAF, some being acquired from the Netherlands Marine Luchtvaartdienst and some being diverted from British contracts—and included eleven Douglas-built DB-73 Boston IIIs (Australian serials A28-1, A28-3 to A28-9, A28-14, A28-21 and A28-22 which had been originally ordered by France but were taken over by the British Purchasing Commission), eleven Boeing-built DB-73 Boston IIIs (A28-2, A28-10 to A28-13, and A28-15 to A28-20 which had a similar origin), nine ex-A-20C-5-DOs (A28-23 to A28-31), nine ex-A-20A-DOs (A28-32 to A28-40), twenty-eight ex-A-20G-DOs (A28-50 to A28-77), and one ex-A-20J-DO (A28-78). In service with No.22 Squadron the Boston IIIs, A-20As and A-20Cs had their glazed nose faired over and mounted a battery of four forward-firing 0·50-in machine-guns supplementing the standard armament. In addition, some aircraft were modified in the field to mount a fixed rear-firing 0·30-in machine-gun in the tail cone; normally firing tracer ammunition, this weapon was primarily intended to deter enemy attack from the rear. Operations began from Ward's Strip, Port Moresby, on 15 November, 1942, and the unit and its crews distinguished themselves during two years of combat operations highlighted by the posthumous Victoria Cross award to Flt Lieut W. E. Hutton who had been beheaded by the Japanese following his capture on 18 March, 1943, when he had to ditch his burning aircraft (A28-3) off Salamaua. By November 1944 the squadron was operating its Bostons from Morotai, Halmahera Islands, and was scheduled to re-equip with Australian-built Beaufighter Mk 21s. Ironically, just before being re-equipped, No.22 Squadron suffered its worst loss when thirteen of its Bostons were destroyed on the ground during an enemy raid at Morotai on 23 November, 1944.

The Netherlands Government had ordered forty-eight DB-7Cs for use in the East Indies. Some twenty of these were unloaded at Tjilatjap Harbour, Java, shortly after the Japanese invasion of this island had begun and only

288

Captured Marine Luchtvaartdienst DB-7C under test in Japan. (*NA & SM*)

one aircraft was assembled in time to take part in the desperate operations against the invading forces. The other aircraft in this shipment were captured in damaged condition by the Japanese but one of them was repaired and later test flown at Tachikawa by the Army. The DB-7Cs which had not yet been delivered to the Dutch were taken over by the USAAF and shipped to the Soviet Union under Lend-Lease while a small number of Bostons and A-20s were delivered in Australia for operations by Dutch crews. However, these crews were re-assigned to No.18 Squadron (NEI) which was flying North American Mitchells, and their Bostons were transferred to No.22 Squadron RAAF.

Even though the Soviet Air Force received more aircraft of the DB-7/A-20 series than any other Service—the United States reserved 3,125 DB-7Bs, DB-73s, DB-7Cs, A-20Bs, A-20Cs, A-20Gs, A-20Hs and A-20Ks for delivery to the USSR under Lend-Lease and 2,901 of these were actually accepted by the Soviet Union while an additional number of Bostons was received from the United Kingdom—little is known about the

Soviet Air Force Boston IIIs. (*S. Kafafyan*)

289

operational career of these aircraft. However, some of the early models with hand-held machine-guns in the dorsal position are known to have been fitted in the USSR with a Russian-made dorsal turret housing a 12·7-mm Beresin BS machine-gun.

Final foreign recipient of the type was the Fôrça Aérea Brasileira which received in 1944–45 some thirty ex-USAAF Havocs (A-20G to A-20K). In Brazil these aircraft saw comparatively little service but at least one A-20 is still on display at the Museu Aeroespacial at Campo dos Afonsos.

Almost one year after the French DB-7s had made their combat début against invading German forces, the A-20A entered service with the 3rd Bombardment Group (Light) at Savannah, Georgia. Soon followed by additional aircraft which equipped the 27th Bombardment Group (Light), the A-20As did not initially give full satisfaction as their engines were prone to overheating and, as a temporary measure, holes had to be cut around the periphery of the cowling just aft of the cylinder baffles. As soon as engine cooling had been improved, Army pilots reported favourably on the aircraft's handling, and the A-20As demonstrated their oustanding qualities during war exercises held at Shreveport, Louisiana, in September 1941. Soon after entering service the USAAF aircraft were named Havocs as intruder and night fighter versions of the related DB-7 series had already been named by the Royal Air Force.

Another unit, the 58th Bombardment Squadron, also received A-20As during 1941 and was based at Hickham Field, Hawaii, when on 7 December, 1941, it lost two of its aircraft during the Japanese attack and thus became the first A-20 unit to be blooded. At that time the 27th Bombardment Group, minus its A-20As, was in the process of being shipped to the Philippines where it was to have been re-established as an A-20 unit. However, no Havocs were available to re-equip the 27th BG and thus the honour of being the first USAAF A-20 unit to fly bombing sorties in the Pacific fell to the 89th Bombardment Squadron, 3rd Bombardment Group, which began operations from Port Moresby on 31 August, 1942. In early 1944, as finally sufficient Havocs were available in the South West Pacific Area, the 3rd BG was joined in New Guinea by the 312th and 417th Bombardment Groups. In this theatre of operations, where the Fifth Air Force had in September 1944 a peak Havoc inventory of 370 aircraft, most sorties were flown at low-level—where the need for a bomb-aimer did not develop—and early Havoc models were fitted with additional forward-firing machine-guns mounted in the faired over nose. At war's end all three Havoc groups of the Fifth Air Force were equipped with the better-suited A-20Gs—the version of the aircraft with which the 312th and 417th BGs had begun combat operations—and A-20Hs and these units were in the process of moving to Okinawa after operating successfully in New Guinea, Leyte, Luzon and Mindoro. On occasions the Fifth Air Force A-20s had their heavy forward-firing armament supplemented by two clusters of three Bazooka-type rocket-launching tubes beneath each wing and, with or without this local field modification, these Havocs did much to justify their name during low-level attacks against Japanese land and sea targets. In Britain, following a sortie flown on 29 June, 1942, by a single crew of the 15th Bombardment Squadron which manned a Boston III from No.226 Squadron, RAF, six crews from this USAAF unit flew Boston IIIs from No.226 Squadron in a 4th of July raid against the Hazebrouck marshalling yards in Belgium. Soon after, the 15th BS acquired its own Boston IIIs from RAF stocks but, in November 1942, was transferred to Algeria where it saw limited action before being assigned to the Northwest African Training Command. More significant to the war effort in this theatre of operations was the contribution made by the 47th Bombardment Group which, after its aircraft had been ferried over the North Atlantic to Britain, flew to French Morocco before flying its first combat mission from Youks-les-Bains, Algeria, on 13 December, 1942. After participating in the North Africa campaign, during which many of its A-20Bs were fitted with additional forward-firing machine-guns in the faired over bomb-aimer's station, this unit moved to Malta, Sicily, Italy, Corsica, France, and then back to Italy where in January 1945 it began re-equipping with Douglas A-26 Invaders.

Following a few sorties flown by the Boston III-equipped 15th Bombardment Squadron, no Douglas light bomber combat unit was operated by the USAAF in the European theatre until March 1944 when the A-20G-equipped 416th Bombardment Group began operations as part of the 97th Combat Bombardment Wing (Light), Ninth Air Force. In April and May 1944 the similarly-equipped 409th and 410th BGs joined the 416th and, led initially by specially field-modified A-20Gs with Boston III glazed noses and later by A-20Js, the Havocs of the 97th Bomb Wing were successfully employed as medium-altitude bombers in the softening up of Festung Europa and in support of the Allied landings in Normandy. Led by the 409th BG which moved to Brétigny on 18 September, 1944, the Havocs of the 97th Bomb Wing followed the advancing US forces into France. However, by then it had been decided to re-equip these three groups with A-26 Invaders and the 409th and 416th BGs converted to the newer Douglas bombers in late 1944. Retaining its Havocs for a longer period, the 410th Bombardment Group began flying night missions during the winter of 1944-45 but even this unit had converted to Invaders by VE-Day.

With the USAAF the night fighter versions of the Havoc, the P-70 Nighthawk series, had an undistinguished career and were primarily used by the 481st Night Fighter Operational Training Group to develop operating procedures and tactics for radar-controlled night interceptions and to train the crews of nineteen night fighter squadrons. However, only five of these squadrons were still equipped with P-70s when they were deployed overseas for combat operations. In Italy, the 427th Night Fighter Squadron actually exchanged its P-70s for Northrop P-61 Black Widows before becoming operational. In the war against Japan, the 6th Night Fighter Squadron began operations from Henderson Field, Guadalcanal,

P-70A-2-DO night-fighter trainer over Florida. (*USAF*)

in February 1943 where it was later supplanted by the 419th N.F.S. whilst the 418th and 421st Night Fighter Squadrons also flew P-70s in New Guinea. Lacking sufficient performance to successfully intercept Japanese night raiders, the P-70s had to be replaced with P-61s as soon as these aircraft could be made available.

Last versions of the Havoc to be used operationally were the photographic-reconnaissance models of the aircraft. Upon completion of their flight trials the YF-3s had been used briefly during 1942 by the 2nd

YF-3-DO (39-748) of the 2nd Photographic Squadron at Ladd Field, Alaska, on 22 August, 1942. (*USAF*)

292

Photographic Mapping Squadron—which deployed at least one to Alaska—but main Service use of reconnaissance versions of the Havoc did not take place until May 1944 when the Ninth Air Force's 155th Photographic Squadron (Night) was equipped with F-3As for night photographic operations in the European theatre.

Following the end of hostilities, the Havocs and the Lend-Leased Bostons became surplus to USAAF requirements. Most of these aircraft were immediately scrapped but surplus Havocs which found their way onto the civil market were modified and used as executive transport aircraft while others saw limited use in dropping fire-retardant chemicals on forest fires. A number of Havocs are now preserved in the United States and Brazil.

A surplus A-20G as an executive transport aircraft. (*MSgt David Menard*)

With a total of 7,478 aircraft built—including the 7B prototype and Boeing-built aircraft—the DB-7/A-20 series was one of the most important types of twin-engined light bombers of World War II, and their American, Australian, Brazilian, British, Canadian, Dutch, French, Russian and South African crews all commented enthusiastically on the aircraft's remarkable handling. For the Douglas Aircraft Company the DB-7s and A-20s started a new line of work which continued with the A-26 Invader and ended during the jet era with the B-66 Destroyer.

Accommodation: Crew of three in separate enclosed cockpits (7B, DB-7, DB-7A, Havoc I (Intruder), Boston I and A-20 to A-20H); two in separate enclosed cockpits (P-70 series and British Havoc night fighters); four in separate enclosed cockpits (F-3 series, A-20J, A-20K, DB-73, and Boston III to V).

	7B	DB-7 Havoc I	DB-7A	DB-7B Boston III	A-20A	A-20C Boston IIIA	A-20G-20-DO	P-70
Span, ft in	61 0	61 3	61 3	61 4	61 4	61 4	61 4	61 4
(m)	(18·59)	(18·67)	(18·67)	(18·69)	(18·69)	(18·69)	(18·69)	(18·69)
Length, ft in	45 5	46 11¾	47 0	47 6	47 7	47 3⅜	47 11⅞	47 7
(m)	(13·84)	(14·32)	(14·33)	(14·48)	(14·50)	(14·42)	(14·63)	(14·50)
Height, ft in	—	15 10	15 10	17 7	17 7	17 7	17 7	17 7
(m)	—	(4·83)	(4·83)	(5·36)	(5·36)	(5·36)	(5·36)	(5·36)
Wing area, sq ft	464	464	464	464	464	464	464	464
(sq m)	(43·107)	(43·107)	(43·107)	(43·107)	(43·107)	(43·107)	(43·107)	(43·107)
Empty weight, lb	—	11,400	13,674	12,200	15,165	15,090	16,993	16,031
(kg)	—	(5,171)	(6,202)	(5,534)	(6,879)	(6,845)	(7,708)	(7,272)
Gross weight, lb	15,200	19,040	19,322	19,750	20,711	21,500	24,127	21,264
(kg)	(6,895)	(8,636)	(8,765)	(8,958)	(9,394)	(9,752)	(10,964)	(9,645)
Wing loading, lb/sq ft	32·8	41	41·6	42·6	44·6	46·3	52	45·8
(kg/sq m)	(159·9)	(200·3)	(203·3)	(207·8)	(217·9)	(226·1)	(254·3)	(223·8)
Power loading, lb/hp	6·9	5·95	6	6·2	6·5	6·7	7·1	6·6
(kg/hp)	(3·1)	(2·7)	(2·7)	(2·8)	(2·9)	(3·0)	(3·2)	(3·0)
Maximum speed, mph at ft	304/5,000	295/13,000	323/12,800	320/11,000	347/12,400	342/13,000	317/10,700	329/14,000
(km/h at m)	(484/1,524)	(475/3,960)	(520/3,900)	(515/3,355)	(558/3,780)	(552/3,960)	(510/3,260)	(529/4,265)
Cruising speed, mph	185	—	275	273	295	280	256	270
(km/h)	(298)	—	(443)	(439)	(475)	(451)	(412)	(435)
Climb rate, ft/min	—	12,000/8	2,420/1	2,000/1	10,000/5·1	10,000/6·3	10,000/8·8	12,000/8
(m/min)	—	(3,658/8)	(738/1)	(610/1)	(3,050/5·1)	(3,050/6·3)	(3,050/8·8)	(3,658/8)
Service ceiling, ft	27,600	25,800	27,680	24,500	28,175	25,320	23,700	28,250
(m)	(8,415)	(7,835)	(8,435)	(7,470)	(8,590)	(7,720)	(7,225)	(8,610)
Combat range, miles	1,555	996	490	1,240	525	745	945	1,060
(km)	(2,503)	(1,603)	(789)	(1,996)	(845)	(1,199)	(1,521)	(1,706)
Maximum range, miles	—	—	—	—	1,000	2,300	2,100	—
(km)	—	—	—	—	(1,609)	(3,701)	(3,380)	—

294

ARMAMENT

Aircraft Versions	Nose (fixed)	Fuselage (fixed)	Dorsal Position (flexible)	Ventral Position (flexible)	Engine Nacelles (fixed)	Tail Turret (flexible)	Bomb Load Normal	Maximum
7B	2 x 0.50 4 x 0.30	-	1 x 0.30	1 x 0.30	-	-	1,560 lb (708 kg)	2,000 lb (908 kg)
DB-7	-	4 x 7.5 mm	1 x 7.5 mm	1 x 7.5 mm	-	-	1,411 lb (640 kg)	1,764 lb (800 kg)
DB-7A	-	4 x 7.5 mm	1 x 7.5 mm	1 x 7.5 mm	2 x 7.5 mm	-	1,411 lb (640 kg)	1,764 lh (800 kg)
DB-7C	(4 x 20 mm)	4 x 0.303	2 x 0.303	1 x 0.303	-	-	1,500 lb (680 kg)	2,000 lb (908 kg)
A-20, A-20A, A-20E, XF-3	-	4 x 0.30	2 x 0.30	1 x 0.30	(2 x 0.30)	-	1,600 lb (726 lb)	
A-20B	-	2 x 0.50	1 x 0.50	1 x 0.30	(2 x 0.30)	-	1,500 lb (680 kg)	2,400 lb (1,089 kg)
A-20C	(6 x 0.50)	4 x 0.30	2 x 0.30	1 x 0.30	-	-	2,000 lb (908 kg)	
XA-20F	(1 x 37 mm)	-	2 x 0.50	2 x 0.50	-	-	1,600 lb (726 lb)	
A-20G-1	4 x 20 mm	-	2 x 0.50	1 x 0.30	-	-	2,000 lb (908 kg)	
A-20G-5 to A-20G-15	6 x 0.50	-	1 x 0.50	1 x 0.30	-	-	2,000 lb (908 kg)	
A-20G-20 to A-20G-45 and A-20H	6 x 0.50	-	2 x 0.50	1 x 0.50	-	-	2,000 lb (908 kg)	4,000 lb (1,816 kg)
A-20J and A-20K and Boston IV and V	-	2 x 0.50	2 x 0.50	1 x 0.50	-	-	2,000 lb (908 kg)	4,000 lb (1,816 kg)
YF-3	-	2 x 0.30	2 x 0.30	1 x 0.30	2 x 0.30	2 x 0.30	-	-
F-3A	-	-	2 x 0.50	1 x 0.50	-	-	-	-
XP-70 and P-70	-	4 x 20 mm	-	-	-	-	-	-
P-70A-1	6 x 0.50	:	-	-	-	-	-	-
P 70A-2 and P 70B-2	-	6 or 8 x 0.50	-	-	-	-	-	-
P-70B-1	-	6 x 0.50	-	-	-	-	-	-
Boston III and Boston IIIA	-	4 x 0.303	2 x 0.303	1 x 0.303	-	-	2,000 lb (908 kg)	
Boston III (Intruder)	-	4 x 0.303 4 x 20 mm	2 x 0.303	1 x 0.303	-	-	1,000 lb (454 kg)	
Havoc I (Intruder)	-	4 x 0.303	1 x 0.303	-	-	-	2,400 lb (1,090 kg)	
Havoc I (Night Fighter)	4 x 0.303	4 x 0.303	-	-	-	-	-	-
Havoc II	12 x 0.303	-	-	-	-	-	-	-

An A-20C-DO (41-19205) was modified as the sole single-seat RA-20C target aircraft. All combat equipment was removed, additional armour panels were fitted around the engines and cockpit, and the fuselage upper decking was cut back. Like Bell RP-63s, the RA-20C was to have been used as a gunnery target against which frangible bullets shattered. (*Air Force Museum*)

The DC-5 prototype (NX21701) on 17 April, 1939, almost two months after its maiden flight. (*MDC*)

Douglas DC-5

The DC-5 was the only Douglas Commercial transport designed and built in the El Segundo plant. The design, entrusted to a team led by Project Engineer Leo Devlin and supervised by Ed Heinemann, was begun during the summer of 1938 in anticipation of a demand for a short-haul feeder transport with performance similar to that of the DC-3s then being used on longer routes with heavier traffic. Benefiting from their own experience with the Northrop Delta series and from their work on the Model 7A and 7B attack bombers, the El Segundo team decided to use a twin-engined high-wing configuration and a fully retractable undercarriage with the main units retracting laterally into the wings outboard of the engine nacelles. The aircraft bore a strong family resemblance to the Model 7B, the only twin-engined aircraft previously designed by this team, which was then about to make its first flight.

As detailed engineering design progressed and construction of a prototype, undertaken as a private venture without airline backing, was initiated, the aircraft began to take shape as an elegant machine. Accommodation for a crew of three and sixteen passengers was planned as standard but provision was made in the design for increasing passenger capacity to twenty-two in high-density configuration. Customers were offered a choice between Wright Cyclone or Pratt & Whitney Hornet engines driving fully-feathering propellers, and two 900 hp Wright Cyclone GR-1820-F62 nine-cylinder air-cooled radials were selected for initial

296

installation on the prototype. In this form the DC-5 (s/n 411, NX21701) was completed in February 1939 and on the 20th of that month Carl Cover took it on its maiden flight. It then appeared that the enterprise was going to be fully rewarded as orders were placed, by KLM for four aircraft, by Pennsylvania-Central for six and by the Colombian airline SCADTA for two, while, shortly after, the Navy Department approved a contract for three of a military version, the R3D-1, for the Navy and for four R3D-2s for the Marine Corps.

Not well known is the fact that the original British Airways, after comparative analyses of the potential of the de Havilland Flamingo and the DC-5 on the London–Berlin route had been prepared during the spring of 1939, had signed on 30 August, 1939, an agreement with Douglas to purchase nine DC-5s and had made an initial down-payment of some 25 per cent towards the price (including ferrying charges to Floyd Bennett Field, New York, lighterage to shipside, ocean freight and import duties, the aircraft unit cost was estimated at £27,912). The first aircraft was scheduled for delivery to New York on 15 December, 1939, the second on 29 December, the third on 22 January, 1940, and the six remaining aircraft were to follow at weekly intervals. In anticipation of their delivery, British Airways' DC-5s were assigned the registrations G-AFYG to G-AFYO inclusive. However, following the outbreak of war, the Air Ministry instructed British Airways to cancel the order and the down-payment funds were transferred towards the purchase of other Douglas types for British military use.

The DC-5's success was, however, short-lived as the aircraft ran into aerodynamic difficulties during its test flight programme when excessive tail buffet was experienced. The trouble was traced to interference between the drag of the high-mounted wings, the engines and the tail surfaces, and to solve this problem the tailplane was given marked dihedral to remove it from the wake created by the wings and engines. Unfortunately, by the time the difficulties had been overcome the war situation in Europe and

A Marine R3D-2 before delivery. (*NA & SM*)

American military build-up made it necessary to concentrate the company's efforts on current military programmes. Furthermore, SCADTA and Pennsylvania-Central Airlines, like British Airways, had withdrawn their orders.

As a result, only five commercial DC-5s, including the prototype, and seven military R3Ds were built. After completion of its trial programme, the first aircraft was re-engined with 1,100 hp Wright R-1820-G102As and, as NC21701 *Rover*, was delivered on 19 April, 1940, to William E. Boeing.

William Boeing's DC-5 at Oakland, California, in 1940. (*Peter M. Bowers*)

The aircraft thus became the second Douglas aircraft to be used by the founder of the Boeing Airplane Company but, less than twenty-two months later, it was impressed by the US Navy and became the only R3D-3 (BuNo 08005). This aircraft was followed by the four R-1820-G102A-powered aircraft which had been ordered by KLM for use on its European routes and tentatively assigned the registrations and names PH-AXA *Alk*, PH-AXB *Bergeend*, PH-AXE *Eend* and PH-AXG *Gruto*. However, the German invasion of The Netherlands forced KLM to divert these aircraft to its overseas operations; two were delivered in May 1940 to KLM (West Indies Division) in Curaçao as PJ-AIW *Wakago* and PJ-AIZ *Zonvogel* while the other two were shipped to Batavia for service with KNILM as PK-ADA and PK-ADB. After serving for a year in the West Indies, PJ-AIW and PJ-AIZ were also shipped to Batavia where they were respectively re-registered PK-ADD and PK-ADC and added to the KNILM fleet, with which they were serving when the Japanese attacked.

The war in the Pacific, rather than ending the already chequered career of these four aircraft, led them to a new and colourful life. PK-ADA's fate was unique. The aircraft had been damaged during a raid on Kemajoran Airport, Batavia, on 9 February, 1942, and after being captured it was repaired and overhauled before being tested at Tachikawa by the Japanese Army and ended its life as an Army radio-navigational trainer. The remaining three DC-5s of KNILM, after helping to evacuate the civil population from Java to Australia, were operated in Australia and New Guinea by Australian National Airways and No.21 Squadron, RAAF, on

PJ-AIW before modification to full production standard, and without tailplane dihedral. The aircraft was eventually impressed into the USAAF as 44-83231, one of three C-110-DEs. (*KLM*)

behalf of the Allied Directorate for Air Transport and were assigned the radio call signs VH-CXA to VH-CXC. These aircraft were impressed in 1944 by the USAAF and, designated C-110-DEs and bearing the serials 44-83230 to 44-83232, were operated by the 374th Troop Carrier Group of the Fifth Air Force. At the end of the war, one of them (s/n 426, ex-PH-AXB, PJ-AIZ, PK-ADC, VH-CXC and 44-83232) was acquired as scrap by Australian National Airways which repaired it and had it registered in September 1946 as VH-ARD. This machine, the last flyable DC-5, was acquired by New Holland Airways in 1947 and finally ended its career at the Tel Aviv Aeronautical Technical School.

In military use the impressed KNILM DC-5s had been preceded by the R3D-1s and R3D-2s which had their fuel capacity increased from 550 US gallons (2,082 litres) to 650 gallons (2,460 litres). Powered by two 1,000 hp

PK-ADA of KNILM during its evaluation by the Japanese Army Air Force at Tachikawa. (*Peter M. Bowers*)

299

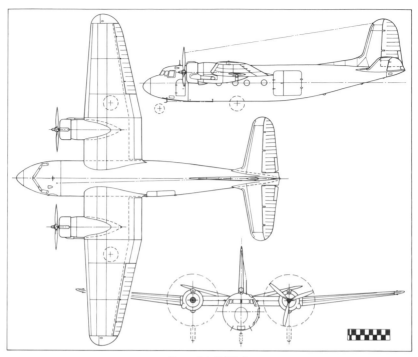

Douglas R3D-2.

Wright R-1820-44 nine-cylinder air-cooled radials, the three R3D-1s (BuNos 1901 to 1903) had been ordered as sixteen-seat personnel transports for US Navy use. However, only two of them were accepted by the Navy in July 1940 as the first one (BuNo 1901) had crashed at Mines Field on 1 June, 1940, before delivery. Supplemented in February 1942 by the only R3D-3, impressed and assigned the BuNo 08005, these aircraft were operated throughout the war and the last two were retired in January 1946.

Four similarly-powered R3D-2s (BuNos 1904 to 1907) were delivered to the Marine Corps in September and October 1940. Fitted as cargo transports, they had a reinforced cabin floor and a 5 ft 6 in by 6 ft 8 in (1·68 m by 2·03 m) door on the port side of the rear fuselage enabling the handling of complete aero-engines on their shipping stands. Alternatively, the R3D-2s could be fitted with twenty-two bucket seats for paratrooper transport. During the war these aircraft were operated within the continental United States and in the Pacific—two R3D-2s were in Hawaii at the time of the Japanese attack and one of these was subsequently shot down off the coast of Australia by a Japanese submarine—and the last three R3D-2s were retained in the Marine inventory until 31 October, 1946.

300

William Boeing's DC-5 shortly after taking-off from the Oakland Municipal Airport, California, in 1940. The outward-retracting main gear is noteworthy. (*Peter M. Bowers*)

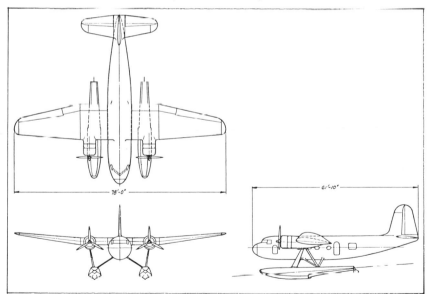

Proposed floatplane version of the DC-5 with Edo Floats. (*Douglas drawing*)

VH-CXC, s/n 426, in Australian National Airways (ANA) markings before being rebuilt as VH-ARD. (*Mervvn W. Prime*)

As an alternative to the standard Wright Cyclone-powered DC-5, Douglas also offered a version powered by four 600 hp Ranger SGV-770 twelve-cylinder inverted-vee air-cooled engines. (*Douglas drawing*)

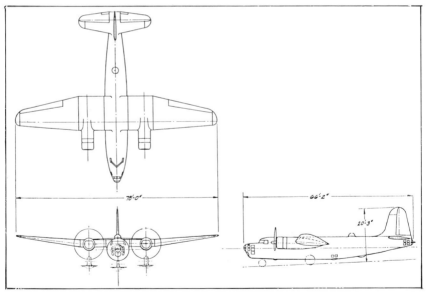

Among proposed DC-5 developments was this 'DB-5' which could be used either as a bomber, with 44 50-lb (22.7-kg) bombs, or as a transport, with 30 troops on canvas seats along the fuselage sides. (*Douglas drawing*)

302

DC-5

Span 78 ft (23·77 m); length 62 ft 2 in (18·96 m); height 19 ft 10 in (6·04 m); wing area 824 sq ft (76·55 sq m). Empty weight 13,674 lb (6,243 kg); loaded weight 20,000 lb (9,072 kg); wing loading 24·3 lb/sq ft (118·5 kg/sq m); power loading 9·1 lb/hp (4·1 kg/hp). Maximum speed 230 mph (370 km/h) at 7,700 ft (2,345 m); cruising speed 202 mph (325 km/h); initial rate of climb 1,585 ft/min (483 m/min); service ceiling 23,700 ft (7,225 m); maximum range 1,600 miles (2,575 km).

R3D-1

Span, length and wing area as DC-5. Height 22 ft 7 in (6·88 m). Empty weight 14,188 lb (6,436 kg); loaded weight 21,000 lb (9,525 kg); wing loading 25·5 lb/sq ft (124·5 kg/sq m); power loading 10·5 lb/hp (4·8 kg/hp). Maximum speed 221 mph (356 km/h) at 5,800 ft (1,770 m); initial rate of climb 1,000 ft/min (305 m/min); service ceiling 19,000 ft (5,790 m); maximum range 1,440 miles (2,315 km).

R3D-2

As R3D-1 except empty weight 13,863 lb (6,288 kg) and maximum range 935 miles (1,505 km).

Douglas B-23 Dragon

It was obvious to Douglas and the Army Air Corps that the performance of the B-18 series was rapidly rendering it obsolete. Accordingly, Douglas proposed improving the bomber's performance by fitting 1,600 hp Wright R-2600-2s to a version of the B-18A which was to be designated B-22. In spite of the substantial increase in available power, the calculated performance fell short of the Air Corps' requirements and development was abandoned. In its place, Douglas proposed a major redesign making use of the stronger wings of the DC-3, a new and better streamlined fuselage, and a large fin and rudder.

B-23 over the Sierra Nevada on 29 August, 1940. (*USAF*)

Designated B-23, the new aircraft was ordered in late 1938 when a Change Order to Contract AC9977 substituted thirty-eight B-23s (s/n 2713 to 2750, serials 39-27 to 39-64) for an equal number of B-18As previously ordered. Although virtually a completely new design, the B-23 was ordered without the usual provision for prototype and Service trials aircraft—which, had they been ordered, would have been designated XB-23 and YB-23 respectively—and all were produced under the simple B-23 designation. The first of these aircraft, powered by two 1,600 hp Wright R-2600-3s, was completed in July 1939 and was first flown at Clover Field, Santa Monica, on the 27th of that month. On this occasion, the aircraft (s/n 2713, 39-27) was fitted with an unglazed nose, whereas production aircraft had a glazed nose housing the bomb-aimer's station and a flexible 0·30-in machine-gun on a ball-socket mount. In service, the B-23s also carried a light machine-gun on a swing mount attached to the aft fuselage bulkhead and firing either through beam hatches or through a swing-down dorsal panel, while a third 0·30-in gun was fired through a ventral hatch. However, the B-23's armament was especially significant due to the mounting of a

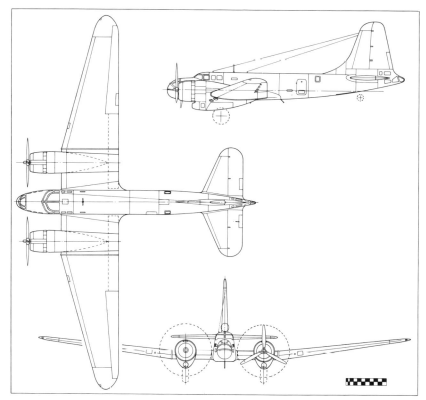

Douglas B-23.

304

A B-23 in service with the 89th Reconnaissance Squadron. (*USAF*)

hand-held 0·50-in machine-gun in a glazed tail gunner's position, the first to be fitted to an American bomber. In addition to its intended role as a bomber, for which a bomb bay capable of accommodating bombs of up to 2,000 lb (908 kg) was fitted behind the pilot's compartment, the B-23 was planned as a photographic reconnaissance aircraft and, consequently, had permanent provision for a camera mounted on the left fuselage side against the forward bulkhead. The crew comprised pilot, bomb-aimer, navigator, radio operator, camera operator and gunner.

After being evaluated by the Materiel Division at Wright Field, Ohio, the B-23s entered service in 1940 with the 89th Reconnaissance Squadron at March Field, California. However, by 1941, even though its top speed of 282 mph (454 km/h) was 66 mph (106 km/h) faster than the B-18A's and its maximum range of 2,750 miles (4,425 km) surpassed that of its forebear, the B-23 was clearly inferior to the B-17E—the first model of the Boeing bomber fully representative of the wartime Flying Fortress. As a twin-engined medium bomber, the B-23 was also slower than the North American B-25 and Martin B-26 and it carried much lighter defensive

C-67 (39-047) used as a staff transport by General C. E. Bradshaw in 1944. (*US National Archives*)

The R-2800 testbed B-23 (39-32) with its port and starboard engines respectively driving three- and four-blade propellers. (*Pratt & Whitney*)

armament than did these newer designs. Consequently, the Douglas bomber was no longer needed in its intended role and the Army Air Forces made it available for conversions and use in special tests.

At least eighteen of these aircraft (known serials 39-29, -31, -34, -35, -39, -41, -43, -44, -47, -54 to -59, -61, -63 and -64) were modified as transports—a class of aircraft which became urgently needed following the start of the war—under the UC-67 designation. Special tests conducted with other B-23s included glider pick-up tests on aircraft 39-28, a method by which a glider's tow line, held off the ground between two poles, was caught by a hook mounted beneath the rear fuselage, thus enabling the B-23 to take the glider in tow without having to land. Emerson Electric also used 39-28 to evaluate various remote gun control and aiming systems. The sixth B-23 (serial 39-32) was handed over to Pratt & Whitney on 20 August, 1940, to be used for accelerated testing of the 1,850 hp R-2800-5 engine in support of the B-26 and XB-28 programme, and was tested with both three-blade and

HC-APV, a civil transport version of the B-23/C-67, which was owned for over ten years by Cia Ecuatoriana de Aviacion. It is seen at Mariscal Sucre International Airport, Quito, in February 1977. (*René J. Francillon*)

four-blade propellers. Finally, 39-53 was operated from Muroc Dry Lake, California, as a control ship for the Culver PQ-8 radio-controlled target.

Following the end of the war, the B-23s and UC-67s were sold as surplus and easily found a market as corporate aircraft. At that time, most of these aircraft were modified for their new role by the Engineering Department of Pan American Airways. As corporate aircraft, they were fitted with a new and longer metal nose and, with a crew of two and full washroom facilities, accommodated twelve passengers in two compartments. Several of these civil B-23s were still flying in the early 1970s and, almost thirty years after having been declared surplus by the Army Air Forces, one aircraft again came to be used in support of a USAF programme. Registered N52327, this aircraft (c/n 2722, ex 39-36) was operated in 1974 by the University of Washington for the Air Force Cambridge Research Laboratory. Heavily instrumented and flown by a crew of seven—pilot, co-pilot and five engineers—, it was used to sample cloud particles as part of a research project sponsored by the Space and Missile Systems Organization, Advanced Ballistic Reentry Systems Program Office.

Span 92 ft (28·04 m); length 58 ft 4¾ in (17·79 m); height 18 ft 5½ in (5·63 m); wing area 993 sq ft (92·253 sq m). Empty weight 19,089 lb (8,659 kg); loaded weight 26,500 lb (12,020 kg); maximum weight 32,400 lb (14,696 kg); wing loading 26·7 lb/sq ft (130·3 kg/sq m); power loading 8·3 lb/hp (3·8 kg/hp). Maximum speed 282 mph (454 km/h) at 12,000 ft (3,660 m); cruising speed 210 mph (338 km/h); climb to 10,000 ft (3,050 m) 6·7 min; service ceiling 31,600 ft (9,630 m); normal range 1,400 miles (2,255 km); maximum range 2,750 miles (4,325 km).

Douglas XB-19

The XB-19 was an experimental long-range bomber stemming from a secret 'Project D' initiated by the US Army Air Corps on 5 February, 1935, and was the largest aircraft produced by the Douglas Aircraft Company. From the onset of 'Project D', the Air Corps stressed the experimental nature of the programme which had been initiated 'in an effort to further the advancement of military aviation by investigating the maximum feasible distance into the future'. Consequently, and in spite of having met all contractual guarantees and substantially exceeded several of them, only the original XB-19 (s/n 2001, serial 38-471) was built.

The Air Corps obtained the necessary administrative and governmental approvals leading to the preparation of Type Specification X-203 by the Matériel Division and to preliminary discussions with Douglas and Sikorsky. During a conference with Douglas representatives on 5 June, 1935, plans were made for this project and the following schedule was elaborated:

Start preliminary design, 31 July, 1935; start detailed design, 31 January, 1936; complete physical article, 31 March, 1938.

This plan, however, suffered numerous delays stemming both from the magnitude of the task and from the lack of sufficient funding, and the XB-19 was eventually completed in May 1941, more than three years behind the original schedule.

A contract covering preliminary and detailed design, mock-up construction and testing of critical components (wing centre section, engine nacelles and undercarriage) was sent to Douglas in October 1935 and finally approved on 18 October. Eventually, following evaluation of the mock-ups submitted by Douglas and Sikorsky, the Douglas design was declared winner of the competition. As time went on, little progress was being made with detailed design and actual construction of the Douglas XBLR-2, as only piecemeal procurement could be obtained because of the limited military budget allowed for Research and Development between December 1935 and November 1937. During that period a number of changes were made in the contract and among other things resulted in the substitution of 2,000 hp Wright R-3350 air-cooled radials for the 1,600 hp Allison XV-3420-1 liquid-cooled engines originally specified. Meanwhile, Douglas obtained on loan from the Air Corps a Douglas OA-4A which was modified to test a tricycle undercarriage, such as had been selected for the XBLR-2. Finally, as funds were made available, construction of a prototype—now re-designated XB-19—was authorized on 8 March, 1938.

The XB-19 displaying its unusually large wing area. (*USAF*)

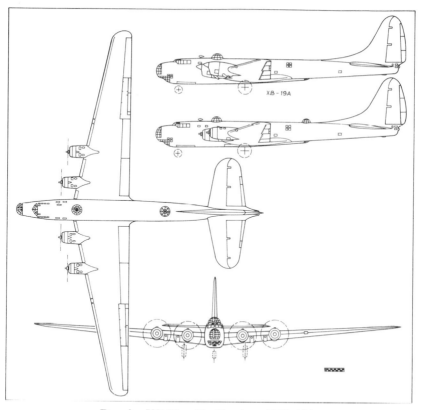

Douglas XB-19, with side view of XB-19A.

Having been forced to spend considerably more of its own funds than had been anticipated and badly needing design personnel to work on other aircraft types having a substantial production future, Douglas temporarily lost interest in the XB-19. Consequently, pointing out that delays suffered during the previous three years had rendered the design obsolete and that weight had increased beyond expectation, on 30 August, 1938, the company recommended cancellation of the contract. The Matériel Division, however, refused to consider the project's abandonment and construction continued slowly. Two years later the Air Corps did indirectly admit that the XB-19 had lost most of its military significance when it removed it from the secret classified list. None the less, at the time of its completion the XB-19 remained a physically and psychologically big aircraft and it was the largest American aircraft until the completion of the Convair B-36 in August 1946.

When completed in May 1941, the XB-19 appeared as a very large, all-metal, stressed-skin low-wing monoplane fitted with a retractable tricycle undercarriage. Its wing span of 212 ft (64·62 m), its maximum gross weight

309

of 162,000 lb (73,482 kg) and its two mainwheels of 8 ft (2·44 m) diameter were particularly impressive at the time. It was powered by four 2,000 hp Wright R-3350-5 eighteen-cylinder radials driving three-blade constant-speed metal propellers of 17 ft (5·18 m) diameter. To obtain the required range, the engines were fed from integral tanks with a capacity of 10,350 US gallons (38,178 litres) while auxiliary tanks with a capacity of 824 gallons (3,119 litres) could be fitted in the bomb bay. With a reduced fuel load a maximum bomb-load of 37,100 lb (16,828 kg) was carried internally and on ten external wing racks while defensive armament—not fitted at the time of completion—included one 37-mm cannon and one 0·30-in machine-gun in the nose and forward dorsal turrets, one 0·50-in machine-gun in each of the following five locations: tail position, rear dorsal turret, ventral turret, and port and starboard positions, and one 0·30-in machine-gun on each side of the bomb-aimer's station and on each side of the fuselage below the tailplane. Normal combat crew consisted of sixteen men but two additional flight mechanics and a six-man relief crew could be accommodated in a special compartment fitted with eight seats and six bunks. To serve this unusually large crew during long flights a complete galley was fitted for inflight preparation of hot meals.

Following completion of the aircraft, initial taxying tests started on 6 May, 1941, but the first flight, scheduled for 17 May, had to be postponed three times due to severe brake difficulties and engine back-firing problems, while the propeller-pitch control system had to be re-wired. Finally, on 27 June, 1941, a crew of seven captained by Major Stanley M. Ulmstead took the XB-19 on its 55-minute maiden flight from Clover Field, Santa Monica, to March Field. This flight was uneventful and won for Donald Douglas a

On 23 January, 1942, the now camouflaged XB-19 was transferred to Wright Field, near which it is seen at the end of the ferry flight from California. (*USAF*)

310

The XB-19 at Wright Field in the spring of 1942. (*USAF*)

congratulatory cable from President Roosevelt. Following this first flight the XB-19 was put through a contractual 30-hour manufacturer's flight-test programme before being tentatively accepted by the Air Corps in October 1941. The Japanese attack on Pearl Harbor imposed a need for special precautions and the aircraft was camouflaged and its guns loaded during the last four test flights in California. However, as an additional safety measure the aircraft was transferred to Wright Field on 23 January, 1942, by which time it had accumulated a total flying time of 70·05 hours.

In June 1942, after minor modifications and installation of improved brakes, the aircraft was accepted and final payment authorized. Total actual contract cost to the US Government was $1,400,064 but in addition the Douglas Aircraft Company had spent almost $4,000,000 in company funds. During the following eighteen months the aircraft and its engines were extensively tested by the USAAF and these tests provided extremely valuable data which were incorporated in the design of other large aircraft, such as the Boeing B-29 and the Convair B-36, which were to be built in substantial numbers and to see considerable service. On test the XB-19 proved relatively trouble-free with the exception of engine cooling difficulties which necessitated keeping the cooling gills opened during long flights, thus reducing maximum speed from 224 mph at 15,700 ft (360 km/h at 4,785 m) to 204 mph (328 km/h) at the same altitude.

Eventually, having outlived its usefulness as a flying laboratory, the aircraft was modified at Wright Field as a cargo aircraft and fitted with four 2,600 hp Allison V-3420-11 twenty-four cylinder liquid-cooled engines, the production version of the powerplant originally specified for the aircraft. Re-designated XB-19A, it reached a top speed of 265 mph (426 km/h) and was no longer plagued by cooling problems. During the next two-and-a-half years the XB-19A was transferred from airfield to airfield within the State of Ohio (from Wright Field to Patterson Field, to Lockbourne Air Base, and to Clinton County Air Base) as its rapidly downgrading importance forced its relegation to less important but less congested airfields. Finally, on 17 August, 1946, the XB-19A made its final flight from Wright Field to Davis-Monthan Field, Arizona, where it was stored until scrapped three years later. Thus ended the aircraft which Major-Gen George H. Brett had called the Douglas Flying Behemoth.

With Allison V-3420-11 liquid-cooled engines, the Douglas experimental bomber was redesignated XB-19A. (*USAF*)

Span 212 ft (64·62 m); length 132 ft 4 in (40·34 m); height 42 ft (12·8 m); wing area 4,285 sq ft (398·091 sq m).

XB-19

Empty weight 86,000 lb (39,009 kg); loaded weight 140,000 lb (63,503 kg); maximum weight 162,000 lb (73,482 kg); wing loading 32·6 lb/sq ft (159·5 kg/sq m); power loading 17·5 lb/hp (7·9 kg/hp). Maximum speed 224 mph (360 km/h) at 15,700 ft (4,785 m); cruising speed 135 mph (217 km/h); initial rate of climb 650 ft/min (198 m/min); service ceiling 23,000 ft (7,010 m); normal range 5,200 miles (8,369 km); maximum range 7,710 miles (12,408 km).

XB-19A

Empty weight 92,400 lb (41,912 kg); loaded weight 140,230 lb (63,607 kg); wing loading 32·7 lb/ sq ft (159·8 kg/sq m); power loading 13·5 lb/hp (6·1 kg/hp). Maximum speed 265 mph (426 km/h) at 20,000 ft (6,095 m); cruising speed 185 mph (298 km/h); service ceiling 39,000 ft (11,885 m); normal range 4,200 miles (6,759 km).

Douglas DC-4 Skymaster

In mid-1939, American, Eastern and United Air Lines and Douglas shared the view that there was a need for an aircraft similar in capacity to the experimental DC-4 but of a lighter and somewhat simpler structure. Agreement was also reached on the need to use less complex systems and to design a cheaper aircraft and one easier to maintain and offering substantially improved operating economics.

The Douglas engineering team, led by A. E. Raymond and E. F. Burton, was aware that there would be little or no benefit in limiting itself to a redesign and decided to design a completely new aeroplane. Confusingly, the new machine was also designated DC-4, thus starting a tradition according to which a DC number became permanently assigned to a given design only when the aircraft was put into quantity production. To avoid the confusion stemming from this practice, the original DC-4 with triple fins and rudders became known as the DC-4E, the E standing for Experimental, under which designation it was described on page 277.

As originally conceived, the new DC-4 was some twenty-five per cent lighter than the DC-4E and had a design gross weight of 50,000 lb (22,680 kg). Its fuselage of circular cross-section had an internal diameter of 118 in

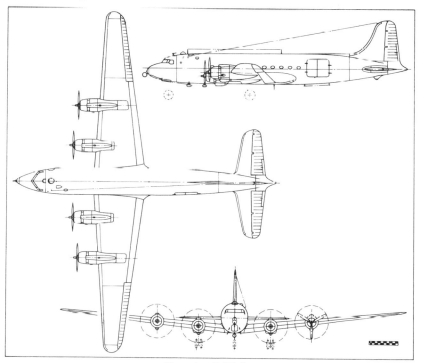

Douglas R5D-2.

313

(3 m), 10 in (25·4 cm) less than that of the DC-4E, and carried a single fin and rudder of clean design. The characteristic DC wings of the DC-4E, with marked sweep on the leading edge, were replaced by considerably smaller wings of higher aspect-ratio, and wing area was reduced from the DC-4E's 2,155 sq ft (200·6 sq m) to 1,457 sq ft (135·4 sq m). The new wings, with constant taper on leading and trailing edges, had a centre-section of typical Douglas/Northrop construction with three spars while their outer panels were of single spar construction. The tricycle undercarriage—one of the most successful features of the original Douglas four-engined transport— was retained for the new DC-4, although in a modified form as the main units retracted forward into the inboard engine nacelles instead of laterally into wing wells. The aircraft, with accommodation for 40 passengers by day—ten rows with two seats on each side of a central aisle—or 28 passengers by night, was initially offered to the airlines with a choice of powerplants: either four 1,000 hp Wright SGR-1820-G205A Cyclone nine-cylinder radials or four 1,050 hp Pratt & Whitney Twin Wasp S1C3-G fourteen-cylinder radials.

Initial reactions from American, Eastern and United were enthusiastic and, after a change in powerplant to four 1,450 hp Pratt & Whitney Twin Wasp (R-2000) 2SD1-G fourteen-cylinder radials had been agreed upon, orders began to come in. For a while, however, it appeared that the DC-4 was doomed before it ever flew. The war in Europe had resulted in increased military orders for Douglas, from the British and French Purchasing Commissions as well as by the US Armed Forces, and the War Department instructed Douglas to concentrate on the design and manufacture of combat aircraft and of the DC-3 and its military derivatives. Donald Douglas was, however, intent on producing his new four-engined transport for which he had received commercial orders for a total of 61 aircraft. After assuring the War Department that the DC-4 programme would not interfere with prompt delivery of military aircraft on order, the Douglas Aircraft Company prepared itself for DC-4 production and went ahead with its construction, albeit at a reduced pace. The Japanese attack affected once again the DC-4 production plans. However, after some uncertainty regarding the eventual disposition of the aircraft already under construction, they were taken over by the US Army Air Forces and designated C-54-DOs and C-54A-DOs.

No DC-4 or C-54 prototype was built, and the first production aircraft, s/n 3050, serial 41-20137, was completed as a C-54-DO in February 1942. Finished in military markings, it made its first flight from Clover Field, Santa Monica, on 14 February with John F. Martin in command. The C-54's successful maiden flight and its trouble-free development trials programme provided the USAAF with a long-range heavy logistic transport, a type urgently needed by the worldwide scale of operations into which the United States had been forced without proper preparation. The need to meet a requirement for longer range on transatlantic and trans-Pacific flights led to the modification of the first twenty-four aircraft—

including the experimental aircraft—to install four auxiliary fuel tanks in the main cabin. With these tanks total capacity increased from 2,012 US gallons (7,616 litres), as planned for the commercial DC-4, to 3,580 US gallons (13,550 litres) for the C-54-DOs, but seating capacity was reduced to twenty-six. However, the C-54-DO was seen only as a stop gap version designed to take advantage of the commercial DC-4 airframes already in an advanced stage of construction and the first true military version of the aircraft was the C-54A-DO which was equipped to carry either troops or cargo.

With the appearance of the C-54A quantity production of the DC-4—although in its military uniform—was finally assured and, to supplement production at Santa Monica, Douglas established a new production line in its Chicago plant. As a result, production of C-54s increased rapidly, with 24 aircraft being delivered in 1942, 74 in 1943, 354 in 1944, 710 in 1945, and, following cancellation of contracts after VJ-Day, one in 1946. The aircraft appeared in the following versions:

C-54-DO: Twenty-four military personnel transports (serials 41-20137 to 41-20145 and 42-32936 to 42-32950) fitted with four long-range auxiliary fuel tanks in the main cabin and with accommodation for 26. All C-54-DOs were received by the USAAF in 1942 and the first accepted was s/n 3060, serial 41-20138, which was delivered on 20 March, 1942, less than five weeks after the first flight of s/n 3050. Four 1,350 hp Pratt & Whitney R-2000-3s. Maximum weight: 65,800 lb (29,846 kg).

C-54A-DO: Fully militarized version equipped to carry either up to 50 troops or up to 32,500 lb (14,515 kg) of cargo. Reinforced cabin floor, 94 in by 67 in (2·38 m by 1·7 m) cargo door in port rear fuselage and built-in twin-boom cargo-loading hoist. Ninety-seven built in the Santa Monica plant (serials 41-37268 to 41-37319 and 42-107426 to 42-107470) in three blocks. Four 1,350 hp R-2000-7s. Maximum weight increased to 73,000 lb (33,122 kg) and reinforced structure. Maximum tank capacity when auxiliary cabin tanks fitted: 3,620 US gallons (13,703 litres).

Bearing the British military serial EW999, this Skymaster I (C-54B-1-DO, 43-17126) served as the personal transport of the Prime Minister, Mr (later Sir) Winston Churchill. (*via MSgt David Menard*)

315

C-54A-DC: One hundred and fifty-five aircraft (42-72165 to 42-72319) identical to the C-54A-DOs but built in four blocks at the Chicago plant. Of the 252 C-54As built in both plants, 56 were transferred to the US Navy as R5D-1s. The first Chicago-built aircraft to be delivered (s/n 10271, serial 42-72166) was accepted by the USAAF on 1 October, 1943.

C-54B-DO: Similar to the C-54A except for the removal of two of the four auxiliary cabin fuel tanks and installation of integral tanks in the outer wing panels. Total fuel capacity: 3,740 US gallons (14,157 litres). One hundred built at Santa Monica in five blocks (43-17124 to 43-17198 and 44-9001 to 44-9025). Early production aircraft were powered by four R-2000-3s while others had R-2000-7s. Cargo-loading hoist not fitted on aircraft from the third block (C-54B-10-DOs). One C-54B-1-DO (s/n 18326, serial 43-17126) was transferred to Britain for use by the Prime Minister, then Mr Winston Churchill, (RAF serial EW999).

C-54B-DC: Chicago-built version of the C-54B of which 120 were delivered (42-72320 to 42-72439) as C-54B-1-DCs. Thirty of the 220 C-54Bs built in both plants were delivered to the US Navy as R5D-2s.

VC-54C-DO: One C-54A-5-DO (s/n 7470, serial 42-107451) specially modified to serve as Presidential transport for President Roosevelt. Named *Sacred Cow*, the aircraft was fitted with a state-room and three conference rooms and had six bunks. Normal accommodation for the President, a staff of fourteen and a crew of seven. Total fuel capacity was increased to 4,510 US gallons (17,034 litres) by fitting integral tanks in the outer wing panels. Electric lift fitted for the President's wheelchair.

C-54D-DC: Built exclusively at the Chicago plant, the C-54D was the Skymaster version delivered in largest number. Including 86 aircraft delivered to the US Navy as R5D-3s, a total of 380 C-54Ds was built (42-72440 to 42-72764 and 43-17199 to 43-17253). Generally similar to the C-54Bs but powered by four 1,350 hp R-2000-11s. Same fuel tank arrangement as C-54B. Modification of existing C-54Ds led to the appearance of several specialized variants. A small number of C-54Ds

City of Las Vegas (C-54D-10-DC, 42-72674), the support aircraft of the 4520th Air Demonstration Squadron, the renowned *Thunderbirds*. (*David Ostrowski*)

SC-54D of the Air Rescue Service, Military Air Transport Service. This ex C-54D-5-DC was one of thirty-six Skymasters modified by Convair for search and rescue missions. (*USAF*)

fitted with special electronic equipment to check airways and air communication equipment were initially designated AC-54Ds but redesignated EC-54Ds in 1962. Nine C-54Ds modified for special duties associated with the recovery of missile nose cones became JC-54Ds. Thirty-eight C-54Ds were modified by Convair for use by MATS Air Rescue Service and were fitted with special radar equipment and observation blisters on the rear fuselage; initially known as SC-54Ds, they were later redesignated HC-54Ds. When modified as multi-engined trainers, the C-54Ds were designated TC-54Ds. Finally, the designation VC-54D was given to some C-54Ds modified as staff transports.

C-54E-DO: Differing from the C-54Ds mainly in having a new fuel tank arrangement in which the remaining two cabin tanks were replaced by collapsible bag-type tanks in the inner wings, total tank capacity 3,520 US gallons (13,324 litres), 125 C-54Es (44-9026 to 44-9150) were built in Santa Monica. Twenty of these went to the US Navy as R5D-4s. Internal cabin arrangement modified to permit rapid conversion from cargo (32,500 lb, 14,515 kg) to troop carriers (50 bucket canvas seats) or to staff transport (44 airline-type seats).

XC-54F-DC: Designation applied to one C-54B-1-DC (s/n 10426, 42-72321) fitted with two paratroop jump doors for use by Troop Carrier Command. Planned C-54F-DC production version was to have been based on C-54D-DC airframes but none was built.

C-54G-DO: Primarily intended as troop carriers, the C-54Gs had similar airframes to the C-54Es but were powered by four R-2000-9s. One hundred and sixty-two C-54Gs (45-476 to 45-637) were built in four blocks at Santa Monica and thirteen were transferred to the US Navy as R5D-5s. After VJ-Day 235 C-54G-20-DOs (45-638 to 45-872) were cancelled and components from these were used by Douglas to produce the civil

317

C-54G-1-DO of the Air Transport Command, USAAF. (*MDC*)

DC-4-1009s. Serial 45-636 (s/n 36090) was the last C-54 delivered and was handed over to the USAAF on 22 January, 1946. The designation VC-54G was given to some C-54Gs modified after delivery to serve as staff transports.

C-54GM: Designation given to the DC-4 derivative built under licence by Canadair.

C-54H-DO: Projected paratroop transport version for Troop Carrier Command which was to have been powered by R-2000-9s. None built.

C-54J-DO: Projected staff transport version which was to be generally similar to the C-54G but without provision for cargo-carrying. None built.

XC-54K-DO: One C-54E-DO experimentally fitted with four 1,425 hp Wright R-1820-HD. Only Skymaster fitted with the nine-cylinder air-cooled Wright Cyclone radials originally offered as an optional powerplant installation for the pre-war DC-4. Not proceeded with.

C-54L-DO: One C-54A-DO modified to test a new fuel system. No production.

C-54M-DO: Designation applied to thirty-eight C-54E-DOs stripped to carry coal during the Berlin Airlift of 1948–49. Payload increased by 2,500 lb (1,134 kg) to 35,000 lb (15,876 kg).

MC-54M-DO: During the Korean War thirty C-54E-DOs were specially modified for aeromedical evacuation for which role they were fitted with 30 stretchers and accommodation for medical attendants.

XC-112: Projected development of the C-54 series with pressurized cabin and four Pratt & Whitney R-2800-22W eighteen-cylinder air-cooled radials. Abandoned in favour of XC-112A (*see* page 410).

XC-114-DO: One prototype (s/n 36327, 45-874) with airframe basically similar to that of the C-54E-DO but with fuselage length increased from

93 ft 10 in (28·6 m) to 100 ft 7 in (30·66 m) and powered by four 1,620 hp Allison V-1710-131 twelve-cylinder vee liquid-cooled engines. Gross weight increased to 80,500 lb (36,514 kg).

XC-115-DO: Projected development of the XC-114 which was to have had four 1,650 hp Packard V-1650-209 twelve-cylinder vee liquid-cooled engines. None built.

XC-116-DO: One aircraft (s/n 36327, 45-875) similar to the XC-114 but fitted with thermal de-icing equipment instead of pneumatic boots.

As indicated above, a number of C-54As, C-54Bs, C-54Ds, C-54Es and C-54Gs—the production of which was covered by contracts from the War Department on behalf of the USAAF—were transferred to the US Navy and the US Marine Corps as R5D-1s to R5D-5s. Designations, including those resulting from the adoption in September 1962 of a new Tri-Service designation system, given to the variants follow:

R5D-1: Fifty-six C-54As transferred to the US Navy (BuNos 39137, 39139, 39141 to 39181, 50840 to 50849, 57988 and 57989, and 91105). The designation R5D-1C was given to a limited number of R5D-1s modified in service by fitting similar fuel tank arrangement to that used by the C-54Bs and their naval counterparts, the R5D-2s. The R5D-1F (VC-54N after September 1962) designation was given to R5D-1s modified as staff transports. The R5D-1Z was an interim designation for the R5D-1F/VC-54N.

R5D-2 (C-54P): Naval version of the C-54B of which thirty were transferred from USAAF contracts (BuNos 50850 to 50868 and 90385 to 90395). R5D-2s modified as staff transports were successively designated R5D-2Fs, R5D-2Zs and VC-54Ps.

R5D-3 (C-54Q): Eighty-six C-54Ds transferred to the US Navy (BuNos 50869 to 50878, 56484 to 56549 and 91994 to 92003). Most surviving R5D-3s were redesignated C-54Qs in 1962 while a few, fitted with photographic equipment, became RC-54Vs. Staff transport variant was designated R5D-3Z and later VC-54Q.

R5D-4: Twenty C-54Es transferred to the US Navy (BuNos 90396 to 90415). The R5D-4R (C-54R) was a personnel transport modification. Other surviving R5D-4s became EC-54Us in 1962 when fitted with electronic countermeasure equipment for training and test purposes.

R5D-5 (C-54S): Naval version of the C-54G series of which at least thirteen were obtained by the Navy Department mainly for use by the US Coast Guard. Some were modified as personnel transports under the designation R5D-5R (VC-54T) while at least one was modified as staff transport under the designation R5D-5Z (VC-54S).

R5D-6: Projected version equivalent to the C-54J. None built.

Among the many projected developments of the C-54/R5D series, one proposal intended to increase range deserves a special mention. For transatlantic and trans-Pacific operations the C-54 had a limited payload-range envelope necessitating either numerous technical stops and/or a sizeable reduction in payload. Room for additional tanks within the

R5D-4R (BuNo 90414), which was assigned to NAS Los Alamitos, California, during a visit to NAAS Corry Field, Pensacola, Florida. (*NA & SM*)

airframe was not available beyond the installation of the collapsible bag-type tanks fitted to the C-54Es, and the only method possible to increase fuel load, without installing cabin tanks which reduced space available for payload, was the use of external tanks. Douglas conceived a novel system of large winged tanks which were to be attached to the wingtips by means of flexible joints linking each wingtip of the aircraft to one of the wingtips of the external tanks. Each tank was fitted, in addition to wings, with a retractable outrigger undercarriage bearing the weight of the tank whilst on the ground. The use of wings on the tanks was planned to reduce total aircraft wing loading, a critical factor once the weight of the tanks and the additional petrol was added to an already fully loaded C-54. While this scheme appeared promising, its development was suspended as newer transport aircraft with increased payload-range capability became available and enabled the US Armed Forces to assign their C-54s/R5Ds to shorter routes. The novel winged tank principle was, however, later used experimentally on the Beech XL-23C Seminole (55-3465).

When war ended and airlines scrambled to rebuild operations, the Skymasters drew the attention of commercial customers. Already, Douglas was anticipating a strong demand for commercial DC-4s incorporating all the improvements progressively introduced in the C-54 series and offered two new versions. The DC-4-1009 had no cargo door and was a passenger transport with accommodation for a crew of five and 44 passengers, baggage and freight for day use, or for 22 passengers, baggage and freight as a sleeper transport. This accommodation was equivalent to first class seating but, later, DC-4-1009s and ex-military C-54s had as many as 86 seats in high-density configuration. The DC-4-1037 was fitted as a commercial cargo transport and retained the large cargo door of the military C-54s on the port side. Both versions were to have Pratt & Whitney Twin Wasp (R-2000) radials rated at 1,450 hp for take-off. Normal fuel capacity was 2,868 US gallons (10,866 litres) but could be increased to 3,592 US gallons (13,596 litres). Cabin pressurization was available for the DC-4-1009s.

Benefiting from cancellation of 235 C-54G-20-DOs which left a large surplus of partially built aircraft and parts, Douglas was able to offer rapid delivery. In spite of this, the new versions did not have much success because cheaper surplus C-54s were available in large numbers. In the event only seventy-nine DC-4-1009s, all unpressurized, were built, the first (s/n 42904, NC10201) being delivered to Western Air Lines on 18 January, 1946, and no DC-4-1037 was ordered by the airlines. The needs of the airlines and foreign air forces were mainly satisfied by modified surplus C-54s and Douglas performed a substantial portion of this conversion in the Santa Monica and El Segundo plants while other aircraft were modified by the airlines themselves and by specialized companies. Finally, DC-4 production was terminated in 1947 following the delivery of the last DC-4-1009 (s/n 43157, ZS-BMH) to South African Airways on 9 August, 1947.

Following acceptance on 20 March, 1942, of their first C-54-DO, the Army Air Forces were able to supplement their makeshift fleet of four-engined transports with a truly effective aeroplane. From late 1942 onward, the C-54s carried an increasing share of US military personnel and cargo between the United States and bases of operations throughout the world, and their payload-range performance enabled them to pioneer inter-continental flights. Flying routinely over the North and South Atlantic, the Pacific and Indian Oceans, across Africa and over the Himalayas, the Skymasters provided the backbone for the long-range operations of Air Transport Command and built up a tremendous reputation for safety and operating reliability (during the war Skymasters completed 79,642 transocean flights with only three ditchings, of which one was a test).

R5D-2 (BuNo 50851) of the US Naval Research Laboratory, Patuxent River, modified as a radar laboratory. (*US National Archives*)

In the midst of their routine operations, the C-54s of Air Transport Command and the R5Ds of Naval Air Transport Service took part in a number of unusual operations. Mission Seventeen (Operation Argonaut) began in January 1945 when Air Transport Command was secretly alerted to prepare to carry American and British representatives to Yalta in the Crimea, where a major Allied conference was to be held. Some flights were to originate in the United States but most were to depart from Malta. As, among the many high-ranking officials, President Roosevelt was to be flown from Malta to Saki—the airfield designated by the Russians as the Soviet terminal for the mission—and as Eastern Europe was still under German control, unusual precautions had to be taken. For example, the presidential VC-54C had its serial number replaced by that of a less noticeable Skymaster, while a route from Malta, south of Sicily to the Ionian Sea, Kithira, Andros, Enez, across western Turkey to Midye, over the Black Sea and on to Saki was carefully planned. Support of the operation was to be assured by a number of Convair C-87s and Curtiss C-46s carrying spare parts, engines and maintenance personnel while Douglas C-47s were to assure a courier service. Finally, on 2 February, 1945, thirty-four four-engined transports—including the VC-54C carrying the President, and several other Skymasters as well as a few Convair C-87s and RAF Avro Yorks—left Malta at short intervals for their 1,360-mile (2,189-km) flight to Saki; from Andros they were escorted by thirty-two Lockheed P-38 Lightnings of the USAAF. All aircraft arrived without difficulty but, before the return flight to Deversoir where President Roosevelt was to meet King Ibn Saud of Saudi Arabia, the VC-54C had to have an unscheduled engine change.

The end of the war with Japan saw the Skymasters at the peak of their activities and 839 C-54s were in service with Air Transport Command. At that time, the C-54s were involved in a number of less routine missions. In particular, on 19 August, 1945, one C-54E-1-DO (s/n 27271, 44-9045) flew the sixteen members of the Japanese surrender delegation led by Lieut-General Kawabe from Ie Shima to Manila. A few days later, 185 Skymasters were assembled at Kadena airfield, Okinawa, with 15 more C-54s in reserve at Manila, Guam and Saipan, to fly the first contingent of US occupation troops to Japan. Between 28 August and 12 September, 1945, these aircraft made 3,646 flights carrying 23,456 troops and military passengers and 2,000 tons of cargo without incident. Meanwhile, following the signing of the Japanese unconditional surrender aboard the battleship USS *Missouri* anchored in Tokyo Bay, a Skymaster carrying films of the ceremony set a new record of 31 hr 25 min between Tokyo and Washington. Also remarkable was the flight around the world made by four Army officers and four press correspondents—including Miss Inez Robb of the International News Service—who, using in relays six Skymasters from Air Transport Command, flew eastbound from Washington National Airport to Washington National Airport between 28 September and 4 October, 1945, to cover 23,279 miles (37,625 km) in 149 hr

44 min (flight time: 116 hr 23 min, average speed: 200 mph, 322 km/h). After this flight, Air Transport Command scheduled a weekly Skymaster round-the-world flight.

The end of the war saw a drastic reduction in C-54s and R5Ds held by the US Armed Forces, with many of their Skymasters being sold as surplus while others were leased to the airlines on a long-term basis by the military Services and the US War Assets Administration. During the post-war period, Skymasters were involved in a number of unusual flights. One C-54D-1-DC (s/n 10566, 42-72461) of the All Weather Flying Center flew, in September 1947, from Stephenville, Newfoundland, to Brize Norton, England, under automatic pilot from take-off to landing, while a year later 42-72734—a C-54D-10-DC, s/n 10839—flew nonstop from Fairbanks to Oslo via the North Pole, covering 6,200 miles (9,978 km) in 22 hours.

The C-54D-1-DC of the All Weather Flying Center which, in September 1947, flew from Newfoundland to England entirely under automatic pilot control. (*USAF*)

Interesting as these peace-time flights were, they were soon forgotten as the Skymasters were called to meet a different challenge. By March 1948, the relations between the former Allies had become strained over the question of access to West Berlin and on 25 June, 1948, all surface traffic to and from Berlin was halted by the Soviet occupation forces. Prior to this, the majority of US military Skymasters had been transferred to MATS which, at the time of its organization, thus had a total of 234 C-54s. To supply the beleaguered city, the western Allies organized an elaborate airlift system. The main US contribution was made by Skymasters and, at the peak of operations, 204 C-54s and 22 R5Ds—with a further 110 Skymasters in training or undergoing maintenance—were operating from Rhein-Main (Frankfurt) to Tempelhof (US zone) and from Fassberg to Gatow (British zone). A record was set on 16 April, 1949, (Easter Sunday) when American and British aircraft, of which C-54s contributed the majority, delivered 12,941 tons of supplies by 1,398 flights. As the main commodity flown was coal, thirty-eight C-54Es of MATS were specially modified as C-54Ms to carry this. Unable to bring the Berliners to their knees, the Russians lifted the blockade on 12 May, 1949, but, as a precautionary measure, the airlift continued until the end of September 1949. During the 15-month operation US military transport aircraft, MATS C-54s assisted by a few Douglas C-47s of MATS and the USAFE, five Fairchild C-82s and one Douglas C-74, carried 1,783,826 tons. Less than nine months later the Skymasters were called upon to meet another challenge. This time the action had shifted from Europe to the Far East where C-54s of the 374th Troop Carrier Group (Heavy) evacuated from South Korea 851 American nationals on 27 and 28 June, 1950. Following the US intervention on behalf of the United Nations, more Skymasters began operating in Korea and provided logistic support for the UN forces. In addition to transporting military personnel and equipment, the C-54s were used for aeromedical evacuations and for that purpose thirty C-54Es were specially modified as MC-54Ms to each carry 30 wounded troops with medical attendants. Following the end of the Korean War, the number of C-54s in US military service was again reduced as more modern aircraft were available to carry the normal peacetime volume of military traffic. However, the type was operated, in small number, during the Vietnamese Conflict. Few Skymasters were still flown in the early seventies by the USAF and the US Navy.

Apart from the US Armed Forces, only the RAF had Skymasters in squadron service and this only during the last year of the war. The first in British service was an ex-C-54B-1-DO (s/n 18326, 43-17126) which was intended for the Prime Minister. Delivered in the autumn of 1944 and assigned the serial number EW999, the aircraft was operated by the VIP Flight of No.246 Squadron but was returned to the United States in late 1945. Twenty-two C-54D-DCs were also delivered to the RAF beginning in February 1945 and, with the serials KL977 to KL986 and KL988 to KL999, served with Nos.232 and 246 Squadrons, No.1332 Heavy Conversion Unit, No.1 Ferry Unit, and Air Command, South East Asia. Being Lend-Lease aircraft, these Skymasters were returned to the United States after the war and no other Skymaster was operated by the Royal Air Force.

After VE-Day but before VJ-Day, France became the third nation to fly C-54s when one C-54E-20-DO (s/n 27374, 44-9148) was presented by the United States as a gift to General de Gaulle. This aircraft was later augmented by a number of surplus C-54s, and Skymasters were operated by the Armée de l'Air and the Aéronavale well into the sixties. Like France, many other nations took advantage of the availability of surplus Skymasters. Eventually, C-54s/DC-4s were operated by the armed forces of at least fifteen nations other than the United States, the United Kingdom and France and, in early 1971, some of these aircraft were still flown by the air forces of fourteen countries.

Over the North Atlantic route a converted C-54 of American Overseas Airlines introduced commercial landplane service on 23 October, 1945, by flying between New York and Hurn, near Bournemouth (then serving

Skymaster (ex-USAAF C-54G-10-DO, 45-601) of the Fôrça Aérea Brasileira. (R. Carson Seely)

London)—with technical stops at Gander and Shannon—in 23 hr 48 min. During the following years, six other airlines, Pan American, KLM, Air France, SAS, Sabena and Swissair, initiated their post-war North Atlantic services with DC-4s. Other intercontinental routes pioneered by DC-4s included trans-Pacific services by Pan American and Australian National Airways, the latter flying on behalf of British Commonwealth Pacific Airlines and making a first experimental flight on 3 May, 1946, before initiating a fortnightly service from Sydney to Vancouver. On the South Atlantic route from South America to Europe the DC-4 was first introduced by Flota Aérea Mercante Argentina (FAMA) beginning on 17 September, 1946. Before that time, following a proving flight which left Amsterdam on 10 November, 1945, KLM and KNILM re-opened with DC-4s their pre-war route linking the Netherlands to the Netherlands East Indies. Later, as more DC-4-1009s were delivered and conversions of surplus C-54s were made at an increasing tempo, DC-4s saw worldwide service with a large number of scheduled and non-scheduled carriers.

On the US domestic route system—the market for which the aircraft had originally been designed—the DC-4 was first operated by its three original sponsors: American Airlines began DC-4 service on the New York–Chicago run in February 1946 and United Air Lines and Eastern Air Lines began DC-4 operations shortly after. On 7 March, 1946, American started DC-4 service between New York and Los Angeles and, while making only one en route stop against three stops for the DC-3, cut the flying time westbound from the DC-3's 17 hr 40 min to 14 hr 30 min and, eastbound, from 16 hr to 13 hr 15 min. Other trunk carriers flying the DC-4 in the United States included Braniff Airways, Capital Airlines, Colonial Airlines, Delta Air Lines, National Airlines, Northwest Airlines (also on Pacific routes), TWA (only on cargo services and mainly on international routes), and Western Air Lines.

C-54D-1-DC (42-72518) making an assisted take-off with JATO units attached beneath the fuselage. (*USAF*)

Among noteworthy highlights in the DC-4's operational life was Braniff's use, in 1949–50, of JATO to enable its flights out of La Paz, Bolivia, to take-off at high gross weights and still comply with CAR regulations in spite of the airport's high altitude—11,800 ft (3,597 m). Some airlines used the DC-4s, beginning with Capital Airlines, in a scheme to deceive uninitiated passengers into believing they were boarding DC-6s; a square of dark paint edged with a white strip was painted around the circular cabin windows. Another interesting use resulted from Sabena's engineering department fitting a swing-tail to an aircraft of Air Congo; so fitted, the aircraft was capable of accepting out-sized cargo loads.

However, the career of the DC-4 on major commercial routes was comparatively short-lived as larger, pressurized, aircraft—such as the Douglas DC-6 and Lockheed Constellation—forced it onto less important routes and to cargo and charter operations. Nevertheless, DC-4s were here to stay and the type is still operated, in fast dwindling numbers, on passenger and cargo scheduled routes, primarily in less-developed countries. Other DC-4s are still flying with non-scheduled carriers.

HC-ARG (ex C-54A-15-DC, 42-72300) of Ecuatoriana at the Mariscal Sucre International Airport, Quito, in August 1974. (*René J. Francillon*)

EI-ARS (ex-C-54E-5-DO, 44-9063) of Aer Turas on lease to the United Nations for use by the High Commissioner for Refugees. It is seen at Juba in the Sudan in June 1973. (*René J. Francillon*)

When in 1944 Canadair Ltd was formed to take over management of the Crown plant at Cartierville, Montreal, its first goal was the development of a Rolls-Royce Merlin-powered version of the Skymaster. Conceived in 1943 by the engineering department of Trans-Canada Air Lines (TCA), the Merlin-powered C-54 was anticipated to meet the requirements of both the Royal Canadian Air Force and of TCA. To save time it was then decided that the first aircraft would use a Douglas-built C-54G unpressurized fuselage and other components while later production aircraft would be entirely built by Canadair and would have a pressurized fuselage incorporating several refinements then being planned by Douglas for the DC-6. The use of Merlins fitted with annular radiators was dictated by the desire to improve performance. Moreover, the selection of these British engines resulted in cost savings as, in accordance with the Commonwealth trade agreement, they could be imported duty-free into Canada whereas the US-produced R-2000 engines would have been subject to customs duties.

The first Canadair aircraft—designated DC-4M-X (Experimental Merlin-powered DC-4), registered CF-TEN-X and bearing the Canadair c/n 101—was powered by four 1,725 hp Merlin 620 liquid-cooled engines and used an airframe generally identical to that of the C-54G-DO. It made its first flight at Cartierville in July 1946, being crewed by Bob Brush of Douglas and Al Lily of Canadair. Although serving as prototype for the Merlin-powered DC-4 version, this aircraft was part of an RCAF order for 24 unpressurized aircraft designated C-54 GMs and named North Stars. Thus, after being retained by the manufacturer until November 1952, this aircraft was taken on strength by the RCAF and received the military serial 17525. In service with the RCAF it was preceded by seventeen North Star Mk Is (military serials 17501 to 17517, c/ns 108 to 124), which were powered by Merlin 620s and taken on strength between September 1947 and April 1948, and by five North Star Mk MIs (military serials 17518 and

C-54GM (serial 17501, Canadair c/n 108) of the RCAF, with unusual fuselage roundel. (*Canadair*)

17520 to 17523, c/ns 102 and 104 to 107), which were powered by Merlin 622s and initially operated by TCA pending availability of the pressurized DC-4M-2s ordered by this airline. Between April 1948 and October 1966, when the last four aircraft of this type were struck off charge, the RCAF North Stars were operated intensively on domestic flights and long overwater logistic flights to Korea—especially during the 1950–53 war in that country—and Europe. On several occasions, the RCAF also flew its North Stars on mercy missions to various parts of the world and on support missions for the United Nations.

Trans-Canada Air Lines, which had originated the planning of the Merlin-powered DC-4 version, ordered twenty DC-4M-2s which, having a pressurized fuselage with square windows, were intended to take full advantage of the better performance at higher altitudes obtained by the use of supercharged Merlin engines. However, as development of the pressurized DC-4M-2 was going to delay its availability, TCA obtained from the RCAF the loan of six unpressurized North Stars (c/ns 102 to 107). Designated DC-4M-1s while in service with TCA, these aircraft (CF-TEK to CF-TEM, and CF-TEO to CF-TEQ) were powered by Merlin 622s and were later fitted with DC-6 type undercarriage to enable certificated gross weight to be increased from 73,000 lb (33,112 kg) to 78,000 lb (35,380 kg). TCA introduced the DC-4M-1 on its Montreal–London route on 15 April, 1947, and, after taking delivery of its own DC-4M-2s, returned the five surviving DC-4M-1s to the RCAF between March and October 1949.

The pressurized aircraft ordered by TCA (CF-TFA to CF-TFT, c/ns 125 to 144) were delivered between October 1947 and June 1948. When powered by Merlin 622s driving three-blade propellers these aircraft were designated DC-4M-2/3s and were certificated at a maximum gross weight of 79,600 lb (36,106 kg) while those powered by Merlin 624s driving four-blade propellers were designated DC-4M-2/4s and were certificated at a maximum weight of 80,200 lb (36,378 kg). Both versions provided accommodation for 40 first-class or up to 62 economy-class passengers. Depending on weight and altitude, the cruising speed exceeded that of the standard DC-4s by 60 to 80 mph (96 to 145 km/h) but the DC-4M-2s were

328

substantially noisier than the Skymasters. Consequently, TCA developed a cross-over exhaust system to reduce cabin noise. With TCA, the DC-4M-2s were used initially on international routes to Europe, the United States and Bermuda, as well as on Canadian transcontinental services. Later, after being replaced on overseas routes by Super Constellations, the DC-4M-2s were operated on TCA's domestic system and as freighters. In the last mentioned role, they were finally withdrawn in June 1961 when TCA disposed of all its remaining DC-4M-2s.

As substitutes for the unsuccessful Avro Tudors, BOAC ordered for its Empire routes twenty-two Canadair C-4s which, powered by four 1,760 hp Merlin 626s, differed from TCA's DC-4M-2s in making maximum use of British equipment to reduce non-sterling payments to about 200,000 dollars per aircraft, and in having a separate crew entrance door. Bearing the c/ns 145, 146, and 151 to 170 and the registrations G-ALHC to G-ALHP, and G-ALHR to G-ALHY, the Canadair C-4s became known as BOAC's Argonaut class. Deliveries took place between March and November 1949 and scheduled service began on 23 August, 1949, on the London–Pakistan–India–Far East route. Later, Argonaut class aircraft were used on services to the Middle East and South America and for several Royal Tours. Eventually, in April 1960 BOAC withdrew its last Argonauts.

The fourth and last original customer for the Merlin-powered Canadair transport aircraft was Canadian Pacific Air Lines which, between May and July 1949, took delivery of four C-4-1s (CF-CPI, CF-CPR, CF-CPJ, and

CF-CPR *Empress of Vancouver*, one of four C-4-1s of Canadian Pacific Air Lines. (*CP Air*)

CF-CPP, c/ns 147 to 150). Differing from the Argonauts only in minor equipment, the C-4-1s were flown by CPAL on routes from Vancouver to New Zealand and Australia, and to Tokyo and Hong Kong until the autumn of 1951 when the three surviving C-4-1s were sold to TCA. These aircraft, together with many of the ex RCAF, TCA and BOAC aircraft, were acquired by a number of operators—including some rather dubious ones—but, by the end of 1975, all but one aircraft had been withdrawn from service.

The RCAF C-5, the only Canadian-built DC-4 derivative to have radial engines.
(*Public Archives of Canada*)

Reverting to Pratt & Whitney radial engines, Canadair produced in 1950 a single pressurized C-5 which was powered by four 2,100 hp R-2800-CA15s. Intended as a VIP transport and long-range crew trainer, this aircraft (c/n 171) was operated by No.412 Squadron, RCAF, and was initially assigned the military serial 17524. Taken on strength on 20 July, 1950, the C-5 was renumbered 10000 on 17 February, 1951, and struck off strength on 5 July, 1967.

In 1959 the specification for a vehicle-ferry aircraft intended to replace the Bristol Superfreighter 32 was laid down for Aviation Traders (Engineering) Ltd by its associated company Channel Air Bridge. From the onset, Freddie Laker, then managing director of Air Charter, Channel Air Bridge and Aviation Traders, was convinced that the cost of a totally new aircraft would be prohibitive due to the small number which could be sold for this rather specialized market. However, as second-hand DC-4/C-54s were available for around $110,000, Laker believed that the conversion of this type would provide the required low first-cost aircraft meeting the Channel Air Bridge specification. Accordingly, Aviation Traders set about designing a DC-4 development for vehicle-ferry operation over relatively short stage lengths.

Seen here in the markings of Air Charter Ltd, G-ANYB *Atalanta* was an ex-C-54B-1-DC. In 1961 it became the first Aviation Traders AT(E)L 98 Carvair.
(*Mervyn Prime*)

Nose-loading was considered essential and Aviation Traders designed an 8 ft 8 in (2·64 m) forward fuselage extension with an hydraulically operated swing nose hinged on the port side. At the same time, the redesigned cockpit was raised 6 ft 10 in (2·08 m) and the nosewheel was made to retract into an external fairing, both modifications contributing to the feasibility of straight-through loading of vehicles. In addition, to offset the increased side area, Aviation Traders was forced to use a fin and rudder of increased height and area. The net result was to increase floor length from 49 ft 10 in (15·19 m) to 80 ft 2 in (24·43 m) and maximum usable volume from 3,691 cu ft (104·5 cu m) to 4,350 cu ft (123·2 cu m). So fitted, the modified DC-4 could carry five cars and 23 passengers in a separate rear cabin; the Superfreighter 32 carried only three cars and 16 passengers.

Following construction of a mock-up using the fuselage of a retired KLM C-54B-1-DC (PH-DBZ, ex 42-72375), in October 1960 Aviation Traders began modification of an Air Charter C-54B-1-DC (G-ANYB, ex 42-72423) to full Carvair standards. Powered by four 1,450 Pratt &

Nose details of an AT(E)L 98 Carvair in service with British United Airways.
(*Aviation Traders*)

Whitney R-2000-7M2s, G-ANYB made its first flight as a Carvair on 21 June, 1961, at Southend. ARB and FAA certification were obtained on 31 January, 1962, in spite of a delay caused by a ground accident in which G-ANYB's rear fuselage was virtually severed by a fork-lift truck. Upon completion of the flight trials, G-ANYB was delivered to Channel Air Bridge and, following demonstration and non-scheduled revenue flights, went into scheduled service on the Southend–Rotterdam route on 1 March, 1962. Three and a half weeks later the second Carvair made its maiden flight. Nineteen other AT(E)L 98 Carvairs, converted from C-54A, C-54B, C-54E and DC-4-1009 airframes, were delivered by Aviation Traders between July 1962 and July 1968 and were operated by airlines in at least ten countries. However, by 1975 only a few Carvairs were still in service.

Powerplants used in civil and military DC-4s

Type	Normal rating	Take-off rating	Aircraft versions
P & W Twin Wasp (R-2000) (14-cyl air-cooled radial)			
2SD1-G	1,100 hp at 17,600 ft (5,180 m)	1,450 hp	DC-4
D3	1,200 hp at 5,000 ft (1,524 m)	1,450 hp	DC-4
D5	1,200 hp at 6,400 ft (1,950 m)	1,450 hp	DC-4
2SD13-G	1,100 hp at 14,000 ft (4,265 m)	1,450 hp	DC-4
7M2		1,450 hp	Carvair
R-2000-3	1,100 hp at 7,000 ft (2,135 m)	1,350 hp	C-54, C-54B, R5D-1
R-2000-4	1,200 hp at 5,000 ft (1,524 m)	1,450 hp	R5D-1, R5D-2, R5D-3, R5D-4
R-2000-7	1,100 hp at 7,000 ft (2,135 m)	1,350 hp	C-54A, C-54B, VC-54C, XC-54F, R5D-1, R5D-2
R-2000-9	1,100 hp at 7,500 ft (2,285 m)	1,450 hp	C-54G, R5D-2, R5D-5
R-2000-11	1,100 hp at 7,500 ft (2,285 m)	1,350 hp	C-54D, C-54E, R5D-3, R5D-4
P & W Double Wasp (R-2800) (18-cyl air-cooled radial)			
R-2800-CA15	1,600 hp at 16,000 ft (4,880 m)	2,100 hp	C-5
Wright Cyclone (R-1820) (9-cyl air-cooled radial)			
R-1820-C9HD	1,200 hp at 5,000 ft (1,525 m)	1,425 hp	XC-54K
Allison V-1710 (12-cyl vee liquid-cooled)			
V-1710-131	1,150 hp at 14,700 ft (4,480 m)	1,620 hp	XC-114, XC-116
Rolls-Royce Merlin (12-cyl vee liquid-cooled)			
Merlin 620	1,160 hp at 10,000 ft (3,050 m)	1,725 hp	C-54GM
Merlin 622	1,420 hp at 18,700 ft (5,700 m)	1,760 hp	DC-4M-1, DC-4M-2/3
Merlin 624	1,420 hp at 18,700 ft (5,700 m)	1,760 hp	DC-4M-2/4
Merlin 626	1,420 hp at 18,700 ft (5,700 m)	1,760 hp	C-4, C-4-1

	C-54A-DO	C-54D-DC	C-54G-DO	XC-114-DO	DC-4-1009	Canadair C-4	AT(E)L Carvair
Span, ft in	117 6	117 6	117 6	117 6	117 6	117 6	117 6
(m)	(35·81)	(35·81)	(35·81)	(35·81)	(35·81)	(35·81)	(35·81)
Length, ft in	93 10	93 10	93 10	100 7	93 10	93 7½	102 7
(m)	(28·66)	(28·60)	(28·60)	(30·66)	(28·60)	(28·54)	(31·27)
Height, ft in	27 5	27 6	27 6	34 0	27 6	27 6 5/16	29 10
(m)	(8·38)	(8·38)	(8·38)	(10·36)	(8·38)	(8·39)	(9·09)
Wing area, sq ft	1,460	1,460	,460	1,464	1,460	1,460	1,462
(sq m)	(135·639)	(135·639)	(135·639)	(136·011)	(135·639)	(135·639)	(135·825)
Empty weight, lb	37,000	38,000	38,930	45,600	43,300	46,832	41,365
(kg)	(16,783)	(17,237)	(17,659)	(20,684)	(19,641)	(21,243)	(18,763)
Loaded weight, lb	62,000	62,000	62,000	71,000	63,500	70,000	73,800
(kg)	(28,123)	(28,123)	(28,123)	(32,206)	(28,804)	(31,751)	(33,475)
Maximum weight, lb	73,000	73,000	73,000	80,500	73,000	82,300	—
(kg)	(33,113)	(33,113)	(33,113)	(36,515)	(33,113)	(37,331)	—
Wing loading, lb/sq ft	42·5	42·5	42·5	48·5	43·5	47·9	50·5
(kg/sq m)	(207·3)	(207·3)	(207·3)	(236·8)	(212·4)	(234·1)	(246·5)
Power loading, lb/hp	12	11·5	10 7	11	10·9	9·9	12·7
(kg/hp)	(5·5)	(5·2)	(4·3)	(5)	(5)	(4·5)	(5·8)
Maximum speed, mph at ft	265/10,000	275/20,000	275/20,000	306/17,500	280/14,000	325/25,200	—
(km/h at m)	(426/3,050)	(442/6,095)	(442/6,095)	(492/5,335)	(451/4,265)	(523/7,680)	—
Cruising speed, mph at ft	192/10,000	203/10,000	190/10,000	198/14,700	227/10,000	289/12,200	184/10,000
(km/h at m)	(309/3,050)	(327/3,050)	(306/3,050)	(319/4,480)	(365/3,050)	(465/3,720)	(296/3,050)
Climb to, ft/min	10,000/14·8	10,000/14·6	10,000/14·6	10,000/11	—	—	—
(m/min)	(3,050/14·8)	(3,050/14·6)	(3,050/14·6)	(3,050/11)	—	—	—
Service ceiling, ft	22,000	22,300	22,330	26,000	—	29,500	—
(m)	(6,705)	(6,795)	(6,795)	(7,925)	—	(8,990)	—
Payload/range, lb/miles	22,000/2,000	14,100/3,100	10,000/4,000	10,000/3,500	11,440/2,500	—	17,635/2,070
(kg/km)	(9,980/3,220)	(6,350/4,990)	(4,535/6,435)	(4,535/5,630)	(5,190/4,025)	—	(8,000/3,330)

Accommodation: Flight crew of four, forty-four passengers and cabin attendants (standard accommodation on DC-4s; high-density seating for up to 86 passengers was later fitted by many carriers); flight crew of four, forty first-class passengers or up to 62 economy-class passengers and cabin attendants (DC-4M-1, DC-4M-2, C-4 and C-4-1); flight crew of four and 50 troops or 32,500 lb (14,742 kg) of cargo (C-54D; other military versions generally similar).

333

The Bowlus XCG-7 (41-29621) nine-seat experimental troop-carrying glider which was built by the El Segundo Division. (*USAF*)

Bowlus XCG-7 and XCG-8

During the late 1930s Al Essig, the head of the advertising agency which handled the Douglas account, prevailed upon Donald Douglas to help finance the fledgling Bowlus Sailplanes Inc. This San Francisco-based company had been founded by William Hawley Bowlus and, at the time, was struggling to find a market for sailplanes. In spite of Donald Douglas's support, Bowlus Sailplanes remained a small company until America's entry into the war. However, William Bowlus had gained a fair reputation as a sailplane designer and thus, when in 1941 the Matériel Division requested proposals for cargo and training gliders, his entries were rewarded by Contract AC-20234 for the XCG-7 and XCG-8 and Purchase Order PO-17694 for the XTG-12 and TG-12A.

Bowlus had the facilities to build the XTG-12 and TG-12A two-seat training sailplanes but was unable to undertake manufacture of the larger XCG-7 and XCG-8. Thus, while proposing that quantity production of the cargo gliders be undertaken by subcontractors in the Midwest, William Bowlus turned to his friend Donald Douglas to provide facilities for manufacturing one static test and one flight test model of both the XCG-7

XCG-7 under tow in the Mojave Desert in 1942. (*MDC*)

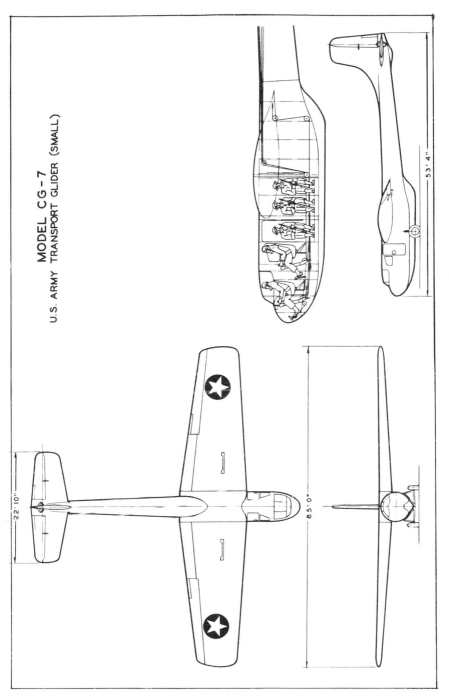

MODEL CG-7
U.S. ARMY TRANSPORT GLIDER (SMALL)

22' 10"

53' 4"

65' 0"

335

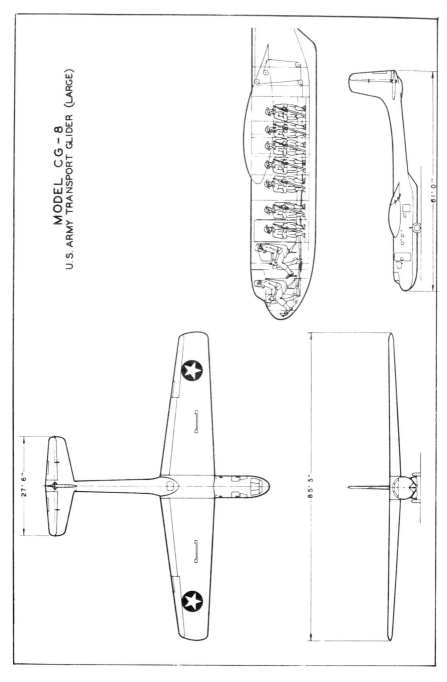

MODEL CG-8
U.S. ARMY TRANSPORT GLIDER (LARGE)

27' 6"

85' 5"

61' 0"

The unsuccessful XCG-8 built in El Segundo for Bowlus Sailplane Inc. (*USAF*)

and XCG-8 which had been ordered on 2 October, 1941. His request for assistance was favourably received and the task of building these four gliders—which were of pod-and-boom configuration, of wooden construction with semi-monocoque tubular tailboom, and had a design towing-speed of 120 mph (193 km/h)—was given to the El Segundo Division.

Designed to meet an Army Air Force specification for a nine-seat troop glider, the two XCG-7s received the El Segundo s/ns 1359 and 1360. The first was intended for flight test and received the USAAF serial 41-29621 whereas s/n 1360 which was to be used for static test only did not receive a USAAF serial number. Similarly, the fifteen-seat XCG-8 troop gliders were s/n 1361, USAAF serial 41-29622 (flight test model) and s/n 1362 (static test article). The first of these to be completed, the static test XCG-7, was delivered to Wright Field on 10 February, 1942, and promptly failed under a structural test. After being repaired, the sailplaine failed again in July 1942 while being subjected to towing loads of 40 to 60 per cent. By then, however, the USAAF requirement for nine-seat troop gliders had been fulfilled by the Waco XCG-3 and further development of the XCG-7 was suspended.

Following the structural failure of the XCG-7, Douglas undertook to strengthen the XCG-8 which had been designed essentially as a scaled-up version of the XCG-7, but it failed to gain acceptance by the Army Air Forces as Wright Field officials seriously doubted the soundness and capacity of the Bowlus Sailplanes' production programme proposal. Consequently, neither Bowlus nor Douglas pursued further development of the XCG-8 and the USAAF adopted the Waco CG-4 as its standard fifteen-seat troop glider.

XCG-7
Span 65 ft (19·81 m); length 53 ft 4 in (16·26 m); wing area 696 sq ft (64·661 sq m). Empty weight 2,870 lb (1,302 kg); loaded weight 4,800 lb (2,177 kg); wing loading 6·9 lb/sq ft (33·7 kg/sq m). Towing speed 120 mph (193 km/h); stalling speed 70 mph (113 km/h).

XCG-8
Span 85 ft 5 in (26·04 m); length 61 ft (18·59 m); wing area 996 sq ft (92·532 sq m). Empty weight 3,895 lb (1,767 kg); loaded weight 5,900 lb (2,676 kg); wing loading 5·9 lb/sq ft (28·9 kg/sq m). Towing speed 120 mph (193 km/h); stalling speed 70 mph (113 km/h).

B-26B-60-DL (44-34564) and B-26C-50-DT (44-35911) of GB I/19 *Gascogne* during *Opération Picardie*, Indo-China, 1953. Both aircraft were delivered to the Armée de l'Air in January 1951 and were returned to the USAF in November 1955. (*ECPA*)

Douglas A-26 (B-26) Invader

The Army Air Corps took an early interest in preliminary design studies undertaken at the El Segundo plant in the autumn of 1940 to develop a common successor to the Douglas A-20, Martin B-26 and North American B-25. Thus, in November 1940 the Bomber Branch of the Experimental Engineering Section at Wright Field assisted Douglas by outlining the following characteristics of the DB-7—the export version of the A-20 series—which had failed to meet the latest requirements of the war in Europe: no interchangeability of crew, insufficient defensive armament, inadequate design strength, and excessive landing and take-off distances.

At the end of January 1941 a team led by Edward Heinemann and Project Engineer Robert Donovan submitted a proposal for the manufacture of two aircraft. The first was to be a twin-engined light bomber, and the second, basically identical to the first, was to be equipped as a night fighter. These experimental aircraft were to be designed for mass production, whilst the extensive use of wind-tunnel testing was proposed to reduce changes required for production models, thereby minimizing delay and total programme costs.

338

From the onset the design team chose to use a mid-mounted wing with laminar flow aerofoil and electrically-operated double-slotted flaps, and to power the aircraft with two 2,000 hp Pratt & Whitney R-2800-27 radials. The aircraft was to have a large bomb bay to carry either 4,000 lb (1,814 kg) of bombs or two torpedoes whilst external racks were to be fitted beneath the outer section of the wing to carry additional bombs. Defensive armament was to be provided by remotely-controlled dorsal and ventral turrets housing twin 0·50-in machine-guns and operated by a gunner located in a separate compartment behind the bomb bay.

Following mock-up inspection between 11 and 22 April, 1941, the War Department approved on 2 June the construction of two prototypes under Contract AC17946, totalling $2,208,390. The first of these, the XA-26-DE, was to be a three-seat attack bomber with a transparent nose providing a station for the navigator/bomb-aimer, while the second aircraft, the XA-26A-DE, was to be a two-seat night fighter with AI radar and heavy forward-firing armament. Three weeks later the contract was amended to add a third prototype, the three-seat XA-26B-DE, to be fitted with an unglazed nose housing one 75 mm cannon.

Production plans for the aircraft had first been put forward by Douglas in a document dated 28 February, 1941, in which it was proposed that 500 aircraft and spares be built in the Santa Monica plant with deliveries beginning twenty months after the contract date. However, the high Douglas bid ($142,250 per aircraft) was initially found excessive by the Matériel Division, and negotiations between the manufacturer and the War Department delayed approval until 31 October, 1941. At that time it was still planned that production aircraft would be manufactured in the Army Air Forces-controlled Santa Monica plant whereas the three prototypes would be built in the Navy-controlled El Segundo plant. However, a later decision by the Army Air Forces to switch production responsibility to the new Douglas plants in Long Beach and Tulsa in order not to disrupt A-20, C-47 and C-54 production in the Santa Monica plant led to more delays.

More production delays resulted from a variety of reasons for which Douglas was frequently blamed by the War Department, but which often were beyond the manufacturer's control and could be traced directly or indirectly to the Army Air Forces. In particular, the AAF showed much indecision in the mix of aircraft between light bombers with transparent nose, ground attack aircraft with unglazed nose housing 75 mm or 37 mm cannon, and attack bombers with unglazed nose housing a battery of forward-firing machine-guns. Thus, as late as 18 July, 1942, Douglas was instructed to install the 75 mm nose cannon in all 500 aircraft on order. This decision, however, was short lived and Douglas was forced to proceed with the development of the transparent nose version whilst diverting much of its design energy to developing alternative forward-firing armament for the proposed unglazed-nose A-26B ground attack version. Alternative nose armament configurations—most of which were later tested on the

One of the gun installations (37 mm cannon, port side, and 75 mm cannon, starboard side) tested on the A-26B. (*MDC*)

XA-26B-DE and on early A-26B-DLs—included either one 75 mm cannon (starboard) and two 0·50-in guns (port); one 75 mm cannon (starboard) and one 37 mm cannon (port); two 37 mm cannon (one on each side of the nose); or one 37 mm cannon (starboard) and two 0·50-in guns (port); four 0·50-in guns (starboard) and one 37 mm cannon (port); or four 0·50-in guns (starboard) and two 0·50-in guns (port). In addition, preliminary studies were made for mounting two quick-firing 37-mm cannon of a new design in a ventral pack with ammunition drums in the bomb bay. Order was restored in the midst of this chaos only at the end of 1944 when it was finally decided that the Long Beach plant would continue to produce exclusively A-26Bs with unglazed-noses housing six or eight 0·50-in machine-guns (earlier this plant had also built five A-26Cs with the transparent nose) whilst, starting in January 1945, the Tulsa plant would discontinue production of A-26Bs to concentrate all of its efforts on manufacturing A-26Cs.

Earlier delays had also been caused by late delivery of undercarriage struts, self-sealing tanks, turrets, and other GFE (Government Furnished Equipment) items such as engines, propellers and generators. Yet, it was Douglas which received much of the blame as the company was accused of having little interest in or little desire to manufacture the A-26, and of diverting too much of its resources to transport programmes of greater value for its postwar future. Specifically, the company was criticised for making insufficient efforts to enrol subcontractors and to provide enough staff to speed production engineering at the Tulsa plant. By 9 October, 1944, this situation had deteriorated so badly that Gen Henry H. Arnold, Chief of Staff of the Army Air Forces, qualified Douglas efforts in the A-26 programme as 'far short from satisfactory and little short of reprehensible'. Indeed, the A-26 required twenty-eight months to proceed from first flight to full-scale combat operations, whereas the heavier and more complex Boeing B-29 Superfortress proceeded from maiden flight to combat operations in only twenty-one months. However, Douglas succeeded in correcting the situation and went on to produce some 2,400 Invaders during the last twenty months of the war.

First flight of the XA-26-DE had originally been scheduled for 15 January, 1942, but delays in obtaining components actually delayed the maiden flight until 10 July when test pilot Ben O. Howard flew the aircraft from Mines Field. Handling and performance met the most sanguine expectations but minor teething troubles and difficulties with engine cooling led to some cowling modifications and to the removal of the propeller spinners on production aircraft. For the initial phase of flight testing, the XA-26-DE was flown without armament but, later on, the dummy dorsal and ventral turrets were replaced with electrically-operated turrets with periscopic sights. The main part of the flight trial programme was done with the XA-26-DE but further testing was done with the 'solid' nose XA-26B-DE and with the XA-26A-DE night fighter. This latter version was not ordered as by then the Northrop P-61 Black Widow, which had similar performance, had already been put into production. Thus, the Invader was built in quantity in only two versions, the A-26B and A-26C.

As in June 1948 the Invader's alpha-numeric designation was changed from A-26 to B-26, when the USAF dropped the A for Attack designator, all versions of the aircraft developed before that date are listed under the original A-26 designations with the later B-26 designations being given in parentheses. Later versions are listed only under their B-26 designations.

XA-26-DE: Bearing the USAAF serial 41-19504 and the El Segundo s/n 1004, the first prototype was fitted with a transparent nose and powered by two 2,000 hp Pratt & Whitney R-2800-27s driving three-blade propellers with large spinners. Defensive armament, not initially installed, comprised

The XA-26-DE during an early flight test. (*NA & SM*)

two forward-firing 0·50-in machine-guns mounted on the starboard side of the nose, and two 0·50-in guns in each of the remotely-controlled dorsal and ventral turrets. Normally operated by the gunner, the upper turret and its two guns could be locked in the forward, no-elevation, position and fired by the pilot. Provision was made for carrying a maximum of 3,000 lb (1,361 kg) of bombs in two fuselage bays and 2,000 lb (907 kg) on four racks beneath the outer wing panels. Alternately, two torpedoes could be carried in the bomb bay and protruded half-way beneath the fuselage. Crew consisted of pilot, navigator/bomb-aimer—who normally sat on a jump seat on the right of the pilot but was provided with a working station in the transparent nose—and gunner. Maximum internal fuel capacity: 1,050 US gallons (3,975 litres).

XA-26A-DE: The two-seat (pilot and radar-operator/gunner) night fighter prototype (41-19505) had an airframe and powerplant installation similar to those of the bomber prototype. It differed from the XA-26-DE in being fitted with centimetric MIT AI-4 radar in a nose radome and in featuring completely revised armament. Armament consisted of four forward-firing 20 mm cannon in a ventral tray beneath the forward bomb bay with their ammunition boxes in the bay, and in one remotely-

The radar-equipped XA-26A-DE night fighter with ventral tub housing four 20 mm cannon. (*US National Archives*)

342

controlled dorsal turret with four 0·50-in machine-guns. For intruder operations 2,000 lb (907 kg) could be carried in the rear bomb bay. Even though its flight trials were successful, the XA-26A-DE was not put into production.

A-26A: Designation given in late 1965 to forty extensively modified aircraft previously designated B-26Ks.

XA-26B-DE: Last Invader built in the El Segundo plant, this aircraft (41-19588) was the attack version prototype and was fitted with an unglazed nose housing a forward-firing 75 mm cannon. The crew consisted of pilot and gun-loader/navigator seated side by side in the forward cockpit and a gunner in the rear cockpit.

A-26B-DL and A-26B-DT (B-26B-DL and B-26B-DT): Initially planned to be fitted with alternate 'solid' nose sections housing a variety of forward-firing weapons as described in a preceding paragraph, the A-26B was tested with several of these weapon combinations but went into service with a nose housing six forward-firing 0·50-in machine-guns. Later, beginning with the A-26B-50-DL block, a new eight-gun nose was fitted. Forward-firing armament could initially be supplemented by eight 0·50-in guns mounted in four twin packages beneath the outer wing panels; however, the A-26B-50-DL block also introduced a change to six internally-mounted wing guns to enable bombs or fourteen 5-in rockets to be carried beneath the wing (note that the modified nose section and outer wing panels were often fitted to earlier A-26B and A-26C variants at the time of major overhauls and, thus, cannot be used as positive identification features). Defensive armament consisted of the remotely-controlled dorsal and ventral turrets, the latter being replaced by a 125-US gallon (473-litre) auxiliary tank in aircraft intended for service in the Pacific with the Fifth and Seventh Air Forces (A-26B-51-DLs, -56-DLs, -61-DLs and -66-DLs). Compared with the prototype, the A-26B had increased maximum bomb load (6,000 lb, 2,723 kg) and internal fuel capacity (initially 1,600 US gallons, 6,057 litres, but later 1,910 gallons, 7,230 litres, or 2,035 gallons, 7,703 litres, when the ventral turret was replaced by an auxiliary tank). Powerplant, housed in slightly revised nacelles and driving three-blade propellers without spinners, consisted of either two 2,000 hp R-2800-27s or (Ford-built) R-2800-71s on early aircraft, or 2,000 hp (Ford-built) R-2800-79s beginning with the A-26B-45-DL block.

During production a number of modifications were progressively introduced, to improve performance by redesigning the oil cooler air inlets on the wing leading edge; to eliminate empennage buffeting by modifying the dorsal turret installation; to improve visibility the original flat top canopy, which opened upward on the right side of the pilot's cockpit, was replaced by a clamshell canopy opening in two frameless elements around hinges on both sides of the pilot's cockpit. The new canopy, which at first was hand-built and fitted to a few early aircraft, was introduced as standard beginning with the A-26B-30-DL block. It enabled the pilot to see over both engine nacelles and towards the tail surfaces as well as to check

Unarmed A-26B-66-DL assigned to the Headquarters, Strategic Air Command, USAF. (*William Balogh*)

whether both main landing wheels were in the down position. This freedom of head movement greatly enhanced formation flying.

As detailed in Appendix B, a total of 1,355 A-26Bs was produced in the Long Beach (1,150 A-26B-1-DLs to A-26B-66-DLs) and Tulsa (205 A-26B-5-DTs to A-26B-25-DTs) plants. In June 1948 these aircraft were redesignated B-26Bs. Furthermore, some were modified as cargo transports (CB-26Bs), target-tugs and advanced trainers with dual controls (TB-26Bs), or staff transports (VB-26Bs).

XA-26C: This designation was given to a projected version which was to have carried four 20 mm cannon in the nose. It was not proceeded with and the A-26C designation was re-assigned to identify the Invaders fitted with a transparent nose.

A-26C-DL and A-26C-DT (B-26C-DL and B-26C-DT): Differing from the A-26B in being fitted with a transparent nose (with two forward-firing 0·50-in machine-guns on the starboard side), the A-26C was originally put into production at both the Long Beach and Tulsa plants. However, the Long Beach plant produced only five A-26C-1-DL and -2-DLs whereas the Tulsa plant concentrated its efforts on this version and delivered 1,086 A-26C-16-DTs to A-26C-55-DTs. Airframe, powerplant installation, defensive armament, and systems were common to both the A-26B and A-26C versions.

Modifications introduced on the A-26B line were also progressively incorporated in the A-26Cs, the principal being the change to the clamshell canopy beginning with the A-26C-30-DT block, and the introduction of R-2800-79 engines, wing panels with internally-mounted guns, increased tank capacity and provision for rockets which were introduced on the A-26C-45-DT block.

The aircraft designation was changed to B-26C in June 1948 whilst a small number of aircraft was modified for night photographic reconnaissance under the designation FA-26C (RB-26C after June 1948). In most instances these aircraft had their remotely-controlled turrets replaced by radomes for electronic reconnaissance equipment. Some aircraft also

344

RB-26C in night camouflage and with all guns removed. (*USAF*)

had a nose radome and/or radar pods beneath the wingtips. Finally, the designation DB-26C identified a small number of B-26Cs modified as directors for target-drone testing, whilst the single EB-26C (44-35300) was used for missile guidance development.

XA-26D-DL: Powered by two 2,100 hp Chevrolet-built R-2800-83s, this aircraft (44-34776) served as prototype for the proposed A-26D version which was to have succeeded the A-26B at Long Beach, but the contract for 750 A-26D-DLs was cancelled after VJ-Day.

XA-26E-DT: During the war a contract was awarded to the Tulsa plant for 1,250 glazed-nosed A-26E-DTs to have been powered by two R-2800-83s to match the A-26D-DL's performance. However, this contract was also cancelled following VJ-Day and only a prototype (44-25563) was flown in 1945 under the designation XA-26E-DT.

XA-26F-DL (XB-26F-DL): To further improve performance, an A-26B-61-DL was modified for two 2,100 hp R-2800-83s, initially driving three-blade propellers, but later fitted with four-blade units with large spinners, and one 1,600 lb (726 kg) thrust General Electric J31 turbojet.

The XA-26F-DL, showing J31 turbojet installation and four-blade propellers driven by R-2800-83 engines. (*US National Archives*)

345

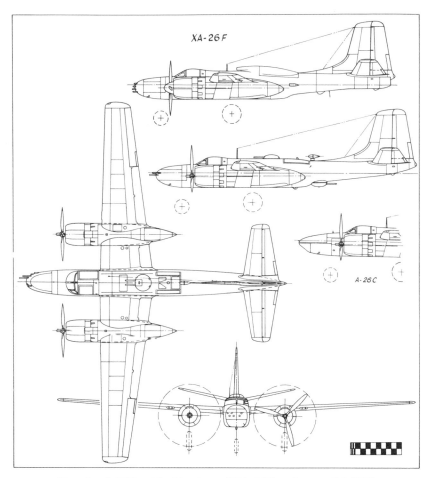

Douglas A-26B, with side view of XA-26F and nose of A-26C.

The turbojet was installed in the rear fuselage with the air intake above the centre portion of the fuselage, in place of the dorsal turret, and exhaust pipe in the tail. With both types of engines operating, the XA-26F-DL reached a top speed of 435 mph at 15,000 ft (700 km/h at 4,570 m), an insufficient gain over the maximum speed of the proposed A-26D-DL to warrant production.

A-26Z: During summer 1945 Douglas proposed the development of the so-called A-26Z for postwar production as the A-26G (unglazed nose) and A-26H (glazed nose). Intended to have the more powerful version of the reliable R-2800, the A-26G and A-26H were to be fitted with a raised pilot's canopy, improved cockpit arrangement, wingtip drop tanks and other improvements dictated by operational experience. In October 1945,

346

however, the USAAF instructed Douglas not to proceed as sufficient numbers of A-26s were already available to equip peacetime units.

JD-1 (UB-26J): Following testing in 1945 of two XJD-1s (BuNo 57990, ex A-26B-45-DL 44-34217, and BuNo 57991, ex A-26C-40-DT 44-35467), the US Navy obtained 150 surplus A-26Cs (BuNos 77139/77224, 80621/80622, and 140326/140377) for use by utility squadrons in the target-towing role. The surviving JD-1s were redesignated UB-26Js in 1962 in accordance with the new Tri-Service designation system.

JD-1 of VU-5 near Guam. (*US National Archives*)

JD-1D (DB-26J): Designation given to JD-1s modified as drone directors and redesignated DB-26Js in 1962.

B-26K (A-26A): See page 350.

RB-26L: Designation given to two RB-26Cs fitted for night photography and carrying Reconofax IV infrared sensors for operations in South Vietnam with the *Farm Gate* Detachment.

The combat debut of the Invader was made in the spring of 1944 by four A-26B-5-DLs which were evaluated under low-altitude combat conditions in New Guinea by crews of the 13th Bombardment Squadron, 3rd BG. However, these aircraft received unfavourable reports as it was noted that they had poor visibility to either side and insufficient forward-firing armament to be used as strafers. A more favourable report was issued by the Ninth Air Force in Europe where in September 1944 18 A-26Bs flew eight medium-altitude combat missions with 553rd Bombardment Squadron, 386th BG, based at Great Dunmow in England. Accordingly, the AAF decided that Invaders would re-equip Ninth and Twelfth Air Forces units in Europe until improved aircraft with clamshell canopy and increased forward-firing armament were available for use by groups of the Fifth and Seventh Air Forces in the Pacific.

The first operational unit to be fully equipped with A-26Bs was the 416th Bombardment Group, Ninth Air Force, which converted from A-20 Havocs to Invaders in November 1944. As deliveries increased, the type was used by the Ninth Air Force to re-equip the 409th, 386th and 391st Bombardment Groups, respectively in February, March and April 1945; a fifth group, the 410th, was converting from Havocs to Invaders when the war ended. Within the Twelfth Air Force in Italy, the 47th BG flew A-26s alongside its A-20s during the last four months of the war. In the Pacific, the 319th BG of the Seventh Air Force was the only unit fully operational with Invaders when the war ended, and the 41st BG (Seventh Air Force) and the 3rd BG (Fifth Air Force) were converting to the type. On all fronts the Invader was regarded as the USAAF's best twin-engined bomber, and plans were in hand to convert all A-20, B-25 and B-26 units to the faster, more manoeuvrable and harder hitting A-26.

When World War II ended, the two outstanding contracts were cancelled on 13 and 27 August, 1945, but the A-26 was selected to equip the light bomber and night reconnaissance squadrons of the much reduced peacetime USAAF, and later of the newly formed USAF. Others equipped light bomber squadrons of the National Guard and units of the Reserve, while many were modified as staff transports or target-towing aircraft, assigned as squadron hacks, or used for special purposes such as drone directors. Additional A-26s were sold as surplus, scrapped, stored for later use, or transferred to the US Navy. Thus, when on 25 June, 1950, the Korean War started, and the United States intervened on behalf of the United Nations, the USAF found itself short of light bombers and the only Invaders immediately available were the twenty-six aircraft of the 3rd Bombardment Group based at Johnson Air Base in Japan.

A B-26B of the 3rd Bombardment Group during a daytime sortie in Korea, January 1951. (*USAF*)

348

Initially flying armed reconnaissance sorties over South Korea, the B-26s of the 3rd BG made the first attack against North Korea on 29 June when they bombed the main military airfield at Pyongyang. Reinforced by the 452nd BG, a Reserve unit called to active duty and flying its first combat mission in October 1950, the 3rd BG increasingly operated interdiction sorties, first by day and later almost exclusively by night, against enemy troops and equipment movements. During the war both units, respectively redesignated 3rd and 17th BWs, flew some 55,000 sorties, mostly at night. They were credited with the destruction of 38,500 vehicles, 3,700 railway carriages, 406 locomotives and seven enemy aircraft, and one pilot, Captain John Wolmsley, was awarded a posthumous Medal of Honor. Their final combat sortie was flown on 27 July, 1953, when, 24 minutes before the signing of the cease-fire at Panmunjon, a B-26 of the 3rd BW dropped the last bombs of the Korean War. Invaders were also used on night reconnaissance by the 162nd Tactical Reconnaissance Squadron (12th TRS after Feb 1951). A few were fitted with APA-64 to locate enemy radar stations.

As peacetime operations were resumed, the USAF had four B-26 and two RB-26 wings but, when the jet-powered Martin B/RB-57 and Douglas B/RB-66 became available in the mid-fifties, Invaders were taken out of front-line service. However, during the 1960s, the 1st Air Commando Group at Eglin AFB, Florida, used B-26s to develop counter insurgency tactics, but wing failures were occurring and forced them out of direct combat. For those remaining active, a strengthening 'wing strap' modification was made along the bottom of the wing spars to prolong service life. The last US military Invader—a VB-26B (44-34160) operated by the National Guard Bureau—was retired in 1972 and was donated to the National Air and Space Museum.

With the US Navy, the JD-1s and JD-1Ds (later UB-26Js and DB-26Js) had been operated into the sixties by five utility squadrons (VU-3, -4, -5, -7, and -10) as target-towing, drone director and general utility aircraft.

The experience of the 1st Air Commando Group led the USAF to order from On Mark Engineering Co of Van Nuys, California—a firm experienced in the modification and remanufacture of B-26s for use as executive aircraft—a prototype of a rebuilt B-26 for use in the counter-insurgency role. On Mark made the following modifications: substitution of 2,500 hp R-2800-103W engines; use of fully reversible, automatic feathering propellers; strengthened wings with steel straps on top and bottom of the spars; use of an enlarged rudder to improve single-engined handling; installation of permanent 165-US gallon (625-litre) wingtip tanks; use of anti-skid braking system, deicer boots and anti-icing devices; modernization of the intrument panel and installation of new electronic equipment; and provision for dual controls. The dorsal and ventral turrets were eliminated and fixed armament consisted of eight 0·50-in machine-guns in the nose. Alternatively, a glazed nose enabled the aircraft to be used for photographic reconnaissance. In addition, the aircraft was to be fitted with eight new wing pylons accommodating a variety of external stores.

B-26K Counter Invader at Edwards AFB, California, in June 1964. (*USAF*)

Modification of a prototype—redesignated YB-26K, renamed Counter Invader, and assigned the new serial 63-5634—was started in October 1962. The first flight of the YB-26K took place on 28 January, 1963. Following extensive evaluation testing at Eglin, in October 1963 the USAF ordered forty B-26s modified to a standard closely matching that of the YB-26K. The main difference between the prototype and production aircraft was the use of 2,500 hp R-2800-52W engines in place of the R-2800-103Ws. Bearing new serial numbers (64-17640/64-17679), the B-26Ks were delivered to the USAF between June 1964 and April 1965. For foreign customers, notably Brazil, other contractors modified additional B-26s to standards approaching that of the B-26K; however, none of these aircraft officially received this designation.

In service with the USAF the Counter Invader was used by the 603rd Special Operations Squadron from Lockbourne and Hurlburt AFBs in the operational training role and, more importantly, by the 606th Air Commando Squadron (later 609th Special Operations Squadron) from Nakhon Phanom Air Base in Thailand. Whilst in Thailand the aircraft were redesignated A-26As since an agreement between the Thai and US Governments prohibited the basing of bombers in the former country (this

Although bearing Vietnamese markings, this Invader belonged to Detachment 2A, 4400th Combat Crew Training Squadron, USAF, and was one of the first aircraft from this Service to be sent to Vietnam in late 1961. [*USAF*)

350

restriction was later rescinded when B-52s were stationed at U Tapao RTNAF), and the A-26As flew night interdiction missions over the Ho Chi Minh Trail until phased out of service in November 1969.

The only foreign air force to receive Invaders during World War II was the Royal Air Force but the type was too late to be placed in squadron service. In the fifties and sixties, however, several nations received B-26s under the Mutual Defense Assistance Program (MDAP) as detailed below:

Brazil: The Fôrça Aérea Brasileira acquired its first Invaders in 1957, and was the largest B-26 operator apart from the United States and France. In 1968 several of the Brazilian Invaders were flown back to Tucson, Arizona, where they were modernized by the Hamilton Aircraft Company. Seven years later, the survivors were still operated by the 1st Esquadrão of the 5th Grupo de Aviação, based at Natal in Rio Grande do Sul, and by another unit based at Cumbica, São Paulo. During 1976 these two units converted to Embraer AT-26 Xavante light strike aircraft and the Invader was phased out after nearly twenty years.

Although designated B-26C and bearing the tail number 5173, this Invader of the Fôrça, Aérea Brasileira was originally an A-26B-61-DL with serial 44-34615. (*Mario Roberto Vax Carneiro*)

Chile: The Fuerza Aérea del Chile has operated one squadron (Grupo 8 at Antofagasta) of B-26B/B-26Cs since the early 1960s.

Colombia: Between 1955 and 1968, the Fuerza Aérea Colombiana operated nineteen B-26Bs, B-26Cs and RB-26Cs, assigned to a light bomber squadron for operations against guerillas.

Dominican Republic: A smaller number of Invaders was operated until the early seventies by one squadron of the Aviación Militar Dominicana.

France: On two separate occasions the Armée de l'Air acquired Invaders to fight colonial wars. Beginning in January 1951 when its GB (Groupe de Bombardement) 1/19 was formed at Tourane, the Armée de l'Air obtained on loan from the USAF one hundred and eleven B-26Bs, B-26Cs and RB-26Cs to equip three bomber groups (GB 1/19 *Gascogne*, 1/25 *Tunisie* and 1/91 *Bourgogne*) and one reconnaissance flight (Escadrille de Reconnaissance Photographique ERP 2/19 *Armagnac*). Twenty-five were

Night fighter Invader (ex-B-26C-50-DT, 44-35926) of Escadrille de Chasse de Nuit 1/71. (*Jean Cuny*)

lost in combat or in flying accidents, one was purchased by the French Government, and the remainder were returned to the United States when the French left Indo-China in 1954. The single aircraft purchased in 1954 was later joined by eight others for use in a variety of trials at the Cazaux gunnery and bombing range, at the Mont de Marsan test centre and at the Melun CEV (Centre d'Essais en Vol). During the Algerian war, eighty-five B-26B/B-26Cs were purchased by France to equip the CIB (Centre d'Instruction au Bombardement) 328 and 329 at Cazaux, and GB 1/91 *Gascogne*, GB 2/91 *Guyenne*, ERP 1/31 *Armagnac*, ERP 2/32 and the Escadrille de Chasse de Nuit 1/71 in Algeria. The last of these was unique as it was equipped with Invaders specially modified as night fighters to intercept light aircraft flying guerilla supplies and cadres across the border with Tunisia. These aircraft were fitted with a di-electric radome housing AI Mk 10 radar taken from surplus Gloster Meteor NF.11s, and were armed with a twin 0·50-in machine-gun package beneath each wing. At the end of the war in Algeria the Armée de l'Air disposed of most of its remaining Invaders but a few were retained for training and ancillary duties—for example, one aircraft was fitted with special tracking radar mounted in a flat nose to test missile tracking systems—until 1968, when the last were scrapped or sold.

Guatemala: The Fuerza Aérea de Guatemala operated Invaders from the mid-fifties until they were replaced by Cessna T-37C armed jet trainers and counter-insurgency aircraft.

Indonesia: To supplement the North American B-25Js equipping its No.1 Squadron, the AURI (Angkatan Udara Republik Indonesia—Air Force of the Republic of Indonesia) acquired a small batch of refurbished B-26Bs in 1960. Both the B-25Js and B-26Bs were replaced later in the decade by Ilyushin Il-28 jet bombers.

Laos: Among the aircraft delivered by the United States to the now defunct Royal Lao Air Force were a small number of A-26As and earlier Invaders.

Nicaragua: The Fuerza Aérea de la Guardia Nacional acquired fourteen B-26Bs and B-26Cs between 1958 and 1963. They were last used from Las Mercedes Airport, Managua, against the Sandinistas in 1978-79.

Peru: Having received its first eight B-26Cs in 1955, the Fuerza Aérea del Peru later acquired additional B-26Bs and B-26Cs and operated them into the sixties until they were replaced by Canberra jet bombers.

Portugal: After arms dealers had attempted unsuccessfully to smuggle in some ten ex civil B-26s during the 1955–56 period, the Fôrça Aérea Portuguesa acquired in the late sixties a sufficient number of Invaders to equip one squadron operating against rebel forces from Luanda in Angola. At least two of these aircraft were left behind when the Portuguese withdrew from Angola in 1976.

Saudi Arabia: In 1955, nine B-26B Invaders achieved the distinction of becoming the first operational aircraft of the Royal Saudi Air Force when they were used to equip No. 3 Squadron at Jeddah.

Turkey: With the Turk Hava Kuvvetleri, the Invader was used primarily in the target-towing role during the late fifties and early sixties.

United Kingdom: Following the testing by the A & AEE (Aeroplane and Armament Experimental Establishment) at Boscombe Down of an A-26B-15-DL (41-39158) on loan from the USAAF from July to November 1944, the Royal Air Force was allotted an initial batch of one hundred and forty A-26C-DTs—designated Invader Is by the RAF and assigned the British military serials KL690/KL829. However, only two aircraft were received before the end of the war but were returned to the US before entering RAF service.

Besides being operated by these air forces, 'civilian' Invaders were used for several covert operations, such as on the 1962 Bay of Pigs operation when CIA-supported anti-Castro Cubans unsuccessfully attempted to regain power in their country, armed air-drops to anti-Duvalier groups in Haiti, anti-Sukarno operations in 1968 from airstrips in the North Celebes, and ground support activities in Biafra where two ex-French aircraft flew a number of sorties against Nigerian forces.

Although the Invader was retained after World War II as the USAAF's main light bomber, a number of A-26s were sold as surplus soon after the end of the war. Among the first on the civil register was an A-26B which, sponsored by industrialist Milton Reynolds and flown by William P. Odon, twice beat Howard Hughes' prewar round-the-world record of 91 hr 41 min. Registered NX67834 and named *Reynolds Bombshell*, the aircraft was first flown around the world between 12 and 16 April, 1947, in 78 hr 55 min 56 sec. Less than four months later, Bill Odon flew the aircraft solo from Chicago to Paris, Cairo, Karachi, Calcutta, Tokyo, Anchorage, Fargo, and back to Chicago, with an elapsed time of 73 hr 5 min 11 sec for a block speed of 269 mph (433 km/h) and an average flying speed of 310·6 mph (498·9 km/h).

Surplus Invaders were quickly acquired by civil operators for a variety of duties including executive transport, aerial photography, geological

On Mark Marketeer of Colorado Oil & Gas Co at Stapleton Airport, Denver, Colorado, in January 1964. (*H. Jay Miller III*)

survey, and aerial fire fighting. While most of these aircraft were modified by a variety of fixed base operators and small companies, others were given semi-production line modifications by the L B Smith Company and by On Mark Engineering Company. Variants developed by L B Smith included the Super 26 which was fitted with wingtip tanks and executive accommodation but otherwise retained the standard Invader structure. The Smith Tempo I (powered by R-2800 B-series engines and with unpressurized fuselage) and Tempo II (with R-2800 C-series engines and full cabin pressurization) both featured wingtip tanks and a new, 9 ft 7½ in (2·93 m) longer fuselage accommodating ten to thirteen passengers. The Smith Biscayne 26 had a still longer fuselage.

Executive transport conversions of the Douglas B-26 developed by On Mark Engineering included the pressurized Marksman A (2,100 hp R-2800-83AM3s), Marksman B (2,100 hp R-2800-83AM4As and wingtip fuel tanks), and Marksman C (2,500 hp R-2800-CB16/17s and internal auxiliary fuel tanks). All versions had a redesigned fuselage, a DC-7 type heated windshield, and improved brakes, deicing, soundproofing, radio/navigation and other systems. They were equipped to carry from six to twelve passengers or cargo, as required. An unpressurized version of the Marksman C was also manufactured as the On Mark Marketeer.

In spite of its initial below standard performance, the Invader went on to be regarded as an outstanding light bomber and to perform dependably in several wars and other less spectacular confrontations. In fact, it came to be considered rightly as one of Douglas's best designs and most successful combat aircraft. More than a third of a century after its first flight, it was still used by a number of the world's smaller air forces and by many civil operators.

	XA-26-DE	A-26B-15-DL	A-26B-60-DL	A-26C-30-DT	XA-26D-DL	XA-26F-DL	B-26K	Marksman C
Span, ft in	70 0	70 0	70 0	70 0	70 0	70 0	71 6	71 6
(m)	(21·34)	(21·34)	(21·34)	(21·34)	(21·34)	(21·34)	(21·79)	(21·79)
Length, ft in	51 2	50 0	50 8	51 3	50 9	50 9	51 7 3/16	53 10
(m)	(15·60)	(15·24)	(15·44)	(15·62)	(15·47)	(15·47)	(15·73)	(16·41)
Height, ft in	18 6	18 6	18 6	18 6	18 6	18 6	19 0	18 6
(m)	(5·64)	(5·64)	(5 64)	(5·64)	(5·64)	(5·64)	(5·79)	(5·64)
Wing area, sq ft	540	540	540	540	540	540	541	541
(sq m)	(50·168)	(50·168)	(50·168)	(50·168)	(50·168)	(50·168)	(50·261)	(50·261)
Empty weight, lb	21,150	22,370	22,362	22,850	22,550	23,000	25,130	24,500
(kg)	(9,593)	(10,147)	(10,143)	(10,365)	(10,229)	(10,433)	(11,399)	(11,113)
Loaded weight, lb	26,700	27,600	26,000	27,600	28,000	33,000	37,000	35,000
(kg)	(12,111)	(12,519)	(11,793)	(12,519)	(12,701)	(14,969)	(16,783)	(15,876)
Maximum weight, lb	31,000	35,000	41,800	35,000	38,000	—	39,250	—
(kg)	(14,061)	(15,876)	(18,960)	(15,876)	(17,237)	—	(17,804)	—
Wing loading, lb/sq ft	49·4	51·1	48·1	51·1	51·9	61·1	68·4	64·7
(kg/sq m)	(241·4)	(249·5)	(235·1)	(249·5)	(253·2)	(298·4)	(333·9)	(315·9)
Power loading, lb/hp	6·7	6·9	6·5	6·9	6·7	—	7·4	7
(kg/hp)	(3)	(3·1)	(2·9)	(3·1)	(3)	—	(3·4)	(3·2)
Maximum speed, mph at ft	370/17,000	355/15,000	322/10,000	355/15,000	403/15,000	435/15,000	327/15,000	—
(km/h at m)	(595/5,180)	(571/4,570)	(518/3,050)	(571/4,570)	(649/4,570)	(700/4,570)	(526/4,570)	—
Cruising speed, mph	212	284	273	284	310	—	310	365
(km/h)	(341)	(457)	(447)	(457)	(499)	—	(499)	(587)
Climb to, ft/min	20,000/10·2	10,000/8·1	1,070/1	10,000/8	10,000/4·3	25,000/13·5	2,050/1	1,700/1
(m/min)	(6,096/10·2)	(3,050/8·1)	(326/1)	(3,050/8)	(3,050/4·3)	(7,620/13·5)	(625/1)	(518/1)
Service ceiling, ft	31,300	22,100	24 500	22,100	31,200	33,000	30,500	25,000
(m)	(9,540)	(6,735)	(7,470)	(6,735)	(9,510)	(10,060)	(9,295)	(7,620)
Normal range, miles	1,800	1,400	1,680	1,400	1,480	—	1,480	2,100
(km)	(2,895)	(2,255)	(2,705)	(2,255)	(2,380)	—	(2,380)	(3,380)
Maximum range, miles	2,500	3,200	2,514	3,200	4,500	—	2,700	2,500
(km)	(4,025)	(5,150)	(4,590)	(5,150)	(7,240)	—	(4,345)	(4,025)

One of the twenty-eight BTD-1s completed before cancellation of the production contract. (*MDC*)

Douglas XSB2D-1 and BTD Destroyer

As tension was building up in the Far East, eight new US fleet carriers—the first ships of the *Essex* class—were ordered in July 1940. To provide the aircraft complement of these new carriers and to modernize that of existing carriers, the Navy boosted its orders for types already in production and initiated development of several new carrier-borne aircraft. Among those ordered during this period were two XSB2D-1 two-seat bombers intended as prototypes for a successor to both the Douglas Dauntless already in service and the new Curtiss SB2C-1 Helldiver then entering production. Contract NOs-88707 covering the design and construction of these two prototypes was awarded to the El Segundo Division on 30 June, 1941.

To achieve the exacting increase in performance and armament specified by the Navy, Ed Heinemann's team designed an aircraft incorporating several features not previously found in naval aircraft. Noteworthy amongst them were the use of laminar-flow aerofoil, tricycle undercarriage and remotely-controlled turrets. In addition, a mid-mounted gull-wing was adopted to provide space beneath its centre section for a large internal bomb bay. Proposed armament consisted of two wing-mounted 20 mm cannon and of dorsal and ventral turrets each housing twin 0·50-in machine-guns, whilst offensive load of up to 4,200 lb (1,906 kg) consisted of either two 1,600-lb (726-kg) bombs in the bomb bay and two 500-lb (227-kg) bombs on wing racks, or of two 2,100-lb (953-kg) torpedoes beneath the fuselage. The powerplant selected for the aircraft was the 2,300 hp Wright R-3350-14 eighteen-cylinder, air-cooled radial driving a three-blade propeller.

356

As the limited staff of the El Segundo Division was almost fully committed to other projects, design and construction of the first XSB2D-1 (s/n 1207, BuNo 03551) progressed slowly and the aircraft, which had been completed on 17 March, 1943, made its first flight on 8 April, more than 21 months after it had been ordered. Flight trials progressed satisfactorily and the XSB2D-1 demonstrated a top speed of 346 mph (557 km/h), exceeding

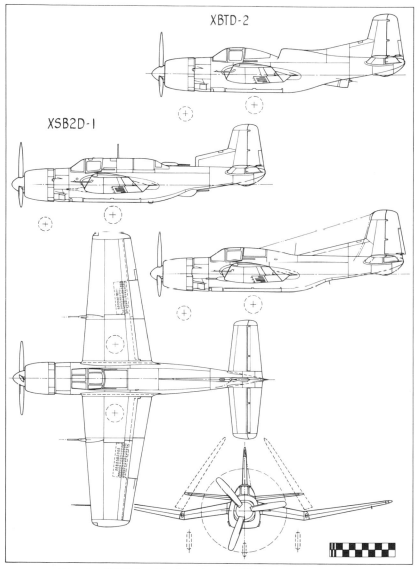

Douglas BTD-1, with side view of XSB2D-1 and XBTD-2.

that of the Curtiss SB2C-1 by 65 mph (105 km/h), and carried almost twice the bombload. Accordingly, the initial production order for thirteen SB2D-1s (BuNos 04959/04971), which had been awarded on 9 April, 1942, was supplemented on 31 August, 1943, by an order for 345 aircraft (BuNos 09048/09392). However, shortly after, the Navy revised its requirements as its air superiority eliminated the need to provide carrier-borne bombers with defensive armament. Henceforth, whilst ordering prototypes of a new series of single-seat carrier bombers (the Curtiss XBTC-1, Kaiser-Fleetwings XBTK-1 and Martin XBTM-1, respectively contracted for in December 1943, March 1944 and May 1944), the Bureau of Aeronautics instructed Douglas to study the feasibility of modifying the XSB2D-1 design to single-seat configuration.

Design modifications were relatively straightforward and the single-seat BTD-1 had a shortened canopy over the pilot's cockpit and an extended dorsal fin instead of the truncated fin made necessary on the XSB2D-1 by the installation of the dorsal turret aft of the gunner's cockpit. Weight saved by removing the turrets and dispensing with the radio-operator/gunner was offset by an increase in maximum fuel capacity from 550 to 640 US gallons (2,082 to 2,423 litres) and in armour. Forward-firing armament, offensive load, powerplant installation, undercarriage design and most of the airframe remained unchanged. Therefore, the switch from SB2D-1 to BTD-1 production could be planned with little loss in time.

While design of the BTD-1 was proceeding Douglas completed the second XSB2D-1 (BuNo 03552) and had undertaken the production of the SB2D-1s. Thus, when the decision was reached not to proceed with the SB2D-1, the construction of the first aircraft (s/n 1363, BuNo 04959) was too far advanced to modify this airframe to BTD-1 standards and the first airframe to be modified during construction was that of s/n 1364, BuNo 04960. Completed on 15 February, 1944, and flown on 5 March, the first BTD-1 was followed by 27 aircraft (BuNos 04961/04971, 09048/09062 and

The first XSB2D-1 at Mines Field in April 1943.
(*Northrop Institute of Technology*)

358

BTD-1 (BuNo 09050) at the Naval Air Test Center, Patuxent River. (*USN*)

04959, this last aircraft bearing the s/n1891 and assuming the BuNo of the uncompleted SB2D-1). In spite of the smooth transition from SB2D-1 to BTD-1, the programme was doomed as the competitive designs, which had been planned from the onset as single-seaters, were anticipated to have superior performance. Consequently, the Navy cancelled the BTD-1 contract and the last aircraft was delivered on 8 October, 1945. Fortunately for Douglas, the company had been able to negotiate a contract for yet another single-seat carrier-borne bomber, the BT2D-1, forerunner of the famous Skyraider series.

At least one BTD-1 was used to test dive-brakes of new design and had its wing-mounted picket-fence brakes replaced by six-segment 'banana peel' brakes on the sides and bottom of the rear fuselage. The use of braking parachute and reversible propeller were also evaluated but were rejected. Of greater historical interest were the two XBTD-2s, the first jet-powered aircraft for Douglas and the US Navy. Retaining their Wright R-3350-14 radial engine, two BTD-1s (BuNos 04962 and 04964) were modified during construction by fitting a jet fuel tank in the bomb bay and by installing a 1,500 lb (680 kg) thrust Westinghouse WE-19XA turbojet in the rear fuselage. Fed by a dorsal intake located behind the pilot's cockpit, the turbojet was mounted behind the bomb bay and exhausted downward at a ten-degree angle from the centreline. Ground tests with the first XBTD-2 began during March 1944 behind a screened enclosure at the Los Angeles Municipal Airport and the first flight was made in May of that year. However, trials proved disappointing as the anticipated 50 mph (80 km/h) increase in combat speed could not be achieved as the turbojet installation proved unsuccessful at speeds in excess of 200 mph (322 km/h). Further development of the XBTD-2 was made unnecessary by the successful testing of the new XBT2D-1 and the programme was cancelled shortly after the end of the war.

XSB2D-1

Span 45 ft (13·72 m); length 38 ft 7 in (11·76 m); height 16 ft 11 in (5·16 m); wing area 375 sq ft (34·839 sq m). Empty weight 12,458 lb (5,651 kg); loaded weight 16,273 lb (7,381 kg); maximum weight 19,140 lb (8,682 kg); wing loading 43·4 lb/sq ft (211·9 kg/sq m); power loading 7·1 lb/hp (3·2 kg/hp). Maximum speed 346 mph (557 km/h) at 16,100 ft (4,905 m); cruising speed 180 mph (290 km/h); initial rate of climb 1,710 ft/min (521 m/min); service ceiling 24,400 ft (7,435 m); normal range 1,480 miles (2,380 km).

BTD-1

Span and length as XSB2D-1. Height 16 ft 7 in (5·05 m); wing area 373 sq ft (34·653 sq m). Empty weight 12,900 lb (5,851 kg); loaded weight 18,140 lb (8,228 kg); maximum weight 19,000 lb (8,618 kg); wing loading 48·6 lb/sq ft (237·4 kg/sq m); power loading 7·9 lb/hp (3·6 kg/hp). Maximum speed 344 mph (554 km/h) at 16,100 ft (4,905 m); cruising speed 188 mph (303 km/h); initial rate of climb 1,650 ft/min (503 m/min); service ceiling 23,600 ft (7,195 m); normal range 1,480 miles (2,380 km); maximum range 2,140 miles (3,445 km).

Douglas XB-42 Mixmaster

Undoubtedly one of Douglas's most ingenious designs, the XB-42 Mixmaster was not put into production as it appeared too late and when the turbojet had shown itself to be the powerplant of the future. None the less, it deserves a special place in aviation history as it was one of the most advanced piston-powered aircraft ever designed, with a truly spectacular performance. For example, on approximately the same power, the XB-42 was as fast as the Mosquito B.XVI but carried twice the maximum bombload (8,000 lb versus 4,000 lb—3,628 kg versus 1,814 kg) over short ranges or a bombload of 3,750 lb (1,701 kg) versus 1,000 lb (454 kg) over a

The Douglas XB-42 was potentially the most formidable piston-powered bomber as it combined high speed and good load/range performance. (*MDC*)

360

The first XB-42, showing the clean wing design and cruciform tail surfaces with protective skid incorporated at the tip of the lower fin. (*MDC*)

range of 1,850 miles (2,977 km). Furthermore, the Mixmaster had a defensive armament of four 0·50-in machine-guns in two remotely-controlled turrets whereas the Mosquito B.XVI was unarmed.

This remarkable aircraft originated as a private venture. Douglas designer E. F. Burton began a study to determine the feasibility of producing a twin-engined aircraft capable of carrying 2,000 lb (908 kg) of bombs to targets within a 2,000 mile (3,220 km) radius and of having a top speed in excess of 400 mph (644 km/h). Burton and his team soon became convinced that, by mounting the engines within the fuselage and using a clean wing, such an aircraft could indeed be built, as drag would be reduced by almost one third. Moreover, when compared with the Boeing B-29 four-engined heavy bomber, this aircraft was estimated to require half the maintenance crew and to be two thirds cheaper. These estimates, together with the supporting documentation, were submitted in May 1943 in an unsolicited proposal.

The XB-42 on take-off from Palm Springs, California. (*NA & SM*)

361

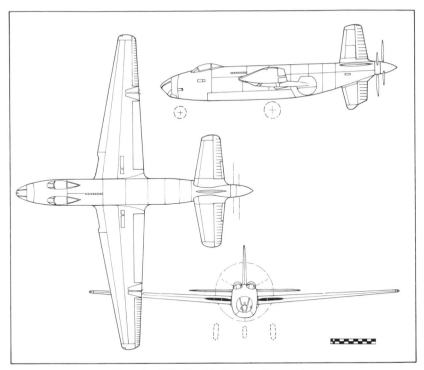

Douglas XB-42 with 'bug-eye' canopies.

The Douglas proposal was received enthusiastically by the Bombardment Branch, Engineering Division, Air Technical Service Command of the Army Air Forces and on 25 June, 1943, the company was awarded Contract AC40188 for two flying prototypes and one static test airframe. In spite of its potential as a long-range medium bomber, the aircraft was classified at that time as an attack bomber and received the designation XA-42. However, on 26 November, 1943, the designation was changed to XB-42. Under the supervision of Ed Burton and of Carlos C. Wood, Chief of the Preliminary Design Division, detail design and construction of the XA-42/XB-42 proceeded swiftly at Santa Monica. The mock-up was inspected and approved in September 1943 and the first aircraft (43-50224) completed in May 1944, only one year after initial submission of the proposal. By completing the XB-42 within ten months from contract award Douglas thus redeemed itself after having been seriously criticized for delays in the A-26 programme.

Several features of the XB-42 were noteworthy. The two 1,325 hp Allison V-1710-125s were installed immediately aft of the pilots' compartment, with the centreline of each at about 20 deg to the vertical, and the engines toed in a few degrees to the rear. Power was transmitted to a gear reduction box in the tail cone through five lengths of shafting, each identical to that

362

The extremely clean lines of the XB-42 make it hard to realize that this aircraft, especially when seen from the rear, was large enough to carry internally up to 8,000 lb of bombs. (*USAF*)

used in the Bell P-39. The three-blade contra-rotating propellers were driven by their own engines, the left powerplant driving the forward propeller and the right the aft. The laminar-flow wing with double-slotted-flaps housed the fuel tanks and the oil and coolant radiators which were fitted with ground cooling fans. In addition, a remotely-controlled General Electric turret with twin 0·50-in machine-guns was installed between the ailerons and flaps. The guns were normally housed within the wing beneath snap-action doors but, in firing position, they covered an area extending 25 deg to either side, 30 deg above and 15 deg below. As the wing was mid-mounted and as it was necessary to provide sufficient clearance for the aft-located propellers, the design of the undercarriage presented some difficulties and led to the adoption of a fuselage-mounted tricycle unit with mainwheels retracting aft into the fuselage sides. A cruciform empennage was fitted as the addition of a lower fin and rudder reduced the size of the upper elements and provided the necessary protection for the propellers. The capacious bomb bay, in which maximum load comprised four 2,000 lb (908 kg) bombs but in which a 10,000 lb (4,536 kg) bomb could be carried by keeping the snap-action doors open six inches (15·2 cm), extended from beneath the cockpit to aft of the wings. The crew of three consisted of a navigator/bomb-aimer in the glazed nose section, and of pilot and co-pilot/gunner in a side-by-side cockpit with small separate canopies.

On 6 May, 1944, Bob Brush took the XB-42 for its maiden flight and soon demonstrated its remarkable potential. Speed was within one percent of prediction, range somewhat exceeded calculations, and rate of climb substantially bettered estimates (in particular, single-engined climb was up 35 per cent). On the negative side, it was found that the 'bug-eye' canopies impaired pilots' communications, and that the aircraft suffered from yaw, excessive propeller vibration—especially when the bomb bay doors were opened—, poor harmonization of control forces, and from limited

The ill-fated second XB-42, with modified canopy as proposed for the projected production version. (*NA & SM*)

efficiency of the cooling ducts. Solutions for most of these problems were found relatively quickly and the aircraft was progressively improved, and it was confidently predicted that remaining difficulties would be solved in production aircraft. All in all the flight trial programme proceeded smoothly, a notable achievement in view of the many novel features incorporated in the aircraft. Shortly after it first flight on 1 August, 1944, the second prototype (43-50225), with -129 engines, was fitted with a single canopy as proposed for production aircraft. In early December 1945 this aircraft was flown by an AAF crew from Long Beach, California, to Bolling Field, DC, in 5 hr 17 min 34 sec at an average speed of 433·6 mph (697·8 km/h). Unfortunately, on the 16th of that month it crashed near Bolling Field, the crew baling out in time.

By that time, however, it had already been decided that the B-42—for which an attack version with forward-firing armament of sixteen 0·50-in machine-guns, or one 75 mm cannon and two 0·50-in guns, or two 37 mm cannon was proposed—would not be put into production as the war's end made it possible for the Army Air Forces to wait for higher performance

The hybrid XB-42A with underslung 19XB-2A turbojets.
(*Northrop Institute of Technology*)

364

jet-powered bombers. Consequently, it was decided to experiment with the remaining Mixmaster by fitting two auxiliary turbojets beneath the wing as originally proposed by Douglas in December 1943. Redesignated XB-42A and powered by two 1,375 hp Allison V-1710-133 liquid-cooled engines and two 1,600 lb (726 kg) thrust Westinghouse 19XB-2A axial-flow turbojets, the aircraft was first flown at Muroc Dry Lake, California, on 27 May, 1947. The hybrid XB-42A was tested over a period of several months and on 30 June, 1949, it was struck off charge. It is now part of the collection of the National Air & Space Museum in Washington.

XB-42

Span 70 ft 6 in (21·49 m); length 53 ft 8 in (16·36 m); height 18 ft 10 in (5·74 m); wing area 555 sq ft (51·561 sq m). Empty weight 20,888 lb (9,475 kg); loaded weight 35,702 lb (16,194 kg); wing loading 64·3 lb/sq ft (314·1 kg/sq m); power loading 13·5 lb/hp (6·1 kg/hp). Maximum speed 410 mph (660 km/h) at 23,440 ft (7,145 m); cruising speed 312 mph (502 km/h); service ceiling 29,400 ft (8,960 m); normal range 1,800 miles (2,895 km); maximum range 5,400 miles (8,690 km).

XB-42A

Span 70 ft 7 in (21·51 m); length 53 ft 10 in (16·41 m). Height and wing area as XB-42. Empty weight 24,775 lb (11,238 kg); loaded weight 39,000 lb (17,690 kg); maximum weight 44,900 lb (20,366 kg); wing loading 70·3 lb/sq ft (343·1 kg/sq m). Maximum speed 488 mph (785 km/h) at 14,000 ft (4,625 m); cruising speed 442 mph (711 km/h); normal range 2,100 miles (3,380 km); maximum range 4,750 miles (7,645 km).

Douglas XTB2D-1 Skypirate

In 1942, when Japanese forces were advancing in the South and Central Pacific, the El Segundo team undertook the design study for a large, single-engined, long-range torpedo bomber capable of operating either from land bases in the defence of the US West Coast or from the very large carriers of the *Midway* class which were then being designed; but, as the Japanese threat receded and as the *Midway*-class carriers would not become operational for a number of years, the Douglas torpedo bomber project was shelved.

The Bureau of Aeronautics was anxious to equip the squadrons of the new carriers with the best possible aircraft. Accordingly, the Douglas project was revived and on 31 October, 1943, four days after construction of the USS *Midway* had begun, the El Segundo Division was awarded a contract for the design, construction and testing of two three/four-seat XTB2D-1s (BuNos 36933 and 36934). With a span of 70 ft (21·34 m) and estimated gross weight of 28,000 lb (12,700 kg) the XTB2D-1 was larger and heavier than the North American B-25B Mitchell, the heaviest aircraft that had flown from the deck of a carrier. The 3,000 hp Pratt & Whitney

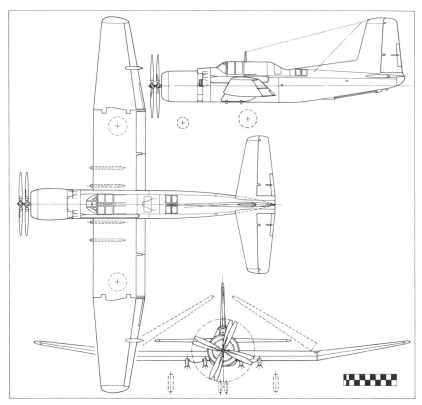

XR-4360-8 twenty-eight-cylinder air-cooled radial engine driving contra-rotating four-blade propellers was chosen to power the aircraft, and it was decided to use a tricycle undercarriage with the single-wheel main units retracting outboard into the wing and the twin-wheel nose unit retracting rearward into the fuselage. Proposed armament consisted of four wing-

The first XTB2D-1 (BuNo 36933) at the time of its completion on 13 March, 1945. (*MDC*)

In spite of its size, the projected TB2D-1 production version was intended to be embarked aboard *Midway*-class carriers, hence the provision for folding wings as illustrated by the first XTB2D-1. (*MDC*)

mounted 0·50 in machine guns, twin 0·50-in guns in a power-operated dorsal turret and single 0·50-in flexible gun in the ventral bath which also housed the torpedo/bomb-aiming gear. Offensive load of up to 8,400 lb (3,810 kg) of torpedoes, bombs or depth-charges could be carried externally on racks mounted two on each inner wing panel between the main undercarriage and the fuselage.

The first of the unarmed prototypes was completed on 13 March, 1945, and first flew early the following month. In spite of its size and weight, the XTB2D-1 soon displayed remarkable performance as it was 73 mph (117 km/h) faster than the Grumman/Eastern TBM-3 Avenger, the Navy's standard torpedo bomber, and could carry two torpedoes 145 miles (233 km) farther than the TBM-3 could carry its single torpedo. However, the end of the war and the development of single-engined, single-seat bombers capable of carrying two torpedoes even when operating from the smaller *Essex*-class carriers rendered the Skypirate redundant and the contract for twenty-three TB2D-1s (BuNos 89097/89119) was cancelled before completion of the first production aircraft.

Span 70 ft (21·34 m); length 46 ft (14·02 m); height 22 ft 7 in (6·88 m); wing area 605 sq ft (56·207 sq m). Empty weight 18,405 lb (8,348 kg); loaded weight 28,545 lb (12,948 kg); maximum weight 34,760 lb (15,767 kg); wing loading 47·2 lb/sq ft (230·4 kg/sq m); power loading 9·5 lb/hp (4·3 kg/hp). Maximum speed 340 mph (547 km/h) at 15,600 ft (4,744 m); cruising speed 168 mph (270 km/h); initial rate of climb 1,390 ft/min (434 m/min); service ceiling 24,500 ft (7,470 m); normal range 1,250 miles (2,010 km); maximum range 2,880 miles (4,635 km).

Three AD-4NAs and one AD-4B of VA-216 bearing the 'O' tail code of Carrier Air Group Twenty-One (CVG-21). (*US National Archives*)

Douglas AD (A-1) Skyraider

When the United States were drawn ino the Second World War, the Navy firmly believed in relying on two basic classes of carrier-borne bombers: two-seat aircraft to equip scouting (VS) and bomber (VB) squadrons, and three-seat aircraft to equip torpedo (VT) squadrons. Already, when Douglas Dauntlesses and Devastators equipped most VB, VS and VT squadrons, the dominance of the Douglas carrier-borne bombers was facing a strong challenge as Grumman Avengers and Curtiss Helldivers were planned, soon to supplement and eventually supplant the Douglas TBD and SBD bombers.

For a while, however, it appeared that Douglas would soon regain its leadership as prototypes of more advanced two-seat scout bombers (XSB2D-1) and three-seat torpedo bombers (XTB2D-1) were respectively ordered from the Santa Monica firm on 30 June, 1941, and 31 October, 1943, but, during 1943, prospects were again bleak as combat experience led the Bureau of Aeronautics to abandon its long-standing support for multi-seat carrier-borne bombers and to initiate the development of single-seat aircraft combining the roles of dive and torpedo bombing. To meet this Douglas developed the BTD-1 and by early 1944 six hundred and twenty-three aircraft of this type were on order. Yet, the BTD-1 did not become operational as in the meantime the Navy had placed orders for prototypes of the Curtiss XBTC-1, Kaiser-Fleetwings XBTK-1 and Martin XBTM-1 single-seat bombers.

Designed from the onset to meet the new BT class requirements, the Curtiss, Kaiser-Fleetwings and Martin designs promised to have better performance than the BTD-1 which was derived from the original XSB2D-1 two-seat design. Consequently, in early July 1944, a team from the El Segundo design group was informed in Washington by the Bureau of Aeronautics that the BTD-1 programme was to be discontinued in favour of the newer XBTC-1, XBTK-1 and/or XBTM-1. Endeavouring to retain a place amongst the major suppliers of the US Navy, the Douglas team— which included Chief Engineer Ed Heinemann, Chief Designer Leo Devlin and Chief Aerodynamicist Gene Root—capitalized on information developed since December 1943 during in-house design studies to produce overnight in their hotel room preliminary sketches and performance estimates for a brand new aircraft. So impressed were the Bureau representatives that, provided Douglas could guarantee that the new aircraft would be completed in time to compete with the entries ordered from one to six months earlier from the other three manufacturers, they authorized the design and manufacture of fifteen XBT2D-1s under an amendment to the existing BTD-1 contract. Ultimately, the night-long efforts of Heinemann, Devlin and Root were rewarded by the production of a total of 3,180 aircraft over a twelve-year period.

Immediately, work began at the El Segundo plant and a target of first flight within one year was set. Soon, however, it looked as if this goal was somewhat unrealistic as the scheduled mock-up completion had to be extended from 24 July to 14 August, 1944. As shown in mock-up form, the XBT2D-1 was characterized by low-mounted, straight-tapered wings. Large dive-brakes were installed on each side of the fuselage behind the

The first XBT2D-1 (BuNos 09085) during an early test flight over Southern California in the spring of 1945. (*USN*)

wing trailing-edge and beneath the rear fuselage. The main legs and wheels of the fully retractable undercarriage retracted backward into wing wells and there was a conventional retractable tailwheel and arrester hook. The powerplant was to be a 2,500 hp Wright R-3350-24W eighteen-cylinder radial. In this form the mock-up was approved by the Board of Inspection with only minor changes being recommended.

Weight soon became a major problem as combat experience indicated that to be successful the aircraft should be fitted with improved protection against anti-aircraft fire and should have significantly greater radius of action, rate of climb and maximum speed, while shorter take-off distance and heavier armament were also recommended. In spite of these demanding requirements, Douglas was able to complete the first XBT2D-1 at a gross weight of 16,372 lb (7,427 kg), some 1,628 lb (738 kg) below the contractual guaranteed design gross weight, and, to offset any potential stability problems resulting from this weight reduction, had to move the wings 4 in (10·16 cm) forward.

Every effort was made to reduce its competitors' lead and to that effect it was decided to use the main undercarriage struts and wheels of the Vought F4U-1 on the first two XBT2D-1s and, due to late availability of the specified 2,500 hp R-3350-24W, to install 2,300 hp R-3350-8s on the first four prototypes. The El Segundo team's experience in naval aircraft design and the energy deployed by the Douglas work force were rewarded when, before the prototype's first flight, the order for fifteen XBT2D-1s was increased to twenty-five in order to keep tooling active and provide additional aircraft for development and evaluation of the basic XBT2D-1 and of contemplated versions specially intended to fill the requirements of Airborne Early Warning, Night Attack, Electronic Countermeasures and other duties. Finally in mid-March 1945, by which time the aircraft had been tentatively named Dauntless II, the first XBT2D-1 was completed. At that time only one of the three other competitors, the Martin XBTM-1, had flown.

On 18 March, 1945, almost four months ahead of the original schedule, the first XBT2D-1 (s/n 1913, BuNo 09085) made its first flight with LaVerne Brown at the controls. During the next three weeks the aircraft completed thirty-one successful test flights and on 7 April the aircraft was delivered to the Navy Proving Ground at Patuxent River. The naval test pilots found the flight characteristics and performance more than satisfactory, rating the XBT2D-1 very high for quality and lacking significant shortcomings. In general, the aircraft was rated superior to any dive-bomber yet tested at Patuxent and the evaluation programme was completed in the record time of five weeks in spite of various engine problems including even a master rod failure.

The official reaction to the unqualified success of the initial flight-trial programme was to prepare authorization for the production contract and on 5 May, 1945, a Letter of Intent for 548 production BT2D-1s was signed. However, following VJ-Day the order was reduced to 377 and shortly after to 277 and these aircraft were delivered as AD-1s and AD-1Qs—the designation change taking place in April 1946 when the Navy overhauled its designation system. The name Skyraider was officially approved for the aircraft in February of the same year.

Meanwhile, deliveries of the XBT2D-1s were slowed down when the Aeroproduct propeller showed questionable vibration and governor characteristics. Other problems were encountered with the powerplant installation, and serious failures of the main undercarriage legs and their supporting structure were disclosed during Service trials at Alameda, California, beginning in May 1946. Consequently, the XBT2D-1s and the first twenty AD-1s had to be returned to the factory for local strengthening and airframe modification. This programme being successfully completed, the Skyraider remained in production until 1957 and, including prototypes, appeared in eight major models and 37 versions.

XBT2D-1: Prototype and Service trials series ordered in July 1944. Twenty-five XBT2D-1s (BuNos 09085 to 09109) were built and accepted by the US Navy between June 1945 and May 1948. Six from this batch were subsequently modified as prototypes for other versions. The first four aircraft were powered by 2,300 hp Wright R-3350-8s—one, BuNo 09088, being tested with a large propeller spinner—but all other aircraft received the 2,500 hp R-3350-24W originally specified. Armament consisted of two wing-mounted 20-mm cannon and up to 8,000 lb (3,629 kg) of bombs, torpedoes, rockets, napalm or smoke canisters, or drop tanks in various combinations. External stores attached to three large pylons, one beneath the fuselage centreline and one beneath each inboard wing panel, and twelve small wing racks.

XBT2D-1N: Two XBT2D-1s (BuNos 09098 and 09099) converted by Douglas as prototypes for a three-seat night attack version. Two radar operators were accommodated within the fuselage aft of the pilot's cockpit and a radar pod was attached beneath the port wing with a searchlight pod beneath the starboard wing. Dive-brakes on fuselage sides not fitted to this variant.

BuNo 09098, the first three-seat XBT2D-1N, at the Naval Air Test Center, Patuxent River, on 27 February, 1948. (*US National Archives*)

AD-1 from Attack Squadron Sixty-Five (VA-65) taking off from the USS *Coral Sea* on 20 May, 1948. (*US National Archives*)

XBT2D-1P: One XBT2D-1 (BuNo 09096) converted by Douglas as prototype for a single-seat photographic reconnaissance version.

XBT2D-1Q: Last XBT2D-1 (BuNo 09109) converted by Douglas as prototype for a two-seat electronic countermeasures aircraft. The ECM operator's station was located within the fuselage and radar and window dispenser pods were attached beneath the wing respectively to port and starboard.

AD-1: First production version of which 242 (BuNos 09110 to 09351) were built. The first AD-1 (s/n 1938, BuNo 09110) flew on 5 November, 1946, and the last was accepted in August 1949. One of these was later modified as an AD-2. Armament and powerplant installation were identical to those of late XBT2D-1s but structural strengthening led to a 415 lb (188 kg) increase in empty weight. Maximum gross weight reached 18,030 lb (8,178 kg), already above the original guaranteed gross weight quoted when the XBT2D-1 was first proposed, but still well under the 25,000 lb (11,340 kg) gross weight of late Skyraider models.

AD-1Q: Thirty-five aircraft (BuNos 09352 to 09386) representing the balance of the original order for 277 BT2D-1s. As two-seat electronic countermeasures aircraft, they carried equipment similar to that of the XBT2D-1Q.

XAD-1W: One XBT2D-1 (BuNo 09107) modified as prototype for a three-seat airborne early warning version. Two radar operators were accommodated aft of the pilot and a large opaque fairing extended behind the pilot's canopy. Search radar was installed in a large fairing beneath the fuselage. This experimental installation later led to the production of 417 airborne early warning Skyraiders in three versions (AD-3W, AD-4W and AD-5W). No 'W' aircraft carried armament.

XAD-2: One XBT2D-1 (BuNo 09108) modified by Douglas to serve as prototype for a more powerful and heavier version of the Skyraider, first proposed under the BT2D-2 designation, and powered by a 2,700 hp Wright R-3350-26W.

AD-2: Following modification by Douglas of one AD-1 (BuNo 09195) as a pilot aircraft for the AD-2 series, a total of 156 AD-2s (BuNos 122210 to 122365) were built and all were accepted by the US Navy during 1948. One AD-2 (BuNo 122226) was first used to demonstrate the improved engine cooling system developed for the AD-3 series and was later fitted with a radome similar to that tested on the XAD-1W. The AD-2 series had wheel-well covers, revised cockpit internal arrangement, an increase in internal fuel capacity from 365 US gallons (1,382 litres) to 380 gallons (1,438 litres) and greater structural strength. In early 1954, Major Warren Schoeder, USMC, demonstrated the potential of the AD-2 as a forest fire-fighting aircraft. For this demonstration which took place at MCAS El Toro, California, the aircraft carried fire retardant chemicals in modified 250-gallon (946-litre) napalm tanks. Although successful, this role was not adopted.

The experimental AD-2W (BuNo 122226) which was used to flight test the ventral radome for the airborne early warning Skyraider.
(*US National Archives*)

AD-2D: Unofficial designation believed to have been applied to two AD-2s used as drones to sample radioactive materials during nuclear tests.

AD-2Q: Two-seat electronic countermeasures version of the AD-2 of which twenty-one were built (BuNos 122366 to 122372 and 122374 to 122387) for delivery between September 1948 and April 1949.

AD-2QU: One aircraft (BuNo 122373) specially built to serve in the target-towing role. Airframe identical to that of the AD-2Q but fitted to carry a Mark 22 aerial target in a container beneath the fuselage.

AD-3: Designation initially given to a projected turbine-powered version. Various engines were considered and included the General Electric TG-100, twin Allison 500, twin Westinghouse 24C, twin Westinghouse 19XB, and a projected Douglas-designed twin turbine. This 1947 project resulted in the XA2D-1 and the AD-3 designation was retained for an improved version of the AD-2.

Line-up of AD-2Qs from VC-33, Composite Squadron Thirty-Three.
(*US National Archives*)

The R-3350-26W powered AD-3 version, of which 125 were built
(BuNos 122729 to 122853), introduced an improved undercarriage with
longer stroke, redesigned cockpit canopy, improved propeller and engine
cooling system, and further local structural strengthening. With these
modifications the aircraft's maximum gross weight rose to 19,664 lb (9,919
kg) but it retained the armament and powerplant of the AD-2. One AD-3
was later modified to AD-4 standard.

AD-3N: Three-seat night attack version of the -3 series of which fifteen
(BuNos 122908 to 122922) were accepted between September 1949 and
May 1950. Subsequently two of these were converted to AD-3S
configuration.

AD-3QU and AD-3Q: Twenty-three aircraft (BuNos 122854 to 122876)
ordered as AD-3QUs for use in the target-towing role. The successful
development of the Mark 22 target tested on the AD-2QU eliminated the
need for this special version and all aircraft were delivered as AD-3Qs for
use as two-seat electronic countermeasures aircraft. For target towing the
AD-3Qs could be quickly adapted to use the Mark 22 aerial target system.

Douglas AD-3W (BuNo 122879) in the markings of the Naval Air Test Center.
(*US National Archives*)

374

AD-3W: First production model of the three-seat airborne early warning configuration first tested on the only XAD-1W. Thirty-one built (BuNos 122877 to 122907). The last two aircraft became AD-3Es.

AD-3E and AD-3S: Two AD-3Ws (BuNos 122906 and 122907) and two AD-3Ns (BuNos 122910 and 122911) were respectively modified as AD-3E (Search) and AD-3S (Attack) to demonstrate the feasibility of using the Skyraider as a 'hunter-killer' team for anti-submarine warfare. Later one AD-3S was fitted with an improved version of the AN/APS-31 radar with larger scanner developed by Douglas and installed in a large store-shaped radome installed under the port wing. The intention was to prove the practicability of combining search and attack capabilities in one aircraft. A tentative proposal to that effect was submitted to the Bureau of Aeronautics in August 1950 but the Navy requested that the first batch of AD-4Ws and AD-4Ns be modified to combine the 'E' and 'S' missions with their basic missions. Eventually all AD-4Ws and AD-4Ns were so modified before delivery or retrofitted.

AD-3S (BuNo 122910) over Boca Chica, Florida, on 31 January, 1950.
(*US National Archives*)

AD-4: Built in larger numbers than any other series of the Skyraider, the AD-4 appeared in eight different versions. The first aircraft to bear the AD-4 designation was an AD-3 (BuNo 122853) which was powered by an improved version of the R-3350, the 2,700 hp R-3350-26WA, and had further improved windscreen, a P-1 automatic pilot and a modified arrester hook. The production AD-4s, of which 372 were built (BuNos 123771 to 123006, 127844 to 127879, and 128917 to 129016), were fitted with APS 19A radar. Later one AD-4 was modified to serve as AD-5 prototype, 63 were modified as AD-4Ls and 28 as AD-4Bs.

AD-4N: Three-seat night attack version of which 307 were built (BuNos 124128 to 124156, 124725 to 124760, 125707 to 125764, 126876 to 127018, and 127880 to 127920). These aircraft were either delivered with the necessary equipment for the 'S' mission or were retrofitted. In addition, 100 became AD-4NAs and 38 AD-4NLs.

AD-4W: Three-seat airborne early warning version of which 168 were built (BuNos 124076 to 124127, 124761 to 124777, 125765 to 125782, 126836 to 126875, and 127921 to 127961). Fifty were transferred to the Royal Navy as Skyraider AEW 1s. Those remaining in service with the US Navy were equipped to also fulfil the 'E' mission in ASW operations.

AD-4Q: Thirty-nine (BuNos 124037 to 124075) two-seat electronic countermeasures aircraft.

AD-4L: Service modification of 63 AD-4s (BuNos 123935, 123952 to 124005, and 127845 to 127852) fitted with anti-icing and de-icing equipment for operations in Korean winter conditions. At the same time the wing-mounted armament was increased to four 20-mm cannon.

AD-4NA (A-1D): One hundred AD-4Ns (BuNos 125742 to 125764, 126876 to 126883, 126903 to 126925, 126947 to 126969, and 126988 to 127010) stripped in service of all night attack gear to enable them to carry heavier bombloads for Korean operations. Wing-mounted armament increased to four 20 mm cannon. Redesignated A-1Ds in September 1962.

AD-4NL: Following modification by Douglas of one AD-4N (BuNo 124153) which was fitted with anti-icing and de-icing equipment, thirty-six AD-4Ns (BuNos 124725 to 124760) were so modified in service. Wing-mounted armament also increased to four 20-mm cannon.

AD-4B: This was an AD-4 version specially strengthened to deliver nuclear weapons by using the toss-bombing, over-the-shoulder, technique and armed with four wing-mounted 20 mm cannon. Twenty-eight AD-4s (BuNos 127854 to 127860, 127866, 127868 to 127872, 128937 to 128943, and 128971 to 128978) were brought up to AD-4B standard following their delivery, and a further 165 aircraft (BuNos 132227 to 132391) were completed at the factory as AD-4Bs.

During a routine delivery flight to the Atlantic Fleet, one of these aircraft (s/n 8471, BuNo 132363) stopped in Dallas on 21 May, 1953, and was

The AD-4B which set a new weight-lifting world's record at NAS Dallas, Texas, on 21 May, 1953. The load of 14,941 lb included three 1,000-lb, six 750-lb and six 500-lb bombs plus racks and fuel. (*MDC*)

loaded with 14,941 lb (6,777 kg) of external stores. Taking off at a weight of 26,739 lb (12,128·6 kg), the aircraft set a new world weight-lifting record for single-engined aircraft.

AD-5 (A-1E): In late 1948 Douglas submitted a proposal for an advanced version of the Skyraider, to be designated AD-5, which was to be powered by a turbo-compound version of the R-3350 engine. This proposal, however, was not accepted by the Navy as this powerplant was larger and heavier—thus necessitating a major airframe redesign—and as at the time production of the Skyraider appeared to be nearing its end, Douglas put a new AD-5 proposal in December 1949. This time the aircraft was offered as an R-3350-26WA powered ASW machine combining the hunter and killer duties in a single airframe and with side-by-side seating. Although the aircraft was favourably regarded by the Bureau of Aeronautics, peacetime military appropriations were too small to authorize production.

A Marine Corps AD-5 aboard the USS *Intrepid* in February 1955.
(*US National Archives*)

The Communist invasion of South Korea suddenly changed the situation and, in addition to ordering an increase in AD-4 production, the Navy ordered an AD-5 prototype after inspecting a mock-up in October 1950. The prototype AD-5 was an AD-4 (BuNo 124006) with a widened forward fuselage to permit side-by-side seating. Major modifications included a 1 ft 11 in (58·4 cm) increase in fuselage length, the deletion of the dive-brakes on the fuselage sides, a 50 per cent increase in the vertical tail surface area, and the installation of improved bomb racks and of four wing-mounted 20-mm cannon. First flown on 17 August, 1951, the prototype AD-5 was followed by 212 production aircraft (BuNos 132478, 132392 to 132476, 132637 to 132686, and 133854 to 133929). These Skyraiders were basically two-seat day attack aircraft (yet were often operated as single-seaters) but conversion kits supplied with the aircraft, fitting in the fuselage below a much enlarged canopy, made it possible to quickly modify the aircraft to fulfil the following secondary missions: aeromedical evacuation with four casualty litters; VIP-transport with four backward-facing seats; twelve-seat troop transport with bench-type seats; utility cargo transport, fitted with a built-in hoist to load up to 2,000 lb (908 kg) of cargo; photographic reconnaissance with five cameras; and target towing.

In 1953 the Navy requested that the AD-5's adaptability be further improved by devising another conversion kit transforming the aircraft into an aerial tanker. This did not prove feasible but Douglas developed an external refuelling store with all necessary power and equipment self-contained. This external refuelling store was adopted for the AD-5 and later Skyraider variants as well as for other aircraft types. In September 1962 the AD-5s were redesignated A-1Es when used in the attack role and UA-1Es when used as utility aircraft.

AD-5N (A-1G): Four-seat night attack version utilizing the basic AD-5 airframe and fitted with search radar and searchlight in pods beneath the wings. Two hundred and thirty-nine AD-5Ns (BuNos 132477, 132480 to 132636, and 134974 to 135054) were built. Redesignated A-1Gs in September 1962.

AD-5W (EA-1E): Four-seat airborne early warning version of the AD-5 series. The aircraft carried a large 'guppy' radome beneath the fuselage and was fitted with a new metal rear canopy. Two hundred and eighteen built (BuNos 132729 to 132792, 133757 to 133776, 135139 to135222, and 139556

AD-5W (BuNo 139605) and AD-6 (BuNo 139769) off the coast of Southern California. (*MDC*)

378

EA-1F (AD-5Q) from Airborne Early Warning Squadron Thirteen (VAW-13), at Cubi Point in the Philippines, on 4 February, 1963. (*USN*)

to 139605). Redesignated EA-1Es under the 1962 Tri-Service designation system.

AD-5S: One experimental ASW aircraft (BuNo 132479) fitted with MAD (Magnetic Anomaly Detector) gear and tested by VX-1 at Key West, Florida.

AD-5Q (EA-1F): Following modification by Douglas of one AD-5N (BuNo 135054) as a four-seat electronic countermeasures aircraft, fifty-three conversion kits were delivered and fitted in service to a like number of AD-5Ns. Aircraft redesignated EA-1Fs in September 1962.

AD-6 (A-1H): Seven hundred and thirteen (BuNos 134466 to 134637, 135223 to 135406, 137492 to 137632, and 139606 to 139821) single-seat day attack aircraft. Basically the AD-6 was an improved AD-4B fitted with

The 3,180th and last Skyraider (BuNo 142081) undergoing final assembly at the El Segundo Division, 22 January, 1957. (*MDC*)

special equipment for low-level attack bombing and the improved types of bomb racks first used on the AD-5. Under the Tri-Service designation system introduced in 1962 the AD-6s became A-1Hs.

AD-7 (A-1J): Final production version of the Skyraider, the AD-7 differed from the AD-6 in being powered by an R-3350-26WB instead of an R-3350-26WA and in having strengthened undercarriage, engine mountings and wing outer panels. Redesignated A-1Js in September 1962, seventy-two AD-7s were built (BuNos 142010 to 142081). The last Skyraider (s/n 11561, BuNo 142081) came off the El Segundo assembly lines on 18 February, 1957.

The Skyraider's military career began in the spring of 1946 when a few XBT2D-1s were delivered to the Pacific Fleet Air Headquarters at NAS

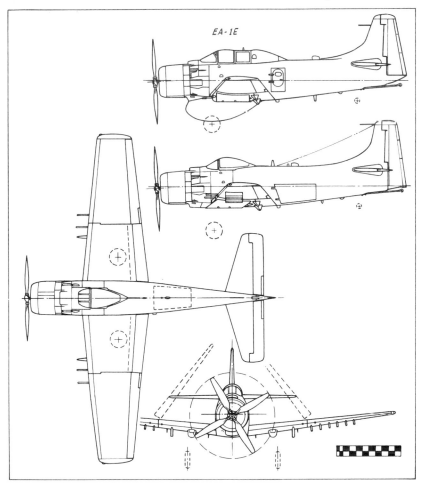

EA-1E

Douglas A1-J and EA-1E.

Alameda for Service trials. Unfortunately, these tests were marred by a series of main undercarriage and wing skin failures. Following a series of tests with three specially instrumented aircraft, it was determined that the original design landing weight of 14,545 lb (6,598 kg) and design limit sinking speed of 14 ft/sec (4·27 m/sec) were far exceeded in a considerable percentage of the landings. A major modification programme was undertaken to increase the aircraft's structural strength and led to increases in sinking speed from 14 ft/sec (4·27 m/sec) for the XBT2D-1, to 19 ft/sec (5·79 m/sec) for the AD-1 and AD-2, 23 ft/sec (7·01 m/sec) for the AD-3 and AD-4, and ultimately to 30 ft/sec (9·14 m/sec) for the AD-5 to AD-7. The success of this programme was amply proven by the fact that in over a quarter of century of service the Skyraider gained the reputation of being extremely strong in spite of a steady growth in maximum take-off and landing weights.

A VA-65 AD-1 Skyraider taxying to take-off position on the deck of the USS *Coral Sea* on 18 April, 1948. (*US National Archives*)

Following completion of the structural strengthening programme, the Skyraider was declared ready for Service use and Attack Squadron VA-19A, Pacific Fleet, became operational on 6 December, 1946. Whereas Pacific Fleet crews had conducted the Skyraider's Service trials, two Atlantic Fleet squadrons, VA-3B and VA-4B, became in June 1947 the first AD units to be fully carrier qualified when, before deployment aboard the USS *Franklin D. Roosevelt* (CVB42), they completed carrier qualification trials aboard the USS *Sicily* (CVE118). As the production of Skyraiders was building up more Navy units were re-equipped with ADs of various models but, as the 1950s began, it appeared that production would soon end. By the end of May 1950, a total of 866 Skyraiders had been accepted by the US Navy and production rate had been reduced to four aircraft a week from a peak of six a week during 1948–49.

Then came the invasion of South Korea, which took place on 25 June, 1950. The Seventh Fleet, after patrolling the Formosa Strait, went into action against targets in Korea and, on 3 July, AD-4s of VA-55 operating from the USS *Valley Forge* gained the distinction of becoming the first Skyraiders to fire their guns in anger, during an attack against Pyongyang airfield. During the next three years Skyraiders were operated by twelve Attack Squadrons, four Composite Squadrons and two Fighter Squadrons of the US Navy from aircraft carriers of the Seventh Fleet, and from land bases by two Marine Attack Squadrons and one Marine Composite Reconnaissance Squadron. The AD, which by now had received the appropriate nickname Able Dog reflecting its official designation, was used in Korea for day and night attacks and radar jamming sorties in support of ground troops as well as for offensive operations against North Korean industrial targets. In addition, beginning on 28 August, 1952, with a mission against the railway bridge at Hungnam, Guided Missile Unit 90 used AD-4Qs to control explosive-laden Grumman F6F-5K drones launched from USS *Boxer* for a series of six attacks against heavily defended North Korean targets. In its more conventional attack role the AD earned a commendable reputation as it was able to carry substantial and varied offensive loads. In particular, it proved to be the only aircraft capable of delivering 2,000 lb (908 kg) bombs with dive-bombing precision against such difficult targets as mountain bridges and hydro-electric dams. It also excelled in the ground support role, and it is said that a hard-pressed ground officer, inquiring to determine the type of stores carried by an AD flight sent to provide air support to his unit, received from the flight leader a fitting reply: 'You name it, we got it!'.

At the El Segundo plant production was stepped up to meet the war's demands and, in spite of delays due to the lack of floor space, production increased markedly, beginning in 1952. During the last year of the war, but

AD-6 from VMA-332, a Marine Corps unit stationed at MCAS Miami, Florida, 2 March, 1956. (*USMC*)

too late to see action, the AD-5 and AD-6 series began to join earlier models in the Navy and Marine Corps.

When in July 1953 the Korean armistice was signed at Panmunjon, Douglas had a large backlog of orders, and production of the Skyraider reached its peak only a year later when fifty-nine aircraft were completed during the month of June 1954. During the same month the XA4D-1—the prototype of the new jet attack aircraft which many thought would soon relegate the AD to museums—made its maiden flight. Yet the Skyraider's ability to penetrate heavily defended targets by flying below the radar, its combat-proven strong structure, its record weight-lifting ability and its adaptability to countless duties kept the aircraft in great demand and the peak Skyraider inventory was reached in 1955 when twenty-nine Navy squadrons and thirteen Marine squadrons were flying ADs. Production continued at El Segundo, albeit at reduced rate, and in March 1956 the 3,000th Skyraider was delivered. Finally, eleven months later, the last AD-7 came off the line.

Following the end of the Korean War, the Skyraider continued to perform splendidly as demonstrated on 26 July, 1954, when two ADs searching for survivors from a Cathay Pacific Airways DC-4 were attacked by two Chinese Communist Lavochkin La-7 fighters and succeeded in shooting them down before returning safely to their carrier. During the remainder of the fifties and the early sixties, Skyraiders took part in many shows of force when tensions in various parts of the world—notably Central America, the Formosa Strait and the Mediterranean—required the presence of the US Fleet. Noteworthy among these operations was the 1958 intervention in Lebanon when ADs of VA-35 and VA-176 provided air support for a Marine amphibious landing. Already the piston-engined Skyraiders had all but disappeared from the Marine Corps—this Service having operated ADs for less than eight years between 1951 and 1958—while, aboard carriers, they were operated alongside jet-powered Skyhawk, Fury and Cougar fighter-bombers.

The August 1964 Gulf of Tonkin Incident, which marked the start of full-scale US intervention in Vietnam, found the Skyraiders still young at heart and A-1Hs of VA-52 and VA-145 were amongst the first US aircraft to take part in combat operations over North Vietnam when they made a retaliatory air strike against motor torpedo boats and their support facilities at five locations along the North Vietnam coast. From Seventh Fleet carriers on Dixie Station, ADs flew close support missions over South Vietnam while from carriers on Yankee Station they flew conventional attack and countermeasures sorties against North Vietnamese targets. For four years these Skyraiders proved very successful as their comparatively slow speed and long endurance made them ideal escort and ground-fire suppression aircraft to accompany helicopters carrying troops or sent to rescue downed American crews in North Vietnam. To add to its legendary operational career the type added a crowning glory when four Skyraiders from VA-25 destroyed a MiG-17 in air combat and discouraged a second one during an action taking place on 20 June, 1965. In a sense, this feat, which was repeated on 9 October, 1966, was the Skyraider's swan song as on 20 February, 1968, another aircraft of VA-25 flew the last combat sortie for Navy single-seat Skyraiders. The last countermeasure sorties were flown on 27 December, 1968, by four-seat EA-1Fs from VAQ-33 Det 11. The last Navy Skyraiders were retired a little over three years later.

Interest in the Skyraider was first shown by the US Air Force in 1949 when an evaluation of aircraft suitable for ground support operations revealed the superiority of the Navy attack aircraft. However, inter-Services rivalry and funding problems combined to prevent Skyraider production for the USAF. More than a decade later, the Air Force acquired more experience with the Skyraider when USAF personnel trained and advised Vietnamese Air Force crews flying A-1Hs and, following the establishment on 27 April, 1962, of the Special Air Warfare Center at Eglin AFB, Florida, the 1st Combat Applications Group tested two Skyraiders lent by the US Navy. The success of this experiment led to the acquisition of a first batch of some 150 surplus A-1Es which were overhauled and modified to meet the special needs of the USAF. The most important modification incorporated in these aircraft was the provision of dual control for use in training Vietnamese pilots and converting USAF jet pilots to tailwheel, piston-engined aircraft. Furthermore, dual control was needed for the special conditions prevailing in Vietnam prior to full-scale US intervention. Allegedly operating only in an advisory capacity, USAF pilots of the 603rd and 604th Fighter Squadrons, 1st Air Commando Wing, were initially required to have Vietnamese co-pilots to take responsibility for identification of targets and for the decision to attack.

In USAF service these A-1Es, later supplemented by A-1Hs, were assigned serial numbers consisting of the original BuNo assigned to the aircraft and prefixed by the last two digits of the Fiscal Year in which they had been originally ordered by the Navy. Thus, for example, the AD-5 (BuNo 132649) ordered by the Navy during Fiscal Year 1952 became the A-1E 52-132649 in USAF service.

Blood, Sweat & Tears, an A-1H of the 1st Special Operations Squadron, 56th Special Operations Wing, operating from Nakhon Phanom, Thailand, on 1 April, 1970. (*USAF*)

A-1E (52-132890) of the USAF over South Vietnam in 1966. (*USAF*)

As American forces began carrying an increasing share in fighting the Vietcong, the A-1Es were flown as single-seaters by USAF pilots, and one of these officers, Major Bernard F. Fisher, earned the Medal of Honor when on 10 March, 1966, to rescue a fellow Skyraider pilot, he landed his A-1E (52-132649, now preserved in the Air Force Museum) in the midst of an attack against the US Special Forces Camp at Ashau.

From the mid-sixties until the early seventies, the well-liked Air Force 'Spads' (A-1Es, A-1Gs, and A-1Hs) performed two basic missions: support of ground forces in South Vietnam, Cambodia, and Laos, and escort and fire suppression for combat SAR helicopter rescue operations over the North and in Laos. The 1st SOS/56th SOW flew the last A-1 rescue escort mission for the Air Force on 7 November, 1972.

The first foreign nation to receive Skyraiders was the United Kingdom which, under the Mutual Defense Assistance Program, received fifty AD-4Ws beginning in November 1951. Intended to provide airborne early warning for the Royal Navy, these aircraft were designated Skyraider AEW 1s and were originally allocated the following British serial numbers: WT943 to WT969, WT982 to WT987, WV102 to WV109 and WV177 to WV185; however, serial numbers were incorrectly applied to five aircraft which respectively appeared as WT097, WT112, WT121, WT761 and WT849 instead of the correct WT943, WT982, WT983, WV108 and WV109. Twenty Skyraider AEW 1s were delivered ex-factory (British serial numbers WT944 to WT963, original BuNos 127942 to 127961) while the remaining thirty came from US Navy stocks.

Skyraider AEW 1s first entered FAA service with No.778 Training Squadron at RNAS Culdrose and this unit conducted British carrier trials with the type aboard HMS *Eagle*. In July 1952, the only operational unit of the Fleet Air Arm to fly Skyraiders, No.849 Squadron, was activated and for the next eight years this unit maintained a Headquarters Flight, permanently based at Culdrose, and four operational Flights which were detached as needed for service aboard carriers at sea. In particular, one of

385

these Flights operated aboard HMS *Bulwark* during the Anglo-French intervention in Egypt in November 1956. By November 1960 the Skyraider AEW 1s had been replaced in first line service by Fairey Gannet AEW 3s but Skyraiders were still operated by the Fleet Air Arm in a training capacity until 1962. Two of these aircraft, WT121 and WV106, are now preserved in the Fleet Air Arm Museum at RNAS Yeovilton.

In late 1962 and early 1963 twelve Skyraider AEW 1s, which had become surplus to Fleet Air Arm requirements, were sold to Svensk Flygtjänst AB for use as target-towing aircraft under Flygvapnet contracts. Refurbished by Scottish Aviation at Prestwick, these aircraft (ex-WT952, WT949, WT962, WT950, WT956, WT957, WT944, WT959, WT947, WV181, WT987 and WT951) had their military equipment—including 'guppy' radome and tail hook—removed and had a large bubble observation window added on both sides of the fuselage behind the rear fuselage entrance door. Two more aircraft, ex-WT945 and WV185, were delivered to Sweden for spares. Receiving the Swedish civil registrations SE-EBA to SE-EBI and SE-EBK to SE-EBM, the twelve fully modified aircraft were used to tow targets for anti-aircraft batteries and some of them were still being operated in the early seventies.

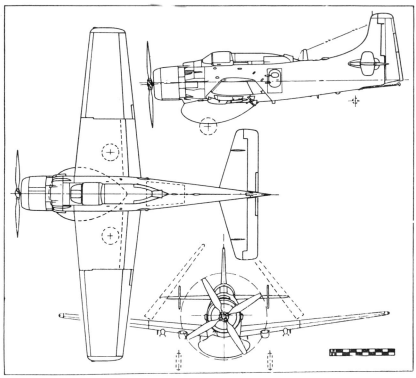

Douglas Skyraider AEW 1.

386

WT951, a Skyraider AEW 1, landing on a Royal Navy carrier.
(*Royal Navy via Alfred Price*)

During the Algerian conflict France's Armée de l'Air had a pressing need for ground attack and counter insurgency aircraft. Amongst the various types acquired to fill this need, France obtained in 1959 ninety-three Skyraiders surplus to US Navy requirements (40 AD-4NAs and 53 AD-4Ns) with which to replace the ageing Republic F-47D Thunderbolts operated by the 20th Escadre. All these aircraft were re-assembled and overhauled by SFERNA at Bordeaux-Mérignac where the AD-4Ns were brought up to AD-4NA standard before delivery to the Armée de l'Air. The first Skyraiders were delivered to Escadron II/20 beginning in February 1960 and subsequently the type was also delivered to I/20 and III/20 of the 20th Escadre for service in Algeria against elements of the FLN (Front de Libération Nationale). Following the granting of independence to Algeria and the reduction in French overseas commitments, Escadron I/20 was reconstituted in 1963 as Escadron I/21 to operate Skyraiders in the French Territory of Afars and Issas (French Somaliland). Shortly after Escadron III/20 became Escadron II/21 to fly Skyraiders in the Malagassy Republic while Escadron II/20 was disbanded. With the exception of a number of aircraft handed over by the French Government to the governments of Cambodia, Chad and Gabon. Skyraiders remained in limited service with the Armée del l'Air until the early seventies and some flew combat sorties during 1970 against Muslim guerillas in the northern section of the Republic of Chad where French forces supported the Bantu-dominated central government.

In 1965 the Kingdom of Cambodia received from France an initial batch of ten Skyraiders. These aircraft, later supplemented by an additional batch of five ex-French AD-4NAs, saw little use until the ousting of the Government of Prince Norodom Sihanouk in 1970 when they were operated against Vietcong guerillas and North Vietnamese troops which had previously been freely operating from Cambodia. Losses to ground fire and sabotage, as well as the lack of a sufficient number of trained ground crews and pilots, contributed to the rapid attrition of this small force of Skyraiders operated by the National Khmer Aviation.

A-1H (BuNo 135281) from the 23rd Tactical Wing, RVNAF, at Tan Son Nhut Air Base, on 19 May, 1970. (*USAF*)

Other ex-Armée de l'Air Skyraiders were handed over to Chad, with six aircraft nominally belonging to the Escadrille Nationale Tchadienne being flown between 1976 and 1984 by French mercenaries in operations against Libyan-backed rebels, and to Gabon, where during the late seventies and early eighties four aircraft were operated for the Garde Présidentielle by French contract personnel.

In the Indo-China peninsula, the US and Cambodian Skyraiders had been preceded by AD-6s delivered to the Republic of Viet-Nam Air Force beginning in late 1961. During the sixties and early seventies a considerable number of A-1Es, A-1Gs and A-1Hs were handed over to South Vietnam

Photographed surreptitiously at the N'Djamena Airport in July 1985, these Skyraiders from the Escadrille Nationale Tchadienne were no longer flyable but otherwise appeared to be in good condition. (*René J. Francillon*)

Ignoring US government objections, France transferred two batches of Skyraiders, one of ten aircraft shown in this delivery line-up in 1965 and one of five aircraft, to Cambodia (*Albert Grandolini via Air Action*)

A-1G (BuNo 132487) of the 518th Fighter Squadron, VNAF, at Bien Hoa Air Base on 15 April, 1970. (*USAF*)

and the type became the numerically most important combat aircraft of the RVNAF. With that Service, Skyraiders were mostly operated in the counter-insurgency role in South Vietnam, where they accounted for a rapidly increasing share of all ground support missions flown against the Vietcong by Vietnamese and US forces. Shortly after the 1964 Gulf of Tonkin Incident they also flew a limited number of combat sorties up to 200 miles north of the de-militarized zone. With the implementation of the Vietnamization policy of the Nixon Administration, the RVNAF Skyraiders were supplemented by jet aircraft. However, the VNAF continued to operate A-1s until the fall of Saïgon in April 1975.

Nearly 40 years after the maiden flight of the XBT2D-1, Skyraiders were still flown in combat by the Escadrille Nationale Tchadienne. This longevity and the fact that in view of combat results serious considerations had been given in 1965 to re-opening the Skyraider's production line—the cost and delays involved in re-tooling being mainly responsible for the decision not to proceed with this new production—are remarkable achievements for an aircraft which was created almost overnight in a hotel.

Carrier-borne or land-based aircraft for day attack, night attack (N), photographic reconnaissance (P), electronic countermeasure (Q), airborne early warning (W), utility (U), ASW search (E), or ASW attack (S) missions.

Pilot in enclosed cockpit (XBT2D-1, XBT2D-1P, AD-1 to AD-4, AD-4B, AD-4L, AD-4NA, AD-6 and AD-7); pilot and one radar operator (Q versions except AD-5Q); pilot and two radar operators (W versions except AD-5W, N versions except AD-5N, AD-3E and AD-3S); pilot and co-pilot (AD-5); pilot, co-pilot and two radar operators (AD-5N, AD-5Q and AD-5W). In addition, the AD-5 could be configured to carry either four passengers, twelve troops, four litter casualties, or 2,000 lb—908 kg—of cargo).

	XBT2D-1	AD-2	AD-2Q	AD-3N	AD-4B	AD-5	AD-6	AD-7
Span, ft in	50 0¼	50 0¼	50 0½	50 0¼	50 0¼	50 9	50 0¼	50 0¼
(m)	(15·25)	(15·25)	(15·25)	(15·25)	(15·25)	(15·47)	(15·25)	(15·25)
Length, ft in	39 5	38 2	38 2	38 2	39 3	40 1	38 10	38 10
(m)	(12·01)	(11·63)	(11·63)	(11·63)	(11·96)	(12·22)	(11·84)	(11·84)
Height, ft in	15 7½	15 7½	15 7½	15 7½	15 8¼	15 10	15 8¼	15 8¼
(m)	(4·76)	(4·76)	(4·76)	(4·76)	(4·78)	(4·83)	(4·78)	(4·78)
Wing area, sq ft	400·33	400·33	400·33	400·33	400·33	400·33	400·33	400·33
(sq m)	(37·192)	(37·192)	(37·192)	(37·192)	(37·192)	(37·192)	(37·192)	(37·192)
Empty weight, lb	10,093	10,546	11,159	11,483	11,783	12,313	11,968	12,094
(kg)	(4,578)	(4,734)	(5,062)	(5,209)	(5,345)	(5,581)	(5,429)	(5,486)
Loaded weight, lb	13,500	16,268	17,140	18,044	18,669	18,799	18,106	22,795
(kg)	(6,124)	(7,379)	(7,775)	(8,185)	(8,468)	(8,528)	(8,213)	(10,340)
Maximum weight, lb	17,500	18,263	19,143	21,180	24,221	25,000	25,000	25,000
(kg)	(7,938)	(8,284)	(8,683)	(9,607)	(10,986)	(11,340)	(11,340)	(11,340)
Wing loading, lb/sq ft	33·7	40·6	42·8	45·1	46·6	47	45·2	56·9
(kg/sq m)	(164·7)	(198·4)	(209·1)	(220·1)	(227·7)	(229·3)	(220·8)	(278·0)
Power loading, lb/hp	5·8	6	6·3	6·7	6·9	7	6·7	8·4
(kg/hp)	(2·7)	(2·7)	(2·9)	(3)	(3·1)	(3·2)	(3)	(3·8)
Maximum speed, mph at ft	375/13,600	321/18,300	317/18,300	296/18,300	320/15,000	311/18,000	322/18,000	343/20,000
(km/h at m)	(604/4,145)	(517/5,580)	(510/5,580)	(476/5,580)	(515/4,570)	(501/5,485)	(518/5,485)	(552/6,095)
Cruising speed, mph	164	198	205	197	196	200	198	195
(km/h)	(264)	(319)	(330)	(317)	(315)	(322)	(319)	(314)
Rate of climb, ft/min	3,680/1	2,800/1	2,590/1	2,260/1	2,980/1	2,300/1	2,850/1	3,230/1
(m/min)	(1,152/1)	(853/1)	(789/1)	(689/1)	(908/1)	(701/1)	(869/1)	(985/1)
Service ceiling, ft	26,000	32,700	26,600	26,500	23,800	26,000	28,500	25,400
(m)	(7,925)	(9,965)	(8,110)	(8,075)	(7,255)	(7,925)	(8,685)	(7,740)
Normal range, miles	1,554	915	1,497	1,496	900	1,202	1,316	1,300
(km)	(2,500)	(1,475)	(2,410)	(2,405)	(1,450)	(1,935)	(2,115)	(2,090)

Armament: Wing-mounted 20-mm cannon: Two: All XBT2D-1 versions, AD-1, AD-1Q, AD-2, AD-2Q, AD-3, AD-3N, AD-3Q, AD-3S, AD-4, AD-4N and AD-4Q. Four: AD-4B, AD-4L, AD-4NA, AD-4NL, AD-5, AD-5N, AD-5Q, AD-6 and AD-7. XAD-1W, AD-3W, AD-4W, and AD-5W were unarmed.

The first C-74-DL (42-65402), with the original twin bubble canopies. (*USAF*)

Douglas C-74 Globemaster I

When in December 1941 the United States became involved in the Second World War, the Army Air Forces had just begun taking delivery of Douglas C-47 and C-53 twin-engined transports. Whilst these aircraft, supplemented by impressed DC-3s and DSTs, proved to be reliable workhorses, they lacked the payload and range required for worldwide logistic support. To meet this new requirement Douglas undertook in January 1942 the preliminary design of a large, four-engined personnel and cargo transport with full transoceanic range. An initial contract for this new type was awarded in June 1942 and eventually covered a total of fifty C-74s (42-65402/42-65451). However, the first C-74 (s/n 13913, 42-65402) did not fly until 5 September, 1945, and, following the mass cancellation of military aircraft contracts after VJ-Day, production was terminated in January 1946 with the delivery of the fourteenth and last Globemaster I.

At the time of its first flight the 86-ton (78 tonne) C-74 was the largest transport landplane yet produced in quantity. Powered by four 3,000 hp Pratt & Whitney R-4360-27 twenty-eight cylinder radials—later replaced by 3,250 hp R-4360-69s—, the Globemaster I had a maximum range of 7,250 miles (11,670 km), sufficient to circumnavigate the globe with only two stops. It was fitted with a laminar-flow wing with full-span Fowler flaps with the outer flap sections acting as ailerons. Initially it was also characterized by the use of separate bubble canopies over the pilots' cockpit but this arrangement was found wanting as it impaired pilot communication, and a conventional canopy and windshield was retrofitted. The capacious fuselage could accommodate either 125 troops, 115 stretchers and medical attendants, or up to 48,150 lb (21,840 kg) of cargo including either ten Wright R-3350 radial engines, fifteen Allison

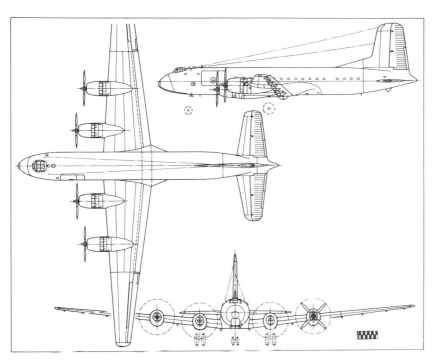

V-1710 inline engines, two T-9E1 light tanks, or two 105-mm howitzers with tractors, ammunition and crews. Loading and unloading operations were facilitated by two onboard travelling cranes with a capacity of 8,000 lb (3,629 kg) and by the installation of a built-in cargo lift consisting of the lower section of the main cabin floor aft of the wing trailing edges.

Service use of the aircraft was relatively limited as the USAF adopted the C-124 Globemaster II—the first of which was obtained by modifying the fifth C-74—as its main heavy logistic cargo transport. Whilst operated by the USAF a C-74 became, on 18 November, 1949, the first aircraft to cross the North Atlantic with more than 100 people on board when it flew from Mobile, Alabama, to Marham, England, with 103 passengers and crew. Earlier that year, as soon as Douglas had completed the modification programme consisting of the replacement of the original double-bubble canopy with a more conventional assembly, C-74s had been assigned to fly three round-trips a week on the Brookely AFB (Alabama)–Bermuda–Azores–Frankfurt route to increase the volume of cargo flown over the North Atlantic and thus free C-54s for use on the short Frankfurt–Tempelhof route as part of the Berlin Airlift.

During the war Douglas had studied the feasibility of adapting the C-74 as a long-range commercial passenger transport and in late 1945 Pan American Airways had placed an order for twenty-six of these aircraft which were designated DC-7s. However, in 1947 Pan American cancelled

393

C-74-DL Globemaster I in the markings of the Atlantic Division, Military Air Transport Service. (*USAF*)

its order for these aircraft as the proposed DC-7—not to be confused with the later DC-7 series aircraft—was then found too large for existing traffic and as production costs had risen substantially due to the reduction in the C-74 contract. Whilst no commercial version of the C-74 was built by Douglas, a number of surplus Globemaster Is saw limited use with cargo charter airlines.

Span 173 ft 3 in (52·81 m); length 124 ft 2 in (37·85 m); height 43 ft 9 in (13·34 m); wing area 2,510 sq ft (233·188 sq m). Empty weight 86,172 lb (39,087 kg); loaded weight 154,128 lb (69,911 kg); maximum weight 172,000 lb (78,018 kg); wing loading 61·4 lb/sq ft (299·8 kg/sq m); power loading 11·9 lb/hp (5·4 kg/hp). Maximum speed 328 mph (528 km/h) at 10,000 ft (3,050 m); cruising speed 212 mph (341 km/h); rate of climb 2,605 ft/min (794 m/min); service ceiling 21,300 ft (6,490 m); normal range 3,400 miles (5,470 km); maximum range 7,250 miles (11,670 km).

HP-379, an ex-C-74-DL (42-65409) of Aeronaves de Panama. (*Mervyn Prime*)

Douglas DC-6

Basically a straightforward development of the DC-4, but with a pressurized cabin, increased accommodation and payload, and higher performance, the DC-6 entered service with the airlines in the spring of 1947. Unfortunately, shortly after, two DC-6s experienced inflight fires, one being fatal, and the type had to be grounded for four months until the cause could be determined and appropriate corrective measures implemented. Once this problem was solved, the DC-6 series became a model of reliability and, particularly in its DC-6A and DC-6B versions, came to be regarded as the ultimate in piston-engined commercial transports. Its operating costs were amongst the lowest recorded until the advent of the more efficient jetliners and, consequently, DC-6s were the most sought-after piston-engined transports during the first twenty-five years of the commercial jet age.

The unmarked XC-112A-DO off the Malibu coast, north of Santa Monica. (*MDC*)

When Douglas had designed its second type to bear the DC-4 designation, the decision had been made to offer this aircraft initially without cabin pressurization. None the less, Douglas had intended to develop this system for later installation. The appearance of the Boeing Stratoliner and Lockheed Constellation, both of which were planned from the beginning to have cabin pressurization, reinforced Douglas's willingness to market pressurized versions of its DC-4. However, wartime pressures were for large quantities of aircraft rather than for more comfortable ones, and the DC-4 was mass-produced as the unpressurized C-54 Skymaster. This short-term requirement, however, did not terminate interest in a pressurized DC-4 development. In particular, American Airlines was increasingly concerned about its anticipated competitive position once the war ended, as its transcontinental rival, TWA, had ordered a substantial fleet of pressurized Lockheed Constellations which were also faster than the DC-4s on which American depended for the resumption of full commercial operations. American Airlines' concern, together with that of United Air Lines to a lesser extent—the third US

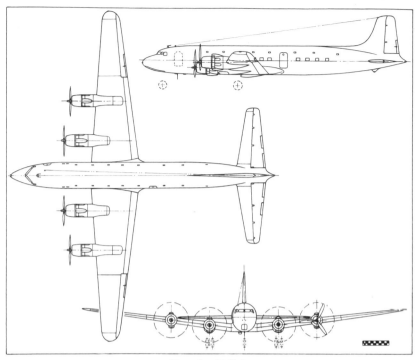

Douglas DC-6.

transcontinental carrier—found receptive ears at Douglas where Arthur Raymond and Ed Burton were intent on developing the DC-4/C-54 into a worthy competitor of the Constellation.

As design and construction of commercial aircraft were stopped during the war, Douglas succeeded in having the prototype of a pressurized development of the C-54E included in an Army Air Forces-funded Skymaster improvement programme, which also included the Allison V-1710 powered XC-114 and XC-116. Designated XC-112A (45-873, s/n 36326), the pressurized prototype was conceived as a much improved aircraft incorporating not only full cabin pressurization but also an 81-inch (2·06-m) longer fuselage with large rectangular windows in place of the circular portholes of the Skymaster, and 2,100 hp Pratt & Whitney R-2800-34 radials. Other systems, such as more powerful de-icing, made necessary by higher operating altitudes, as well as the radio and navigation equipment were improved. The net result was a substantial improvement in all-round performance.

Flight tests, which began at Santa Monica on 15 February, 1946, when a crew captained by John F. Martin took the aircraft on its maiden flight, confirmed the most sanguine expectations. However, postwar curtailments had temporarily eliminated the prospect of having the new aircraft ordered in quantity by the Army Air Forces but freed Douglas to proceed with the marketing of the previously thinly disguised DC-6 commercial variant. Already, more than fifteen months before the first flight of the XC-112A, Douglas had received from American Airlines an order for fifty DC-6s, and the first of these commercial aircraft began its flight trials on 29 June, 1946, only four and a half months after the military prototype. Subsequent civil and military orders kept the DC-6 production line open until the end of 1958.

DC-6: Initially powered by four 2,100 hp Double Wasp CA15 radials, with other R-2800 versions being fitted later, the DC-6 was the first Douglas transport to have cabin pressurization. Normal accommodation was for 48–52 passengers in single-class configuration but the aircraft could seat up to 86 passengers in high-density layout. The DC-6 retained the DC-4 wing with a span of 117 ft 6 in (35·81 m) and area of 1,463 sq ft (135·918 sq m) but had an 81-in (2·06-m) longer fuselage and maximum gross take-off weight increased from 73,000 lb (33,113 kg) for the DC-4-1009 to 97,200 lb (44,089 kg). The DC-6 made its first flight on 29 June, 1946, and was certificated nine months later. Deliveries to American Airlines and United Air Lines began simultaneously on 20 November, 1946, and the 175th and last DC-6 was delivered to Braniff on 2 November, 1951. Subsequently, a number of DC-6s phased out of passenger service were modified as freighters and fitted with a C-54 type cargo door aft of the wing on the port side.

DC-6 of American Airlines over Long Island on 16 March, 1947. At that time the DC-6 had not yet received its certificate of airworthiness, hence the NX registration. (*American Airlines*)

397

PH-TGA *Dr Ir M. H. Damme*, showing the two main-deck cargo doors which were a feature of the DC-6A. (*KLM*)

DC-6A: The availability of more powerful versions of the Double Wasp engine with water-methanol injection, together with the favourable results of structural analyses, led Douglas in 1948 to plan a further stretch of the DC-6 to provide increased cabin volume, payload and operating weights. This was first applied to an all-cargo version which, initially powered by four 2,400 hp Double Wasp CB16s, had a 5-ft (1·52-m) longer fuselage. Designated DC-6A, this version retained cabin pressurization, had a reinforced cabin floor, no fuselage windows, and two upward-opening freight doors—one forward and one aft of the wing—on the port side. The electrical system was upgraded, maintainability was improved and typical fuel capacity was increased from 4,260 to 5,525 US gallons (16,125 to 20,915 litres). Cargo capacity was 28,188 lb (12,786 kg). The first DC-6A (N30006, s/n 42901) was flown on 29 September, 1949, and the 74th and last DC-6A was delivered to the Brazilian carrier Loide Aereo Nacional on 10 February, 1959. Some DC-6As were subsequently converted to passenger use by removing the metal plugs normally fitted over the cabin windows, whilst others—designated DC-6Cs—were built with the normal cabin windows to enable rapid conversion from cargo to passenger configurations and vice-versa.

Originally delivered to Japan Air Lines as JA-6206, this DC-6B (s/n 44432) was in service with Compania de Aviacion Faucett SA from May 1966. It is seen here at Jorge Chavez Airport, Lima, in May 1977. (*René J. Francillon*)

DC-6B: Dimensionally identical to the DC-6A, the DC-6B was a passenger transport without the reinforced floor and main deck cargo doors. Initially, normal accommodation was provided for 54 passengers but in high-density layout up to 102 passengers could be carried. Like the DC-6As, the DC-6Bs were powered by either 2,400 hp Double Wasp CB16s or 2,500 hp Double Wasp CB17s driving three-blade fully-reversible propellers. Produced in larger numbers than any other version in the DC-6 series, the DC-6B was first flown on 2 February, 1951, (N37547, s/n 43257) and was certificated in April of that year. The 704th and last aircraft in the DC-6 series, the 288th DC-6B, was delivered to JAT-Jugoslovenski Aerotransport on 17 November, 1958.

One of the two DC-6Bs fitted with a cargo-loading swing tail by the Engineering Department of Sabena. (*Kar-Air O/Y*)

After being taken out of service by the major air carriers, a substantial number of DC-6Bs were modified—by Pacific Airmotive Corp, airlines, or specialized contractors—as freighters by installation of cargo doors and reinforced floors. These modified aircraft became known unofficially as DC-6AB, DC-6AC, DC-6A(C) or DC-6BF. Two DC-6Bs (s/n 44434, EC-BBK, and s/n 45202, OH-KDA) were modified by Sabena's Engineering Department by installation of a cargo-loading swing tail for use respectively by Spantax in Spain and Kar-Air O/Y in Finland. Other DC-6Bs were modified as tankers for use against forest fires in the United States and Canada.

DC-6C: Designation given to a passenger/cargo convertible version of the DC-6A produced by Douglas and included in the total number of DC-6As delivered.

XC-112A: The military prototype of the DC-6 series was first flown on 15 February, 1946, on the day when the rival Lockheed Constellation was introduced into commercial service by TWA. Initially powered by 2,100 hp R-2800-34s, this aircraft was later redesignated YC-112A. Upon com-

C-118-DO *The Independence*, the US Presidential aircraft. (*USAF*)

pletion of military trials, the aircraft was briefly used by the USAAF before being sold to Conner Air Lines. After passing through the hands of various US, Ecuadorian, Spanish and Canadian operators, it was acquired in 1968 by Mercer Airlines. On 8 February, 1976, it crashed on take-off at Van Nuys Airport, California, whilst still in service with Mercer.

C-118-DO: On 1 July, 1947, the USAF took delivery of the 29th DC-6 for use as a Presidential aircraft. Named *The Independence*, after the Missouri home town of President Truman, the aircraft (46-505) was donated twenty years later to the National Air & Space Museum.

C-118A-DO: For use as personnel and logistic transports by MATS (Military Air Transport Service, later MAC, Military Airlift Command), the USAF ordered 101 aircraft (51-3818/51-3835, and 53-3223/53-3305) similar to the commercial DC-6As but fitted with military equipment and powered by four 2,500 hp R-2800-52Ws. The USAF also acquired forty ex-USN R6D-1s which later had their BuNos replaced by USAF serials (50-1843/50-1844, 51-17626/51-17661, and 51-17667/51-17668). Capacity was 74 troops or 27,000 lb (12,247 kg) of cargo.

R6D-1 (C-118B): Preceding the USAF, the USN ordered 65 DC-6As which received the BuNos 128423/128433 and 131567/131620. These were initially designated R6D-1s when equipped as logistic transports, or R6D-1Zs when configured as VIP/staff transports. Forty of these aircraft were transferred to the USAF and, in 1962, those remaining in USN and USMC service were re-designated C-118Bs and VC-118Bs.

Simultaneous DC-6 delivery was made on 24 November, 1946, to American Airlines and United Air Lines but, as the type had not yet received its certificate of airworthiness, the two airlines had to use their DC-6s for crew training and route proving for five months. Finally, on 27 April, 1947, by which time a total of twenty-two DC-6s had been delivered to these two airlines and to Panagra, American inaugurated DC-6 service on the New York–Chicago route. Over the competitive US transcontinental routes American and United pitted their DC-6s against the Constellations of TWA whilst United also began on 1 May, 1947, to use DC-6s on routes to Hawaii.

Douglas R6D-1 (BuNo 131578) assigned to NAS Los Alamitos, California.
(*USN*)

The first of the two inflight fires which led to the early grounding of the DC-6 involved s/n 42875, N37510, of United Air Lines which crashed in Bryce Canyon National Park, Utah, with the loss of 52 passengers and crew. More fortunate was a DC-6 of American Airlines which, on 11 November, 1947, burst into flames but was successfully landed at Gallup, New Mexico. Exhaustive tests revealed that the fires were caused by fuel venting into the cabin heater intakes and modifications were made to prevent the recurrence of this problem. Services were resumed on 21 March, 1948, and the DC-6 and its derivatives were then operated without difficulty.

Other US airlines purchasing new DC-6s included Panagra, which used them on routes from Panama to various points in South America; National Airlines, which flew them primarily on east coast routes to Miami: Delta, which operated them on routes linking Atlanta with Chicago, Miami and New York; and Braniff, which had DC-6s operating from its Texas base. The last of these airlines to fly DC-6s was United Air Lines which disposed of its last aircraft at the end of 1968.

The first foreign operator was Sabena which acquired five aircraft for use on its routes to New York and the Congo. Seven other foreign airlines— BCPA (British Commonwealth Pacific Airlines), FAMA (Flota Aérea Mercante Argentina, later nationalized as Aerolineas Argentinas), KLM, LAI (Linee Acree Italiane), Mexicana (Compania Mexicana de Aviación), PAL (Philippine Air Lines), and SAS (Scandinavian Airlines System)— purchased a total of forty-three DC-6s. Later, many other airlines acquired second-hand DC-6s, with a number being modified as freighters by installation of either C-54 sideways-opening cargo doors or DC-6A upward-opening doors. Cargo configured DC-6s were still operated in 1977.

DC-6s modified as freighters had been preceded in service by the specially-designed DC-6As. The first of these cargo aircraft had been put into service on 16 April, 1951, by Slick Airways, of San Francisco, whilst on 5 January, 1952, Pan American had used one to operate its first commercial, all-cargo flight over the North Atlantic. On this last-mentioned route, Pan American was followed initially by several European

401

Linee Aeree Italiane DC-6s I-LOVE and I LUCK at Ciampino, Rome, in January 1951. (*John Stroud*)

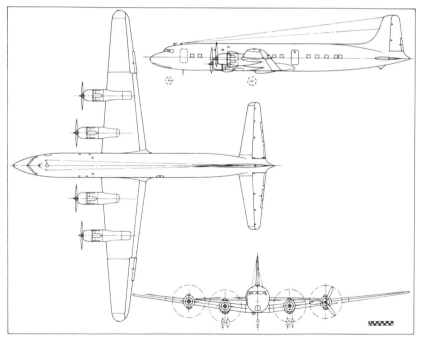

Douglas DC-6B.

flag carriers including KLM, Sabena and Swissair. Other carriers, operating scheduled as well as non-scheduled services, initially flew DC-6As on US domestic routes and on trans-Pacific services. Later, as the true DC-6A freighters were supplemented by modified DC-6Bs which had cargo doors added after being phased out of passenger operations, the type was extensively operated in all parts of the world. Many still remain in service with small operators.

Among the many unusual uses of the DC-6As, mention must be made of that assigned to two second-hand aircraft (s/n 45227 and 45368). Fitted in 1960 with special radar and instrumentation, they were flown by the Weather Bureau of the US Department of Commerce in a hurricane research programme. Finally, two noteworthy DC-6As were s/n 44889 and 45110 which, also in 1960, were modified as airborne TV transmission and relay stations to broadcast instructional programmes to sparsely populated areas of the US midwest.

Even though the first DC-6B did not fly until sixteen months after the DC-6A's maiden flight, the all-passenger DC-6B was put into service during the same month as its freighter counterpart when, on 29 April, 1951, American Airlines began substituting DC-6Bs for DC-6s on the competitive US transcontinental route. Subsequently, all US trunk carriers, with the exception of TWA, became DC-6B operators. US flag carriers operating DC-6Bs included Panagra and Braniff with routes to South America, and Pan American which selected it to inaugurate tourist-class service over the North Atlantic along with its first-class service operated with Boeing Stratocruisers and Lockheed Constellations. The lower seat-mile costs of the DC-6B rendered it ideal for this purpose, and the type was operated by many of the world's major flag carriers. Noteworthy among these airlines were Swissair, which in July 1951 became the first non-US DC-6B operator; Canadian Pacific, which in June 1955 began operating DC-6Bs on the Vancouver–Edmonton–Søndre Strømfjord–Amsterdam polar route; SAS, which flew DC-6Bs on polar routes linking Scandinavia with Los Angeles and Tokyo; and Japan Air Lines, which introduced DC-6Bs on its Tokyo–San Francisco route in February 1954, to begin its phenomenal growth into one of the world's major airlines.

The introduction into service of the Boeing 707 and Douglas DC-8 jetliners during the late fifties progressively but rapidly relegated the DC-6B to lesser routes, and the appearance in the mid-sixties of large numbers of medium- to short-range jetliners finally forced its retirement from the fleets of the major carriers. None the less, the low initial cost of used DC-6Bs, together with their favourable operating costs and reputation for high reliability, ensured them a new future. Many were modified as freighters or as passenger/cargo convertible aircraft and, over the years, underwent many changes of owners. These aircraft not only saw service with cargo airlines, charter operators and airlines of developing nations, but were acquired by many of the world's air forces, often from their respective flag carriers.

A number of used DC-6Bs were also modified as aerial tankers for use against forest fires. For this role, the aircraft were fitted with a large external tank beneath the fuselage, with a capacity of 2,500 to 3,000 US gallons (9,463 to 11,356 litres) of fire retardant chemicals to cover an area 90 ft (27 m) wide and 2,750 ft (840 m) long. These tankers were operated mostly in the western part of the United States and Canada during summer and autumn. On occasions, however, some were operated in Chile and Peru during the rest of the year when fire hazard was minimal in the northern hemisphere but high in the southern hemisphere.

N37565, s/n 43562, an ex-United Air Lines DC-6B modified as a firefighting aerial tanker, at Santa Rosa, California, in January 1975.
(*Mariette J. Francillon*)

The ex-airline DC-6A/DC-6B/DC-6Cs operated by air forces in Europe and Latin America had been preceded into military service by the aircraft bought new by the USAF and the USN. The first to be used for any length of time was the C-118-DO which, in July 1947, became the Presidential aircraft. Equivalent to the commercial DC-6 version but fitted with VIP accommodation and special communications equipment, this aircraft was followed into service by sixty-five R6D-1s ordered by the Navy and one hundred and one C-118As purchased by the Air Force, both versions being generally similar to the DC-6A. The USAF initially operated its C-118As—including forty ex-USN aircraft—as the main personnel and logistic transport aircraft of its Military Air Transport Service (MATS). When jet transports became available to the Military Airlift Command, as MATS had been renamed, the C-118As continued in USAF service as aeromedical and staff transports. Similar uses were made by the Navy of their remaining C-118Bs (R6D-1s). In addition, at least one C-118A was transferred to NASA whilst another (53-3281) went to the Department of Justice, to be based at Brownsville, Texas, and operated by the US Border Patrol, to repatriate 'wetbacks', the Mexican nationals who illegally entered the United States to seek work and, when caught, had to be expelled.

404

C-118A-DO (51-3833) of the 63rd Military Airlift Wing at Norton AFB, California, on 27 February, 1972. (*Peter Mancus*)

Thirty years after the maiden flight of the XC-112A prototype, almost three out of ten DC-6s built between 1946 and 1958 were still in service with airlines—which accounted for some 130 aircraft, primarily operated in cargo configuration—air forces, government agencies, air tanker contractors and other operators. By comparison, the DC-6's arch-rival—the Constellation/Super Constellation series—had by then almost become extinct with only four aircraft remaining in commercial service. Considering that many types of piston-engined transports became obsolete because of the appearance of jetliners, this achievement is a strong testimony to the excellence of the DC-6 series.

DC-6

Span 117 ft 6 in (35·81 m); length 100 ft 7 in (30·66 m); height 29 ft 1 in (8·86 m); wing area 1,463 sq ft (135·918 sq m). Empty weight 53,623 lb (24,323 kg); maximum gross take-off weight 97,200 lb (44,089 kg); wing loading 66·4 lb/sq ft (324·4 kg/sq m); power loading 11·6 lb/hp (5·2 kg/hp). Typical cruising speed 328 mph (528 km/h); rate of climb 900 ft/min (274 m/min); service ceiling 29,000 ft (8,840 m); maximum payload range, 3,340 miles (5,375 km) with 21,300 lb (9,662 kg); maximum fuel range 3,915 miles (6,300 km).

DC-6A

Span and wing area as DC-6. Length 105 ft 7 in (32·18 m); height 28 ft 8 in (8·74 m). Empty weight 49,767 lb (22,574 kg); maximum gross take-off weight 107,000 lb (48,534 kg); wing loading 73·1 lb/sq ft (357·1 kg/sq m); power loading 11·1 lb/hp (5·1 kg/hp). Typical cruising speed 315 mph (507 km/h); rate of climb 1,010 ft/min (307 m/min); maximum payload range 2,925 miles (4,710 km) with 28,188 lb (12,786 kg); maximum fuel range 4,720 miles (7,595 km).

DC-6B

Dimensions as DC-6A. Empty weight 55,357 lb (25,110 kg); maximum gross take-off weight 107,000 lb (48,534 kg); wing loading 73·1 lb/sq ft (357·1 kg/sq m); power loading 11·1 lb/hp (5·1 kg/hp). Typical cruising speed 315 mph (507 km/h); rate of climb 1,120 ft/m (341 m/min); maximum payload range 3,005 miles (4,835 km) with 24,565 lb (11,142 kg); maximum fuel range 4,720 miles (7,595 km).

The first XB-43 at the Muroc Army Air Base in May 1946. (*MDC*)

Douglas XB-43

Though the XB-43 was the first US jet bomber, and thus ought to have a special place in the annals of American aviation, it is one of Douglas's least known aircraft. Its development, which was facilitated by the fuselage-mounted engines and clean wing configuration of the XB-42, was first seriously considered in October 1943 when the Air Matériel Command discussed with Douglas the feasibility of fitting turbojets in the XB-42 Mixmaster instead of the inline piston engines. Preliminary studies proved the practicability of the scheme and, on 31 March, 1944, Douglas received a Change Order to Contract AC-40188 (the original XB-42 contract), which called for the design, construction and testing of two jet-powered XB-43s (44-61508 and 44-61509).

44-61509, the second XB-43, with test camera ports on the side and below its plywood nose cone. (*USAF*)

406

The first XB-43 landing at Muroc Dry Lake. (*USAF*)

The modifications devised to install two 3,750 lb (1,678 kg) thrust General Electric TG-180 turbojets (redesignated J35-GE-3s in their production form) were simplicity itself and consisted of mounting the turbojets in the forward fuselage bays previously occupied by the Allison V-1710s of the XB-42. Flush air intakes were incorporated in the upper fuselage sides immediately behind the two-seat pressurized cockpit, and long tail-pipes took the hot gases to side-by-side openings in the tail. At the same time, as there was no need for propeller protection in the instance of a belly landing, the lower fin of the XB-42 was dispensed with whilst, to maintain positive directional control, the area of the upper fin was enlarged. As so few changes were required to turn the XB-42 into a jet-powered aircraft, it was decided that time and money could be saved by modifying the static XB-42 airframe into the first XB-43.

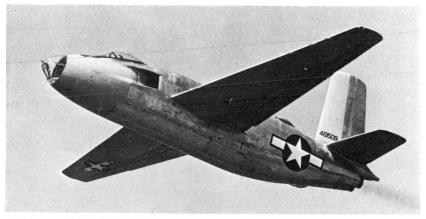

The second XB-43 (44-61509), showing flush air intakes and twin tail-pipes. (*MDC*)

407

In spite of this time-saving approach, the first XB-43 was not flown until more than two years after contract award. Part of the delay was due to the slowdown which followed the end of the war whilst late delivery of the turbojets combined with engine teething troubles during ground testing accounted for several more months. Turbojet unreliability had occurred in October 1945 when during an engine run-up test at Clover Field the starboard engine shed some first-stage compressor blades, causing instantaneous separation of all blades in all stages. Some of the blades punctured the engine casing and fuselage skin and injured a member of the ground crew, and the first flight had to be delayed another seven months. Finally, after being trucked to Muroc Army Air Base in the Mojave Desert, the first XB-43 made its maiden flight on 17 May, 1946, in the hands of test pilot Bob Brush and engineer Russell Thaw.

Before the aircraft's first flight, production plans had been discussed between the AAF and Douglas, consideration being given to ordering an initial production batch of 50, whilst Douglas submitted a proposal calling for the company to tool up for an eventual production rate of two hundred B-43s a month. These production aircraft were planned to be fitted with a conventional canopy in place of the small bug-eye canopies of the first XB-43, and were to be built in two versions: a bomber with transparent nose and maximum bomb load of 6,000 lb (2,722 kg), and an attack aircraft with unglazed nose and an armament of sixteen forward-firing 0·50-in machine-guns and thirty-six 5-in rockets. Both versions were to be fitted with a remotely-controlled, radar-directed tail turret with twin 0·50-in guns. However, by the time of its first flight, the XB-43 was already superseded in AAF thinking by the four-engined North American B-45 jet bomber and the XB-43 programme had been reduced to the status of flying testbed.

Problems associated with cracking of the Plexiglass nose led to the installation of a plywood nose cone on the second XB-43. (*USAF*)

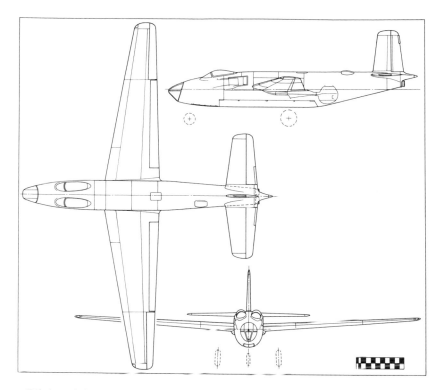

Flight trials were generally satisfactory but the aircraft was found to be somewhat underpowered, whilst its Plexiglass nose cracked due to temperature changes and had to be replaced by a plywood cone. The second aircraft, which had also been delayed by late engine deliveries, was fitted with a single canopy as proposed for the production aircraft. It was delivered to Muroc in May 1947 and was used as an engine testbed. For this purpose, 44 61509 had one of its J35s replaced by a General Electric J47 and was kept flying by cannibalizing the first XB-43 which had been damaged on 1 February, 1951. In late 1953, the second XB-43 was retired and is now, minus wings, part of the collection of the National Air & Space Museum.

Span 71 ft 2 in (21·69 m); length 51 ft 2 in (15·6 m); height 24 ft 3 in (7·39 m); wing area 563 sq ft (52·305 sq m). Empty weight 21,775 lb (9,877 kg); loaded weight 37,000 lb (16,783 kg); maximum weight 39,533 lb (17,932 kg); wing loading 65·7 lb/sq ft (320·9 kg/sq m); power loading 4·9 lb/lb. Maximum speed at sea level 515 mph (829 km/h); cruising speed 420 mph (676 km/h); service ceiling 38,500 ft (11,735 m); normal range 1,100 miles (1,770 km); maximum range 2,840 miles (4,585 km).

Douglas Cloudster II

The concept of placing the propeller of an otherwise conventional aeroplane aft of the empennage was first applied in 1939 at Douglas by Edward F. Burton to a proposed high-performance Army fighter aircraft. It was later incorporated in the XB-42 Mixmaster bomber which was powered by two engines buried in the fuselage and driving propellers by means of extension shafts. Initial flight trials had confirmed that, compared with the conventional twin-engined layout, this arrangement resulted in a 30 per cent reduction in drag and eliminated single-engine controllability problems. Consequently, this configuration was adopted for a five-seat private aircraft combining the speed, range and reliability of contemporary twin-engined transports with the handling of single-engined aircraft.

A project group under Charles S. Glascow was organized in May 1945 and designed the Model 1015 Cloudster II, accommodating a pilot and a co-pilot/passenger in separate seats and three passengers on a bench-type seat behind, in a cabin located well forward of the wing. Access was by means of a 15-in step and a car-type door on the port side. Two 250 hp Continental E-250 six-cylinder air-cooled engines were installed within the fuselage, behind the cabin, canted inward to the line of flight, and drove a two-blade pusher propeller via a three-section drive-shaft. Cooling air was admitted through large intakes on each side of the fuselage and exhausted beneath the fuselage, aft of the wing. The aircraft had a low-mounted wing with laminar-flow aerofoil, was fitted with a fully-retractable under-carriage, and had a lower fin incorporating a skid to prevent propeller damage in the event of excessive rotation on take-off or nose-high landing.

The prototype Cloudster II (s/n 43113, NX8000H) was first flown at Santa Monica on 12 March, 1947, with Bob Brush at the controls. Inflight handling and performance were most satisfactory but the aircraft suffered from excessive vibration due to transmission shaft problems and from ground cooling difficulties. Neither difficulty was solved during the following months and in late 1947 the project was shelved owing to necessary postwar retrenchment, the uncertainty of the future of luxury-type private flying, and the very extensive research and development needed in a design incorporating many structural and mechanical innovations. Furthermore, the selling price had risen from the original estimate of $30,000 per aircraft to some $68,000.

Span 35 ft 4½ in (10·78 m); length 39 ft 9⅜ in (12·13 m); height 12 ft (3·66 m). Empty weight 3,200 lb (1,451 kg); loaded weight 5,085 lb (2,307 kg); power loading 10·2 lb/hp (4·6 kg/hp). Maximum speed 229 mph (369 km/h) at 1,200 ft (365 m); cruising speed 200 mph (322 km/h); rate of climb 1,500 ft/min (457 m/min); service ceiling 22,200 ft (6,765 m); normal range 950 miles (1,530 km); maximum range 1,175 miles (1,890 km).

NX8000H, Douglas's last venture in the private aircraft market. (*MDC*)

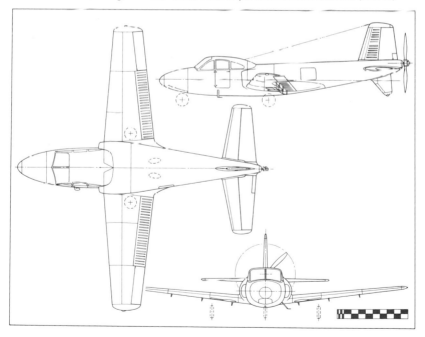

Douglas D-558-1 Skystreak

During two conferences held on 15 March, 1944, at NACA's Langley Laboratory, representatives of the Army Air Technical Service Command, the Navy's Bureau of Aeronautics and NACA agreed on the need for research aircraft to explore problems associated with speeds approaching and exceeding the speed of sound. The Navy and NACA further agreed to work together in preparing joint specifications, a task made difficult by the Navy's desire to obtain an aircraft capable of eventually meeting military requirements whereas NACA wanted a pure research aircraft. In spite of the conflicting requirements, which in part were offset by an early agreement on the use of a turbojet as powerplant, the two organizations concluded in the latter part of 1944 that the aircraft should be (1) unencumbered by military requirements, (2) capable of taking-off and landing on its own power, (3) designed to carry a pilot and up to 500 lb (227 kg) of test instrumentation, and (4) able to obtain the maximum speed possible with existing powerplants. The Navy and NACA, however, were still not yet ready to circulate official specifications. None the less, L. Eugene Root—Chief Aerodynamicist for Douglas El Segundo—was able to obtain preliminary information during a routine visit to the Bureau of Aeronautics in late 1944.

The information was of considerable interest and Douglas decided to submit a proposal to the Bureau of Aeronautics. Under the general supervision of Ed Heinemann and Leo Devlin, a team led by Project Engineer Robert Donovan prepared a preliminary proposal for the smallest aircraft which could be designed around the most powerful engine then available, the General Electric TG-180 turbojet, and still meet Navy and NACA requirements. In February 1945 engineering proposals for the Douglas Model 558 High Speed Test Airplane were transmitted. Two months later, on 13 April, Douglas submitted a contract proposal covering six aircraft, recommending that four TG-180 powered aircraft (three with side air intakes and one with nose intake) be completed with wings using a NACA aerofoil having a 10 per cent thickness-chord ratio, while the last two aircraft, also powered by a TG-180 and fitted with side air intakes, were to have respectively thinner and thicker aerofoils. Douglas further proposed that at a later stage two of the aircraft be modified by replacing the original TG-180 engine with a smaller Westinghouse 24C turbojet and by adding a rocket engine. The initial models were intended to investigate the region between Mach 0·75 and 0·85 from sea level to approximately 40,000 ft (12,195 m) whereas the modified aircraft were to test the Mach 0·85 to 1·0 envelope and reach higher altitudes. Furthermore, fearing that a pilot would not survive a conventional ejection, Douglas designed a jettisonable nose section, including the cockpit, from which the pilot could bale out once the nose section reached slower speeds after its separation from the crippled aircraft.

Photographed over Muroc Dry Lake, this Skystreak (BuNo 37972) is seen fitted with the 50-gallon wingtip tanks. (*MDC*)

Following NACA's and BuAer's favourable review of the Model 558 proposal, Douglas was awarded on 22 June, 1945, a Letter of Intent under Contract NOa(s) 6850, three development phases being covered. Phase One called for the design, construction and testing of six TG-180 powered aircraft; Phase Two specified the modification of two aircraft for turbojet-cum-rocket powerplant; and Phase Three concerned the proposed design and mock-up of a combat type.

Initial mock-up inspection took place between 2 and 4 July, 1945, and resulted in NACA requesting that the canopy be redesigned and that side air intakes no longer be considered. A follow-on mock-up inspection was held during 14–17 August and, at that time, the programme was redirected to provide for two separate projects. The initial D-558-1 project, based on the original straight-wing, turbojet-powered design and intended for transonic research, was now to be followed by a D-558-2 design with swept-wing and turbojet-cum-rocket power for research in the supersonic regime. From that point on, the design of the two D-558 models proceeded separately. Details of the D-558-2 are included in a separate chapter.

To reduce risks and uncertainties, the design of the D-558-1 was kept as conventional as possible and, upon being completed in April 1947, the aircraft emerged as a low-wing, unswept, monoplane with a cylindrical-section fuselage designed around a nose air intake, a bifurcated air duct around the cockpit and straight-through jet exhaust. The 5,000 lb (2,268 kg) thrust J35-A-11 engine, an Allison-built version of the General Electric-designed TG-180 turbojet, was installed in the centre fuselage and was fed from integral wing tanks with 230-US gallon (871-litre) capacity. In addition, provision was made for two 50-gallon (189-litre) wingtip tanks. Other notable design characteristics included the use of specially designed, high-pressure tyres, the mounting of the inflight-adjustable

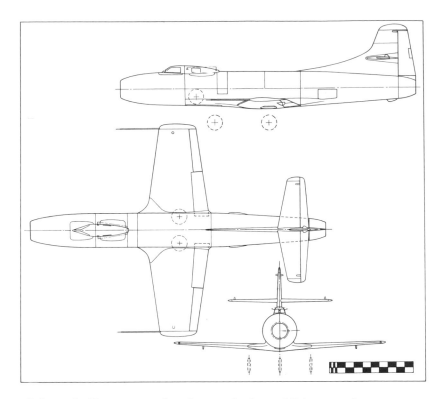

tailplane half-way up the fin, and the addition—a last moment modification requested by the test pilots—of speed-brakes mounted externally on either side of the fuselage just aft of the wing.

Painted scarlet and named Skystreak, the first D-558-1 (s/n 6564, BuNo 37970) was trucked to Muroc Dry Lake in April 1947 for the first phase of its manufacturer's trials. On 15 April, Eugene F. May took the aircraft on its first flight but immediately had to cut the test short due to a partial power loss. On landing, the aircraft's left wheel brake disintegrated. Six days later, a second attempt ended with similar troubles and the unlucky prototype was grounded for four weeks. On its return to flight status, it continued to run into troubles as it was plagued with persistent undercarriage retraction problems. Finally, however, the various deficiencies were remedied and by mid-July 1947 the aircraft was ready for general handling and high-speed trials. At that time, the original clear canopy was replaced by a hooded covering with a flat V windshield.

In early August 1947, by which time BuNo 37970 had reached a top speed of Mach 0·85, the second D-558-1 (BuNo 37971) was ready to join in the trials, and Service pilots began to share the task of flying the aircraft. As flight time slowly built up while the aircraft's handling characteristics and performance were systematically explored, confidence in the Skystreak

414

increased steadily and the Navy decided to use the aircraft for an attempt on a new world airspeed record. Accordingly, Cdr Turner Caldwell, the Navy project officer, flew BuNo 37970 on 20 August, 1947, and averaged 640·663 mph (1,031·049 km/h) during four passes over a low-level 3-km course to break the 623·738 mph (1,003·811 km/h) record set a month earlier by Col Albert Boyd in the specially modified Lockheed P-80R. However, Caldwell's record held for only five days as, on 25 August, Major Marion Carl, a Marine pilot, flying the second Skystreak averaged 650·796 mph (1,047·356 km/h).

Following these record flights, the first D-558-1 was returned to its contractor programme and completed a total of 101 flights prior to being delivered to NACA on 21 April, 1949. However, BuNo 37970 was never flown by NACA but was used by this agency to provide spares needed to support the trials of the third D-558-1. The second Skystreak, the holder of the world airspeed record, completed 27 flights in the hands of Navy and Marine and company pilots before being handed over to NACA on 23 October, 1947. Upon being fitted by NACA with special instrumentation, BuNo 37971 made two further flights in November 1947 with NACA's pilot Howard C. Lilly at the controls, but winter flooding of the runway and the need for engine maintenance resulted in an eleven-week grounding. Preceded by a single flight during the month of February, the intensive flight trial programme planned by NACA began on 31 March but, within five weeks, the aircraft crashed and Howard Lilly was killed. This accident, the first in which a NACA pilot lost his life while on duty, occurred on 3 May, 1948, when during the aircraft's 46th flight the engine compressor disintegrated shortly after take-off.

The crash of the second Skystreak and the death of its pilot delayed the NACA research programme by almost a year, although the third D-558-1 (BuNo 37972) had been delivered in November 1947 and had been flown four times by Douglas pilots before being handed over to NACA. During most of 1948 and into April 1949, the third Skystreak remained grounded

The first D-558-1 (BuNo 37970), in its scarlet finish, with original canopy and rounded windshield. (*NA & SM*)

The high-speed canopy fitted to the D-558-1 after completion of the initial low-speed trials was so narrow that pilots had to wear helmets covered with chamois leather to prevent scratching the transparency. (*MDC*)

while the accident to BuNo 37971 was being investigated. Eventually, the inquiry exonerated the Skystreak and BuNo 37972 was returned to flight status, making its first NACA flight on 22 April, 1949. A total of 77 additional flights were made by seven NACA pilots, enabling the agency to obtain and quantify much useful data on high-subsonic handling. Finally, the aircraft made its 82nd and final flight on 10 June, 1953, to complete the Skystreak's four-and-a-quarter years of active research flying.

The first and third Skystreaks are still in existence and are held respectively at the Naval Aviation Museum in Pensacola, Florida, and at MCAS Quantico, Virginia.

Span 25 ft (7·62 m); length 35 ft 8½ in (10·88 m); height 12 ft 1$\frac{11}{16}$ in (3·7 m); wing area 150·7 sq ft (14 sq m). Loaded weight 9,750 (4,423 kg); maximum weight 10,105 lb (4,584 kg); wing loading 64·7 lb/sq ft (315·9 kg/sq m); power loading 1·95 lb/lb. Maximum speed at sea level 651 mph (1,047 km/h).

BuNo 37972, the third Skystreak, bearing the winged NACA logo across its vertical tail surfaces. (*NASA*)

416

A VF-14 Skyknight (F3D-2, BuNo 127072) during carrier operations on 9 November, 1954. (*US National Archives*)

Douglas F3D (F-10) Skyknight

In the history of US Naval aviation 1944 was eventful, with major offensive air-sea battles being fought in the Pacific and European war theatres while significant technical developments were taking place in the United States. For Douglas, then a major supplier of naval aircraft, 1944 not only saw the completion of SBD Dauntless production but also the realization of the company's first jet-powered aircraft, the XBTD-2, although delivery of Douglas jet combat aircraft to Navy operational units did not take place until almost seven years later when F3D-1 Skynights were delivered to Composite Squadron Three (VC-3).

Late in 1945 BuAer representatives began discussing with Curtiss, Douglas, Fleetwings and Grumman the Navy requirement for a jet-powered, two-seat, carrier-borne night fighter capable of detecting enemy aircraft flying at 500 mph (805 km/h) and 40,000 ft (12,190 m) from a distance of 125 miles (201 km). These discussions led to the placing on 3 April, 1946, of an order for three Douglas XF3D-1s while shortly after Grumman was awarded a contract for the XF9F-1. Eventually, however, the Grumman design evolved into a single-seat day fighter and Douglas was left to develop the world's first carrier-borne jet night fighter. Designed at the El Segundo Division by a team led by Ed Heinemann, the XF3D-1 was a mid-wing design, with two 3,000 lb (1,361 kg) thrust Westinghouse J34-WE-24 axial-flow turbojets installed in semi-external nacelles beneath the fuselage centre section. The crew of two sat side by side in a cockpit located well forward of the wing. As the operation of contemporary ejector seats was not compatible with this seating arrangement, Douglas designed a novel escape system consisting of a ventral tunnel through which the crew members slid, one at a time, feet first and facing aft. In common with other contemporary jet night fighters, the XF3D-1 was a large and heavy aircraft (its empty weight substantially exceeded the normal loaded weight of carrier-borne single-seat jet fighters). Armament consisted of four forward-firing 20-mm cannon, and Westinghouse APQ-35 search and target acquisition radar was housed in the plastic nose section.

The second XF3D-1 (BuNo 121458) experimentally fitted to carry four Sparrow guided missiles beneath its wings, as adopted for the F3D-1Ms. (*USN*)

The maiden flight of the first XF3D-1 (s/n 6670, BuNo 121457) was made on 23 March, 1948, at El Segundo with Russell Thaw as pilot, and company tests continued until October when the three prototypes were transferred to Edwards AFB for government trials. During this time the aircraft were also tested by the USAF but its contemplated procurement failed to materialize. However, the production future of the aircraft had already been assured with the placing in June 1948 of an order for twenty-eight F3D-1 Skyknights for delivery to the US Navy and Marine Corps.

F3D-1 (F-10A): Externally identical to the prototype, twenty-eight F3D-1s (BuNos 123741 to 123768) were built at El Segundo with first flight of a production aircraft taking place on 13 February, 1950. Internal equipment was revised and additional electronic gear installed resulting in an increase in gross weight of some 5,362 lb (2,434 kg). On delivery these aircraft were powered by two 3,000 lb (1,361 kg) thrust Westinghouse

J34-WE-32 turbojets but maximum static thrust was later increased to 3,250 lb (1,474 kg) at which time the engines were redesignated J34-WE-34s. In September 1962 the F3D designation was replaced under the Tri-Service system by the F-10 designation and surviving F3D-1s became F-10As.

F3D-1M (MF-10A): Designation applied to a least twelve F3D-1s which were modified after delivery to test Sparrow guided missiles. Four racks were fitted beneath the outer wing panels to carry the missiles.

F3D-2 (F-10B): Second production version of the Skyknight ordered in August 1949 and intended to be powered by two 4,600 lb (2,087 kg) thrust Westinghouse J46-WE-3s in enlarged nacelles. However, when on 14 February, 1951, the first F3D-2 (BuNo 124595) flew it was powered by two 3,400 lb (1,542 kg) thrust Westinghouse J34-WE-36s as the J46 was experiencing major teething troubles. Eventually all F3D-2s were powered by J34-WE-36s as production of J46s was abandoned but the larger engine nacelles were retained. In addition to engine change, the F3D-2s differed from the first production model in having improved cockpit air conditioning system, electronic equipment and windshield and in being fitted with an automatic pilot and wing spoilers. A total of 237 F3D-2s (BuNos 124595 to 124664, 125783 to 125882, and 127019 to 127085) were built with final delivery taking place on 23 March, 1952. Several of these aircraft were later modified as detailed anon.

F3D-2B: One F3D-2 experimentally fitted with special armament was so designated in 1952.

F3D-2M (MF-10B): Sixteen F3D-2s were modified as missile-armed fighters with guns removed, APQ-36 radar in an extended nose cone, and four wing-mounted Sparrows.

F3D-2Q (EF-10B) Thirty-five F3D-2s were modified as electronic countermeasures aircraft with their radar replaced with specialized ECM equipment.

F3D-2T: Five F3D-2s were modified as night fighter trainers.

F3D-2 Skyknight from the Marine Corps at MCAS Quantico, Virginia.
(*NA & SM*)

419

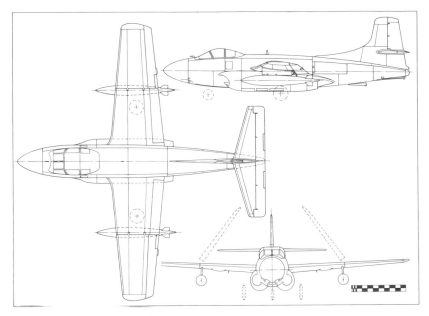

Douglas F3D-2 Skyknight

F3D-2T2 (TF-10B): Designation applied to fifty-five F3D-2s used as radar-operator trainers.

F3D-3: Projected development of the F3D-2 which was to have been powered by two J46-WE-3s and to have swept wings. As the J46 programme had been discontinued and as calculated performance with J34 engines was insufficient to warrant production of this model, contracts for 287 aircraft (BuNos 125883 to 125892 and 130463 to 130739) were cancelled in February 1952.

Following Service trials—which began in December 1950 and were conducted at Moffett Field, California, by Composite Squadron Three (VC-3)—the F3D-1s were assigned to Marine Fighter Squadron VMF(N)-542. Even though the Korean War was making heavy demands on the limited resources of the USN and USMC, the F3D-1s were retained in the United States for continued testing and for training pilots and radar operators of squadrons to be equipped with fully operational F3D-2s.

After completing their training at MCAS El Toro, California, crews from VMF(N)-542 deployed to Korea in the spring of 1952 to begin combat operations from K-2 airfield at Taegu. Almost immediately, however, crews and Skyknights were transferred to VMF(N)-513 at Kunsan (K-8). Mainly flying night escort missions for Air Force B-29 bombers, VMF(N)-513 crews soon had opportunities to tangle with enemy jet

The penultimate F3D-1 (BuNo 123767) in the markings of VMF(N)-542 during the unit's training period before deploying to Korea with F3D-2s. (*USAF*)

fighters. History was made during the night of 2 November, 1952, when Maj William Stratton, pilot, and MSgt Hans Hoagland, radar operator, shot down a North Korean Yak-15 to make the first kill in a jet versus jet night action. In addition to flying fighter sorties, during which they were credited with the destruction of another Yak-15 and of six MiG-15s, VMF(N)-513 crews also flew some night strike and interdiction sorties. In 14 months of combat operations in Korea, no Skyknights were lost to enemy fighters but two aircraft and their crews were lost to unknown causes.

With the return of peace, the Skyknights continued well into the sixties to perform valuable service with Marine Corps units. With Navy units, particularly VFAW-3, Skyknights had a much shorter life as front line fighters as their performance was not very impressive. Rapidly replaced in first line units by nimbler single-seat all-weather fighters, the Navy Skyknights were used for training and experimental purposes. In this latter role, the Skyknight had been first used in July 1949 when an XF3D-1 had completed initial flight test evaluation of Douglas-designed low-drag external stores (with two low-drag 2,000 lb—908 kg—bombs the aircraft reached a top speed 51 kt (96 km/h) greater than when carrying two conventional 2,000 lb bombs). F3D-1Ms and F3D-2Ms were also used by

F3D-2T2 (BuNo 125824) from VFAW-3.
(*Arnold Photograph from AAHS collection*)

421

BuNo 124630, one of the Skyknights bailed to Raytheon and flown with US Army markings, at Holloman AFB, New Mexico, on 4 May, 1980. (*Mike J. Kasiuba*)

TF-10B experimentally fitted with an A-4E nose at NOTS China Lake in 1967. (*Peter B. Lewis*)

Air Development Squadron Four (VX-4) at the Navail Air Missile Test Center, Point Mugu, California, to conduct operational evaluation tests for the Sparrow air-to-air missile. Other R&D naval facilities which flew Skyknights during the sixties include the Naval Parachute Facility at El Centro, California; the Naval Air Ordnance Test Station at Chincoteague, Virginia; the Naval Air Development Unit at South Weymouth, Massachusetts; and the Naval Ordnance Test Station at China Lake, California. The latter, eventually redesignated Naval Weapons Center, was a long-term Skyknight operator and frequently had special nose sections grafted to its F3D-2T2s (EF-10Bs) and F3D-2Ms (MF-10Bs) to test radar, missile guidance systems, and other electronic equipment. Test and development of missile components and guidance systems were also tasks undertaken during the seventies and early eighties by three Skyknights bailed to Raytheon and flown with US Army markings mainly from Holloman AFB, New Mexico.

EF-10B (BuNo 124663) of VMCJ-3 at McClellan AFB. (*Peter B. Lewis*)

Don Walker, was credited with making on 12 August, 1957, the first automatic carrier landing on the USS *Antietam*. In the training role, F3D-2T2s (TF-10Bs) were used by VF-101 to train F-4 crews.

In its EF-10B electronic countermeasures version, the Skyknight was still operated by Marine Composite Reconnaissance Squadrons One, Two, and Three (VMCJ-1, -2, and -3) at the time of America's active participation in air operations over North Vietnam. To ferret out North Vietnamese radar (*Fogbound* missions) and provide tactical jamming for strike aircraft flying over the North, VMCJ-1 deployed an EF-10B detachment to Da Nang AB, South Vietnam, in April of 1965. Never having more than ten EF-10Bs on strength, the Marine detachment compiled an enviable record before being brought back to the States in 1969. The last Marine EF-10Bs were finally retired on 31 May, 1970. By then the only flyable Skyknights were the three aircraft bailed to Raytheon. Two of them lasted into the early eighties.

Span 50 ft (15·24 m); length 45 ft 5 in (13·87 m); height 16 ft 1 in (4·9 m); wing area 400 sq ft (37·161 sq m).

XF3D-1
Empty weight 12,683 lb (5,753 kg); loaded weight 18,668 lb (8,472 kg); maximum weight 21,500 lb (9,752 kg); wing loading 46·7 lb/sq ft (228 kg/sq m); power loading 3·11 lb/lb. Maximum speed 543 mph (874 km/h) at 11,000 ft (3,355 m); cruising speed 330 mph (531 km/h); initial rate of climb 4,420 ft/min (1,347 m/min); service ceiling 42,800 ft (13,045 m); normal range 717 miles (1,154 km); maximum range 1,120 miles (1,802 km).

F3D-2
Empty weight 18,160 lb (8,237 kg); loaded weight 23,575 lb (10,693 kg); maximum weight 27,681 lb (12,556 kg); wing loading 58.9 lb/sq ft (287.8 kg/sq m); power loading 3·47 lb/lb. Maximum speed 565 mph (909 km/h) at 20,000 ft (6,095 m); cruising speed 390 mph (628 km/h); initial rate of climb 4,000 ft/min (1,219 m/min); service ceiling 38,200 ft (11,675 m); maximum range 1,540 miles (2,478 km).

Douglas D-558-2 Skyrocket

Between 14 and 17 August, 1945, when other Douglas departments were enjoying a special holiday to celebrate VJ-Day, the D-558 design team remained on duty to participate in the second mock-up inspection of the original straight-wing, transonic research project. On this occasion, Navy and NACA representatives asked Douglas for initial design studies for a more advanced research aircraft capable of supersonic speeds. As a result of research into captured German aerodynamic reports by the Douglas engineers who had joined the Naval Technical Mission in Europe in May 1945, the new aircraft, the D-558-2, was designed around swept wings. Furthermore, to supplement the insufficient thrust of available turbojets, a rocket engine with enough fuel for two minutes' operation at 4,000 lb (1,814 kg) thrust was to be installed.

Douglas first considered developing a version of the D-558-1 fitted with swept wing and tail surfaces. However, while low-speed wind-tunnel tests

The first Skyrocket, BuNo 37973, as completed in the autumn of 1947. (*MDC*)

424

BuNo 37973 on 27 October, 1949, after installation of the XLR-8-RM5 rocket engine. (*MDC*)

gave satisfactory results, it soon became clear that the D-558-1 fuselage would be too small to house a turbojet, a rocket engine and rocket fuel tanks. Consequently, a complete redesign of the fuselage was undertaken while the wing design was refined to combine the required high-speed performance with low-speed handling equal to those of the straight-wing D-558-1. As this redesign progressed satisfactorily, Douglas was granted on 29 January, 1946, preliminary authorization to develop the aircraft. This led to inspection of the swept-wing mock-up on 18 and 19 March, 1946, and finally, on 27 January, 1947, to a formal change order substituting three D-558-2 Skyrockets for the last three D-558-1 Skystreaks which had been ordered under Contract NOa(s) 6850.

Designed by a team supervised by Ed Heinemann and led by aerodynamicist Kerwin E. Van Every, the supersonic aircraft emerged with a circular-section fuselage of greater diameter and length than that of the D-558-1. It contained not only the pilot's jettisonable compartment but also the 3,000 lb (1,361 kg) thrust Westinghouse J34-WE-40 turbojet, provision for installation of a 6,000 lb (2,722 kg) thrust Reaction Motors XLR-8-RM-5 four-chamber rocket engine, fuel tanks for both engines, and the tricycle undercarriage. The turbojet was mounted in the centre fuselage, was fed by side air intakes and exhausted beneath the fuselage. The rocket engine was to be installed in the rear fuselage. Fuel for the turbojet consisted of 250 US gallons (946 litres) of aviation gasoline contained in two tanks which were located above the wing centre section. The rocket engine, not installed for initial low-speed trials, was to be fed from a 195-

425

gallon (738-litre) alcohol tank in the rear fuselage and from a 180-gallon (681-litre) liquid oxygen tank in the forward fuselage. In addition, an 11-gallon (42-litre) hydrogen peroxide tank was provided to supply the turbine pump feeding the rocket engine, while seven small helium tanks were fitted to pressurize the rocket fuel tanks.

Other design features of interest included the narrow-track under-carriage with all members retracting into the fuselage, the wing with a sweep of 35 deg and the tailplane with 40 deg sweep. The wing had a thickness-chord ratio increasing from 10 per cent at the root to 12 per cent at the tip and, to improve stall characteristics, was fitted with fences and Handley Page automatic leading-edge slats.

On 10 December, 1947, the first D-558-2 (s/n 6567, BuNo 37973) was trucked to the test centre at Muroc Dry Lake where its J34-WE-40 turbojet was fitted and where it was prepared for manufacturer's trials. These began on 4 February, 1948, when John F. Martin flew the Skyrocket on its maiden flight. Test data collected during the initial phase indicated that with only the turbojet installed the aircraft had a sluggish performance, particularly on take-off, that visibility from the cockpit was poor, and that directional stability was inadequate. Consequently, the original clamshell-type clear canopy which did not protrude above the fuselage top line was replaced by a raised cockpit with a flat V windshield, and the height of the vertical tail surfaces was increased from 11 ft 6 in (3·51 m) to 12 ft 8 in (3·86 m). After being modified, BuNo 37973 was retained by Douglas for tests at subsonic speeds (maximum speed was Mach 0·825 at 20,000 ft, 6,095 m) until the summer of 1949 when its 6,000 lb (2,722 kg) thrust XLR-8-RM-5 rocket unit was installed.

Still operated in the conventional take-off mode but now powered by the turbojet/rocket combination, the first D-558-2 was tested by Douglas from October 1949 until August 1951. From its first flight on 4 February, 1948,

BuNo 37973 with its original canopy. Details of the intake for the J34-WE-30 turbojet are clearly visible. (*MDC*)

426

The Skyrocket at low altitude over the Mojave Desert. (*NASA*)

until delivered to NACA on 31 August, 1951, the aircraft made a total of 122 flights in Douglas pilots' hands. Upon delivery to NACA's High Speed Flight Station, the aircraft was renumbered NACA 143 but was not flown by this agency which kept it in storage until 1954. At that time, it was returned to Douglas to be modified to the air-launched, all-rocket configuration first devised for the second D-558-2. In this form, and powered solely by a 6,000 lb (2,722 kg) thrust XLR-8-RM-6 rocket engine, the aircraft was intended to be used by NACA for testing the shape of external stores at supersonic speeds. However, the aircraft was flown only once by NACA, on 17 September, 1956, before being officially retired in March 1957.

BuNo 37974, the second D-558-2, was also initially delivered without rocket engine and on 2 and 7 November, 1948, Gene May completed its two demonstration flights for Douglas. The aircraft, still powered only by the J34-WE-40 turbojet, was delivered to NACA on 1 December, 1948, and NACA pilots made twenty-one turbojet-powered flights between 24 May, 1949, and 6 January, 1950. It was then returned to Douglas to be modified for high-speed, air-launched flights and fitted with an XLR-8-RM-6 rocket engine and additional rocket fuel tanks replacing the turbojet.

The decision to modify BuNo 37974 and, later, BuNo 37973 to the air-launched configuration was made by NACA and the Navy on the basis of the flight-test results with BuNo 37975. This aircraft, the third D-558-2, had been fitted from the beginning with both the J34-WE-40 turbojet and XLR-8-RM-5 rocket engine and had made its first flight, on turbojet power alone, on 8 January, 1949. A little over six weeks later, on 25 February, it was used for the Skyrocket's first turbojet-cum-rocket flight. Testing of the mixed-power third D-558-2 continued until November 1949 and, in the course of its fifteen-flight manufacturer's trial programme, the aircraft exceeded Mach 1·0 for the first time on 24 June, 1949. However, the

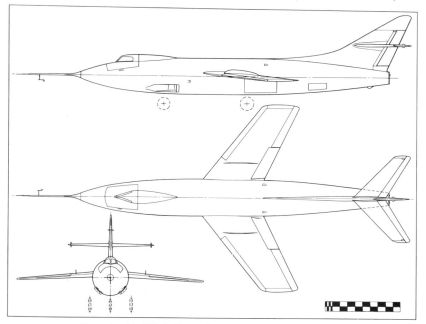

Douglas D-558-2 Skyrocket with modified canopy.

428

The second Skyrocket, in its all-rocket configuration, beneath the fuselage of its parent Boeing P2B-1S. (*MDC*)

conventional take-off test mode proved unsatisfactory as (1) the take-off with the aircraft heavily laden with highly explosive rocket propellants was dangerous, (2) insufficient fuel could be lifted to give the aircraft adequate endurance at full power as part of the fuel had to be burned while operating the rocket engine during take-off and climb, and (3) the aircraft could only reach a top speed of Mach 1·08 (720 mph, 1,159 km/h) at 40,000 ft (12,190 m) before running out of fuel. On the other hand, the USAF Bell X-1 had demonstrated the practicality of air-launched operations. Accordingly, in November 1949 the Bureau of Aeronautics instructed Douglas to modify BuNo 37975 to air-launched configuration with the original turbojet-cum-rocket powerplant installation, BuNo 37974 to air-launched configuration with rocket engine only, and a Boeing P2B-1S (BuNo 84029, ex-USAAF B-29-95-BW serial 45-21787, later renumbered NACA 137) as a launch aeroplane.

Modification of the third Skyrocket was limited to the installation of retractable mounts for the launch hooks, and in September 1950 it was ready to make captive flights in the belly of the P2B-1S. On 8 September, with William B. Bridgeman as its pilot, BuNo 37975 was launched at 24,850 ft and 225 mph (7,575 m and 362 km/h) from the P2B-1S captained by George Jansen, for a flight on turbojet power alone. Three additional flights on turbojet power and two flights on turbojet-cum-rocket power were made by Bridgeman before 15 December, 1950, when the aircraft was delivered to NACA which designated it NACA 145. Between 22 December, 1950, and 28 August, 1956, the third D-558-2 was flown 66 times by NACA, USAF and USMC pilots to perform a variety of tests including evaluation of high-speed handling with wing slats fully or partially opened and with slats replaced with chord extension over the outer 32 per cent of the wing panels, and with external stores. Some time after being retired after completion of its NACA test programme, bringing its total number of flights to 87, the third Skyrocket was mounted on a pedestal at the Antelope Valley College, Lancaster, California, where it could still be seen in 1977.

During the first ten months of 1950, the second D-558-2 was extensively modified by Douglas. The original turbojet and rocket engines were removed, the turbojet's air intakes and exhaust faired over, and a 6,000 lb (2,722 kg) thrust XLR-8-RM-6 four-chamber rocket engine installed. Intended for research at maximum speed, the aircraft had to have endurance increased and, to that effect, it was fitted with additional liquid oxygen and diluted ethyl alcohol tanks bringing total capacity of these two chemicals up from 170 to 345 gallons (644 to 1,306 litres) and from 192 to 378 gallons (727 to 1,431 litres), respectively. Upon completion of its modification programme, the aircraft was ferried in the belly of the P2B-1S to Edwards AFB where the company made three unsuccessful launch attempts during December 1950. On 26 January, 1951, Bill Bridgeman and the Skyrocket almost came to grief when, about to abort on a fourth attempt, a communication failure between Bridgeman and the P2B-1S captain resulted in an accidental launch. In spite of a drop in fuel pressure, Bridgeman climbed the D-558-2 to 40,000 ft (12,190 m) and then dived back towards Edwards AFB. In the process, the Skyrocket reached a top speed of Mach 1·28 at 38,890 ft (11,855 m), the highest Mach number it had yet achieved. During six additional manufacturer's flights, Bill Bridgeman began to explore the Skyrocket's maximum performance and successively reached the following milestones: Mach 1·79 at 64,000 ft (19,510 m) on 11 June, 1951; Mach 1·85 at 63,000 ft (19,200 m) on 23 June; Mach 1·88 at 66,000 ft (20,165 m) on 7 August; and a maximum altitude of

Drawing of the projected D-558-3 hypersonic research aircraft. (*NA & SM*)

74,494 ft (22,705 m) on 15 August. Thus, when on 31 August, 1951, BuNo 37974 was handed over to NACA, it was the aircraft which had flown fastest and highest.

Renumbered NACA, 144, the second Skyrocket made another 75 flights while piloted by NACA, Marine and Air Force pilots during a 63-month test programme. While most were strictly for research purposes, two resulted in new records. On 21 August, 1953, Lt-Col Marion Carl, the Marine officer who had gained the world's speed record whilst flying the second Skystreak, reached an altitude of 83,235 ft (25,370 m) to set a new unofficial world's record. Three months later, on 20 November, NACA's pilot A. Scott Crossfield pushed the D-558-2 into a dive from 72,000 ft (21,945 m) and reached a speed of Mach 2·005—approximately 1,291 mph, 2,078 km/h—at 62,000 ft (18,900 m), thus becoming the first man to travel at twice the speed of sound. Subsequent flights, which provided much useful data, were less spectacular and culminated on 20 December, 1956, with the 105th flight of the second D-558-2, the last Skyrocket to be flown. Appropriately, this record-setting aircraft is now kept in the National Air & Space Museum.

The D-558 research programme might have been continued beyond the last Skyrocket flight as in June 1953 Kermit E. Van Every, chief of the aerodynamics section at El Segundo, had launched a design study for a Mach 9·0 hypersonic research aircraft. Tentatively designated D-558-3, this projected vehicle was to have had a very thin, straight wing and been powered by a rocket engine. Its maximum design speed and altitude were respectively 8,870 ft per second (approximately 6,050 mph, 9,735 km/h) and 750,000 ft (228,600 m). However, lack of funds and a multi-agency agreement to pool efforts on the North American X-15 led to the cancellation of the study by the Office of Naval Research.

Even without the contribution which the D-558-3 could have made, the achievements of the D-558 programme in general and of the D-558-2 in particular were both highly useful and truly spectacular. While very different in nature from the better known Douglas achievements, they contributed most brilliantly to the Douglas share in the development of aviation. It is not surprising, therefore, to note that the Skyrocket programme won for Ed Heinemann the 1951 Sylvanus Albert Reed award of the American Institute of Aeronautical Sciences and for Bill Bridgeman the 1953 Octave Chanute award.

Span 25 ft (7·62 m); length 42 ft (12·8 m); height 12 ft 8 in (3·86 m); wing area 175 sq ft (16·258 sq m). Launch weight 10,572 lb (4,795 kg) with turbojet only, 15,266 lb (6,925 kg) with mixed power, 15,787 lb (7,161 kg) with rocket only. Wing loadings, respectively, 60·4 lb/sq ft (294·9 kg/sq m), 87·2 lb/sq ft (425·9 kg/sq m), 90·2 lb/sq ft (440·5 kg/sq m). Maximum speed 585 mph (941 km/h) at 20,000 ft (6,095 m) on turbojet only, 720 mph (1,159 km/h) at 40,000 ft (12,190 m) on mixed power with conventional take-off, 1,250 mph (2,010 km/h) at 67,500 ft (20,575 m) on rocket power only when air-launched.

The first DC-3S, originally built as a C-47-DL with USAAF serial 41-18656, during its flight-trials. (*MDC*)

Douglas Super DC-3 and R4D-8

No sooner had production of the DC-3 ended than a search for its successor began. Understandably, Douglas had a vital interest in finding the replacement, and some preliminary work was done during 1947. Later, the threat of impending Civil Air Regulations, too stringent to allow renewed airworthiness certificates for the standard DC-3s and converted C-47s, lent a new urgency to the project.

To save engineering time and cost and to reduce price while providing new life for the large number of DC-3s and derivatives which were menaced by expiry of their airworthiness certificates in 1952, Douglas decided to concentrate its efforts on modernizing existing aircraft rather than designing an entirely new machine. After initial design work had been done by a team comprising many of the DC-3's original designers, the project was transferred to a special group led by M. K. Oleson. To meet the new Civil Air Regulations, the aircraft's stability, single-engined performance and take-off had to be improved, and competitive pressures made it necessary to improve its speed.

Using two aircraft which had been bought second-hand—an ex C-47-DL, s/n 6017, serial 41-18656, and an ex DC-3, s/n 4122, NC15579—, Douglas undertook to build two prototypes of the DC-3S better known as the Super DC-3. The fuselage structure was strengthened, a 3 ft 3 in (99 cm) section with an extra window on each side was added to the fuselage forward of the front wing spar—thus increasing normal seating capacity to thirty—and the passenger door, now also acting as an integral airstair, was moved forward. New vertical and horizontal tail surfaces with squared tips and increased area were fitted and the dorsal fin area was substantially increased to improve single-engined handling. The wing centre section was left unchanged but new outer panels with squared tips and 15·5 deg sweep on the leading edge and 4 deg sweep on the trailing edge replaced the original wing outboard sections. Span was reduced from the 95 ft (28·96 m) of the standard DC-3 to 90 ft (27·43 m) and wing area was cut from its 986 sq ft (91·696 sq m) to 969 sq ft (90·023 sq m). New, smoother, engine nacelles with doors fully enclosing the strengthened undercarriage were designed to accommodate either 1,475 hp Wright Cyclone R-1820-C9HE nine-cylinder radials or 1,450 hp Pratt & Whitney R-2000-D7 fourteen-cylinder radials driving fully-feathering propellers.

After completion of the extensive modernization programme, s/n 6017 emerged as the first DC-3S and was given new serial and registration numbers: s/n 43158, N30000. Powered by two Wright R-1820-C9HE engines, the aircraft made its first flight at Clover Field on 23 June, 1949, with John F. Martin at the controls. Flight test results exceeded expectations and there was little doubt that the Super DC-3 would meet all Civil Air Regulations requirements while offering increased payload and

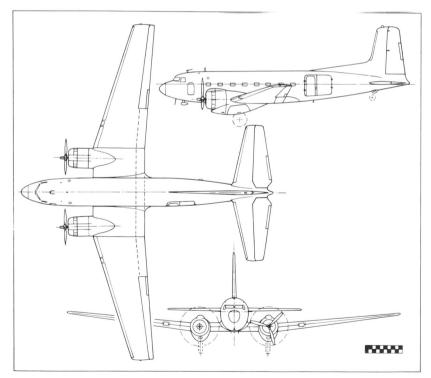

Douglas R4D-8.

434

improved performance. Compared with the DC-3C, maximum speed increased from 230 mph (368 km/h) to 270 mph (432 km/h), cruising speed from 207 mph (331 km/h) to 251 mph (401 km/h), and initial rate of climb from 1,130 ft/min (345 m/min) to 1,300 ft/min (396 m/min). Following completion of the flight trial programme the aircraft was used by Douglas for a sales tour of the United States. Meanwhile, the second DC-3S—s/n 43159, ex s/n 4122—was completed and flown with Pratt & Whitney R-2000-D7 engines.

In spite of offering markedly improved performance, the commercial Super DC-3 programme proved a failure and, as a result of the sales tour, only Capital Airlines' interest in the aircraft was converted into an order for three R-1820-C9HE powered machines, while the second prototype was acquired by a construction company. Major airlines preferred the more modern and faster Convair-Liner series with pressurized cabins. Smaller airlines, including the US local service airlines which had been the prime sales targets, found the Super DC-3 too expensive for their tight budgets and in any case were finally able to retain current airworthiness certificates on their large holdings of standard DC-3s.

US Navy R4D-8 (BuNo 50784, ex-R4D-6 and C-47B-10-DK 43-49152) at NAS Quonset Point, Rhode Island. (*Roger Besecker*)

Having failed to sell the Super DC-3 to the airlines, Douglas sold the first prototype of the aircraft to the USAF which assigned to it the serial 51-3817 and the designation YC-129, this being later changed to YC-47F. Following trials, the USAF decided not to adopt the YC-47F and the aircraft was transferred to the US Navy as the R4D-8X (BuNo 13820). At last Douglas had found a customer for the Super DC-3, the US Navy awarding the manufacturers a contract to modify one hundred R4D-5s, R4D-6s and R4D-7s to R4D-8 configuration.

Powered by two 1,475 hp Wright R-1820-80s, the modernized aircraft were assigned new factory serial numbers (43301 to 43400) but retained their original Bureau Numbers. Some of the aircraft in this batch were modified to fulfil a variety of missions and were especially redesignated as follows: R4D-8T (TC-117D after 1962) trainers, R4D-8Z (VC-117D) staff

A VC-117D from Headquarters & Maintenance Squadron Twenty-Seven (H & MS-27). (*Jim Sullivan*)

transports and R4D-8L (LC-117D) transports modified for cold-weather operation. All standard R4D-8s became C-117Ds in 1962 and the type remained in naval service until retired by the USMC in July 1976.

Accommodation: Crew of three, cabin attendants and 30-38 passengers (DC-3S), three crew and 33 passengers (R4D-8)

Span 90 ft (27·43 m); length 67 ft 9 in (20·75 m); height 18 ft 3 in (5·56 m); wing area 969 sq ft (90·023 sq m). Empty weight 19,537 lb (8,870 kg); maximum weight 31,000 lb (14,075 kg); wing loading 32 lb/sq ft (156·2 kg/sq m); power loading 10·5 lb/hp (4·8 kg/hp). Maximum speed 270 mph (432 km/h) at 5,900 ft (1,800 m); cruising speed 251 mph (401 km/h); initial rate of climb 1,300 ft/min (396 m/min); maximum range 2,500 miles (4,025 km).

Weights and performance for R4D-8.

Douglas C-124 Globemaster II

To take full advantage of the C-74's load-carrying ability over short ranges and to enable the airlifting of heavy ground forces equipment, such as heavy tanks and bulldozers, Douglas and the USAF agreed that the fifth C-74 (42-65406) should be modified to serve as prototype for a heavy strategic cargo transport. Retaining the wings, tail surfaces and 3,500 hp Pratt & Whitney Wasp Major R-4360-49 engines of the Globemaster I, the YC-124 made its first flight at Long Beach on 27 November, 1949. Externally the new aircraft was characterized by its double-deck fuselage of rectangular cross-section and by its impressive rounded nose which incorporated clamshell loading doors and a built-in double ramp. Vehicles could be driven in and out of the aircraft under their own power and additional cargo loaded by means of the amidship lift as fitted to the C-74. When used to carry ground forces equipment, the aircraft could also accommodate the equipment crews on its upper deck. Alternately, the aircraft could be equipped to carry either 200 fully-equipped troops, or 123 litter patients, 45 ambulatory patients and 15 medical attendants. Normal crew was five and maximum payload 74,000 lb (33,565 kg).

As the YC-124 was a modification of the proven C-74 flight trials proceeded smoothly, the only significant modification being the substitution of 3,500 hp R-4360-35A engines for the original R-4360-49s. Construction of a production prototype (48-795) and of a first batch of twenty-eight C-124As (49-232/49-259) began almost immediately with initial delivery of C-124As commencing in May 1950. Initially these aircraft differed from the YC-124 only in minor equipment details and in being powered by four 3,500 hp R-4360-20WAs but, over the years, they were progressively upgraded. Subsequent contracts covered an additional one hundred and twenty-five C-124As (50-083/50-118, 50-1255/50-1268, 51-073/51-182, and 51-5173/51-5187), and most of these aircraft, as well as some in the initial production batch, were subsequently modified by addition of APS-42 weather radar in a nose thimble radome and of combustion heaters which were housed in wingtip pods. These provided cabin heating and wing and tail surface de-icing.

Entering squadron service with the Military Air Transport Service and the Troop Carrier Command at the start of the Korean War, the C-124A proved a valuable and timely addition to USAF airlift capability. Unfortunately, its service debut was soon marred by two major accidents, each resulting in the then largest number of people killed in a single aircraft accident. The first of these took place on 20 December, 1950, when a C-124A crashed on take off from Moses Lake, Washington, killing 86 out of the 116 men on board. Seven months later, on 18 June, 1951, another C-124 crashed near Tokyo with the loss of all 129 occupants. Luckily, these were isolated occurrences, and the Globemaster II gave many years of

C-124-DL (51-131) in service with the Pacific Division of MATS. The aircraft had been retrofitted with combustion heaters in wingtip pods but not with APS-42 weather radar. (*USAF*)

C-124C-DL Globemaster II over San Francisco on 15 February, 1955. The famous Golden Gate bridge is seen above the port wingtip. (*USAF*)

valuable service, first with regular squadrons and, from 1961, with reserve and ANG units.

In 1951 Douglas began the development of a propeller-turbine powered version of the Globemaster II intended as a tanker. The use of 5,550 eshp Pratt & Whitney YT34-P-1 turbines was anticipated to substantially boost the ceiling and cruise performance of the proposed YKC-124B and thus

The propeller-turbine powered YC-124B-DL (51-072) which was originally intended to serve as a prototype for a projected tanker version. (*Pratt & Whitney*)

438

render it highly suitable for inflight refuelling of high-performance jet combat aircraft. Much to the chagrin of Douglas, however, the USAF decided to standardize its tanker fleet on the lower-performance Boeing KC-97. Redesignated YC-124B, the turbine-powered Globemaster II (51-072) was first flown on 2 February, 1954, and served as an engine testbed until October 1956 when it was retired and shipped to the Redstone Arsenal at Huntsville, Alabama, for training personnel in missile loading techniques. During its 32 months of evaluation, the YC-124B provided much useful data which were incorporated in the design of the next Douglas heavy cargo aircraft, the C-133 Cargomaster.

The second production version of the Globemaster II was the C-124C of which 243 (51-5188/51-5213, 51-7272/51-7285, 52-939/52-1089, and 53-001/53-052) were built until May 1955. Powered by four 3,800 hp R-4360-63As, the C-124C had increased fuel capacity and operating weights, and was fitted from the beginning with the nose radome and combustion heaters in wingtip fairings. For experimental use in support of the projected Douglas C-132, one C-124C (52-1069) was fitted with a 16,000 eshp Pratt & Whitney XT57-P-1 propeller-turbine in the nose.

Although the C-124As and C-124Cs remained in production for only five years, they had a long and useful Service life as, until the advent of the

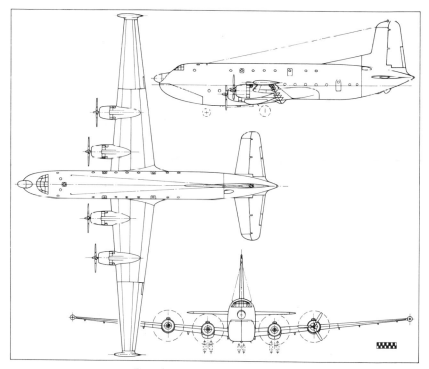

Douglas C-124 Globemaster II.

JC-124C-DL (52-1069) serving as flying testbed for the 16,000 eshp XT57-P-1.

Lockheed C-5A they were the only USAF cargo aircraft, with the exception of the C-133 Cargomaster, capable of airlifting most of the US Army equipment. Thus regular and reserve squadrons, as well as ANG groups, played a major part in the airlift made necessary by combat operations in Southeast Asia. In a more peaceful role, Globemaster IIs were frequently used to carry food and other emergency supplies to disaster stricken parts of the world. At the end of a quarter of a century of reliable service, the C-124s were retired and many ended their life in neat rows at the Davis-Monthan AFB storage facility.

	C-124A	C-124C
Span, ft in	173 3	174 1½
(m)	(52·81)	(53·07)
Length, ft in	127 2	130 5
(m)	(38·76)	(39·75)
Height, ft in	48 3	48 3½
(m)	(14·71)	(14·72)
Wing area, sq ft	2,506	2,506
(sq m)	(232·816)	(232·816)
Empty weight, lb	—	101,165
(kg)	—	(45,888)
Loaded weight, lb	175,000	185,000
(kg)	(79,379)	(83,915)
Maximum weight, lb	—	194,500
(kg)	—	(88,224)
Wing loading, lb/sq ft	69·8	73·8
(kg/sq m)	(341)	(360·4)
Power loading, lb/hp	25	24·3
(kg/hp)	(11·3)	(11)
Maximum speed, mph at ft	298/20,800	304/20,800
(km/h at m)	(480/6,340)	(489/6,340)
Cruising speed, mph	264	230
(km/h)	(425)	(370)
Rate of climb, ft/min	800	760
(m/min)	(244)	(232)
Service ceiling, ft	22,050	21,800
(m)	(6,720)	(6,645)
Payload/range, lb/miles	50,000/2,300	26,375/4,030
(kg/km)	(22,680/3,700)	(11,963/6,485)
Maximum range, miles	6,280	6,820
(km)	(10,105)	(10,975)

Douglas A2D-1 Skyshark

On 25 June, 1945, barely three months after the XBT2D-1 had first flown, Douglas was asked by BuAer to prepare design studies for propeller-turbine powered carrier aircraft. During the next eighteen months, the company submitted three designs intended to lead to the development of an XBT3D-1. The Model D-557A was to be powered by two General Electric TG-100 turbines in wing nacelles whereas the D-557B was to have nose-mounted twin TG-100 engines driving contra-rotating propellers and the D-557C was conceived around a single Westinghouse 25D turbine. The project proceeded past the mock-up stage to the modification of an XBT2D-1 airframe as prototype for the propeller-turbine aircraft. However, before completion of this modification programme, the project was cancelled due to engine development problems. Further studies followed and were based on either twin Allison 500 turbines or a projected Douglas-designed powerplant consisting of twin Westinghouse 24C turbojets mounted side by side with their exhaust driving a large turbine which, in turn, drove contra-rotating propellers. None of these studies proceeded beyond the preliminary conceptual design phase.

Meanwhile, the Power Plant Section of the Bureau of Aeronautics had satisfied itself that the propeller-turbine would have a lower specific fuel consumption than the pure turbojet. To obtain reliable flight-test data, BuAer thus sought funds to fit a propeller-turbine to an existing aircraft. The modified machine was to serve not only as a testbed but was also to have the necessary development potential for eventual production as an attack aircraft. Logically, the Douglas studies and the Navy requirements were merged and on 11 June, 1947, Douglas received a Letter of Intent for the preparation of preliminary layouts, wind-tunnel testing and construction of a mock-up. The latter was inspected in September 1947 and on the 25th of that month Douglas was awarded a contract for two XA2D-1s (BuNos 122988/122989) to be powered by twin Allison XT40-A-2 turbines.

The first XA2D-1 (BuNo 122988) over the Mojave Desert. (*USN*)

441

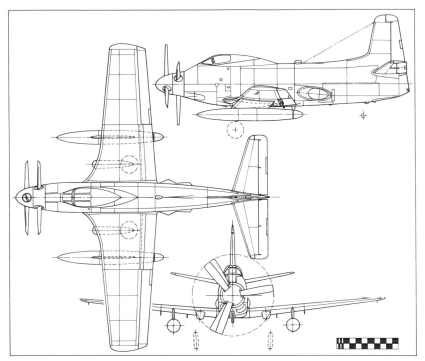

Douglas A2D-1 Skyshark.

Initially the project contemplated a fairly straightforward conversion of the AD airframe to fit the new engine. However, it soon became obvious that in order to derive the full benefit of the increased power (the XT40 was more than twice as powerful as the R-3350 fitted to the Skyraider) a major redesign would be necessary. The result was virtually a new aeroplane bearing only a close family resemblance to its forebear. The wing planform remained unchanged but its root thickness was reduced from 17 per cent to 12 per cent. The tail surfaces were also new and the height and area of the vertical surfaces were further increased after completion of the aircraft's initial trials. The main undercarriage was of similar design but was strengthened and had increased stroke. The 5,100 eshp Allison XT40-A-2 was mounted inside the fuselage above the wing and consisted of two Allison T38s driving contra-rotating propellers through a common gearbox. In cruise, one of the T38s could be shut down to further increase range and endurance at the expense of speed but with handling unaffected. The cockpit was moved forward, was pressurized and fitted with an ejector seat.

First flight at Edwards AFB, California, was made on 26 May, 1950, by George Jansen, and flight trials were conducted with the two prototypes and with six of the ten production Skysharks (BuNos 125479/125488).

With the exception of top speed, which fell some ten per cent below estimates, performance and handling were promising and the A2D Skyshark offered substantial improvements over the Skyraider. In particular, it had a 50 per cent better performance in terms of bomb load per mile per hour than the AD's while having a 160 per cent faster rate of climb, a 50 per cent higher service ceiling, and a 170 mph (275 km/h) greater top speed. Unfortunately, the Skyshark suffered from protracted powerplant teething troubles which in particular affected the gearbox. The engine's lack of reliability resulted in numerous incidents and in two accidents, with BuNo 122988 and its Navy pilot being lost on 19 December, 1950, whilst on 5 August, 1954, George Jansen was able to eject when BuNo 125480 was lost. Furthermore, the A2D performance promised to be overshadowed by that of its new stablemate, the XA4D-1 Skyhawk. Accordingly, BuNos 125485/125488 were completed but not flown, and 339 A2D-1s (BuNos 127962/128042, 132793/133042, and 134438/134445) which were on order were cancelled, the programme terminating with the delivery of the sixth production aircraft.

Span 50 ft $0\frac{3}{16}$ in (15·24 m); length 41 ft $2\frac{13}{32}$ in (12·56 m); height 17 ft $0\frac{3}{4}$ in (5·2 m); wing area 400 sq ft (37·161 sq m). Empty weight 12,944 lb (5,871 kg); loaded weight 18,720 lb (8,491 kg); maximum weight 22,966 lb (10,417 kg); wing loading 46·8 lb/sq ft (228·5 kg/sq m); power loading 3·7 lb/eshp (1·7 kg/eshp). Maximum speed 501 mph (806 km/h) at 25,000 ft (7,620 m); cruising speed 276 mph (444 km/h); rate of climb 7,290 ft/min (2,222 m/min); service ceiling 48,100 ft (14,660 m); combat range 637 miles (1,025 km); maximum range 2,200 miles (3,540 km).

Armament. Four wing-mounted 20-mm cannon. Maximum external load 5,500 lb (2,495 kg) of bombs, napalm tanks or rockets on three main racks and 10 auxiliary racks.

Dimensions, weights and performance for XA2D-1.

Douglas F4D (F-6) Skyray

After losing to Chance Vought a 1946 design competition calling for the development of a carrier-based interceptor fighter capable of reaching a top speed of 600 mph at 40,000 ft (966 km/h at 12,190 m), the engineering team at the El Segundo Division was given another chance in 1947 when the Navy opened a new design competition. Analyses of data captured in Germany towards the end of the Second World War had resulted in considerable interest in the work of Dr Alexander Lippisch on delta and modified delta wing planforms. Believing that this wing geometry offered particular promise in the design of fast climbing interceptor fighters, the Navy invited the US aircraft industry to submit proposals for aircraft embodying this design feature.

On 17 June, 1947, the Navy Bureau of Aeronautics selected the Douglas proposal for further studies and awarded a contract covering the preliminary design phase. As work under the direction of E. H. Heinemann

The first XF4D-1 at El Segundo on 9 October, 1950. The BuNo appears on the fin as 184586; it should have been 124586. (*MDC*)

and C. S. Kennedy advanced, the design was progressively revised and eventually the basic delta planform was abandoned in favour of low aspect-ratio highly swept, mid-mounted wings with round tips. The tricycle undercarriage was supplemented by a small tailwheel—made necessary by the aircraft's high angle of incidence—which retracted into a rear fuselage fairing. Provision was made in the wings for four 20 mm cannon, mounted outboard of the mainwheels and wing drop tanks and with their muzzles located slightly below and behind the wing leading edges. The wing outer panels folded hydraulically upward to facilitate carrier storage. The cockpit was in the front of the fuselage well forward of the bifurcated air intakes in the wing roots. In common with many other contemporary naval types, the aircraft was to be powered by a Westinghouse J40 axial-flow turbojet, and use of an afterburner to increase maximum thrust was already contemplated during the early design phase. With this powerplant performance estimates included a maximum speed slightly in excess of Mach 1 in level flight while the rate of climb was to exceed that of all other contemporary types to enable the aircraft to reach from a standing start enemy bombers flying at 40,000 ft (12,190 m) and before reaching their dropping point for nuclear weapons. On the strength of these calculations Douglas was awarded on 16 December, 1948, a contract for the construction and testing of two XF4D-1 Skyrays.

Construction of the prototypes at El Segundo progressed slowly and the first aircraft was not completed until two years after the award of the contract. However, construction of the airframes had outpaced engine development and the 7,000 lb (3,175 kg) thrust Westinghouse XJ40-WE-6 intended for the XF4D-1 was not ready to be installed for flight trials. Rather than delaying the programme further, Douglas and the Bureau of Aeronautics chose a 5,000 lb (2,268 kg) thrust Allison J35-A-17 turbojet for the first aircraft (s/n 7463, BuNo 124586). With this powerplant installed

444

the XF4D-1 was transferred by road to the flight test centre at Edwards AFB in the Mojave Desert where, on 23 January, 1951, Robert Rahn took it on its maiden flight. Soon after, the similarly-powered second prototype (BuNo 124587)—which was the only Skyray fitted with a sliding canopy whereas the first XF4D-1 and all production F4D-1s had clamshell canopies—joined BuNo 124586 in the flight-trial programme and both machines were used to evaluate handling. The full performance envelope could not, however, be tested as with the Allison J35 engine the aircraft was seriously underpowered and, even without full military load, could not reach its design top speed.

As development of the engine originally intended for the Skyray was progressing slowly, the prototypes were successively re-engined with the 7,000 lb (3,175 kg) thrust non-afterburning XJ40-WE-6 and with the 11,600 lb (5,262 kg) thrust afterburning XJ40-WE-8. Although both versions of the J40 proved rather temperamental they enabled contractors' and Service pilots to explore the high-speed characteristics. The results proved sufficiently promising, particularly when the afterburning XJ40-WE-8 had been fitted, to warrant an attempt against the British-held world's speed record. For this attempt, made with BuNo 124587, Lt-Cdr James B. Verdin took off on 3 October, 1953, from the Naval Auxiliary Air Station at El Centro, California. Flying over a three-kilometre course above the Salton Sea and taking advantage of a 98·5 deg F (36·9 deg C) ambient temperature, Verdin broke the record at an average speed of 752·944 mph (1,211·487 km/h) and thus the XF4D-1 became the first carrier-borne aircraft to hold the absolute world's speed record. Thirteen days later, the same aircraft, flown this time by Douglas test pilot Bob

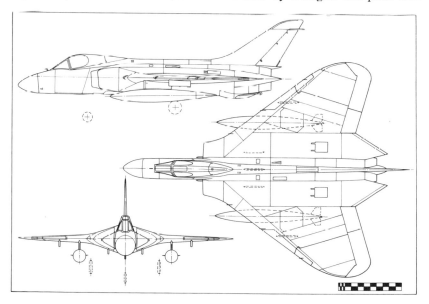

445

Rahn, was used to break the 100-kilometre closed course world's speed record at an average speed of 728·11 mph (1,171·53 km/h) over Muroc Dry Lake.

In spite of these spectacular feats, the J40-powered Skyray was not intended to go into production as its persistent troubles with the J40 led to the cancellation of the engine programme. Fortunately for Douglas, the Skyray could be adapted to take the new Pratt & Whitney J57 axial-flow turbojet which was not only more reliable but also more powerful and the F4D-1 powered by a 9,700 lb (4,400 kg) thrust* J57-P-2 was ordered into production in March 1953. In October 1953, while work on the J57-powered production version was progressing, the J40-powered XF4D-1 was used for carrier qualification trials aboard the USS *Coral Sea*.

F4D-1 (BuNo 130747) on XC-7 catapult at NATC Patuxent River; the aircraft carries two drop tanks and four rocket pods. (*US National Archives*)

On 5 June, 1954, the first production F4D-1 (BuNo 130740) exceeded the speed of sound in level flight during its maiden flight, thus justifying the basic design and the substitution of the Pratt & Whitney J57-P-2. The type, however, ran into further troubles. Not enough time had been available effectively to adapt the new powerplant to the basic airframe, and engine stall was frequently encountered at near sonic speed above 40,000 ft (12,190 m). To solve this problem it was found necessary to modify the geometry of the air intakes and to add an airflow baffle plate ahead of each intake, while changes had to be made in the geometry of the fairing around the afterburner exhaust duct to smooth the airflow. Thus no time was saved by proceeding with the J57 installation concurrently with construction of the first production aircraft and Skyrays could not be delivered to Service units until more than twenty-two months after the first flight of the J57-powered F4D-1. Late production aircraft had the J57-P-8, P-8A or P-8B which developed 10,200 lb (4,627 kg) thrust dry and 16,000 lb (7,257 kg) with afterburning.

*14,800 lb (6,713 kg) thrust with reheat.

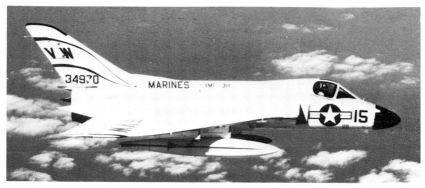

A Skyray from VMF-314 operating from MCAS El Toro, California, on 12 May, 1958. (*USMC*)

On 16 April, 1956, Composite Squadron Three (VC-3) at NAS Moffett, California, became the first Navy unit to be equipped with Skyrays when it received an initial complement of F4D-1s for Service evaluation. By then production of the type was in full swing—a total of 419 production F4D-1s were built (BuNos 130740 to 130750, 134744 to 134973, and 139030 to 139207) with the last one being delivered to the Navy on 22 December, 1958, whilst at least 230 others (BuNos 136163 to 136392) were cancelled—and Navy Skyrays first became operational in mid-1956 with VF-74 at NAS Oceana, Virginia. Less than a year later F4D-1s entered service with the Marine Corps when they were delivered to VMF-115 at MCAS Cherry Point, North Carolina. In service the aircraft, which in its production version was fitted with an Aero 13F fire control system, proved to be a very effective interceptor fighter and Maj Edward N. LeFaivre, USMC, demonstrated its spectacular climb by breaking five world's time-to-height

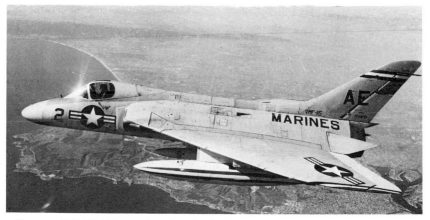

Skyray of VMF-115 over Los Angeles harbour and the Palos Verdes peninsula. (*USMC*)

447

records. On 22 and 23 May, 1958, Maj LeFaivre, flying BuNo 130745 from the Naval Air Missile Test Center at Point Mugu, California, climbed to 3,000 m (9,842·5 ft) in 44·39 sec, to 6,000 m(19,685 ft) in 1 min 6·13 sec, to 9,000 m (29,527·5 ft) in 1 min 29·81 sec, to 12,000 m (39,370 ft) in 1 min 51·23 sec and to 15,000 m (49,212·5 ft) in 2 min 36·05 sec.

Not surprisingly in the light of the superlative climb of the F4D-1, which had been so brilliantly demonstrated by Maj LeFaivre, the Skyray-equipped VFAW-3 based at NAS North Island, California, became the only Navy unit assigned to the North American Air Defense Command. In the more conventional naval fighter role, F4D-1s were used operationally from carriers and land bases by a total of eleven first-line Navy squadrons and six operational Marine fighter squadrons as well as by three reserve squadrons and a number of specialized units. In addition, the Skyray was used for flight research by NASA whilst, beginning on 18 July, 1961, an F4D-1 was used at the Naval Missile Center, Point Mugu, for a series of ten unguided rocket launches. Intended to be used as an economic sounding research rocket and using two Sparrow air-to-air missile rocket motors, the Sparroair rocket launched by the F4D-1 reached an altitude of 64 miles (103 km).

Colourful F4D-1 (BuNo 139162) from VFAW-3.
(*Arnold Photograph from AAHS collection*)

In September 1962, less than four years after the last Skyray had been delivered, the F4D-1s were re-designated F-6As under the new Tri-Service designation system, although, by that time only three front-line squadrons (VFAW-3, VMF-114 and VMF-531) and three reserve units (VF-881, VF-882 and VMF-215) were still equipped with Skyrays since the type lacked the multi-mission capability desired by the Navy.

The Skyray had been nicknamed the 'Ten-minute killer' as its primary mission consisted of a fast climb to altitude, interception and destruction of enemy bombers—the whole sortie lasting only a few minutes. The aircraft never had to fire its guns in anger but, in a twist of fate, contributed to more peaceful developments. Loaned in 1958 to General Electric, the second XF4D-1 (BuNo 124587) was used by this company initially to flight-test its

The second Skyray prototype serving as a testbed for the CJ805-3 turbojet. (*General Electric*)

J79 military engine and later its 11,000 lb (4,990 kg) thrust CJ805-3 turbojet which was being developed to power the Convair 880 jet transport.

A progressive development of the Skyray with improved all-weather capability was studied as the F4D-2N but was eventually built in prototype form as the F5D-1 Skylancer. Though relatively short-lived, and finally retired in 1964, the F4D remains none the less a significant type as, in addition to breaking five world's time-to-height records and the world's 100-kilometre closed-circuit speed record, it became the first carrier-borne fighter to break the world's absolute speed record and the first Navy fighter capable of Mach 1 performance in level flight.

Span 33 ft 6 in (10·21 m); length 45 ft 3 in (13·79 m); height 13 ft (3·96 m); wing area 557 sq ft (51·747 sq m). Empty weight 16,024 lb (7,268 kg); loaded weight 22,008 lb (9,983 kg); maximum weight 27,116 lb (12,300 kg); wing loading 39·5 lb/sq ft (192·2 kg/sq m); power loading with J57-P-8 1·4 lb/lb. Maximum speed 722 mph (1,162 km/h) at sea level and 695 mph (1,118 km/h) at 36,000 ft (10,975 m); cruising speed 520 mph (837 km/h); initial rate of climb 18,300 ft/min (5,580 m/min); service ceiling 55,000 ft (16,765 m); normal range 700 miles (1,127 km); maximum range 1,200 miles (1,931 km).

Armament. Four wing-mounted 20-mm cannon. External stores up to 4,000 lb (1,814 kg) of bombs, rocket pods or Sidewinder air-to-air guided missiles or seven wing and fuselage points or two 150-US gallon (568-litre) or 300-US gallon (1,136-litre) drop tanks.

F4D-1 Skyray, BuNo 9162, in the colourful markings of All-Weather Fighter Squadron Three (VFAW-3). (*AAHS collection*)

The Stiletto. (*USAF*)

Douglas X-3 Stiletto

Conceived as a research vehicle to obtain experience for the design of future high-speed combat aircraft, the X-3 had one of the longest gestation periods of any Douglas-designed aircraft. As early as 1941, at the request of the USAAF, Douglas had begun to investigate supersonic flight and on 30 December, 1943, the company had been specifically asked to determine the feasibility of designing an aeroplane capable of flying at sustained speeds beyond Mach 1. Following a series of conferences held throughout 1944 between Air Technical Service Command and Douglas representatives, a Phase I proposal was submitted in January 1945. With this proposal plans were made to undertake initial design, prepare preliminary specifications, conduct wind-tunnel model testing, build a mock-up and draft detailed specifications for this research aircraft. However, even though this proposal was endorsed by the USAAF on 30 May and a contract signed by the Secretary of War on 20 June, 1945, the aircraft did not fly until 20 September, 1952.

The basic performance requirements included a top speed of Mach 2 at 30,000 ft (9,145 m) and an endurance of 30 minutes, while from the onset it was felt that the aircraft should not be catapulted or carried aloft by a mother aeroplane but should be able to take-off and land under its own power on a conventional runway. The task thus facing the design team led by Frank N. Fleming was particularly arduous and many configurations and powerplant installations were proposed and studied until the late summer of 1948 when a final configuration was selected. During this three-year initial design phase several powerplant alternatives were evaluated, including single- and twin-jet configurations with or without thrust augmentation by means of either main engine reheat, auxiliary rocket engines, pulse jets or ramjets during the transonic regime. Wing configurations under consideration included delta and low aspect ratio designs while fuselage cross-section was kept at a minimum to reduce aerodynamic drag and kinetic heating. Difficulties slowing progress stemmed from the limited endurance of most of the proposed configurations, from inexperience in designing structures capable of absorbing the heat generated during sustained flight at twice the speed of sound and from the need to devise a safe means of emergency escape for the pilot.

Finally, the Douglas Model 499C configuration showed considerable promise and in August 1948 the USAF authorized construction of a detailed full-size mock-up. At this stage the aircraft was anticipated to have a gross weight of around 23,000 lb (10,433 kg) and was to be powered by two 4,500 lb (2,041 kg) thrust—6,000 lb (2,722 kg) thrust with afterburner—Westinghouse XJ46-WE-1 turbojets with which a 10-minute endurance at Mach 2 and 35,000 ft (10,670 m) was considered possible. It was also planned that the aircraft would be fitted with a jettisonable nose and pressurized cockpit section to facilitate emergency pilot escape at high speeds.

Mock-up inspection took place between 6 and 9 December, 1948, by which time the jettisonable nose section, which in wind-tunnel tests had been found to create aircraft instability, had been replaced by a conventional nose section with downward-operating pilot ejector seat. The mock-up inspection team, which included Maj Charles E. Yeager who on 14 October, 1947, had become the first pilot to exceed the speed of sound in level flight, was impressed by the quality of workmanship and great detail shown in the mock-up, these being indicative of the amount of research and engineering effort expended during the course of the initial Phase I contract. There were 96 comments submitted by the inspection team but

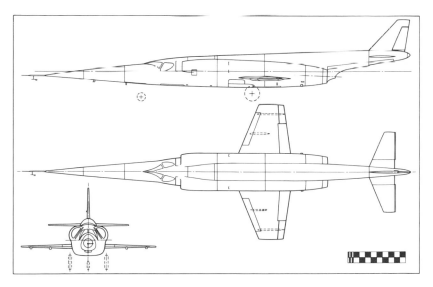

The camera angle accentuates the diminutive span of the X-3's thin wings.
(*MDC*)

this was not considered excessive in view of the complexity and experimental nature of the aircraft. On the basis of the mock-up inspection team's report and from additional data submitted by the manufacturers, the USAF approved on 30 June, 1949, Phase II of the project and ordered two flying prototypes (49-2892 and 49-2893) and one fatigue and structural test airframe.

During the course of the next year there were several developments affecting the future of the programme. The most significant change was that the developed Westinghouse J46 required an increase in diameter beyond the limits imposed by the narrow cross-section of the X-3 fuselage. Consequently, it was decided to install a pair of 3,370 lb (1,529 kg) thrust— 4,900 lb (2,223 kg) thrust with afterburner—Westinghouse XJ34-WE-17 turbojets on the first prototype and to suspend work temporarily on the second. The reduction in total available thrust of just over 18 per cent became a source of major concern and NACA (National Advisory Committee for Aeronautics) were asked to study ways of increasing the power of the XJ34-WE-17. Studies were made of water injection and liquid ammonia injection systems but neither proved successful enough for adoption and, consequently, the X-3 was left seriously underpowered. NACA contribution to the X-3 programme was, however, not limited to powerplant improvement studies but also included free-fall tests with a quarter-scale model which disclosed the need to modify and strengthen the boom supporting the tail surfaces. While all this work was being done Douglas suggested and obtained approval for the substitution of 629 lb (285 kg) of titanium instead of the 1,024 lb (464 kg) of stainless steel in various critical airframe components.

Construction of the single X-3 prototype—the second test vehicle being cancelled due to powerplant problems—was begun in early 1950 and completed in September 1951, seven years and nine months after initial discussions. The aircraft had a slender fuselage with an extremely long tapered nose containing most of the 1,200 lb (544 kg) of instrumentation, much of it specially designed for the X-3 and supplied by NACA. The pressurized cockpit was fitted with a downward ejector seat which was also an electrically-operated lift for the pilot's use on the ground. For emergency evacuation on the ground the side cockpit windows could be jettisoned by the pilot or ground crew. The two turbojets were mounted side by side midway in the fuselage and were fed from two fuel tanks, one behind the pilot and beneath the air ducts and one located in the tail boom above the downward sloping afterburners. The diminutive wings had a span of only 22 ft 8¼ in (6·91 m), an aspect ratio of 3 and a 4½ per cent thick modified diamond aerofoil, and were fitted with split trailing-edge flaps. The tricycle undercarriage retracted into the fuselage.

Due to a number of problems, particularly leakages in the fuel system, flight trials were delayed a further year following the completion of the aircraft. Finally, the X-3 (49-2892) was transferred to the flight test centre at Edwards AFB where, on 20 September, 1952, Douglas test pilot William

E. Bridgeman took it on an 18-minute first flight. From then until 30 June, 1953, the contractor's demonstration programme was conducted at Edwards AFB. Few technical problems were encountered during this period but, due to the insufficient thrust developed by the two Westinghouse XJ34-WE-17s, the aircraft failed to reach its design maximum speed and was found to be only slightly supersonic in a dive (a maximum of Mach 1·21 was reached on 28 July, 1953). In level flight top speed was only 706 mph at 20,000 ft (1,136 km/h at 6,095 m)—·987 Mach. As little or no hope of improving the X-3 performance existed, the USAF cancelled its programme after only six flights with the aircraft and the X-3 was transferred to the High Speed Flight Station of NACA at Edwards AFB where a total of 20 research flights were made by NACA pilots between 23 August, 1953, and 23 May, 1956. Finally, the X-3 was transferred to Wright-Patterson AFB for permanent display at the Air Force Museum.

The X-3 landing at Edwards AFB, California, with braking parachute deployed.
(*NA & SM*)

In spite of its disappointing performance, the X-3 contributed greatly to development of high-speed aircraft, and data obtained with this aircraft were distributed by NACA throughout the United States aerospace industry. X-3 influence was found in the Lockheed F-104 which featured diminutive straight wings, long pointed fuselage, undercarriage retracting into the fuselage and, at least initially, downward ejector seat, items which were all reminiscent of features characterizing the earlier Douglas research aeroplane. However, the X-3's most significant contribution to the advancement of the state-of-the-art was the pioneering by Douglas of fabrication and construction techniques with titanium.

Span 22 ft 8¼ in (6·91 m); length 66 ft 9 in (20·35 m); height 12 ft 6$\frac{5}{16}$ in (3·82 m); wing area 166·5 sq ft (15·468 sq m). Empty weight 14,345 lb (6,507 kg); loaded weight 20,800 lb (9,435 kg); maximum weight 22,400 lb (10,160 kg); wing loading 124·9 lb/sq ft (609·9 kg/sq m); power loading 2·1 lb/lb. Maximum speed 706 mph (1,136 km/h) at 20,000 ft (6,095 m); initial rate of climb 19,000 ft/min (5,790 m/min); absolute ceiling 38,000 ft (11,580 m); endurance 1 hr at 590 mph (950 km/h) at 30,000 ft (9,145 m).

A tanker-configured A-3B (BuNo 142656) from VAH-11 during a refuelling exercise over the Caribbean Sea in March 1964. (*USN*)

Douglas A-3 (A3D) Skywarrior

Biggest and heaviest aircraft ever designed for routine use from an aircraft carrier, the Skywarrior was the Navy's first twin-jet nuclear bomber and has been in service for over thirty yers. Design of this truly great aircraft was undertaken in early 1947 in answer to an RFP (Request for Proposals) circulated to selected aircraft manufacturers by the Bureau of Aeronautics. At that time the aircraft was intended for use aboard the new super carrier being planned by the Navy, and the RFP specified that the bomber was to be capable of carrying a 10,000-lb (4,536-kg) nuclear device a distance of 2,000 naut miles (3,700 km) and then return to its carrier. Furthermore, gross weight was not to exceed 100,000 lb (45,360 kg) and power was to be supplied by two new turbojets in the 10,000 lb (4,536 kg) thrust class.

The main constraint confronting the design team led by Project Engineer Harry Nichols and supervised by Ed Heinemann and Leo Devlin was the need to provide a large internal bomb bay accessible from the cockpit, as the nuclear device had to be armed in flight. This requirement led to the selection of a swept wing configuration with the wing mounted above the capacious bomb bay, with the crew of three grouped in a single cockpit immediately behind and above the nose radome housing the navigation and bombing radar. Two other early design decisions concerned the location of the undercarriage and powerplant. As the wing, which had a quarter-chord sweep of 36 deg and a thickness/chord ratio of 10 per cent at the root and $8\frac{1}{4}$ per cent at the tip, was shoulder mounted, it was necessary to use a narrow-track undercarriage with the main units retracting

455

rearward into the fuselage. The two engines were to be installed in individual pods ahead of and below the wing and fed from integral fuel tanks in the wing inner sections and from large tanks fore and aft of the bomb bay.

Ed Heinemann, always weight conscious, strove even harder to keep the aircraft weight well below the 100,000 lb limit as he was convinced that construction of the super carrier would be cancelled as a result of the power struggle between the USAF and USN. The result was soon evident as in mid-1948 Douglas submitted a proposal for a 68,000 lb (30,844 kg) aircraft capable of operating from *Midway*-class carriers whilst the Curtiss proposed design weighed close to 100,000 lb. The third competitor, North American, had already dropped out of contention as it did not believe that the Navy's requirements could be met by an aircraft weighing less than 100,000 lb. Although doubting that Douglas could build an aircraft two-thirds the weight of its rival, the Navy gave Curtiss and Douglas a three-month preliminary design contract to enable them to refine their proposals. Soon it became evident that indeed Ed Heinemann and his team would be able to realize their promise, and on 31 March, 1949, Douglas was awarded a contract for two XA3D-1s and a static test airframe.

Detailed design proceeded apace during the next two years under the watchful eyes of Ed Heinemann who continued his fight against excess weight. In the process, the decision was made to install a crew escape chute similar to that fitted on the F3D Skyknight as the use of ejector seats would have resulted in a 3,500 lb (1,589 kg) increase in gross weight (although this decision was wise at the time, the lack of ejector seats later led to the filing against Douglas of a $2·5 million damage suit by the widow of Lt-Cdr Charles Parker who had been unable to abandon his crippled EKA-3B during a mission over Vietnam on 21 January, 1973). Much attention was

XA3D-1 landing with tail bumper in the down position. (*MDC*)

also paid to the problems of wing flutter and of interference between the engine pod, pylon and wing and, as a result of computer calculations and wind-tunnel testing, the wing structure was strengthened whilst the pylons were extended and cambered. Meanwhile, the Navy was considering the fitting of the British-devised angled deck and steam catapult to its *Essex*- and *Midway*-class carriers. The adoption of these carrier improvements and Heinemann's success in the fight against increases in aircraft weight paid off handsomely as, before the first flight of the XA3D-1, it became evident that the new carrier bomber would be able to operate from the smaller carriers at a weight exceeding its design gross weight and would thus have a substantial growth potential.

When ordering the XA3D-1 the Navy had specified that the aircraft should be powered by Westinghouse J40s. Accordingly, Douglas fitted two 7,000 lb (3,175 kg) thrust XJ40-WE-3 engines to the XA3D-1 and proposed using 7,500 lb (3,042 kg) J40-WE-12s on the production A3D-1 Skywarriors. Powered by two of the ill-starred Westinghouse engines, the first XA3D-1 (s/n 7588, BuNo 125412) was trucked to Edwards AFB, where on 28 October, 1952, George Jansen took it up for its maiden flight. During the following months, as the higher portion of the speed envelope was progressively explored, the XA3D-1 ran into flutter problems. Fortunately for Douglas, as the use of J40s would also have resulted in the production A3D-1s being markedly underpowered, that engine's development had by then run into serious teething troubles and a proposal to fit the more powerful Pratt & Whitney J57 two-spool turbojet on the A3D-1s was endorsed by the Navy. Initially mounted on the first of fifty A3D-1s (BuNos 130352/130363 and 135407/135444), which was redesignated YA3D-1 and first flew at El Segundo on 16 September, 1953, the 9,700 lb (4,400 kg) thrust dry (11,600 lb (5,262 kg) thrust with water injection) J57-P-6 turbojets were housed in modified pods located further forward. The revised powerplant installation solved the flutter problem, and the increased thrust and reduced fuel consumption enabled the YA3D-1 to live up to expectations. Company and Service trials continued for the next two and a half years whilst additional orders were placed for the bomber version, as well as for trainer, electronic reconnaissance and counter measures, and photographic reconnaissance models.

XA3D-1: The two prototypes (BuNos 125412 and 125413) were initially powered by two XJ40-WE-3s but were later re-engined with J57-P-1s. Twin 20-mm cannon not initially installed in Westinghouse turret.

YA3D-1: Production prototype (BuNo 130352) with two Pratt & Whitney J57-P-1s. The electronic pod mounted at the top of the XA3D-1's vertical tail surfaces was dispensed with. Westinghouse tail turret originally fitted but later removed when the aircraft, by then redesignated YA-3A, was used for a variety of tests, notably from the Naval Missile Center.

A-3A (A3D-1): First production version of which 49 were built (BuNos 130353/130363 and 135047/135444). Like the XA3D-1s and the YA3D-1, the A-3As were fitted with a radar-controlled tail turret and carried a crew

A3D-1 from VAH-1 on 31 March, 1956, when this unit, the first to be equipped with Skywarriors, received its first aircraft. (*USN*)

of three (pilot, bombardier/navigator, third crewman/gunner). Two 10,000 lb (4,536 kg) thrust J57-P-1s, P-6As or P-6Bs and provision for up to six 4,500 lb (2,041 kg) thrust Aerojet JATO bottles clipped on each side of the rear fuselage (the combined thrust of the turbojets and JATOs—74,000 lb, 33,566 kg—enabled the aircraft to take off at maximum weight from the deck of an *Essex*-class carrier without being catapulted). One A3D-1 became the YA3D-1P, five were modified as YA3D-1Q/A3D-1Qs, and BuNo 130355 was experimentally fitted in 1958 with a pair of 15,800 lb (7,167 kg) thrust Pratt & Whitney J75-P-2 turbojets to serve as a test bed for the power plant selected for the Martin P6M-2 flying-boat. In 1956, BuNo 130353 became the first Skywarrior to be fitted with a refuelling probe. The A3D-1s were redesignated A-3As in 1962 and a few used for a variety of tests then became NA-3As.

NRA-3A (YA3D-1P): In 1954, an A3D-1 (BuNo 130358) was fitted by Douglas with a photographic-reconnaissance kit installed in the bomb bay and was redesignated YA3D-1P. The crew consisted of pilot, photo-navigator/assistant pilot, and photo technician/gunner. It eventually became the sole NRA-3A.

EA-3A (A3D-1Q): In 1955, five A3D-1s (BuNos 130356, and 130360/ 130363) were modified by O&R Norfolk, the Navy's Overhaul and Repair facility in Virginia, as electronic reconnaissance aircraft. Specialized equipment was fitted in the bomb bay, in a ventral fairing, and in a cheek radome on each side of the forward fuselage. The first of these aircraft was designated YA3D-1Q and two became EA-3As in 1962 with one of the two EA-3As being subsequently redesignated NEA-3A while serving with the Naval Missile Center at NAS Point Mugu, California. In addition to the standard cockpit crew, the A3D-1Qs had four ECM operators in the unpressurized bomb bay compartment.

BuNo 135411, one of the two A3D-1s used during carrier suitability trials aboard the USS *Forrestal* (CVA-59) in April 1956. (*US National Archives*)

A-3B (A3D-2): The first 123 A3D-2s (BuNos 138902/138976, 142236/142255, 142400/142407, and 142630/142649) initially differed from the A3D-1s in having a strengthened airframe (load factor of 3.4 g versus 2.67 g for the first model) and in being powered by 10,500 lb (4,763 kg) thrust J57-P-10s. The next 20 (BuNos 142650/142665, and 144626 to 144629) were fitted with a refuelling probe extending forward of the nose on the port side, removable HRU (hose reel unit) refuelling equipment, and CLE (cambered leading edge) wings incorporating inboard slats and increasing wing area from 779 to 812 sq ft (72.37 to 75.44 sq m). The HRU tanker package, which was tested in the autumn of 1966 on BuNo 138903 after the earlier installation of a rigid 'flying pipe' refuelling device had proved unsatisfactory, was fitted in the rear of the bomb bay with the drogue pod attached beneath the fuselage. The final twenty-one A3D-2s (BuNos 147648/147668) had an AN/ASB-7 bomb director system beneath a flat panel nose radome in lieu of the original AN/ASB-1A beneath a pointed radome and had the tail turret replaced with DECM (defensive electronic counter measures) equipment in a dovetail fairing. Refuelling package, nose refuelling probe, flat panel nose radome, and DECM in dovetail fairing were progressively retrofitted to most early production A3D-2s. Ninety A-3Bs were modified as KA-3Bs or EKA-3Bs in 1967-69 and two test aircraft were redesignated NA-3Bs.

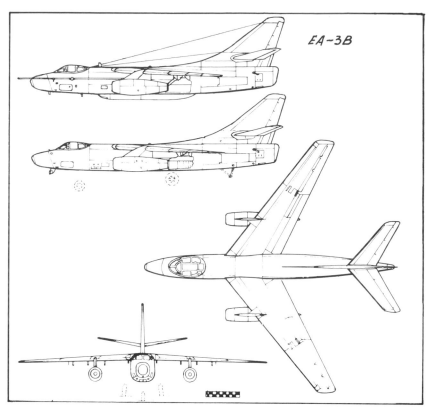

Douglas A-3B and EA-3B.

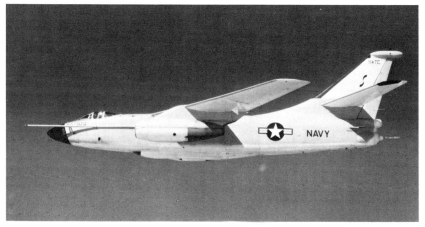

A3D-2Q (BuNo 142672) during evaluation by the Naval Air Test Center, Patuxent River, on 10 March, 1960. (*USN*)

EA-3B (A3D-2Q): This model, the only Skywarrior variant specially produced for used in the TASES (Tactical Signal Exploitation System) role, differed mainly from the A-3B in having a pressurized compartment in place of the bomb bay. This compartment, which provided accommodation for an evaluator and three ECM operators in port-facing seats, and the cockpit with reinforced canopy, were pressurized to 7.5 psi differential over flight pressure versus 3.3 psi for the bomber variants. The cockpit crew consisted of pilot, navigator/assistant pilot, and ECM operator/gunner. Electronic equipment included numerous receivers, signal analyzers, recorders, and direction finders. The A3D-2Q/EA-3Bs were distinguished externally by the installation of a ventral 'canoe' fairing housing some of the electronic equipment and square windows on the fuselage sides.

The YA3D-2Q (BuNo 142670 which was first flown on 10 December, 1958) and the first eleven A3D-2Qs (BuNos 142671/142673 and 144848/144855) were built with standard wings and gun turret, and were retrofitted with DECM in dovetail fairing. The next twelve (BuNos 146448/146459) were delivered with CLE wings and DECM. With the exception of the YA3D-2Q which initially had a test boom in place of the refuelling probe, all were delivered with the refuelling probe. Most had their original pointed nose radome replaced by the flat panel radome as fitted to late production A3D-2s. BuNo 142672 became the only A3D-2Z.

EKA-3B: Designation given in 1967 to A-3Bs modified by NARF Alameda, the Naval Air Rework Facility in northern California, as combination ECM/tanker aircraft. The HRU installation was similar to that of tanker-configured A-3Bs. The ECM equipment was in the forward portion of the bomb bay, atop the fin, in the DECM tail cone, and in external fairings beneath the fuselage and on both sides of the fuselage fore

A3D-2P from VCP-61 over the Chocolate Mountains, California, on 12 November, 1959. (*USN*)

461

and aft of the wing. NARF delivered five aircraft as EKA-3Bs and subsequently modified thirty-four KA-3Bs into EKA-3Bs. After 1975, most EKA-3Bs had their electronic gear and external fairings removed and were redesignated KA-3Bs. The crew consisted of pilot, navigator/assistant pilot/ECM operator, and third crewman/ECM operator.

ERA-3B: Designation given to eight RA-3Bs (BuNos 142668, 144827, 144832, 144838, 144841, 144846, and 146446/146447) modified for service with VAQ-33 and VAQ-34 as 'electronic aggressors.' To exercise naval defences by simulating electronically enemy aircraft, missiles, and ships, the ERA-3Bs were fitted with ECM equipment and chaff dispensers in a modified tail cone, a ventral 'canoe' fairing, a fin cap cylindrical fairing, and wing pods. Two ram-air turbines were fitted on each side of the fuselage to generate power for the ECM equipment. The crew consisted of pilot, navigator, and plane captain in the cockpit and two ECM evaluators in the pressurized fuselage cabin.

KA-3B: Designation initially given in 1967 to 85 A-3Bs permanently modified as tankers by NARF Alameda by removal of bombing equipment and upgrading of their fuel management and transfer systems. Thirty-four KA-3Bs were subsequently brought up to EKA-3B standards but most were later returned to the KA-3B configuration.

NA-3A and NA-3B: Designations given to A-3As and A-3Bs used for sundry tests.

NRA-3B: Designation given to RA-3Bs modified to a variety of test configurations.

RA-3B (A3D-2P): Like the EA-3B, the RA-3B photographic reconnaissance version had cabin pressurization increased from 3.3 to 7.5 psi. Twelve camera positions and mounts were provided in a pressurized compartment located in the forward portion of the bomb bay and accessible in flight so that the photo-technician could change film or adjust cameras. For night photography the aircraft carried photo-flash bombs or cartridges in the rear half of the bomb bay. The crew consisted of pilot, photo-navigator/ assistant pilot, and photo technician/gunner-ECM operator. Douglas built thirty A3D-2Ps (BuNo 142256, which was initially designated YA3D-2P and first flew on 22 July, 1958, and BuNos 142666/142669, 144825/144847, and 146446/146447). Only the last two had CLE wings, most were eventually fitted with the DECM tail cone, and all had a refuelling probe. Externally, the A3D-2Q/RA-3Bs were characterized by a camera 'jowl' fairings on both sides of the forward fuselage and a circular porthole on each side of the fuselage.

Over the years, six RA-3Bs were modified as NRA-3Bs for use as test-bed aircraft, mainly from the Pacific Missile Test Center at Point Mugu, California. After serving at Point Mugu, one of these NRA-3Bs, BuNo 144834, was again modified and became the sole TNRA-3B. Another RA-3B (144843) was bailed to Raytheon and flown in US Army markings during test and evaluation of the Patriot surface-to-air missile. Eight other RA-3Bs became ERA-3Bs as detailed above.

EKA-3B from Tactical Electronics Warfare Squadron 130 (VAQ-139) operating from the USS *Franklin D. Roosevelt* in August 1969. (*USN*)

KA-3B *Luck of the Irish* from VAH-10, CVW-21, USS *Hancock*, at NAS Alameda on 15 April, 1970. (*Peter Lewis*)

A transport-configured TA-3B from the Department of the Navy's VIP Flight at NAS Alameda, California, on 24 September, 1971.
(*Peter Mancus*)

TA-3B (A3D-2T): Bombardier-navigator trainer with pressurized cabin in place of bomb bay as in A3D-2Q and crew consisting of a pilot, an assistant pilot, and a trainee in the cockpit (with the seat aft of that of the pilot facing forward instead of aft as in other Skywarrior versions) and an instructor and four bombardier-navigator trainees in forward-facing seats in the fuselage compartment. Bomb damage assessment cameras and recorders were housed in a turret-like tail fairing and a training shape for nuclear stores or a practice bomb dispenser was carried beneath each wing outer panel. The first aircraft flew on 29 August, 1959, and twelve A3D-2T/TA-3Bs (BuNos 144856/144867) were built with CLE wings, refuelling probe, and pointed nose radome. Most had this radome replaced by the flat panel radome as fitted to late production A3D-2s and were retrofitted with the dovetail fairing.

Five (BuNos 144857, 144860, and 144863/144865) were modified as VIP/staff transports with galleys, tables and airline-type seats or bunks installed in the fuselage. For most of their service life they retained the TA-3B designation; however, two of these transport-configured TA-3Bs were redesignated UA-3Bs in 1987.

In 1957, Pan American Airways seriously contemplated purchasing two demilitarized A3D-2Ts to gain experience with high-speed high-altitude jet aircraft before the entry into service of its Boeing 707s and Douglas DC-8s. However, as Douglas could not deliver these aircraft before 707s became available, the deal fell through.

TNRA-3B: Designation given in 1985 to BuNo 144834 after its conversion as a pilot training aircraft. However, this aircraft was not fitted with dual controls before to being assigned to VQ-2.

UA-3B: Designation given in 1987 to BuNos 144857 and 144865, the last two transport-configured TA-3Bs.

VA-3B: BuNo 142672, the fourth A3D-2Q, was modified in 1958-59 by O&R Norfolk as the first VIP-configured Skywarrior. Although it was to have been redesignated A3D-2Z, this aircraft retained its A3D-2Q designation until after the 1962 Tri-Service designation system came into being; it then became the sole VA-3B.

Deliveries to a fleet squadron began on 31 March, 1956, when five A3D-1s were ferried from NAS Patuxent, Maryland, to NAS Jackonsville, Florida, for assignment to Heavy Attack Squadron One (VAH-1) and soon the new carrier-borne bomber showed its might. The first public demonstration of the Skywarrior's performance was given exactly four months after its entry into service when Lt-Cdrs P. Harwood and A. Henson and Lt R. Miears flew 3,200 miles (5,150 km) nonstop and without inflight refuelling from Honolulu to Albuquerque, New Mexico, in 5 hr 40 min at an average speed of 565 mph (909 km/h). The range capability of the A3D-1 was further exhibited during the first three days of September 1956 when aircraft of VAH-1 were launched from the USS *Shangri-la* whilst the carrier was steaming the Pacific from Mexico to Oregon and flew without refuelling to their Florida homebase at NAS Jacksonville.

The following year saw the service debut of the A3D-2, the main production variant of the Skywarrior which was first delivered to VAH-2, and as more A3D squadrons were formed the US Navy acquired a new role as part of the overall strategic deterrent concept. The year was also marked by a number of spectacular Skywarrior flights including that made by Cdr Dale Cox and his crew who during a single flight on 21 March, 1957, broke the westbound US transcontinental record with a time of 5 hr 12 min 39·24 sec and the Los Angeles–New York–Los Angeles record with a time of 9 hr 31 min 35·4 sec. Two and half months later, on 6 June, two Skywarriors landed aboard the USS *Saratoga* off the east coast of Florida 4 hr 1 min after having been launched from the USS *Bon Homme Richard* off the California coast. Record flights between the San Francisco bay area and Hawaii were made twice during 1957, two A3D-2s of VAH-2 covering the distance in 4 hr 45 min on 16 July whilst on 11 October a VAH-4 Skywarrior covered the distance in 4 hr 29 min 55 sec.

Joined in the late fifties by the specialized electronic reconnaissance (A3D-2Q), photographic reconnaissance (A3D-2P) and trainer (A3D-2T) versions, the A3Ds grew in importance until a peak of eighteen squadrons was reached shortly after the last Skywarrior was delivered in January 1961. Eleven of the thirteen Heavy Attack Squadrons equipped with Skywarriors—VAH-1, VAH-2, VAH-4 to VAH-11, and VAH-13—flew A3D-2s primarily in the strategic bombing role whilst VAH-3 (redesignated RVAH-3 in 1964) and VAH-123 flew A3D-1s and A3D-2Ts in the training role. Beginning in August 1961, when VAH-7 converted to North American A3J-1s, seven Heavy Attack Squadrons exchanged their Skywarriors for Vigilantes whilst RVAH-3 flew Vigilantes alongside A3D-2T/

EA-3B, BuNo 146453, of VQ-2, at NARF Alameda, California, on 3 June 1981.
(*L. S. Smalley*)

TA-3Bs between 1961 and 1979. The remaining Heavy Attack Squadrons continued to fly Skywarriors until they were either disestablished (VAH-8 in 1968 and VAH-123 in 1971) or redesignated (VAH-2 and VAH-4 respectively becoming VAQ-132 and VAQ-131 in 1968 and VAH-10 becoming VAQ-129 in 1970).

Preceded by A3D-1Qs in service with VQ-1 and VQ-2, the long-lived A3D-2Q/EA-3Bs have been operated continuously since 1959 by these two Fleet Air Reconnaissance Squadrons. In the photographic-reconnaissance role A3D-2P/RA-3Bs equipped VAP-61 for 12 years beginning in 1959, VAP-62 between 1959 and 1969, and VCP-63 between 1959 and 1961. Normally land-based, both the EA-3B squadrons and the RA-3B squadrons have all along provided carrier detachments as required, with VQ-1 and VQ-2 continuing to do so during the late 1980s.

Progressively the Skywarrior's role evolved as the Navy relinquished its strategic bombing role and began emphasizing the use of carriers and their aircraft in the context of limited wars such as the new conflict then flaring up in Vietnam. Fortunately, the A-3 (the A3D-1 and -2 had been redesignated A-3A and A-3B in September 1961 in accordance with the new Tri-Service designation system) was a remarkably adaptable aircraft and, after flying a few conventional bombing missions over both North and South Vietnam in 1965, A-3Bs were used as tankers even before being modified into KA-3Bs and EKA-3Bs. In the tanking role, Skywarriors proved invaluable not only during the course of routine combat operations but also when refuelling aircraft about to run out of fuel short of their carrier or having sustained battle damage to their fuel system. In the process, they saved scores of lives and several hundred million dollars in equipment. Beginning in late 1967, KA-3Bs nd EKA-3Bs, the latter proving better as tankers than as ECM platforms, served first with VAW-13 and then equipped seven Tactical Electronic Warfare Squadrons (VAQ-129 to VAQ-135). During the war, EA-3Bs from VQ-1 provided much valuable

Bailed to Raytheon for use in the development programme for the SAM-D Patriot, this RA-3B in US Army markings was photographed at Fairchild AFB, Washington, on 19 May 1985. (*D. Remington via Norm Taylor*)

BuNo 142667, one of the NRA-3Bs of the Pacific Missile Test Center. The aircraft has a modified tail cone and pylons on the forward fuselage. (*L. S. Smalley*)

information on the North Vietnamese radar system while RA-3Bs from VAP-61, supplemented by crews and aircraft detached from VAP-62, were the main night reconnaissance aircraft covering the Ho Chi Minh Trail.

Following the end of the Southeast Asia War, the KA-3Bs and EKA-3Bs were rapidly phased out from Fleet squadrons but at the beginning of 1987, nearly 14 years after the war had ended, 53 Skywarriors were still operational. VQ-1 and VQ-2 then still used EA-3Bs to gather electronic intelligence, VAQ-33 and VAQ-34 were flying ERA-3Bs in the electronic aggressor role, and two reserve squadrons, VAK-208 and VAK-308, flew KA-3B tankers. In addition, other Skywarriors were operated by the Pacific Missile Center and the Naval Weapons Center or were bailed to civilian contractors (notably to Hughes which was modifying a TA-3B as a test bed for the Grumman F-14D radar). In spite of its age the Skywarrior then looked set for more years of service. However, in early 1988, following the loss of four aircraft (two EA-3Bs, one ERA-3B, and one KA-3B) in one year, the Navy appeared to be planning a faster phase-out for the venerable A-3. As retirement day approached, the Skywarrior remained the heaviest aircraft ever to be operated from a carrier, a record take-off weight of 84,000 lb (38,102 kg)—still well below the original Navy limited which Ed Heinemann had succeeded in bettering by a fantastic margin—having been demonstrated on 25 August, 1959, during suitability trials preceding the commissioning of the USS *Independence*.

Span 72 ft 6 in (22·1 m); length 76 ft 4 in (23·27 m); height 22 ft 9½ in (6·95 m); wing area 812 sq ft (75·438 sq m). Empty weight 39,409 lb (17,876 kg); loaded weight 70,000 lb (31,751 kg); maximum weight 82,000 lb (37,195 kg); wing loading 86·2 lb/sq ft (420·9 kg/sq m); power loading 2·8 lb/lb. Maximum speed 610 mph (982 km/h) at 10,000 ft (3,050 m); cruising speed 520 mph (837 km/h); service ceiling 41,000 ft (12,495 m); normal range 2,100 miles (3,380 km); maximum range 2,900 miles (4,665 km).

Dimensions, weights and performance for A-3B.

Offensive load of up to 12,000 lb (5,443 kg) in internal bomb bay—A-3A and A-3B only.

DC-7C, F-BIAR, of TAI—Transports Aériens Intercontinentaux. This aircraft, s/n 45466, was one of three Seven Seas later modified for use by the Armée de l'Air in support of the French missile and space programme. (*UTA*)

Douglas DC-7

Even though the 1945–58 period saw the debut of turbine-powered commercial transports, it was essentially dominated by well established and constantly improved piston-engined transports. Thus, in the medium- and long-range markets, the Douglas DC-4/DC-6/DC-7 series and the Lockheed Constellation/Super Constellation/Starliner series virtually had a monopoly. The superiority of the Douglas and Lockheed four-engined transports was partially the result of the fierce competition between the two rivals. The DC-7, the last of the Douglas piston-engined transports, was the product of this competition and represented the ultimate development of the basic DC-4 design.

In the late 1940s, the Wright R-3350 eighteen-cylinder radial, which in its civil form developed up to 2,500 hp, had been developed into the R-3350 Turbo-Compound series by the addition of an exhaust-driven turbine coupled to the engine crankshaft. As the development of the Turbo-Compound engine had been partially funded by the US Navy, Lockheed had first fitted two of these engines to a new version of its P2V Neptune land-based patrol bomber. Furthermore, as the new powerplant initially offered some 30 per cent more power, Lockheed saw the opportunity of improving its Constellation by fitting four of these engines to a faster, longer-ranged and stretched version of its airliner, the L.1049 Super Constellation. TWA immediately ordered Super Constellations and, thus, placed its transcontinental rivals, American and United, at a marked

468

disadvantage as the new aircraft would be able to operate across the country nonstop regardless of headwinds, a feat not within the reach of the DC-6B, yet to be introduced into service.

To meet this new challenge, American Airlines and its president, C. R. Smith, in 1951 set out to convince Douglas of the need to develop a competitive aircraft powered by four of the new 3,250 hp Wright R-3350 Turbo-Compound engines. Donald Douglas, Arthur Raymond, Ed Burton and the design team were not enthusiastic as they doubted whether a market existed for it and, thus, its design and construction would drain profit away from the well-established DC-6 line. However, American Airlines offered in January 1952 to pay $40 million for 25 of the new aircraft to supplement its fleet of fifty DC-6s, six DC-6As and twenty-five DC-6Bs. With most of the development costs paid for from the American Airlines' order, Douglas committed the new aircraft to production and resurrected for it the DC-7 designation which had not been used when the civil version of the C-74 had been cancelled. In time, the company realized a substantial profit by selling a total of 338 DC-7s, DC-7Bs and DC-7Cs, which were produced at the Santa Monica plant on the same line as the DC-6As and DC-6Bs. For the airlines, on the other hand, the DC-7 series was not quite so successful as its timing and the unreliability of its engines clearly showed that it had been developed too far from a basic design tracing its origins to the late 1930s.

DC-7: Sold exclusively to US trunk carriers (United, 57; American, 34; Delta, 10; and National, 4), the 105 DC-7s were direct developments of the DC-6B with the fuselage stretched 40 in (1·02 m) to add one row of seats. All of these aircraft were powered by four 3,250 hp Wright R-3350-18DA-2 Turbo-Compound engines driving four-blade propellers, and retained the fuel tank arrangement of the DC-6B (maximum capacity: 5,525 US

N303AA, s/n 44124, the third DC-7 acquired by American Airlines.
(*American Airlines*)

gallons, 20,914 litres). Design changes introduced on the DC-7 included the use of titanium for added fire resistance in the engine nacelles, and of a strengthened undercarriage which could be lowered at higher speeds to be used as air-brakes during rapid descent. Maximum gross take-off weight increased from 107,000 lb (48,534 kg) for the DC-6B to 122,200 lb (55,429 kg) for the DC-7. The first DC-7 (s/n 44122) was flown on 18 May, 1953, and, following receipt of its type certificate, entered service with American Airlines on 29 November, 1953.

During the 1959–60 period, Douglas modified a number of DC-7s—as well as DC-7Bs and DC-7Cs—as freighters by fitting reinforced flooring and cargo doors. Other aircraft in the DC-7 series were modified as freighters by other contractors.

DC-7B of Braniff International Airways, showing the extended engine nacelles of this version of Douglas's last piston-engined commercial transport. (*Braniff*)

DC-7B: Externally identical to the DC-7, with the exception of longer engine nacelles, the 112 DC-7Bs were powered by four 3,250 hp R-3350-18DA-4 radials and were certificated at a higher MGTOW (126,000 lb, 57,153 kg). The added weight came mostly from increased fuel tankage (up to 6,460 US gallons, 24,453 litres) obtained by extending the engine nacelles to form saddle tanks. However, the DC-7Bs delivered to US domestic trunk carriers and to Panagra were not fitted with the extra tanks but this feature was incorporated into the aircraft bought by Pan American and South African Airways. The first flight of the DC-7B was made in October 1954 (s/n 44435, later certificated and delivered to Delta as a DC-7) and Pan American introduced the DC-7B into service on 13 June, 1955, on nonstop New York to London services.

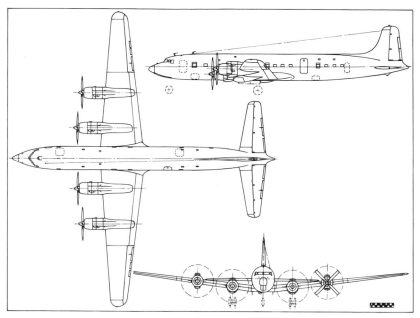

Douglas DC-7B.

DC-7C: Developed to meet Pan American's requirement for an aircraft fully capable of scheduled nonstop transatlantic services in either direction and even against prevailing winds (the DC-7B could not fly nonstop westbound against average winds), the DC-7C became the world's first truly long-range commercial transport and, thus, fully deserved its name Seven Seas which had been derived from its alpha-numeric designation within the DC series. To achieve the required range, span was increased 10 ft (3·05 m) by adding sections between the fuselage and inner nacelles. This modification not only enabled total fuel to be increased to 7,825 US gallons

OO-SFK, s/n 45945, a Seven Seas of Sabena on take-off. (*Sabena*)

471

(29,620 litres) but also moved the engines further outboard to reduce noise and vibration in the passenger cabins, an important consideration for long flights. Furthermore, the fuselage length was further increased by 42 in (1·10 m) to a total of 112 ft 3 in (34·21 m), as compared to only 93 ft 10 in (28·60 m) for the original DC-4. Maximum gross take-off weight was increased to 143,000 lb (64,864 kg) and all DC-7Cs were powered by 3,400 hp R-3350-18EA-1 radials driving four-blade propellers. The first Seven Seas (s/n 44872) was flown on 20 December, 1955, and Pan American introduced the type into service on 1 June, 1956. A total of 121 DC-7Cs were sold to US and foreign airlines and, after being phased out of passenger service, many were converted as freighters.

DC-7D: Proposed propeller-turbine powered development of the DC-7C which was to have been obtained either through production of new aircraft or through modification of existing airframes. The 5,800 eshp Rolls-Royce Tyne was the favoured engine for this programme but the sudden emergence of the 707 and DC-8 jetliners rendered it obsolete.

The DC-7's claim to fame stems from its use in developing scheduled, nonstop, long-range commercial operations across the United States, over the Atlantic and Pacific, and over the North Pole. When first introduced by American Airlines the DC-7 made possible a feat not previously feasible commercially: scheduled nonstop US transcontinental service with elapsed time reduced by 2 hr to 2 hr 15 min over the time achieved by one-stop DC-6B service (eastbound: 8 hr versus 10 hr, and westbound: 8 hr 45 min versus 11 hr). Later supplemented by DC-7Bs, the American Airlines DC-7s were joined on transcontinental routes by DC-7s of United Air Lines, which also flew the type on its Hawaiian service. Other US carriers

With DC-7Bs, such as ZS-DKE, South African Airways operated a 21-hour Johannesburg–London service. (*South African Airways*)

472

flying DC-7s and DC-7Bs on domestic routes were Eastern, Continental, Delta and National. Panagra, the only US airline operating wholly outside the United States, flew DC-7Bs between Panama and points in South America. The only non-US original DC-7B customer was South African Airways which operated it on its services from Johannesburg to London and to Australia.

After buying an interim fleet of seven DC-7Bs, offering nonstop eastbound transatlantic service, Pan American acquired twenty-five DC-7Cs to provide nonstop transatlantic flights in both directions. The appeal of these services forced several foreign flag carriers—including BOAC which had to acquire DC-7Cs when its propeller-turbine Britannia 312s ran into teething troubles, and KLM which had to switch from Super Constellations to Seven Seas, as well as Alitalia, Sabena, SAS and Swissair which were DC-6B operators—to follow Pan American's lead over the

JA6302 *City of Honolulu*, a DC-7C of Japan Air Lines. (*JAL*)

North Atlantic. Across the Pacific, Seven Seas were operated by Japan Air Lines, Northwest and Pan American. Perhaps more significant than these relatively routine operations was SAS's development of DC-7C 'polar' services from Copenhagen to Tokyo (beginning on 24 February, 1957) and to Los Angeles. Later, polar Seven Seas services were offered by Japan Air Lines (Japan to Europe), KLM (Amsterdam–Anchorage–Tokyo–Biak), and Pan American (Los Angeles–San Francisco–London).

When the major airlines began in 1958 to equip with pure-jet fleets, DC-7s were first relegated to lesser and lesser routes until either modified as freighters (unofficially designated DC-7F, DC-7BF, DC-7C(F) or DC-7CF), sold to smaller operators or traded in for jetliners. As the discarded DC-7s had relatively low operating time, initially they were absorbed rapidly by supplemental, all-cargo or smaller airlines. However, as their operating costs were higher (primarily due to engine unreliability) than those of the DC-6A/DC-6Bs, the R-3350-powered DC-7s had a shorter life than their stablemates powered by the reliable Pratt & Whitney R-2800s.

Whilst most of the DC-7s were finally scrapped, a small number found other applications including air racing (at least one aircraft was used in pylon races in the US), aerial firefighting, and tracking of satellites. In the firefighting role, the DC-7 had first been evaluated in 1953 when, during a test flight of the DC-7 prototype, the Douglas crew decided to jettison the 1,300 gallons (4,921 litres) of water ballast. This was done over the runway at Palm Springs Airport and produced a strip of water 200 ft (61 m) wide and almost a mile (1·6 km) long—so impressive that Douglas saw the potential and offered the aircraft to the Los Angeles County Fire Department for a measured test. For this purpose, a DC-7 (N301AA) was equipped with six 400-gallon (1,514-litre) tanks, water pumps and three 6-in (15·24-cm) holes in the lower left-hand side of the fuselage. Demonstrations were given at Rosamund Dry Lake in December 1953 but, although successful, the DC-7 was not adopted for this specialized role as it was then too expensive. However, when used DC-7s became available at low prices, the scheme was revived and a few aircraft were converted as aerial firefighters.

Another unique use of the type was made in France where the government had acquired three used DC-7Cs in 1963–64. Registered F-ZBCA (s/n 45061, ex-Swissair HB-IBK and SAS LN-MOG), F-ZBCB (s/n 45367, ex-TAI/UTA F-BIAQ) and F-ZBCC (s/n 45466, ex-TAI/UTA F-BIAR), they were operated under contract by the French independent

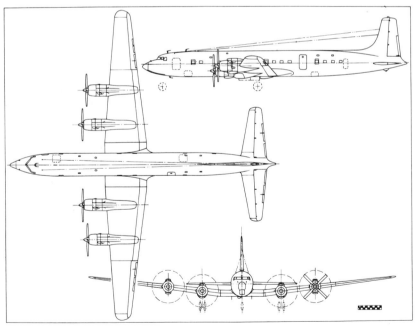

Douglas DC-7C.

474

DC-7 AMOR (ex F-BIAQ of TAI/UTU) in service with GAM 85, Armée de
l'Air. (*ECPA*)

airline UTA in support of nuclear testing operations in the Pacific Atomic
Testing Area. During 1966 these aircraft were modified by UTA for use in
the French space programme in the satellite-launcher tracking and re-entry
observation roles. To suit them to their new role, the aircraft were fitted
with a large radome above the fuselage centre, another radome beneath the
forward fuselage, a Doppler radar beneath the rear fuselage, and
additional direction-finding equipment on the port wingtip. Highly
accurate clocks and timing equipment were installed in the fuselage while

DC-7 N6322C *Mainliner Waipahu* of United Airlines passing Diamond Head, near
Honolulu. (*United Airlines*)

475

five visual observation stations were provided (one on each side of the fuselage fore and aft of the wings, and one on top). Carrying a normal crew consisting of two pilots, one navigator, one radio-operator, and two flight engineers, these aircraft provided accommodation in the forward fuselage for the six technicians operating the special tracking and timing equipment. The rear fuselage had crew rest facilities and seats for nineteen passengers. As a result of these modifications, the aircraft had an empty weight of 37,334 kg (82,307 lb), a maximum weight of 64,863 kg (142,988 lb), and a maximum operating endurance of 20 hr at 240 kt (445 km/h).

The first flight of the modified aircraft, which was designated DC-7 AMOR (Avion de Mesure et d'Observation au Réceptacle), was made on 14 September, 1966. They were initially flown by personnel of the CEV (Centre d'Essais en Vol) for the benefit of the CES (Centre d'Etudes Spatiales). Later they were operated by the Groupement Aérien Mixte GAM85 from Tahiti-Hao in French Polynesia.

The last aircraft in the DC-7 series to be delivered was a Seven Seas (s/n 45549, PH-DSR) which was handed over to KLM on 10 December, 1958. By then, however, the Boeing 707 was already in service and the first two DC-8s were undergoing tests. None the less, in its relatively brief career with major carriers, and in spite of the unreliability of its engines, the type pioneered many new routes for the new breed of jetliners.

	DC-7	DC-7B	DC-7C
Span, ft in	117 6	117 6	127 6
(m)	(35·81)	(35·81)	(38·86)
Length, ft in	108 11	108 11	112 3
(m)	(33·2)	(33·2)	(34·21)
Height, ft in	28 7	28 7	31 10
(m)	(8·71)	(8·71)	(9·7)
Wing area, sq ft	1,463	1,463	1,637
(sq m)	(135·918)	(135·918)	(152·083)
Empty weight, lb	66,306	67,995	72,763
(kg)	(30,076)	(30,842)	(33,005)
MGTOW, lb	122,200	126,000	143,000
(kg)	(55,429)	(57,153)	(64,864)
Wing loading, lb/sq ft	83·5	86·1	87·4
(kg/sq m)	(407.8)	(420·5)	(426·5)
Power loading, lb/hp	9·4	9·7	10·5
(kg/hp)	(4·3)	(4·4)	(4·8)
Typical crusing speed, mph	359	360	355
(km/h)	(578)	(579)	(571)
Rate of climb, ft/min	1,760	—	—
(m/min)	(536)	—	—
Service ceiling, ft	27,900	—	21,700
(m)	(8,505)	—	(6,615)
Range with maximum payload			
lb/miles	20,000/2,850	21,516/3,280	23,350/4,605
(kg/km)	(9,075/4,585)	(9,759/5,280)	(10,591/7,410)
Range with maximum fuel, miles	4,340	4,920	5,640
(km)	(6,985)	(7,920)	(9,075)

A-4B assigned to a reserve unit operating from NAS Los Alamitos, California. This aircraft, BuNo 142084, carries a buddy refuelling tank beneath its fuselage. (*USN*)

Douglas A-4 (A4D) Skyhawk

In production from 1954 until 1979, the Skyhawk has had a longer production life than any other type of combat aircraft in the Free World. Affectionately know as Heinemann's Hot Rod, Tinker Toy, Bantam Bomber, Mighty Mite, Ford and Scooter, the diminutive A-4 Skyhawk was the standard light attack carrier-borne aircraft of the US Navy for almost twenty years and provided the bulk of its striking power during much of the Southeast Asia War. With the US Marine Corps, A4D-1s entered service at the beginning of 1957 and at press time single-seat A-4Ms were expected to serve with the Fleet Marine Force until the end of 1989. Moreover, foreign A-4s and US two-seat Skyhawks will remain in service well into the 1990s. Quite an achievement for a combat aircraft conceived in the early fifties!

During the early phase of the Korean War Heinemann became increasingly concerned about the rising weight of contemporary fighters and the resultant performance degradation and increased cost. Trying to reverse this trend, he set his team to design as a private venture a light fighter with a thrust/weight ratio exceeding unity (as a comparison, it should be noted that the corresponding ratio for two contemporary fighters, the USAF-86A Sabre and the USN F9F-2 Panther, respectively was only 0·36:1 and 0·39:1!). When the results of this preliminary design study were presented to the Bureau of Aeronautics early in January 1952 the Navy showed much interest but, as the Service was already sponsoring several new fighter designs, Heinemann was encouraged to apply his philosophy to the design of a carrier-borne jet attack bomber. Requirements for this aircraft, intended for the nuclear strike role, included a top speed of 500 mph (805 km/h), a combat radius of 345 miles (555 km), a 2,000 lb (908 kg) weapon load, and a maximum gross weight of less than 30,000 lb (13,608 kg). Two weeks later, Heinemann was back in Washington with an almost unbelievable preliminary design for a carrier-borne aircraft which bettered every requirement by a substantial margin (normal loaded weight was less than half the limited specified by the Navy while top speed and combat radius respectively exceeded requirements by 100 mph (161 km/h) and 115 miles (185 km). Though considerable doubts regarding the project's feasibility were expressed by some BuAer members, Douglas was authorized to proceed with additional design work. The Skyhawk saga had begun.

Stressing design simplicity, Ed Heinemann and Project Engineer Ben Collins instructed their team to re-examine carefully each item in the airframe and, wherever possible, to cut down weight while preserving structural strength. Key to their endeavour was the design of a wing of modified delta planform with a quarter-chord sweep of 33 deg and a span of only 27 ft 6 in (8·38 m) which eliminated the need for wing folding mechanism and saved much weight. Though it was small and light, the wing was strong, its design load factor of $7\frac{1}{2}$ exceeding the value of 7 required by the Navy, and it was fitted with automatic leading-edge slats and split flaps on the trailing edge. The selected engine was a licence-built version of the Armstrong Siddeley Sapphire which was anticipated to give a thrust of 8,000 lb (3,629 kg) and was installed in the fuselage centre with air intakes on both sides aft of the cockpit and straight-through exhaust in the tail. Internal fuel capacity was set at 770 US gallons (2,915 litres) carried in integral wing tanks and a self-sealing cell aft of the cockpit. Other characteristic features included a tall undercarriage with the main units retracting forward into fairings protruding below the wing, and a tailplane and elevator of modified delta planform set at the rear of the dorsal fin. Preliminary mock-up inspection took place in February 1952.

The work performed during the first half of 1952 was rewarded on 21 June when Douglas was awarded a contract for one XA4D-1 (s/n 10709, BuNo 137812) and one static test airframe. Final mock-up inspection followed during October 1952—by which time a contract for nine pre-production aircraft, soon increased to nineteen (BuNos 137813/137831), had been received—and detailed design progressed swifly. However, construction of the first aircraft, which was built with production tooling, was delayed by teething troubles with the special milling machine used to produce the continuous tip-to-tip spars. Further delays resulted from the late delivery of the 7,200 lb (3,266 kg) thrust Wright J65-W-2 turbojet, and the XA4D-1, which had been rolled out in February 1954, remained grounded for four months. Finally, on 22 June, 1954—two years and one day after it had been ordered—the XA4D-1 was first flown at Edwards AFB by Robert Rahn. Less than two months later, on 14 August, the prototype was joined by the first A4D-1 and flight trials were soon shared between these aircraft and additional pre-production aircraft.

Although the initial Wright J65s, which came from existing USAF inventory and included a number of overhauled engines, were less powerful than anticipated and not completely reliable, the flight test programme progressed smoothly and revealed the need for only three minor modifications. To correct a wing buffet tendency at high speed and high altitude, two rows of vortex generators were installed on the wing upper surface near the tip of the leading-edge slats and in front of the ailerons, whilst a sugar scoop fairing was added above and behind the engine exhaust to smooth the air flow. Both modifications were devised during the flight trials and were adopted for installation on all production aircraft. The third modification, which consisted of replacing the standard rudder with one made of a single skin with external ribs, was devised to cure rudder buzzing but was not adopted as standard until the A4D-2 model. During the trials, the second pre-production aircraft (BuNo 137814) was used by Lt Gordon Grey on 15 October, 1955, to set a new 500-km (310·7-mile) closed-circuit world's record at an average speed of 695·163 mph (1,118·759 km/h).

A4D-1 from VA-94 carrying two wing drop tanks and a multiple rack beneath the fuselage. (*US National Archives*)

After manufacturer's and Bureau of Inspection and Survey trials, including the initial carrier qualification conducted on board the USS *Ticonderoga* in September 1955, the A4D-1 was cleared for delivery to Service squadrons and so began its long operational career in many forms and under several flags. The A4D-1s and A4D-2s were built with these designations but, in September 1962, they became A-4As and A-4Bs. The change of designation took place during production of the A4D-2N/A-4C version, and all subsequent Skyhawks, with the exception of eight A4D-5s, were delivered with A-4 designations. These changes are reflected in the following production history.

XA4D-1: Powered by a 7,200 lb (3,266 kg) thrust Wright J65-W-2 turbojet, the single XA4D-1 (BuNo 137812) was first flown on 22 June, 1954. No armament was installed and, initially, only the centreline rack was fitted. A large test probe extended from the nose.

A4D-1 (A-4A): A total of 165 A4D-1s (BuNos 137813/137831, 139919/ 139970, and 142142/142235) was built until 1957. These aircraft were powered by 7,700 lb (3,493 kg) thrust J65-2-4 or -W-4B turbojets and were armed with two 20-mm cannon in the wing roots. Three external racks, one beneath the fuselage and one beneath each wing outboard of the undercarriage, could be used to carry either a normal weapon load of 5,000 lb (2,268 kg) or up to three drop tanks with a combined capacity of 800 US gallons (3,028 litres). The electronic and avionic equipment was installed in the nose cone. Externally and structurally the A4D-1s were identical to the XA4D-1.

An early A4D-2, with refuelling probe beneath the starboard wing, on the flight ramp, 6 August, 1957. (*MDC*)

A4D-2 (A-4B): Characterized by the use of the new single-skin rudder with dual hydraulic boost, strengthened rear fuselage structure, single-point refuelling, and changes in the cockpit and gunsight, the A4D-2s were powered by 7,800 lb (3,538 kg) thrust J65-W-16A turbojets. The first A4D-2 flew on 26 March, 1956, and production began in parallel with that of the A4D-1. After a few had been built, the A4D-2s were fitted with an inflight probe-and-drogue refuelling system. The refuelling probe was first experimentally attached beneath the starboard wing just outboard of the undercarriage fairing, but a probe location on the starboard side of the fuselage nose was adopted for production aircraft. At the same time the centreline rack was adapted to carry a 300-US gallon (1,136-litre) buddy refuelling tank with built-in drogue and hose. A total of 542 A4D-2s was built and these aircraft were assigned BuNos 142082/142141, 142416/ 142423, 142674/142953, and 144868/145061. Several A-4Bs surplus to Navy requirements were later refurbished and sold to foreign air forces as detailed under the A-4P, A-4Q and A-4S designations.

A4D-2N (A-4C): Until the introduction of the A4D-2N, the first of which flew on 21 August, 1959, the Skyhawk had been limited to daytime operations in clear weather. To expand its capability the A4D-2N version was developed and was distinguished by the installation of terrain

A4D-2N (BuNo 148483) fitted with dual-wheel main undercarriage and drag parachute in a canister beneath the rear fuselage, for evaluation by the US Army in 1961. (*US Army*)

clearance radar in a 9 in (22·9 cm) longer nose, autopilot, angle of attack indicating system, LABS (Low Altitude Bombing System) and improved low-level ejector seat. The A4D-2Ns initially retained the 7,800 lb (3,538 kg) thrust J65-W-16A turbojets but later many received J65-W-20s with take-off rating increased to 8,400 lb (3,810 kg) thrust. A total of 638 A4D-2Ns (BuNos 145062/145146, 147669/147849, 148304/148317, 148435/148612, 149487/149646, and 150581/150600) was built up to the end of 1962.

During its last year of production, this version became the first to be produced under the A-4 designation, as well as the first to be built on a

A4D-2N from Marine Attack Squadron 225 (VMA-225) deployed aboard the USS *Shangri La* in May 1961. (*USN*)

481

different production line. This change in production facilities from the old El Segundo plant to the Long Beach plant (with some components being built in Torrance, California, and final assembly and delivery at a government-owned facility in Palmdale, California) came as a result of the company's desire to reduce expenses by closing the El Segundo plant where only the Skyhawk remained in production. The move was planned in 1961 and executed in several stages during 1962.

Much later a number of A-4Cs being phased out of fleet squadrons were refurbished and modifed as A-4Ls for delivery to reserve squadrons. Other surplus A-4Cs were made available for sale overseas, while the second A4D-2N (BuNo 145063) was used to test the five weapon racks configuration adopted for the A-4E and subsequent Skyhawk models. Two A4D-2Ns were modified in 1961 for evaluation by the US Army in competition with the Northrop N-156—the prototype of the F-5 Freedom Fighter—and the Fiat G.91 R. Fitted with a drag chute in a canister beneath the rear fuselage, and low-pressure, twin-wheel main undercarrige retracting into enlarged fairings beneath the wing, these aircraft were tested at Fort Rucker, Alabama. However, the Army agreed to relinquish to the USAF full responsibility for providing air support to ground troops, and thus had no need for aircraft such as the modified A4D-2Ns. The two aircraft were then converted back to standard configuration and delivered to the US Navy.

A4D-3: Preceding the A4D-2N, the A4D-3 was designed during 1957 as an all-weather attack aircraft powered by an 8,500 lb (3,856 kg) thrust Pratt & Whitney J52-P-2. Four development aircraft were ordered but the project was cancelled before any could be completed. In its place, the Navy ordered development of the cheaper A4D-2N which retained the existing engine.

A4D-4: Design project not proceeded with.

A-4D: Model designation not used to avoid confusion with the pre-1962 A4D basic aircraft designation.

A-4E (A4D-5): While development and production of this version were undertaken in the days of the old designation system, all but eight of the 499 aircraft built (BuNos 148613/148614, 149647/149666, 149959/150138, 150122/151201, and 151984/152100) were delivered with the A-4E designation. Powered by an 8,500 lb (3,856 kg) thrust Pratt & Whitney J52-P-6A, the A-4E also differed from the A-4C in having an improved ejector seat. Range was substantially increased as a result of the J52's 27 per cent lower fuel consumption. Two additional stores pylons, one under each outboard wing panel, resulted in an increase in weapon load to a maximum of 8,200 lb (3,719 kg) and marked a mission change from nuclear strike—for which the original Skyhawks had been optimized—to air support and conventional bombing. The first A4D-5 was flown on 12 July, 1961, and this version remained in production until April 1966. In service the aircraft were retrofitted with humped avionic compartment, many received 9,300 lb (4,218 kg) J52-P-8s, and some had the straight refuelling

A-4F Skyhawk from VA-22 during operations in the Gulf of Tonkin, August 1969. (*USN*)

probe replaced by the canted probe of the A-4M. Some also had the cockpit and canopy modified to approximate that of the A-4M. Twenty-eight surplus A-4Es were transferred to Israel in 1973.

A4D-6: Proposed development of the Skyhawk, with enlarged airframe and 11,500 lb (5,216 kg) thrust Pratt & Whitney TF30 turbofan, entered by Douglas in the light attack (VAL) design competition won in February 1964 by the LTV A-7 Corsair II.

TA-4E: Two production prototypes (BuNos 152102 and 152103) of a two-seat advanced trainer were ordered in 1964 and first flew on 30 June, 1965. They retained most of the airframe, the engine and the armament of the A-4E but were fitted with a 2 ft 6 in (0·76 m) longer fuselage incorporating a second cockpit with raised seat. Both cockpits were enclosed under a large canopy and both crew sat on zero-zero ejector seats. Internal fuel capacity was reduced by 140 US gallons (530 litres) due to the installation of the second cockpit.

A-4F: Last attack version for the US Navy, the A-4F differed from the A-4E in being powered by a 9,300 lb (4,218 kg) thrust J52-P-8A, and in having a zero-zero ejector seat, nosewheel steering and wing spoilers. Additional avionics were fitted in a humped compartment atop the fuselage, behind the cockpit. The A-4F first flew on 31 August, 1966, and a total of 147 Skyhawks of this model (BuNos 152101, 154172/154217, and 154970/155069) was built. Many re-engined with the 11,200 lb (5,080 kg) thrust J52-P-408.

TA-4F: Production version of the TA-4E powered by an uprated J52-P-8A rated at 9,300 lb (4,218 kg) thrust on take-off. A total of 238 TA-4Fs (BuNos 152846/152878, 153459/153531, 153660/153690, 154287/154343, and 154614/154657) were built with deliveries beginning in May 1966. Most TA-4Fs were modified as TA-4Js, a few became EA-4F 'electronic aggressors', and 23 became OA-4Ms.

A-4G: Generally similar to the A-4E but powered by the 9,300 lb (4,218 kg) thrust J52-P-8A, this version was ordered by the Royal Australian Navy. Assigned the BuNos 154903/154910 during construction, these eight aircraft retained these serials while in RAN service but had the added prefix N13 (*eg* 154903 became N13-154903). Deliveries were made during 1967.

TA-4G: Also delivered to the Royal Australian Navy during 1967, the two TA-4Gs (BuNos 154911/154912 with prefix N13 added in Australian service) were generally similar to the TA-4Fs of the US Navy.

A-4H: Specially designed for Israel's Heyl Ha'Avir to operate from land bases, this version was basically similar to the A-4E but was powered by a 9,300 lb (4,218 kg) thrust J52-P-8A and fitted with modified, square-tipped vertical tail surfaces. The A-4H also had a ribbon-type drag chute housed in a canister beneath the rear fuselage and was armed with two 30 mm DEFA cannon in place of the 20-mm weapons fitted to all previous Skyhawk versions. The aircraft were later retrofitted in Israel with the humped avionics compartment and extended jetpipe. Produced under USN contracts, the ninety A-4Hs were assigned BuNos 155242/155289,

An A-4P from the Fuerza Aérea Argentina on the ramp at the Tulsa plant. (*MDC*)

157395/157428, and 157918/157925. Delivery began in 1967 after the Six-Day War.

TA-4H: Two-seat trainer version of the A-4H of which ten were delivered to Israel (BuNos 157429/157434, and 157926/157929).

TA-4J: Whereas the TA-4Fs retained the complete armament and electronic equipment of the single-seat Skyhawk attack aircraft, the TA-4Js ordered for the US Naval Air Advanced Training Command had some of the tactical systems, such as air-to-air and air-to-ground missile launch equipment, omitted. They were powered by the 8,500 lb (3,856 kg) thrust J52-P-6. In service built-in armament was limited to one 20-mm cannon but this was often omitted. Beginning in June 1969, 293 TA-4Js were delivered wih the BuNos 155070/155119, 156891/156950, 158073/158147, 158453/ 158527, 158712/158723, 159099/159104, 159546/159556, and 159795/ 159798. Most TA-4Fs were redesignated TA-4Js after being modified.

A-4K: Deliveries of ten single-seat Skyhawks with square-tipped fin and rudder, drag chute beneath the fuselage and J52-P-8A engine were made to the RNZAF beginning in January 1970. The ten A-4Ks were assigned the BuNos 157904/157913 and became NZ6201/NZ6210 in New Zealand

TA-4J from Training Squadron 21 (VT-21) aboard the uss *Wasp* on 10 February, 1969. (*USN*)

485

service. The Skyhawk modernization programme is described in the New Zealand paragraph on page 496.

TA-4K: Four two-seat TA-4Ks (BuNos 157914/157917, NZ6251/NZ6254) completed the RNZAF order and were fitted with the square-tipped tail and braking chute.

A-4KU: Ordered by the Kuwait Government in November 1974, thirty A-4KUs (BuNos 160180/160209) are generally similar to the A-4M with 11,200 lb (5,443 kg) thrust J52-408A, square-tipped tail and braking chute.

TA-4KU: Designation identifying six two-seat trainers (BuNos 160210/160215) for Kuwait.

A-4L: When the A-4Cs were phased out of fleet squadrons, a number of them were overhauled for use by reserve squadrons. Fitted with improved instrumentation and humped avionics compartment, they were standardized on the uprated J65-W-20 with 8,400 lb (3,810 kg) thrust for take-off.

A-4M (BuNo 158161) from VMA-324 at MCAS Beaufort, South California, on 15 June, 1972. (*Frank MacSorley*)

A-4M: First flown on 10 April, 1970, this was a special version for the Marine Corps and introduced a number of major improvements including the installation of an 11,200 lb (5,443 kg) thrust J52-P-408A, enlarged canopy for improved visibility, doubled ammunition capacity (from 100 to 200 rpg), self-contained electrical engine starter, and electrical power generating capacity increased by 60 per cent. The A-4M was also fitted with a modified refuelling probe angled to starboard to prevent interference with the electronic equipment in the nose. The square-tipped tail surfaces and drag chute were also retained. A total of 158 (BuNos 158148/158196, 158412/158435, 159470/159493, 159778/159790, 160022/160045, and 160241/160264) were built, including the last Skyhawk which was delivered on 27 February, 1979. In 1973, thirteen early A-4Ms were transferred to Israel where they were brought up to A-4N standards. Most A-4Ms remaining in Marine service were retrofitted with a head-up display and a

486

Hughes ARBS (Angle/Rate Bombing System) featuring television and laser tracking modes.

OA-4M: Between 1978 and 1980, twenty-three TA-4Fs (BuNos 152856, 152874, 153507, 153510, 153527, 153529, 153531, 154294, 154306/154307, 154328, 154333, 154335/154336, 154340, 154623/154624, 154628, 154630, 154633, 154638, 154645, and 154651) were modified at NARF Pensacola to serve with Marine squadrons in the TACA (Tactical Air Coordinator, Airborne) role. They were fitted with an avionics hump, nose and fin caps, TACAN, ECM, and additional nav/com equipment.

A-4N: Retaining the basic airframe and uprated engine of the A-4M version, the A-4N Skyhawk II for Israel was fitted with a new navigation/weapons delivery system including a Lear Siegler digital computer, Singer-Kearfott intertial platform, and an Elliott Automation head-up display which greatly improved accuracy. In common with earlier Israeli Skyhawks, the A-4Ns substituted 30 mm DEFA cannon for the 20-mm guns of the US aircraft. First flown on 12 June, 1972, 117 A-4Ns have been built with BuNos 158726/158743, 159035/159052, 159075/159098, 159515/159545, and 159799/159824.

A-4P: A first batch of 25 ex-US Navy A-4Bs was refurbished in Tulsa, Oklahoma, by Douglas before delivery in October 1966 to the Fuerza Aérea Argentina. The first of these aircraft, which were redesignated A-4Ps, flew at Tulsa on 31 December, 1965. Subsequent purchases of A-4Ps included a batch of 25 aircraft, also refurbished by Douglas in Tulsa and delivered in 1969, and a batch of 25 aircraft refurbished by Lockheed Aircraft Service Company at Ontario, California, and delivered in 1975. Aircraft in this last batch were fitted before delivery with the Ferranti D126R Isis weapons aiming sight and most of the earlier aircraft have since received this sight. Argentine serials assigned to these A-4Ps were C-201 to C-275.

A-4PTM: As part of an ambitious expansion programme for the Tentera Udara Diraja Malaysia (TUDM, or Royal Malaysian Air Force), the Malaysian Government initiated in 1979 the acquisition of 25 A-4Cs and 63 A-4Ls surplus to USN requirements. Subsequently, budgetary constraints forced the TUDM to reduce from 68 to 40 the number of these aircraft which were to be refurbished and to scale down the planned A-4 upgrade. In the end, Singapore Engine Overhaul refurbished 52 J65 engines and Grumman modified 34 aircraft as A-4PTMs (Peculiar To Malaysia) by fitting them with a TACAN, a modern nav/com equipment, an attitude heading system, a lead computing sight, and an improved ejector seat. The first A-4PTM modified at the Grumman plant in St Augustine, Florida, first flew on 12 April, 1984. The A-4PTMs have been given the Malaysian serials M32-07 to M32-40.

TA-4PTM: As part of its Malaysian contract Grumman also modified six A-4C/A-4L airframes as two-seat trainers. Canopy and tandem seating arrangements were generally similar to those of Douglas-built TA-4s. The first TA-4PTM first flew in St Augustine on 28 August, 1984. The six

TA-4PTMs were given the Malaysian serials M32-01 to M32-06.

A-4S: In 1972 the Government of Singapore purchased forty surplus US Navy A-4Bs, held in storage at Davis-Monthan AFB, and awarded Lockheed Aircraft Service Company a contract for their overhaul and modernization, consisting of a complete inspection and repair of the airframe as well as several major modifications including the installation of solid state electronics for the communication, radio and navigation systems, redesign of the cockpit to accommodate new instrumentation and control boxes, substitution of an angled A-4M type flight-refuelling probe for the original straight probe, installation of a drag chute housed in a canister beneath the rear fuselage, the fitting of 30-mm Aden cannon in

The first A-4S for the Singapore Air Defence Command.
(*Lockhead Aircraft Service Co*)

place of the A-4B's 20-mm cannon, and the overhauling and upgrading of the J65 engine. Redesignated A-4S, eight Skyhawks (serials 600 to 607) were overhauled and modified by LAS—the first being completed in October 1973—before being delivered to NAS Lemoore, California, for use in training crews of the Singapore Air Defence Command. The last thirty-two aircraft (serials 608 to 639) were modified by LAS at Singapore,—with the first of these A-4S being delivered in April 1974.

Aircraft which were retrofitted by SAI (Singapore Aircraft Industries) with new avionics and sturdier pylons were given the A-4S-1 designation. Still later, one of these upgraded aircraft was re-engined by SAI with an 11,000 lb (4,990 kg) General Electric F404-GE-100D turbofan and was first flown in October, 1986. With the new engine, climb rate and acceleration are said to have been improved respectively by 35 and 40 per cent and field length is claimed to be reduced by 30 per cent. At press time, in early 1988, it appeared likely that all A-4S-1s and TA-4S-1s would be similarly re-engined and would also be fitted with modernized systems.

TA-4S: Ordered in 1975 for use in the Singapore Air Defense Command's pilot training programme at NAS Lemoore, the seven TA-4S (serials 651 to 657) were modified by LAS from surplus A-4B airframes. Whereas all other two-seat Skyhawks have a continuous canopy, over both cockpits, the TA-4S are unique in having separate tandem cockpits and canopies.

A-4Y: Designation initially planned but not actually used to identify A-4Ms fitted with the Hughes ARBS.

Delivery of A4D-1s to the fleet started on 26 September, 1956, when VA-72 received its first. Based at NAS Quonset Point, Rhode Island, this Atlantic Fleet unit shared with the Pacific Fleet's VF(AW)-3 at NAS Moffett Field, California, responsibility for the intensive Flight Indoc'rination Program. At its conclusion, VA-72 and VA-93 respectively became the first operational squadrons in the Atlantic and Pacific Fleets, while VA-125 was designated as the Replacement Air Group (RAG) to train Skyhawk personnel. The first Marine Corps unit to fly A4D-1s was VMA-224 at MCAS El Toro, California, which received its first aircraft during January 1957.

As production increased and new models were introduced, additional squadrons were formed while later Skyhawk models replaced the A4D-1s in the early squadrons. Thus, the A4D-2 became operational with VMA-211 in September 1957 and was followed by the A4D-2N, which entered service with VMA-225 in March 1960, and by the A-4E, which in December 1962 replaced the A-4B as the equipment of VA-23. Throughout this period Skyhawks spent most of their time in routine training interspaced with regular deployment aboard carriers of the Atlantic and Pacific Fleets, including numerous cruises in the western Pacific and Mediterranean. The least routine of these cruises was when aircraft were embarked aboard the USS *Essex* to provide air cover for the US Marine's amphibious landing in Lebanon in July 1958. It was also during one of the Mediterranean cruises that VA-34 became in August 1959 the first A4D

The seventh A4D-1 (BuNo 137819), fitted with an instrumented nose probe for use in the aircraft's evaluation programme. (*MDC*)

489

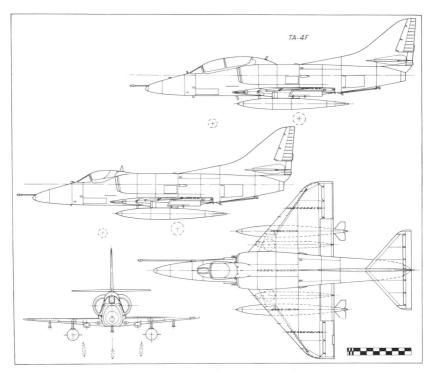

Douglas A-4E Skyhawk and TA-4F.

squadron to be deployed overseas with aircraft fitted to carry up to three Bullpup air-to-ground missiles, the new weapon which considerably increased the Skyhawk's striking power. A little over three years later, Skyhawks aboard the *Enterprise, Independence, Essex* and *Randolph* took part in the blockade of Cuba. Other noteworthy events in the Skyhawk's early operational life were the nonstop, non-refuelled, flight from El Toro, California, to Cherry Point, North Carolina (2,082 miles, 3,351 km, in 4 hr 25 min) by two aircraft of the Second Marine Air Wing, and a two-way crossing of the Atlantic between MCAS Cherry Point and NS Rota, Spain, which was made between 8 and 17 October, 1962, by sixteen A-4Cs of VMA-225 with inflight refuelling and intermediate stops in Bermuda (eastbound) and Lajes, Azores (westbound).

On 2 August, 1964, North Vietnamese torpedo-boats attacked the destroyer USS *Maddox*, initiating the infamous Gulf of Tonkin Incident. On the following day when, on orders from President Lyndon Johnson, aircraft from the carriers *Constellation* and *Ticonderoga* attacked torpedo-boats and their supporting facilities, the Skyhawk became one of the most important types in the Southeast Asia War. Throughout the war, carrier operations were in two areas, strikes against targets in North Vietnam being flown from carriers on Yankee Station in the Gulf of Tonkin while air

490

support missions over South Vietnam and Cambodia were mounted from Dixie Station south of the DMZ (de-militarized zone separating North and South Vietnams). Operations in the south were also supported by land-based Marine and Navy Skyhawk squadrons (with occasional strikes north of the DMZ and over Laos), and A-4s of VMA-211 at Chu Lai, South Vietnam, became the first unit to use for combat purposes the new SATS (Short Airfield Tactical Support) system. The SATS basically comprised a 2,210 ft (674 m) aluminium runway and required JATO take-offs and cable arresting gear for landings.

Operations in the north fell into two basic categories: major strikes and interdiction sorties. The first involved more than one squadron and a variety of aircraft, and were flown against predetermined targets such as industrial facilities, main bridges, airfields, fuel depots and the like; the second, often involving only a couple of aircraft at a time, were primarily directed against the North Vietnamese road and rail network and other targets of opportunity. In the north, the A-4s were often attacked by MiGs but their manoeuvrability proved a major asset. Flying an A-4C from VA-76 off the USS *Bon Homme Richard*, Lt-Cdr Ted Swartz even succeeded on 1 May, 1967, in helping the North Vietnamese celebrate May Day by shooting down one of their MiG-17s with Zuni air-to-ground rockets.

Initially, low-level approach to avoid detection by radar was favoured, but it was soon found that the required zoom before release resulted in an unacceptable loss in speed and manoeuvrability. Accordingly, targets were later approached at high-altitude and high-speed, SAM 2 missiles being relatively easy to dodge, and were bombed in shallow diving attacks with greater accuracy. Accuracy was also greatly improved through the use of increasingly sophisticated weapons such as Bullpup air-to-ground missiles, Walleye television guided missiles, and so-called smart bombs. None the less, the A-4 squadrons took heavy losses, especially during the initial offensive against the North.

Probably the most dangerous missions flown by A-4s over North Vietnam were those mounted to suppress flak and destroy enemy ground-to-air guided missiles. For this purpose, Skyhawks were armed with Shrike anti-radiation missiles homing on the radar guiding missiles and directing guns, and with cluster bombs to obliterate anti-aircraft gun sites.

The war in Vietnam greatly increased the need for naval pilots and led to the development of the two-seat Skyhawk. The TA-4Fs, which retained the full combat capability of the single seaters, were delivered from May 1966 and subsequently were operated in small numbers by a variety of Navy and Marine units, the primary user being the A-4 Combat Readiness Air Group (CRAG), VA-125 at NAS Lemoore. A number of TA-4Fs were later modified by installation of ECM equipment and redesignated EA-4Fs, while others were used as forward air controllers (FAC) by the Marines. The TA-4Js, on the other hand, were primarily intended for use as advanced trainers and for gunnery and deck-landing training, mostly being operated by squadrons of the Naval Air Training Command, such as VT-4

-7, -21, -22, -23, -24, -25, and -26, and by the Jet Transition Training Unit.

The single-seat A-4s were also operated by VSF squadrons to provide fighter protection for anti-submarine carriers since they required less deck space than contemporary fighter aircraft. The A-4's manoeuvrability, especially when armament and other equipment were removed to reduce weight, also led the Fighter Weapons School and several attack, fighter, and composite squadrons to use the Skyhawk as an 'aggressor' for air combat training. In 1974, the same quality also resulted in the selection of A-4Fs to replace the F-4Js of the Navy Flight Demonstration Squadron, the *Blue Angels*. In this much publicized role, A-4Fs were exchanged for F/A-18As in 1987.

Beginning in December 1967, the A-4s were progressively phased out of operations with fleet squadrons, the last carrier units to fly A-4Fs being VA-55, VA-164 and VA-212 which were decommissioned at the end of 1975 at the same time as the last of the modified *Essex*-class carriers, the USS *Hancock*. Single-seat A-4s remained in service with Navy reserve squadrons until the late seventies and by the mid-eighties only a few were used as aggressors. In service with the Navy, TA-4s fared much better and in late 1987 were still equipping seven training squadrons (VT-4, -7, -21, -22, -24, -25, and -86, with which they were expected to remain operational until replaced by McDonnell Douglas T-45 Goshawks during the early 1990s), flew as aggressors with VF-45, VF-126, VA-127 and the Fighter Weapons School and as 'electronic aggressors' with VAQ-33, and served in a variety of support roles with composite squadrons. With the Marine Corps A-4Ms are expected to remain in first-line service until the end of 1989 before replacing A-4Fs in reserve squadrons.

Ten years after the A4D-1 entered service with the US Navy, refurbished A-4Bs were delivered to the Fuerza Aérea Argentina, and during the following year the first Skyhawks specially built for overseas customers became operational with the Royal Australian Navy and the Heyl Ha'Avir. Brief summaries of foreign deliveries and service history are given here in chronological order of entry into service.

Argentina: Receiving its first twenty-five A-4Ps in the autumn of 1966, the Fuerza Aérea Argentina at the end of 1977 operated four squadrons of Skyhawks: the I and II Escuadrones de Caza-Bombaredo, IV Brigada Aérea, at the Plumerillo Air Base, Mendoza, and the IV and V Escuadrones de Caza-Bombardeo, V Brigada Aérea, at the General Pringles Air Base, Villa Reynolds, San Luis.

The Comando de Aviación Naval Argentina followed its sister Service and acquired sixteen refurbished A-4Bs in 1971. Redesignated A-4Qs and equipping the I Escuadron de Ataque, these aircraft are normally based at the Comandante Espora Base with regular deployment aboard the carrier ARA *25 de Mayo*.

When war started in the South Atlantic following the Argentine invasion of the Falklands (or, as seen from the other side, when the Malvinas were liberated) in the spring of 1982, the Fuerza Aérea Argentina (FAA) still had

For use by the *Blue Angels*, A-4Fs had their armament removed, their J52-P-8As replaced by more powerful J52-P-408As, and smoke generating cannisters installed. BuNo 154983 was photographed at NAS Memphis, Tennessee, in 1976.
(*Fred Harl via Jay Miller*)

twenty operational A-4Ps with the IV Brigade Aérea at El Plumerillo and twenty-six with the V Brigade Aérea at Villa Reynolds whilst the 3ª Escuadrilla Aeronaval de Caza y Ataque, Comando de Aviación Naval (CANA), had three A-4Qs at Puerto Belgrano (Comandante Espora) and eight A-4Qs aboard the ARA *25 de Mayo*. During the brief but costly war, gallant FAA and CANA pilots flew their Skyhawks at the limit of their range and were credited with sinking HMS *Ardent*, HMS *Antelope*, and HMS *Coventry*, and damaging several other Royal Navy ships. Their losses, however, were grievous, with Sea Harriers, surface-to-air missiles, and operational accidents resulting in the loss of nineteen A-4Ps and three A-4Qs.

Notwithstanding post-Falklands War reports according to which the FAA and CANA were to receive up to thirty second- or third-hand Skyhawks from Israel, it appears that none of these aircraft reached Argentina. Hence, by the mid-eighties all remaining FAA Skyhawks, about twenty aircraft, were assigned to the V Brigade Aérea and the CANA had but a handful of flyable A-4Qs.

Australia: The Fleet Air Arm Group of the Royal Australian Navy operated two squadrons of Skyhawks from RANAS Nowra, New South Wales. VF-805 was an operational squadron which was regularly deployed aboard the carrier HMAS *Melbourne* whereas VC-724 was a training squadron. Over the years, these two squadrons were equipped with eight A-4Gs and two TA-4Gs delivered in July 1967, and eight ex-US Navy A-4Fs (BuNos 155051/155052, 155055, 155060/155063, and 155069) and two ex-USN TA-4Fs (BuNos 154647 and 154648) delivered in August 1961. After HMAS *Melbourne* was withdrawn from service in June 1982, the surviving RAN Skyhawks were briefly operated by VC-724 before being sold to New Zealand.

TA-4G (N13-154911) of VC-724, a Royal Australian Navy training squadron based at RANAS Nowra, New South Wales. (*RAN*)

Israel: Largest operator of Skyhawks outside the United States, the Heyl Ha'Avir has acquired at least 258 A-4s and TA-4s since the autumn of 1967. Aircraft received by this Service include 90 A-4Hs, 10 TA-4Hs and 117 A-4Ns which it had ordered, plus at lest 28 A-4Es and 13 A-4Ms delivered as part of the American emergency aid during the Yom Kippur War of 1973. During that conflict, the Skyhawks provided most of the short-range striking power on the Sinai and Golan Heights fronts, and emerged victorious in several encounters with fighters. However, losses to ground fire and guided missiles were quite high, especially during the first week when the Heyl Ha'Avir was fighting defensively. The situation improved markedly when Israel took the offensive and neutralized most of the Egyptian and Syrian Soviet-built radar-guided anti-aircraft guns and missiles through intensive use of ECM techniques.

A-4H Skyhawks of the Heyl Ha'Avir. The lead aircraft is BuNo 155246.
(*Heyl Ha'Avir*)

494

A quartet of A-4Gs from VF-805 on the aft deck of HMAS *Melbourne* in April 1972. (*RAN*)

Although over the years Israeli Skyhawks have been upgraded, notably by installation of extended jetpipes for infra-red suppression and of various ECM systems, they began losing some of their importance for the Heyl Ha'Avir following the entry into service of the IAI Kfir in 1975. Consequently, some A-4Es and TA-4Hs were made available for export. Nevertheless, Israeli A-4s took part in major operations in Lebanon in 1982 and since then have continued to fly retaliatory strikes against 'guerilla' bases in Lebanon. The A-4 was to have been replaced by the IAI Lavi but after this indigenous project was abandoned in 1987 it appeared that the Skyhawk would remain in service with the Heyl Ha'Avir until the mid-1990s.

An Israeli A-4N landing at an air base in the Sinai with drag chute deployed and spoilers in the up position. (*Heyl Ha'Avir*)

495

New Zealand: The RNZAF took delivery of the first of its ten A-4Ks and four TA-4Ks on 16 January, 1970. Initially assigned to an operational unit, No. 75 Squadron at Ohakea, and to a training unit, No. 14 Squadron, all remaining aircraft were later assigned to No. 75 Squadron.

Following the acquisition of ex-Australian aircraft, eight single-seaters and two two-seaters, the RNZAF re-formed No. 2 Squadron at Ohakea in December 1984 to act as a conversion unit and to develop operational tactics and procedures. A major upgrading programme was initiated in the mid-eighties and 22 RNZAF Skyhawks were due to be modified before the end of 1989. In the process they will be fitted with a Westinghouse APG-66NZ radar (similar to that used on the General Dynamics F-16 but optimized for maritime search and track modes), a Ferranti head-up display, HOTAS (hands-on-throttle-and-stick) control, a radar warning receiver, and a chaff/flare dispenser. They may also later be re-engined with the F404 turbofan.

NZ6205, one of ten A-4K Skyhawks delivered to the RNZAF in 1970, seen in service with No. 75 Squadron. (*RNZAF*)

Singapore: Following the delivery of eight A-4S and three TA-4S rebuilt in California, the Singapore Air Defence Command took delivery of 32 additional A-4S and four TA-4S refurbished in Singapore. Pilot training began in 1974 with US modified aircraft at NAS Lemoore, and the first operational unit, No.142 Squadron, was formed at Changi in 1975, with No. 143 Squadron following a year later. These two squadrons moved to Tengeh where they were joined in 1982 by the newly formed No. 145 Squadron.

Kuwait: In 1975 the Kuwait Air Force ordered thirty A-4KUs and six TA-4KUs to equip two squadrons. The first aircraft were delivered in 1976 for initial crew training at NAS Lemoore under USN supervision. The surviving aircraft have been reported stored since 1984 at the Ahmad al

Jabar Air Base.

Indonesia: In 1979, the TNI-AU first ordered an initial batch of refurbished Skyhawks (fourteen A-4Es with extended jetpipes and two TA-4Hs) from Israel to equip Skwadron Udara 11 at Maidun. A similar repeat order enabled Skwadron Udara 12 to be equipped at Pakanbaru in 1985.

Malaysia: The thirty-four A-4PTMs and six TA-4PTMs refurbished by Grumman from surplus A-4C and A-4L airframes have been used by the TUDM to equip No. 6 Squadron, from 1985, and No. 9 Squadron, from 1986, both based at Kuantan.

OA-4M, BuNo 154306, of H&MS-32 flying over the North California coast in December 1981. (*USMC*)

Data for A-4A, A-4E, TA-4F and A-4M appear on page 498.

497

	A-4A	A-4E	TA-4F	A-4M
Span, ft in	27 6	27 6	27 6	27 6
(m)	(8·38)	(8·38)	(8·38)	(8·38)
*Length, ft in	39 4¾	40 1½	42 7¼	40 3¾
(m)	(12·01)	(12·23)	(12·99)	(12·29)
Height, ft in	15 0	15 2	15 3	15 0
(m)	(4·57)	(4·62)	(4·65)	(4·57)
Wing area, sq ft	260	260	260	260
(sq m)	(24·155)	(24·155)	(24·155)	(24·155)
Empty weight, lb	8,400	9,853	10,602	10,465
(kg)	(3,810)	(4,469)	(4,809)	(4,747)
Loaded weight, lb	14,875	16,216	15,783	—
(kg)	(6,747)	(7,355)	(7,159)	—
Maximum weight, lb	20,000	24,500	24,500	24,500
(kg)	(9,072)	(11,113)	(11,113)	(11,113)
Wing loading, lb/sq ft	57·2	62·4	60·7	—
(kg/sq m)	(279·3)	(304·5)	(296·4)	—
Power loading, lb/lb st	1·9	1·9	1·7	—
Maximum speed, mph at				
sea level	664	673	660	670
(km/h)	(1,069)	(1,083)	(1,062)	(1,078)
Rate of climb, ft/min	—	5,750	—	8,440
(m/min)	—	(1,753)	—	(2,573)
Service ceiling, ft	—	—	38,700	—
(m)	—	—	(11,795)	—
Normal range, miles	—	1,160	1,350	—
(km)	—	(1,865)	(2,175)	—
Maximum range, miles	—	2,525	2,200	2,055
(km)	—	(4,065)	(3,540)	(3,305)

*Excluding flight refuelling probe

Douglas B-66 Destroyer

Conceived as a straightforward development of the A3D Skywarrior and intended as a tactical light bomber and reconnaissance aircraft to succeed to the obsolete B-26 Invader, the B/RB-66 Destroyer evolved into a substantially redesigned machine which proved particularly successful in the late sixties as an electronic countermeasures (ECM) aircraft.

Initial B-26 operations in Korea had made it painfully clear that the USAF had an urgent need for a tactical jet bomber capable of day and night operations and possessing substantially improved performance. To meet this requirement, the USAF showed interest in the XA3D-1 carrier-borne twinjet bomber which was then still one year from entering flight trials. The idea was to order a land-based version of the aircraft which would incorporate minimum changes to adapt it to its new role. Accordingly, in February 1952 the USAF awarded Douglas an initial contract for five pre-production RB-66As. Additional Air Force alterations changed this planned 'off-the-shelf buy' into virtually a new project bearing only a strong family resemblance to its naval ancestor.

Redesign of the aircraft was entrusted to a Long Beach Division team under the leadership of John C. Buckwalter and work began in early 1952. Some twenty-seven months later the first RB-66A (52-2828) was rolled out and, although looking much like a development of the Skywarrior, differed from its forebear in many and important respects affecting not only items of equipment but also structural and aerodynamic features. All items of naval equipment, such as powered wing folding mechanism, arrester hook and specially strengthened undercarriage, were dispensed with, and the Pratt & Whitney J57 turbojets were replaced by Allison J71s. The wing had a revised planform to reduce thickness/chord ratio at the root, new ailerons and flaps, and a 2 per cent reduction in incidence. The revised fuselage incorporated a new cockpit with the pilot sitting centrally forward and the navigator and gunner/camera operator immediately aft under a new canopy and with upward-operating ejector seats in place of the chute used in the Skywarrior. Main new types of equipment included a battery of four cameras in the centre fuselage bay, thermal de-icing, APS-27 and K-5 bombing and navigation radar, and a new remotely-controlled General Electric tail turret with twin 20-mm cannon.

First flight, from Long Beach to Edwards AFB, was made on 28 June, 1954, with George R. Jansen in command, and production, at the Long Beach and Tulsa plants, totalled 209 aircraft in five versions. Many of these aircraft were later modified to produce the models described below.

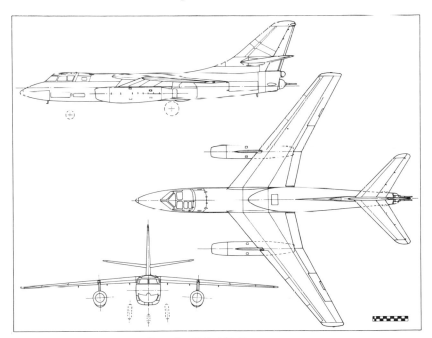

Douglas RB-66B Destroyer.

499

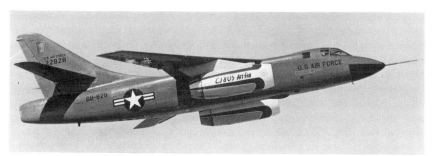

The first RB-66A-DL (52-2828), serving as a testbed for the CJ805-23 aft-fan engine. (*General Electric*)

RV-66A-DL: Pre-production version of which five were built (52-2828/52-2832) in the Long Beach plant and fitted as reconnaissance aircraft with four cameras and carrying photo-flash bombs and cartridges. Two 9,570 lb (4,341 kg) thrust Allison YJ71-A-9 turbojets in underslung nacelles powered this version. None of these aircraft were used operationally but the first RB-66A was subsequently bailed out to General Electric to flight-test first the 11,200 lb (5,080 kg) thrust CJ805-3 turbojet and then the 16,000 lb (7,257 kg) thrust CJ805-23 aft-fan engine in support of the Convair 880 and 990 commercial transport programmes.

B-66B-DL: Design began in September 1952 and, first flown on 4 January, 1955, the B-66B was the only bomber version of the Destroyer and 72 of these aircraft (53-482/53-507, 54-477/54-505, 54-548/54-551, and 55-303/55-314) were built in the Long Beach plant. An additional 69 B-66Bs (55-315/55-383) were cancelled. Initially powered by 10,200 lb (4,627 kg) thrust Allison J71-A-11s but later fitted with improved J71-A-13s of similar rating, the B-66B retained the crew of three and the tail turret of the RB-66A but carried up to 15,000 lb (6,804 kg) of bombs in place of the cameras. Subsequent modifications resulted in the EB-66B and NB-66B.

B-66B-DL (54-479) at the Air Force Flight Test Center, Edwards AFB, California, on 26 November, 1957, (*USAF*)

500

EB-66B-DL: During the early phase of the war in Southeast Asia, thirteen B-66Bs (53-482, 53-484/53-487, 53-489, 53-491/53-493, and 53-495/53-498) were modified to serve in the ECM role as radar jammers. The tail turret and provision for carrying bombs were dispensed with and an electronic warfare officer (EWO) replaced the bomb-aimer/gunner. Automatic jamming equipment was fitted in the nose, in the tail (in the space previously occupied by the turret), and in the bomb bay. Numerous antennae protruded from the aircraft and chaff dispensing pods were carried.

NB-66B-DL: As part of an R & D programme jointly funded by the Air Force, Army and Navy, two B-66Bs (53-488 and 54-481) were modified for high-altitude parachute drops of heavy items such as Gemini and Apollo space capsules. The bomb bay doors were removed and the large items to be para-dropped were carried semi-externally beneath the fuselage.

RB-66B-DL: Also built in the Long Beach plant, the RB-66B was the production version of the RB-66A from which it differed in being powered by Allison J71-A-11 or -A-13 turbojets, in being fitted with a removable flight-refuelling probe on the right side of the forward fuselage, and in minor equipment details. The first of 145 RB-66Bs (53-409/53-481, 54-417/54-446, and 54-506/54-547) was flown in March 1955 and this version was the numerically most important variant. Later fifty-two of these aircraft were modified as EB-66Es.

One RB-66B (53-412) was modified to test the radar and control system of the Boeing Bomarc ground-to-air missile and was fitted with a pointed radome protruding forward. Another RB-66B (53-421) was used to test the Pratt & Whitney TF33 turbofan and the nacelle developed by Douglas to house the JT3D civil version in the DC-8-50. In this configuration the aircraft was first flown on 2 March, 1961. Fourteen months later, the 17,000 lb (7,711 kg) thrust TF33-P-3 on the starboard side was replaced by a 21,000 lb (9,525 kg) thrust TF33-P-7. At the conclusion of its test programme, the aircraft was refurbished by Pratt & Whitney and returned to the USAF.

RB-66B-DL (53-421) experimentally fitted with two 17,000 lb thrust TF33-P-3 turbofans. (*Pratt & Whitney*)

501

EB-66C-DT: Redesignated RB-66Cs with upgraded ECM equipment.

RB-66C-DT: Built in the Tulsa plant, which had been selected as a second production source at the time of the Korean War, the RB-66Cs were seven-seat electronic reconnaissance and countermeasures aircraft fitted with specialized equipment to locate and identify the function and frequency of enemy radar. The crew consisted of pilot, navigator and EWO in the cockpit and four additional EWOs in the pressurized compartment which replaced the bomb/camera bay of the B/RB-66B. Powered by two J71-A-11 or -A-13 turbojets, thirty-six RB-66Cs (54-447/54-476, and 55-384/55-389) were built and this model was first flown on 29 October, 1955. ECM equipment was carried in wingtip pods, in the nose and, later, in place of the tail turret. Chaff dispensing pods could be fitted beneath the wing outboard of the engine nacelles in place of the drop tanks carried by other versions.

EB-66C-DT (54-469) from the 42nd Tactical Electronic Warfare Squadron, 355th Tactical Fighter Wing, operating from Takhli Air Base, Thailand, in March 1970. (*USAF*)

WB-66D-DT: Final production version of the Destroyer, the WB-66D was built in the Tulsa plant as a weather reconnaissance aircraft to be used in combat areas. It thus retained the flight-refuelling probe and the tail turret with its associated MD-1A fire control system of earlier production models but had no provision for bombs or cameras. The flight crew consisted of pilot, navigator and gunner in the front cockpit, and was supplemented by two weather equipment operators who shared the pressurized bomb bay compartment with their specialized equipment. Powered by two J71-A-13s, thirty-six aircraft of this model were built (55-390/55-425) and the WB-66D was first flown on 26 June, 1957. The last Destroyer, a WB-66D, was delivered in June 1958. The first WB-66D (55-390) was modified in the early seventies to flight test the Hughes APG-63 radar intended for the McDonnell Douglas F-15 Eagle. Two other WB-66Ds (55-408 and 55-410) were modified by Northrop as X-21A-NOs.

EB-66E-DL: To supplement the EB-66Bs as active radar jammers, fifty-two RB-66Bs (53-479/53-480, 54-417, 54-419/54-420, 54-423/54-424,

502

The first Northrop X-21A (ex-WB-66D-DT) during its flight trials programme. (*Northrop Corporation*)

54-426/54-427, 54-429, 54-431, 54-434/54-435, 54-438/54-443, 54-445/ 54-446, 54-506/54-511, 54-514/54-516, 54-519/54-529, 54-531/54-534, 54-536/54-537, 54-539/54-540, 54-542, and 54-546) were modified in the mid-sixties. The crew and most of the ECM equipment was similar to that fitted to the EB-66Bs.

X-21A-NO: To demonstrate the laminar flow control system developed by Dr Werner Pfenninger, a Swiss-born scientist on its staff, Northrop undertook to modify extensively two WB-66Ds (55-408 and 55-410) for use in a series of test flights. First flown on 18 April, 1963, the X-21A was fitted with a completely new wing of substantially increased span and area (see technical data table), sweep reduced from 35 deg to 30 deg, and incorporating span-wise slots through which the turbulent boundary air was sucked by means of bleed burn turbines housed in underwing fairings and driven by bleed air from the J79 engines. The two 9,490 lb (4,305 kg) thrust General Electric XJ79-GE-13 turbojets were mounted à la Caravelle on the sides of the rear fuselage. The X-21A crew consisted of a pilot and two flight engineers in the front cockpit, and two flight test engineers, together with their instrumentation and camera recording equipment, in the centre fuselage bay beneath the wing. The two X-21As proved the feasibility of Dr Pfenninger's laminar flow control system which resulted in a substantially increased range. The system was proposed for design of extreme long-range aircraft but maintenance difficulties, associated with the need to keep the minute slots on the wing surface spotlessly clean, proved to be too costly for practical application.

Following the delivery of the first RB-66B on 1 February, 1956, the B/RB-66s were operated by USAFE, TAC and PACAF squadrons. Besides its regular peacetime operations with light bomber and all-weather reconnaissance squadrons, the Destroyer was used in its RB-66C version to locate Soviet radar sites. In this role, which often entailed crossing into communist territory due to alleged navigational error or equipment

503

EB-66E-DL (55-440) of the 42nd TEWS, 355th TFW, at Takhli Air Base, Thailand, in December 1968. (*USAF*)

malfunction, several of these aircraft were shot down. The Destroyer distinguished itself during a number of unusual flights, including one in March 1956 when two RB-66Bs averaged 700 mph (1,127 km/h) between Tucson, Arizona, and Crestview, Florida. Five months later, B-66Bs using flight-refuelling were delivered nonstop from the US to Europe. During 1957, B 66Bs took part in Operation Redwing by flying in the midst of an H-bomb test at Bikini to evaluate their survivability. In the autumn of that year B-66Bs, on a training Composite Air Strike Force deployment to the Far East, were flying practice bombing missions in the Philippines 17 hours after they had been alerted at their US base.

After seven years in squadron service, the bomber and photographic reconnaissance versions of the Destroyer were already obsolescent; as an ECM aircraft, however, the Destroyer was still without equal and, as the war in Southeast Asia increased the need for this type of weapon, the USAF modified thirteen B-66Bs and fifty-two RB-66Bs as EB-66Bs and EB-66Es. In addition to equipping one USAFE squadron, the 39th TEWS (Tactical Electronic Warfare Squadron) at Spangdahlen AB, and partially equipping a training unit, the 363rd Tactical Reconnaissance Wing at Shaw

RB-66C, 54-467, of the 42nd Tactical Reconnaissance Squadron, 10th Tactical Reconnaissance Wing, USAFE. (*David W. Menard*)

504

AFB, South California, the ECM configured Destroyers saw active service over North Vietnam with the 41st and 42nd TEWS of the 355th Tactical Fighter Wing based at Takhli.

The EB-66Cs, operating with or without fighter escort, were used to locate North Vietnamese radar sites, determine their functions (early warning, gun laying, missile control, etc) and identify their frequency, the data thus obtained enabling the preparation of an enemy radar order of battle and the selection of somewhat safer routes for the strike aircraft. The EB-66Bs and EB-66Es, on the other hand, joined strike aircraft to jam enemy radar either electronically or by dropping chaff. Extensive, but most useful, use of the ECM versions of the Destroyer took its toll of the elderly aircraft and, after the end of the war in Southeast Asia, fatigue problems and excessive maintenance requirements forced their retirement.

Accommodation: RB-66A and RB-66B—pilot, navigator and gunner/camera operator; B-66B—pilot, navigator and gunner/bomb-aimer; EB-66B and EB-66E—pilot, navigator and electronic warfare officer; RB/EB-66C—pilot, navigator and five electronic warfare officers; WB-66D—pilot, navigator, gunner and two equipment operators; X-21A—pilot and four flight engineers.

	B-66B	RB-66	RB-66C	X-21A
Span, ft in	72 6	72 6	74 7	93 6
(m)	(22·10)	(22·10)	(22·73)	(28·50)
Length, ft in	75 2	75 2	75 2	76 3½
(m)	(22·91)	(22·91)	(22·91)	(23·25)
Height, ft in	23 7	23 7	23 7	23 7
(m)	(7·19)	(7·19)	(7·19)	(7·19)
Wing area, sq ft	780	780	781	1,250
sq m)	(72·465)	(72·465)	(72 558)	(116·129)
Empty weight, lb	42,549	43,476	43,966	—
(kg)	(19,300)	(19,720)	(19,943)	—
Loaded weight, lb	57,800	59,550	64,085	—
(kg)	(26,218)	(27,011)	(29,068)	—
Maximum weight, lb	83,000	83,000	82,420	83,000
(kg)	(37,648)	(37,648)	(37,385)	(37,648)
Wing loading, lb/sq ft	74·1	76·3	82·1	—
(kg/sq m)	(361·8)	(372·7)	(400·6)	—
Power loading, lb/lb st	2·8	2·9	3·1	—
Maximum speed, mph at ft	631/6,000	631/6,000	640/sea level	—
(km/h at m)	(1,015/1,830)	(1,015/1,830)	(1,030/—)	—
Cruising speed, mph	528	525	532	—
(km/h)	(850)	(845)	(856)	—
Rate of climb, ft/min	5,000	4,840	5,000	—
(m/min)	(1,524)	(1,475)	(1,524)	—
Service ceiling, ft	39,400	38,900	39,200	—
(m)	(12,010)	(11,855)	(11,950)	—
Combat radius, miles	900	925	1,440	—
(km)	(1,450)	(1,490)	(2,320)	—
Maximum range, miles	2,470	2,425	2,935	—
(km)	(3,975)	(3,905)	(4,725)	—

Armament: Two 20 mm cannon in remotely-controlled tail turret (RB-66, B-66, WB-66). Bomb load: B-66B only—15,000 lb (6,804 kg) in internal bomb bay.

505

The first F5D-1 six weeks after beginning trials. (*MDC*)

Douglas F5D-1 Skylancer

Shortly after the J57-powered F4D-1 Skyray had been ordered into production in March 1953, the El Segundo design team led by Ed Heinemann and C. S. Kennedy and the Bureau of Aeronautics agreed to proceed with its development to take full advantage of the increased thrust made available by the substitution of the Pratt & Whitney J57-P-2 for the Westinghouse J40-WE-8 initially specified for production F4D-1s. At the same time it was further agreed that it would be fitted with more comprehensive electronic equipment to increase all-weather capability whilst fuel capacity would be increased to improve upon the limited endurance of the F4D-1.

Designated F4D-2N when two prototypes (BuNos 139208 and 139209) of the carrier-borne interceptor were ordered, the aircraft was initially conceived as a progressive development of the F4D-1. However, as engineering design progressed it became necessary to depart substantially from this concept and, to reflect this change, the new type was re-designated F5D-1 and named Skylancer. Retaining the wing planform of the F4D-1, the F5D-1 had wings of much reduced thickness/chord ratio and a longer fuselage housing additional fuel tanks bringing total internal fuel capacity up from the 640 US gallons (2,423 litres) in the F4D-1 to 1,333 gallons (5,408 litres). While, initially at least, the four wing-mounted 20 mm cannon were to have been retained, armament was revised and was to have primarily consisted of four Sidewinder or two Sparrow air-to-air guided missiles and/or spin-stabilized unguided 2-in rockets. Other changes included a redesign of the air intakes, the use of a two-piece, V-shaped, forward canopy, and a taller fin and rudder. In this form, and powered by a 10,200 lb (4,627 kg) thrust—16,000 lb (7,257 kg) with

506

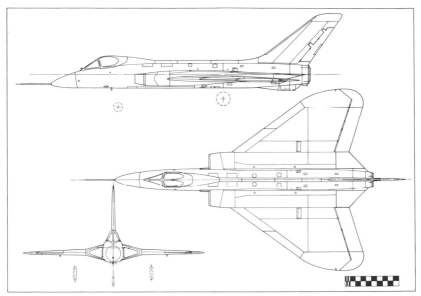

Douglas F5D-1 Skylancer.

The four Skylancers (from front to rear BuNos 139209, 142349, 142350 and 139208) on the ramp at the El Segundo Division on 15 July, 1957. (*MDC*)

afterburner—Pratt & Whitney J57-P-8 turbojet, the first F5D-1 made its maiden flight at Edwards AFB, on 21 April, 1956.

By that time nine Service evaluation machines (BuNos 142349 to 142357) and fifty-one production F5D-1s (BuNos 143393 to 143400, and 145159 to 145201) had already been ordered and it was planned that initial production aircraft would be powered by a 10,700 lb (4,853 kg) thrust— 16,900 lb (7,666 kg) with afterburner—Pratt & Whitney J57-P-14 and later production aircraft would have the still more powerful General Electric J79 (to test this proposed turbojet installation the second XF4D-1 was fitted with a J79 engine). However, although the two J57-P-8 powered prototypes and the similarly-powered first and second Service trial F5D-1s (BuNos 142349 and 142350) performed satisfactorily during their flight trial programme, the decision was made to suspend production as the F5D-1's performance was similar to that of the Chance Vought F8U-1 which had entered service with VF-32 in March 1957.

NASA 212, the Skylancer used to test-fly a modified wing of ogee planform.
(*NASA*)

In 1961, after serving as military test-beds, BuNos 139209 and 142349 were grounded and the other two transferred to the NASA's Flight Research Center at Edwards AFB. NASA 212 (ex-139208) was mostly flown in support of the US supersonic transport programme and, before being sent to the Ames Laboratory in 1963, was fitted with wings of modified ogee planform. NASA 213 (ex-142350) was used mainly to simulate abort procedures for the Boeing X-20A Dyna-Soar. Both were retired in 1970.

Span 33 ft 6 in (10·21 m); length 53 ft 9¾ in (16·4 m); height 14 ft 10 in (4·52 m); wing area 557 sq ft (51·747 sq m). Empty weight 17,444 lb (7,912 kg); loaded weight 24,445 lb (11,088 kg); maximum weight 28,072 lb (12,733 kg); wing loading 43·9 lb/sq ft (214·3 kg/sq m); power loading 1·5 lb/lb. Maximum speed 749 mph (1,205 km/h) at sea level, 1,098 mph (1,767 km/h) at 10,000 ft (3,050 m) and 990 mph (1,593 km/h) at 44,000 ft (13,410 m); cruising speed 637 mph (1,025 km/h); initial rate of climb 20,820 ft/min (6,346 m/min); service ceiling 57,500 ft (17,525 m); combat range 1,334 miles (2,147 km).

Full-size mock-up of the proposed C-132 which, if it had been built, would have been the largest US propeller-turbine powered aircraft. (*USAF*)

Douglas C-133 Cargomaster

Solidly established as the USAF's main supplier of heavy cargo transports, Douglas received in the early fifties development contracts for two new heavy strategic freighters powered by propeller-turbines. The C-132, the largest of the two projects, traced its origin to a January 1951 USAF request for the preliminary design of a heavy cargo aircraft and progressed in stages to the submission in February 1954 of design data for an aircraft suitable for use as either a logistic transport or tanker. The proposed aircraft had a high-mounted wing with 25 deg sweepback, span of 186 ft 8 in (56·90 m) and area of 4,201 sq ft (390·3 sq m). The double-deck fuselage with rear loading ramp had a length of 183 ft 10 in (56·03 m). The pod-mounted main undercarriage had eight wheels and there were twin nosewheels. Power was to be supplied by four 15,000 eshp Pratt & Whitney T57-P-1s driving 20-ft (6·10 m) diameter four-blade propellers. In cargo configuration, for which a maximum take-off weight of 389,500 lb (176,674 kg) was calculated, the C-132 was to be capable of carrying 137,000 lb (62,142 kg) for 2,530 miles, or 74,700 lb (33,883 kg) for 5,180 miles (8,335 km). In tanker configuration, for which maximum weight was increased to 469,225 lb (212,837 kg), the aircraft was capable of transferring 19,550 US gallons (74,000 litres) of jet fuel within a radius of 2,475 miles (3,985 km). A full-scale mock-up was built but the C-132 project was cancelled in 1956.

The smaller and less ambitious C-133 Cargomaster was more successful and achieved an initial contract for twelve aircraft (54-135/54-146). Detailed design of this aircraft, for which no prototype was built, had been initiated in February 1953 to meet the requirements of the USAF Logistic Carrier Supporting System SS402L. When rolled out three years after start of design, the first C-133 appeared as a large aircraft with shoulder-

509

The third C-133A Cargomaster, at Da Nang Air Base, South Vietnam, in April 1966. (*USAF*)

mounted straight wing of high aspect ratio with four underslung 5,700 eshp Pratt & Whitney T34-P-3 propeller-turbines. Its circular section fuselage, with external pods housing the four twin-wheel main undercarriage units and an auxiliary power unit, could accommodate 96 per cent of all US Army vehicles. Vehicle loading was accomplished by way of a built-in ramp and multi-section cargo door in the lower aft fuselage while other cargo could be loaded through an upward-opening door on the forward port side.

The C-133A, the first USAF transport specified for propeller-turbine power, was first flown on 23 April, 1956, by a crew captained by J. C. Armstrong. As a result of flight tests, the size of the dorsal fin was increased and this was retained for all production aircraft. Deliveries began in August 1957 and C-133As were initially operated by the 39th ATS (Air Transport Squadron) at Dover AFB, Delaware, and 84th ATS at McChord, Washington. During production the C-133As were progressively improved and, beginning with the eighth aircraft (54-142), a redesigned flat beaver tail replaced the original tail cone, while the 33rd to 35th C-133As (57-1613/57-1615) had a new clamshell-type rear loading door to add three feet (0·91 m) to usable hold length for transporting fully assembled Atlas ICBMs or Thor and Jupiter IRBMs. Late production C-133As were also fitted with 7,100 eshp T34-P-7W propeller-turbines with water injection in place of the original 5,700 eshp T34-P-3s.

Incorporating the new clamshell loading door and powered by four 7,500 eshp T34-P-9Ws, fifteen C-133Bs were produced between October 1959 and April 1961 to bring total Cargomaster production to fifty aircraft. Compared with the early C-133As, the C-133Bs carried 52,000 lb (23,587 kg) instead of 42,000 lb (19,051 kg) over a distance of 4,000 miles (6,435 km). Plans were also made for a version powered by four 7,500 eshp Allison T54 propeller-turbines but not proceeded with. The Cargomasters remained in service with three USAF squadrons for ten years. However, owing to fatigue problems, the C-133As and C-133Bs were withdrawn from MAC (Military Airlift Command) service during 1971 and placed in storage at Davis-Monthan AFB, Arizona.

510

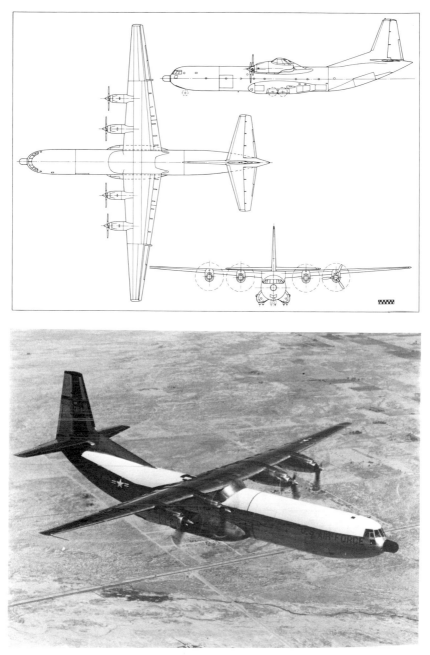

C-133A flying over the Mojave Desert during a test flight from Edwards AFB. (*USAF*)

511

C-133B, with open clamshell doors, at Edwards AFB on 25 April, 1960. (*USAF*)

In 1973 the non-profit Foundation for Airborne Relief acquired four surplus C-133As (N136AR, N199AR, N201AR and N202AR, respectively ex 54-136, 56-1999, 56-2001 and 56-2000) for modification as flying hospitals to be used in worldwide disaster relief operations. The aircraft were to be fitted with intensive care and surgery wards, laboratories and medical clinic, and were to carry a small helicopter for rescue operations. However, the Federal Aviation Administration judged that the fatigue problems precluded the granting of even a limited type certificate and the project was abandoned. Three years later, Northern Air Cargo obtained a surplus C-133B for use in airlifting equipment for the trans-Alaska pipeline construction. Registered N133B, this aircraft was restricted to the transport of government agencies equipment.

Accommodation: Pilot, co-pilot, flight engineer, navigator and loadmaster plus provision for relief crew. Up to 110,000 lb (49,895 kg) of assorted cargo such as ballistic missiles, or two 40,000-lb (18,144-kg) scrapers, or sixteen loaded jeeps.

Span 179 ft 7¾ in (54·78 m); length 157 ft 6½ in (47·01 m); height 48 ft 3 in (14·7 m); wing area 2,673 sq ft (248·331 sq m). Empty weight 120,263 lb (54,550 kg); loaded weight 275,000 lb (124,738 kg); maximum weight 286,000 lb (129,727 kg); wing loading 102·9 lb/sq ft (502·3 kg/sq m); power loading 9·2 lb/hp (4·2 kg/hp). Maximum speed 359 mph (578 km/h) at 8,700 ft (2,650 m); cruising speed 323 mph (520 km/h); rate of climb 1,280 ft/min (390 m/min); service ceiling 29,950 ft (9,140 m); payload/range 52,000 lb (23,587 kg) over 4,000 mile (6,435 km) stage. Weights and performance for C-133B.

The former 54-136, the first Cargomaster for the Foundation for Airborne Relief at Mojave, California. (*Peter Lewis*)

512

N8008D, the first of 556 DC-8s, in its original configuration. (*MDC*)

Douglas DC-8

Several months after the maiden flight of the de Havilland Comet, the world's first jet transport, Donald W. Douglas and Arthur W. Raymond, his Vice President for Engineering, publicly expressed their concern over the market potential for a turbojet transport, being convinced that the market was too limited.

The Boeing Aircraft Company, however, capitalizing on the experience gained with the design of its six-engined B-47 Stratojet and eight-engined B-52 Stratofortress jet bombers, decided on 20 May, 1952, (eighteen days after the entry into service of the Comet 1) to undertake as a private-venture the development and construction of a prototype of a turbojet-powered aircraft from which could be developed a military tanker and/or a commercial passenger transport.

Although Douglas had made low-priority studies of pure-jet transport designs, the company favoured propeller-turbine developments of its existing piston-engined aircraft. However, Douglas was keen to retain its privileged role as the world's leading supplier of commercial transport aircraft and the Boeing challenge could not be ignored. Thus, on 7 June, 1955, more than one year after the Boeing 367-80 prototype jet transport had been rolled out, Douglas formally announced its intention to produce a jet successor to the DC-7 and immediately began an intensive sales drive to obtain for its DC-8 a major share of the market.

The project team led by Art Raymond and Ed Burton produced a basic design remarkably similar to that of the Boeing 367-80, with four turbojets underslung from the wing in individual nacelles, and decided to use a three-spar wing with only 30 deg sweep-back for better low-speed lift and handling.

In designing its first jet transport aircraft, Douglas was early to recognize the full impact on air transport made possible by the introduction in 1952 of the tourist class fare on the North Atlantic routes. Consequently, the DC-8 had a fuselage diameter of sufficient width to accommodate six-abreast economy class seating as against the Boeing's five-abreast layout. Fortunately for Douglas, the airlines endorsed the wider DC-8.

Initially Douglas proposed an aircraft with an MGTOW (maximum gross take-off weight) of 257,000 lb (116,573 kg)—already up 22 per cent from the original estimate of 211,000 lb (95,708 kg)—, a span of 134 ft (40·84 m) and a length of 140 ft (42·67 m). The aircraft was to be powered by four 11,000 lb (4,989 kg) thrust Pratt & Whitney JT3 turbojets. With this powerplant, however, the aircraft would have had insufficient range for North Atlantic crossings against strong winds. Furthermore, at maximum gross weight the aircraft would have excessive take-off field length requirements in high temperatures or at high-elevation airports. Consequently, Douglas soon moved to offer its DC-8 with either the JT3 engines or the 45 per cent more powerful Pratt & Whitney JT4. With the JT4 improvements in take-off field length could be traded for more range by increasing both fuel capacity and gross weight. Douglas thus began to offer a JT3-powered DC-8 for US domestic routes, a JT4-powered domestic version with improved field performance, and a JT4-powered series with longer range for intercontinental routes.

The DC-8-30, the intercontinental version, became the first to be ordered when in September 1955 Pan American World Airways signed a contract for twenty-five. Secrecy surrounding this historic order was lifted on 13 October, 1955, when Pan American officially announced it. Although Pan American had already ordered early delivery of twenty Boeing 707-120s in time to meet the introduction of BOAC's Comet 4s over the North Atlantic, it was clear that at that time Pan American favoured the Douglas product. Yet, dissatisfied with the initial failure of the DC-8-30 to meet guaranteed range performance, Pan American never re-ordered the DC-8. Before the end of 1955, however, orders for the DC-8 totalled 98 aircraft for seven carriers (Eastern, KLM, JAL, National, Pan American, SAS and United) against 73 aircraft for six carriers for the 707. However, within a year Boeing had overtaken Douglas and, from September 1956 onward, the 707 order book exceeded that of the DC-8.

As its design was frozen, the DC-8 appeared as a larger and heavier aircraft than originally proposed. Span and length had respectively been increased to 139 ft 7 in (42·55 m) and 150 ft 6 in (45·87 m) and MGTOW was anticipated to be 265,000 lb (120,200 kg) for the JT3C-powered domestic version—later designated DC-8 Series 10—and 287,500 lb

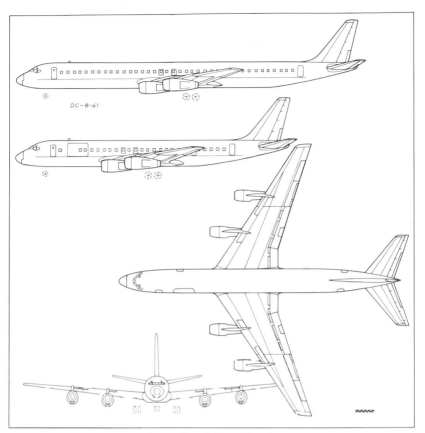

Douglas DC-8-50CF and DC-8-61.

(130,400 kg) for the JT4A-powered long-range DC-8 Series 30. A fourth model, powered by Rolls-Royce Conway bypass engines but otherwise similar to the DC-8-30, was also introduced and was first ordered in May 1956 by Trans-Canada Air Lines, now Air Canada.

Initial assembly of the first aircraft—no prototype was built—began on 18 February, 1957, in new facilities at Long Beach. This aircraft (N8008D) was built to Series 10 standard and was rolled out on 9 April, 1958. On 30 May, 1958, a crew captained by A. G. Heimerdinger took the DC-8 on its 2 hr 7 min maiden flight from Long Beach to Edwards AFB where the initial trials were conducted. At that time the aircraft differed somewhat from production aircraft and, in particular, was fitted with fuselage air-brakes, mounted just aft of the wing fillets; in production these were replaced by a Douglas-designed ejector-type thrust reverser and engine noise suppression system.

Striving to minimize Boeing's time lead, Douglas implemented an accelerated flight trial programme leading to full certification of the

515

DC-8-11 on 31 August, 1959 (time between first flight and certification date was fifteen months for the DC-8 compared with fifty-one months for the 707-120—based on the first flight of the 367-80—or ten months—based on the first 707 flight). Like N8008D, the second DC-8 to fly was powered by four 12,500 lb (5,670 kg) thrust (with water injection) JT3C-4 turbojets. Initially registered N8018D, this aircraft was first used for structural testing and later was tested with four 16,800 lb (7,620 kg) thrust (dry) JT4A-9s before being delivered to United Air Lines as a DC-8-21 (N8001U). It was also used to evaluate two modifications to improve low-speed flight characteristics—wing leading-edge slots were incorporated inboard of each engine pylon and covered by flush-fitting doors which opened when the flaps were extended—and to increase range by fitting new wingtips which increased span to 142 ft 5 in (43·41 m) and reduced drag. Two other Series 10 aircraft for United followed and preceded the first JT4A-12-powered DC-8 Series 30 for Pan American (first flown on 20 February, 1959). Finally, the first DC-8 Series 40 (N6577C during tests and CF-TJA upon delivery to TCA) powered by 17,500 lb (7,938 kg) thrust Rolls-Royce Conway R. Co. 12 engines, the ninth airframe produced, made its maiden flight on 23 July, 1959.

DC-8s with standard fuselage length were produced until November 1968 in five series and sixteen models as:

Series 10: The basic domestic version was powered by four 13,000 lb—5,897 kg—(with water injection) JT3C-6 turbojets and was certificated as the DC-8-11 on 31 August, 1959. This model had an MGTOW of 265,000 lb (120,202 kg), maximum high-density accommodation for 176 economy class passengers, typical accommodation in mixed class for 124, and a maximum payload of 39,100 lb (17,735 kg). With wingtip profile changed and addition of wing leading-edge slots, the otherwise identical DC-8-12 was certificated at an MGTOW of 273,000 lb (123,831 kg). A total of twenty-eight Series 10 aircraft were built for United and Delta Air Lines and these two carriers began in 1963 to modify their Series 10 aircraft to Series 50 (Delta and United) or Series 20 (United only) standards. No DC-8-11 or -12 still exists.

Series 20: Specifically tailored for operations from hot and high airfields, the domestic Series 20 differed from the Series 10 in having more powerful JT4A turbojets (15,800 lb—7,167 kg—JT4A-3 typical). The JT4A's greater thrust was achieved without water injection and resulted in a reduction in FAR take-off field length from 9,800 ft (2,990 m)* for the DC-8-12 to 8,900 ft (2,715 m)* for the DC-8-21. The airframe of the DC-8-21, the only model in the Series 20, was similar to that of the -12 but the new engine increased the MGTOW to 276,000 lb (125,192 kg). Thirty-four DC-8-21s were built for Aeronaves de Mexico, Eastern, National and United and, in addition, United modified fifteen of its Series 10 aircraft to DC-8-21 standard.

Series 30: Retaining the basic DC-8 airframe, the JT4A-powered (16,800 lb—7,620 kg—JT4A-9 typical) Series 30 was specially tailored to intercontinental operations. To achieve range, fuel capacity was increased

DC-8-21 of Eastern Air Lines. This carrier advertised this version of the Douglas jet transport under the unofficial designation DC-8B.

from 17,500 US gallons (66,243 litres) for the DC-8-21 to 23,400 gallons (88,577 litres) for the DC-8-33 while MGTOW increased from 276,000 lb (125,192 kg) for the DC-8-21, to 300,000 lb (136,078 kg) for the DC-8-31, 310,000 lb (140,614 kg) for the DC-8-32, and 315,000 lb (142 882 kg) for the DC-8-33. Maximum seating capacity remained unchanged but maximum payload was increased by 6,300 lb (2,858 kg) to 43,800 lb (19,867 kg) for the DC-8-33. Range with maximum payload was increased by 650 naut miles (1,205 km) to 4,700 naut miles (8,710 km). However, these increases were obtained at the expense of FAR take-off field length which increased to 10,500 ft (3,200 m).* The DC-8-31 had the same wing configuration as the DC-8-21 but the DC-8-32 and -33 had drooped flaps to limit increases in field length requirements in spite of increases in MGTOW.

*At sea level and 15 deg C.

DC-8-32 (F-BIUY, s/n 45569) before delivery to TAI. (*UTA*)

To improve range, a recontouring of the leading edge increasing chord by 4 per cent and wing area by 112 sq ft (10·406 sq m) to 2,883 sq ft (267·841 sq m) was introduced during the course of production and was retrofitted to some early Series 20, 30 and 40 aircraft. Production of DC-8 Series 30 for JAL, KLM, Northwest, Panagra, Pan American, Panair do Brasil, SAS, Swissair, TAI and UAT totalled 57 aircraft. Some of these were later converted to Series 50 standard.

Series 40: The DC-8-41, -42, and -43 respectively corresponded to the -31, -32 and -33 from which they differed in being powered by four 17,500 lb (7,938 kg) thrust Rolls-Royce Conway R.Co. 12 bypass engines. A total of thirty-two Series 40s were built for Alitalia, Canadian Pacific and Trans-Canada.

N109RD fitted with experimental nacelles housing JT3D turbofans; the aircraft was subsequently delivered with conventional nacelles as a Jet Trader. (*MDC*)

Series 50: The new Pratt & Whitney JT3D turbofan engine, a development of the JT3C with a new fan section located in front and forming an integral part of the low-pressure compressor, enabled Douglas to offer a much improved DC-8. Housed in new nacelles with exhaust louvres on each side of the cowling, the JT3D engines were first fitted to the original DC-8, N8008D. In this form, the aircraft was first flown on 20 December, 1960, and was used to obtain, on 1 May, 1961, FAA certification for the Series 50.

The DC-8-51 was a domestic version with MGTOW limited to 276,000 lb (125,192 kg) in spite of the added power offered by its four 17,000 lb (7,711 kg) thrust JT3D-1 turbofans. The DC-8-52, -53 and -55 were long-range intercontinental versions powered by either four 17,000 lb JT3D-1s (DC-8-52 only), or 18,000 lb (8,165 kg) JT3D-3s, or JT3D-3Bs (DC-8-52, -53 or -55) respectively with MGTOW of 300,000 lb (136,078 kg), 315,000 lb (142,882 kg) and 325,000 lb (147,418 kg). At a gross weight of 325,000 lb,

The first DC-8 after installation of JT3D turbofans. (*MDC*)

the DC-8-55 carried the heaviest payload (51,700 lb, 23,450 kg) of any standard passenger models in the DC-8 family. Fuel capacity for the turbofan powered DC-8-55 was identical to that of the corresponding turbojet-powered DC-8-33 but the lower fuel consumption rate resulted in an increase in payload-range (*eg* maximum range without load increased by 700 naut miles, 1,300 km, to 5,920 naut miles, 10,970 km). Without change in external fuselage dimensions, maximum high-density capacity was increased on late production aircraft from 176 seats to 189 by relocation of the aft bulkhead. In addition to eighty-eight Series 50 production aircraft, six Series 10 (including the prototype already mentioned) and four Series 30 aircraft were brought up to the same standard.

DC-8-55 (PI-C-803, s/n 45937) landing at the Long Beach Municipal Airport. (*MDC*)

Series 50CF: Announced in April 1961 and certificated on 29 January, 1963, this version was a convertible passenger/cargo aircraft with a 140 in by 85 in (3·56 m by 2·16 m) cargo door on the left side of the forward fuselage and with a reinforced floor incorporating a cargo-handling and tie-down system. The engines were 18,000 lb (8,165 kg) thrust JT3D-3 or -3B turbofans. Two versions were produced: the DC-8-54CF with an MGTOW of 315,000 lb (142,882 kg) and the DC-8-55CF with an MGTOW of 325,000 lb (147,418 kg). When carrying freight, the DC-8-55CF had a maximum payload of 88,730 lb (40,247 kg) versus only 51,700 lb (23,450 kg) for the all-passenger DC-8-55. Sometimes called Jet Trader, thirty-nine Series 50CFs were built. In addition, during 1975 Douglas set up in the Tulsa plant modification facilities to bring to Series 50CF standard a number of DC-8-30s, -40s and -50s no longer needed for passenger service. One of the DC-8-54CFs (s/n 45674, N109RD) built for Riddle Airlines was used by Douglas before delivery for flight testing new engine nacelles. The tests were not successful and led Douglas to entrust Rohr Industries Inc with the design of the new nacelles for the Series 62 and 63.

All-cargo DC-8-54AF of United Air Lines. On this version most of the cabin windows were covered over. (*United Airlines*)

Series 50AF: Fifteen all-freighter DC-8-54AF (first delivered on 30 January, 1964) were built for United Air Lines and the last of these was the last DC-8 with standard fuselage length to be delivered. Powered by four 18,000 lb (8,165 kg) thrust JT3D-3B turbofans and grossing 315,000 lb (142,882 kg), the DC-8-54AF had no cabin windows, galleys or other passenger amenities.

The DC-8 had been designed with substantial growth potential, and in particular incorporated long undercarriage struts, placing the main cabin floor 2 ft 5 in (0·74 m) higher from the ground than that of the 707, and a fuselage with a more pronounced upward sweep at the rear. Thus, when traffic growth and airport/airway congestion dictated larger capacity transports, the DC-8 could easily be stretched by inserting fuselage plugs fore and aft of the wings without encountering rotation problems. Douglas capitalized on this and development of the Super Sixty family revitalized the sagging DC-8 sales.

Between 1966 and 1972 Douglas produced 262 Series 60 DC-8s in four all-passenger, three convertible passenger/cargo, and two all-cargo models.

Model 61: Primarily intended for use on the longest and busiest US domestic routes (*eg* New York–Los Angeles, and Los Angeles–Honolulu), the DC-8-61 was a minimum change aircraft retaining the wing, tail surfaces, powerplant and fuel capacity of the DC-8-55. It was characterized by its 36 ft 8 in (11·18 m) fuselage stretch (240-in forward and 200-in aft of the wing) which resulted in increases in maximum high-density seating from 189 to 259, in belly-hold baggage and cargo volume from 1,390 to 2,500 cu ft (39·4 to 70·8 cu m), and in maximum payload from 51,700 to 71,900 lb (23,450 to 32,613 kg). Other changes included the use of a 30 kW solid-state alternator system in place of the older 20kW system, local strengthening of the airframe, improvements in the flap system, and new anti-skid brakes.

This view of a Delta Air Lines DC-8-61 shows to advantage the longer fuselage of the Series 61 and 63. (*MDC*)

Having the same MGTOW as the DC-8-55, the DC-8-61 traded weight of fuel for additional payload. Thus, range with full passenger load and no cargo decreased from the DC-8-55's 5,000 naut miles (9,260 km) with 189 passengers to 3,450 naut miles (6,390 km) with 259 passengers. The first DC-8-61 made its maiden flight on 14 March, 1966, and a total of seventy-eight Model 61s were built for Air Canada, Delta, Eastern, JAL, National and United.

Model 61CF: Convertible passenger/cargo version with forward main-deck cargo door and reinforced floor with cargo-handling and tie-down system. It had the same MGTOW of 325,000 lb (147,418 kg) as the

521

The first DC-8-61CF of Trans International Airlines in its original markings. (*MDC*)

DC-8-55CF but had a 17 per cent greater combined main deck and belly-hold capacity. Ten DC-8-61CFs were built, for Saturn, Trans Caribbean, TIA and Universal.

Model 62: Specially developed from the DC-8-55 for use on extra long stages (*eg* Los Angeles–Copenhagen, and Rome–Buenos Aires), the DC-8-62 had a number of aerodynamic improvements designed to reduce drag. These included (1) 3-ft (0·91-m) wingtip extension; (2) engine pods of new design, augmenting installed thrust and ducting fan air throughout the nacelle; and (3) recontoured pylons. In addition, a number of system changes were introduced whilst fuel capacity was increased to 24,275 US gallons (91,889 litres). The fuselage was stretched 6 ft 8 in (2·03 m) by inserting two 40-in plugs, one forward and one aft of the wing.

Powered by either four 18,000 lb (8,165 kg) thrust JT3D-3B or 19,000 lb (8,618 kg) thrust JT3D-7 turbofans, the Model 62 was produced in two variants: the -62 with a gross weight of 335,000 lb (151,953 kg) and the -62H with an MGTOW of 350,000 lb (158,757 kg). The -62H's heavier maximum take-off weight enabled it to carry either 70 per cent more payload with maximum fuel or to have a greater range with a given payload. Compared with corresponding figures for the DC-8-55, max-

JA8031 *Awaji*, the first DC-8-62 of Japan Air Lines, which was delivered on 19 April, 1968. (*MDC*)

522

imum seating capacity and payload remained unchanged. However, over distances of up to 5,300 naut miles (9,815 km) the -62H carried more payload than the -55, due to its better performance in terms of miles per pound of fuel, Production of the DC-8-62 for Alitalia, Braniff, JAL, Swissair, United and UTA totalled twenty-nine aircraft while twenty-two -62Hs were built for Alitalia, JAL and United. The DC-8-62 first flew on 29 August, 1966.

Model 62AF: Six all-cargo DC-8-62AFs, which were fitted with a 140 in by 85 in (3·56 m by 2·16 m) main-deck cargo door and reinforced flooring, were built for JAL and SAS and respectively had MGTOW of 350,000 lb (158,757 kg) and 335,000 lb (151,953 kg). Both variants dispensed with all passenger amenities and windows.

Model 62 CF: Like the 62AF, the DC-8-62CF retained the airframe and powerplant installation of the all-passenger -62 and was fitted with a cargo door and reinforced flooring. However, the -62CF retained passenger amenities, enabling it to be operated in all-passenger, all-cargo or mixed

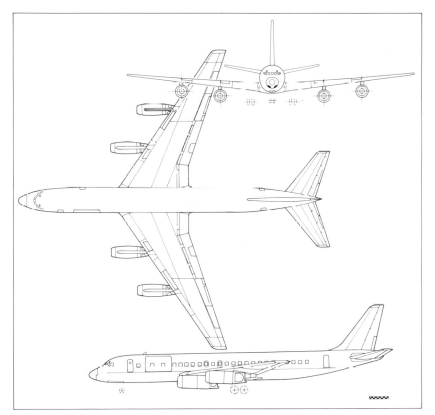

Douglas DC-8-62CF.

523

HB-IDH *Piz Bernina*, a DC-8-62CF of Swissair, showing its 140 in by 85 in main-deck cargo door. (*Swissair*)

passenger-cargo configuration. Eight -62CFs with MGTOW of 335,000 lb were built for Braniff, Finnair, SAS and Swissair, and two aircraft with MGTOW of 350,000 lb were delivered to Alitalia.

Model 63: Combining the stretched fuselage of the DC-8-61 with the wing and powerplant installation of the DC-8-62, the Model 63 was designed for transatlantic operations. In practice, it was limited to sectors, such as Amsterdam to New York (great circle distance, uncorrected for winds: 3,160 naut miles, 5,850 km), since it lacked sufficient range to carry a commercial load over longer transatlantic routes, such as Rome to New York (great circle distance, uncorrected for winds: 3,720 naut miles, 6,890 km). Carrying up to 259 passengers in high-density seating or a maximum passenger/cargo load of 71,260 lb (32,323 kg), the -63 had a maximum take-off weight of 350,000 lb (158,757 kg). The first -63 made its maiden flight on 10 April, 1967, and was followed by 40 similar aircraft which were delivered to Air Canada, Canadian Pacific, Iberia, KLM, SAS and VIASA.

DC-8-63, PH-DEB *Christoforus Columbus*, of KLM Royal Dutch Airlines. (*MDC*)

524

DC-8-63CF of Cargolux, the Luxembourg-based cargo airline. (*Cargolux*)

Model 63AF: The DC-8-63AF was an all-cargo version with cargo handling and loading facilities similar to those of the -62AF. The wing structure and undercarriage were reinforced to permit an increase in maximum landing weight from 245,000 lb (111,130 kg) for the DC-8-63 to 255,000 lb (124,738 kg) for the DC-8-63AF (the new maximum landing weight represented an increase of more than 42 per cent over the landing weight at which the DC-8-11 had originally been certificated). All seven DC-8-63AFs produced were delivered to Flying Tiger and could carry a maximum payload of 114,700 lb (52,027 kg), the highest of any DC-8 variants and exceeded that of its rival, the Boeing 707-320C, by more than 21 per cent. MGTOW of the DC-8-63AF was 355,000 lb (161,025 kg).

Model 63CF: Most numerous of the Super Sixty series, the DC-8-63CF was a passenger/cargo version with the same reinforced features as the -63AF. It was certificated at gross weights of 350,000 lb (158,757 kg) and 355,000 lb (161,025 kg) and 53 were delivered to Air Afrique, Air Congo, Airlift, American Flyers, Capitol, Flying Tiger, Iberia, ONA, Seaboard World, TIA and World Airways.

The DC-8-63PF was the last version of the DC-8 to be put into production. Only six of this version were built, all for Eastern Air Lines. (*Eastern Air Lines*)

525

Model 63PF: This specialized all-passenger version, of which six were built for Eastern Air Lines, combined the fuselage and powerplant of the DC-8-63 with the reinforced main-deck flooring, wing and undercarriage of the DC-8-63AF and -63CF, but was not fitted with the main-deck door and other cargo handling devices.

While the DC-8 production ended on 12 May, 1972, with the delivery of the 556th aircraft—the DC-8-63, s/n 46163, SE-DBL of SAS—, Douglas had not abandoned the development of the DC-8 without first trying to market more advanced versions. However, competitive pressure from the Boeing 747 and the L-1011 Tri-Star forced Douglas not to pursue the proposed Series 70 and 80. The Series 70 (not to be confused with the Cammacorp Super 70 as described later) was intended to meet various requirements, and one version, making use of the 22,500 lb (10,205 kg) thrust JT3D-15 turbofan and offering a 1,400 US gallons (5,300 litres) increase in fuel capacity, was planned as a longer range version of the DC-8-63. Another version was projected as a short- to medium-range 'Airbus' transport. The aircraft was to have had lower weights and reduced fuel capacity, with a DC-8-63 fuselage and wing, and four 15,000 lb (6,804 kg) thrust Pratt & Whitney JT8D-11 turbofans.

Studies of advanced DC-8-63 versions with increased range, capacity and comfort were stepped up. Planned to be powered by 28,000 lb (12,700 kg) thrust advanced turbofans with high bypass ratio, these projected variants included the DC-8-84 using the wing, lower fuselage lobe and tail section of the DC-8-63 combined with a new upper fuselage lobe of wider diameter. Another proposal foresaw an aircraft retaining the fuselage cross-section of earlier DC-8 variants but obtaining increased capacity through use of a further stretch in fuselage length (overall length was to be increased from 187 ft 4 in—57·10 m—for the DC-8-63 to 212·4 ft—64.74 m—for the proposed DC-8-83). Wing area was to be substantially increased while span was to go from 148 ft 5 in—45·24 m—for the DC-8-63 to 158·4 ft—48·28 m for the DC-8-83.

Even though Pan American World Airways had been the first airline to order the DC-8—the purchase contract was officially executed on 11 October, 1955—this carrier had to wait until 7 February, 1960, to take delivery of its first aircraft (s/n 45256, N803PA) as it had ordered the longer-ranged, JT4A-powered Series 30. Meanwhile, other airlines, which had placed their orders after Pan American, took delivery of their JT3C- and JT4A-powered domestic DC-8s ahead of Pan American. Thus, the honour of putting the DC-8 into scheduled commercial service was shared by Delta Air Lines—which had become the eighth DC-8 customer and took delivery of its first DC-8-11, s/n 45408, on 21 July, 1959—and United Air Lines—which was the second DC-8 customer but which became the first to accept a DC-8 when it took delivery of s/n 45281 on 29 May, 1959. Following the granting on 31 August, 1959, of the FAA certificate for the DC-8-11, these two domestic carriers began DC-8 service on 18

DC-8-11 of Delta Air Lines taking-off with sound-suppressor rings slid aft of its JT3C nacelles. (*Delta Air Lines*)

September—some eleven months after Boeing 707-120 and de Havilland Comet 4 operations over the North Atlantic—with flights between Atlanta and New York (Delta) and between San Francisco and New York (United). Two other US trunk carriers, Eastern and National, also preceded Pan American as they respectively began DC-8-21 service on the New York–Miami route on 24 January and 18 February, 1960.

At last Pan American put the DC-8-30 into service on the New York–Bermuda route on 27 March, 1960, and, one month later, on the New York–London route. However, Pan American was dissatisfied with the payload-range performance of the DC-8-30. Already in May 1956 Pan American had transferred title to four of its previously ordered DC-8s to its affiliated company, Panagra, for use on the South American route network. This transfer was followed in March 1960 by the transfer of two additional DC-8-30s to another affiliated company, Panair do Brasil. Thus, Pan American World Airways took delivery of only 19 of the 25 aircraft ordered in October 1955 and, with serious consequences for Douglas, never reordered. Its fleet was standardized around various models of Boeing jets, and Pan American disposed of its last DC-8-30 in May 1971.

American Airlines never bought any DC-8s; however, it briefly became the owner of a small number of DC-8s and Super DC-8s when it absorbed Trans Caribbean Airways. Northwest Airlines, having ordered five DC-8-30s in July 1958 and received its first aircraft in May 1960, switched to Boeings and sold its DC-8-30s. At the other end of the scale, the all-cargo Flying Tiger Line became a DC-8 customer in 1966–67 when DC-8-63AFs and -63CFs were acquired to replace the previously operated Boeing 707-320Cs which proved to be space limited when compared to the stretched DC-8 freighters. Douglas was also successful when Braniff

International, a Boeing customer, merged with Panagra and decided to retain its DC-8-62s as they had better airfield performance than the 707-320Bs when operating from the high-elevation airports at La Paz and Quito.

Many airlines became enthusiastic operators of DC-8s. United Air Lines, having placed an initial order for thirty DC-8s in November 1955, eventually bought fifty standard DC-8s (DC-8-11, -12, -21, and -52), fifteen DC-8-54AF freighters and forty Super DC-8s (DC-8-61 and -62), and acquired eleven used DC-8-31, -32 and -33s from other airlines to become the largest operator of DC-8s.

Forty-five per cent of the standard DC-8s and 44 per cent of the Super DC-8s were first sold to customers outside the United States. With the exception of Trans-Canada Air Lines, Canadian Pacific Air Lines and Alitalia which initially ordered Conway-powered DC-8-40s, and Aeronaves de Mexico (later Aeromexico) which first bought a DC-8-21, foreign customers concentrated on the Series 30, 50 and 50CF and on the Super DC-8. The first non-US airline to order the DC-8 was KLM, a longtime Douglas customer, placing an initial order for eight DC-8-30s on 9 December, 1955, and eventually taking delivery of seven DC-8-32s, nine DC-8-53s, two DC-8-55s, five DC-8-55CFs, and eleven DC-8-63s.

The colourful, but somewhat gaudy, livery of this Braniff DC-8-62 (N1805 *Flying Colors*) was designed by Alexander Calder, the noted American artist. (*Braniff*)

On 20 December, 1955, SAS had become the second overseas DC-8 customer, with an order for seven DC-8-32s. This carrier, which had pioneered the polar routes, initially used its DC-8s on routes linking Scandinavia—with Copenhagen as the main gateway—to New York and, over the polar region, to Los Angeles and Tokyo. However, on the long polar flights the DC-8-32s proved to have insufficient range when carrying heavy loads; Douglas therefore developed the DC-8-62.

Another airline which remained a major Douglas customer was Japan Air Lines which, after operating DC-4s, DC-6Bs and DC-7Cs, ordered its first DC-8s in February 1956. Eventually, JAL acquired a total of forty-four DC-8s—including aircraft bought new from Douglas and second-hand from various sources—to become the largest non-US operator of DC-8s. Air Canada, which as TCA had placed the first order for Conway-powered Series 40s on 18 July, 1956, and the first DC-8F order on 29 December, 1961, ranked a close second behind JAL with its fleet of forty-two DC-8s and Super DC-8s. It began DC-8-40 service on 1 April, 1960, on the Montreal–Toronto–Vancouver route and started transatlantic service two months later. On 2 March, 1963, this carrier put its first DC-8-54CF into service on the Montreal–Prestwick–London route in a four-pallet and 117-economy class configuration.

The Douglas sales efforts in the Middle East, Africa, Asia and the United Kingdom met with little or no success. In Great Britain, for example, Douglas failed to sell a single standard DC-8 but managed to sell in September 1966 a DC-8-63CF to Lloyd International Airways. However, even this order was cancelled before delivery and the first DC-8s to appear on the United Kingdom register were the DC-8CFs acquired second-hand by IAS Cargo Airlines.

DC-8s are or have been operated by almost all US supplemental and scheduled all-cargo airlines including Airlift International, Flying Tiger, Seaboard World, American Flyers, Capitol, ONA, Saturn, TIA and World Airways. For these two groups, several of which were already operating standard DC-8s and DC-8 freighters, the Super DC-8 convertible freighters proved ideal for passenger charters the first use of the DC-8-61CF being made on 11 June, 1967, by TIA for a charter flight originating in Long Beach, California—and for freight operations, including military airlift support the Vietnam War.

In service the Super DC-8s demonstrated the lowest operating costs of any conventional jets and, as early as 1967, McDonnell Douglas began to worry about the probable impact the type would have upon the potential DC-10 market. Ideally, the company would have liked to continue producing the DC-8-60s in parallel with the DC-10; however, the resulting production rate for each type was forecast to be too low to result in profitable operation and, in 1971, the decision was reached to stop accepting DC-8 orders. The last of these aircraft—s/n 46163, a DC-8-63 for SAS—was delivered on 12 May, 1972. Second-hand DC-8s—especially the convertible models—continued to find a brisk market and during 1975 the

Tulsa plant of McDonnell Douglas began to overhaul and market standard passenger DC-8s with reinforced main deck flooring, large cargo door on the port side and, in some cases, substitution of JT3D turbofans for the turbojets fitted to early DC-8 models. In so doing the company took advantage of the DC-8's extremely strong structure which has enabled it to have a safe life equivalent to at least 80,000 flying hours. A similar conversion programme was also undertaken by Aeritalia in Italy. Moreover, after new ICAO and FAA noise regulations came into force during the eighties, several small firms developed hush kits for still sprightly DC-8s.

Noteworthy are the following records and unusual flights made by the DC-8, including a brief supersonic dive by s/n 45608, N9608Z—a DC-8-53 ordered by Philippine Air Lines but temporarily retained by Douglas—to become in the spring of 1962 the first commercial airliner to exceed the speed of sound. A little over a year later s/n 45408, N801E—the aircraft with which Delta had made the first DC-8 revenue flight—was returned to Douglas to be re-engined with JT3D turbofans and, before going back into service, was fitted with high-altitude photographic equipment to record the total eclipse of the sun over North America on 20 July, 1963. A different type of unofficial record was set in April 1969 by a DC-8-63 of Iberia which carried 346 passengers from Bata to Las Palmas and Madrid when evacuating Spanish nationals following the granting of independence to Equatorial Guinea.

Military uses of the DC-8 began in December 1965 when the Armée de l'Air took delivery of a new DC-8-55F. Subsequently, France acquired additional Series 30, 50, and 62 aircraft on the second-hand market for use in the long-range transport role by Escadron de transport 3/60 'Estérel' and in the electronic reconnaissance role (with large wingtip SLAR, Side-Looking Airborne Radar, pods) by Escadron électronique 51 'Aubrac'. Next, in 1981, the Fuerza Aérea del Peru obtained two ex-Swissair DC-8-62s for its Escuadrón 3, Grupo de Transporte 51. In the early eighties, other military operators included the Fuerza Aérea Espanola (two DC-8-52s designated T.15s and serving with Escuadrón 401) and the Thai

DC-8-55 (F-RAFB, s/n 45692) from Escadron 3/60 *Estérel*. (*ECPA*)

530

F-RAFG, one of the three DC-8-72CFs operated by Escadron de transport 3/60 *Estérel*, landing at Nellis AFB, Arizona, on 13 February, 1987. (*René J. Francillon*)

Air Force (three DC-8-62AFs with No. 601 Squadron). At press time, confirmation was received that the USN has acquired a DC-8-54F which, designated EC-24A, has been modified to serve as an 'electronic aggressor' with FEWSG (Fleet Electronic Warfare Support Group).

A total of 556 DC-8s—294 standard DC-8s and 262 Super DC-8s—were built in Long Beach as follows.

1	prototype	4	DC-8-41	15	DC-8-54CF	10	DC-8-62CF
23	DC-8-11	8	DC-8-42	8	DC-8-55	41	DC-8-63
5	DC-8-12	20	DC-8-43	24	DC 8 55CF	7	DC-8-63AF
34	DC-8-21	30	DC-8-51	78	DC-8-61	53	DC-8-63CF
4	DC-8-31	25	DC-8-52	10	DC 8 61CF	6	DC-8-63PF
42	DC-8-32	25	DC-8-53	51	DC-8-62		
11	DC-8-33	15	DC-8-54AF	6	DC-8-62AF		

Data for various DC-8 versions appear on pages 532 and 533.

Accommodation: Flight crew of three and five to eight cabin attendants.

| | Passenger models | | | AF or CF models |
	High-density configuration (no. of seats)	Mixed-class configuration (no. of seats)		Maximum structural weight limited cargo load (lb/kg)
Series 10, 20, 30 and 40	176	120 to 140		—
Series 50	189	130 to 150		—
DC-8-54AF	—	—		92,950/42,160
DC-8-55CF	189	130 to 150	or	88,730/40,247
DC-8-61 and -63	259	180 to 220		—
DC-8-61CF	259	180 to 220	or	88,910/40,330
DC-8-62	189	140 to 165		—
DC-8-62AF	—	—		90,825/41,195
DC-8-62CF	189	140 to 165	or	86,460/39,220
DC-8-63	—	—		114,700/52,027
DC-8-63CF	259	180 to 220	or	102,990/46,715

Powerplant: The following types of turbojets and turbofans were fitted to DC-8s:

Engine type	Take-off thrust (lb/kg)	Aircraft versions
P & W JT3C (axial-flow turbojet)		
JT3C-4	11,200/5,080 (Dry) 12,500/5,670 (Wet)	DC-8 prototype
JT3C-6	11,200/5,080 (Dry) 13,000/5,897 (Wet)	DC-8-11, DC-8-12
JT3C-10	10,200/4,627 (Dry) 13,000/5,897 (Wet)	DC-8-11, DC-8-12
P & W JT4A (axial-flow turbojet)		
JT4A-3	15,800/7,167	Sr 20 and 30
JT4A-5	15,800/7,167	Sr 20 and 30
JT4A-9	16,800/7,620	Sr 20 and 30
JT4A-10	16,800/7,620	Sr 20 and 30
JT4A-11	17,500/7,938	Sr 20 and 30
JT4A-12	17,500/7,938	Sr 20 and 30
P & W JT3D (turbofan)		
JT3D-1	17,000/7,711	DC-8-51, DC-8-52
JT3D-3	18,000/8,165	Sr 50 and DC-8-61
JT3D-3B	18,000/8,165	Sr 50, DC-8-61, -62 and -63
JT3D-7	19,000/8,618	DC-8-62 and DC-8-63
Rolls-Royce Conway (bypass turbojet)		
R.Co.12	17,500/7,938	Sr40

	DC-8-11	DC-8-21	DC-8-32	DC-8-43	DC-8-54AF	DC-8-61	DC-8-62CF	DC-8-63AF
Span, ft in	142 5	142 5	42 5	142 5	142 5	142 5	148 5	148 5
(m)	(43·41)	(43·41)	(43·41)	(43·41)	(43·41)	(43·41)	(45·24)	(45·24)
Length, ft in	150 6	150 6	150 6	150 6	150 6	187 4	157 5	187 4
(m)	(45·87)	(45·87)	(45·87)	(45·87)	(45·87)	(57·10)	(47·98)	(57·10)
Height, ft in	43 4	43 4	43 4	43 4	43 4	43 0	43 5	43 0
(m)	(13·21)	(13·21)	(13·21)	(13·21)	(13·21)	(13·11)	(13·23)	(13·11)
Wing area, sq ft	2,771	2,771	2,771	2,883	2,883	2,883	2,927	2,927
(sq m)	(257·435)	(257·435)	(257·435)	(267·841)	(267·841)	(267·841)	(271·928)	(271·928)
Empty weight, lb	123,300	130,000	134,000	137,700	128,700	148,900	139,300	146,300
(kg)	(55,928)	(58,957)	(60,781)	(62,460)	(58,377)	(67,540)	(63,185)	(66,361)
Loaded weight, lb	265,000	276,000	310,000	315,000	315,000	325,000	335,000	355,000
(kg)	(120,202)	(125,192)	(140,614)	(142,882)	(142,882)	(147,418)	(151,953)	(161,025)
Maximum payload, lb	39,100	38,000	42,500	43,105	92,950	71,900	90,700	114,700
(kg)	(17,735)	(17,367)	(19,278)	(19,552)	(42,161)	(32,613)	(41,141)	(52,027)
Wing loading, lb/sq ft	95·6	99·6	111·9	109·3	109·3	112·7	114·5	121·3
(kg/sq m)	(466·9)	(486·3)	(546·2)	(533·5)	(533·5)	(550·4)	(558·8)	(592·2)
Power loading, lb/lb st	5·3	4·4	4·6	4·5	4·4	4·5	4·4	4·7
Maximum cruising speed, mph	559	599	588	585	593	581	587	596
(km/h)	(900)	(964)	(946)	(941)	(954)	(935)	(945)	(959)
Long-range cruising speed, mph	—	500	—	535	532	529	524	514
(km/h)	—	(805)	—	(861)	(856)	(851)	(843)	(827)
Payload/range, lb/miles	39,100/4,330	38,000/4,660	42,500/4,605	43,105/4,375	92,950/2,760	71,900/2,930	90,700/3,440	114,700/2,140
(kg/km)	(17,735/6,950)	(17,367/7,500)	(19,278/7,410)	(19,552/7,040)	(42,161/4,440)	(32,613/4,715)	(41,141/5,535)	(52,027/3,445)
Payload/range, lb/miles	27,800/4,680	26,600/5,095	25,500/6,045	25,500/5,410	32,000/5,595	18,660/5,725	49,000/5,755	41,585/5,480
(kg/km)	(12,610/7,530)	(12,066/8,200)	(11,567/9,725)	(11,567/8,705)	(14,515/9,000)	(8,464/9,210)	(22,226/9,260)	(18,863/8,820)

Piaggio-Douglas PD-808 (I-PIAL) at Genoa.
(*Industrie Aeronautiche e Meccaniche Rinaldo Piaggio*)

Piaggio PD-808

The last attempt by Douglas to develop an aircraft for the civil, non-commercial market met with little success and it was not built by the company; however, the design was acquired by Industrie Aeronautiche e Meccaniche Rinaldo Piaggio SpA and the aircraft was produced in Genoa between 1964 and 1973 as the PD-808 (Piaggio-Douglas 808) twinjet light transport and trainer for the Italian Air Force.

The PD-808 originated with a design study undertaken in 1957 at the El Segundo Division by a team led by Project Engineer Floyd C. Newton Jr. At the time, the aircraft was conceived as a six- to ten-seat executive type powered by either two General Electric CJ610-1 or Bristol Siddeley Viper 20 turbojets set into the rear fuselage sides to reduce control problems under engine-out conditions, and had its tailplane set relatively low to prevent deep stall problems. This design study, which had been undertaken as a private venture, proceeded at a slow pace until 1961 when an agreement was reached between Douglas and Piaggio to continue jointly the development of this aircraft, with Piaggio responsible for detail design, manufacturing and testing of the aircraft, whilst Douglas assisted in an advisory capacity. Furthermore, the Italian Government was to assist by buying the two prototypes and providing test facilities.

Built in Genoa and powered by two 3,000 lb (1,360 kg) thrust Viper 525s, the first prototype flew on 29 August, 1964. The second PD-808 was first flown on 14 June, 1966, and differed from the original prototype in having an enlarged dorsal fin, wingtip tanks of increased capacity, and revised canopy with 'bug-eye' windshield. Italian and US Federal Aviation Administration certifications were obtained in November 1966. Both aircraft were subsequently re-engined with 3,360 lb (1,524 kg) thrust Viper 526s built under licence by Piaggio and this engine was retained for two seven-seat civil executive PD-808s and for the 25 aircraft ordered in 1965 by the Italian Air Force. Twelve of these aircraft were equipped for checking airways and navaids, three were fitted out for electronic countermeasures with a crew consisting of two pilots and three ECM operators, four were six-seat VIP transports, and six were completed as nine-seat communications and navigation trainer aircraft. The last PD-808 was completed in 1973. A projected version with 3,500 lb (1,587 kg) thrust AiResearch TFE-731-2 turbofans was not proceeded with.

A total of twenty-nine PD-808s—including two prototypes, two civilian aircraft and twenty-five military aircraft—were built by Piaggio in Genoa, Italy, between 1964 and 1973.

Span 43 ft 3½ in (13·2 m); length 42 ft 2 in (12·8 m); height 15 ft 9 in (4·8 m); wing area 225 sq ft (20·903 sq m). Empty weight 10,650 lb (4,830 kg); maximum take-off weight 18,000 lb (8,165 kg); wing loading 80 lb/sq ft (390·6 kg/sq m); power loading 2·7 lb/lb. Maximum speed 529 mph (852 km/h) at 19,500 ft (5,945 m); cruising speed 449 mph (722 km/h); initial rate of climb 5,400 ft/min (1,650 m/min); service ceiling 45,000 ft (13,715 m); normal range 1,322 miles (2,128 km).

Douglas DC-9

Excluding 45 aircraft built for military customers and those later redesignated MD-80s, Douglas built 831 DC-9s. Thus, in spite of stiff competition, initially from the later versions of the Aérospatiale Caravelle and the BAC One-Eleven, and then from the Boeing 737, the DC-9 became the most successful of the Douglas Commercial aircraft. This remarkable success was largely due to the fact that the DC-9 was superior to the Caravelle, with lower operating costs and the ability to carry cargo as well as passengers (the Caravelle had only limited underfloor cargo capacity), had better growth potential than the BAC One-Eleven which was handicapped by the limited thrust of its Spey engines, and was produced ahead of the Boeing 737. The latter, however, eventually overcame the DC-9. Fortunately for McDonnell Douglas, the DC-9 got a new lease on life as, after an initially slow start, the Series 80/MD-80 gained wide acceptance. At press time, 23 years after the first DC-9 flight in 1965, the MD-80 was set to remain in production well into the early 1990s.

In the search for a short- to medium-range jetliner to complement its long-range, large capacity, DC-8, Douglas first asked various airlines for their views on a proposal for a medium-range, four-engined design with about two-thirds the capacity of the DC-8. This proposed aircraft—closely comparable to the Convair 880, one of the commercially least successful jetliners—did not gain acceptance; and Douglas entered into a two-year contract with Sid-Aviation to market jointly the Caravelle in the Americas, but the arrangement failed to result in any sales.

YV-C-AVR, a DC-9-14, of the Venezuelan domestic carrier Avensa. (*MDC*)

With the needs of the long-range market satisfied by the 707 and DC-8 and the medium-range market met by the 727, it remained for Douglas to tackle the specific needs of short-range operators who required an aircraft that would bring the dependability, speed, comfort and operating economics of the larger jetliners to the shorter-haul segments. Douglas therefore designed an aircraft with moderate wing sweep, rear-mounted turbofans, T-tail, integral stairs, built-in APU (auxiliary power unit) for quick turn-round with minimum use of ground handling equipment, and five-abreast seating arrangement. Other design parameters included short field length requirement and an MGTOW of less than 80,000 lb (36,287 kg), enabling the use of a two-man flight crew (the FAA later relaxed the requirements for a three-man flight crew to operate aircraft with an MGTOW exceeding 80,000 lb, and DC-9 versions with take-off weight exceeding this limit by more than fifty per cent are now commonly operated by two crew). Furthermore, Douglas incorporated freight holds large enough to carry cargo, in addition to baggage and mail (for example, the holds of the original DC-9-10 had a total volume of 600 cu ft, 17 cu m, compared with only 375 cu ft, 10·7 cu m, for the holds of the Caravelle VIR). Finally, the aircraft was carefully adapted to the needs of local and regional airlines and its high maximum landing weight was adopted to enable it to fly several segments without refuelling, as frequently done by these airlines.

Though there had been no order for the DC-9, Douglas announced on 8 April, 1963, that development and production of its second jetliner would proceed. The first order for fifteen aircraft was received from Delta Air Lines in May 1963 and was followed during the same year by orders from Bonanza and Air Canada. Sales, however, were slow as the airline industry was then in the midst of a recession. Thus, by the time of the first flight only fifty-eight DC-9s had been ordered by six airlines whereas sales of the DC-8 had reached a total of 127 aircraft for 14 airlines at the comparable point in the programme. Fortunately, 1965 saw substantial increases in traffic, and orders for the DC-9 went from 58 to 228 aircraft during the ten months between its maiden flight and its entry into service with Delta. Since that time sales have increased steadily and reached a total of 978 civil and military DC-9s ordered or on option by the spring of 1978. However, the success of the DC-9 has been partially limited by the later appearance of the Boeing 737 which has a wider fuselage with six-abreast seating arrangement. Although preferable for passenger operations, the narrower DC-9 fuselage does not suit freighter or convertible versions of the aircraft as well as the wider 737 fuselage and, at one point, Douglas considered offering a wide-fuselage version of its twinjet. This project did not materialize but the DC-9 has been stretched to meet the needs of airlines with steadily growing traffic. With the exception of Series 80 aircraft, which are described in Volume II, details of the original and stretched versions of the DC-9 developed for civil and military purposes follow:

Series 10: Powered by two 12,000 lb (5,443 kg) thrust Pratt & Whitney JT8D-5 turbofans, the first DC-9 (s/n 45695, registered N9DC during tests and N1301T upon delivery to Trans-Texas/Texas International) made its maiden flight from Long Beach to Edwards AFB on 25 February, 1965, under the command of George R. Jansen. Four additional Series 10 aircraft were used in the trial and certification programme which concluded on 23 November, 1965, with the award of the FAA Type Approval. Two weeks later, on 8 December, Delta Air Lines put the DC-9 into service. A total of 137 Series 10 DC-9s were built for US and foreign airlines, the last being delivered to Aeronaves de Mexico on 27 November, 1968. Four all-passenger models and two convertible passenger/cargo models were produced. All have the same external dimensions (span of 89 ft 5 in, 27·25 m, and length of 104 ft 5 in, 31·82 m). In passenger configuration Series 10 aircraft have high-density seating for 90, but MGTOW and engines vary as shown overleaf:

After completing its flight evaluation programme the first DC-9 (originally N9DC) was refurbished and delivered to Trans-Texas Airlines as N1301T. (*Texas International*)

Model	MGTOW	Engines and static thrust
DC-9-11	77,700 lb/35,244 kg	12,000 lb/5,443 kg JT8D-5
DC-9-12	85,700 lb/38,873 kg	14,000 lb/6,350 kg JT8D-1 or JT8D-7
DC-9-14	76,300 lb/39,100 kg	12,000 lb/5,443 kg JT8D-5, or
		14,000 lb/6,350 kg JT8D-1
DC-9-15	90,700 lb/41,141 kg	14,000 lb/6,350 kg JT8D-1 or JT8D-7

The DC-9-15MC (Multiple Change) and DC-9-15RC (Rapid Change) convertible passenger/cargo versions were produced for Trans-Texas Airways and Continental Air Lines, respectively. Both models had a 90,700 lb (41,141 kg) MGTOW, but the MC was powered by JT8D-1 engines, whereas the RC had JT8D-7 engines. Differences in the methods used to achieve convertibility from passenger to cargo configuration accounted for the different designations (the MC had folding passenger seats which were carried in the rear of the aircraft with cargo in the front, whereas the RC had removable seats on pallets). Both models had a reinforced main cabin floor and an 81 in by 136 in (2·06 m by 3·45 m) upward-hinged cargo door on the left forward side of the fuselage.

Series 20: Specially intended for operations from short runways, the DC-9-21 had a take-off runway length requirements at sea level on a standard 15 deg C day of only 5,600 ft (1,707 m) versus 7,300 ft (2,225 m) for the DC-9-15. Introduced after the Series 30, the Series 20 combined the fuselage and capacity of Series 10 aircraft with the long span, slatted wings of Series 30 aircraft. Powered by two 14,500 lb (6,577 kg) thrust JT8D-9 or 15,000 lb (6,804 kg) JT8D-11 turbofans, the DC-9-21 was certificated at an MGTOW of 100,000 lb (45,359 kg), although SAS—the only customer for this model, for its intra-Scandinavia network—limited the MGTOW to 87,000 lb (39,463 kg). The first of ten DC-9-21s for SAS was first flown on 18 September, 1968, and this model was put into service in January 1969. The tenth and last DC-9-21 was delivered in May 1969.

Two DC-9-21s for Scandinavian Airlines System undergoing final check at Long Beach. (*SAS*)

538

DC-9-31 (VH-CZB, s/n 47004), the 81st Douglas twinjet transport was delivered to Ansett-ANA on 11 April, 1967. This aircraft was acquired by the USN in 1982 and became BuNo 162391. (*MDC*)

Series 30: From the onset of the DC-9 programme, the aircraft had been planned for substantial growth as its MGTOW was initially limited to less than 80,000 lb to fit within the then current FAA restrictions for operations by a two-man crew whilst it had to use JT8D turbofans derated from their normal take-off thrust of 14,000 lb (6,350 kg) to 12,000 lb (5,443 kg). Thus, during negotiations with Eastern Air Lines Douglas first offered a version with a fuselage stretch of 9 ft 6 in (2·90 m). This was soon superseded by a version stretched by 15 ft (4·57 m) to add five rows of seats (maximum seating capacity: 115) and to increase belly-hold volume by almost 50 per cent. To limit the increase in take-off field length requirements, wing span was increased by 4 ft (1·22 m) at the tips, full-span leading-edge slats were added, and uprated engines were fitted. The first flight was made on 1 August, 1966, and Eastern put the DC-9-31 into service in February 1967.

A total of 621 Series 30s were built, the last being delivered to USAir in April 1982, with the following engine and MGTOW options:

Model	MGTOW	Engines and static thrust
DC-9-31	98,000 lb/44,444 kg	14,000 lb/6,350 kg JT8D-1 or JT8D-7
DC-9-32	108,000 lb/48,988 kg	14,000 lb/6,350 kg JT8D-7, or
		14,500 lb/6,577 kg JT8D-9, or
		15,000 lb/6,804 kg JT8D-11, or
		15,500 lb/7,031 kg JT8D-15
DC-9-34	121,000 lb/54,885 kg	16,000 lb/7,257 kg JT8D-17

The DC-9-32 (MGTOW of 108,000 lb/48,988 kg) and DC-9-33 (MGTOW of 114,000 lb/51,710 kg) have been offered in Rapid Change (RC), Convertible Freighter (CF) and All Freight (AF) versions. All are powered by two 14,500 lb (6,577 kg) thrust JT8D-9s or 15,000 lb (6,804 kg) thrust JT8D-11s. The Italian and Kuwait air forces have acquired some of these aircraft. A DC-9-32 (s/n 47649) was tested in 1975 with two JT8D-109 refanned experimental engines to develop a quieter installation for possible retrofit.

N8901 (s/n 45826), the first DC-9-15RC for Continental Airlines. The fourth and eleventh windows have been removed to install the cargo door on the port side. (*Continental Airlines*)

DC-9-32CF of Hawaiian Airlines on the apron at Honolulu International Airport. (*Hawaiian Airlines*)

I-DIBK *Ercole,* an all-cargo DC-9-32F of Alitalia. (*Alitalia*)

DC-9-41 (LN-RLJ, s/n 47287) of Scandinavian Airlines System. (*Erik Collin*)

Series 40: Designed to meet SAS requirements for a high-capacity, short-range aircraft, the Series 40 traded range and runway length requirement for increased seating capacity and payload. First flown on 28 November, 1967, this version had a fuselage stretched an additional 6 ft 2 in (1·88 m) to 125 ft 7 in (38·27 m) and could accommodate up to 125 passengers in high-density configuration. Certificated at an MGTOW of 114,000 lb (57,710 kg), -40s have been fitted with either two 14,500 lb (6,577 kg) thrust JT8D-9s, two 15,000 lb (6,804 kg) JT8D-11s, or two 15,500 lb (7,031 kg) JT8D-15s. Seventy-one Series 40 aircraft were built for SAS and Toa Domestic Airlines of Japan—with the last being delivered to SAS in March 1979—but several have since appeared in the markings of seven other carriers. Late production DC-9-40s have been fitted with additional nacelle sound-proofing and have been certificated to meet FAR (Federal Aviation Regulations) Part 36 noise standards.

Series 50: Still retaining the long-span, slatted wing first introduced on the Series 30, the DC-9-50 introduced yet another fuselage stretch bringing overall length to 133 ft 7 in (40·71 m)—a 28 per cent increase over the DC-9-10's fuselage length—and maximum accommodation up to 139 passengers. However, having the more powerful JT8D-17 (16,000 lb/7,257

A Swissair DC-9-51 landing at Zurich Airport. (*Swissair*)

541

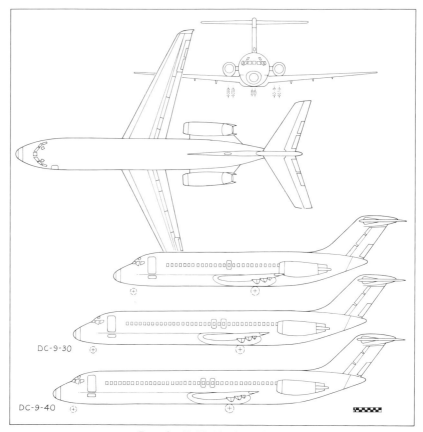

Douglas DC9-10, -30 and -40.

kg take-off thrust), it had an increased MGTOW of 121,000 lb (54,885 kg) and a range comparable to that of the Series 30. It was first flown on 17 December, 1974, and became the first version to be certificated from the onset to FAR Part 36 noise standards. A total of 96 DC-9-50s were built, the last being delivered to Finnair in April 1981.

Series 80: Launched in October 1977, the Series 80 is characterized by the use of refanned Pratt & Whitney JT8D-200 series turbofans. It is fully described under the McDonnell Douglas MD-80 heading in the companion volume dealing with aircraft and events since the 1967 merger which resulted in the organization of the McDonnell Douglas Corporation.

C-9A Nightingale: Aeromedical evacuation version developed for the USAF from the DC-9-32CF. This military version retains the 81 in by 136 in (2·06 m by 3·45 m) forward door but also has a built-in stretcher loading ramp and specialized equipment. Up to the end of 1976 twenty-one C-9As (67-22583/67-22586, 68-8932/68-8935, 68-10958/68-10961, and 71-874/

The first C-9A at the Long Beach plant. The folding ramp designed to ease the loading and unloading of litters is noteworthy. (*MDC*)

71-882) had been built. All are powered by 14,500 lb (6,577 kg) thrust JT8D-9s.

C-9B Skytrain II: Military logistic version of the DC-9-32CF operated by the USN and USMC. Powered by JT8D-9 turbofans, seventeen C-9Bs (BuNos 159113/159120, 160046/160051, 161266, and 161529/161530) were built by Douglas for the Department of the Navy. BuNo 161530, which was delivered on 28 October, 1982, was the 976th and last DC-9. In addition to the 17 new aircraft, the Navy has obtained six ex-airline DC-9s which have received the following BuNos: 162390/162393 (ex-Australian DC-9-31s) and 162753/162754 (ex-Dutch DC-9-33RCs).

VC-9C: VIP-transport version of the Series 30 of which three (73-1681/73-1683) had been delivered to the USAF by the end of 1976.

After a rapid test and certification programme, the DC-9-10 entered scheduled service with Delta Air Lines on 8 December, 1965, a mere nine and a half months after its maiden flight. This version, the smallest in the DC-9 family, was initially purchased by four US trunk carriers

C-9B Skytrain II (BuNo 160047) in service with the US Marine Corps. (*Peter Mancus*)

VC-9C, 73-1682, of the 89th Military Airlift Wing at Andrews AFB, Maryland. (*USAF*)

(Continental, 1; Delta, 14; Eastern, 15; and TWA, 20), seven US local carriers (Allegheny, 1; Bonanza, 3; Hawaiian, 2; Ozark, 6; Southern, 6; Trans-Texas, 2; and West Coast, 4), seven foreign airlines (Aeronaves de Mexico, 9; Air Canada, 6; Avensa, 2; KLM, 6; LAV, 1; Saudia, 3; and Swissair, 5), and two private operators (W. J. Brennan and Tracey Investment Corp, each with one). In addition, Continental bought nineteen DC-9-15RCs and Trans-Texas five DC-9-15MCs. Amongst these early DC-9 operators, TWA was particularly notable as it had not been a Douglas customer since the DC-4 days; unfortunately, TWA never re-ordered DC-9s. In service with these airlines, the DC-9-10s proved to be very reliable but their operating costs per aircraft-mile were somewhat higher than those of the competitive BAC One-Elevens whilst their operating costs per seat-mile were less attractive than those of their stretched versions. Consequently, many of the early DC-9 operators switched to Series 30 aircraft and DC-9-10s quickly became available on thes second-hand market. Several of these changed hands several times and in 1976 one of these Series 10s was leased by British Midland Airways, the first United Kingdom operator of the DC-9.

The Series 20, which had been specially developed to operate in and out of airports with relatively short runways, was acquired only by SAS which accepted ten aircraft between December 1968 and May 1969. Although having high seat-mile costs, the DC-9-20s have proved quite successful in filling the specialized Scandinavian requirements.

Accounting in its civil and military versions for seven out of ten DC-9s sold to the end of 1976, the Series 30 entered service with Eastern Air Lines in February 1967. With this carrier DC-9-30s have been, and continue to be, used not only on regular routes but also on the shuttle service between New York and Washington, and between New York and Boston. With aircraft-mile costs only marginally higher than those of the DC-9-10s but carrying up to 25 additional passengers, the DC-9-30s achieved remarkably low seat-miles costs over short sectors. This version thus met with considerable success and eight airlines ordered twenty or more new DC-9-30s each (Delta, 77; Eastern, 72; Air Canada, 44; Alitalia, 38; Allegheny, 37; Iberia, 35; and North Central and Swissair, 20 each). In addition, operators of DC-9-30s, in passenger or passenger/cargo convertible versions, have included not only scheduled airlines on all continents but also supplemental/charter carriers, private operators and the Italian, Kuwaiti and US armed forces. The Series 30 was superseded by the Series 50 and 80 which offered increased capacity over similar stage lengths whilst achieving a marked reduction in noise. Consequently, the DC-9-30 was phased out of production, which ended in April 1982.

Like the Series 20, the Series 40 was developed to meet SAS requirements and, for many years, met with little success with other operators as it lacked the range of the shorter Series 30. However, over short sectors, the -40 offered still better seat-mile costs as it carried ten more passengers. SAS initially ordered ten SC-9-41s and this version entered service in the spring of 1968. The Scandinavian carrier, which also operated five leased DC-9-32s and two DC-9-33AFs, later increased its order to cover a total of forty-five Series 40 aircraft of which four were temporarily leased to Swissair and two were operated by Thai Airways between January 1970 and April 1972. Toa Domestic Airlines became the second customer for this version when it ordered fourteen DC-9-41s which were delivered from March 1974.

Taking advantage of the availability of the higher rated JT8D-17 engines, Douglas announced in July 1973 the development of the Series 50 which combines the range capability of the Series 40 with a further increase in fuselage stretch and passenger capacity. Swissair became the first DC-9-51 customer and put this version into service during the summer of 1975. Since then it has been ordered by previous DC-9 operators as well as by a new customer, British West Indian Airways, which became the fiftieth DC-9 user when in 1976 it acquired one convertible Series 30 and two Series 50s.

The USAF received its first C-9A on 8 August, 1968, and since then Nightingales have been operated by the 375th Aeromedical Airlift Wing in the US, the 7111th Operations Squadron and 55th Aeromedical Airlift Squadron in Germany, and the 20th Aeromedical Airlift Squadron in the Philippines. The Special Air Mission (ie, VIP transport) VC-9Cs have been operated since the mid-seventies by the 89th Military Airlift Wing at Andrews AFB, on the outskirts of Washington, DC. In naval service, C-9Bs are operated by eight Navy transport squadrons (VR-51 and VR-55 to VR-61) and by the Marines from MCAS Cherry Point, North Carolina.

Data for DC-9 Series appear on page 546.

	DC-9-15	DC-9-21	DC-9-33CF	DC-9-41	DC-9-51
Span, ft in	89 5	93 5	93 5	93 5	93 5
(m)	(27·25)	(28·47)	(28·47)	(28·47)	(28·47)
Length, ft in	104 5	104 5	119 5	125 7	133 7
(m)	(31·82)	(31·82)	(36·39)	(38·27)	(40·71)
Height, ft in	27 6	27 6	27 6	28 1	28 1
(m)	(8·38)	(8·38)	(8·38)	(8·56)	(8·56)
Wing area, sq ft	934·3	1,000·7	1,000·7	1,000·7	1,000·7
(sq m)	(86·796)	(92·965)	(92·965)	(92·965)	(92·965)
Operating weight empty, lb	49,160	52,640	—	59,130	65,000
(kg)	(22,299)	(23,877)		(26,821)	(29,484)
MGTOW, lb	90,700	100,000	114,000	114,000	121,000
(kg)	(41,141)	(45,359)	(51,710)	(51,710)	(54,885)
Wing loading, lb/sq ft	97·1	99·9	113·9	113·9	120·9
(kg/sq m)	(474)	(487·9)	(556·2)	(556·2)	(590·4)
Power loading, lb/lb st	3·2	3·4	3·0	3·7	3·8
Maximum speed, mph	575	581	575	564	564
(km/h)	(925)	(935)	(925)	(908)	(908)
Cruising speed, mph	495	495	495	506	506
(km/h)	(797)	(797)	(797)	(814)	(814)
Range with maximum payload, lb/miles	24,840/690	25,360/1,150	—	36,360/670	33,000/805
(kg/km)	(11,270/1,110)	(11,505/1,850)	—	(16,495/1,080)	(14,970/1,295)
Range with maximum fuel, lb/miles	17,000/1,670	21,000/1,670	—	31,000/1,245	21,400/2,150
(kg/km)	(7,710/2,690)	(9,525/2,690)	—	(14,060/2,005)	(9,705/3,460)
Ferry range, miles	1,955	2,015	2,070	1,725	2,475
(km)	(3,145)	(3,245)	(3,330)	(2,775)	(3,985)

DC-9 PRODUCTION SUMMARY: Excluding DC-9-80s and MD-80s, a total of 976 DC-9s were built in the Long Beach plant between 1965 and 1982. This total comprises 113 Series 10s, 19 Series 15RCs, 5 Series 15MCs, 10 Series 20s, 584 Series 30s, 6 Series 30AF, 17 Series 30CFs, 14 Series 30RCs, 71 Series 40s, 96 Series 50s, and 41 C-9s.

The last of these aircraft a C-9B, was delivered 28 October, 1982, but production of MD-80s will continue well into the 1990s.

Powered by CFM56-2-C turbofans, the DC-8 Super 72 offers exceptional range performance. With maximum passenger load, 200 in all-tourist configuration, this re-engined DC-8-62 can fly 7,220 miles (11,620 km) nonstop. (*Cammacorp*)

Cammacorp DC-8 Super 70

In 1965, after Boeing had announced the launching of its 747 programme, Douglas seriously considered countering with a development of the stretched DC-8 Series 60 powered by advanced turbofans. While some of its systems would not have been as advanced as those of the Boeing 747, the proposed aircraft had several things in its favour as pointed out in a memorandum to management written by the author in October 1965. Firstly, the use of advanced turbofans would give the aircraft the required range characteristics (whereas, for example, Swissair felt that the DC-8-63 lacked the range for full payload operations between Zürich and New York), lower noise characteristics, reduced pollutant emission, and improved take-off and climb performance. Secondly, the aircraft would enable airlines to control capacity increase by going from 707s and DC-8s with 140 seats in mixed-class configuration, to stretched and re-engined DC-8s with 210 seats in a similar configuration, and only then to 747s with 350 to 430 seats, thus avoiding the excess capacity which was bound to result from wide-body jet operations. Finally, the development of this aircraft by Douglas would place Boeing in a difficult situation by forcing it to choose between either pushing forward with the development of the 747, then too capacious for the market, or undertaking a costly development programme to redesign the wing and undercarriage of the 707 to match the size of the proposed re-engined stretched DC-8.

Notwithstanding these advantages, Douglas concluded that a re-engined DC-8-63 would provide insufficient work for its engineering staff and preferred to attempt developing a double-deck, wide-bodied aircraft with maximum accommodation for up to 650 passengers. When that overly ambitious 'DC-10' project failed to attract airline interest, it was not just the engineering staff but the entire Douglas staff which found itself without sufficient work outside of the DC-9 programme. Moreover, failure to provide airline customers with a viable alternative to the 747 contributed to Douglas being forced into a merger. Be that as it may, the advanced turbofan stretched DC-8 concept remained dormant for nearly 12 years. Finally, in 1977, five years after the production of JT3D-powered DC-8s had ended in Long Beach, a group of former Douglas executives resurrected the idea and organized Cammacorp for the express purpose of marketing DC-8 Series 61, 62, 63 aircraft re-engined with either CFM International CFM56 high-bypass-ratio turbofans or Pratt & Whitney JT8D-209 refanned engines. In April 1979, after United Airlines became the first airline to confirm its interest and selected the CFM56 to re-engine its thirty DC-8-61s, further work on the proposed JT8D-powered version was discontinued.

On the strength of United's order and of almost simultaneous commitments from Delta and Flying Tigers, Cammacorp was able to proceed with the programme. However, lacking personnel and facilities to engineer, manufacture, test, and support the re-engined aircraft, it was forced to subcontract these tasks. The Douglas Aircraft Company was retained to design the necessary modifications in Long Beach, to undertake the testing of the aircraft at its flight test facility in Yuma, Arizona, and to manufacture components in Tulsa, Oklahoma. Grumman Corporation was selected to design and built the engine nacelles and perform other related work. Furthermore, while aircraft needed for the certification programme were to be converted by Douglas in Tulsa, Cammacorp proposed from the onset that other aircraft be re-engined either in Tulsa or in engineering and maintenance facilities of major airlines.

Whether converted from Series 61, 62 or 63 airframes, all aircraft were to be re-engined with 22,000 lb (9,979 kg) thrust CFM International CFM56-2C turbofans housed in Grumman-designed nacelles and fitted with 'cut-back' underwing pylons as orginally developed for Series 62 and 63 aircraft. Thus, the conversion of DC-8-61s required more work, including the installation of new wing leading-edge segments, but yielded greater improvements in performance.

The first aircraft to be converted was a United DC-8-61, N8093U, which was redesignated DC-8-71 and first flew in Tulsa on 15 August, 1981. However, following certification of the DC-8-71 in April 1982, it was Delta Air Lines which placed the type in service on 24 April. By then, the DC-8-72 (re-engined DC-8-62) and DC-8-73 (re-engined DC-8-63) were already undergoing trials after first flying respectively on 5 December, 1981, and 4 March, 1982. Both of these models entered service shortly after being certificated in May 1982. All three Super 70 models were certificated in passenger, convertible, and all-cargo variants and could be fitted with up to three easily removable fuel tanks in baggage holds.

The use of CFM56s to re-engine DC-8 Series 50 aircraft was also proposed but proved unattractive to airlines. Coming too late, the DC-8 re-engining programme proved less successful overall than anticipated by Cammacorp and only 110 of the 262 DC-8 Series 60 aircraft were modified as DC-8 Super 70s by Air Canada (9 aircraft), Delta Air Lines (48 aircraft), Douglas (44 aircraft), and UTA Industries (9 aircraft). Models and serial numbers of the re-engined aircraft are listed below:

DC-8-71: The following 43 DC-8-61s were re-engined: 45810/45813, 45849, 45907, 45914/45915, 45941, 45944/45947, 45970/45971, 45973/45979, 45983, 45993/45998, 46014, 46018, 46029/46030, 46039/46040, 46048, 46055/46056, 46064/46066, 46072, and 46099.

DC-8-71CF: The following ten DC-8-61CFs were re-engined: 45897/45898, 45900, 45902, 45938/45939, 45948/45950, and 45952.

This DC-8-73CF, s/n 45991, was built as a DC-8-63CF and, registered N781FT, entered service with Flying Tigers in July 1968. It was re-engined with CFM56-2s during the spring of 1984 and has since been operated by German Cargo as D-ADUI. (*H. L. James*)

DC-8-72: The following four DC-8-62s were re-engined: 46067, 46081/46082, and 46084.

DC-8-72CF: The following three DC-8-62CFs were re-engined: 46013, 46043, and 46130.

DC-8-73: One DC-8-63, 46063, was re-engined.

DC-8-73AF: The following six DC-8-63AFs were re-engined: 46003/46004, 46006/46008, and 46044.

DC-8-73CF: The following 33 DC-8-63CFs were re-engined: 45936, 45966/45968, 45990/45991, 46001/46002, 46045/46047, 46051/46053,

46059, 46062, 46073, 46086, 46089/46091, 46094, 46101, 46103/46104, 46106, 46108/46109, 46112, 46117, 46133, 46140, and 46149.

DC-8-73F: The following eight DC-8-63s were re-engined and fitted with a main-deck cargo door: 46019, 46033, 46076, 46080,46100, and 46123/46125.

DC-8-73PF: The following two DC-8-63PFs were re-engined: 46074 and 46095.

Having obtained 13 and 29 DC-8-71s respectively in 1982-83, Delta and United became the main operators of passenger-configured Super 70s. The principal operator of cargo-configured aircraft was United Parcel Service which by the end of 1987 had acquired 42 aircraft including several DC-8-71CFs, -73AFs, and -73CFs, as well as two DC-8-73Fs and one DC-8-73PF. Other DC-8-70s went to such diverse operators as the Sultan of Oman (one DC-8-73CF), NASA (one DC-8-72 based at the Ames Research Center, Moffett Field, California, and used for medium-altitude land and ocean sciences research), and the French Air Force (three DC-8-72CFs).

Dimensions and maximum take-off weight of the DC-8-71, DC-8-72, and DC-8-73 were the same as those of DC-8 Series 61, 62 and 63. The only exception was the DC-8-71CF which was certificated at a maximum take-off weight of 350,000 lb (158,757 kg) versus 325,000 lb (147,418 kg) for the corresponding DC-8-61CF. Likewise, DC-8 Super 70 maximum and cruising speeds were similar to those of the DC-8 Super but take-off field length and payload/range were substantially improved as shown in this table:

	Take-off field length	Range with maximum passenger load
DC-8-71	8,950 ft/2,730 m	4,650 mi/7,485 km
DC-8-61	9,880 ft/3,040 m	3,750 mi/6,035 km
Percentage reduction/increase	− 11.3 per cent	+ 24.0 per cent
DC-8-72	9,700 ft/2,955 m	7,220 mi/11,620 km
DC-8-62	9,780 ft/2,980 m	6,000 mi/9,640 km
Percentage reduction/increase	− 0.8 per cent	+ 20.3 per cent
DC-8-73	10,050 ft/3,065 m	5,560 mi/8,950 km
DC-8-63	11,500 ft/3,505 m	4,500 mi/7,240 km
Percentage reduction/increase	− 12.6 per cent	+ 23.6 per cent

Production Summary

The table summarizes by plants the total production for all aircraft designed and/or built by the Davis-Douglas Company, the Douglas Company, the Douglas Aircraft Company and the Northrop Corporation. It includes also the aircraft of their design built under licence by other contractors and the aircraft built by these companies under licence from other contractors.

Only the general types are identified in this summary (*eg*, under the designation DC-3 and derivatives are included not only the true commercial DC-3 models, but also all military variants and licence-built versions). Full details by models and variants are provided in the main text and in Appendices B and C.

In this table, aircraft shown as produced in Santa Monica include those manufactured in the original facilities at the Koll Planning Mill and in the Wilshire Boulevard plant.

DOUGLAS PLANTS

AIRCRAFT TYPES	USAAF/USAF PLANT DESIGNATORS						OTHER CONTRACTORS	TOTAL
	Santa Monica DO	El Segundo DE	Long Beach DL	Tulsa DT	Chicago DC	Oklahoma City DK		
Davis-Douglas Cloudster	1	—	—	—	—	—	—	1
Douglas DT	46	—	—	—	—	—	44	90
Curtiss HS-2L	2	—	—	—	—	—	—	2
Douglas World Cruiser	11	—	—	—	—	—	—	11
Douglas Observation Biplanes	879	—	—	—	—	—	6	885
Douglas C-1	26	—	—	—	—	—	—	26
Douglas Mailplanes (M Series)	59	—	—	—	—	—	—	59
Douglas Commuter	1	—	—	—	—	—	—	1
Douglas T2D and P2D	30	—	—	—	—	—	—	30
Douglas DA-1	1	—	—	—	—	—	—	1
Douglas PD-1	25	—	—	—	—	—	—	25
Douglas Sinbad and Dolphin	59	—	—	—	—	—	—	59
Douglas Observation Monoplanes	127	—	—	—	—	—	—	127
Douglas 0-35 and B-7	14	—	—	—	—	—	—	14
Douglas XT3D	1	—	—	—	—	—	—	1
Northrop Gamma	—	61	—	—	—	—	—	61
Douglas XFD-1	1	—	—	—	—	—	—	1
Northrop Delta	—	13	—	—	—	—	19	32
Douglas DC-1	1	—	—	—	—	—	—	1
Northrop XFT	—	1	—	—	—	—	—	1
Douglas X02D-1	1	—	—	—	—	—	—	1
Douglas DC-2	193	—	—	—	—	—	5	198

DOUGLAS PLANTS

AIRCRAFT TYPES	USAAF/USAF PLANT DESIGNATORS						OTHER CONTRACTORS	TOTAL
	Santa Monica DO	El Segundo DE	Long Beach DL	Tulsa DT	Chicago DC	Oklahoma City DK		
Douglas YOA-5 and XP3D	2	—	—	—	—	—	—	2
Douglas TBD Devastator	130	—	—	—	—	—	—	130
Douglas B-18 Bolo	370	—	—	—	—	—	—	370
Northrop 3A	—	1	—	—	—	—	—	1
Northrop A-17 and Douglas 8A	—	351	—	—	—	—	102	453
Northrop BT-1	—	54	—	—	—	—	—	54
Northrop 5	—	3	—	—	—	—	—	3
Douglas DC-3 and Derivatives	960	—	4,285	—	—	5,409	2,500+	13,154+
Douglas DF	4	—	—	—	—	—	—	4
Douglas SBD and A-24 Dauntless	—	5,323	—	615	—	—	—	5,938
Douglas DC-4E	1	—	—	—	—	—	—	1
Douglas DB-7 and A-20 Havoc/Boston	5,998	101	999	—	—	—	380	7,478
Douglas DC-5	—	12	—	—	—	—	—	12
Douglas B-23 Dragon	38	—	—	—	—	—	—	38
Douglas XB-19	1	—	—	—	—	—	—	1
Douglas DC-4 Skymaster	589	—	—	—	655	—	71	1,315
Bowlus XCG-7 and XCG-8	—	4	—	—	—	—	—	4
B-17-DL and B-24-DT	—	—	3,030	962	—	—	—	3,962
Douglas A-26 Invader	—	3	1,157	1,292	—	—	—	2,452
Douglas XSB2D-1 and BTD Destroyer	—	30	—	—	—	—	—	30
Douglas XB-42 Mixmaster	2	—	—	—	—	—	—	2
Douglas XTB2D-1 Skypirate	—	2	—	—	—	—	—	2

553

DOUGLAS PLANTS

AIRCRAFT TYPES	USAAF/USAF PLANT DESIGNATORS						OTHER CONTRACTORS	TOTAL
	Santa Monica DO	El Segundo DE	Long Beach DL	Tulsa DT	Chicago DC	Oklahoma City DK		
Douglas AD Skyraider	–	3,180	–	–	–	–	–	3,180
Douglas C-74 Globemaster I	–	–	14	–	–	–	–	14
Douglas DC-6	704	–	–	–	–	–	–	704
Douglas XB-43	2	–	–	–	–	–	–	2
Douglas D-558-1 Skystreak	–	3	–	–	–	–	–	3
Douglas Cloudster II	1	–	–	–	–	–	–	1
Douglas F3D Skyknight	–	268	–	–	–	–	–	268
Douglas D-558-2 Skyrocket	–	3	–	–	–	–	–	3
Douglas Super DC-3	105	–	–	–	–	–	–	105
Douglas C-124 Globemaster II	–	–	448	–	–	–	–	448
Douglas A2D-1 Skyshark	–	12	–	–	–	–	–	12
Douglas F4D Skyray	–	421	–	–	–	–	–	421
Douglas X-3 Stiletto	1	–	–	–	–	–	–	1
Douglas A-3 Skywarrior	–	283	–	–	–	–	–	283
Boeing B-47	–	–	–	262	–	–	–	262
Douglas DC-7	338	–	–	–	–	–	–	338
Douglas A-4 Skyhawk	–	1,168	1,792	–	–	–	–	2,960
Douglas B-66 Destroyer	–	–	222	72	–	–	–	294
Douglas F5D-1 Skylancer	–	4	–	–	–	–	–	4
Douglas C-133 Cargomaster	–	–	50	–	–	–	–	50
Douglas DC-8	–	–	556	–	–	–	–	556
Douglas DC-9	–	–	976	–	–	–	–	976
TOTALS	10,724	11,301	13,499	3,203	655	5,409	3,127	47,918

Flagship San Francisco, s/n 2263, was the penultimate DST ordered by American Airlines. (*American Airlines*)

The second XA2D-1, BuNo 122989, with the taller tail surfaces retrofitted during trials. (*Air Force Flight Test Center*)

HZ-AEA, s/n 47000, one of three DC-9-15s operated by Saudi Arabian Airlines between 1967 and 1976. (*MDC*)

555

APPENDIX B

Production Details and Douglas Serial Numbers

This Appendix contains the following data for each type of aircraft produced by the Davis-Douglas Company, the Douglas Company, the Douglas Aircraft Company Inc, and the Douglas Aircraft Division of the McDonnell Corporation:

Column 1—Factory serial numbers (s/ns)
Column 2—Aircraft model
Column 3—Original customer
Column 4—Original military serial numbers or civil registrations
Column 5—Number of aircraft in each batch of factory serial numbers

These data are arranged by aircraft type in the same chronological sequence as used in the main text. Within each aircraft type, the data are listed in the numerical sequence of the factory serial numbers assigned to each batch of aircraft.

Due to the large number of aircraft produced by Douglas Aircraft and their forebears, only the original military serial numbers or civil registrations are given and no attempt has been made to list subsequent changes in identity.

Factory serial numbers preceded by an asterisk are serial numbers assigned to aircraft from the Northrop/El Segundo Division production line.

```
DOUGLAS CLOUDSTER (Number built:  1)
100              Cloudster        D. R. Davis              --              1

DOUGLAS DT (Number built:  90, including 46 by Douglas and 44 by licensees)
101              DT-1             USN             A6031                    1
102/103          DT-2             USN             A6032/A6033              2
106/123          DT-2             USN             A6405/A6422             18
124/143          DT-2             USN             A6563/A6582             20
149              DT-2B            Norway          --                      1
253/254          DTB              Peru            --                      2
384/385          DTB              Peru            --                      2

CURTISS HS-2L (Number rebuilt by Douglas:  2)
104/105          HS-2L            Pacific Marine  551/552                 2

DOUGLAS WORLD CRUISER (Number built:  11)
144              DWC              USAAS           23-1210                  1
145/148          DWC              USAAS           23-1229/23-1232          4
151/156          DOS (0-5)        USAAS           24-2/24-7                6

DOUGLAS OBSERVATION BIPLANES (Number built:  885, including 879 by Douglas and
                                       6 by licensee)
157              XO-2             USAAS           23-1251                  1
167              XO-2             USAAS           23-1254                  1
168              O-2A             USAAS           25-387                   1
170/214          O-2              USAAS           25-335/25-379           45
215              XA-2             USAAS           25-380                   1
216/221          O-2B             USAAS           25-381/25-386            6
222/238          O-2A             USAAS           25-388/25-404           17
239/241          O-7              USAAS           25-405/25-407            3
242              O-8              USAAS           25-408                   1
243              O-9              USAAS           25-409                   1
265              O-2BS            James McKee     C 236                    1
266/277          O-2C             USAAC           26-386/26-397           12
278/279          OD-1             USMC            A7203/A7204              2
280/297          O-2C             USAAC/NG        26-400/26-417           18
298/299          O-2D             USAAC           26-419/26-420            2
300              O-2E             USAAC           26-418                   1
301/302          O-2C             USAAC           26-398/26-399            2
343/356          O-2C             USAAC/NG        26-001/26-014           14
358/365          O-2C             Mexico          --                      8
386/395          O-2H             USAAC           27-288/27-297           10
405              O-2J             USAAC           28-127                   1
406/465          O-2H             USAAC           28-128/28-187           60
466              O-2J             USAAC           28-188                   1
467/476          O-2H             NG              28-349/28-358           10
477              XO-14            USAAC           28-194                   1
504/508          O-2K             USAAC           29-179/29-183            5
509              Y10-29           USAAC           29-184                   1
510/533          O-2K             USAAC           29-185/29-208           24
534              O-2J             USAAC           29-209                   1
535/542          O-2K             USAAC           29-210/29-217            8
543              O-32             USAAC           29-218                   1
544-549          O-2H             USAAC           29-158/29-163            6
550              O-25             USAAC           29-164                   1
551/564          O-2H             USAAC           29-165/29-178           14
565/574          O-2H             NG              29-342/29-351           10
575/604          O-2H             NG              29-375/29-404           30
605/606          O-22             USAAC           29-371/29-372            2
607              YO 34            USAAC           29-373                   1
608/616          O-2M             Mexico          --                      9
617/636          O-2K             NG              29-413/29-432           20
637/666          O-32A            USAAC           30-196/30-225           30
667              O-25A            USAAC           30-160                   1
```

668/670	O-25B	USAAC	30-161/30-163	3
671/702	O-25A	USAAC	30-164/30-195	32
704/720	O-25A	USAAC	30-354/30-370	17
723/868	BT-2B	USAAC	31-1/31-146	146
869	O-38A	NG	30-407	1
370/881	O-38	NG	30-408/30-419	12
882/912	O-38	NG	31-349/31-379	31
915/924	O-2MC	China	--	10
925/926	O-2M-2	Mexico	--	2
946	O-2M-2	Mexico	--	1
947/948	O-38	NG	31-406/31-407	2
949/968	BT-2C	USAAC	31-439/31-458	20
969/998	O-38B	USAAC	31-409/31-438	30
1004/1033	O-25C	USAAC	32-181/32-210	30
1034/1048	O-38B	NG	32-102/32-116	15
1049/1068	O-2MC-2	China	--	20
1090/1107	O-38B	NB	32-325/32-342	18
1120	O-38C	USAAC	32-394	1
1121	O-38S	Co owned	X12267	1
1127/1131	O-2MC-3	China	--	5
1141/1146	O-38P	Peru	--	6
1147/1161	O-38E	NG	33-002/33-016	15
1162/1173	O-2MC-4	China	--	12
1175/1182	O-38F	NG	33-322/33-329	8
1213/1234	O-38E	NG	34-001/34-022	22
1336/1347	O-2MC-5	China	--	12
1379/1400	O-2MC-6	China	--	22
?	O-2MC-10	China	--	1

DOUGLAS C-1 (Number built: 26)
158/166	C-1	USAAS	25-425/25-433	9
366/372	C-1C	USAAC	26-421/26-427	7
373/382	C-1C	USAAC	27-203/27-212	10

DOUGLAS MAILPLANES (Number built: 59)
169	DAM-1	Co owned	--	1
244/245	M-2	WAE	C150/C151	2
246/248	M-2	WAE	C1489/C1491	3
252	M-2	WAE	C1512	1
255/264	M-3	US Post Office	--	10
303/342	M-4	US Post Office	--	40
357	M-4A	WAE	C1475	1
383	M-4S	NAT	C7163	1

DOUGLAS COMMUTER (Number built: 1)
| 150 | Commuter | Co owned | -- | 1 |

DOUGLAS T2D AND P2D (Number built: 30)
249/251	XT2D-1	USN	A7051/A7053	3
396/404	T2D-1	USN	A7587/A7595	9
928/945	P2D-1	USN	A8644/A8661	18

DOUGLAS DA-1 (Number built: 1)
| 503 | DA-1 | Ambassador AW | X7281 | 1 |

DOUGLAS PD-1 (Number built: 25)
| 478/502 | PD-1 | USN | A7979/A8003 | 25 |

DOUGLAS SINBAD AND DOLPHIN (Number built: 59)
703	Sinbad	Co owned	X145Y	1
999	Dolphin 1	Wilmington-Catal	NC967Y	1
1000	XRD-1	USN	A8876	1
1101	Dolphin 3	Powell Crosley	NC982Y	1
1002	Dolphin 1	Wilmington-Catal	NC12212	1

1003	Dolphin 1 Sp	Co owned	NC12243	1
1075/1082	Y1C-21	USAAC	32-279/32-286	8
1083/1084	Y1C-26	USAAC	32-396/32-397	2
1122	RD-2	USCG	29	1
1123/1126	Y1C-26A	USAAC	32-403/32-406	4
1132/1135	Y1C-26A	USAAC	32-407/32-410	4
1138/1140	RD-2	USN	9347/9349	3
1183/1184	C-29	USAAC	33-292/33-293	2
1185/1188	C-26B	USAAC	33-294/33-297	4
1262/1267	RD-3	USN	9528/9533	6
1268/1277	RD-4	USCG	130/139	10
1278	Dolphin 113	Armand Esders	NC14203	1
1279	Dolphin 114	Philip Wrigley	NC14204	1
1280	Dolphin 117	William Boeing	NC14205	1
1281	Dolphin	Armada Argentina	T-203	1
1282	Dolphin 136	S.O. New Jersey	NC14286	1
1283	Dolphin 119	A G Vanderbilt	NC14207	1
1284	Dolphin 119	W K Vanderbilt	NC14208	1
1348/1349	Dolphin 129	Pan American	NC14239/NC14240	2

DOUGLAS OBSERVATION MONOPLANES (Number built: 127)

721	XO-31	USAAC	30-229	1
722	YO-31	USAAC	30-230	1
1069/1072	YO-31A	USAAC	31-604/31-607	4
1073	YO-31C	USAAC	31-608	1
1074	YO-31B	NG	32-231	1
1085/1089	Y1O-43	USAAC	32-291/32-295	5
1189/1211	O-43A	USAAC	33-268/33-290	23
1212	XO-46	USAAC	33-291	1
1423/1493	O-46A	USAAC	35-161/35-231	71
1528/1544	O-46A	USAAC	36-128/36-144	17
1558/1559	O-46A	NG	36-147/36-148	2

DOUGLAS O-35 AND B-7 (Number built: 14)

913	XO-35	USAAC	30-227	1
914	XB-7	USAAC	30-228	1
1108/1114	Y1B-7	USAAC	32-308/32-314	7
1115/1119	Y1O-35	USAAC	32-315/32-319	5

DOUGLAS XT3D (Number built: 1)

| 927 | XT3D-1 | USN | A8730 | 1 |

NORTHROP GAMMA (Number built: 61)

* 1	Gamma 2A	Texas Co	X12265	1
* 2	Gamma 2B	Lincoln Ellsworth	X12269	1
* 5	Gamma 2C	Co owned	X12291	1
* 8/10	Gamma 2D	TWA	X13757/X13758/NC13759	3
* 11	Gamma 2G	J Cochran	X13761	1
* 12	Gamma 2H	M P Guggenheim	X2111	1
* 14	Gamma 2E	China	--	1
* 15/16	Gamma 2ED	China	--	2
* 17/22	Gamma 2EC	China	--	6
* 23/27	Gamma 2ED	China	--	5
* 30/37	Gamma 2ED	China	--	8
* 44	Gamma 2F	Co owned	--	1
* 45	Gamma 2EC	China	--	1
* 46	Gamma 2E	China	--	1
* 47	Gamma 2ED-C	Co owned	X13760	1
* 48/72	Gamma 2E	China	--	25
* 186	Gamma 2J	Co owned	X18148	1
* 347	Gamma 2L	Bristol	G-AFBT	1

```
DOUGLAS XFD-1 (Number built:  1)
1136              XFD-1            USN              9223                    1

NORTHROP DELTA (Number built:  32, including 13 by Douglas and 19 by licensee)
*  3             Delta 1A         TWA              X12292                   1
*  4             Delta 1B         Pan American     X236Y                    1
*  7             Delta 1C         ABA              SE-ADI                   1
* 28             Delta 1D         Richfield Oil    NC13777                  1
* 29             Delta 1F         ABA              X13755                   1
* 38             Delta 1D-1       Powell Crosley   NC14241                  1
* 39             Delta 1D-2       Hal Roach        NC14242                  1
* 40             Delta 1D-3       W H Danforth     NC14265                  1
* 41             Delta 1D-4       Morton May       NC14266                  1
* 42             Delta 1D-5       G F Harding      NC14267                  1
* 73             Delta 1D-6       B Dodson         NC14220                  1
* 74             RT-1             USCG             382                      1
* 185            Delta 1D-8       Canada           --                       1

DOUGLAS DC-1 (Number built:  1)
1137             DC-1             TWA              X223Y                    1

NORTHROP XFT (Number built:  1)
*  6             XFT-1            USN              9400                     1

DOUGLAS XO2D-1 (Number built:  1)
1236             XO2D-1           USN              9412                     1

DOUGLAS DC-2 (Number built:  198, including 193 by Douglas and 5 by licensee)
1237/1256        DC-2-112         TWA              NC13711/NC13730         20
1257/1260        DC-2-112         General AL       NC13731/NC13734          4
1261             DC-2-112         Eastern          NC13735                  1
1286/1290        DC-2-112         Eastern          NC13736/NC13740          5
1291/1292        DC-2-112         Eastern          NC13781/NC13782          2
1293/1300        DC-2-112         TWA              NC13783/NC13790          8
1301/1306        DC-2-118A/B      PAA/PAA Grace    NC14268/NC14273          6
1307/1316        DC-2-120         American         NC14274/NC14283         10
1317             DC-2-115A        Fokker           NC14284                  1
1318             DC-2-115D        Fokker           PH-AKF                   1
1319             DC-2-115B (DC-2A) Avio Linee Ital  I-EROS                  1
1320             DC-2-115D        Austrian Gov'mt  A-500                    1
1321/1322        DC-2-115B        Swissair         HB-ITI & HB-ITE          2
1323             DC-2-123         Nakajima         NC14284                  1
1324             DC-2-124         Swiftlite Corp   NC1000                   1
1325/1327        R2D-1 (DC-2-125) USN              9620/9622                3
1328             DC-2A-127 (DC-2A) Standard Oil     NC14285                 1
1329             DC-2-115B        Swissair         HB-ITA                   1
1330             DC-2-115D        LAPE             EC-XAX                   1
1331/1332        DC-2-115D/F      Swissair         HB-ISI & HB-ITO          2
1333             DC-2-115B        French Gov'mt    F-AKHD                   1
1334             DC-2-115B        LAPE             EC-AAY                   1
1335             DC-2-115E        KLM              PH-AKG                   1
1350/1352        DC-2-118B/A      PAA/PAA Grace    NC14290/NC14292          3
1354/1365        DC-2-115E        KLM              PH-AKH/PH-AKS           12
1366             DC-2-115H (DC-2A) KLM              PH-AKT                  1
1367/1370        DC-2-118D/A      PAA/PAA Grace    NC14295/NC14298          4
1371             DC-2-118B        PAA              NC14950                  1
1372/1373        DC-2-171         Eastern          NC14969/NC14970          2
1374/1376        DC-2-115G        KNILM            PK-AFJ/PK-AFL            3
1377/1378        DC-2-115F (DC-2B) LOT              SP-ASK/SP-ASL           2
1401/1403        DC-2-120         American         NC14921/NC14923          3
1404/1405        R2D-1 (DC-2-142) USN              9993/9994                2
1406             DC-2-120         American         NC14966                  1
1407             DC-2             American         Parts only              --
1408/1409        DC-2-172         TWA              NC14978/NC14979          2
```

```
1410/1411    DC-2-120          American          NC14924/NC14925        2
1412         DC-2              American          Parts only            --
1413         DC-2-152          Amtorg (USSR)     NC14949 (URSS-M25)     1
1414         XC-32 (DC-2-153)  USAAC             36-1                   1
1415         YC-34 (DC-2-173)  USAAC             36-345                 1
1416         YC-34 (DC-2-346)  USAAC             36-346                 1
1417         DC-2-115J         LAPE              EC-EBB                 1
1418/1422    DC-2              Nakajima          Parts only            --
1503/1520    C-33 (DC-2-145)   USAAC             36-70/36-87           18
1521         DC-2-115J         LAPE              EC-BBE                 1
1527         DC-2-115M         Fokker            --                     1
1560         DC-2-192          China             --                     1
1561         DC-2-199          Holyman's AW      VH-UXJ                 1
1562         DC-2-200          CLS               OK-AIC                 1
1563         DC-2-210          ANA               VH-UYB                 1
1564         DC-2-211          Fokker            PH-ALZ                 1
1565         DC-2-211          CLS               OK-AID                 1
1566         DC-2-210          ANA               VH-UYC                 1
1567/1568    DC-2-221          CNAC              --                     2
1580         DC-2-185          Holyman's AW      VH-USY                 1
1581/1582    DC-2-115K         CLS               OK-AIA/OK-AIB          2
1583/1585    DC-2-115L         KLM               PH-ALD/PH-ALF          3
1586         DC-2-190          Capt G Whittell   NC16048                1
1598         DC-2-193          China             --                     1
1599         DC-2-172          TWA               NC16049                1
1600         DC-2              CNAC              Parts only            --
2053         C-41 (DC-2-253)   USAAC             38-502                 1
2057/2059    C-39 (DC-2-243)   USAAC             38-499/38-501          3
2060         C-42 (DC-2-267)   USAAC             38-503                 1
2061/2092    C-39 (DC-2-243)   USAAC             38-504/38-535         32

DOUGLAS YOA-5 AND XP3D (Number built:  2)
1174         YOA-5             USAAC             33-17                  1
1235         XP3D-1            USN               9613                   1

DOUGLAS TBD DEVASTATOR (Number built:  130)
1285         XTBD-1            USN               9720                   1
1750/1863    TBD-1             USN               0268/0381            114
2273/2287    TBD-1             USN               1505/1519             15

DOUGLAS B-18 BOLO (Number built:  370)
1353         DB-1              Co owned          --                     1
1630/1649    Digby             RCAF              738/757               20
1650/1731    B-18              USAAC             36-262/36-343         82
1732/1747    B-18              USAAC             36-431/36-446         16
1748/1749    B-18              USAAC             37 1/37-2              2
1864/1894    B-18              USAAC             37-3/37-33            31
1950         DB-2              USAAC             37-34                  1
2458/2634    B-18A             USAAC             37-458/37-634        177
2635/2659    B-18A             USAAC             38-585/38-609         25
2660/2674    B-18A             USAAC             39-12/39-26           15

NORTHROP 3A (Number built:  1)
*  184       3A                Co owned          --                     1

NORTHROP A-17 AND DOUGLAS 8A (Number built:  453, including 351 by Douglas and
                                             102 by licensee)
*  75/183    A-17              USAAC             35-052/35-160        109
*  189/288   A-17A             USAAC             36-162/36-261        100
*  289/290   A-17AS            USAAC             36-349/36-350          2
*  348/377   8A-2              Argentina         --                    30
*  378       8A-1              Sweden            7001                   1
*  381/409   A-17A             USAAC             38-327/38-355         29
*  410       8A-1              Sweden            7002                   1
```

```
  *  412/421       8A-3P              Peru                 --             10
  *  531/548       8A-3N              Netherlands          381/398        18
  *  613/627       8A-4              Iraq                 --             15
  *  715/750       8A-5              Norway               --             36

NORTHROP BT-1 (Number built:  54)
  *  43            XBT-1              USN                  9745            1
  *  293/329       BT-1              USN                  0590/0626      37
  *  331/346       BT-1              USN                  0628/0643      16

NORTHROP 5 (Number built:  3)
  *  187           5A                Co owned             X14997          1
  *  188           5B                Co owned             NR14998         1
  *  291           5D                Co owned             X16091          1

DOUGLAS DC-3 AND DERIVATIVES (Number built:  10,654 by Douglas plus some 2,500
                                             under license)
  1494            DST-144            American             NX14988         1
  1495/1500       DST-144            American             NC16001/NC16006 6
  1545/1548       DC-3-178           American             NC16009, NC16030,
                                                          NC16011, NC16012 4
  1549            DST-144            American             NC16007         1
  1551/1557       DC-3-178           American             NC16013/NC16019 7
  1588            DC-3-178           American             NC16008         1
  1589            DC-3-196           USSR                 --              1
  1590            DC-3-194           KLM                  PH-ALI          1
  1900/1909       DC-3A-191          United               NC16060/NC16069 10
  1910/1914       DC-3A-197          United               NC16070/NC16074 5
  1915/1916       DC-3-201           Eastern              NC16094/NC16095 2
  1917/1921       DC-3-178           American             NC17331/NC17335 5
  1922/1924       DC-3B-202          TWA                  NC17312/NC17314 3
  1925/1929       DC-3A-197          United               NC16086/NC16090 5
  1930/1934       DC-3B-202          TWA                  NC17315/NC17319 5
  1935/1944       DC-3-194B          KLM                  PH-ALH, -ALN, -ALO,
                                                          -ALR/-ALW       10
  1945/1946       DC-3-216           Swissair             HB-IRA, HB-IRI  2
  1947            DC-3A-214          ABA                  SE-BAA          1
  1948/1949       DC-3-201           Eastern              NC16081/NC16082 2
  1951/1958       DST-A-207          United               NC18103/NC18110 8
  1959/1960       DST-A-207          Western              NC18101/NC18102 2
  1961/1964       DC-3-208           American             NC17326/NC17329 4
  1965            DC-3-194B          KLM                  PH-ALP          1
  1966/1970       DC-3-209           TWA                  NC17320/NC17324 5
  1971            DC-3-201           Eastern              NC16083         1
  1972            DC-3A-214          ABA                  SE-BAB          1
  1973            DC-3-220           CLS                  OK-AIH          1
  1974            DC-3-227           USSR                 --              1
  1975            DC-3A-214          ABA                  SE-BAC          1
  1976            DST-217            American             NC18144         1
  1977/1978       DST-A-207A         United               NC18145/NC18146 2
  1979            DC-3-237A          Mitsui               --              1
  1980/1982       DC-3-194C          KLM                  PH-ARB, -ARE, -ARG 3
  1983/1984       DC-3A-197          United               NC18611/NC18612 2
  1985/1986       DC-3-227           Lares                YR-PIF, YR-PAF  2
  1987/1988       DC-3-227           USSR                 --              2
  1989/1994       DC-3-228           Pan American         NC18113/NC18118 6
  1995            DC-3-229           Panagra              NC18119         1
  1996/2000       DC-3-201           Eastern              NC18120/NC18124 5
  2002/2003       DC-3-232           AL of Australia      VH-UZJ, VH-UZK  2
  2004/2008       DC-3A-197B         United               NC18938/NC18942 5
  2009            DC-3A-237A         Mitsui               --              1
  2010            DC-3A-197B         United               NC18943         1
  2011            DC-3-229           Panagra              NC18936         1
  2012            DC-3-228           Pan American         NC18937         1
```

2013/2016	DC-3-209A	TWA	NC18949/NC18952	4
2017	DC-3A-197B	United	NC18944	1
2018	DC-3A-191B	United	NC18945	1
2019/2022	DC-3-194B	KLM	PH-ARW/-ARZ	4
2023/2024	DC-3-220A	CLS	OK-AIE, OK-AIF	2
2025/2026	DC-3-237A	Mitsui	--	2
2027/2028	DC-3B-202A	TWA	NC18953/NC18954	2
2029/2030	DC-3-232A	AL of Australia	VH-ABR, VH-ACB	2
2031/2035	DC-3-196A	USSR	--	5
2036	DC-3-194E	KLM	PH-ASK	1
2037/2041	DC-3A-237B	Mitsui	--	5
2042/2047	DC-3-196A	USSR	--	6
2048	DC-3A-237D	Mitsui	--	1
2049/2052	DC-3-237C	Mitsui	--	4
2054	DC-3-227A	Swissair	HB-IRO	1
2055/2056	DC-3A-237D	Mitsui	--	2
2093/2094	DC-3-227B	Sabena	OO-AUH/OO-AUI	2
2095	DC-3-220B	CLS	OK-AIG	1
2096/2101	DC-3-260	Nakajima	--	6
2102	DC-3-201A	Eastern	NC21743	1
2103/2107	DC-3-208A	American	NC21745/NC21749	5
2108	DC-3-201A	Eastern	NC21744	1
2109/2111	DC-3-194F	KLM	PH-ASP, -ASR, -AST	3
2112/2117	DC-3-196B	USSR	--	6
2118/2120	DC-3-209B	TWA	NC14931/NC14933	3
2121	DC-3-276	Swissair	HB-IRE	1
2122	DC-3-294	Air France	F-ARQJ	1
2123/2125	DC-3A-269	Northwest	NC21711/NC21713	3
2126/2127	DC-3-270	Can Colonial	NC21750/NC21751	2
2128	DC-3-228A	Pan American	NC21717	1
2129/2131	DC-3A-269	Northwest	NC21714/NC21716	3
2132	DC-3-268	Swissair	HB-IRU	1
2133	DC-3-268	ABA	SE-BAF	1
2134	DC-3-279	Panagra	NC21718	1
2135	DC-3-228B	CNAC	--	1
2136/2140	DC-3-277	American	NC16096, NC18141/ NC18143, NC17340	5
2141	DC-3-201B	Eastern	NC21729	1
2142	DC-3-194G	KLM	PH-ASM	1
2143/2144	DC-3-201B	Eastern	NC21727/NC21728	2
2145	C-41A-DO	USAAC	40-70	1
2146	DC-3A-253A	Northwest	NC21777	1
2147	DC-3-194H	KLM	PH-AXH	1
2148	DC-3-294A	Fokker	--	1
2149	DST-217A	American	NC21769	1
2165	DST-217A	American	NC21752	1
2166/2167	DC-3-277A	American	NC21767/NC21768	2
2168/2173	DC-3-313	Penn Central	NC21780/NC21785	6
2174/2177	DC-3A-197C	United	NC25677/NC25680	4
2178	DC-3-268B	Aer Lingus	EI-ACA	1
2179/2182	DC-3-314	Braniff	NC21773/NC21776	4
2183/2185	DC-3A-269B	Northwest	NC25608/NC25610	3
2186/2189	DC-3-313	Penn Central	NC21787/NC21790	4
2190/2192	DC-3A-279A	Panagra	NC14967, NC14996, NC25652	3
2193/2197	DC-3A-228C	Pan American	NC25653/NC25657	5
2198/2215	DC-3-277B	American	NC21793/NC21795, NC21797/NC21799, NC25658, NC25660/ NC25661, NC25663/ NC25665, NC25670/ NC25673, NC25676 and NC25684	18
2216/2217	DST-217B	American	NC25685, NC25686	2

2218/2220	DC-3-322	Chicago & So	NC25625/NC25627	3
2221	DC-3A-197C	United	NC25681	1
2222/2223	DST-A-207B	United	NC25682/NC25683	2
2224/2226	DST-318	Eastern	NC25649/NC25651	3
2227	DC-3A-269B	Northwest	NC25621	1
2228/2232	DC-3A-228C	Pan American	NC25641/NC25645	5
2233	DC-3-322	Chicago & So	NC25628	1
2234/2236	DC-3-201C	Eastern	NC25646/NC25648	3
2237/2238	DC-3-270A	Can Colonial	NC21758/NC21759	2
2239/2242	DC-3-314A	Braniff	NC25666/NC25669	4
2243/2245	DC-3-277C	American	NC15589/NC15591	3
2246/2247	DC-3-201D	Eastern	NC15595/NC15596	2
2248/2254	DC-3-277C	American	NC15592, NC15629, NC19974, NC28310, NC28321, NC28323 and NC28324	7
2255	DC-3-322A	Chicago & So	NC19977	1
2256	DC-3-313A	Penn Central	NC25691	1
2257/2260	DC-3-201D	Eastern	NC15597/NC15599, NC19963	4
2261	DC-3-268C	Fokker	--	1
2262	DC-3-313A	Penn Central	NC25692	1
2263/2264	DST-217A	American	NC28325, NC28350	2
2265	DC-3A-343	Western	NC19964	1
2266/2267	DC-3-313A	Penn Central	NC25693, NC28343	2
2268/2269	DC-3-201E	Eastern	NC28391/NC28392	2
2270	DC-3A-269C	Northwest	NC25622	1
2271/2272	DC-3-270B	Can Colonial	NC28360, NC25694	2
3250/3251	DST-318A	Eastern	NC28394, NC28393	2
3252/3254	DC-3-201E	Eastern	NC19968/NC19970	3
3255	DC-3A-197D	United	NC25611	1
3256	C-48-DO	USAAF	41-7681	1
3257/3262	DC-3A-197D	United	NC25613/NC25618	6
3263/3264	DST-A-207C	United	NC25619/NC25620	2
3265	DST-A-207D	United	NC25621	1
3266/3269	DC-3-362	TWA	NC1941/NC1944	4
3270/3274	C-49-DO	USAAF	41-7685/41-7689	5
3275	DC-3A-363	Swiflite	NC1000	1
3276	DC-3A-269C	Northwest	NC25623	1
3277/3279	DC-3-357	Delta	NC28340/NC28342	3
3280	C-49D-DO	USAAF	42-65584	1
3281	DC-3-357	Delta	NC28344	1
3282	C-49A-DO	USAAF	41-7690	1
3283	DC-3A-343A	Western	NC28379	1
3284	DC-3A-393	Panagra	NC28380	1
3285	DC-3-322B	Chicago & So	NC28378	1
3286/3288	DC-3A-367	Northeast	NC33621/NC33623	3
3289	C-51-DO	USAAF	41-7702	1
3290/3293	DC-3A-228D	Pan American	NC28301/NC28304	4
3294/3296	DC-3-362	TWA	NC1945/NC1947	3
3297	C-49-DO	USAAF	41-7694	1
3298/3299	DC-3-362	TWA	NC1948/NC1949	2
4080	DC-3A-348	CAA	NC14	1
4081/4082	DC-3-313B	Penn Central	NC25696/NC25697	2
4083	C-50C-DO	USAAF	41-7695	1
4084	C-50D-DO	USAAF	41-7696	1
4085/4088	DC-3A-228D	Pan American	NC28305/NC28308	4
4089/4093	DC-3-201F	Eastern	NC28381/NC28385	5
4094/4096	C-49B-DO	USAAF	41-7691/41-7693	3
4097/4098	R4D-2	USN	4707/4708	2
4099	DC-3-313C	Penn Central	NC25689	1
4100/4105	DC-3A-228F	Pan American	NC33609/NC33614	6
4106/4108	DC-3-314B	Braniff	NC28362/NC28364	3
4109/4111	C-50B-DO	USAAF	41-7703/41-7705	3

4112	C-52-DO	USAAF	41-7708	1
4113/4114	DST-A-207D	United	NC33641/NC33642	2
4115/4118	DC-3-277D	American	NC33651, NC33653/	
			NC33655	4
4119/4122	C-50-DO	USAAF	41-7697/41-7700	4
4123	DC-3A-197E	United	NC33644	1
4124	DC-3A-399	Panagra	NC33645	1
4125/4126	DC-3A-197E	United	NC33646/NC33647	2
4127/4128	C-52B-DO	USAAF	41-7706/41-7707	2
4129	DST-406	Eastern	NC33643	1
4130	DC-3-313D	Penn Central	NC33675	1
4131	C-50D-DO	USAAF	41-7709	1
4132/4133	DC-3-313D	Penn Central	NC33677/NC33678	2
4134/4135	C-50D-DO	USAAF	41-7712/41-7713	2
4136	C-52C-DO	USAAF	41-7701	1
4137/4140	DC-3-201G	Eastern	NC33631/NC33635	4
4141/4145	C-49D-DO	USAAF	41-7716/41-7720	5
4146/4148	C-48A-DO	USAAF	41-7682/41-7684	3
4170/4172	C-48C-DO	DSC	42-38332/42-38334	3
4173/4174	C-68-DO	USAAF	42-14297/42-14298	2
4175/4176	C-48C-DO	DSC	42-38335/42-38336	2
4177	Undesignated	DSC	--	1
4178	C-48C-DO	DSC	42-38337	1
4179/4181	Undesignated	DSC	--	3
4182	C-48C-DO	DSC	42-38338	1
4183	Undesignated	DSC	--	1
4200/4203	C-47-DL	USAAF	41-7722/41-7725	4
4204	R4D-1	USN	3131	1
4205/4221	C-47-DL	USAAF	41-7726/41-7742	17
4222/4229	R4D-1	USN	3132/3139	8
4230/4279	C-47-DL	USAAF	41-7743/41-7792	50
4280/4283	R4D-1	USN	3140/3143	4
4284	R4D-1	USN	4692	1
4285/4299	C-47-DL	USAAF	41-7793/41-7807	15
4300/4306	R4D-1	USN	4693/4699	7
4307/4359	C-47-DL	USAAF	41-7800/41-7860	53
4360/4366	R4D-1	USN	4700/4706	7
4367/4368	R4D-1	USN	01648/01649	2
4369/4374	C-47-DL	USAAF	41-7861/41-7866	6
4375/4432	C-47-DL	USAAF	41-18337/41-18394	58
4433/4441	R4D-1	USN	01977/01985	9
4442/4444	C-47-DL	USAAF	41-18395/41-18397	3
4445/4459	C-47-DL	USAAF	41-38564/41-38578	15
4460/4527	C-47-DL	USAAF	41-18398/41-18465	68
4528/4549	C-47-DL	USAAF	41-38579/41-38600	22
4550/4554	R4D-1	USN	01986/01990	5
4555/4557	R4D-1	USN	05051/05053	3
4558/4628	C-47-DL	USAAF	41-18466/41-18536	71
4629/4653	C-47-DL	USAAF	41-38601/41-38625	25
4654/4661	R4D-1	USN	05054/05061	8
4662/4728	C-47-DL	USAAF	41-18537/41-18603	67
4729/4753	C-47-DL	USAAF	41-38626/41-38650	25
4754/4764	R4D-1	USN	05062/05072	11
4765/4799	C-47-DL	USAAF	41-18604/41-18638	35
4800/4801	DC-3A-279B	Panagra	NC28334/NC28335	2
4802/4803	DC-3-277D	American	NC33656/NC33657	2
4804/4805	C-50A-DO	USAAF	41-7710/41-7711	2
4806/4808	DC-3A-375	Inter Island AL	NC33606/NC33608	3
4809	DC-3A-408	Douglas	NC30000	1
4810	C-53-DO	USAAF	41-20045	1
4811/4812	DC-3A-343B	Western	NC33670/NC33671	2
4813	C-52A-DO	USAAF	41-7714	1
4814/4815	C-49C-DO	USAAF	41-7715, 41-7721	2
4816/4906	C-53-DO	USAAF	41-20046/41-20136	91

4907/4956	C-53-DO	USAAF	42-6455/42-6504	50
4957/4959	Undesignated	DSC	--	3
4960/4961	C-53-DO	USAAF	43-14404/43-14405	2
4962	R4D-4	USN	07000	1
4963	Undesignated	DSC	--	1
4964/4967	C-53C-DO	USAAF	43-2018/43-2021	4
4968	Undesignated	DSC	--	1
4969/4976	C-53C-DO	USAAF	43-2025/43-2032	8
4977	Undesignated	DSC	--	1
4978/4980	C-53C-DO	USAAF	43-2022/43-2024	3
4981	Undesignated	DSC	--	1
4982/4986	C-49K-DO	USAAF	43-1995/43-1999	5
4987/4992	C-49J-DO	USAAF	43-1962/43-1967	6
4993/4995	C-49J-DO	USAAF	43-1969/43-1971	3
4996	C-49J-DO	USAAF	43-1961	1
4997	C-49J-DO	USAAF	43-1968	1
4998	C-49J-DO	USAAF	43-1974	1
4999	C-49J-DO	USAAF	43-1979	1
5000	C-49J-DO	USAAF	43-1982	1
6000/6033	C-47-DL	USAAF	41-18639/41-18672	34
6034/6058	C-47-DL	USAAF	41-38651/41-38675	25
6059/6070	C-47-DL	USAAF	43-30628/43-30639	12
6071/6078	C-47-DL	USAAF	41-38676/41-38683	8
6078/6105	C-47-DL	USAAF	41-18673/41-18699	27
6106/6142	C-47-DL	USAAF	41-19463/41-19499	37
6143/6222	C-47-DL	USAAF	41-38684/41-38763	80
6223/6258	C-47-DL	USAAF	42-5635/42-5670	36
6259/6261	C-49J-DO	USAAF	43-1983/43-1985	3
6262	C-49J-DO	USAAF	43-1987	1
6263/6264	C-49J-DO	USAAF	43-1980/43-1981	2
6313/6314	C-49J-DO	USAAF	43-1972/43-1973	2
6315/6318	C-49J-DO	USAAF	43-1975/43 1978	4
6319/6323	C-49J-DO	USAAF	43-1990/43-1994	5
6324	C-49K-DO	USAAF	43-2012	1
6325/6336	C-49K-DO	USAAF	43-2000/43-2011	12
6337/6341	C-49K-DO	USAAF	43-2013/43-2017	5
6342	C-49J-DO	USAAF	43-1986	1
6343/6344	C-49J-DO	USAAF	43-1988/43-1989	2
6345	R4D-4	USN	07001	1
6346/6347	C-53C-DO	USAAF	43-2033/43-2034	2
6348/6349	R4D-4	USN	07002/07003	2
6350/6355	R4D-4	USN	33815/33820	6
7313/7324	C-53-DO	USAAF	42-47371/42-47382	12
7325/7364	C-53-DO	USAAF	42-15530/42-15569	40
7365/7386	C-47-DL	USAAF	42-5671/42-5692	22
7387/7411	C-53-DO	USAAF	42-15870/42-15894	25
9000/9011	C-47-DL	USAAF	42-5693/42-5704	12
9012/9149	C-47-DL	USAAF	42-32786/42-32923	138
9150/9161	C-47A-DL	USAAF	42-32924/42-32935	12
9162/9208	C-47A-1-DL	USAAF	42-23300/42-23346	47
9209/9217	C-47A-5-DL	USAAF	42-23347/42-23355	9
9218/9241	C-47A-10-DL	USAAF	42-23356/42-23379	24
9242/9274	C-47A-15-DL	USAAF	42-23380/42-23412	33
9275/9399	C-47A-20-DL	USAAF	42-23413/42-23537	125
9400/9442	C-47A-25-DL	USAAF	42-23538/42-23580	43
9443/9649	C-47A-30-DL	USAAF	42-23581/42-23787	207
9650/9824	C-47A-35-DL	USAAF	42-23788/42-23962	175
9825/9947	C-47A-40-DL	USAAF	42-23963/42-24085	123
9948/9999	C-47A-45-DL	USAAF	42-24086/42-24137	52
10000/10183	C-47A-50-DL	USAAF	42-24138/42-24321	184
10184/10199	C-47A-55-DL	USAAF	42-24322/42-24337	16
10200/10269	C-47A-60-DL	USAAF	42-24338/42-24407	70
11620/11778	C-53D-DO	USAAF	42-68693/42-68851	159
11779/11846	C-47A-DK	USAAF	42-92024/42-92091	68

566

11847/12170	C-47A-1-DK	USAAF	42-92092/42-92415	324
12171/12327	C-47A-5-DK	USAAF	42-92416/42-92572	157
12328/12498	C-47A-10-DK	USAAF	42-92573/42-92743	171
12499/12678	C-47A-15-DK	USAAF	42-92744/42-92923	180
12679/12913	C-47A-20-DK	USAAF	42-92924/42-93158	235
12914/12920	C-47A-DK	USAAF	42-108794/42-108800	7
12921/12956	C-47A-1-DK	USAAF	42-108801/42-108836	36
12957/12974	C-47A-5-DK	USAAF	42-108837/42-108854	18
12975/12993	C-47A-10-DK	USAAF	42-108855/42-108873	19
12994/13013	C-47A-15-DK	USAAF	42-108874/42-108893	20
13014/13039	C-47A-20-DK	USAAF	42-108894/42-108919	26
13040	C-47B-DK	USAAF	42-93159	1
13041/13164	C-47A-20-DK	USAAF	42-93160/42-93283	124
13165/13704	C-47A-25-DK	USAAF	42-93284/42-93823	540
13705/13718	C-47A-20-DK	USAAF	42-108920/42-108933	14
13719/13778	C-47A-25-DK	USAAF	42-108934/42-108993	60
13779/13790	C-47A-60-DL	USAAF	42-24408/42-24419	12
13791/13912	C-47A-DL	USAAF	43-30640/43-30761	122
18899/19098	C-47A-65-DL	USAAF	42-100436/42-100635	200
19099/19298	C-47A-70-DL	USAAF	42-100636/42-100835	200
19299/19498	C-47A-75-DL	USAAF	42-100836/42-101035	200
19499/19898	C-47A-80-DL	USAAF	43-15033/43-15432	400
19899/20098	C-47A-85-DL	USAAF	43-15433/43-15632	200
20099/20598	C-47A-90-DL	USAAF	43-15633/43-16132	500
20599/20898	C-47B-1-DL	USAAF	43-16133/43-16432	300
25224/25532	C-47A-30-DK	USAAF	43-47963/43-48262	300
25524/25639	C-47B-1-DK	USAAF	43-48263/43-48378	116
25640	C-47B-2-DK	USAAF	43-48379	1
25641/25766	C-47B-1-DK	USAAF	43-48380/43-48505	126
25767	C-47B-2-DK	USAAF	43-48506	1
25768/25823	C 47B-1-DK	USAAF	43-48507/43-48562	56
25824/25866	C-47B-5-DK	USAAF	43-48563/43-48605	43
25867	C-47B 7 DK	USAAF	43-48606	1
25868/25896	C-47B-5-DK	USAAF	43-48607/43-48635	29
25897	C-47B-7-DK	USAAF	43-48636	1
25898/25901	C-47B-5-DK	USAAF	43-48637/43-48640	4
25902	TC-47B-5-DK	USAAF	43-48641	1
25903/25946	C-47B-5-DK	USAAF	43-48642/43-48685	44
25947	C-47B-6-DK	USAAF	43-48686	1
25948/25958	C-47B-5-DK	USAAF	43-48687/43-48697	11
25959/25963	C-47B-9-DK	USAAF	43-48698/43-48702	5
25964/25996	C-47B-5-DK	USAAF	43-48703/43-48735	33
25997	C-47B-6-DK	USAAF	43 48736	1
25998/26018	C-47B-5-DK	USAAF	43-48737/43-48757	21
26019	C-47B-8-DK	USAAF	43-48758	1
26020/26066	C-47B-5-DK	USAAF	43-48759/43-48805	47
26067	C-47B-7-DK	USAAF	43-48806	1
26068/26076	C-47B-5-DK	USAAF	43-48807/43-48815	9
26077	C-47B-6-DK	USAAF	43-48816	1
26078/26146	C-47B-5-DK	USAAF	43-48817/43-48885	69
26147	C-47B-7-DK	USAAF	43-48886	1
26148/26166	C-47B-5-DK	USAAF	43-48887/43-48905	19
26167	C-47B-6-DK	USAAF	43-48906	1
26168/26173	C-47B-5-DK	USAAF	43-48907/43-48912	6
26174/26182	C-47B-10-DK	USAAF	43-48913/43-48921	9
26183	C-47B-13-DK	USAAF	43-48922	1
26184/26192	C-47B-10-DK	USAAF	43-48923/43-48931	9
26193	C-47B-13-DK	USAAF	43-48932	1
26194/26212	C-47B-10-DK	USAAF	43-48933/43-48951	19
26213	C-47B-13-DK	USAAF	43-48952	1
26214/26266	C-47B-10-DK	USAAF	43-48953/43-49005	53
26267	C-47B-13-DK	USAAF	43-49006	1
26268/26276	C-47B-10-DK	USAAF	43-49007/43-49015	9
26277	C-47B-13-DK	USAAF	43-49016	1

26278	C-47B-10-DK	USAAF	43-94017	1
26279	C-47B-11-DK	USAAF	43-49018	1
26280/26283	C-47B-10-DK	USAAF	43-49019/43-49022	4
26284	C-47B-11-DK	USAAF	43-49023	1
26285/26288	C-47B-10-DK	USAAF	43-49024/43-49027	4
26289	C-47B-11-DK	USAAF	43-49028	1
26290/26293	C-47B-10-DK	USAAF	43-49029/43-49032	4
26294	TC-47B-10-DK	USAAF	43-49033	1
26295/26337	C-47B-10-DK	USAAF	43-49034/43-49076	43
26338	C-47B-11-DK	USAAF	43-49077	1
26339	C-47B-10-DK	USAAF	43-49078	1
26340	C-47B-14-DK	USAAF	43-49079	1
26341/26342	C-47B-10-DK	USAAF	43-49080/43-49081	2
26343	C-47B-11-DK	USAAF	43-49082	1
26344/26347	C-47B-10-DK	USAAF	43-49083/43-49086	4
26348	C-47B-11-DK	USAAF	43-49087	1
26349/26358	C-47B-10-DK	USAAF	43-49088/43-49097	10
26359	C-47B-11-DK	USAAF	43-49098	1
26360/26368	C-47B-10-DK	USAAF	43-49099/43-49107	9
26369	C-47B-11-DK	USAAF	43-49108	1
26370/26378	C-47B-10-DK	USAAF	43-49109/43-49117	9
26379	C-47B-11-DK	USAAF	43-49118	1
26380/26388	C-47B-10-DK	USAAF	43-49119/43-49127	9
26389	C-47B-11-DK	USAAF	43-49128	1
26390/26398	C-47B-10-DK	USAAF	43-49129/43-49137	9
26399	C-47B-11-DK	USAAF	43-49138	1
26400/26406	C-47B-10-DK	USAAF	43-49139/43-49145	7
26407	C-47B-13-DK	USAAF	43-49146	1
26408/26442	C-47B-10-DK	USAAF	43-49147/43-49181	35
26443	C-47B-11-DK	USAAF	43-49182	1
26444	C-47B-10-DK	USAAF	43-49183/43-49191	9
26453	C-47B-11-DK	USAAF	43-49192	1
26454/26462	C-47B-10-DK	USAAF	43-49193/43-49201	9
26463	C-47B-11-DK	USAAF	43-49202	1
26464/26472	C-47B-10-DK	USAAF	43-49203/43-49211	9
26473	C-47B-11-DK	USAAF	43-49212	1
26474/26482	C-47B-10-DK	USAAF	43-49213/43-49221	9
26483	C-47B-11-DK	USAAF	43-49222	1
26484/26486	C-47B-10-DK	USAAF	43-49223/43-49225	3
26487	C-47B-13-DK	USAAF	43-49226	1
26488	C-47B-11-DK	USAAF	43-49227	1
26489/26492	C-47B-10-DK	USAAF	43-49228/43-49231	4
26493	C-47B-11-DK	USAAF	43-49232	1
26494/26497	C-47B-10-DK	USAAF	43-49233/43-49236	4
26498	C-47B-11-DK	USAAF	43-49237	1
26499/26502	C-47B-10-DK	USAAF	43-49238/43-49241	4
26503	C-47B-11-DK	USAAF	43-49242	1
26504/25507	C-47B-10-DK	USAAF	43-49243/43-49246	4
26508	C-47B-11-DK	USAAF	43-49247	1
26509/26512	C-47B-10-DK	USAAF	43-49248/43-49251	4
26513	C-47B-11-DK	USAAF	43-49252	1
26514/26516	C-47B-10-DK	USAAF	43-49253/43-49255	3
26517	C-47B-13-DK	USAAF	43-49256	1
26518	C-47B-11-DK	USAAF	43-49257	1
26519/26522	C-47B-10-DK	USAAF	43-49258/43-49261	4
26523	C-47B-11-DK	USAAF	43-49262	1
26524/26528	C-47B-15-DK	USAAF	43-49263/43-49267	5
26529	TC-47B-15-DK	USAAF	43-49268	1
26530	C-47B-16-DK	USAAF	43-49269	1
26531/26532	C-47B-15-DK	USAAF	43-49270/43-49271	2
26533/26534	C-47B-16-DK	USAAF	43-49272/43-49273	2
26535	C-47B-15-DK	USAAF	43-49274	1
26536/26537	C-47B-18-DK	USAAF	43-49275/43-49276	2
26538/26589	C-47B-15-DK	USAAF	43-49277/43-49328	52

568

26590	C-47B-16-DK	USAAF	43-49329	1
26591/26593	C-47B-15-DK	USAAF	43-49330/43-49332	3
26594	C-47B-18-DK	USAAF	43-49333	1
26595/26596	C-47B-15-DK	USAAF	43-49334/43-49335	2
26597	C-47B-16-DK	USAAF	43-49336	1
26598	C-47B-15-DK	USAAF	43-49337/43-49339	3
26601	C-47B-18-DK	USAAF	43-49340	1
26602/26604	C-47B-15-DK	USAAF	43-49341/43-49343	3
26605	C-47B-16-DK	USAAF	43-49344	1
26606/26608	C-47B-15-DK	USAAF	43-49345/43-49347	3
26609	TC-47B-15-DK	USAAF	43-49348	1
26610/26611	C-47B-15-DK	USAAF	43-49349/43-49350	2
26612	TC-47B-15-DK	USAAF	43-49351	1
26613/26615	C-47B-15-DK	USAAF	43-49352/43-49354	3
26616	C-47B-16-DK	USAAF	43-49355	1
26617/26619	C-47B-15-DK	USAAF	43-49356/43-49358	3
26620	C-47B-18-DK	USAAF	43-49359	1
26621/26622	C-47B-15-DK	USSAF	43-49360/43-49361	2
26623	C-47B-16-DK	USAAF	43-49362	1
26624/26626	C-47B-15-DK	USAAF	43-49363/43-49365	3
26627	C-47B-18-DK	USAAF	43-49366	1
26628/26629	C-47B-15-DK	USSAF	43-49367/43-49368	2
26630	C-47B-16-DK	USAAF	43-49369	1
26631/26632	C-47B-15-DK	USAAF	43-49370/43-49371	2
26633	C-47B-16-DK	USAAF	43-49372	1
26634/26635	C-47B-15-DK	USAAF	43-49373/43-49374	2
26636	TC-47B-15-DK	USAAF	43-49375	1
26637/26668	C-47B-15-DK	USAAF	43-49376/43-49407	32
26669	C-47B-16-DK	USAAF	43-49408	1
26670/26671	C-47B-15-DK	USAAF	43-49409/43-49410	2
26672	C-47B-16-DK	USAAF	43-49411	1
26673	C-47B-15-DK	USAAF	43-49412/43-49415	4
26677	C-47B-16-DK	USAAF	43-49416	1
26678/26873	C-47B-15-DK	USAAF	43-49417/43-49612	196
26874/26900	C-47B-20-DK	USAAF	43-49613/43-49639	27
26901	C-47B-23-DK	USAAF	43-49640	1
26902/26963	C-47B-20-DK	USAAF	43-49641/43-49702	62
26964	TC-47B-20-DK	USAAF	43-49703	1
26965/27005	C-47B-20-DK	USAAF	43-49704/43-49744	41
27006	C-47B-23-DK	USAAF	43-49745	1
27007/27020	C-47B-20-DK	USAAF	43-49746/43-49759	14
27021	TC-47B-20-DK	USAAF	43-49760	1
27022/27035	C-47B-20-DK	USAAF	43-49761/43-49774	14
27036	C-47B-23-DK	USAAF	43-49775	1
27037/27050	C-47B-20-DK	USAAF	43-49776/43-49789	14
27051	TC-47B-20-DK	USAAF	43-49790	1
27052/27062	C-47B-20-DK	USAAF	43-49791/43-49801	11
27063	C-47B-23-DK	USAAF	43-49802	1
27064/27068	C-47B-20-DK	USAAF	43-49803/43-49087	5
27069	TC-47B-20-DK	USAAF	43-49808	1
27070/27074	C-47B-20-DK	USAAF	43-49809/43-49813	5
27075	TC-47B-20-DK	USAAF	43-49814	1
27076/27086	C-47B-20-DK	USAAF	43-49815/43-49825	11
27087	C-47B-23-DK	USAAF	43-49826	1
27088/27092	C-47B-20-DK	USAAF	43-49827/43-49831	5
27093	TC-47B-20-DK	USAAF	43-49832	1
27094/27105	C-47B-20-DK	USAAF	43-49833/43-49844	12
27106	C-47B-23-DK	USAAF	43-49845	1
27107/27112	C-47B-20-DK	USAAF	43-49846/43-49851	6
27113	TC-47B-20-DK	USAAF	43-49852	1
27114/27119	C-47B-20-DK	USAAF	43-49853/43-49858	6
27120	C-47B-23-DK	USAAF	43-49859	1
27121/27133	C-47B-20-DK	USAAF	43-49860/43-49872	13
27134	C-47B-23-DK	USAAF	43-49873	1

27135/27140	C-47B-20-DK	USAAF	43-49874/43-49879	6
27141	TC-47B-20-DK	USAAF	43-49880	1
27143/27147	C-47B-20-DK	USAAF	43-49881/43-49886	6
27148	C-47B-23-DK	USAAF	43-49887	1
27149/27158	C-47B-20-DK	USAAF	43-49888/43-49897	10
27159	C-47B-23-DK	USAAF	43-49898	1
27160/27163	C-47B-20-DK	USAAF	43-49899/43-49902	4
27164	TC-47B-20-DK	USAAF	43-49903	1
27165/27167	C-47B-20-DK	USAAF	43-49904/43-49906	3
27168	C-47B-23-DK	USAAF	43-49907	1
27169/27176	C-47B-20-DK	USAAF	43-49908/43-49915	8
27177	C-47B-23-DK	USAAF	43-49916	1
27178/27181	C-47B-20-DK	USAAF	43-49917/43-49920	4
27182	TC-47B-20-DK	USAAF	43-49921	1
27183/27185	C-47B-20-DK	USAAF	43-49922/43-49924	3
27186	C-47B-23-DK	USAAF	43-49925	1
27187/27194	C-47B-20-DK	USAAF	43-49926/43-49933	8
27195	C-47B-23-DK	USAAF	43-49934	1
27196	C-47B-20-DK	USAAF	43-49935/43-49938	4
27200	TC-47B-20-DK	USAAF	43-49939	1
27201/27203	C-47B-20-DK	USAAF	43-49940/43-49942	3
27204	C-47B-23-DK	USAAF	43-49943	1
27205/27212	C-47B-20-DK	USAAF	43-49944/43-49951	8
27213	C-47B-23-DK	USSAF	43-49952	1
27214/27216	C-47B-20-DK	USAAF	43-49953/43-49955	3
27217	TC-47B-20-DK	USAAF	43-49956	1
27218/27221	C-47B-20-DK	USAAF	43-49957/43-49960	4
27222	C-47B-23-DK	USAAF	43-49961	1
27223	C-47B-20-DK	USAAF	43-49962	1
32527	C-47B-25-DK	USAAF	44-76195	1
32528/32529	C-47B-27-DK	USAAF	44-76196/44-76197	2
32530/32534	C-47B-25-DK	USAAF	44-76198/44-76202	5
32535	C-47B-28-DK	USAAF	44-76203	1
32536/32537	C-47B-25-DK	USAAF	44-76204/44-76205	2
32538	TC-47B-25-DK	USAAF	44-76206	1
32539/32541	C-47B-25-DK	USAAF	44-76207/44-76209	3
32542	C-47B-28-DK	USAAF	44-76210	1
32543/32545	C-47B-25-DK	USAAF	44-76211/44-76213	3
32546	TC-47B-25-DK	USAAF	44-76214	1
32547/32550	C-47B-25-DK	USAAF	44-76215/44-76218	4
32551	C-47B-28-DK	USAAF	44-76219	1
32552/32554	C-47B-25-DK	USAAF	44-76220/44-76222	3
32555	TC-47B-25-DK	USAAF	44-76223	1
32556/32558	C-47B-25-DK	USAAF	44-76224/44-76226	3
32559	C-47B-28-DK	USAAF	44-76227	1
32560/32567	C-47B-25-DK	USAAF	44-76228/44-76235	8
32568	C-47B-28-DK	USAAF	44-76236	1
32569/32571	C-47B-25-DK	USAAF	44-76237/44-76239	3
32572	TC-47B-25-DK	USAAF	44-76240	1
32573/32575	C-47B-25-DK	USAAF	44-76241/44-76243	3
32576	C-47B-28-DK	USAAF	44-76244	1
32577/32579	C-47B-25-DK	USAAF	44-76245/44-76247	3
32580	TC-47B-25-DK	USAAF	44-76248	1
32581/32583	C-47B-25-DK	USAAF	44-76249/44-76251	3
32584	C-47B-28-DK	USAAF	44-76252	1
32585	C-47B-25-DK	USAAF	44-76253	1
32586	C-47B-27-DK	USAAF	44-76254	1
32587/32588	C-47B-25-DK	USAAF	44-76255/44-76256	2
32589	TC-47B-25-DK	USAAF	44-76257	1
32590/32592	C-47B-25-DK	USAAF	44-76258/44-76260	3
32593	C-47B-28-DK	USAAF	44-76261	1
32594/32596	C-47B-25-DK	USAAF	44-76262/44-76264	3
32597	TC-47B-25-DK	USAAF	44-76265	1
32598/32600	C-47B-25-DK	USAAF	44-76266/44-76268	3

32601	C-47B-28-DK	USAAF	44-76269	1
32602/32604	C-47B-25-DK	USAAF	44-76270/44-76272	3
32605	TC-47B-25-DK	USAAF	44-76273	1
32606/32608	C-47B-25-DK	USAAF	44-76274/44-76276	3
32609	C-47B-28-DK	USAAF	44-76277	1
32610/32613	C-47B-25-DK	USAAF	44-76278/44-76281	4
32614	TC-47B-25-DK	USAAF	44-76282	1
32615/32617	C-47B-25-DK	USAAF	44-76283/44-76285	3
32618	C-47B-28-DK	USAAF	44-76286	1
32619/32621	C-47B-25-DK	USAAF	44-76287/44-76289	3
32622	TC-47B-25-DK	USAAF	44-76290	1
32623	C-47B-25-DK	USAAF	44-76291	1
32624	C-47B-27-DK	USAAF	44-76292	1
32625	C-47B-25-DK	USAAF	44-76293	1
32626	C-47B-28-DK	USAAF	44-76294	1
32627/32629	C-47B-25-DK	USAAF	44-76295/44-76297	3
32630	TC-47B-25-DK	USAAF	44-76298	1
32631/32633	C-47B-25-DK	USAAF	44-76299/44-76301	3
32634	C-47B-28-DK	USAAF	44-76302	1
32635/32637	C-47B-25-DK	USAAF	44-76303/44-76305	3
32638	TC-47B-25-DK	USAAF	44-76306	1
32639/32641	C-47B-25-DK	USAAF	44-76307/44-76309	3
32642	C-47B-28-DK	USAAF	44-76310	1
32643/32645	C-47B-25-DK	USAAF	44-76311/44-76313	3
32646	TC-47B-25-DK	USAAF	44-76314	1
32647/32649	C-47B-25-DK	USAAF	44-76315/44-76317	3
32650	C-47B-28-DK	USAAF	44-76318	1
32651/32653	C-47B-25-DK	USAAF	44-76319/44-76321	3
32654	TC-47B-25-DK	USAAF	44-76322	1
32655/32657	C-47B-25-DK	USAAF	44-76323/44-76325	3
32658	C-47B-28-DK	USAAF	44-76326	1
32659/32661	C-47B-25-DK	USAAF	44-76327/44-76329	3
32662	TC-47B-25-DK	USAAF	44-76330	1
32663/32665	C-47B-25-DK	USAAF	44-76331/44-76333	3
32666	C-47B-28-DK	USAAF	44-76334	1
32667/32669	C-47B-25-DK	USAAF	44-76335/44-76337	3
32670	TC-47B-25-DK	USAAF	44-76338	1
32671/32673	C-47B-25-DK	USAAF	44-76339/44-76341	3
32674	C-47B-28-DK	USAAF	44-76342	1
32675	C-47B-25-DK	USAAF	44-76343	1
32676	C-47B-27-DK	USAAF	44-76344	1
32677	C-47B-25-DK	USAAF	44-76345	1
32678	TC-47B-25-DK	USAAF	44-76346	1
32679/32681	C-47B-25-DK	USAAF	44-76347/44-76349	3
32682	C-47B-28-DK	USAAF	44-76350	1
32683/32685	C-47B-25-DK	USAAF	44-76351/44-76353	3
32686	TC-47B-25-DK	USAAF	44-76354	1
32687/32689	C-47B-25-DK	USAAF	44-76355/44-76357	3
32690	C-47B-28-DK	USAAF	44-76358	1
32691/32693	C-47B-25-DK	USAAF	44-76359/44-76361	3
32694	TC-47B-25-DK	USAAF	44-76362	1
32695/32697	C-47B-25-DK	USAAF	44-76363/44-76365	3
32698	C-47B-28-DK	USAAF	44-76366	1
32699/32701	C-47B-25-DK	USAAF	44-76367/44-76369	3
32702	TC-47B-25-DK	USAAF	44-76370	1
32703/32705	C-47B-25-DK	USAAF	44-76371/44-76373	3
32706	C-47B-28-DK	USAAF	44-76374	1
32707/32709	C-47B-25-DK	USAAF	44-76375/44-76377	3
32710	TC-47B-25-DK	USAAF	44-76378	1
32711/32713	C-47B-25-DK	USAAF	44-76379/44-76381	3
32714	C-47B-28-DK	USAAF	44-76382	1
32715/32717	C-47B-25-DK	USAAF	44-76383/44-76385	3
32718	TC-47B-25-DK	USAAF	44-76386	1
32719/32721	C-47B-25-DK	USAAF	44-76387/44-76389	3

571

32722	C-47B-28-DK	USAAF	44-76390	1
32723/32725	C-47B-25-DK	USAAF	44-76391/44-76393	3
32726	TC-47B-25-DK	USAAF	44-76394	1
32727	C-47B-27-DK	USAAF	44-76395	1
32728/32729	C-47B-25-DK	USAAF	44-76396/44-76397	2
32730	C-27B-28-DK	USAAF	44-76398	1
32731/32733	C-47B-25-DK	USAAF	44-76399/44-76401	3
32734	TC-47B-25-DK	USAAF	44-76402	1
32735/32737	C-47B-25-DK	USAAF	44-76403/44-76405	3
32738	C-47B-28-DK	USAAF	44-76406	1
32739/32741	C-47B-25-DK	USAAF	44-76407/44-76409	3
32742	TC-47B-25-DK	USAAF	44-76410	1
32743/32745	C-47B-25-DK	USAAF	44-76411/44-76413	3
32746	C-47B-28-DK	USAAF	44-76414	1
32747/32749	C-47B-25-DK	USAAF	44-76415/44-76417	3
32750	TC-47B-25-DK	USAAF	44-76418	1
32751/32753	C-47B-25-DK	USAAF	44-76419/44-76421	3
32754	C-47B-28-DK	USAAF	44-76422	1
32755/32761	C-47B-25-DK	USAAF	44-76423/44-76429	7
32762	TC-47B-25-DK	USAAF	44-76430	1
32763/32769	C-47B-25-DK	USAAF	44-76431/44-76437	7
32770	TC-47B-25-DK	USAAF	44-76438	1
32771/32777	C-47B-25-DK	USAAF	44-76439/44-76445	7
32778	TC-47B-25-DK	USAAF	44-76446	1
32779/32780	C-47B-25-DK	USAAF	44-76447/44-76448	2
32781	C-47B-27-DK	USAAF	44-76449	1
32782/32785	C-47B-25-DK	USAAF	44-76450/44-76453	4
32786	TC-47B-25-DK	USAAF	44-76454	1
32787/32793	C-47B-25-DK	USAAF	44-76455/44-76461	7
32794	TC-47B-25-DK	USAAF	44-76462	1
32795/32801	C-47B-25-DK	USAAF	44-76463/44-76469	7
32802	TC-47B-25-DK	USAAF	44-76470	1
32803/32809	C-47B-25-DK	USAAF	44-76471/44-76477	7
32810	TC-47B-25-DK	USAAF	44-76478	1
32811/32817	C-47B-25-DK	USAAF	44-76479/44-76485	7
32818	TC-47B-25-DK	USAAF	44-76486	1
32819/32825	C-47B-25-DK	USAAF	44-76487/44-76493	7
32826	TC-47B-25-DK	USAAF	44-76494	1
32827/32833	C-47B-25-DK	USAAF	44-76495/44-76501	7
32834	TC-47B-25-DK	USAAF	44-76502	1
32835/32841	C-47B-25-DK	USAAF	44-76503/44-76509	7
32842	TC-47B-25-DK	USAAF	44-76510	1
32843/32849	C-47B-25-DK	USAAF	44-76511/44-76517	7
32850	TC-47B-25-DK	USAAF	44-76518	1
32851/32855	C-47B-25-DK	USAAF	44-76519/44-76523	5
32856	TC-47B-25-DK	USAAF	44-76524	1
32857/32865	C-47B-30-DK	USAAF	44-76525/44-76533	9
32866	TC-47B-30-DK	USAAF	44-76534	1
32867/32873	C-47B-30-DK	USAAF	44-76535/44-76541	7
32874	TC-47B-30-DK	USAAF	44-76542	1
32875/32881	C-47B-30-DK	USAAF	44-76543/44-76549	7
32882	TC-47B-30-DK	USAAF	44-76550	1
32883/32884	C-47B-30-DK	USAAF	44-76551/44-76552	2
32885	TC-47B-30-DK	USAAF	44-76553	1
32886/32889	C-47B-30-DK	USAAF	44-76554/44-76557	4
32890	TC-47B-30-DK	USAAF	44-76558	1
32891/32897	C-47B-30-DK	USAAF	44-76559/44-76565	7
32890	TC-47B-30-DK	USAAF	44-76566	1
32899/32905	C-47B-30-DK	USAAF	44-76567/44-76573	7
32906	TC-47B-30-DK	USAAF	44-76574	1
32907/32909	C-47B-30-DK	USAAF	44-76575/44-76577	3
32910	TC-47B-30-DK	USAAF	44-76578	1
32911/32913	C-47B-30-DK	USAAF	44-76579/44-76581	3
32914	TC-47B-30-DK	USAAF	44-76582	1

572

32915/32919	C-47B-30-DK	USAAF	44-76583/44-76587	5
32920	TC-47B-30-DK	USAAF	44-76588	1
32921/32924	C-47B-30-DK	USAAF	44-76589/44-76592	4
32925	TC-47B-30-DK	USAAF	44-76593	1
32926/32929	C-47B-30-DK	USAAF	44-76594/44-76597	4
32930	TC-47B-30-DK	USAAF	44-76598	1
32931/32937	C-47B-30-DK	USAAF	44-76599/44-76605	7
32938	TC-47B-30-DK	SAAF	44-76606	1
32939/32943	C-47B-30-DK	USAAF	44-76607/44-76611	5
32944	TC-47B-30-DK	USAAF	44-76612	1
32945/32949	C-47B-30-DK	USAAF	44-76613/44-76617	5
32950	TC-47B-30-DK	USAAF	44-76618	1
32951/32956	C-47B-30-DK	USAAF	44-76619/44-76624	6
32957	TC-47B-30-DK	USAAF	44-76625	1
32958/32963	C-47B-30-DK	USAAF	44-76626/44-76631	6
32964	TC-47B-30-DK	USAAF	44-76632	1
32965/32969	C-47B-30-DK	USAAF	44-76633/44-76637	5
32970	TC-47B-30-DK	USAAF	44-76638	1
32971/32976	C-47B-30-DK	USAAF	44-76639/44-76644	6
32977	TC-47B-30-DK	SAAF	44-76645	1
32978/32983	C-47B-30-DK	USAAF	44-76646/44-76651	6
32984	TC-47B-30-DK	USAAF	44-76652	1
32985/32989	C-47B-30-DK	USAAF	44-76653/44-76657	5
32990	TC-47B-30-DK	USAAF	44-76658	1
32991/32994	C-47B-30-DK	USAAF	44-76659/44-76662	4
32995	TC-47B-30-DK	USAAF	44-76663	1
32996/32999	C-47B-30-DK	USAAF	44-76664/44-76667	4
33000	TC-47B-30-DK	USAAF	44-76668	1
33001/33006	C-47B-30-DK	USAAF	44-76669/44-76674	6
33007	TC-47B-30-DK	USAAF	44-76675	1
33008/33011	C-47B-30-DK	USAAF	44-76676/44-76679	4
33012	TC-47B-30-DK	USAAF	44-76680	1
33013/33017	C-47B-30-DK	USAAF	44-76681/44-76685	5
33018	TC-47B-30-DK	USAAF	44-76686	1
33019/33022	C-47B-30-DK	USAAF	44-76687/44-76690	4
33023	TC-47B-30-DK	USAAF	44-76691	1
33024/33027	C-47B-30-DK	USAAF	44-76692/44-76695	4
33028	TC-47B-30-DK	USAAF	44-76696	1
33029/33031	C-47B-30-DK	USAAF	44-76697/44-76699	3
33032	TC-47B-30-DK	USAAF	44-76700	1
33033/33036	C-47B-30-DK	USAAF	44-76701/44-76704	4
33037	TC-47B-30-DK	USAAF	44-76705	1
33038/33042	C-47B-30-DK	USAAF	44-76706/44-76710	5
33043	TC-47B-30-DK	USAAF	44-76711	1
33044/33047	C-47B-30-DK	USAAF	44-76712/44-76715	4
33048	TC-47B-30-DK	USAAF	44-76716	1
33049/33053	C-47B-30-DK	USAAF	44-76717/44-76721	5
33054	TC-47B-30-DK	USAAF	44-76722	1
33055/33060	C-47B-30-DK	USAAF	44-76723/44-76728	6
33061	TC-47B-30-DK	USAAF	44-76729	1
33062/33065	C-47B-30-DK	USAAF	44-76730/44-76733	4
33066	TC-47B-30-DK	USAAF	44-76734	1
33067/33070	C-47B-30-DK	USAAF	44-76735/44-76738	4
33071	TC-47B-30-DK	USAAF	44-76739	1
33072/33075	C-47B-30-DK	USAAF	44-76740/76743	4
33076	TC-47B-30-DK	USAAF	44-76744	1
33077/33079	C-47B-30-DK	USAAF	44-76745/44-76747	3
33080	TC-47B-30-DK	USAAF	44-76748	1
33081/33084	C-47B-30-DK	USAAF	44-76749/44-76752	4
33085	TC-47B-30-DK	USAAF	44-76753	1
33086/33089	C-47B-30-DK	USAAF	44-76754/44-76757	4
33090	TC-47B-30-DK	USAAF	44-76758	1
33091/33094	C-47B-30-DK	USAAF	44-76759/44-76762	4
33095	TC-47B-30-DK	USAAF	44-76763	1

33096/33099	C-47B-30-DK	USAAF	44-76764/44-76767	4
33100	TC-47B-30-DK	USAAF	44-76768	1
33101	C-47B-30-DK	USAAF	44-76769/44-76772	4
33105	TC-47B-30-DK	USAAF	44-76773	1
33106/33109	C-47B-30-DK	USAAF	44-76774/44-76777	4
33110	TC-47B-30-DK	USAAF	44-76778	1
33111/33120	C-47B-30-DK	USAAF	44-76779/44-76788	10
33121	TC-47B-30-DK	USAAF	44-76789	1
33122/33125	C-47B-30-DK	USAAF	44-76790/44-76793	4
33126	TC-47B-30-DK	USAAF	44-76794	1
33127/33132	C-47B-30-DK	USAAF	44-76795/44-76800	6
33133	TC-47B-30-DK	USAAF	44-76801	1
33134/33143	C-47B-30-DK	USAAF	44-76802/44-76811	10
33144	TC-47B-30-DK	USAAF	44-76812	1
33145/33154	C-47B-30-DK	USAAF	44-76813/44-76822	10
33155	TC-47B-30-DK	USAAF	44-76823	1
33156/33159	C-47B-30-DK	USAAF	44-76824/44-76827	4
33160	TC-47B-30-DK	USAAF	44-76828	1
33161/33169	C-47B-30-DK	USAAF	44-76829/44-76837	9
33170	TC-47B-30-DK	USAAF	44-76838	1
33171/33179	C-47B-30-DK	USAAF	44-76839/44-76847	9
33180	TC-47B-30-DK	USAAF	44-76848	1
33181/33185	C-47B-30-DK	USAAF	44-76849/44-76853	5
33186	TC-47B-30-DK	USAAF	44-76854	1
33187/33191	C-47B-35-DK	USAAF	44-76855/44-76859	5
33192	TC-47B-35-DK	USAAF	44-76860	1
33193/33200	C-47B-35-DK	USAAF	44-76861/44-76868	8
33201	TC-47B-35-DK	USAAF	44-76869	1
33202/33205	C-47B-35-DK	USAAF	44-76870/44-76873	4
33206	TC-47B-35-DK	USAAF	44-76874	1
33207/33215	C-47B-35-DK	USAAF	44-76875/44-76883	9
33216	TC-47B-35-DK	USAAF	44-76884	1
33217/33229	C-47B-35-DK	USAAF	44-76885/44-76894	10
33227	TC-47B-35-DK	USAAF	44-76895	1
33228/33231	C-47B-35-DK	USAAF	44-76896/44-76899	4
33232	TC-47B-35-DK	USAAF	44-76900	1
33233/33240	C-47B-35-DK	USAAF	44-76901/44-76908	8
33241	TC-47B-35-DK	USAAF	44-76909	1
33242/33250	C-47B-35-DK	USAAF	44-76910/44-76918	9
33251	TC-47B-35-DK	USAAF	44-76919	1
33252/33255	C-47B-35-DK	USAAF	44-76920/44-76923	4
33256	TC-47B-35-DK	USAAF	44-76924	1
33257/33266	C-47B-35-DK	USAAF	44-76925/44-76934	10
33267	TC-47B-35-DK	USAAF	44-76935	1
33268	C-47B-35-DK	USAAF	44-76936/44-76942	7
33275	TC-47B-35-DK	USAAF	44-76943	1
33276/33282	C-47B-35-DK	USAAF	44-76944/44-76950	7
33283	TC-47B-35-DK	USAAF	44-76951	1
33284/33290	C-47B-35-DK	USAAF	44-76952/44-76958	7
33291	TC-47B-35-DK	USAAF	44-76959	1
33292/33298	C-47B-35-DK	USAAF	44-76960/44-76966	7
33299	TC-47B-35-DK	USAAF	44-76967	1
33300/33304	C-47B-35-DK	USAAF	44-76968/44-76972	5
33305	TC-47B-35-DK	USAAF	44-76973	1
33306/33313	C-47B-35-DK	USAAF	44-76974/44-76981	8
33314	TC-47B-35-DK	USAAF	44-76982	1
33315/33321	C-47B-35-DK	USAAF	44-76983/44-76989	7
33322	TC-47B-35-DK	USAAF	44-76990	1
33323/33328	C-47B-35-DK	USAAF	44-76991/44-76996	6
33329	TC-47B-35-DK	USAAF	44-76997	1
33330/33336	C-47B-35-DK	USAAF	44-76998/44-77004	7
33337	TC-47B-35-DK	USAAF	44-77005	1
33338/33344	C-47B-35-DK	USAAF	44-77006/44-77012	7
33345	TC-47B-35-DK	USAAF	44-77013	1

33346/33350	C-47B-35-DK	USAAF	44-77014/44-77018	5
33351	TC-47B-35-DK	USAAF	44-77019	1
33352/33358	C-47B-35-DK	USAAF	44-77020/44-77026	7
33359	TC-47B-35-DK	USAAF	44-77027	1
33360/33366	C-47B-35-DK	USAAF	44-77028/44-77034	7
33367	TC-47B-35-DK	USAAF	44-77035	1
33368/33516	C-47B-35-DK	USAAF	44-77036/44-77184	149
33517/33626	C-47B-40-DK	USAAF	44-77185/44-77294	110
34129/34132	C-117A-1-DK	USAAF	45-2545/45-2548	4
34133	C-117A-5-DK	USAAF	45-2549	1
34134/34135	C-47B-45-DK	USAAF	45-876/45-877	2
34136	C-117A-1-DK	USAAF	45-2550	1
34137/34144	C-47B-45-DK	USAAF	45-878/45-885	8
34145	C-117A-1-DK	USAAF	45-2551	1
34146/34167	C-47B-45-DK	USAAF	45-886/45-907	22
34168	C-117A-1-DK	USAAF	45-2552	1
34169/34190	C-47B-45-DK	USAAF	45-908/45-929	22
34191	C-117A-1-DK	USAAF	45-2553	1
34192/34211	C-47B-45-DK	USAAF	45-930/45-949	20
34212	C-117A-1-DK	USAAF	45-2554	1
34213/34233	C-47B-45-DK	USAAF	45-950/45-970	21
34234	C-117A-1-DK	USAAF	45-2555	1
34235/34249	C-47B-45-DK	USAAF	45-971/45-985	15
34250	C-117A-1-DK	USAAF	45-2556	1
34251/34263	C-47B-45-DK	USAAF	45-986/45-998	13
34264	C-117A-1-DK	USAAF	45-2557	1
34265/34277	C-47B-45-DK	USAAF	45-999/45-1011	13
34278	C-117A-1-DK	USAAF	45-2558	1
34279/34290	C-47B-45-DK	USAAF	45-1012/45-1023	12
34291	C-117A-1-DK	USAAF	45-2559	1
34292/34304	C-47B-45-DK	USAAF	45-1024/45-1036	13
34305	C-117A-1-DK	USAAF	45-2560	1
34306/34317	C-47B-45-DK	USAAF	45-1037/45-1048	12
34318	C-117A-1-DK	USAAF	45-2561	1
34319/34325	C-47B-45-DK	USAAF	45-1049/45-1055	7
34326/34409	C-47B-50-DK	USAAF	45-1056/45-1139	84
42954	DC-3D	Dutch Air Force	DT993	1
42955	DC-3D	Pacific Northern	N37465	1
42956/42957	DC-3D		N37466/N37467	2
42958	DC-3D	Colonial AL	N37468	1
42959/42960	DC-3D	Pacific Northern	N37469/N37470	2
42961	DC-3D	Swiftlite	NC3000	1
42962/42963	DC-3D	SAS	OY-DCO, OY-DCU	2
42964	DC-3D	Colonial AL	N34968	1
42965	DC-3D	--	NC34969	1
42966	DC-3D	Pacific Northern	N34970	1
42967	DC-3D	Braniff	N34971	1
42968	DC-3D	Sabena	OO-UAL	1
42969	DC-3D	Swissair	HB-IRB	1
42970/42972	DC-3D	Air France	F-BAXA/F-BAXC	3
42973	DC-3D	Sabena	OO-AUM	1
42974	DC-3D	Piedmont	N34978	1
42975	DC-3D	Air France	F-BAXD	1
42976	DC-3D	SAS	OY-DCY	1
42977	DC-3D	Sabena	OO-AUN	1
42978	DC-3D	Swissair	HB-IRC	1
42979/42980	DC-3D	Navigacao Aerea	PP-NAL, PP-NAM	2
42981	DC-3D	Texas Co.	N1624	1
43073	DC-3C	W.W. West	N27W	(1)
43074	DC-3C	Pacific Northern	N33676	(1)
43075	DC-3C	Tenn. Gas	N33692	(1)
43076	DC-3C	--	N355M	(1)
43077/43079	DC-3C	TACA Venezuela	YV-C-AZY, -AZF, -AZA	(3)
43080	DC-3C	Seaboard Oil	N1822	(1)

43081	DC-3C	United Aircraft	N13300	(1)
43082	DC-3C	Johns Manville	N34916	(1)
43083	DC-3C	--	--	(1)
43084	DC-3C	Gulf Oil	N37497	(1)
43085	DC-3C	Creole Petroleum	N37499	(1)
43086	DC-3C	Chase Nat'l Bk	N67125	(1)
43087/43092	DC-3C	Sabena	OO-AUV, -AUX, -AUZ, -AWG, -CBJ	(6)
43154	DC-3C	Sabena	OO-AWH	(1)

DOUGLAS DF (Number built: 4)

--	DF-151	Japan	J-ANES, J-ANET	2
--	DF-195	USSR	CCCP-H-205, CCCP-H-206	2

DOUGLAS SBD AND A-24 DAUNTLESS (Number built: 5,938)

* 330	XBT-2	USN	0627	1
* 549/584	SBD-1	USN	1596/1631	36
* 585/605	SBD-1	USN	1735/1755	21
* 628/714	SBD-2	USN	2102/2188	87
* 751/801	SBD-3	USN	4518/4568	51
* 802/956 (even #)	A-24-DE	USAAF	41-15746/41-15823	78
* 803/955 (odd #)	SBD-3	USN	4569/4645	77
* 957/1002	SBD-3	USN	4646/4691	46
* 1003	SBD-3	USN	2109	1
* 1007/1206	SBD-3	USN	03185/03384	200
* 1209/1228	SBD-3A	USN (USAAF)	42-6682/42-6701	20
* 1229/1282	SBD-3	USN	06492/06545	54
* 1283	SBD-5	USN	10957	1
* 1284/1313	SBD-3A	USN (USAAF)	42-6702/42-6731	30
* 1314/1358	SBD-3	USN	06546/06590	45
* 1376/1403	SBD-3	USN	06591/06618	28
* 1404/1433	SBD-3A	USN (USAAF)	42-6732/42-6761	30
* 1434/1516	SBD-3	USN	06619/06701	83
* 1517/1526	SBD-3A	USN (USAAF)	42-6762/42-6771	10
* 1527/1546	A-24A-DE	USAAF	42-6772/42-6791	20
* 1547/1651	SBD-4	USN	06702/06806	105
* 1652/1681	A-24A-DE	USAAF	42-6792/42-6821	30
* 1682/1801	SBD-4	USN	06807/06926	120
* 1802/1811	A-24A-DE	USAAF	42-6822/42-6831	10
* 1812/1831	A-24A-DE	USAAF	42-60772/42-60791	20
* 1832/1875	SBD-4	USN	06927/06970	44
* 2221/2235	SBD-4	USN	06971/06985	15
* 2236/2240	SBD-5	USN	10807/10811	5
* 2241/2246	SBD-4	USN	06986/06991	6
* 2247/2324	SBD-4	USN	10317/10394	78
* 2325/2354	A-24A-DE	USAAF	42-60792/42-60821	30
* 2355/2518	SBD-4	USN	10395/10558	164
* 2519/2548	A-24A-DE	USAAF	42-60822/42-60851	30
* 2549/2646	SBD-4	USN	10559/10656	98
* 2647/2656	SBD-5	USN	10812/10821	10
* 2657/2698	SBD-4	USN	10657/10698	42
* 2699/2728	A-24A-DE	USAAF	42-60852/42-60881	30
* 2729/2732	SBD-4	USN	10699/10702	4
* 2733/2752	SBD-5	USN	10822/10841	20
* 2753/2786	SBD-4	USN	10703/10736	34
* 2787/2806	SBD-5	USN	10842/10861	20
* 2807/2830	SBD-4	USN	10737/10760	24
* 2831/2860	SBD-5	USN	10862/10891	30
* 2861/2884	SBD-4	USN	10761/10784	24
* 2885/2914	SBD-5	USN	10892/10921	30
* 2915/2934	SBD-4	USN	10785/10804	20

* 2935/2968	SBD-5	USN	10922/10955	34
* 2969/2970	SBD-4	USN	10805/10806	2
* 3236/3265	SBD-5A	USAAF (USN)	09693/09722	30
* 3266	SBD-5	USN	10956	1
* 8367/3360	SBD-5	USN	10958/11051	94
* 3361/3390	SBD-5A	USAAF (USN)	09723/09752	30
* 3391/3405	SBD-5	USN	11052/11066	15
* 3406/4176	SBD-5	USN	28059/28829	771
* 4177	XSBD-6	USN	28830	1
* 4178/4560	SBD-5	USN	28831/29213	383
* 4561/5060	SBD-5	USN	35922/36421	500
* 5061/5560	SBD-5	USN	36433/36932	500
* 5564/6113	SBD-5	USN	54050/54599	550
* 6114/6563	SBD-6	USN	54600/55049	450
17124/17238	A-24B-1DT	USAAF	42-54285/42-54399	115
17239/17298	A-24B-5-DT	USAAF	42-54400/42-54459	60
17299/17488	A-24B-10-DT	USAAF	42-54460/42-54649	190
17489/17738	A-24B-15-DT	USAAF	42-54650/42-54899	250

DOUGLAS DC-4E (Number built: 1)

1601	DC-4	Co owned	NX18100	1

DOUGLAS DB-7 AND A-20 HAVOC/BOSTON (Number built: 7,478, including 7,098 by Douglas and 380 by licensee)

* 292	7A	Co owned	Not completed	--
* 379	7B	Co owned	--	1
* 431/530	DB-7	Armee de l'Air	No. 1/No. 100	100
2288/2457	DB-7	Armee de l'Air	No. 101/No. 270	170
2950/3049	DB-7A	Armee de l'Air	--	100
3300/3449	DB-7B	RAF	W8252/W8401	150
3450/3599	DB-7B	RAF	Z2155/Z2304	150
3600/3839	DB-73	Armee de l'Air	--	240
4149	DB-7B	RAF	AH740	1
6265/6312	DB-7C	Kon Marine	DO-101/DO-148	48
--	A-20A-DO	USAAC	39-721/39-734	14
--	A-20-DO	USAAC	39-735	1
--	P-70-DO	USAAC	39-736/39-740	5
--	XF-3-DO	USAAC	39-741	1
--	P-70-DO	USAAC	39-742/39-744	3
--	YF-3-DO	USAAC	39-745	1
--	P-70-DO	USAAC	39-746/39-747	2
--	YF-3-DO	USAAC	39-748	1
--	P-70-DO	USAAC	39-749/39-797	49
--	A-20A-DO	USAAC	40-71/40-179	109
--	A-20A-DO	USAAC	40-3143/43-3162	20
5001/5999	A-20B-DL	USAAC	41-2671/41-3669	999
--	A-20C-DO	USAAC	41-19088/41-19462	375
--	A-20C-1-DO	USAAF	42-32951/42-33050	100
--	A-20C-5-DO	USAAF	42-33051/42-33200	150
--	A-20C-10-DO	USAAF	42-33201/42-33383	183
--	A-20G-1-DO	USAAF	42-53535/42-53784	250
--	A-20G-5-DO	USAAF	42-53785/42-53834	50
--	A-20G-10-DO	USAAF	42-53835/42-54134	300
--	A-20G-15-DO	USAAF	42-54135/42-54284	150
--	A-20G-20-DO	USAAF	42-86563/42-86912	350
--	A-20G-25-DO	USAAF	43-9038/43-9229	192
--	A-20J-1-DO	USAAF	43-9230	1
--	A-20G-25-DO	USAAF	43-9231/43-9437	207
--	A-20J-5-DO	USAAF	43-9438/43-9457	20
--	A-20G-30-DO	USAAF	43-9458/43-9637	180
--	A-20J-5-DO	USAAF	43-9638/43-9664	27
--	A-20G-30-DO	USAAF	43-9665/43-9837	173
--	A-20G-35-DO	USAAF	43-9838/43-9856	19
--	A-20J-10-DO	USAAF	43-9857/43-9880	24

--	A-20G-35-DO	USAAF	43-9881/43-9909	29
--	A-20J-10-DO	USAAF	43-9910/43-9917	8
--	A-20G-35-DO	USAAF	43-9918/43-10104	187
--	A-20J-10-DO	USAAF	43-10105/43-10144	40
--	A-20G-35-DO	USAAF	43-10145/43-10237	93
20899/21078	A-20G-40-DO	USAAF	43-21252/43-21431	180
21079/21118	A-20J-15-DO	USAAF	43-21432/43-21471	40
21119/21198	A-20G-40-DO	USAAF	43-21472/43-21551	80
21199/21228	A-20J-15-DO	USAAF	43-21552/43-21581	30
21229/21348	A-20G-40-DO	USAAF	43-21582/43-21701	120
21349/21398	A-20J-15-DO	USAAF	43-21702/43-21751	50
21399/21474	A-20G-45-DO	USAAF	43-21752/43-21827	76
21475/21524	A-20J-20-DO	USAAF	43-21828/43-21877	50
21525/21634	A-20G-45-DO	USAAF	43-21878/43-21987	110
21635/21794	A-20J-20-DO	USAAF	43-21988/43-22147	160
21795/21898	A-20G-45-DO	USAAF	43-22148/43-22251	104
23224/23231	A-20H-1-DO	USAAF	44-1/44-8	8
23232	A-20K-1-DO	USAAF	44-9	1
23233/23248	A-20H-1-DO	USAAF	44-10/44-25	16
23249/23288	A-20H-5-DO	USAAF	44-26/44-65	40
23289/23323	A-20K-5-DO	USAAF	44-66/44-100	35
23324/23421	A-20K-10-DO	USAAF	44-101/44-198	98
23422/23551	A-20H-10-DO	USAAF	44-199/44-328	130
23552/23629	A-20K-10-DO	USAAF	44-329/44-406	78
23630/23759	A-20H-10-DO	USAAF	44-407/44-536	130
23760/23773	A-20K-10-DO	USAAF	44-537/44-550	14
23774/23841	A-20K-15-DO	USAAF	44-551/44-618	68
23842/23929	A-20H-15-DO	USAAF	44-619/44-706	88
23930/24048	A-20K-15-DO	USAAF	44-707/44-825	119

DOUGLAS DC-5 (Number built: 12)

* 411	DC-5	Co owned	NX21701	1
* 422/423	DC-5-518	Penn Central	Not completed	--
* 424	DC-5-510	KLM (West Indies)	PJ-AIW	1
* 425	DC-5-535	SCADTA (Colombia)	Not completed	--
* 426	DC-5-535	KLM (West Indies)	PJ-AIZ	1
* 427	DC-5-518	Penn Central	Not completed	--
* 428	DC-5-511	KNILM	PK-ADB	1
* 429	DC-5-518	Penn Central	Not completed	--
* 430	DC-5-511	KNILM	PK-ADA	1
* 606/608	R3D-1	USN	1901/1903	3
* 609/612	R3D-2	USMC	1904/1907	4

DOUGLAS B-23 DRAGON (Number built: 38)

2713/2750	B-23	USAAC	39-27/39-64	38

DOUGLAS XB-19 (Number built: 1)

2001	XB-19	USAAC	38-471	1

DOUGLAS DC-4 SKYMASTER (Number built: 1,315, including 1,244 by Douglas and 71 by licensee)

3050	C-54-DO	USAAF	41-20137	1
3051/3052	C-54-DO	USAAF	41-20139/42-20140	2
3053	C-54-DO	USAAF	41-20144	1
3054/3059	C-54-DO	USAAF	41-37268/41-37273	6
3060	C-54-DO	USAAF	41-20138	1
3061/3062	C-54-DO	USAAF	41-20141/41-20142	2
3063	C-54-DO	USAAF	41-20145	1
3064/3074	C-54-DO	USAAF	41-37274/41-37284	11
3075	C-54-DO	USAAF	41-20143	1
3076/3110	C-54-DO	USAAF	41-37285/41-37319	35
3111/3125	C-54-DO	USAAF	42-32936/42-32950	15
7445/7464	C-54A-1-DO	USAAF	42-107426/42-107445	20
7465/7489	C-54A-5-DO	USAAF	42-107446/42-107470	25

578

10270/10279	C-54A-1-DC	USAAF	42-72165/42-72174	10
10280/10304	C-54A-5-DC	USAAF	42-72175/42-72199	25
10305/10344	C-54A-10-DC	USAAF	42-72200/42-72239	40
10345/10424	C-54A-15-DC	USAAF	42-72240/42-72319	80
10425/10544	C-54B-1-DC	USAAF	42-72320/42-72439	120
10545/10644	C-54D-1-DC	USAAF	42-72440/42-72539	100
10645/10744	C-54D-5-DC	USAAF	42-72540/42-72639	100
10745/10844	C-54D-10-DC	USAAF	42-72640/42-72739	100
10845/10869	C-54D-15-DC	USAAF	42-72740/42-72764	25
18324/18326	C-54B-1-DO	USAAF	43-17124/43-17126	3
18327/18348	C-54B-5-DO	USAAF	43-17127/43-17148	22
18349/18373	C-54B-10-DO	USAAF	43-17149/43-17173	25
18374/18398	C-54B-15-DO	USAAF	43-17174/43-17198	25
22149/22203	C-54D-15-DC	USAAF	43-17199/43-17253	55
27227/27251	C-54B-20-DO	USAAF	44-9001/44-9025	25
27252/27276	C-54E-1-DO	USAAF	44-9026/44-9050	25
27277/27301	C-54E-5-DO	USAAF	44-9051/44-9075	25
27302/27326	C-54E-10-DO	USAAF	44-9076/44-9100	25
27327/27371	C-54E-15-DO	USAAF	44-9101/44-9145	45
27372/27376	C-54E-20-DO	USAAF	44-9146/44-9150	5
35929/35978	C-54G-1-DO	USAAF	45-476/45-525	50
35979/36028	C-54G-5-DO	USAAF	45-526/45-575	50
36029/36078	C-54G-10-DO	USAAF	45-576/45-625	50
36079/36090	C-54G-15-DO	USAAF	45-626/45-637	12
36327	XC-114-DO	USAAF	45-874	1
36328	YC-116-DO	USAAF	45-875	1
42904	DC-4-1009	Western	NC10201	1
42905	DC-4-1009	SILA	SE-BBA	1
42906	DC-4-1009	SABENA	OO-CBD	1
42907	DC-4-1009	National	NC33679	1
42908	DC-4-1009	KLM	PH-TAT	1
42909	DC-4-1009	Air France	F-BBDA	1
42910	DC-4-1009	ANA	VH-ANA	1
42911	DC-4-1009	Northwest	NC6402	1
42912	DC-4-1009	Air France	F-BBDB	1
42913/42914	DC-4-1009	Northwest	NC6403/NC6404	2
42915	DC-4-1009	Waterman AL	NC33691	1
42916	DC-4-1009	ANA	VH-ANE	1
42917/42918	DC-4-1009	Western	NC10202/NC10203	2
42919/42922	DC-4-1009	National	NC33680/NC33683	4
42923/42925	DC-4-1009	KLM	PH-TAR, - TAS, - TAP	3
42926/42927	DC-4-1009	SILA	SE-BBC/SE-BBD	2
42928/42930	DC-4-1009	ABA	SE-BBE/SE-BBG	3
42931	DC-4-1009	DDL	OY-DFI	1
42932/42933	DC-4-1009	SABENA	OO-CBE/OO-CBF	2
42934	DC-4-1009	SAA	ZS-AUA	1
42935/42943	DC-4-1009	Air France	F-BBDC/F-BBDK	9
42948/42950	DC-4-1009	ANA	VH-ANB/VH-AND	3
42951/42952	DC-4-1009	Iberia	EC-DAO/EC-DAP	2
42982/42983	DC-4-1009	Western	NC10204/NC10205	2
42984/42985	DC-4-1009	SAA	ZS-AUB/ZS-AUC	2
42986	DC-4-1009	SABENA	OO-CBG	1
42987	DC-4-1009	DDL	OY-DFO	1
42988	DC-4-1009	Iberia	EC-DAQ	1
42989/42992	DC-4-1009	Air France	F-BBDL/F-BBDO	4
42993/42994	DC-4-1009	DNL	LN-IAD/LN-IAE	2
42995/42996	DC-4-1009	KLM	PH-TCE/PH-TCF	2
43065/43068	DC-4-1009	TAA	VH-TAA/VH-TAD	4
43071	DC-4-1009	National	NC37684	1
43072	DC-4-1009	Swissair	HB-ILA	1
43093	DC-4-1009	Swissair	HB-ILE	1
43094	DC-4-1009	Aramco	NC1625	1
43095/43096	DC-4-1009	SABENA	OO-CBH/OO-CBI	2
43097/43098	DC-4-1009	Swissair	HB-ILI & HB-ILO	2

```
43099/43101    DC-4-1009        SABENA      OO-CBP/OO-CBR              3
43102          DC-4-1009        National    NC74685                   1
43155/43157    DC-4-1009        SAA         ZS-BMF/ZS-BMH             3
```

BOWLUS XCG-7 AND XCG-8 (Number built: 4)
```
*  1359/1360    XCG-7           USAAF       41-29221 & no serial      2
*  1361/1362    XCG-8           USAAF       41-29622 & no serial      2
```

WARTIME HEAVY BOMBERS (Number built: 3,962 by Douglas, including 3,000 B-17-DLs
                      and 962 B-24-DTs)
```
7900/7902      B-17F-1-DL       USAAF       42-2964/42-2966           3
7903/7914      B-17F-5-DL       USAAF       42-2967/42-2978          12
7915/7939      B-17F-10-DL      USAAF       42-2979/42-3003          25
7940/7974      B-17F-15-DL      USAAF       42-3004/42-3038          35
7975/8009      B-17F-20-DL      USAAF       42-3039/42-3073          35
8010/8084      B-17F-25-DL      USAAF       42-3074/42-3148          75
8085/8124      B-17F-30-DL      USAAF       42-3149/42-3188          40
8125/8164      B-17F-35-DL      USAAF       42-3189/42-3228          40
8165/8219      B-17F-40-DL      USAAF       42-3229/42-3283          55
8220/8274      B-17F-45-DL      USAAF       42-3284/42-3338          55
8275/8329      B-17F-50-DL      USAAF       42-3339/42-3393          55
8330/8358      B-17F-55-DL      USAAF       42-3394/42-3422          29
8359/8384      B-17F-60-DL      USAAF       42-3423/42-3448          26
8385/8418      B-17F-65-DL      USAAF       42-3449/42-3482          34
8419/8439      B-17F-70-DL      USAAF       42-3483/42-3503          21
8440/8498      B-17F-75-DL      USAAF       42-3504/42-3562          59
8499           B-17G-5-DL       USAAF       42-3563                   1
8500/8501      B-17F-80-DL      USAAF       42-37714/42-37715         2
8502           B-17G-10-DL      USAAF       42-37716                  1
8503/8506      B-17F-85-DL      USAAF       42-37717/42-37720         4
8507/8589      B-17G-10-DL      USAAF       42-37721/42-37803        83
8590/8679      B-17G-15-DL      USAAF       42-37804/42-37893        90
8680/8774      B-17G-20-DL      USAAF       42-37894/42-37988        95
8775/8869      B-17G-25-DL      USAAF       42-37989/42-38083        95
8870/8999      B-17G-30-DL      USAAF       42-38084/42-38213       130
15514/15516    B-24D-DT         USAAF       41-11754/41-11756         3
15517          B-24D-DT         USAAF       41-11864                  1
15518/15520    B-24D-DT         USAAF       41-23725/41-23727         3
15521/15523    B-24D-DT         USAAF       41-23756/43-27758         3
15524/15531    B-24E-1-DT       USAAF       41-28409/41-28416         8
15532/15559    B-24E-10-DT      USAAF       41-28417/41-28444        28
15560/15591    B-24E-15-DT      USAAF       41-28445/41-28476        32
15592/15615    B-24E-20-DT      USAAF       41-28477/41-28500        24
15616/15688    B-24E-25-DT      USAAF       41-28501/41-28573        73
15689/15754    B-24H-1-DT       USAAF       41-28574/41-28639        66
15755/15783    B-24H-5-DT       USAAF       41-28640/42-28668        29
15784/15867    B-24H-10-DT      USAAF       41-28669/41-28752        84
15868/16056    B-24H-15-DT      USAAF       41-28753/41-28941       189
16057/16121    B-24H-20-DT      USAAF       41-28942/41-29006        65
16122/16148    B-24H-20-DT      USAAF       42-51077/42-51103        27
16149/16226    B-24H-25-DT      USAAF       42-51104/42-51181        78
16227/16270    B-24H-30-DT      USAAF       42-51182/42-51225        44
16271/16337    B-24J-1-DT       USAAF       42-51226/42-51292        67
16338/16440    B-24J-5-DT       USAAF       42-51293/42-51395       103
16441/16475    B-24J-10-DT      USAAF       42-51396/42-51430        35
21899/22148    B-17G-35-DL      USAAF       42-106984/42-107233     250
22224/22348    B-17G-40-DL      USAAF       44-6001/44-6125         125
22349/22473    B-17G-45-DL      USAAF       44-6126/44-6250         125
22474/22723    B-17G-50-DL      USAAF       44-6251/44-6500         250
22724/22848    B-17G-55-DL      USAAF       44-6501/44-6625         125
22849/22973    B-17G-60-DL      USAAF       44-6626/44-6750         125
22974/23098    B-17G-65-DL      USAAF       44-6751/44-6875         125
23099/23223    B-17G-70-DL      USAAF       44-6876/44-7000         125
31877/32001    B-17G-75-DL      USAAF       44-83236/44-83360       125
```

32002/32126	B-17G-80-DL	USAAF		44-83361/44-83485	125
32127/32226	B-17G-85-DL	USAAF		44-83486/44-83585	100
32227/32326	B-17G-90-DL	USAAF		44-83586/44-83685	100
32327/32526	B-17G-95-DL	USAAF		44-83686/44-83885	200

DOUGLAS A-26 (B-26) INVADER (Number built: 2,452)

* 1004	XA-26-DE	USAAC		41-19504	1
* 1005	XA-26A-DE	USAAC		41-19505	1
* 1006	XA-26B-DE	USAAC		41-19588	1
6813/6817	A-26B-1-DL	USAAF		41-39100/41-39104	5
6818/6832	A-26B-5-DL	USAAF		41-39105/41-39119	15
6833/6852	A-26B-10-DL	USAAF		41-39120/41-39139	20
6853/6864	A-26B-15-DL	USAAF		41-39140/41-39151	12
6865	A-26C-1-DL	USAAF		41-39152	1
6866/6905	A-26B-15-DL	USAAF		41-39153/41-39192	40
6906	A-26C-2-DL	USAAF		41-39193	1
6907	A-26B-15-DL	USAAF		41-39194	1
6908	A-26C-2-DL	USAAF		41-39195	1
6909/6911	A-26B-15-DL	USAAF		41-39196/41-39198	3
6912/6913	A-26C-2-DL	USAAF		41-39199/41-39200	2
6914/7012	A-26B-20-DL	USAAF		41-39201/41-39299	99
7013/7062	A-26B-25-DL	USAAF		41-39300/41-39349	50
7063/7137	A-26B-30-DL	USAAF		41-39350/41-39424	75
7138/7212	A-26B-35-DL	USAAF		41-39425/41-39499	75
7213/7312	A-26B-40-DL	USAAF		41-39500/41-39599	100
18399/18413	A-26B-5-DT	USAAF		43-22252/43-22266	15
18414/18448	A-26B-10-DT	USAAF		43-22267/43-22301	35
18449/18450	A-26B-16-DT	USAAF		43-22302/43-22303	2
18451	A-26C-16-DT	USAAF		43-22304	1
18452/18454	A-26B-15-DT	USAAF		43-22305/43-22307	3
18455/18459	A-26C-16-DT	USAAF		43-22308/43-22312	5
18460/18492	A-26B-15-DT	USAAF		43-22313/43-22345	33
18493/18496	A-26C-16-DT	USAAF		43-22346/43-22349	4
18497/18546	A-26B-15-DT	USAAF		43-22350/43-22399	50
18547/18600	A-26B-20-DT	USAAF		43-22400/43-22453	54
18601/18613	A-26D-25-DT	USAAF		43-22454/43-22466	13
18614/18640	A-26C-15-DT	USAAF		43-22467/43-22493	27
18641/18711	A-26C-20-DT	USAAF		43-22494/43-22564	71
18712/18898	A-26C-25-DT	USAAF		43-22565/43-22751	187
27377/27496	A-26B-45-DL	USAAF		44-34098/44-34217	120
27497/27565	A-26B-50-DL	USAAF		44-34218/44-34286	69
27566	A-26B-51-DL	USAAF		44-34287	1
27567/27575	A-26B-50-DL	USAAF		44-34288/44-34296	9
27576/27577	A-26B-51-DL	USAAF		44-34297/44-34298	2
27578/27601	A-26B-50-DL	USAAF		44-34299/44-34322	24
27602	A-26B-51-DL	USAAF		44-34323	1
27603/27605	A-26B-50-DL	USAAF		44-34324/44-34326	3
27606	A-26B-51-DL	USAAF		44-34327	1
27607/27609	A-26B-50-DL	USAAF		44-34328/44-34330	3
27610	A-26B-51-DL	USAAF		44-34331	1
27611	A-26B-50-DL	USAAF		44-34332	1
27612/27613	A-26B-55-DL	USAAF		44-34333/44-34334	2
27614	A-26B-56-DL	USAAF		44-34335	1
27615/27617	A-26B-55-DL	USAAF		44-34336/44-34338	3
27618	A-26B-56-DL	USAAF		44-34339	1
27619/27621	A-26B-55-DL	USAAF		44-34340/44-34342	3
27622	A-26B-56-DL	USAAF		44-34343	1
27623/27625	A-26B-55-DL	USAAF		44-34344/44-34346	3
27626	A-26B-56-DL	USAAF		44-34347	1
27627/27629	A-26B-55-DL	USAAF		44-34348/44-34350	3
27630	A-26B-56-DL	USAAF		44-34351	1
27631/27642	A-26B-55-DL	USAAF		44-34352/44-34363	12
27643	A-26B-56-DL	USAAF		44-34364	1
27644/27646	A-26B-55-DL	USAAF		44-34365/44-34367	3

27647	A-26B-56-DL	USAAF	44-34368	1
27648/27650	A-26B-55-DL	USAAF	44-34369/44-34371	3
27651	A-26B-56-DL	USAAF	44-34372	1
27652/27655	A-26B-55-DL	USAAF	44-34373/44-34376	4
27656	A-26B-56-DL	USAAF	44-34377	1
27657/27660	A-26B-55-DL	USAAF	44-34378/44-34381	4
27661	A-26B-56-DL	USAAF	44-34382	1
27662/27665	A-26B-55-DL	USAAF	44-34383/44-34386	4
27666	A-26B-56-DL	USAAF	44-34387	1
27667/27671	A-26B-55-DL	USAAF	44-34388/44-34392	5
27672	A-26B-56-DL	USAAF	44-34393	1
27673/27677	A-26B-55-DL	USAAF	44-34394/44-34398	5
27678	A-26B-56-DL	USAAF	44-34399	1
27679/27683	A-26B-55-DL	USAAF	44-34400/44-34404	5
27684	A-26B-56-DL	USAAF	44-34405	1
27685/27687	A-26B-55-DL	USAAF	44-34406/44-34408	3
27688	A-26B-56-DL	USAAF	44-34409	1
27689/27691	A-26B-55-DL	USAAF	44-34410/44-34412	3
27692	A-26B-56-DL	USAAF	44-34413	1
27693/27695	A-26B-55-DL	USAAF	44-34414/44-34416	3
27696	A-26B-56-DL	USAAF	44-34417	1
27697/27698	A-26B-55-DL	USAAF	44-34418/44-34419	2
27699	A-26B-56-DL	USAAF	44-34420	1
27700/27701	A-26B-55-DL	USAAF	44-34421/44-34422	2
27702	A-26B-56-DL	USAAF	44-34423	1
27703/27751	A-26B-55-DL	USAAF	44-34424/44-34472	49
27752/27756	A-26B-60-DL	USAAF	44-34473/44-34477	5
27757	A-26B-61-DL	USAAF	44-34478	1
27758/27759	A-26B-60-DL	USAAF	44-34479/44-34480	2
27760	A-26B-61-DL	USAAF	44-34481	1
27761/27762	A-26B-60-DL	USAAF	44-34482/44-34483	2
27763	A-26B-61-DL	USAAF	44-34484	1
27764/27765	A-26B-60-DL	USAAF	44-34485/44-34486	2
27766	A-26B-61-DL	USAAF	44-34487	1
27767/27768	A-26B-60-DL	USAAF	44-34488/44-34489	2
27769	A-26B-61-DL	USAAF	44-34490	1
27770/27771	A-26B-60-DL	USAAF	44-34491/44-34492	2
27772	A-26B-61-DL	USAAF	44-34493	1
27773/27774	A-26B-60-DL	USAAF	44-34494/44-34495	2
27775	A-26B-61-DL	USAAF	44-34496	1
27776/27777	A-26B-60-DL	USAAF	44-34497/44-34498	2
27778	A-26B-61-DL	USAAF	44-34499	1
27779/27780	A-26B-60-DL	USAAF	44-34500/44-34501	2
27781	A-26B-61-DL	USAAF	44-34502	1
27782/27783	A-26B-60-DL	USAAF	44-34503/44-34504	2
27784	A-26B-61-DL	USAAF	44-34505	1
27785/27786	A-26B-60-DL	USAAF	44-34506/44-34507	2
27787	A-26B-61-DL	USAAF	44-34508	1
27788/27789	A-26B-60-DL	USAAF	44-34509/44-34510	2
27790	A-26B-61-DL	USAAF	44-34511	1
27791/27792	A-26B-60-DL	USAAF	44-34512/44-34513	2
27793	A-26B-61-DL	USAAF	44-34514	1
27794/27795	A-26B-60-DL	USAAF	44-34515/44-34516	2
27796	A-26B-61-DL	USAAF	44-34517	1
27797/27798	A-26B-60-DL	USAAF	44-34518/44-34519	2
27799	A-26B-61-DL	USAAF	44-34520	1
27800	A-26B-60-DL	USAAF	44-34521	1
27801/27864	A-26B-61-DL	USAAF	44-34522/44-34585	64
27865	XA-26F-DL	USAAF	44-34586	1
27866/27896	A-26B-61-DL	USAAF	44-34587/44-34617	31
27897/28032	A-26B-66-DL	USAAF	44-34618/44-34753	136
28055	XA-26D-DL	USAAF	44-34776	1
28477/28636	A-26C-30-DT	USAAF	44-35198/44-35357	160
28637/28836	A-26C-35-DT	USAAF	44-35358/44-35557	200

582

28837/28841	A-26C-40-DT	USAAF	44-35558/44-35562	5
28842	XA-26E-DT	USAAF	44-35563	1
28843/28934	A-26C-40-DT	USAAF	44-35564/44-35655	92
28935/29061	A-26C-45-DT	USAAF	44-35656/44-35782	127
29062/29216	A-26C-50-DT	USAAF	44-35783/44-35937	155
29217/29226	A-26C-55-DT	USAAF	44-35938/44-35947	10
29232	A-26C-55-DT	USAAF	44-35953	1
29234	A-26C-55-DT	USAAF	44-35955	1
29236/29275	A-26C-55-DT	USAAF	44-35957/44-35996	40

DOUGLAS XSB2D-1 AND BTD DESTROYER (Number built: 30)

*	1207/1208	XSB2D-1	USN	03551/03552	2
*	1364/1375	BTD-1	USN	04960/04971	12
*	1876/1890	BTD-1	USN	09048/09062	15
*	1891	BTD-1	USN	04959	1

DOUGLAS XB-42 MIXMASTER (Number built: 2)

	XB-42-DO	USAAF	43-50224/43-50225	2

DOUGLAS XTB2D-1 SKYPIRATE (Number built: 2)

*	5561/5562	XTB2D-1	USN	36933/36934	2

DOUGLAS AD (A-1) SKYRAIDER (Number built: 3,180)

*	1913/1937	XBT2D-1	USN	09085/09109	25
*	1938/2179	AD-1	USN	09110/09351	242
*	2180/2214	AD-1Q	USN	09352/09386	35
*	6673/6828	AD-2	USN	122210/122365	156
*	6829/6835	AD-2Q	USN	122366/122372	7
*	6836	AD-2QU	USN	122373	1
*	6837/6850	AD-2Q	USN	122374/122387	14
*	6851/6975	AD-3	USN	122729/122853	125
*	6976/6998	AD-3Q	USN	122854/122876	23
*	6999/7029	AD-3W	USN	122877/122907	31
*	7030/7044	AD-3N	USN	122908/122922	15
*	7077/7312	AD-4	USN	123771/124006	236
*	7343/7381	AD-4Q	USN	124037/124075	39
*	7382/7433	AD-4W	USN	124076/124127	52
*	7434/7462	AD-4N	USN	124128/124156	29
*	7535/7570	AD-4N	USN	124725/124760	36
*	7571/7587	AD-4W	USN	124761/124777	17
*	7600/7657	AD-4N	USN	125707/125764	58
*	7658/7675	AD-4W	USN	125765/125782	18
*	7676/7818	AD-4N	USN	126876/127018	143
*	7819/7858	AD-4W	USN	126836/126875	40
*	7859/7894	AD-4	USN	127844/127879	36
*	7895/7935	AD-4N	USN	127880/127920	41
*	7936/7976	AD-4W	USN	127921/127961	41
*	8235/8334	AD-4	USN	128917/129016	100
*	8335/8499	AD-4B	USN	132227/132391	165
*	8872	AD-5N	USN	132477	1
*	8873	AD-5	USN	132478	1
*	8874	AD-5S	USN	132479	1
*	8875/9031	AD-5N	USN	132480/132636	157
*	9325/9388	AD-5W	USN	132729/132792	64
*	9389/9408	AD-5W	USN	133757/133776	20
*	9409/9493	AD-5	USN	132392/132476	85
*	9494/9543	AD-5	USN	132637/132686	50
*	9544/9619	AD-5	USN	133854/133929	76
*	9695/9866	AD-6	USN	134466/134637	172
*	9867/10050	AD-6	USN	135223/135406	184
*	10051/10131	AD-5N	USN	134974/135054	81
*	10216/10299	AD-5W	USN	135139/135222	84
*	10568/10708	AD-6	USN	137492/137632	141
*	10838/11053	AD-6	USN	139606/139821	216

```
*   11054/11103   AD-5W              USN            139556/139605           50
*   11490/11561   AD-7               USN            142010/142081           72

DOUGLAS C-74 GLOBEMASTER I (Number built:  14)
13913/13926      C-74-DL            USAAF          42-65402/42-65415       14

DOUGLAS DC-6 (Number built:  704)
36326            XC-112A-DO         USAAF          45-873                   1
42854/42865      DC-6               American       N90701/N90712           12
42866/42075      DC 6               United         N37501/N37510           10
42876/42878      DC-6               Panagra        N90876/N90878            3
42879/42880      DC-6               American       N90713/N90714            2
42881            VC-118-DO          USAAF          46-505                   1
42882/42896      DC-6               American       N90715/N90729           15
42897/42899      DC-6               Delta          N1903M/N1905M            3
42900            DC-6               KLM            PH-TPW                    1
42901            DC-6A              Co owned       N30006                   1
42902/42903      DC-6               PAL            PI-C 293/PI-C 294         2
43000/43024      DC-6               United         N37511/N37535           25
43025/43029      DC-6               United         N37537/N37541            5
43030/43034      DC-6               FAMA           LV-ADR/LV-ADV            5
43035/43054      DC-6               American       N90730/N90749           20
43055/43058      DC-6               National       N90891/N90894            4
43059/43060      DC-6               PAL            PI-C 290/PI-C 291         2
43061            DC-6               United         N37536                   1
43062/43064      DC-6               Sabena         OO-AWA/OO-AWC            3
43103/43104      DC-6               Panagra        N8103H/N8104H            2
43105/43110      DC-6               Braniff        N90881/N90886            6
43111/43112      DC-6               KLM            PH-TPJ & PH-TKW           2
43114/43118      DC-6               KLM            PH-TPJ, -TPM, -TPT,       5
                                                   -TPB, -TPP
43119/43128      DC-6               ABA (SAS)      SE-BDA/SE-BDI           10
43129/43131      DC-6               SILA (SAS)     SE-BDL/SE-BDM and         3
                                                   SE-BDO
43132/43133      DC-6               DDL (SAS)      OY-AAE/OY-AAF            2
43134/43135      DC-6               DNL (SAS)      LN-LAG/LN-LAH            2
43136            DC-6               FAMA           LV-ADW                    1
43137            DC-6               American       N90750                    1
43138            DC-6               PAL            PI-C 292                  1
43139/43140      DC-6               Delta          N1901M/N1902M            2
43141            DC-6               Panagra        N6141C                    1
43142            DC-6               Delta          N1906M                    1
43143/43147      DC-6               United         N37542/N37546            5
43148/43149      DC-6               Sabena         OO-AWU & OO-AWW           2
43150/43151      DC-6               National       N90895/N90896            2
43152            DC-6               LAI            I-LIKE                    1
43206/43210      R6D-1              USN            128423/128427            5
43211/43213      DC-6               Mexicana       XA-JOR/XA-JOT            3
43214            DC-6               National       N90897                    1
43215/43217      DC-6               LAI            I-LUCK, -LADY, -LOVE     3
43218            DC-6               National       N90898                    1
43219            DC-6               Delta          N1907M                    1
43257/43262      DC-6B              United         N37547/N37552            6
43263/43273      DC-6B              American       N90751/N90761           11
43274/43275      DC-6B              Swissair       HB-IBA & HB-IBE           2
43276            DC-6B              United         N37555                    1
43291/43292      DC-6B              United         N37553/N37554            2
43293/43295      DC-6               Braniff        N6887/N6889              3
43296/43297      DC-6A              Slick          N90807/N90808            2
43298/43300      DC-6B              United         N37556/N37558            3
43401/43405      R6D-1              USN            128428/128432            5
43517            R6D-1              USN            128433                    1
43518/43535      DC-6B              Pan American   N6518C/N6535C           18
43536/43537      DC-6B              Panagra        N6536C/N6537C            2
```

43538/43542	DC-6B	United	N37559/N37563	5
43543/43544	DC-6B	American	N90765/N90766	2
43545/43547	DC-6B	American	N90762/N90764	3
43548/43549	DC-6B	SAS	OY-KMA & LN-LML	2
43550/43551	DC-6B	KLM	PH-TFH/PH-TFI	2
43552/43556	DC-6B	KLM	PH-TFK/PH-TFO	5
43557/43558	DC-6B	PAL	PI-C 295/PI-C 296	2
43559/43560	DC-6B	Aramco	N708A/N709A	2
43561/43563	DC-6B	United	N37564/N37566	3
43564	DC-6B	American	N90767	1
43565/43582	C-118A-DO	USAF	51-3818/51-3835	18
43670/43723	R6D-1	USN	131567/131620	54
43738/43743	DC-6B	National	N8221H/N8226H	6
43744/43749	DC-6B	SAS	OY-KME, LN-LMO, LN-LMP, SE-BDP, SE-BDR, SE-BDS	6
43750	DC-6B	Swissair	HB-IBI	1
43817/43819	DC-6A	Slick	N90809/N90811	3
43820/43821	DC-6B	National	N8227H/N8228H	2
43822/43826	DC-6B	Western	N91302/N91306	5
43827/43832	DC-6B	Sabena	OO-SDF, OO-SDH, OO-CTH, OO-CTI, OO-CTK, OO-CTL	6
43833/43835	DC-6B	TAI	F-BGOB/F-BGOC	3
43836/43837	DC-6B	Mexicana	XA-KIQ, XA-KIR	2
43838	DC-6B	Pan American	N6538C	1
43839/43841	DC-6A	American	N90776/N90778	3
43842/43844	DC-6B	Can Pacific	CF-CUO/CF-CUQ	3
43845/43847	DC-6B	American	N90768/N90770	3
44056/44060	DC-6B	American	N90771/N90775	5
44061	DC-6B	Pan American	N4061K	1
44062	DC-6B	Can Pacific	CF-CUR	1
44063/44064	DC-6A	Can Pacific	CF-CUS/CF-CUT	2
44069/44075	DC-6A	Flying Tiger	N34953/N34959	7
44076	DC-6A	KLM	PH-TGA	1
44080/44081	DC-6B	United	N37567/N37568	2
44082/44083	DC-6B	Continental	N90960 & N90962	2
44087/44089	DC-6B	Swissair	HB-IBO, - IBU, -IBZ	3
44102	DC-6B	Pan American	N8102H	1
44103/44117	DC-6B	Pan American	N6103C/N6117C	15
44118/44121	DC-6B	Pan American	N5118V/N5121V	4
44165/44170	DC-6B	SAS	SE-BDT, OY-KMI, LN-LMS, SE-BDU, OY-KMU, LN-LMT	6
44175/44176	DC-6B	Sabena	OO-CTM, OO-CTN	2
44251/44254	DC-6B	Alitalia	I-DIMA, -DIME, -DIMO	4
44255/44256	DC-6B	Panagra	N6255C/N6256C	2
44257	DC-6A	KLM	PH-TGB	1
44258/44260	DC-6A	Pan American	N6258C/N6260C	3
44417/44419	DC-6B	LAI	I-LYNX, -LINE, -LAND	3
44420/44421	DC-6A	Sabena	OO-CTO, OO-CTP	2
44424/44428	DC-6B	Pan American	N5024K/N5028K	5
44429/44431	DC-6B	Western	N91307/N91309	3
44432/44433	DC-6B	Japan AL	JA6205/JA6206	2
44434	DC-6B	Western	N91310	1
44594/44676	C-118A-DO	USAF	53-3223/53-3305	83
44677/44678	DC-6A	Flying Tiger	N34953/N34954	2
44687/44688	DC-6B	Trans American	N6120C/N6121C	2
44689	DC-6B	Continental	N90961	1
44690/44692	DC-6B	LAN-Chile	CC-LDD/CC-LDF	3
44693/44694	DC-6B	ANA	VH-INH, VH-INU	2
44695	DC-6B	Sabena	OO-SDQ	1
44696/44697	DC-6B	TAI	F-BHEE/F-BHEF	2
44698/44699	DC-6B	Northwest	N569/N570	2

44871	DC-6B	UAT	F-BGSN	1
44888	DC-6B	Alitalia	I-DIMU	1
44889	DC-6A	Airwork	G-AOFX	1
44890	DC-6A	Northwest	N571	1
44891/44892	DC-6B	Can Pacific	CF-CZE/CF-CZF	2
44893/44902	DC-6B	United	N37569/N37578	10
44905/44909	DC-6A	United	N37590/N37594	5
44913	DC-6B	Alitalia	I-DIMB	1
44914/44917	DC-6A	American	N90779/N90782	4
45058	DC-6A	Airwork	G-AOFY	1
45059	DC-6B	Aramco	N710A	1
45060	DC-6B	Western	N93117	1
45063/45067	DC-6B	Western	N93111/N93112, N93114/N93116	5
45075	DC-6B	LAI	I-LEAD	1
45076/45077	DC-6B	ANA	VH-INS/VH-INT	2
45078/45079	DC-6B	Can Pacific	CF-CZQ/CF-CZR	2
45107/45109	DC-6B	Trans American	N3022C/N3024C	3
45110	DC-6A	Slick	N6815C	1
45131/45137	DC-6B	United	N37579/N37585	7
45173/45179	DC-6B	Western	N93118/N93124	7
45197/45202	DC-6B	Northwest	N572/N577	6
45216/45225	DC-6B	Northeast	N6580C/N6589C	10
45226/45227	DC-6A	Trans Caribbean	N6538C/N6539C	2
45243	DC-6A	Slick	N6118C	1
45319/45320	DC-6B	Northwest	N578/N579	2
45321/45324	DC-6B	Western	N93125/N93128	4
45326/45329	DC-6B	Can Pacific	CF-CZS/CF-CZV	4
45368/45369	DC-6A	Trans Caribbean	N6540C/N6541C	2
45372	DC-6A	Riddle	N7780B	1
45373/45375	DC-6A	American	N90783/N90785	3
45457	DC-6A	Slick	N7818C	1
45458	DC-6A	Belgian Air Force	OT-CDA	1
45472/45473	DC-6B	Trans American	N3025C/N3026C	2
45474/45476	DC-6A	Overseas National	N630NA, N640NA and N650NA	3
45478/45479	DC-6B	UAT	F-BIAM,F-BIAO	2
45480/45481	DC-6A	Los Angeles Air Service	N6579C/N6580C	2
45491/45494	DC-6B	United	N37586/N37589	4
45496	DC-6B	Cathay Pacific	VR-HFK	1
45497	DC-6A	Maritime Central	CF-MCK	1
45498/45500	DC-6A	Can Pacific	CF-CZZ, CF-CPB, CF-CPF	3
45501/45502	DC-6B	Northwest	N581/N582	2
45503/45504	DC-6A	Nevada Aero Transport	N6575C/N6576C	2
45505	DC-6B	Can Pacific	CF-CZY	1
45506	DC-6B	Maritime Central	CF-MCL	1
45513/45516	DC-6B	LAN-Chile	CC-CCG/CC-CCJ	4
45517/45520	DC-6A	Slick	N6119C, N7820C/ N7822C	4
45521/45522	DC-6A	United	N37595/N37596	2
45523/45524	DC-6B	Ethiopian	ET-T-25/ET-T-26	2
45527/45530	DC-6A	Loide Aereo Nacional	PP-LFA/PP-LFD	4
45531/45532	DC-6A	Hunting Clan	G-APNO/G-APNP	2
45533	DC-6B	Ethiopian	ET-T-27	1
45534/45538	DC-6B	Western	N93129/N93133	5
45539/45540	DC-6B	Olympic	SX-DAD/SX-DAE	2
45543	DC-6B	Olympic	SX-DAF	1
45544	DC-6B	Co owned	N6574C	1
45550	DC-6B	CAT	B-1006	1
45551	DC-6A	Swissair	HB-IBB	1

```
45563/45564      DC-6B              JAT          YU-AFA/YU-AFB         2

DOUGLAS XB-43 (Number built:  2)
                 XB-43-DO           USAAF        44-61508             1
                 YB-43-DO           USAAF        44-61509             1

DOUGLAS D-558-1 SKYSTREAK (Number built:  3)
*  6564/6566     D-558-1            USN          37970/37972          3

DOUGLAS CLOUDSTER II (Number built:  1)
43113            Cloudster II       Co owned     NX8000H              1

DOUGLAS F3D SKYKNIGHT (Number built:  268)
*  6670/6671     XF3D-1             USN          121457/121459        3
*  7047/7074     F3D-1              USN          123741/123768       28
*  7465/7534     F3D-2              USN          124595/124664       70
*  7977/8076     F3D-2              USN          125783/125882      100
*  8087/8143     F3D-2              USN          127019/127085       67

DOUGLAS D-558-2 SKYROCKET (Number built:  3)
*  6567/6569     D-558-2            USN          37973/37975          3

DOUGLAS SUPER DC-3 (Number built:  105)
43158/43159      DC-3S              Co owned     N30000, N15579       2
43191/43193      DC-3S              Capital      N16019, N16016,      3
                                                 N16012
43301/43400      R4D-8              USN          See main text      100

DOUGLAS C-124 GLOBEMASTER II (Number built:  448)
                 C-124A-DL          USAF         48-795               1
                 C-124A-DL          USAF         49-232/49-259       28
43221/43256      C-124A-DL          USAF         50-083/50-118       36
43277/43290      C-124A-DL          USAF         50-1255/50-1268     14
43406            YC-124D-DL         USAF         51-072               1
43407/43516      C-124A-DL          USAF         51-073/51-182      110
43583/43597      C-124A-DL          USAF         51-5173/51-5187     15
43598/43623      C-124C-DL          USAF         51-5188/51-5213     26
43724/43737      C-124C-DL          USAF         51-7272/51-7285     14
43848/43998      C-124C-DL          USAF         52-939/52-1089     151
                 C-124C-DL          USAF         53-001/53-052       52

DOUGLAS A2D-1 SKYSHARK (Number built:  12)
*  7045/7046     XA2D-1             USN          122988/122989        2
*  7590/7599     A2D-1              USN          125479/125488       10

DOUGLAS F4D (F-6) SKYRAY (Number built:  421)
*  7463/7464     XF4D-1             USN          124586/124587        2
                 F4D-1              USN          130740/130750       11
                 F4D-1              USN          134744/134973      230
                 F4D-1              USN          139030/139207      178

DOUGLAS X-3 STILETTO (Number built:  1)
                 X-3-DO             USAF         49-2892              1

DOUGLAS A-3 (A3D) SKYWARRIOR (Number built:  283)
*  7588/7589     XA3D-1             USN          125412/125413        2
                 A3D-1              USN          130352/130363       12
                 A3D-1              USN          135407/135444       38
*  10763/10837   A3D-2              USN          138902/138976       75
                 A3D-2              USN          142236/142255       20
                 A3D-2P             USN          142256               1
                 A3D-2Q             USN          142257               1
                 A3D-2              USN          142400/142407        8
                 A3D-2              USN          142630/142665       36
```

587

```
               A3D-2P              USN          142666/142669       4
               A3D-2Q              USN          142670/142673       4
               A3D-2               USN          144626/144629       4
  *  12071/12093  A3D-2P           USN          144825/144847      23
  *  12094/12101  A3D-2Q           USN          144848/144855       8
  *  12102/12113  A3D-2T           USN          144856/144867      12
               A3D-2P              USN          146446/146447       2
               A3D-2Q              USN          146448/146459      12
               A3D-2               USN          147648/147668      21


BOEING B-47 STRATOJET (Number built by Douglas:  262)
  43624/43633   B-47B-35-DT        USAF         51-2141, -2150,    10
                                                -2155, -2160, -2165,
                                                -2170, -2175, -2180,
                                                -2185 and -2190
  43634/43643   B-47E-1-DT         USAF         52-019/52-028      10
  43644/43656   B-47E-5-DT         USAF         52-029/52-041      13
  43657/43669   B-47E-10-DT        USAF         52-042/52-054      13
  43751/43754   B-47E-10-DT        USAF         52-055/52-058       4
  43755/43777   B-47E-15-DT        USAF         52-059/52-081      23
  43778/43807   B-47E-20-DT        USAF         52-082/52-111      30
  43808/43816   B-47E-25-DT        USAF         52-112/52-120       9
  44000/44030   B-47E-25-DT        USAF         52-146/52-176      31
  44031/44055   B-47E-30-DT        USAF         52-177/52-201      25
  44149/44161   B-47E-35-DT        USAF         53-2028/53-2040    13
  44436/44449   B-47E-40-DT        USAF         53-2090/53-2103    14
  44450/44463   B-47E-45-DT        USAF         53-2104/53-2117    14
  44464/44477   B-47E-50-DT        USAF         53-2118/53-2131    14
  44478/44490   B-47E-55-DT        USAF         53-2132/53-2144    13
  44491/44503   B-47E-60-DT        USAF         53-2145/53-2157    13
  44504/44516   B-47E-65-DT        USAF         53-2158/53-2170    13


DOUGLAS DC-7 (Number built:  338)
  44122/44146   DC-7               American     N301AA/N325AA      25
  44171/44174   DC-7               National     N8205H/N8208H       4
  44261/44264   DC-7               Delta        N4871C/N4874C       4
  44265/44289   DC-7               United       N6301C/N6325C      25
  44435         DC-7B              Co owned     N70D                1
  44679/44684   DC-7               Delta        N4875C/N4880C       6
  44700/44704   DC-7B              Panagra      N51700/N51704       5
  44852/44863   DC-7B              Eastern      N801D/N812D        12
  44864/44870   DC-7B              Pan American N771PA, N777PA, and  7
                                                N772PA/N776PA
  44872         DC-7C              Co owned     N70C                1
  44873/44887   DC-7C              Pan American N731PA/N745PA      15
  44903/44904   DC-7               United       N6326C/N6327C       2
  44910/44912   DC-7B              SAA          ZS-DKD/ZS-DKF       3
  44921/44925   DC-7B              American     N381AA, N385AA,     5
                                                N387AA, N390AA,
                                                N394AA
  44926/44933   DC-7C              SAS          OY-KNA, LN-MOB,     8
                                                SE-CCA, OY-KNB,
                                                LN-MOD, SE-CCB,
                                                OY-KNC, LN-MOE
  45061/45062   DC-7C              Swissair     HB-IBK, HB-IBL      2
  45068/45074   DC-7C              Braniff      N5900/N5906         7
  45082/45089   DC-7B              Eastern      N813D/N820D         8
  45090/45097   DC-7C              Pan American N746PA/N753PA       8
  45098/45106   DC-7               American     N326AA/N334AA       9
  45111/45120   DC-7C              BOAC         G-AOIA/G-AOIJ      10
  45121         DC-7C              Pan American N754PA              1
  45122         DC-7C              Panair do Brasil PP-PDL          1
  45123         DC-7C              Pan American N755PA              1
  45124/45125   DC-7C              Panair do Brasil PP-PDM, PP-PDN  2
```

45127/45130	DC-7C	Mexicana	XA-LOB/XA-LOE	4
45142/45156	DC-7	United	N6328C/N6342C	15
45157/45162	DC-7C	Sabena	OO-SFA/OO-SFF	6
45180/45189	DC-7C	KLM	PH-DSA/PH-DSI, and	
			PH-DSK	10
45190/45191	DC-7C	Swissair	HB-IBM, HB-IBN	2
45192	DC-7B	Continental	N8210H	1
45193/45196	DC-7B	Continental	N8210H/N8213H	4
45203/45210	DC-7C	Northwest	N284/N291	8
45211/45215	DC-7C	SAS	OY-KND, LN-MOF and	5
			SE-CCD/SE-CCF	
45228/45231	DC-7C	Alitalia	I-DUVA, -DUVE,	4
			-DUVI, -DUVO	
45232/45239	DC-7B	American	N335AA/N342AA	8
45244	DC-7B	Panagra	N51244	1
45308/45310	DC-7C	Sabena	OO-SFG, -SFH, -SFJ	3
45311/45314	DC-7B	Delta	N4882C/N4885C	4
45325	DC-7C	SAS	SE-CCC	1
45330/45349	DC-7B	Eastern	N821D/N840D	20
45350/45355	DC-7B	Delta	N4886C/N4891D	6
45356/45361	DC-7	United	N6343C/N6348C	6
45362/45365	DC-7B	National	N6201B/N6204B	4
45366/45367	DC-7C	TAI	F-BIAP, F-BIAQ	2
45397/45407	DC-7B	American	N344AA/N350AA,	11
			N357AA, N359AA,	
			N362AA and N365AA	
45446	DC-7C	TAI	F-BIAR	1
45447/45456	DC-7B	Eastern	N841D/N850D	10
45462/45467	DC-7C	Northwest	N292/N297	6
45468/45471	DC-7C	Japan Air Lines	JA6301/JA6303 and	4
			JA6305	
45477	DC-7B	SAA	ZS-DKG	1
45482/45490	DC-7	United	N6349C/N6357C	9
45495	DC-7C	Sabena	OO-SFK	1
45525	DC-7B	Continental	N8214H	1
45541/45542	DC-7C	Alitalia	I-DUVU, I-DUVB	2
45545/45549	DC-7C	KLM	PH-DSM/PH-DSP,	5
			PH-DSR	
45553	DC-7C	Swissair	HB-IBP	1

DOUGLAS A-4 (A4D) SKYHAWK (Number built. 2,960)

* 10709	XA4D-1	USN	137812	1
* 10710/10728	A4D-1 (A-4A)	USN	137813/137831	19
* 11284/11335	A4D-1 (A-4A)	USN	139919/139970	52
* 11336/11395	A4D-2 (A-4B)	USN	142082/142141	60
* 11396/11489	A4D-1 (A-4A)	USN	142142/142235	94
* 11601/11608	A4D-2(A-4B)	USN	142416/142423	8
* 11736/12015	A4D-2 (A-4B)	USN	142674/142953	280
* 12114/12307	A4D-2 (A-4B)	USN	144868/145061	194
* 12308/12392	A4D-2N (A-4C)	USN	145062/145146	85
* 12433/12613	A4D-2N (A-4C)	USN	147669/147849	181
* 12614/12627	A4D-2N (A-4C)	USN	148304/148317	14
* 12628/12805	A4D-2N (A-4C)	USN	148435/148612	178
* 12806/12807	A4D-5(A-4E)	USN	148613/148614	2
* 12812/12971	A4D-2N (A-4C)	USN	149487/149646	160
* 12972/12991	A4D-5 (A-4E)	USN	149647/149666	20
* 12992/13011	A4D-2N (A-4C)	USN	150581/150600	20
* 13012/13191	A4D-5 (A-4E)	USN	149959/150138	180
* 13192/13371	A4D-5 (A-4E)	USN	151022/151201	180
* 13372/13488	A-4E	USN	151984/152100	117
* 13489	A-4F	USN	152101	1
* 13490/13491	TA-4E	USN	152102/152103	2
* 13492/13524	TA-4F	USN	152846/152878	33

589

TA-4F	USN	153459/153531	73
TA-4F	USN	153660/153690	31
A-4F	USN	154172/154217	46
TA-4F	USN	154287/154343	57
TA-4F	USN	154614/154657	44
A-4G	RAN	154903/154910	8
TA-4G	RAN	154911/154912	2
A-4F	USN	154970/155069	100
TA-4J	USN	155070/155119	50
A-4H	Israel	155242/155289	48
TA-4J	USN	156891/156950	60
A-4H	Israel	157395/157428	34
TA-4H	Israel	157429/157434	6
A-4K	RNZAF	157904/157913	10
TA-4K	RNZAF	157914/157917	4
A-4H	Israel	157918/157925	8
TA-4H	Israel	157926/157929	4
TA-4J	USN	158073/157147	75
A-4M	USMC	158148/158196	49
A-4M	USMC	158412/158435	24
TA-4J	USN	158453/158527	75
TA-4J	USN	158712/158723	12
A-4N	Israel	158726/158743	18
A-4N	Israel	159035/159052	18
A-4N	Israel	159075/159098	24
TA-4J	USN	159099/159104	6
A-4M	USMC	159470/159493	24
A-4N	Israel	159515/159545	31
TA-4J	USN	159546/159556	11
A-4M	USMC	159778/159790	13
TA-4J	USN	159795/159798	4
A-4N	Israel	159799/159824	26
A-4M	USMC	160022/160045	24
A-4KU	Kuwait	160180/160209	30
TA-4KU	Kuwait	160210/160215	6
A-4M	USMC	160241/160264	24

DOUGLAS B-66 DESTROYER (Number built: 294)

RB-66A-DL	USAF	52-2828/52-2832	5
RB-66B-DL	USAF	53-409/53-481	73
B-66B-DL	USAF	53-482/53-507	26
RB-66B-DL	USAF	54-417/54-446	30
RB-66C-DT	USAF	54-447/54-476	30
B-66B-DL	USAF	54-477/54-505	29
RB-66B-DL	USAF	54-506/54-547	42
B-66B-DL	USAF	54-548/54-551	4
B-66B-DL	USAF	55-302/55-314	13
RB-66C-DT	USAF	55-384/55-389	6
WB-66D-DT	USAF	55-390/55-425	36

DOUGLAS F5D-1 SKYLANCER (Number built: 4)

F5D-1	USN	139208/139209	2
F5D-1		142349/142350	2

DOUGLAS C-133 CARGOMASTER (Number built: 50)

44705	C-133A-DL	USAF	54-135	1
44706/44708	C-133A-1-DL	USAF	54-136/54-138	3
44709/44712	C-133A-5-DL	USAF	54-139/54-142	4
44713/44716	C-133A-10-DL	USAF	54-143/54-146	4
	C-133A-15-DL	USAF	56-1998/56-2002	5
	C-133A-20-DL	USAF	56-2003/56-2007	5
	C-133A-25-DL	USAF	56-2008/56-2011	4
	C-133A-30-DL	USAF	56-2012/56-2014	3
	C-133A-35-DL	USAF	57-1610/57-1615	6

45573/45587	C-133B-DL	USAF	59-522/59-536	15

DOUGLAS DC-8 (Number built: 556)

45252	DC-8-11	Co owned	N8008D	1
45253/45271	DC-8-31	Pan American	N800PA/N818PA	19
45272/45273	DC-8-33	Panair do Brasil	PP-PDS, PP-PDT	2
45274/45277	DC-8-31	Panagra	N8274/N8277	4
45278	DC-8-21	United	N8001U	1
45279	DC-8-12	United	N8002U	1
45280/45290	DC-8-11	United	N8003U/N8013U	11
45291	DC-8-21	United	N8018U	1
45292/45298	DC-8-21	United	N8023U/N8029U	7
45299/45300	DC-8-21	United	N8031U/N8033U	2
45301/45303	DC-8-52	United	N8034U/N8036U	3
45304/45307	DC-8-12	United	N8037U/N8040U	4
45376/45382	DC-8-32	KLM	PH-DCA/PH-DCG	7
45383	DC-8-53	KLM	PH-DCH	1
45384/45390	DC-8-32	SAS	OY-KTA, LN-MOA, SE-DBA, OY-KTB, LN-MOT, SE-DBB, SE-DBC	7
45391/45393	DC-8-21	National	N6571C/N6573C	3
45408/45413	DC-8-11	Delta	N801E/N802E	6
45416/45417	DC-8-32	Swissair	HB-IDA, HB-IDB	2
45418/45420	DC-8-32	Japan AL	JA8001/JA8003	3
45421	DC-8-32	Japan AL	JA8005	1
45422/45431	DC-3-21	Eastern	N8601/N8610	10
45432	DC-8-21	Aeromexico	XA-SAS	1
45433/45437	DC-8-21	Eastern	N8612/N8615 and N8617	5
45442/45445	DC-8-41	Air Canada	CF-TJA/CF-TJD	4
45526	DC-8-32	Swissair	HB-IDC	1
45565/45566	DC-8-42	Air Canada	CF-TJE, CF-TJF	2
45567/45568	DC-8-32	UAT (UTA)	F-BJLA, F-BJLB	2
45569	DC-8-32	TAI (UTA)	F-BIUY	1
45570	DC-8-33	TAI (UTA)	F-BIUZ	1
45588/45591	DC-8-11	United	N8014U/N8017U	4
45592/45593	DC-8-11	United	N8019U/N8020U	2
45594/45595	DC-8-21	United	N8021U/N8022U	2
45596/45597	DC-8-21	United	N8030U, N8032U	2
45598/45601	DC-8-42	Alitalia	I-DIWA, -DIWE, -DIWT, -DIWO	4
45602/45606	DC-8-32	Northwest	N801US/N805US	5
45607	DC-8-53	KLM	PH-DCR	1
45608	DC-8-53	PAL	PI-C 001	1
45609/45610	DC-8-42	Air Canada	CF-TJG, CF-TJH	2
45611/45612	DC-8-43	Air Canada	CF-TJI, CF-TJJ	2
45613/45616	DC-8-53	KLM	PH-DCI, -DCK, -DCL and -DCM	4
45617/45619	DC-8-52	Iberia	EC-ARA/EC-ARC	3
45620/45623	DC-8-43	Canadian Pacific	CF-CPF, -CPH, -CPI, -CPG	4
45624/45625	DC-8-43	Alitalia	I-DIWU, I-DIWB	2
45626	DC-8-33	Japan AL	JA8006	1
45627	DC-8-33	TAI (UTA)	F-BJUV	1
45628	DC-8-51	Trans Caribbean	N8780R	1
45629	DC-8-53	KLM	PH-DCN	1
45630/45631	DC-8-43	Alitalia	I-DIWF, I-DIWD	2
45632	DC-8-53	KLM	PH-DCO	1
45633	DC-8-51	Aeromexico	XA-NUS	1
45634/45635	DC-8-51	National	N774C, N875C	2
45636/45637	DC-8-43	Alitalia	I-DIWP, I-DIWR	2
45638	DC-8-43	Air Canada	CF-TJK	1
45640	DC-8-54CF	Air Canada	CF-TJL	1

45641/45644	DC-8-51	National	N876C, N877C, N278C, N779C	4
45645/45646	DC-8-51	Delta	N807E, N808E	2
45647	DC-8-53	Japan AL	JA8007	1
45648	DC-8-51	Trans Caribbean	N8781R	1
45649/45650	DC-8-51	Delta	N809E, N810E	2
45651	DC-8-53	Japan AL	JA8010	1
45652	DC-8-51	Aeromexico	XA-PEI	1
45653/45655	DC-8-54CF	Air Canada	CF-TJM/CF-TJO	3
45656	DC-8-53	Swissair	HB-IDD	1
45657/45659	DC-8-52	Iberia	EC-AUM, -ATP, -ASN	3
45660	DC-8-43	Alitalia	I-DIWG	1
45661	DC-8-43	Canadian Pacific	CF-CPJ	1
45662	DC-8-53	Japan AL	JA8009	1
45663	DC-8-54CF	Airlift	N108RD	1
45664	DC-8-53	Japan AL	JA8011	1
45665/45666	DC-8-43	Alitalia	I-DIWS, I-DIWT	2
45667	DC-8-54CF	Trans Caribbean	N8782R	1
45668	DC-8-54CF	Capitol	N4904C	1
45669	DC-8-54CF	TIA	N8008F	1
45670/45671	DC-8-53	Air Afrique	TU-TCA/TU-TCB	2
45672/45673	DC-8-51	Delta	N811E, N812E	2
45674	DC-8-54CF	Airlift	N109RD	1
45675/45677	DC-8-54AF	United	N8041U/N8043U	3
45678	DC-8-55CF	Japan AL	JA8014	1
45679	DC-8-54CF	Air Canada	CF-TJP	1
45680/45681	DC-8-53	Japan AL	JA8012, JA8013	2
45682	DC-8-43	Alitalia	I-DIWL	1
45683	DC-8-55CF	KLM	PH-DCS	1
45684	DC-8-54CF	Trans Caribbean	N8783R	1
45685	DC-8-51	Aeromexico	XA-PIK	1
45686	DC-8-54CF	Air Canada	CF-TJQ	1
45687/45690	DC-8-51	Delta	N814E, N813E, N815E, N816E	4
45691	DC-8-55CF	KLM	PH-DCT	1
45692	DC-8-55CF	Seaboard	N801SW	1
45693/45694	DC-8-52	United	N8060U/N8061U	2
45750/45752	DC-8-52	Air New Zealand	ZK-NZA/ZK-NZC	3
45753	DC-8-55	SAS	SE-DBD	1
45754	DC-8-55CF	TIA	N3325T	1
45755	DC-8-43	Alitalia	I-DIWN	1
45756/45759	DC-8-52	United	N8065U, N8062U/ N8064U	4
45760	DC-8-51	Eastern	N8779R	1
45761	DC-8-43	Canadian Pacific	CF-CPK	1
45762	DC-8-55CF	PAL	PI-C 802	1
45763/45764	DC-8-55	Japan AL	JA8015/JA8016	2
45765	DC-8-55	Garuda	PK-GJD	1
45766	DC-8-55	KLM	PH-DCV	1
45767	DC-8-55	SAS	LN-MOH	1
45768	DC-8-53	VIASA	YV-C-VID	1
45769	DC-8-54CF	Trans Caribbean	N8784R	1
45800/45802	DC-8-54AF	United	N8044U/N8046U	3
45803	DC-8-55CF	Trans Caribbean	N8785R	1
45804	DC-8-55CF	SAS	OY-KTC	1
45805	DC-8-55CF	Capitol	N4905C	1
45806/45808	DC-8-51	Delta	N819E, N817E, N818E	3
45809	DC-8-53	Canadian Pacific	CF-CPM	1
45810/45813	DC-8-61	United	N8070U/N8071U	4
45814	DC-8-52	Iberia	EC-BAV	1
45815	DC-8-51	Delta	N820E	1
45816/45818	DC-8-55CF	Seaboard	N804SW, N805SW, N802SW	3
45819	DC-8-55CF	UTA	F-BNLD	1

45820	DC-8-55CF	Armee de l'Air	F-RAFA	1
45821	DC-8-55CF	Seaboard	N803SW	1
45822/45823	DC-8-62	SAS	LN-MOD, SE-DBE	2
45824	DC-8-55CF	Overseas National	N851F	1
45848	DC-8-61	Eastern	N8778	1
45849	DC-8-61	United	N8074U	1
45850/45853	DC-8-52	United	N8066U/N8067U	4
45854	DC-8-55	Japan AL	JA8017	1
45855	DC-8-51	Aeromexico	XA-SIB	1
45856	DC-8-55CF	Overseas National	N852F	1
45857	DC-8-55CF	Air Afrique	TU-TCC	1
45858	DC-8-55CF	Panagra	N1509U	1
45859	DC-8-55CF	KLM	PH-DCU	1
45860/45861	DC-8-54CF	Air Canada	CF-TJR/CF-TJS	2
45862	DC-8-55CF	Capitol	N4906C	1
45877	DC-8-51	Delta	N821R	1
45878	DC-8-51	Aeromexico	XA-SIA	1
45879	DC-8-53	VIASA	YV-C-VIC	1
45880/45881	DC-8-54AF	United	N8047U, N8048U	2
45882	DC-8-55CF	Japan AL	JA8018	1
45883	DC-8-55CF	Seaboard	N806SW	1
45884/45886	DC-8-54AF	United	N8050U, N8051U, N8049U	3
45887/45889	DC-8-61	Eastern	N8777, N8776, N8775	3
45890/45893	DC-8-61	Air Canada	CF-TJT/CF-TJW	4
45894	DC-8-61	Eastern	N8774	1
45895/45896	DC-8-62	Braniff (Panagra)	N1803, N1804	2
45897/45898	DC-8-61CF	Trans Caribbean	N8786R, N8787R	2
45899	DC-8-62	Braniff (Panagra)	N1805	1
45900	DC-8-61CF	TIA	N8962T	1
45901	DC-8-63	KLM	PH-DEB	1
45902	DC-8-61CF	TIA	N8961T	1
45903	DC-8-63	KLM	PH-DEA	1
45904	DC-8-62CF	Braniff (Panagra)	N1807	1
45905/45906	DC-8-62	SAS	SE-DBF, OY-KTD	2
45907	DC-8-61	Delta	N822E	1
45908	DC-8-61	National	N45090	1
45909/45910	DC-8-62H	Alitalia	I-DIWN, I-DIWV	2
45911	DC-8-62	Braniff (Panagra)	N1806	1
45912/45913	DC-8-61	Eastern	N8770, N8771	2
45914/45915	DC-8-61	Delta	N823E, N824E	2
45916	DC-8-55	Japan AL	JA8019	1
45917/45918	DC-8-62	UTA	F-BNLE, F-BOLF	2
45919/45920	DC-8-62	Swissair	HB-IDE, HB-IDF	2
45921	DC-8-62	SAS	SE-DBG	1
45922	DC-8-62CF	SAS	OY-KTE	1
45923/45924	DC-8-63	SAS	LN-MOU, SE-DBH	2
45925	DC-8-62	Swissair	HB-IDG	1
45926/45929	DC-8-63	Canadian Pacific	CF-CPO/CF-CPQ and CF-CPS	4
45930/45931	DC-8-63	Iberia	EC-BMX, EC-BMY	2
45932	DC-8-52	Air New Zealand	ZK-NZD	1
45933/45934	DC-8-53	Air Canada	CF-TIH, CF-TII	2
45935	DC-8-51	Aeromexico	XA-SID	1
45936	DC-8-63CF	Seaboard	N8631	1
45937	DC-8-55	PAL	PI-C 803	1
45938	DC-8-61CF	TIA	N8960T	1
45939	DC-8-61CF	Universal	N801U	1
45940/45941	DC-8-61	United	N8075U, N8076U	2
45942/45943	DC-8-61	Eastern	N8773, N8772	2
45944	DC-8-61	Delta	N825E	1
45945/45947	DC-8-61	United	N8077U/N8079U	3
45948/45949	DC-8-61CF	Saturn	N8955U, N8956U	2
45950	DC-8-61CF	Universal	N802U	1

45951	DC-8-63CF	TIA	N4863T	1
45952	DC-8-61CF	Trans Caribbean	N8788R	1
45953/45956	DC-8-62	Japan AL	JA8031/JA8034	4
45960/45961	DC-8-63CF-H	Alitalia	I-DIWC, I-DIWQ	2
45962	DC-8-53	Air Canada	CF-TIJ	1
45963/45964	DC-8-61	Air Canada	CF-TJX, CF-TJY	2
45965	DC-8-55CF	Iberia	EC-BMY	1
45966	DC-8-63CF	Seaboard	N8632	1
45967/45968	DC-8-63CF	Capitol	N4907C/N4908C	2
45969	DC-8-63CF	Airlift	N6161A	1
45970/45978	DC-8-61	United	N8080U/N8088U	9
45979	DC-8-61	Delta	N826E	1
45980	DC-8-61	Air Canada	CF-TJZ	1
45981	DC-8-61	National	N45191	1
45982/45983	DC-8-61	Eastern	N8769, N8768	2
45984	DC-8-62CF	Swissair	HB-IDH	1
45985	DC-8-52	Air New Zealand	ZK-NZE	1
45986	DC-8-62H	Alitalia	I-DIWJ	1
45987	DC-8-62	UTA	F-BOLG	1
45988	DC-8-63CF	Iberia	EC-BMZ	1
45989/45991	DC-8-63CF	Flying Tiger	N779FT/N781FT	3
45992	DC-8-61	Eastern	N8767	1
45993/45998	DC-8-61	United	N8089U/N8094U	6
45999/46000	DC-8-63	KLM	PH-DEC, PH-DED	2
46001	DC-8-63CF	Overseas National	N863F	1
46002	DC-8-63CF	Flying Tiger	N782FT	1
46003/46008	DC-8-63AF	Flying Tiger	N783FT/N788FT	8
46009/46012	DC-8-54AF	United	N8052U/N8055U	4
46013	DC-8-62CF	Finnair	OH-LFR	1
46014	DC-8-61	Delta	N1300L	1
46015/46017	DC-8-61	Eastern	N8766, N8765, N8764	3
46018	DC-8-61	Delta	N1301L	1
46019	DC-8-63	KLM	PH-DEE	1
46020/46021	DC-8-63CF	Seaboard World	N8633/N8634	2
46022	DC-8-62AF	Japan AL	JA8036	1
46023/46024	DC-8-62	Japan AL	JA8035, JA8037	2
46026/46027	DC-8-62H	Alitalia	I-DIWZ, I-DIWY	2
46028	DC-8-62	UTA	F-BOLH	1
46029/46030	DC-8-61	Delta	N1302L/N1303L	2
46031/46032	DC-8-61	Japan AL	JA8038/JA8039	2
46033/46036	DC-8-63	Air Canada	CF-TIK/CF-TIN	4
46037/46038	DC-8-61	Eastern	N8763, N8762	2
46039/46040	DC-8-61	United	N8095U/N8096U	2
46041	DC-8-63	SAS	OY-KTF	1
46042	DC-8-63	VIASA	YV-C-VIA	1
46043	DC-8-62CF	Finnair	OH-LFS	1
46044	DC-8-63AF	Flying Tiger	N790FT	1
46045/46047	DC-8-63CF	Flying Tiger	N791FT/N793FT	3
46048	DC-8-61	Delta	N1304L	1
46049/46053	DC-8-63CF	Seaboard World	N8639 and N8635/ N8638	5
46054	DC-8-63	SAS	LN-MOY	1
46055/46056	DC-8-61	Delta	N1306L/N1307L	2
46057	DC-8-62	Japan AL	JA8040	1
46058	DC-8-63PF	Eastern	N8759	1
46059	DC-8-63CF	TIA	N4864T	1
46060	DC-8-63CF	Capitol	N4909C	1
46061/46062	DC-8-63CF	Airlift	N6162A/N6163A	2
46063	DC-8-63	VIASA	YV-C-VIB	1
46064/46066	DC-8-61	United	N8097U/N8099U	3
46067/46071	DC-8-62H	United	N8966U/N8970U	5
46072	DC-8-61	Delta	N1305L	1
46073	DC-8-63CF	TIA	N4865T	1
46074	DC-8-63PF	Eastern	N8760	1

46075	DC-8-63	KLM	PH-DEH	1
46076	DC-8-63	Air Canada	CF-TIO	1
46077	DC-8-62	Swissair	HB-IDI	1
46078	DC-8-62CF	Swissair	HB-IDK	1
46079	DC-8-63	Iberia	EC-BQS	1
46080	DC-8-63	KLM	PH-DEF	1
46081	DC-8-62H	United	N8971U	1
46082	DC-8-62H	Alitalia	I-DIWK	1
46084/46085	DC-8-62H	United	N8972U/N8973U	2
46086	DC-8-63CF	Flying Tiger	N794FT	1
46087/46088	DC-8-63CF	Overseas National	N864F/N865F	2
46089/46091	DC-8-63CF	TIA	N4866T/N4868T	3
46092	DC-8-63	KLM	PH-DEG	1
46093	DC-8-63PF	Eastern	N8758	1
46094	DC-8-63CF	Capitol	N4910C	1
46095/46097	DC-8-63PF	Eastern	N8757, N8756, N8755	3
46098	DC-8-62H	Alitalia	I-DIWW	1
46099	DC-8-61	Japan AL	JA8041	1
46100	DC-8-63	Air Canada	CF-TIP	1
46101	DC-8-63CF	Seaboard World	N8630	1
46102	DC-8-62	SAS	LN-MOG	1
46103/46104	DC-8-63CF	Flying Tiger	N795FT/N796FT	2
46105	DC-8-62	Braniff	N1808E	1
46106	DC-8-63CF	Seaboard World	N8641	1
46107	DC-8-62	Braniff	N1809E	1
46108	DC-8-63CF	American Flyers	N123AF	1
46109	DC-8-63CF	Seaboard World	N8642	1
46110/46111	DC-8-62H	United	N8974U/N8975U	2
46112	DC-8-63CF	Overseas National	N866F	1
46113/46115	DC-8-63	Air Canada	CF-TIU, -TIW, -TIX	3
46116	DC-8-63	Iberia	EC-BSD	1
46117	DC-8-63CF	TIA	N4869T	1
46121/46122	DC-8-63	PAL	PI-C 827/PI-C 829	2
46123/46126	DC-8-63	Air Canada	CF-TIQ/CF-TIS, CF-TIV	4
46127/46128	DC-8-61	Japan AL	JA8042/JA8043	2
46129	DC-8-62CF	SAS	SE-DBI	1
46130	DC-8-62CF	Finnair	OH-LFY	1
46131	DC-8-62	SAS	LN-MOW	1
46132	DC-8-62H	Alitalia	I-DIWH	1
46133	DC-8-63CF	Airlift	N6165A	1
46134	DC-8-62	Swissair	HB-IDL	1
46135	DC-8-63CF	Air Afrique	TU-TCF	1
46136	DC-8-63	SAS	SE-DBK	1
46137	DC-8-63CF	Atlantis	D-ADIX	1
46139	DC-8-62AF	Japan AL	JA8044	1
46140	DC-8-63CF	American Flyers	N124AF	1
46141	DC-8-63	KLM	PH-DEM	1
46142	DC-8-62H	Alitalia	I-DIWX	1
46143	DC-8-63CF	Atlantis	D-ADIY	1
46144	DC-8-63CF	Airlift	N6164A	1
46145	DC-8-63CF	Atlantis	D-ADIZ	1
46146	DC-8-63CF	Airlift	N6166A	1
46147	DC-8-63CF	Air Zaire	9Q-CLH	1
46148	DC-8-62AF	Japan AL	JA8054	1
46149	DC-8-63CF	Airlift	N6167A	1
46150	DC-8-62AF	SAS	LN-MOC	1
46151	DC-8-63CF	Air Zaire	9Q-CLG	1
46152/46153	DC-8-62H	Japan AL	JA8051/JA8052	2
46154	DC-8-62AF	Japan AL	JA8055	1
46155	DC-8-63	Iberia	EC-BSE	1
46157/46160	DC-8-61	Japan AL	JA8045/JA8048	4
46161	DC-8-62H	Japan AL	JA8053	1
46162	DC-8-62AF	Japan AL	JA8056	1

46163	DC-8-63	SAS	SE-DBL	1

DOUGLAS DC-9 (Number built: 976 excluding DC-9-80s and MD-80s)

45695	DC-9-14	Co owned	N9DC	1
45696/45709	DC-9-14	Delta	N3301L/N3314L	14
45710	DC-9-32	Delta	N3315L	1
45711/45713	DC-9-14	Air Canada	CF-TLB/CF-TLD	3
45714/45716	DC-9-14	TWA	N1051T/N1053T	3
45717	DC-9-15	Hawaiian	N901H	1
45718/45723	DC-9-15	KLM	PH-DNA/PH-DNF	6
45724	DC 9 15	Hawaiian	N902H	1
45725/45727	DC-9-14	Air Canada	CF-TLE/CF-TLG	3
45728/45730	DC-9-11	Bonanza	N945L/N947L	3
45731/45732	DC-9-15	Swissair	HB-IFA/HB-IFB	2
45733/45734	DC-9-31	Eastern	N8916E/N8917E	2
45735/45741	DC-9-15	TWA	N1054T/N1060T	7
45742/45749	DC-9-14	Eastern	N8901E/N8908E	8
45770/45771	DC-9-14	Eastern	N8909E/N8910E	2
45772/45773	DC-9-15	Ozark	N9702/N9712	2
45774	DC-9-32	THY	TC-JAB	1
45775/45784	DC-9-15	TWA	N1061T/N1070T	10
45785/45787	DC-9-15	Swissair	HB-IFC/HB-IFE	3
45788/45793	DC-9-32	Swissair	HB-IFF/HB-IFL	6
45794/45796	DC-9-14	West Coast	N9101/N9103	3
45797	DC-9-15	Northeast	N8953U	1
45798/45799	DC-9-15	Standard	N490SA	2
45825	DC-9-14	Eastern	N8911E	1
45826	DC-9-15RC	Continental	N8901	1
45827	DC-9-15	Korean	HL7201	1
45828	DC-9-15	Continental	N8918	1
45829/45832	DC-9-14	Eastern	N8912E/N8915E	4
45833/45840	DC-9-31	Eastern	N8918E/N8925E	8
45841	DC-9-15	Ozark	N972Z	1
45842/45844	DC-9-14	Continental	N8961/N8963	3
45845/45846	DC-9-32	Air Canada	CF-TLH/CF-TLI	2
45847	DC-9-32	Swissair	HB-IFM	1
45863/45876	DC-9-31	Eastern	N8926E/N3929E, N8952E/N8953E, N8960E/N8965E and N8968E/N8969E	14
47000/47002	DC-9-15	Saudia	HZ-AEA/HZ-AEC	3
47003/47005	DC-9-31	Ansett	VH-CZA/VH-CZC	3
47006	DC-9-31	PSA	N891PS	1
47007/47009	DC-9-31	Trans-Australia	VH-TJJ/VH-TJL	3
47010/47018	DC-9-15RC	Continental	N8902/N8907, N8909, N8911 and N8913	9
47019/47024	DC-9-32	Air Canada	CF-TLJ/CF-TLO	6
47025/47032	DC-9-32	Delta	N3316L/N3323L	8
47033/47035	DC-9-15	Ozark	N973Z/N975Z	3
47036	DC-9-31	Eastern	N8973E	1
47037	DC-9-32	Iberia	EC-BIG	1
47038/47039	DC-9-32	Alitalia	I-DIKA, I-DIKE	2
47040/47041	DC-9-32CF	Overseas National	N931F/N932F	2
47042	DC-9-31	Southern	N89S	1
47043	DC-9-14	Texas Int'l	N1302T	1
47044/47045	DC-9-15MC	Texas Int'l	N1303T/N1304T	2
47046/47047	DC-9-32	Alitalia	I-DIKI, I-DIKO	2
47048	DC-9-15	Continental	N8964	1
47049	DC-9-14	Bonanza	N948L	1
47050/47052	DC-9-31	Allegheny	N970VJ/N972VJ	3
47053/47054	DC-9-31	Northeast	N970NE/N971NE	2
47055	DC-9-15MC	Texas Int'l	N1305T	1
47056	DC-9-14	Avensa	YV-C-AVM	1

47057/47058	DC-9-31	Northeast	N972NE/N973NE	2
47059	DC-9-15	Aeromexico	XA-SOA	1
47060	DC-9-14	Avensa	YV-57C	1
47061/47062	DC-9-15MC	Texas Int'l	N1306T/N1307T	2
47063/47064	DC-9-15	Southern	N91S/N92S	2
47065	DC-9-31	Ansett	VH-CZD	1
47066	DC-9-31	Northeast	N974NE	1
47067	DC-9-31	North Central	N951N	1
47068/47071	DC-9-32	Air Canada	CF-TLP/CF-TLS	4
47072	DC-9-31	Trans-Australia	VH-TJM	1
47073	DC-9-31	North Central	N952N	1
47074	DC-9-31	Eastern	N8974E	1
47075	DC-9-31	Northeast	N975NE	1
47076/47077	DC-9-32	Iberia	EC-BIH/EC-BII	2
47078	DC-9-15	Southern	N93S	1
47079/47080	DC-9-32	Iberia	EC-BIJ/EC-BIK	2
47081	DC-9-14	West Coast	N9104	1
47082	DC-9-31	Northeast	N976E	1
47083	DC-9-31	North Central	N953N	1
47084	DC-9-32	Iberia	EC-BIL	1
47085	DC-9-15	Aeromexico	XA-SOB	1
47086/47087	DC-9-15RC	Continental	N8915, N8917	2
47088/47093	DC-9-32	Iberia	EC-BIM/EC-BIR	6
47094	DC-9-32	SAS/Swissair	SE-DBZ	1
47095/47097	DC-9-31	Northeast	N977NE/N979NE	3
47098	DC-9-31	Caribair	N938PR	1
47099	DC-9-31	Allegheny	N973VJ	1
47100	DC-9-15	Aeromexico	XA-SOC	1
47101	DC-9-32	Alitalia	I-DIKU	1
47102	DC-9-32	KLM	PH-DNG	1
47103/47109	DC-9-32	Delta	N3324L/N3330L	7
47110/47113	DC-9-32	SAS/Swissair	OY-KGU, LN-RLS, SE-DBY, OY-KGW	4
47114/47117	DC-9-41	SAS	SE-DBX, OY-KGA, LN-RLK, SE-DBW	4
47118	DC-9-32	Alitalia	I-DIKB	1
47119	DC-9-31	Eastern	N8975E	1
47120/47121	DC-9-31	Caribair	N939PR, N967PR	2
47122/4/127	DC-9-15	Aeromexico	XA-SOD/XA-SOI	6
47128/47129	DC-9-32	Alitalia	I-DIKC/I-DIKD	2
47130	DC-9-31	Allegheny	N974VJ	1
47131/47133	DC-9-32	KLM	PH-DNH/PH-DNI, PH-DNK	3
47134/47137	DC-9-31	Northeast	N980NE/N983NE	4
47138	DC-9-31	West Coast	N9330	1
47139/47145	DC-9-31	Eastern	N8930E/N8936E	7
47146	DC-9-31	Allegheny	N975VJ	1
47147/47148	DC-9-32CF	Overseas National	N933F/N934F	2
47149/47150	DC-9-31	Hawaiian	N903H, N905H	2
47151	DC-9-15	W R Grace	N228Z	1
47152/47156	DC-9-15RC	Continental	N8908, N8910, N8912, N8914, N8916	5
47157/47158	DC-9-31	Eastern	N8959E, N8937E	2
47159/47160	DC-9-31	North Central	N954N/N955N	2
47161/47167	DC-9-31	Eastern	N8938E/N8944E	7
47168/47170	DC-9-32	KLM	PH-DNS/PH-DNT, PH-DNV	3
47171	DC-9-31	Hawaiian	N906H	1
47172/47177	DC-9-32	Delta	N331L/N3336L	6
47178/47180	DC-9-41	SAS	OY-KGB, LN-RLC, SE-DBU	3
47181/47189	DC-9-31	Eastern	N8945E/N8951E, N8954E/N8955E	9
47190	DC-9-32	KLM	PH-DNL	1

47191/47194	DC-9-33RC	KLM	PH-DNM/PH-DNP	4
47195/47200	DC-9-32	Air Canada	CF-TLT, CF-TLU/ CF-TLY	6
47201	DC-9-32	KLM	PH-DNW	1
47202	DC-9-31	Ansett	VH-CZE	1
47203	DC-9-31	Trans-Australia	VH-TJN	1
47204/47206	DC-9-15	Southern	N94S/N96S	3
47207/47212	DC-9-31	Allegheny	N984VJ/N989VJ	6
47213	DC-9-32	THY	TC-JAC	1
47214/47217	DC-9-31	Eastern	N8956E/N8958E, N8966E	4
47218/47219	DC-9-32	Suedflug	D-ACEB/D-ACEC	2
47220/47221	DC-9-32F	Alitalia	I-DIKF/I-DIKG	2
47222/47238	DC-9-32	Alitalia	I-DIKJ, I-DIKL/ I-DIKN, I-DIKP/ I-DIKT, I-DIKV, I-DIKY, I-DIBC/ I-DIBD, I-DIBJ, I-DIBQ, I-DIBO, I-DIZA	17
47239	DC-9-32	InexAdria	YU-AHJ	1
47240	DC-9-15	Continental	N8919	1
47241/47242	C-9A	USAF	67-22583/67-22584	2
47243	DC-9-32	Avensa	YV-C-AVD	1
47244/47245	DC-9-31	Southern	N90S, N97S	2
47246/47247	DC-9-31	Air West	N9333/N9334	2
47248/47250	DC-9-31	Ozark	N976Z/N978Z	3
47251	DC-9-31	PSA	N982PS	1
47252/47256	DC-9-31	North Central	N956N/N960N	5
47257/47262	DC-9-32	Delta	N1262L/N1267L	6
47263/47264	DC-9-31	Air West	N9331/N9332	2
47265/47266	DC-9-32	Air Canada	CF-TLZ, CF-TMA	2
47267/47272	DC-9-31	Eastern	N8967E, N8970E/ N8972E, N8976E/ N8977E	6
47273/47278	DC-9-32	Delta	N3337L/N3340L, N5341L/N5342L	6
47279	DC-9-33RC	KLM	PH-DNR	1
47280	DC-9-31	Southern	N1334U	1
47281/47282	DC-9-32	Swissair	HB-IFT/HB-IFU	2
47283	DC-9-32	Alitalia	I-DIKW	1
47284/47285	DC-9-32	Delta	N1268L/N1269L	2
47286/47288	DC-9-41	SAS	OY-KGC, LN-RLJ, SE-DET	3
47289/47290	DC-9-32	Air Canada	CF-TMB/CF-TMC	2
47291	DC-9-33RC	Martinair	PH-MAN	1
47292/47294	DC-9-32	Air Canada	CF-TMD/CF-TMF	3
47295/47300	C-9A	USAF	67-22585/67-22586, 68-8932/68-8935	6
47301/47308	DC-9-21	SAS	LN-RLL, OY-KGD, SE-DBS, LN-RLM, OY-KGE, SE-DBR, LN-RLO, OY-KGF	8
47309	DC-9-14	Aeropostal	YV-OIC	1
47310	DC-9-31	Allegheny	N991VJ	1
47311	DC-9-32	Alitalia	I-DIKZ	1
47312/47314	DC-9-32	Iberia	EC-BIS/EC-BIU	3
47315/47316	DC-9-31	Texas Int'l	N1308T/N1309T	2
47317/47324	DC-9-32	Delta	N1261L, N1270L/ N1276L	8
47325	DC-9-31	Ansett	VH-CZF	1
47326	DC-9-31	Trans-Australia	VH-TJO	1
47327/47331	DC-9-31	Eastern	N8978E/N8982E	5
47332/47336	DC-9-31	Allegheny	N993VJ/N997VJ	5

598

47337/47338	DC-9-31	Air West	N9335/N9336	2
47339	DC-9-32	Alitalia	I-DIBN	1
47340/47342	DC-9-32	Air Canada	CF-TMG/CF-TMI	3
47343/47345	DC-9-31	Ozark	N979Z/N981Z	3
47346/47347	DC-9-31	Air West	N9337/N9338	2
47348/47350	DC-9-32	Air Canada	CF-TMJ/CF-TML	3
47351/47352	DC-9-32	Air Jamaica	6Y-JGA/6Y-JGB	2
47353/47354	DC-9-32	Air Canada	CF-TMO/CF-TMP	2
47355	DC-9-32F	Alitalia	I-DIBK	1
47356/47359	DC-9-32	Delta	N1277L/N1280L	4
47360/47361	DC-9-21	SAS	SE-DBP, SE-DBO	2
47362	DC-9-31	Hawaiian	N907H	1
47363	DC-9-33RC	Martinair	PH-MAO	1
47364/47365	DC-9-32	Iberia	EC-BPF/EC-BPG	2
47366/47367	C-9A	USAF	68-10958/68-10959	2
47368	DC-9-32	Iberia	EC-BPH	1
47369/47370	DC-9-31	Hawaiian	N1798U/N1799U	2
47371/47375	DC-9-31	Allegheny	N978VJ/N979VJ, N964VJ/N965VJ, N967VJ	5
47376	DC-9-32	Purdue	N394PA	1
47377/47381	DC-9-32	Delta	N1281L/N1285L	5
47382	DC-9-31	Air West	N9339	1
47383	DC-9-32	Swissair	HB-IFV	1
47384	DC-9-33F	Swissair	HB-IFW	1
47385/47386	DC-9-32	Garuda	PK-GNA/PK-GNB	2
47389/47391	DC-9-31	Air West	N9340/N9342	3
47392	DC-9-32	Purdue	N393PA	1
47393	DC-9-31	Southern	N1335U	1
47394	DC-9-32	Playboy	N950PB	1
47395/47396	DC-9-41	SAS	OY-KGG, LN-RLD	2
47397	DC-9-32	THY	TC-JAK	1
47399/47403	DC-9-31	Eastern	N8983E/N8987E	5
47404	DC-9-31	Hawaiian	N1332U	1
47405/47406	DC-9-31	North Central	N961N/N962N	2
47407/47409	DC-9-33CF	Overseas National	N935F/N937F	3
47410	DC-9-33RC	Martinair	PH-MAR	1
47411/47412	DC-9-31	Ozark	N983Z/N984Z	2
47413/47414	DC-9-33F	SAS	SE-DBN, LN-RLW	2
47415/47417	DC-9-31	North Central	N963N/N965N	3
47418/47419	DC-9-31	Trans-Australia	VH-TJP/VH-TJQ	2
47420/47421	DC-9-31	Allegheny	N966VJ, N969VJ	2
47422/47424	DC-9-32	Air Canada	CF-TMQ/CF-TMS	3
47425	DC-9-32	JAT	YU-AHL	1
47426/47427	DC-9-32	Delta	N1286L/N1287L	2
47428	DC-9-33RC	Iberia	EC-BYK	1
47429	DC-9-31	Allegheny	N968VJ	1
47430	DC-9-32	East African	5H-MOI	1
47431	DC-9-32	ATI	I-ATIA	1
47432/47435	DC-9-32	Alitalia	I-DIZI, I-DIZU, I-DIZB/I-DIZC	4
47436/47438	DC-9-32	ATI	I-ATIE, I-ATIO, I-ATIU	3
47439/47441	DC-9-31	Air West	N9343/N9345	3
47442	DC-9-32	THY	TC-JAG	1
47443/47445	DC-9-32	Delta	N1288L/N1290L	3
47446/47447	DC-9-32	Iberia	EC-BQT/EC-BQU	2
47448/47449	C-9A	USAB	68-10960/68-10961	2
47450	DC-9-32	Atlantis	D-ADIT	1
47451	DC-9-32	THY	TC-JAF	1
47452/47456	DC-9-32	Iberia	EC-BYI, EC-BQV, EC-BQX/EC-BQZ	5
47457	DC-9-32	Atlantis	D-ADIU	1
47458	DC-9-32	Austrian	OE-LDF	1

47459	DC-9-32	Atlantis	D-ADIS	1
47460	DC-9-32	JAT	YU-AHV	1
47461	DC-9-32	Iberia	EC-BYJ	1
47462	DC-9-33	KLM	PH-DNY	1
47463	DC-9-32	Garuda	PK-GND	1
47464	DC-9-41	SAS	SE-DAN	1
47465	DC-9-33CF	Balair	HB-IDN	1
47466	DC-9-32	Delta	N1291L	1
47467	C-9A	USAF	71-874	1
47468	DC-9-32	East African	5Y-ALR	1
47469/47470	DC-9-32	JAT	YU-AHM/YU-AHN	2
47471	C-9A	USAF	71-875	1
47472/47473	DC-9-32	JAT	YU-AHO/YU-AHP	2
47474	DC-9-32	ATI	I-ATIX	1
47475	C-9A	USAF	71-876	1
47476	DC-9-33	KLM	PH-DNZ	1
47477	DC-9-32	ATI	I-ATIK	1
47478	DC-9-32	East African	5X-UVY	1
47479/47480	DC-9-32	Swissair	HB-IFZ, HB-IDO	2
47481	DC-9-32	Garuda	PK-GNC	1
47482	DC-9-32	JAT	YU-AHT	1
47484	DC-9-32	Austrian	OE-LDG	1
47485	DC-9-32	Air Canada	CF-TMX	1
47486	DC-9-32	Delta	N1293L	1
47487	DC-9-31	Texas Int'l	N1310T	1
47488/47489	DC-9-32	THY	TC-JAD/TC-JAE	2
47490	DC-9-31	Texas Int'l	N1311T	1
47491	DC-9-31	Ozark	N985Z	1
47492/47494	DC-9-41	SAS	SE-DAK, OY-KGH, OY-KGI	3
47495	C-9A	USAF	71 877	1
47496	DC-9-32	Iberia	EC-BYM	1
47497/47499	DC-9-41	SAS	LN-RLB, SE-DAL, SE-DAM	3
47500	DC-9-32	Dominicana	HI-177	1
47501	DC-9-31	Ansett	VH-CZG	1
47502	DC-9-32	Alitalia	I-DIZE	1
47503	DC-9-32	Inex Adria	YU-AHR	1
47504	DC-9-32	Iberia	EC-BYE	1
47505/47508	DC-9-31	Allegheny	N960VJ/N963VJ	4
47509/47513	DC-9-41	SAS	SE-DAO, OY-KGK, LN-RLU, SE-DAP, LN-RLX	5
47514	DC-9-32	Martinair	PH-MAX	1
47516	DC-9-32	Delta	N1294L	1
47517	DC-9-31	Hawaiian	N908H	1
47518/47519	DC-9-32	Alitalia	I-DIZO, I-DIZF	2
47520/47521	DC-9-32	Austrian	OE-LDC, OE-LDA	2
47522	DC-9-32	Iberia	EC-BYD	1
47523	DC-9-32	Swissair	HB-IDP	1
47524	DC-9-32	Austrian	OE-LDB	1
47525	DC-9-32	Delta	N1295L	1
47526/47527	DC-9-31	Ansett	VH-CZH/VH-CZI	2
47528	DC-9-31	Trans-Australia	VH-TJR	1
47529	DC-9-32	Delta	N1292L	1
47530	DC-9-33CF	Inex Adria	YU-AHW	1
47531	DC-9-32	Austrian	OE-LDE	1
47532	DC-9-32	JAT	YU-AHU	1
47533	DC-9-32	ATI	I-ATIW	1
47534	DC-9-32	THY	TC-JAL	1
47535	DC-9-32	Swissair	HB-IDR	1
47536/47538	C-9A	USAF	71-878/71-880	3
47539	DC-9-32	Austrian	OE-LDD	1
47540/47541	C-9A	USAF	71-881/71-882	2

600

47542/47543	DC-9-32	Iberia	EC-BYF/EC-BYG	2
47544	DC-9-32	ATI	I-ATIJ	1
47545	DC-9-33RC	Iberia	EC-BYL	1
47546	DC-9-32	Air Canada	CF-TMF	1
47547/47549	DC-9-31	Ansett	VH-CZJ/VH-CZL	3
47550/47552	DC-9-31	Trans-Australia	VH-TJS/VH-TJU	3
47553	DC-9-32	ATI	I-ATIH	1
47554	DC-9-32	Air Canada	CF-TMU	1
47555	DC-9-32	Austrian	OE-LDH	1
47556	DC-9-32	Iberia	EC-BYH	1
47557	DC-9-32	Air Canada	CF-TMV	1
47559	DC-9-32	Austrian	OE-LDI	1
47560	DC-9-32	Air Canada	CF-TMW	1
47561	DC-9-32	Garuda	PK-GNE	1
47562/47563	DC-9-32	JAT	YU-AJH/YU-AJI	2
47564	DC-9-31	Allegheny	N950VJ	1
47565	DC-9-33RC	Iberia	EC-BYN	1
47566	DC-9-31	North Central	N949N	1
47567/47568	DC-9-32	JAT	YU-AJJ/YU-AJK	2
47569	DC-9-32	Garuda	PK-GNF	1
47570	DC-9-32	Pan Adria	YU-AJF	1
47571	DC-9-32	JAT	YU-AJL	1
47572/47573	DC-9-31	North Central	N940N, N967N	2
47574	DC-9-31	Allegheny	N952VJ	1
47575	DC-9-32	ATI	I-ATIY	1
47576	DC-9-31	Allegheny	N951VJ	1
47577/47578	C-9B	USN	159113, 159119	2
47579	DC-9-32	Inex Adria	YU-AJN	1
47580/47581	C-9B	USN	159116/159117	2
47582	DC-9-32	JAT	YU-AJM	1
47583	DC-9-31	Allegheny	N953VJ	1
47584/47587	C-9B	USN	159114, 159118, 159120, 159115	4
47588	DC-9-31	Allegheny	N956VJ	1
47589	DC-9-31	Ozark	N98GZ	1
47590	DC-9-31	Allegheny	N954VJ	1
47591	DC-9-32	ATI	I-ATIQ	1
47592	DC-9-32	Air Canada	CF-TMY	1
47593	DC-9-31	Allegheny	N955VJ	1
47594	DC-9-32	Aeromexico	XA-DEJ	1
47595	DC-9-32	AMI	SM012	1
47596/47597	DC-9-41	SAS	SE-DAR, OY-KGL	2
47598	DC-9-32	Air Canada	CF-TMZ	1
47599	DC-9-41	SAS	LN-RLA	1
47600	DC-9-32	AMI	SM013	1
47601	DC-9-32	Garuda	PK-GNG	1
47602	DC-9-32	Aeromexico	XA-DEK	1
47603/47606	DC-9-41	Toa	JA8423/JA8426	4
47607	DC-9-32	Aeromexico	XA-DEL	1
47608	DC-9-41	Toa	JA8427	1
47609	DC-9-32	Aeromexico	XA-DEM	1
47610	DC-9-41	SAS	SE-DAS	1
47611	DC-9-32	Air Canada	C-FTMM	1
47612/47620	DC-9-41	Toa	JA8428/JA8430, JA8432/JA8437	9
47621/47622	DC-9-32	Aeromexico	XA-DEN/XA-DEO	2
47623/47634	DC-9-41	SAS	LN-RLS, OY-KGM, SE-DAT, LN-RLT, SE-DAU, OY-KGN, SE-DAW, LN-RLN, SE-DAX, OY-KGO, SE-DBM, LN-RLZ	12
47635/74636	DC-9-32	Garuda	PK-GNH/PK-GNI	2
47637	DC-9-32	Aviaco	EC-CGN	1

47638	DC-9-31	Texas Int'l	N3504T	1
47639	DC-9-32	Air Jamaica	6Y-JIJ	1
47640	DC-9-32	Aviaco	EC-CGO	1
47641	DC-9-32	ATI	I-ATJA	1
47642/47645	DC-9-32	Aviaco	EC-CGP/EC-CGS	4
47646	DC-9-41	SAS	OY-KGP	1
47647	DC-9-31	North Central	N943N	1
47648	DC-9-32	ALM	PJ-SNA	1
47649	DC-9-32	Inex Adria	YU-AJR	1
47650	DC-9-32	Aeromexico	XA-DEI	1
47651/47652	DC-9-51	Austrian	OE-LDK/OE-LDL	2
47653	DC-9-32	ATI	I-ATJB	1
47654/47663	DC-9-51	Swissair	HB-ISK/HB-ISP, HB-ISR/HB-ISU	10
47664	DC-9-31	North Central	N945N	1
47665	DC-9-31	Allegheny	N923VJ	1
47666	DC-9-32	ALM	PJ-SNB	1
47667	DC-9-32	ATI	I-ATJC	1
47668•	VC-9C	USAF	73-1681	1
47669	DC-9-32	ALM	PJ-SNC	1
47670/47671	VC-9C	USAF	73-1682/73-1683	2
47672/47673	DC-9-32	Garuda	PK-GNJ/PK-GNK	2
47674	DC-9-32	THY	TC-JBK	1
47675	DC-9-32	Aviaco	EC-CLD	1
47676/47677	DC-9-51	Hawaiian	N609HA, N619HA	2
47678	DC-9-32	Aviaco	EC-CLE	1
47679	DC-9-51	Hawaiian	N629HA	1
47680	DC-9-32	Garuda	PK-GNL	1
47681	C-9B	USN	160048	1
47682/47683	DC-9-51	Allegheny	N920VJ/N921VJ	2
47684	C-9B	USN	160046	1
47685/47686	DC-9-51	Allegheny	N922VJ, N925VJ	2
47687	C-9B	USN	160047	1
47688	DC-9-51	Allegheny	N924VJ	1
47689	DC-9-51	Hawaiian	N639HA	1
47690/47691	DC-9-32CF	Kuwait AF	160750, 160749	2
47692/47693	DC-9-51	Allegheny	N926VJ/N927VJ	2
47694/47696	DC-9-51	Finnair	OY-LYN/OH-LYP	3
47697	DC-9-51	Inex Adria	YU-AJT	1
47698/47700	C-9B	USN	160049/160051	3
47701	DC-9-32	Garuda	PK-GNM	1
47702	DC-9-34CF	Aviaco	EC-CTR	1
47703	DC-9-51	LAV	YV-22C	1
47704	DC-9-34CF	Aviaco	EC-CTS	1
47705	DC-9-51	LAV	YV-20C	1
47706/47707	DC-9-34CF	Aviaco	EC-CTT/EC-CTU	2
47708/47710	DC-9-51	North Central	N760NC/N762NC	3
47711	DC-9-34CF	Balair	HB-IDT	1
47712/47715	DC-9-51	Hawaiian	N649HA, N659HA, N669HA, N679HA	4
47716/47718	DC-9-51	North Central	N763NC/N765NC	3
47719/47720	DC-9-51	LAV	YV-21C, YV-23C	2
47721	DC-9-31	LAV	YV-25C	1
47722	DC-9-32	Garuda	PK-GNN	1
47723	DC-9-32	THY	TC-JBL	1
47724	DC-9-51	North Central	N767NC	1
47725	DC-9-41	SAS	OY-KGR	1
47726	DC-9-51	Austrian	OE-LDM	1
47727	DC-9-31	LAV	YV-24C	1
47728	DC-9-51	Eastern	N991EA	1
47729	DC-9-51	North Central	N768NC	1
47730	DC-9-32	Garuda	PK-GNO	1
47731/47733	DC-9-51	Eastern	N992EA/N994EA	3
47734	DC-9-32	Ozark	N920L	1

47735	DC-9-51	Austrian	OE-LDN	1
47736/47738	DC-9-51	Finnair	OH-LYR/OH-LYT	3
47739	DC-9-51	North Central	N766NC	1
47740/47741	DC-9-32	Garuda	PK-GNP/PK-GNQ	2
47742/47743	DC-9-51	BWIA	9Y-TFG, 9Y-TFH	2
47744	DC-9-32	Garuda	PK-GNR	1
47745/47746	DC-9-51	Eastern	N995EA/N996EA	2
47747/47748	DC-9-41	SAS	SE-DDP, LN-RLH	2
47749	DC-9-51	Eastern	N997EA	1
47750	DC-9-41	SAS	SE-DDR	1
47751	DC-9-51	Eastern	N998EA	1
47752	DC-9-34CF	BWIA	9Y-TFI	1
47753	DC-9-51	Eastern	N417EA	1
47754	DC-9-51	Inex Adria	YU-AJU	1
47755	DC-9-51	Ghana Airways	9G-ACM	1
47756	DC-9-51	Austrian	OE-LDO	1
47757/47758	DC-9-51	North Central	N769NC/N770NC	2
47759/47762	DC-9-41	Toa	JA8439/JA8442	4
47763/47764	DC-9-51	Hawaiian	N699HA, N709HA	2
47765	DC-9-32	Texas Int'l	N3506T	1
47766	DC-9-41	SAS	OY-KGS	1
47767/47768	DC-9-41	Toa	JA8448/JA8449	2
47769	DC-9-51	North Central	N771NC	1
47770	DC-9-51	LAV	YV-32C	1
47771/47773	DC-9-51	Finnair	OH-LYU/OH-LYV, N8714Q	3
47774/47776	DC-9-51	North Central	N772NC/N774NC	3
47777/47779	DC-9-41	SAS	SE-DDS, LN-RLP, SE-DDT	3
47780/47781	DC-9-41	Toa	JA8450/JA8451	2
47782	DC-9-51	LAV	YV-33C	1
47783/47784	DC-9-51	Swissair	HB-ISV/HB-ISW	2
47785/47787	DC-9-51	North Central	N775NC/N777NC	3
47788	DC-9-32	Texas Int'l	N3507T	1
47789/47795	DC-9-32	Garuda	PK-GNS/PK-GNY	7
47796	DC-9-51	BWIA	9Y-TGC	1
47797/47799	DC-9-32	Texas Int'l	N3508T/N3510T	3
48100/48102	DC-9-51	Republic	N778NC/N780NC	3
48103/48106	DC-9-34	Aviaco	EC-DGB/EC-DGE	4
48107/48110	DC-9-51	Republic	N782NC/N785NC	4
48111/48113	DC-9-32	Texas Int'l	N3512T/N3514T	3
48114/48117	DC-9-31	Allegheny	N934VJ/N937VJ	4
48118/48120	DC-9-31	US Air	N929VJ, N938VJ/N939VJ	3
48121	DC-9-51	Republic	N781NC	1
48122	DC-9-51	BWIA	9Y-TGP	1
48123/48124	DC-9-34	Ozark	N927L/N928L	2
48125/48130	DC-9-32	Aeromexico	XA-AMA/XA-AMF	6
48131	DC-9-31	US Air	N928VJ	1
48132/48133	DC-9-32	KLM	PH-DOA/PH-DOB	2
48134/48136	DC-9-51	Finnair	OH-LYX/OH-LYZ	3
48137	C-9B	USN	161266	1
48138/48147	DC-9-31	US Air	N918VJ/N926VJ, N976VJ	10
48148/48149	DC-9-51	Republic	N786NC/N787NC	2
48150/48151	DC-9-32	Aeromexico	N1003P, N1003U	2
48154/48159	DC-9-31	US Air	N927VJ, N977VJ, N980VJ/N983VJ	6
48165/48166	C-9B	USN	161529/161530	2

Selected Projects

In forty-seven years of existence as an independent company, Douglas prepared a vast number of preliminary designs which, for a variety of reasons, were not built. Due to space limitations, only a few representative projects can be described and illustrated in the following pages.

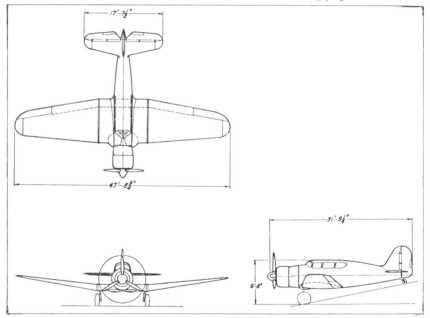

Douglas drawing

Douglas DT-202

The Douglas DT-202 was a six-seat light transport proposal derived from the A-17A. Conceived at the El Segundo Division during the late thirties, the DT-202 was to have been powered by either a Wright R-1820-G103A or a Pratt & Whitney Twin Wasp S3C3-G. Principal characteristics were: span 47 ft 8¾ in (14·55 m); length 31 ft 9¼ in (9·68 m); empty weight 5,700 lb (2,585 kg); and loaded weight 8,075 lb (3,665 kg). With the Twin Wasp radial, calculated performance included a maximum speed of 262 mph (422 km/h) and a maximum range of 1,500 miles (2,400 km).

Douglas 1939 VTB Proposal

In August 1939, Douglas and five other manufacturers submitted proposals for three-seat **VTB** (carrier-based torpedo bomber) aircraft which the Navy needed to replace the TBD-1 Devastator. Powered by a 1,600 hp Wright R-2600 radial engine, the Douglas proposal differed from those of its competitors in being fitted with a tricycle undercarriage and in being armed with a pair of forward-firing 20 mm cannon. Bombs or a single torpedo were to have been carried internally as specified by the Bureau of Aeronautics. The Navy, however, lacked experience with the novel undercarriage and was not yet ready to accept this feature for carrier-based aircraft. Consequently, Douglas lost out to Grumman, which produced the TBF Avenger, and to Vought, which developed the less successful TBU. The Douglas design had a span of 47 ft (14.33 m) and a length of 38 ft $1\frac{11}{16}$ in (11·63 m).

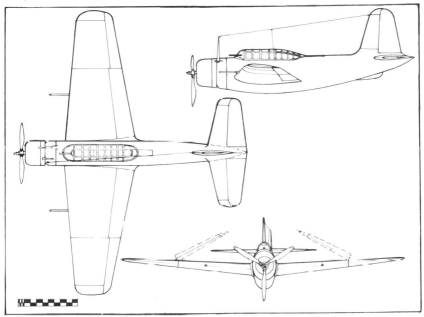

Based on Douglas drawing

605

Douglas XP-48

During 1939 the Santa Monica design team proposed to the Army Air Corps its Model 312 lightweight fighter which was to have been powered by a 525 hp Ranger SGV-770 twelve-cylinder engine driving a three-blade propeller. The projected fighter introduced a number of novel features including a high aspect ratio wing with a span of 32 ft (9·75 m) and an area of 92 sq ft (8·547 sq m), and a tricycle undercarriage with the main units

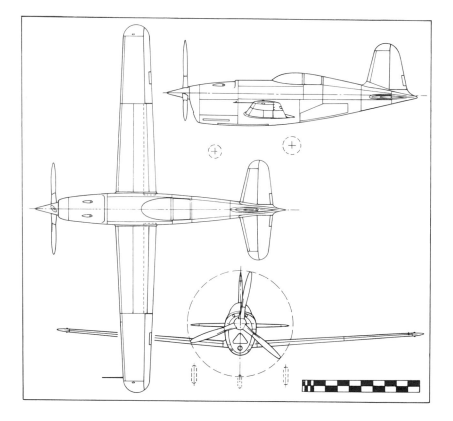

attached to the fuselage and retracting aft into the fuselage sides. Overall length and loaded weight were 21 ft 9 in (6·63 m) and 3,400 lb (1,542 kg), respectively, and armament was to have consisted of one 0·50-in and one 0·30-in forward-firing guns in the engine cowling. Calculated performance was judged by the Army Air Corps to be optimistic and development of the XP-48 was not funded.

Douglas XB-31

Initially designed in competition with the Boeing XB-29, Lockheed XB-30 and Convair XB-32, the Douglas Model 423 was a projected long-range heavy bomber powered by four 3,000 hp Pratt & Whitney R-4360 twenty-eight-cylinder radials driving three-blade propellers. Larger and heavier than the B-29 Superfortress, the XB-31 was to have had a span of 207 ft (63·09 m), a length of 117 ft 3 in (35·74 m), a wing area of 3,300 sq ft

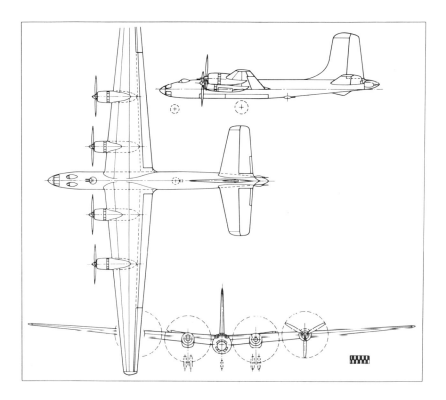

(306·581 sq m), an empty weight of 109,200 lb (49,532 kg), and a maximum weight of 198,000 lb (89,811 kg). The pilot and co-pilot were to be seated under separate double bubble canopies as later fitted to the C-74, and six other crew members were to be accommodated at separate stations. Defensive armament was to have consisted of twin 0·50-in guns in remotely-controlled dorsal and ventral turrets and of two 37-mm cannon in the tail, while a maximum bombload of 25,000 lb (11,340 kg) was to have been carried in two fuselage bays. In spite of its potential, the development of the XB-31 was cancelled in late 1941 as by then the Boeing B-29 had already been ordered into production.

Douglas D-557

The D-557 design study was originated in 1946 to investigate possible configurations for a propeller-turbine powered attack aircraft. The D-557A was planned around two General Electric TG 100 engines in conventional nacelles. The D-557B had its two TG 100 engines mounted side-by-side in the forward fuselage and driving contra-rotating propellers. The D-557C, as illustrated, was designed around a single Westinghouse X25D2 turbine mounted in the rear of the fuselage and driving contra-rotating propellers. All three variants were to be armed with two 20 mm cannon and were to have carried bombs of up to 2,000 lb (908 kg) externally. Provision was made in the D-557C design for the installation of an ASV radar in a wingtip pod. Principal characteristics and estimated performance of the D-557C were: span 46 ft 6 in (14·17 m); length 42 ft (12·80 m); empty weight 11,700 lb (5,307 kg); loaded weight 21,430 lb (9,720 kg); maximum speed at sea level 405 mph (652 km/h); radius of action with 2,000 lb bomb 230 miles (370 km).

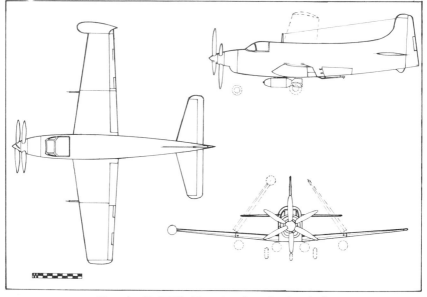

Douglas D-557C. (*Based on Douglas drawing*)

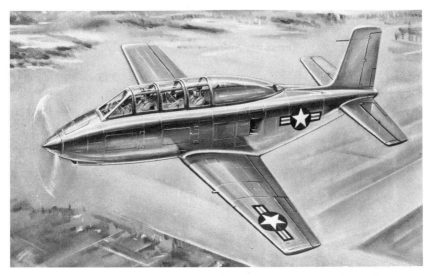

Drawing of the XT-30 with R-1300 engine mounted in the fuselage aft of the cockpit. (*USAF*)

Douglas XT-30

Intended as a successor to the T-6 Texan, the XT-30 was a projected advanced trainer offered to the USAF in 1948 in competition with the North American T-28. Its 800 hp Wright R-1300 engine was to be located in the fuselage, immediately aft of the tandem cockpit, and drive a three-blade propeller by means of extension shafts. The XT-30 was to have had a span of 36 ft 4 in (11·07 m), a length of 36 ft 9½ in (11·21 m), and a design gross weight of 5,999 lb (2,721 kg). Calculated performance included a top speed of 286 mph (460 km/h), an endurance of 6½ hr at 190 mph (306 km/h), and a service ceiling of 29,600 ft (9,020 m). The USAF, however, selected the less complex North American T-28 and the XT-30 was not built.

Douglas DC-8

Shortly after the end of World War Two Douglas offered to the airlines a twin-engined short- to medium-range transport using the novel powerplant installation developed for the XB-42. Compared wih the experimental bomber, the proposed DC-8 was to have had its two 1,375 hp Allison V-1710s relocated slightly forward to a position immediately aft and below the pilots' cockpit. Its contra-rotating propellers were to be driven by extension shafts located beneath the cabin floor. The wing was moved lower to provide room for a pressurized cabin with accommodation for 40 to 48 passengers. Performance was calculated to exceed markedly that of conventional twin-engined airliners. However, development costs and sales price were substantially higher, and the airlines, which were also worried about added maintenance costs stemming from the use of long extension

The first aircraft to bear, although only tentatively, the DC-8 designation was this proposed derivative of the XB-42. (*MDC via Aero Digest*)

shafts, ordered the less risky Convair 240/440 and Martin 2-0-2/4-0-4 series, forcing Douglas to abandon development of the first airliner to bear the DC-8 designation.

Douglas 603 and 604

Designed in answer to a request for proposals issued by the Bureau of Aeronautics in 1949, the Models 603 and 604 were twin-engined carrier-

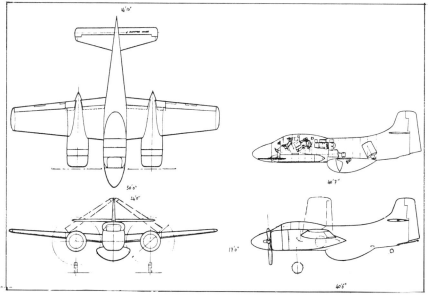

Douglas drawing

610

based aircraft combining search and attack capability in the anti-submarine role. In the configuration illustrated by the accompanying drawing, the aircraft was to have been fitted with AN/APS-20 radar in a large ventral radome and to have carried a retractable AN/APS-38 radar further aft in the fuselage. Two 20 mm cannon were fitted in the nose and sonobuoys and offensive stores were carried in a forward fuselage bay and externally beaneath the wings. Power was provided by a pair of 1,525 hp Wright R-1820 radial engines. Span was 50 ft (15.24 m) and length 40 ft 7 in (12.37 m). The Models 603 and 604 lost out to the Grumman G-89 which was produced in large quantity as the S2F Tracker.

Douglas DC-9

Among the many projected airliners tentatively designated DC-9s, Douglas proposed between 1957 and 1959 a series of scaled-down DC-8s with four pod-mounted engines. One of these designs, which had a calculated MGTOW of 120,000 lb (54,431 kg), was to have been powered by four 8,250 lb (3,742 kg) thrust Pratt & Whitney JTF10A-1 turbofans and

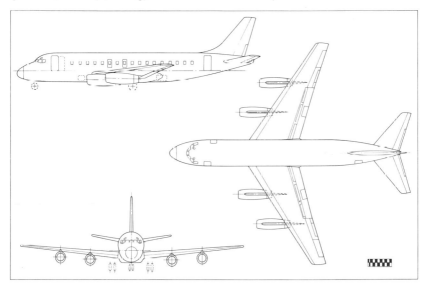

carry from 68 to 92 passengers on sectors of up to 2,500 miles (4,025 km). Preliminary dimensions included a span of 94 ft (28·65 m), a length of 103 ft (31·39 m), and a wing area of 1,285 sq ft (119·381 sq m). This project did not materialize and the DC-9 designation was finally bestowed on the now familiar short-range jetliner with two rear mounted turbofans.

611

Douglas DC-10

Whereas the aircraft which went into production under the DC-10 designation is a wide-bodied trijet, the first project tentatively designated DC-10 was a much smaller aircraft with shoulder-mounted wing and four 1,500 shp Lycoming LTS4A-1 propeller-turbines. Intended as a DC-3 replacement for use on short-haul operations, this 1957 project (Model

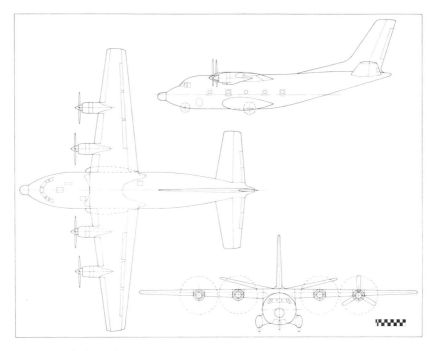

1940) was derived from a projected assault transport (Model 1906) for the Marine Corps. Providing accommodation for 35 to 50 passengers, the Model 1940 had a span of 102 ft 6 in (31·24 m) and a length of 92 ft 6 in (28·19 m). However, neither it nor its military forebear progressed beyond the preliminary design phase.

Douglas F6D Missileer.

Douglas F6D Missileer

In 1959, after awarding to a Bendix/Grumman team a development contract for the XAAM-N-10 Eagle long-range air-to-air missile, the Navy requested from the industry proposals for a carrier-borne aircraft to be used as a launch platform for the new weapon. The launch vehicle could be either a development of existing aircraft or a new design optimized for this role. Six companies submitted proposals and in July 1960 Douglas was selected to develop its all-new D-9766 design into the F6D Missileer. Bearing a family resemblance to the F3D Skyknight, the F6D design was for a large aircraft powered by two 10,000 lb (4,536 kg) thrust Pratt & Whitney TF30-P-2 turbofans underslung beneath the fuselage. Weighing some 50,000 lb (22,680 kg) on take-off and fitted with a straight wing, it had a design maximum speed of Mach 0·9 and an endurance on station of four to six hours. The F6D was to carry a three-man crew (pilot, co-pilot and missile control operator), to be fitted with high-power pulse-Doppler and a track-while-scan missile control system, and have a normal armament consisting of six Eagle missiles beneath the wings; under overload conditions, two additional missiles could have been carried beneath the fuselage. However, the single-role subsonic Missileer was deemed not to be cost effective and its development was abandoned within less than one year of contract award.

Douglas D-906

Before being invited to be one of the three companies submitting proposals for the USAF C-5 cargo transport, for four years Douglas had actively studied the requirements for a heavy logistics aircraft capable of efficiently deploying Army units and carrying outsize objects for which there was an airlift requirement. Under the generic designation CX-4 and the Air Force acronym CX-HLS (Experimental Cargo-Heavy Logistics Support), a number of designs were studied in some detail. Typical of those was the

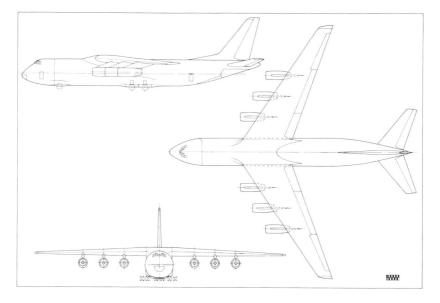

Model D-906. Capable of carrying up to 195,000 lb (88,450 kg) of cargo for up to 3,750 miles (6,035 km), this aircraft was planned around the use of six 30,000 lb (13,608 kg) thrust advanced turbofans and was to have weighed 606,000 lb (274,877 kg) on take-off. The shoulder-mounted wing had a span of 192 ft 2½ in (58·59 m) and an area of 4,920 sq ft (457·085 sq m), and overall length was 190 ft 8½ in (58·13 m).

An impression of the D-920 submitted in April 1965 to the USAF as Douglas's entry in the C-5 competition. (*MDC*)

Douglas D-920

In answer to a December 1964 RFP (Request for Proposals), in April 1965 Douglas submitted its Model D-920 which had been designed to meet the USAF requirement for a heavy logistics aircraft. Like its Lockheed competitor, which five months later was selected for production as the C-5A Galaxy, the Douglas project featured a shoulder-mounted wing and was to have been powered by four 40,000 lb (18,144 kg) thrust high bypass-ratio turbofans then being developed by General Electric and Pratt & Whitney. Its characteristics and performance were similar to those of the Lockheed design as both types had been designed to meet the same stringent USAF specifications. Both proposals had a rear loading ramp but instead of the Lockheed's visor-type nose loading door, the Model D-920 had a swing nose opening with the entire forward fuselage section— including the cockpit—hinged on its starboard side.

Douglas D-966

To meet an American Airlines' requirement for a twin-engined wide-bodied jetliner capable of carrying 250 passengers over sectors of up to 1,750 naut miles (3,250 km), in 1966 Douglas prepared preliminary design studies. By mid-1967, the company was looking at two- and three-engined configurations including the Model D-966. This aircraft featured a raised cockpit, to facilitate nose-loading of containers into a proposed freighter version, and a lower-deck lounge or cabin. With seating accommodation in the lower cabin, the D-966 was to carry a maximum of 332 passengers. It was to be powered by two 47,000 lb (21,319 kg) thrust turbofans and to

615

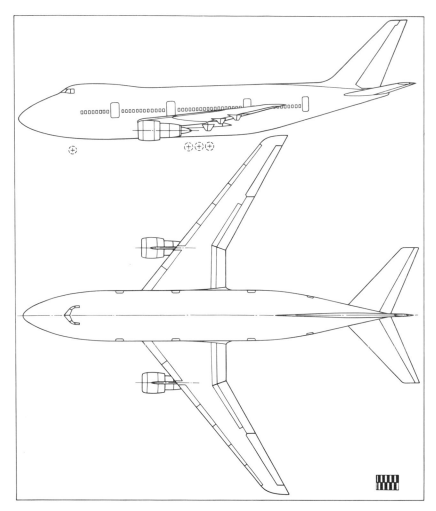

have an MGTOW of 331,000 lb (150,139 kg). Its span was 160 ft 6 in (48·92 m) and its length 184 ft 6 in (56·24 m). In parallel, Douglas proposed a trijet version with 32,000 lb (14,515 kg) thrust turbofans, from which the DC-10 eventually evolved.

Douglas D-974

Ever since losing the C-5A competition, Douglas has made low-keyed efforts to produce eventually a family of purely commercial cargo aircraft, believing that operating costs would be substantially lower than those of freighters derived either from passenger transports or from military cargo aircraft. One such aircraft proposed in 1967 was the D-974 which was to have been powered by six 50,000 lb (22,680 kg) thrust turbofans to carry a maximum payload of 412,000 lb (186,880 kg). Weighing up to 1,245,000 lb (564,723 kg) on take-off, this aircraft was to have had a span of 248 ft 2½ in (75·65 m) and a length of 256 ft (78·03 m). However, development costs of such an aircraft are too high to be amortized on a relatively small production run and derivatives of passenger aircraft will remain more economic until such time as the cargo market reaches a sufficient size to support its development.

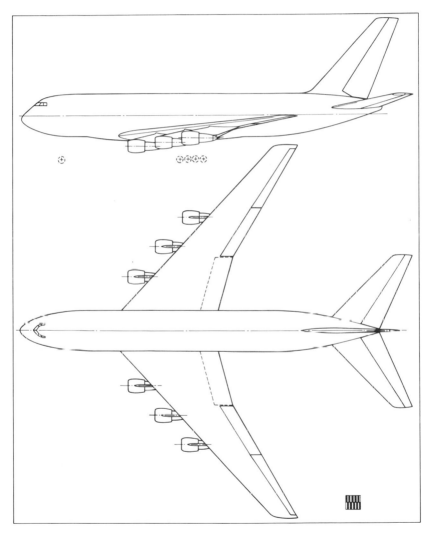